D1132855

SIGNIFICANT ACCOUNTING ESSAYS

Edited by

MAURICE MOONITZ
University of California

A. C. LITTLETON
University of Illinois

SIGNIFICANT
ACCOUNTING ESSAYS

PRENTICE-HALL, INC., Englewood Cliffs, New Jersey

Library of Congress Catalog Card No. 65–16940

Printed in the United States of America C–80996

PRENTICE-HALL INTERNATIONAL, INC., *London*
PRENTICE-HALL OF AUSTRALIA, PTY., LTD., *Sydney*
PRENTICE-HALL OF CANADA, LTD., TORONTO
PRENTICE-HALL OF INDIA (PRIVATE) LTD., *New Delhi*
PRENTICE-HALL OF JAPAN, INC., *Tokyo*

This book is intended to give the reader some perspective on the development of accounting thought in the United States since 1900 and to stimulate his own exploration of the subject. In the last 35 years, the volume of literature has increased tremendously; however, in the first 30 years of this century, much less material was published. Because access to the original sources is limited, even for those living close to the large collections of published works on accounting, a book of readings is especially useful.

The editors of this book followed certain rules in selecting the items to be included and tried to distribute them among various topical areas, such as history, postulates and principles, price-level changes, cost analysis, depreciation, etc. We favored articles that are "significant" because they are well-written statements of topics or view points of lasting interest to students in the field. A few items also represent some of the leading names in the field.

We further circumscribed the total area surveyed by using the *Journal of Accountancy* and *The Accounting Review* as the primary but not exclusive sources. Articles dealing mainly with taxes and management services (including systems) were excluded because those fields are technical and distinct enough to deserve books devoted exclusively to them. Also excluded were materials published after 1955 because the volume of recent literature obscures perspective and because the original sources are probably readily available to almost everyone. Finally, the number of articles for any one author was limited; only a few author's are represented by two items.

Each selection should be considered in view of the period when it was written. Some are enlightening because of the "advanced" ideas held by the authors; others because the views expressed highlight the development since the turn of the century. Each selection contains a headnote which gives a brief biographical sketch of the author and a short statement about why the item was included.

Most of the essays selected were published in the 1930's and the 1940's and center around the related topics of postulates, principles, and price-level changes. These concerns reflect the high level of activity in the struggle to establish the "principles" of accounting. These essays, therefore, become helpful background for readers following the rapid growth of the literature since 1955.

This volume begins with Henry Rand Hatfield's "An Historical Defense of Bookkeeping" (1924) and closes with Walter A. Staub's "Mode of Conducting an Audit" (1904) and Robert H. Montgomery's "Professional Standards: A Plan for Co-operation Among Accountants" (1905). Hatfield's "Defense" is a fine exposition of the reasons why a simple, early recording technology could evolve toward its present level of sophistication. Staub's article was an indication of the essence of the distinction between the professional approach to accounting in the U.S.A. and in Britain, an indication strengthened by Montgomery's text on auditing in 1912. Montgomery's "Professional Standards" article shows early evidence of his leadership qualities that culminated in the final consolidation of the American profession into the present Institute in the 1930's. That firm foundation lies beneath the growth in the service capacity of the profession that is so evident today.

M. M.
A. C. L.

CONTENTS

Part One: History

Part Two: Postulates and Principles

Part Three: Price-Level Changes

Part Four: Cost Analysis

Part Five: Accounting Under Regulation

Part Six: Specialized Topics

SIGNIFICANT ACCOUNTING ESSAYS

Part One

History

Henry Rand Hatfield

AN HISTORICAL DEFENSE
OF BOOKKEEPING

Henry Rand Hatfield *(1866–1945) received a bachelor's degree from North-western in 1892 and a Ph.D. from Chicago in 1897. He spent four years in the bond business (1886–1890), but otherwise his career was entirely aca-demic, covering four years on the faculty at Washington University, two years at Chicago, and more than forty years at California. He also gave the Dickinson Lectures at Harvard in 1942, served as president of the American Association of University Instructors in Accounting (now the American Accounting Association) in 1918, as vice-president of the American Economic Association the same year, and as a Senator of Phi Beta Kappa, 1923–1928.*
He published his Modern Accounting *in 1908, and a revision in 1927 under the title* Accounting: Its Principles and Problems. *He was coauthor of* A Statement of Accounting Principles *(1938) with Thomas H. Sanders of Harvard and Underhill Moore of Yale, a work that was financed by the Haskins and Sells Foundation and published by the American Institute of C.P.A. His Dickinson Lectures were published under the title* Surplus and Dividends *(1942). He had a deep interest in the history of accounting—the Hatfield Collection of early works on accounting, housed in the library of the University of California, gives tangible evidence of this interest.*
The essay reprinted here reflects Hatfield's wit, learning, and deep love of accounting. His own academic credentials were flawless. He served not only as a professor of accounting and as a dean of a college of commerce but also as dean of the faculties at the University of California. He was consulted frequently by members of the legal profession and worked closely with Henry W. Ballantine, a leading authority in the field of corporation law, in completely redrafting the California Corporation Law, adopted in 1931. He also established excellent relations with the professional accountants, es-pecially in the San Francisco Bay Area, and let it be known to his colleagues and students that he expected them to do the same. All of this, and more, is in this essay, which is the envy of all who aspire to write and the delight of all who read. It is indeed a classic.

A paper read before the American Association of University Instructors in Accounting, December 29, 1923. Reprinted from *The Journal of Accountancy* (April, 1924), pp. 241–53, by permission.

3

I am sure that all of us who teach accounting in the universities suffer from the implied contempt of our colleagues, who look upon accounting as an intruder, a Saul among the prophets, a pariah whose very presence detracts somewhat from the sanctity of the academic halls. It is true that we ourselves speak of the science of accounts, or of the art of accounting, even of the philosophy of accounts. But accounting is, alas, only a pseudoscience unrecognized by J. McKeen Cattell; its products are displayed neither in the salon nor in the national academy; one finds it discussed by neither realist, idealist nor phenomenalist. The humanists look down upon us as beings who dabble in the sordid figures of dollars and cents instead of toying with infinities and searching for the elusive soul of things; the scientists and technologists despise us as able only to record rather than to perform deeds.

We suffer perhaps in silence, even, as Carlyle says, "consuming our own choler as some chimneys consume their own smoke," perhaps in public denying that we suffer at all, but here—in a meeting not of accountants, but of university instructors in accounting—we can admit among ourselves that at times this academic attitude does get under our skins.

The contempt for accounting is not limited to university circles, but is well-nigh universal. It is evidenced by ignorance of the subject, by condescension toward its devotees, by their exclusion from polite literature.

And how abysmal that ignorance! I give two instances. The university speaker who said, "If you do so and so your ledger [speaking figuratively, of course] will show a debit balance." Would he have spoken of an equation with unequal numbers? And the distinguished writer in the October *Atlantic*, thesaurus of culture, supposedly barred to academic solecisms, who says, "In most sections of America the fact that a man or woman has been divorced . . . is something to be set down . . . on the debit side of the account," ignorant that likely as not a debit (as for instance in the bank account) means the imputation of additional value—which, I take it, is quite contrary to what Mrs. Gerould intended.

But the contempt for accounting is even more clearly shown by a constantly repeated phrase, a phrase which of all phrases is to me the most exacerbating—because of the combination of ignorance and supercilious condescension. This phrase, which I could quote from uncounted sources, is: "That is a mere bookkeeping entry." One might as well say, "That is a mere algebraic equation," or, "That is a mere statement of discovered fact," or, "That is the formulation of a mere axiom." Mere truth, mere fact, mere sanctity, mere virtue. Do you wonder that I lose my temper every time I see the phrase? Of course, one may make a misstatement in bookkeeping, just as one may lie either in Greek or in German: But that merits some adjective more invidious than "mere."

And remember how accounting has been slighted in literature. The public eye has generally, both in history and in fiction, been turned on the man on horseback, but nevertheless at times there comes upon the stage a more prosaic figure. Great masterpieces have grouped themselves about a scholar as Faust, about a carpenter as Adam Bede, about a manufacturer as in *Les Miserables,* about a sailor as Robinson Crusoe, about courtesans, thieves and beggars beyond recital. Even a horse and a dog have been made the heroes in *Black Beauty* and in *Rab and His Friends.* But never, so far as I recollect, has a bookkeeper been made the hero of novel, play or poem. The bookkeeper is not even honored by being made a noteworthy villain.

Long ago Sir Roger de Coverley assumed that "little that is truly noble can be expected from one who is ever poring on his cashbook or balancing his accounts." Literature has maintained this attitude ever since, and the bookkeeper has reached his apogee in the gentle and pathetic figure of Tim Clerkenwell. Compare him for a moment with the military hero. The latter appears mounted on a horse, leading, to the music of bugle and drum, his martial columns in charges against the foe, brandishing a reeking sword, and wearing on his brow the victor's wreath of laurel. The bookkeeper too is mounted, but on a quadrupedal stool, he too marshals columns, but of figures to the accompaniment of a clicking Burroughs, his charges are those on the debit side of the ledger, his brow is encircled but by a green eye shade, he brandishes only the humble rival of the sword, guiltless doubtless of his country's blood, and incarnadined only with Carter's cardinal ink.

But it is not good for a man's soul always to suffer under the inferiority complex. Let us no longer bear in humility the lash of contumely. Let us face our contemners, be they classicists, philosophers or scientists.

> No matter if he is a houn',
> They gotta quit kicking my dog aroun'.

Let us boldly raise the question whether accounting, the late chaimant for recognition as a profession, is not entitled to some respect, or must it consort with crystal-gazing, sociology, chiropractic, pedagogy and palm-reading.

Three elements, if not conclusively proving, at least presumptively establish, respectability. These are, first, parentage and lineage; second, the company one keeps; and, third, the services which one renders the community. Let us examine accounting in these aspects.

Without raising the question as to accounting in antiquity, we look upon the Franciscan monk Paciolo as the father of modern accounting, as his *Summa,* published in 1494, which was the first printed work dealing with algebra, also contained the first text on bookkeeping, a slender tractate entitled *De Computis et Scripturis.*

Not much can be said of Paciolo,[1] aside from his writings, but his academic credentials are flawless. He was an important if not a great mathematician. His first appointment to teach in a university was at Perugia. In less than

---

[1] H. Staigmüller, "Lucas Paciuolo, eine biographische Skizze," in *Zeitschrift für Mathematik und Physik,* Bd. 34, Historisch-literarische Abtheilung. pp. 81–102, 121–128.

a year his request for an increase of salary was granted. The reason stated in the official records has a singularly modern sound. It reads: "because he has already taught for two months and has shown himself to be a man of highest learning, and because it appears that he manifestly cannot live on such a meagre stipend." Again in less than six months he was promoted, this time with a more permanent tenure as well as increase of salary. Soon afterward he left the university, probably devoting himself to the study of philosophy and theology. He returned to Perugia in 1487, and while he had previously signed himself "Brother Luke," in his later writings he was wont to describe himself as a "humble professor of sacred theology." He held many other university positions, at various times teaching at Naples, at Pisa, at Florence and at Bologna. He ended his career with his highest honor, for in 1514 Pope Leo X appointed him professor of mathematics in the *Sapienza* at Rome, a position in the "university of the highest standing in all Christendom."

In 1496 he was called to Milan by the reigning duke, Ludovico il Moro, whose court was a center of light and learning, and to be established there was a signal honor. Adams in China, Hollander in Puerto Rico, Bogart in Persia, Paciolo in Milan—all indications of deserved recognition of professorial eminence—all doubtless to be kept in mind for at least 427 years.

At Milan, Paciolo was brought into contact with many prominent persons, the most significant being Leonardo da Vinci, perhaps the most eminent man of his day. Between the two there grew up an intimate friendship. Da Vinci himself tells that he hastened to buy a copy of Paciolo's *Summa* as it came off the press, and he collaborated with Paciolo on a later book, the *Divina Proportione*, for which Paciolo furnished the text and Da Vinci the illustrations. Honor indeed for a university professor! Would not the most eminent mathematician of today rejoice if the greatest man of his time, say Roosevelt or Henry Ford, had hastened to buy one of his treatises (even though it contained the adventitious attraction of some chapters on bookkeeping)? Would not even one so eminent as William James have been flattered if in his psychology the somatic reactions of the emotions could have been illustrated by the master hand of the creator of Mutt and Jeff?

I need not outline to you the nature of Paciolo's treatise, with which you are familiar, at least through Geijsbeek's somewhat paraphrastic translation.* Have any of you not read this you will be interested in it, not merely as a piece of technical literature, but because of its quaintness of expression, its naïve attention to detail, its exuberance of piety, its flavor of mediævalism.

It is seldom the case that a first book on a subject has so dominated its literature as was the case with Paciolo's *De Computis et Scripturis*. It is

---

* John B. Geijsbeek, *Ancient Double-Entry Bookkeeping* (Denver: 1914). Other translations are now available: Pietro Crivelli, *Original Translation of the Treatise on Double-Entry Bookkeeping* by Lucas Pacioli (London: 1924); R. Gene Brown and Kenneth S. Johnston, *Paciolo on Accounting* (New York: 1963).

nearly true to say that for a hundred years the texts appearing in England, France, Germany, Italy and the low countries were "at the best revisions of Paciolo, at the worst servile transcriptions without even the courtesy of referring to the original author." But further than that many little matters of bookkeeping technique were followed for at least four centuries, merely because they were inculcated by Paciolo, persisting like buttons on our coat sleeves, long after their significance had disappeared. I need not mention these to you, but may I refer to a peculiar instance relating rather to a matter of general form?

Whether it was because of his churchly connections or because it conformed to the customs of his day, Paciolo's book is replete with gems of moral and religious advice. I know not how it may be in the higher branches, such as sociology or Americanization—but in the elementary textbooks, such as algebra or chemistry, we do not today find the thread of the discourse interrupted by bits of proverbial philosophy or moral exhortation. But in bookkeeping this has continued down until today. I might cite instances from many of the high school texts used today, from practically all used so lately as ten years ago. But let me take a single extreme example. Soule's book is still in vogue in this country. At the foot of nearly every one of his 749 pages, he has a line quite in keeping with Paciolo. The statement in the earlier writer, "Who does nothing makes no mistakes, who makes not mistakes learns nothing," is matched by Soule's "Our greatest glory is not in never falling but in rising every time we fall." "It costs more to make a good merchant than to make a doctor of laws," is matched with "Experience is not a free school, we all pay for our tuition." But even a fifteenth-century monk cannot rise quite to the level of the twentieth-century practical American who tells us "The only amaranthine flower on earth is virtue, the the only lasting treasure truth." Bookkeeping was spread throughout the world by a series of plagiarisms and imitations of Paciolo. The habit of imitation became so fixed that in bookkeeping it has persisted throughout the centuries, and even the foibles of Brother Luke are reproduced in the treatises of today.

Let those who vaunt the superior merits of other disciplines remember that this first presentation made by Paciolo was not crude and incorrect but contains the essentials of bookkeeping as we know it today, despite the fact that it was written at a time when chemistry partook of the vagaries of alchemy, biology was a weird collection of errors, and medicine had more in common with the medicine man than it has even today. It may be well to see how this discipline—I do not venture to call it science—compares in its antiquity with the more arrogant natural sciences. In neither case do I go back to the feeble beginnings and adumbrations of learning but compare the position of bookkeeping, as it was first formulated in print by a university professor, with the formulation of natural sciences—not by some dim groper in far-off antiquity—but by the first vice-president of Harvard College. A comparison, thus made, is, I am sure, more than generous to the natural sciences, despite their illiberal attitude toward the social sciences, with which, in general, they admit of no kinship.

Charles Morton, who, like Paciolo, was at once distinguished teacher and cleric, was brought to Harvard from England almost two hundred years after Paciolo had formulated bookkeeping. If not professor, he was at least made vice-president, and his work on science was used as a textbook in the college.[2]

But he explained the problem of the migration of birds by saying that each autumn they flew to the moon, 200,000 miles distant, a two months' journey, and in his textbook, earthquakes are explained as follows: "They come from choking up of wind below, fermenting, bursting out, causing trembling and strokes." Or dropping into verse:

> In subterranean caverns winds do frolic
> When Mother Earth is troubled with the colic.

How marked a contrast to the teachings of the geologist at the University of California. It is told that when he appeared in court as an expert witness, the opposing lawyer foolishly attempting to ridicule his pretension of knowledge, said: "And do you pretend to know what is going on in the bowels of the earth?" To this the geologist replied: "I do not know that the earth has any bowels."

Only two hundred years ago science—in the leading American college— was a futile and ludicrous display of ignorance. More than four hundred years ago, in the very first book published on the subject, bookkeeping was outlined in a form which still prevails around the entire world. Cannot bookkeeping claim an honorable and ancient lineage? Is it indeed an upstart as compared with geology, and chemistry, and landscape gardening, and social psychology, and business English, and olericulture, and otorhino-laryngology, and other cherished subjects of the university curriculum? Founded, like San Francisco, by a follower of St. Francis of Assisi, cradled in mathematics with algebra as a twin, established under the ægis of a great university—surely this is an origin sufficiently academic to give respectability to this our "houn' dog." Perhaps I should adopt the language appropriate to the kennel and speak of bookkeeping as having been sired four hundred years ago by a monk, and today damned by thousands of university students, and yet, despite certain questions which the frivolous might raise to a celibate paternity and the extremely puzzling biological enigma of such a multiple maternity, bookkeeping is thoroughly respectable.

But many a house founded by a great man has degenerated and the descendants have been of quite inferior clay. Has the later entourage of bookkeeping been made up of a fair number of respectable persons?

---

[2] The authority for the following statements is found in Meriwether, *Our Continental Curriculum,* pp. 188ff.

The second book on bookkeeping was also written by a man of distinction, Grammateus or Schreiber. He, like Paciolo, combined algebra and book-keeping, and his book, dated 1518, was the first work published in Germany dealing with either of these subjects. On the authority of Cantor, he stands, as a mathematician, unquestionably in the front rank of his time.

Almost immediately following Grammateus was Jerome Cardan, that picturesque scapegrace and brilliant scholar, astrologer, physician, scientist, mathematician, professor of medicine first at Pavia, later at Bologna. He, too, wrote a book combining algebra and bookkeeping. This work, says Richard Garnett, marks an era in the history of mathematics, being the first in which the principle of cubic equations was fully explained. Everett says it is one of the most valuable contributions to the literature of algebra. As a physician he was so eminent that he was called to Scotland, no mean journey in those days, to attend an archbishop; he was famous enough as an astrologer to visit the court of Edward VI to cast the king's nativity. But his chief claim to distinction is his general scientific attitude, so far in advance of his times. Says Garnett: "Alike intellectually and morally, Cardan is one of the most interesting personages connected with the revival of science in Europe. He possessed the true scientific spirit in perfection. As a mathematician he effected most important advances, and to complete the catalogue of his accomplishments he is no contemptible poet." And to add pictur-esqueness to his career, he became involved in difficulties, was addicted to gaming, imprisoned for debt, banished from Milan, was later deposed from his professorship, imprisoned, released, prohibited from further teaching, but spent his latter years in Rome as a prisoner of the pope.

Out of the first six writers three are thus seen to be men of eminent distinction—in fields other than that of bookkeeping, as judged by persons who are not themselves particularly interested in bookkeeping. Surely the early days—if not the unknown origin of bookkeeping—are sufficiently respectable so that we need not be ashamed.

Extending somewhat the field of survey, we find that Brown lists only 150 names of writers on bookkeeping before 1800. But even the reduced list of those who have reputations in fields other than bookkeeping is too long to repeat in detail. These are not a group of narrow specialists. One finds there authorities on algebra (as is to be expected), on navigation, on optics, a commissioner to settle the foreign exchange, the author of the French code of 1763 (who not only had this great code named after him, the Code Savary, but is perhaps even more distinguished by having had seventeen children who also bore his name), astronomers, a French grammarian, an authority on gunpowder and the historian of the Baptist church. To find these names in the *Encyclopaedia Britannica* one does not look under ac-counting or bookkeeping—these articles are scant and unsatisfactory and both contain misstatements concerning the history of the subject—but under the following rubrics: algebra, camera obscura, deaf and dumb, earth figure, fortification and siege craft, gravitation, infinitesimal calculus, insurance, logarithms, mathematical tables, Napier, and navigation.

Perhaps I may be pardoned if I mention more specifically three of the names. There is Simon Stevin. Cantor styles him a Dutch mathematician, but says his claims to fame are varied. He invented a horseless carriage which worked, he was first to solve some problems regarding polyhedra, he proved the law of equilibrium on an inclined plane, he discovered the hydrostatic paradox, he explained the tides by the moon, he devised new forms of fortification, was many times public officer, a soldier and statesman, and the first to introduce decimals. Yet he thought it well worth while, in 1602, to write an extended treatise on bookkeeping for the express purpose of training his royal pupil, the prince of Orange.

There was Charles Hutton, a colliery boy, who became teacher of mathematics at eighteen and later professor at the royal academy at Woolwich, fellow and foreign secretary of the Royal Society (three others in the brief list were also fellows of that distinguished body), perhaps most famous for his computation of the density of the earth, an achievement recognized by Laplace and said by various competent critics to show ingenious and important methods, which can hardly be improved upon, author too of a work on conic sections said by Montucla to be a model of precision and clarity, receiver of the Copley medal for his paper on gunpowder, and doctor of laws of Edinburgh. And yet this man, who could weigh the earth as in a balance, condescended to write a textbook on bookkeeping, a subject which many think worthy the attention only of writing masters and proprietors of business colleges.

There was Robert Hamilton, who after some years' experience as a banker, betook himself to teaching, and was professor first of natural philosophy and later of mathematics at Aberdeen; famed, however, more as an economist, for it was he who exposed the economic fallacies of Pitt's policy of the sinking fund. Yet this man, banker, merchant, mathematician, capable of confuting England's master statesman, thought it not beneath his dignity also to write on bookkeeping.

I have limited this survey to writers before 1800. I will mention only two persons since then. Augustus De Morgan, whose eminence needs no description, was so far interested in bookkeeping that one of the best elementary books ever written on the subject acknowledges that it is based on the suggestions of De Morgan. And finally Arthur Cayley, who thirty years ago turned aside from his duties as professor of mathematics at Cambridge long enough to write a most excellent work, entitled *The Principles of Double-entry Bookkeeping*.

I have cited illustrious men who have written on bookkeeping rather than illustrious writers on bookkeeping. I did this merely to establish the argument that bookkeeping is a subject worthy the attention of men of ability— not to be relegated to the ordinary business college.

But not all who have attempted to write on the subject have succeeded. He may, like Grammateus, stand high as a mathematician, and yet, as a writer on bookkeeping "deserve no praise beyond that of being the first German who ventured to write on that difficult subject," producing a book, which Row Fogo says is "so confused that it is extremely improbable that he himself knew much about what he was attempting to teach." He may, like Cardan, show originality and genius in science, yet as a writer on bookkeeping be worse than banal. He may, like Collins, hold an honorable position in the Royal Society, yet produce a work on bookkeeping which receives no particular mention by the historian of the subject. He may, like Hamilton, deserve the encomium of McCullough, that he succeeded in the impossible task of opening the mind of the British public on an economic question, and yet have the *Encyclopaedia Britannica* say that his work on bookkeeping is now forgotten. A man of distinction may write on book-keeping; his work in that line is not necessarily distinguished. Would it be fair to say that it takes a peculiar genius to make a success in that subject?

The third presumptive evidence of respectability is that one performs some important service in the world. Can this be said of accounting? Perhaps this can best be answered by showing that bookkeeping appeared, not as a chance phenomenon, but distinctly in response to a world need. This is true not only of the days of Paciolo, but, as I hope to show, of that more important, almost present-day, revival.

It is not without significance that bookkeeping appeared at the end of the fifteenth century, nor that its birthplace was in the Italian republics. We all know of the marvelous awakening of that period, and particularly of the sudden expansion of commerce. Sieveking, one of the few historians who has paid attention to the subject, says that bookkeeping arose as a direct result of the establishment of partnerships on a large scale, a feature of the expanding commerce.

But bookkeeping dozed for several centuries, and it was not until just about four hundred years after Paciolo's book that a startling awakening took place. New works in unheard-of abundance and of a new quality began to appear, and again the universities seriously undertook instruction in a subject which had fallen into academic disrepute.

Why this new prominence in a subject taught before 1500? The answer is so obvious that I offend by explanation. The end of the nineteenth, even more than the end of the fifteenth century, was marked by a most extraordinary expansion of business. Then was the period of the organization of the great corporations (ordinarily called trusts), a phenomenon common to America, England and Germany. Then came that new appearance, the billion-dollar corporation, and just then—not a curious coincidence but a necessary response—accountants woke up. Garcke and Fells started the list of works on cost-accounts, Pixley first and then Dicksee began their voluminous writings dealing with the more refined problems of corporation accounts,

England chartered the Institute of Chartered Accountants, New York set the example, since followed by every American state, of granting the title of "certified public accountant," the adding machine was invented, logarithms were placed beside the ledger, books were written, conventions were held, accounting was.

In part the new significance of accounting is due to subdivision of ownership and the severance of ownership and control so characteristic of the corporate form of business organization. If the substitution of a small partnership for the individual trader called for improvement in bookkeeping methods, how much more was improvement needed when the partnership was displaced by the corporation with its owners numbered by the tens of thousands.

But still more significant has been the great investment of fixed capital characteristic of modern production and made possible by the organization of corporations. The use of fixed capital on a large scale increases incalculably the difficulty of determining the profits earned in any given year. Paciolo made no serious effort to do this. Business in his day was a congeries of disconnected ventures. A ship went here, a caravan there, a joint venture was undertaken with Messer Juan Antonio in French wool, and a flyer was taken in *ginger michini*. As these ventures fell in, the profit gained in the completed transaction was ascertained, somewhat roughly, it is true, but fairly satisfactorily. But no attempt was made to deal with unfinished operations.

But today business is a continuum. Machinery serves for many years, the factory building stands for a generation, the railroad is built to last forever. The industrial process is made up of a never-ending stream of raw materials, goods in process and finished commodities. Expenses are incurred in common and not like the expenses of a caravan solely in connection with one parcel of goods. But man is strangely agricultural in his tradition, even though society has become industrial. Time was when the recurring cycle of the year was of immense significance to him, for seed-time and harvest each came in connection with the course of the earth around the sun. And man still thinks that he must reckon results in terms of the accidental period involved in such a circuit. We demand to know how much a concern makes in a year. We must know, because the reciprocal rights of preferred and common stockholders may be altogether changed, depending on whether profit is to be attributed to the month of December or to the following January. We must know in order to satisfy the demands of the income-tax collector. And so accountants are asked to perform the hopeless task of taking this economic continuum, of chopping it up into arbitrary and meaningless lengths called a year and apportioning to each such year a proper part of the cost of a building which will last fifty years, of a machine which will be used for twenty years, of a blast furnace which will last ten, and of a stock of coal bought in December which will all be consumed before spring again appears.

Progress in the science seems slow. There stand out, however, two contributions of present-day accountants, one of practical, the other of theoretical importance. The first, made by America, consists of innumerable little devices for saving work in the handling of great masses of figures. Cumbersome and needless forms, surviving as tradition from the past centuries in England, and still more on the continent, have been discarded in America and new forms have been introduced by which results can be obtained with less labor. The other contribution has been the attempt to ascertain the exact cost of producing objects or parts of objects or for carrying on processes in continuous manufacture. Manufacturers now must know not only what it costs to make a machine but what is the cost of each separate wheel, pinion and screw in that machine; what is the cost not merely of a yard of cloth, but of carding, of roving, of spinning, of weaving, of dyeing, of finishing, of selling that yard of cloth. This has been the characteristic scientific contribution of recent years.

Progress is being made. What better evidence is there than that even lawyers and courts are coming to appreciate that there are such things as accounting principles? No longer is it possible for the supreme Court of the United States to declare that "the public...rarely ever take into account the depreciation of the building in which the business is carried on."[3] Never again, I believe, with the Supreme Court of California repeat the statement regarding depreciation:[4] "The theory is...that a sum should be set aside to be handed to the stockholders upon the sad occasion of the company's demise as an alleviating salve to their sorrow, but such a thing is all wrong. The theory cannot be tolerated for a moment that such a fund is to be stowed away to make glad the hearts of the stockholders."

I have tried to remove the stigma attached to accounting by showing that in its origin it is respectable, nay even academic; that despite its present disrepute it has from time to time attracted the attention of men of unquestioned intellectual attainment; that it justifies itself in that it has arisen to meet a social need. Its functions are to locate responsibility, to prevent fraud, to guide industry, to determine equities, to solve the all-essential conundrum of business: "What are my profits?"; to facilitate the government in its fiscal operations, to guide the business manager in the attempt to secure efficiency. Are not these efforts worthy of any man's attention? And so I close this paper with quotations from men whom all must respect: Scott, the romanticist, declared the profession of accounting "respectable"; Goethe, the universal genius, speaks of bookkeeping as "one of the fairest inventions of the human mind"; and Cayley, scientist beyond question, even more significantly declared "Bookkeeping is one of the two perfect sciences." With these I rest the defense of my houn' dog.

---

3 *Eyster* v. *Centennial Board of Finance*, 94 U.S. 503.
4 *San Diego Water Co.* v. *San Diego*, 118 Cal. 556.

Stanley E. Howard

PUBLIC RULES
FOR PRIVATE ACCOUNTING
IN FRANCE, 1673 AND 1807

Stanley Edwin Howard *was born in Quebec in 1888, received a bachelor's degree from Bates (1910) and a Ph.D. from Princeton (1916). He taught Latin and Greek in the public schools of Pennington, New Jersey (1910–12), economics and sociology at Mt. Holyoke College (1913–14), and economics at Dartmouth (1917–18) and at Princeton (1918–48).*
This essay reports on an important chapter in the legal regulation of accounting records, a kind of regulation that is virtually unknown in the United States, except in the public-utility field, but is familiar to many Europeans.

Accounting Rules
of the Ordinance of 1673

In March, 1673, Louis XIV promulgated his Ordinance *"Pour le Commerce,"* the framework upon which was completed the structure of Napoleon's *Code de Commerce* of 1807. Title III of the Ordinance bears the descriptive heading: "Concerning the Books and Registers of Tradesmen, Merchants, and Bankers." This Title III contains ten articles. Their provisions are so briefly stated that they can best be presented here in full translation.[1]

---

[1] This passage and others from French books and documents are in this paper presented in English translation by the present writer.

Translation in this instance has been from an official edition of the Ordinance published in 1709. The title page reads: *Ordonnance de Louis XIV. Roy de France et de Navarre. Pour le Commerce. Donnée à S. Germain en Laye au mois de Mars 1673. Nouvelle Edition. Augmentée des Edits, Déclarations, Arrests + Réglements concernans la même matière. A Paris, Chez les Associez choisis par ordre de Sa Majesté pour l'impression de ses nouvelles Ordonnances. M.DCC.IX.*

For a general statement of the relationship between the Ordinance of 1673 and the Code of 1807, see Levasseur, E., *Histoire du Commerce de la France,* pt. 1, p. 300.

Reprinted from *The Accounting Review* (June, 1932), pp. 91–102, by permission.

I. Tradesmen and merchants at wholesale and at retail shall have a book (*livre*), which shall contain all their business, their bills of exchange, their accounts receivable and payable (*dettes actives et passives*), and the monies employed for the expense of their [domestic] establishment [s].

II. Dealers in exchange, and bankers shall keep a journal (*livre journal*), in which shall be entered all the affairs negotiated by them, to have recourse to it in case of dispute.

III. The books of tradesmen and merchants both at wholesale and at retail shall be signed on the first page and on the last by one of the consuls in the cities where there is consular jurisdiction, and in the others by the mayor or one of the aldermen, without cost or fee, and the pages shall be initialed and numbered from first to last by the hand of those who shall have been commissioned by the consuls or mayor and aldermen, notation of which shall be made on the first page.

IV. The books of dealers in exchange and bankers shall be signed and initialed [or "flourished"] by one of the consuls on each page, and notation shall be made on the first [page] of the name of the dealer in exchange or bankers; of the kind of book [that it is], whether it is to serve as a journal or as the cash book; and whether it is the first, second, or [some] other [book], notation of which shall be made in the register at the office of the consular jurisdiction or at the city hall.

V. Journals shall be written up consecutively by order of date[s] without any blank space, [shall be] interrupted at each item and at the end; and nothing shall be written in the margin.

VI. All tradesmen, merchants, and dealers in exchange, and bankers shall be held within six months of the publication of our present Ordinance to make new journals and registers signed, numbered, and initialed [or "flourished"] as it is above ordered; into which they may, if it seems good to them, transfer the copies of their former books.

VII. All tradesmen and merchants both at wholesale and at retail shall file the letters which they shall receive, and shall put in a register the copy of those which they shall write.

VIII. All merchants shall be held to make in the same period of six months an inventory under their signature of all their effects, real and personal, and of their accounts receivable and payable (*dettes actives et passives*), [and] the same shall be remade and revised every two years.

IX. The presentation (*représentation*) or production (*communication*) of journals, registers, and inventories cannot be required or ordered in [a court of] justice, except [in cases involving] succession, *communauté*, and dissolution of a partnership (*société*) in case of failure.

X. In case, nevertheless, that a tradesman or merhcant wishes to serve himself by means of his journals and registers, or that the [other] party should offer to give credence to them, their presentation (*représentation*) may be ordered, to extract from them that which concerns the point in dispute.

Thus the Ordinance required these designated classes of business men to "keep books." Public regulation, "on paper" at least, extended to the making of rules as to the books to be kept, forms to be observed in the making of entries, authentication by a public official as a means to the prevention of the crudest kind of falsifications, the making of periodic inventories, and the preservation of correspondence. The rules for authentication of the books of exchange dealers and bankers appear a little more strict than those for the authentication of the books of tradesmen and merchants. An attempt was made in the last two articles of the title to define the status of accounting records in suits at law.

The Livre Journal and Other Books

It is quite clear from the wording of Article II that the *livre* required to be kept by exchange dealers and bankers was a journal in the modern sense, a *livre journal* or formal book of original entry. The wording of Article I, applicable to tradesmen and merchants, is ambiguous; for there the word *livre* appears unmodified by an adjective. Nevertheless, literature of the period puts it beyond doubt that the *livre* of Article I is also a *livre journal*. In the *Dictionnaire Universel de Commerce* published in 1723 we read:[2]

> It is the *Livre Journal* of which the Ordinance of the month of March 1673 intends to speak, when it is said in Title 3, Articles 1, 3, and 5 that tradesmen and merchants both at wholesale and at retail shall have a *livre* which shall contain all their business, their letters of exchange, their accounts receivable and payable, etc.

The *livre journal* and its use are described in the same article in the *Dictionnaire*.[3]

> The name of this book makes clear enough its use, that is to say that one writes in it day by day all the transactions as rapidly as they occur.
>
> Each item that one enters in this book should be composed of seven parts, which are the date, the debtor, the creditor, the sum, the quantity and kind [of goods], the *action* or how payable, and the price.
>
> Ordinarily this book is a register in *folio*, of five or six *mains* of paper, numbered, and ruled with one line on the side of the margin and with three [lines] on the other [side] for extending the sums.[4]

Although the debit and credit analysis of each transaction was customarily indicated in the *livre journal*, the modern spatial arrangement to clarify this

---

[2] The *Dictionnaire Universel de Commerce* was published in 1723 (Vols. I and II) and 1730 (Vol. III). It was known as Savary's *Dictionnaire*. The title page reads: *Dictionnaire Universel de Commerce, contenant tout ce qui concerne le commerce, ...* [etc., etc.] *Ouvrage posthume du Sieur Jacques Savary des Bruslons, Inspecteur général des Manufactures, pour le Roy, à la Doüane de Paris, Continué sur les Mémoires de l'auteur, et donné au Public par M. Philémon Louis Savary, Chanoine de l'Eglise Royale de S. Maur des Fossez, son Frère. A Paris, chez Jacques Estienne, rue Saint Jacques, à la Vertu. M.DCC.XXIII. Avec Privilège du Roy.*

The Jacques Savary here referred to and his brother Philémon Louis were the sons of Jacques Savary the elder (1622–1690) who is credited with the most active part in the Council of Reform which drafted the Ordinance of 1673.

The present quotation is from columns 570–571, Vol. II.

[3] *Ibid.*, Vol. II, col. 570.

[4] These lines were to provide three columns: one for *livres* ("pounds," not "books"); one for *sols* (there were twenty to the pound); and one for *deniers* (there were twelve to the *sol*). *Ibid.*, col. 568.

analysis was lacking. Below is a sample entry taken from the *Dictionnaire*.[5]

February 19, 1708

Wine debit by[6] Cash—£1600:—
bought of Duval for cash 16 *Muids*
of Burgundy wine at £100 . . . .£1600

It is interesting thus to note that public regulation of private commercial accounting should have selected this one book, a general journal, or primary book of formal entry as the point of attack. The Ordinance made no mention of a book (*livre memorial*) or books of informal original entry on the one hand, or of the ledger (*grand livre, livre extrait,* or *livre de raison*) on the other hand. Both of these groups of record books were, of course, well known and in use. Good accounting practice also recognized the desirability of introducing specialized journals and ledgers.

In 1675, Jacques Savary the elder, principal author of the Ordinance of 1673, published *Le Parfait Négociant*—"The Complete Tradesman"—a book of explanation of and commentaries upon the provisions of the Ordinance and of suggestions and instructions to business men and young men contemplating entrance into business. In it we find instructive information concerning the subject of this paper.[7] There is set forth *inter alia* a list of the books which a merchant of substance should keep. These are the items of the list.

1. A purchases book (*livre d'achat*).
2. An accounts payable subsidiary ledger (*livre extrait du livre d'achat*).
3. A sales journal, designated simply as the *livre journal,* but described by Savary as the book in which one enters everything sold on credit.
4. A subsidiary accounts receivable ledger (*livre extrait du journal*).
5. A journal (*livre de vente*) in which to handle exclusively cash sales of merchandise.
6. A journal (*livre d'argent payé*) in which to handle cash payments exclusively.
7. A cash book which appears to have been a ledger account for cash based upon items 5 and 6 above, called the *livre de caisse* and referred to as being in effect *l'extrait du livre de vente au comptant et du livre d'argent payé.*

---

[5] *Ibid.,* col. 571.

[6] *"Doit à."* The significance of *doit* is reserved for later discussion.

[7] From the date of its first publication until the Revolution, *Le Parfait Négociant* was in great demand not only in France but in England and on the continent generally. It was translated into English, Italian, Dutch, and German. The seventh edition appeared in 1713, brought out by the son Jacques (who died in 1716). The eighth edition was brought out in 1721 by the son Philémon Louis. The writer of this paper has used and translated from the French edition of 1777. The title page reads: *Le Parfait Négociant, ou Instruction Générale pour ce qui regarde le commerce des Marchandises de France + des Pays Entrangers. Par le Sieur Jacques Savary, Enrichi d'augmentations par le Sieur Jacques Savary des Bruslons; et après lui, par M. Philémont-Louis Savary, Chanoine de l'Eglise Royal de S. Maur, son Fils. Paris. Chez les Frères Estienne, Librairies rue Saint Jacques, à la Vertu. M. DCC. LXXVII Avec privilége du Roi,* See p. 275ff.: in particular, for the list of nine books, pp, 278–279.

8. A book called the *livre de numero,* a detailed running inventory of merchandise kept in ledger account form.

9. Savary suggested also the keeping of a *livre de teinture,* or book of dyeing; but this was because the merchant of substance of Savary's illustration was considered to be running a dyeing, as well as a mercantile, enterprise. It would be well to generalize from Savary's suggestion to the effect that it was considered to be good accounting to keep a special record of manufacturing of producing operations whenever there were any such.

Savary recommended also the keeping of a *carnet* or notebook of detailed informal memoranda, particularly those relating to instalment payments; but he did not list this book with the other nine items just presented.[8]

Such a set of books as that suggested by the first seven items of Savary's list, exceeded, of course, in its refinement of specialization and organization the conditions presupposed by the stipulations of the Ordinance—the keeping of a simple *livre journal.* This fact raises the question of the application of the rules of the Ordinance, such as those respecting authentication, to a system of specialized journals and specialized (perhaps subsidiary) ledgers. Savary indicated that the requirements of the law would be met by authentication of books of primary entry alone. The *livre d'achat* should be authenticated, but not the *livre extrait du livre d'achat;* the *livre journal,* but not the *livre extrait du journal.*[9]

Not only was it true that these first seven books recommended by Savary exceeded the minimum requirements of the Ordinance; they exceeded also the minimum requirements of many merchants, those engaged in what Savary called *commerce mediocre.* These business men, he said, might advantageously condense the seven books into three: (1) a *livre d'achat,* (2), a *livre journal de vente à crédit,* and (3) a *livre de caisse.* The first two, like items 1, 3, 5, and 6 of the list of seven books, were not to be kept in debit and credit *form.* The last, the *livre de caisse,* like items 2, 4, and 7, were to employ this technical form.

Savary advocated the use of the ledger; but in the event of its non-use he suggested an interesting method of journal procedure, as for example in the *livre d'achat.* An alphabetical list of persons dealt with would precede or accompany the journal record proper. As each entry was made in the journal there would be entered following the name of the person involved (as it appeared in the alphabetical "index") the journal page number. In addition, whenever the effect of a journal entry was to put in balance the personal account in question, there would be entered in the index the letter "S." This, meaning *solde* (balance), would facilitate periodic or occasional verification of the condition of any particular personal account.

For the conditions of petty trade, Savary thought it might sometimes be advantageous to combine the first two of the three books into one, using the

---

8 For another list of specialized records which were in use in this general period, see the *Dictionnaire de Commerce,* Vol. II, col. 570.

9 *Le Parfait Négociant,* pp. 278–279.

left-hand pages consecutively as a *livre d'achat* and the right-hand pages as a *livre journal de vente à crédit*. If this were done, the formal authentication of the two journal records must be independently performed for each series of pages.

The language of the Ordinance made no mention of double entry book-keeping; but Savary appears to have assumed its use or at least the desir-ability of its use. His instructions in *Le Parfait Négociant,* which was intended not only to inform men of the business classes as to the require-ments of the law but also to stimulate them in the matter of compliance with the law, include models of bookkeeping form and explanations as to pro-cedure. One of these discussions relates to the ledger and to the meanings of debit and credit entries. As it throws some light on the contemporary "philosophy" of debit and credit entries, a short digression from our main theme may be justified. Savary said:[10]

> The ledger (*livre extrait ou de raison*) is kept in debit and credit; that is to say, that the merchandise which one shall have sold should be written on the debit side, where one enters "So-and-so should give" (*un tel doit donner*); and on the other side, opposite, which is the credit [side], where one enters "The said So-and-so [should] have (*avoir*)," one writes the money which one receives from his debtor.
>
> [As to] the merchandise which one purchases from anyone, one must give credit to him [i.e., the seller] on the side where one enters "The said gentleman [should] have (*avoir ledit sieur*)" and when one pays for that which one has bought, it is necessary to write it on the debit side, where it is ⌊written⌋ "He should give (*doit donner*)."

Whatever lack of clarity inheres in these statements is in part, if not wholly, removed by Savary's illustrative examples or *formules*. In one of these, exhibiting the account of a fictitious Mr. Pierre Arnaut, we find as the heading of the left-hand page:

> Mr. Pierre Arnaut should give (*doit donner*).

And as the heading of the right-hand page:

> The said gentleman [should] have (*avoir*).

Apparently there is an ellipsis in the French expression *"doit et avoir."* One finds confirmation of this in Savary's *formule* for the *livre de caisse*.[11] There the headings appear in full. Over the debit page we read:

> Cash should give (*Caisse doit donner*).

and over the credit page:

> Cash should have (*Caisse doit avoir*).

It is interesting to note that the French expression for "debit and credit" arbitrarily employs in the one case the less significant, finite part (*doit*) of

---

10 *Ibid.,* p. 297.
11 *Ibid.,* p. 296.

the full verbal expression which is implied; while in the other case the infinitive form (*avoir*) alone appears.[12]

Accounting Rules
of the Commercial Code of 1807

Out of the disorders and reconstructive measures of the Revolution there finally came the five Napoleonic *Codes*.[13] In Title II of Book I of the *Code de Commerce,* we find rules for the keeping and use of business records which strongly resemble those of the Ordinance of 1673. Of the ten articles under the caption *Des Livres du Commerce,* four deal with bookkeeping rules, including the requirements of authentication of certain books; the remaining six articles are concerned with the use of the books in the event of litigation.

The first four articles, rendered into English, read thus:

8. Every business man (*commerçant*) is required to have a journal which presents day by day his accounts receivable and payable, the operations of

---

12 In connection with this topic, see Littleton, A. C., *Early Transaction Analysis,* THE ACCOUNTING REVIEW, Vol. VI, no. 3 (Sept. 1931), pp. 179–183, especially the note on p. 180.

13 These were the *Code Civil,* the *Code de Procédure Civile,* the *Code de Commerce,* the *Code d'Instruction Criminelle,* and the *Code Pénal.* The present writer has used in referring to codes other than the *Code de Commerce* an early French edition entitled *Les Cinqs Codes Français. Edition nouvelle, conforme au Bulletin des Lois; Augmentée de la Charte, constitutionelle, de la Loi sur l'abolition du Divorce, et terminée par une Table des Chapitres.* Paris. 1816.

In this edition the 648 articles of the *Code de Commerce* are numbered consecutively and cumulatively throughout the four "Books." Book I has the descriptive heading "Concerning Commerce in General." Title II of this book bears the caption *"Des Livres du Commerce,"* which may be rendered "Concerning the Books of Commerce," or, more freely, "Concerning Business Records." The ten articles of this title are, in the numbering system used both for this Book and for the whole Code in the edition above described, those numbered 8 to 17 inclusive.

Because of better typography it is more convenient to use the text of the *Code de Commerce* as it appeared first in the *Bulletin des Lois* under a series of dates from Sept. 10 to Sept. 25, 1807. *Bulletin des Lois,* No. 164 (in that volume of the 4th series of *Bulletins* covering the period August, 1807-June, 1808) pp. 161–284. The text of the *Code de Commerce* is published as [Law] No. 2804; that of the imperial decree declaring the *Code* to be effective Jan. 1, 1808 is published as [Law] No. 2805. Title II of Book I is found on pp. 163–164. The numbering of articles in this edition is consecutive and cumulative only within each Book.

There are English translations of the *Code de Commerce.* Two which have been used by the present writer in seeking to secure an insight into the provisions of this body of law are: (1) Mayer, Sylvain. *The French Code of Commerce, as revised to the end of 1886; and an Appendix containing later statutes in connection therewith. Rendered into English, with explanatory notes and copious index.* London. Butterworth's, 1887. (2) Goirand, Léopold. *The French Code of Commerce and Most Usual Commercial Laws, with a theoretical and practical commentary, and a compendium of the judicial organisation and of the course of procedure before the tribunals of commerce, together with the text of the law: the most recent decisions of the courts, and a glossary of French judicial terms.* London. Stevens and Sons, 1880. The text of the Code is found on pp. 561–700.

his business, his transfers, acceptances and endorsements of commercial paper, and in general everything which he receives and pays, under whatever head it may be; and which makes known month by month the sums employed for the expense of his [domestic] establishment: all [of which is required] independently of the other books used in business, but which are not indispensable.

He is required to file the letters which he receives, and to copy in a register those which he sends.

9. He is required to make every year under private signature an inventory of his property, real and personal, and of his accounts receivable and payable, and to copy it year by year in a special register devoted to this [use].

10. The journal and the book of inventories shall be initialed.

The book of copies of letters shall not be subjected to this formality.

All [of them] shall be kept by order of dates, without blank spaces, gaps, or runnings over into the margin.

11. The books the keeping of which is ordered by articles 8 and 9 above shall be numbered, initialed [or "flourished"] and authenticated (visés) either by one of the judges of the courts of commerce, or by the mayor or an assistant [of the mayor] in ordinary form and without cost. Business men shall be required to preserve these books for ten years.

Thus, in the Code of 1807, the journal continued to receive the first and principal emphasis. In must be complete in its record of business transactions; the entries must be made chronologically and with some formality; the book must be duly authenticated, and it must be preserved for a period of ten years.

The former requirement of a biennial inventory of all assets and liabilities became, under the Code, an annual requirement. The inventory, when taken, must be copied into a book, and the book must be preserved for ten years. This book of inventories must be authenticated.

As hitherto, business letters received must be filed. Copies of outgoing letters must be copied in a register or letter-book, which need not be authenticated. The language of Article 11 would seem to require the preservation of the letter-book for a period of ten years; but that of Article 10, distinguishing between the journal and the book of inventories on the one hand and the letter-book on the other, casts some doubt upon the intention of the drafters of the Code in the matter of the preservation of correspondence.

The provisions of these four articles and of the others in Title II were applicable to *commerçants* (or in the contemporary spelling, *commerçans*), and no use was made in this part of the Code of the words *négociants* (tradesmen), *marchands* (merchants), *agents de change* (dealers in exchange), and *agents de banque* (bankers), as in the old Ordinance. In Title V of Book I, however, there are special provisions, not simply as to bookkeeping, applicable to *agents de change* (translated by Mayer as "stockbrokers"), and *courtiers* (translated by Mayer as "brokers"). By reason of this segregation for special treatment in the Code, and by reason of the special rules laid down in the Code, it seems quite clear that the businesses of stockbrokers, mercantile brokers, insurance brokers, interpreting and ship brokers, and land and water carriage brokers were looked upon as in some way or ways peculiarly "affected with a public interest." As to the rules for bookkeeping in such enterprises, they were in principle similar to those for *commerçants;* in practice somewhat more minutely prescriptive of detail. Article 84 (in Section II of Title V) reads:[14]

> Stockbrokers and brokers are bound to keep a book in the manner described in Article 11. They are bound to enter in this book, every day, and in order of date, without erasures, interlineations, or transpositions, and without abbreviations or figures, all the conditions of the sales, purchases, insurances, negotiations, and in general of all business carried out by them.

But who are, or were, the *commerçants* to whom the requirements of Title II of Book I of the Code of 1807 were applicable? "Those are *commerçans*," said the Code, who habitually perform *"actes de commerce."*[15] Then in that part of the Code which deals with the jurisdiction of the courts or tribunals of commerce, *actes de commerce* are itemized.[16]

> Every purchase of produce or goods, either raw or manufactured for resale, or simply to let out on hire; any manufacturing trade, business on commission, or carriage by land or water; any undertaking to supply goods; agencies, business offices, establishments for sales by auction, and places of public amusement; any exchange, banking or commission transaction; all transactions with or concerning public banks, all contracts between merchants and bankers; and transactions in relation to bills of exchange or remittances of money from place to place between all persons.
>
> Any undertaking to build, and all purchases, sales, and resales of vessels for interior and exterior navigation, maritime transport of all kinds; any sale or purchase of rigging, apparel, or stores for vessels; the chartering of vessels, and bottomry and respondentia bonds; all insurance and other contracts concerning maritime commerce; all agreements and arrangements for the pay of the crew; any engagement of seamen for the merchant service.

However unsatisfactory these lists of *actes de commerce* may be for purposes other than the determination of questions of jurisdiction in law suits, it seems quite clear that the substitution of the word *commerçant* for the four more specific terms of the Ordinance of 1673 was not intended to restrict more narrowly the application of the accounting requirements of the law. Rather, we may conclude, the field of application was intended to be enlarged; and the rules laid down for stockbrokers and brokers were intended to be superimposed upon, rather than substituted for, the general rules for all *commerçants* or "business men."

---

14 As translated by Mayer, *op. cit.,* p. 18.

15 Book I, Title I, Art. 1.

16 Book IV, Title II, Arts. 18 and 19 (of the title) or 632 and 633 (in the cumulative numbering of the whole Code). The passages quoted in the text are from Mayer's translation, *op. cit.,* pp. 175–176.

The Problem of Enforcement

Direct public control of accounting methods in private business enterprises seems so radical a policy that the question arises as to how and to what extent the bookkeeping rules of the Ordinance and of the Code were obeyed or enforced. One cannot read Savary's *Le Parfait Négociant* without feeling that this principal author of the Ordinance of 1673 appreciated both the public and private advantages which might be derived from the use of systematic bookkeeping methods by merchants and other business men, and the difficulty which would probably be encountered in the public enforcement of such use. Savary lost no opportunity to urge upon business men and upon young men contemplating a business career the importance of good bookkeeping. In his *formules* of *commandite* partnership articles, of which there appear three in *Le Parfait Négociant,* he inserted as an article of agreement among or between the partners a stipulation that there should be kept good and faithful books of account in accordance with the requirements of the Ordinance.[17] Possibly it was his view that the accounting requirements set forth in the Ordinance were in advance of the times and of current business practice; that there was need of commercial education as well as of commercial legislation.[18]

The Ordinance of 1673 and the Code of 1807 were weak in that they established no administrative machinery or procedure for the constructive enforcement of the prescribed accounting rules; which means that for the most part the exercise of public authority, if made effective at all, must take place after the fact of violation rather than as a means of preventing the violation of the law. There were, at least "on paper," penalties for non-observance of the law's requirements; but they were not set forth in the title on bookkeeping. If a merchant became bankrupt, then there was brought

---

[17] For example, in model articles between de la Mare, a silk manufacturer of Lyon, the Langlois Brothers, bankers of Lyon, and Fournier, a Paris merchant, it was set forth that: "The said de la Mare shall be bound to keep good and faithful books, as well as journals for giving the silks to the dyers...sales books and ledgers, as well as others which are considered to be necessary to be kept in the accustomed manner in the city of Lyon; the which sales journal shall be initialed by messieurs the judges and conservators of the city of Lyon, according to the Ordinance." *Le Parfait Négociant,* p. 392. Fournier also, who was the sales representative in Paris, was bound to keep proper accounts. Rules were set forth in the articles of agreement covering the taking of periodic inventories. For other articles in similar hypothetical agreements, see *Le Parfait Négociant,* pp. 401 and 405. The principal accounting discussions in *Le Parfait Négociant* are found in Part I, Book IV, Chs. IV, V, IX, and X.

[18] This notion seems to have been held by Bédarride, the commentator of the Napoleonic commercial code, nearly two hundred years later. "The keeping of business records is an art which is not given to everybody to understand and to practice. Bookkeeping by double entry...is very accurate and very exact, [it] requires special understanding, which one does not find among many honest tradesmen." Bédarride, J., *Droit Commercial. Commentaire du Code de Commerce. Titre I. Des Commercants. Titre II. Des Livres de Commerce.* (Both titles are discussed in one volume.) Paris. 2nd ed., 1879, p. 341.

in question the showing of the condition of his business and its history as represented on his bookkeeping records. According to the Ordinance, if it could be established that he had failed to keep books properly authenticated and as otherwise required by the articles of the Ordinance, he would be declared not merely a bankrupt, but a fraudulent bankrupt and subject to the penalty of death.[19] That this was, in the language of the commentator Bédarride, a case of fulfilling "too energetically" the obligation which the framers of the Ordinance apparently felt of "attaching a penal sanction to the violation of the law" would hardly be denied by most modern students.[20] If there were no other factors to consider, there would be this: that the very severity of the prescribed penalty would deter from law enforcement. Capital punishment for violation of bookkeeping regulations is worse than an absurdity. It was a step in the right direction when in the Napoleonic codes the severity of the law was somewhat diminished. In the *Code de Commerce* it was provided[21] that a business man who failed was to be adjudged a fraudulent bankrupt if he concealed his books; that he might be prosecuted as a fraudulent bankrupt, if he had not kept books or if his books did not show his correct asset and liability position.[22] There was no guilt of fraud attached to the non-observance of those provisions of the Code which required public authentication of record books. In the *Code Pénal* the rigor of the law was softened. Fraudulent bankrupts were declared to be punishable by a period of forced labor.[23]

Since, then, no administrative machinery of enforcement was provided by the Ordinance or by the Code, and since the criminal penalties, at least those provided by the Ordinance, were not such as to give promise of efficacy, it is not surprising that, to employ the somewhat formal French expression, the law fell into desuetude, or in modern English figure of speech became a dead letter. There is some testimony, also, to the effect that a stamp tax placed upon books of account furnished an incentive to the evasion of the law's requirements.[24]

The commentator Jousse is authority for the statement that the formalities

---

19 Ordinance of 1673, Title XI, Arts. XI, XII.

20 Bédarride, *op. cit.*, p. 332.

21 Book III, Title IV, ch. II, art. 593, sub-section 7.

22 In Art. 594.

23 *Code Pénal, Book* III, Title II, ch. II, sec. II, sub-section I, Art. 402.

24 An *arrêt du conseil* of April 3, 1675, ordered the writing of the journal on stamped paper subject to a penalty of 1000 *livres* and "nullity" of the journal. There is testimony to the effect that this requirement was honored more in the breach than in the observance. Bédarride, *op. cit.*, p. 320, citing as authority Jousse (1704–1781) whose commentary on the Ordinance of 1673 appeared in 1757.

In the Revolutionary period, the law of 13 *brumaire* of the year VII imposed a stamp tax on books of account and forbade the public authentication of unstamped paper. Letter-books were exempted from this burden, but the other books were not. At the time of the revision of the commercial law an attempt was made, but unsuccessfully, to have the tax removed. Each year the enforcement of Articles 10 and 11 of the Code became more difficult. Tax receipts from this item fell to ridiculously small sums, and finally the tax was repealed by Article 4 of the Law of July 20, 1837. Bédarride, *op. cit.*, p. 351. See also Lacour, Léon, and Bouteron, Jacques, *Précis de Droit Commercial*. Paris. 2nd ed., 1921, Vol. I, p. 88.

of authentication were hardly ever observed in practice in the era of the Ordinance; that there was official toleration of this non-observance of the law; that unauthenticated books otherwise in good order were allowed to be used in court as evidence by parties of good personal and business reputation.[25]

In the face of this ignoring of the law the commission which drafted the Code of 1807 insisted on renewing the old requirements. They said:[26]

> The former laws prescribed imperiously the authentication of business records. It should not be concluded from their failure of exception that this [authentication] was not necessary. The abuses which have been tolerated do not justify the abuses; they add to the necessity of checking them.
>
> The cause which has, perhaps, rendered these abuses too common and the failure of execution of the former laws almost general is that, in prescribing these obligations, they did not impose any penalty upon those who have infringed them. We have felt how necessary this guarantee [of authenticity] is, and we have not only prescribed the inadmissibility of unauthenticated books, but we have declared to those who would neglect to conform to the wish of the law that, in the event of failure, this violation would be a presumption of fraud which would authorize a criminal suit against them.[27]

The Council of State likewise looked upon the formalities of authentication as "indispensable for putting to an end the disorders which have been introduced into trade."[28] In the face of a record of ineffectiveness of the prescribed formalities the government persisted in the continuation of the policy of requiring them. It was the testimony of Bédarride in the latter part of the nineteenth century that properly authenticated books were exceptional.[29]

The Use of Private
Accounting Records in Litigation

Articles IX and X of Title III of the Ordinance of 1673 dealt with the status and use in court of the accounting records of tradesmen, merchants, dealers in exchange, and bankers. Perhaps the provisions of these articles may properly be looked upon as an indirect means for the enforcement of the law; for the interests of litigating parties might be affected by the recognition or non-recognition of the showing of their accounting records. Success or failure of a party to a law suit might hinge upon the right of presenting his bookkeeping record in evidence, or of demanding of his opponent the production of *his* books, or upon the right of the court to insist upon the production of books by either party or by both parties. Whether

---

[25] Bédarride, *op. cit.*, p. 347. Bédarride also quotes authority to the effect that the consuls at Paris accepted evidence in the form of unauthenticated books.

[26] *Ibid.*, p. 348.

[27] It is difficult to understand the basis for the statement that no penalty had been prescribed for violation of the Ordinance.

[28] Bédarride, *op. cit.*, p. 350.

[29] *Ibid.*, pp. 350–351. See also Lacour and Bouteron, *op cit.*, Vol. I, p. 88.

or not the insertion of these two articles was motivated by the desire to facilitate the enforcement of the bookkeeping rules of the Ordinance we do not know. Nevertheless, it is quite clear that there would arise, sooner or later, such questions as have been presented above. It is by no means surprising that the framers of the Ordinance made an attempt to deal with them.

To repeat, these articles of the old Ordinance read:

IX. The presentation (*représentation*) or production (*communication*) of journals, registers and inventories cannot be required or ordered in [a court of] justice, except [in cases involving] succession, *communauté*, and dissolution of a partnership (*société*) in case of failure.

X. In case, nevertheless, that a tradesman or merchant wishes to serve himself by means of his journals and registers, or that the [other] party should offer to give credence to them, their presentation (*représentation*) may be ordered to extract from them that which concerns the point in dispute.

To be compared or contrasted with these are Articles 12–17 inclusive of the Code of 1807.

12. Business records, regularly kept, can be admitted by the judge to offer proof between business men in business matters.

13. Books which persons engaging in business are required to keep, and for which they shall not have observed the formalities above prescribed, may not be presented (*représentés*) and may not offer proof in [a court of] justice to the advantage of those who shall have kept them; without prejudice in respect of that which shall be ordered in the book [i.e., of the Code] "Concerning Failures and Bankruptcies."

14. The production (*communication*) of books and inventories in [a court of] justice cannot be ordered except in cases of succession, *communauté*, dissolution of a [business] company (*société*), and in case of failure.

15. In the course of a dispute the presentation (*représentation*) of the books can be ordered by the judge by virtue of his office for the purpose of extracting from them that which concerns the point at issue.

16. In the event that the books whose presentation (*représentation*) is offered, requested or ordered should be in places remote from the court having jurisdiction over the case, the judges can address an order of inquiry to the court of commerce of the place, or can delegate a justice of the peace to acquaint himself with the matter, prepare a report of the content [i.e., of the record], and transmit it to the court having jurisdiction over the case.

17. If the party to whose books it is proposed to give credence refuses to present (*représenter*) them, the judge can accept the sworn statement of the other party.

The language of both the Ordinance and the Code makes it quite clear that French law has hesitated to allow a party in litigation to require his opponent to produce his private business records. The statements of Article IX of Title III of the Ordinance and of Article 14 of the Code are negative statements. "This thing cannot be done, except...etc." The reason is not far to seek. It is found in the principle of privacy and in the practical danger that private records produced in court many inadvertently or otherwise be examined by the requiring party for business secrets not related to the point immediately at issue. The sanctity of business secrets was recognized and to some extent protected.[30] The exceptions to these prohibitory provisions of both the Ordinance and the Code are substantially the same: cases involving succession, *communauté* (or property held in common by parties to the marriage contract), dissolution of a partnership or other business company, and business failure.[31] In all of these exceptional cases the relations between the parties concerned are so close and are so clearly dependent upon business records for fair and successful determination as to warrant less respect for the principle or privilege of privacy.

In one matter at least Article IX of Title III of the Ordinance and Article 14 of the Code are different. In the former both the *représentation* and the *communication* of business records are declared not to be subject to the demand or request of an opposing party; in the latter we find only the word *communication*. The difference of wording is an important one.

> That which distinguishes the *communication* of books from their *représentation* is that, in the first case, the business man divests himself of his books in favor of the interested parties, [who arc] free after that to examine them and look them over in all their parts. In the second case, on the contrary, the business man is authorized not to divest himself of them, not to let them out of his sight; he is not bound to present (*représenter*) them except [in the sense that] in his presence and with his concurrence there may be extracted that which concerns the point in dispute.[32]

Thus, except in the specific cases noted, the Ordinance dealt very strictly with litigants who attempted to compel the production of the bookkeeping records of their opponents. This strictness was such as to deny the right to compel either *communication* or *représentation*.

In the Code, on the other hand, Article 14 denied to each party to a dispute only the right to compel *communication* of his opponent's book. *Représentation* was dealt with in Articles 15, 16 and 17. In Article 15 we find one of the most significant provisions of the new law, that which gave to a judge the right *même d'office* (officially, *ex-officio*, by virtue of his office) to order the *représentation* of the books of either or both of the parties.[33] In the most obvious sense this provision was an innovation. In

---

[30] On this point see Bédarride, *op. cit.*, pp. 415–421.

[31] The forms of *société commerciale* recognized in the Ordinance were partnerships; in the Code, both partnerships and corporations (*société anonymes*). The term "business company" would perhaps be a good rendering of the word *société* as used in the accounting provisions of both the Ordinance and the Code.

[32] Bédarride, *op. cit.*, pp. 483–484.

[33] Goirand's rendering of Article 15 is very free, the freedom of translation apparently being designed to emphasize the point of distinction between *communication* and *représentation*. "In the course of an action the production of one or more entries upon a particular point may be ordered by the judge, even of his own accord, to the end that extracts may be taken of such entries as relate to the question in dispute." Goirand, *op. cit.*, p. 563.

At another place (pp. 54–55) the same writer says that when there is *représentation* the owner of the books produces them in a certain place "where no person has access to them but the Court." On the other hand, "*communication* is the handing over of the books with liberty to examine all parts thereof."

another sense it was not an innovation, for it merely gave expression in the
form of a written code to a practice which had already been approved by the
highest court in France, the *Cour de Cassation*.[34]

Under the Ordinance, then, either party to an action might wish his
opponent's books produced in court or an extract made from them to serve
as evidence. He could not demand either of these procedures. Under the
Code, on the other hand, the judge might, even if both parties were unwilling,
order the *représentation,* but not the *communication,* of the books of either
party or of both parties.

Article 16 of the Code covers a practical matter of procedure in the
représentation of books which are remote from the court having jurisdiction in a particular case. The practical advantage of a procedure of inspection of such books by a deputy and report by him in writing requires no
discussion. That which is of particular interest is the history of the device.
The provision of the Code found its precedent in the terms of an old
ordinance of February 18, 1578, applicable to the fairs at Lyon.

> Merchants may not be divested of their books and papers of account, nor
> bound to exhibit them and present (*représenter*) them in [a court of]
> justice, nor carry them outside their establishments for an extract to be
> made from them; and the extracts, and the comparison [i.e., of records],
> if there is need of such, shall not be made except from the parts in which
> the said books shall make mention of the things which are found to be in
> litigation and in controversy, and in their said establishments.[35]

Bédarride says of this old ordinance that, while it applied originally to the
fairs at Lyon, its rules became generally applied after the promulgation of

---

34 The leading case appears to be that involving a bankrupt, Lerat, and his creditors,
among the latter two brothers named Manuel, who were in partnership. When Lerat filed
his schedule in bankruptcy he showed a liability to the Manuel brothers amounting to
some 7000 *livres*. The Manuel brothers, on the other hand, put in a claim for a sum very
much larger than this, offering to verify the claim, if necessary, by their book record.
The other creditors of Lerat, impressed by the discrepancy between the acknowledged
liability and the asserted claim, asked the Manuel brothers to make a *représentation of*
their books. The latter declined, said that they had never kept books showing dealings
with Lerat, and offered rather to substantiate their claims on Lerat by a written
acknowledgment of Lerat for a sum smaller than the amount of their first claim but
larger than the amount of liability admitted by Lerat.

This did not satisfy the other creditors of Lerat, and they pressed proceedings for the
représentation of the Manuel brothers' books. This *représentation* was ordered by the
Court of Commerce of Dijon, from which appeals were taken to the Court of Appeal
at Dijon, and ultimately to the Court of Cassation. The last named body handed down
a decision on 12 *floreal* of the year XII, in which the right of the lower court to demand
the *représentation* of the books of the Manuel brothers was upheld.

Note that the books whose *représentation* was involved were not those of the bankrupt
Lerat, but those of a creditor concern. The Court of Cassation, in formulating its
decision, relied to some extent upon a *"déclaration"* of Sept. 13, 1739 which required
creditors of a bankrupt to submit documentary proof of the validity of their claims.
This case is discussed rather fully by Bédarride, *op. cit.,* pp. 456–463.

35 Bédarride, *op. cit.,* pp. 489–490. Regarding this point see also Brésard, Marc, *Les
Foires de Lyon aux XVe et XVIe Siècles.* Paris, 1914. pp. 107–109.

the Ordinance of 1673, so that they became "the common law of all France."[36]

Article X of Title III of the Ordinance of 1673 contained a provision somewhat peculiar in its wording and significance. The case referred to is that of two contending traders of whom the one is willing to submit his books, or rather the *représentation* of his books, to the court, while the other offers to give credence to what this *représentation* reveals concerning the point at issue. Under such circumstances, said the article of the Ordinance, the *représentation* can be "ordered" to extract that which concerns the matter in dispute. From the wording of this article, its significance would not at first thought seem to be very great; but simply that litigants might by agreement and voluntarily use their books of account as evidence. There may have been an added meaning, less clearly apparent but more important. Bédarride states that the rules of the Ordinance were modified by those of the Code by "the suppression of the condition imposed on the [second or opposing] party, namely the offer to give credence to [the showing of] the books whose *représentation* he asks."[37] That is to say: if X and Y are in litigation, and X willingly makes a *représentation* of his books at Y's request, then (under the old Ordinance) Y is bound without further question to accept as conclusive the showing on X's records. This, thought Bédarride, was an unfortunate stipulation, and we may well agree with him. For the *représentation* of the bookkeeping entries, while important, may in a particular instance be less conclusive than evidence of some other sort or from some other source.[38]

Article 12 of the Code seems to be in effect a substitute for Article X of Title III of the Ordinance. If there was in the Ordinance a rule of acceptance of the bookkeeping evidence offered, it is clear that it formed no part of the provisions of the Code.

Article 13 purported to restrict the application of Article 12 to those books which have been properly authenticated. We have already noted that the rules of authentication fell into desuetude.

The final article (17) of Title II of Book I of the Code contrasts strongly with Article X of Title III of the old Ordinance. Here the point of view is shifted. X and Y, let us say, are in litigation. The former offers to give credence to Y's bookkeeping record, but Y refuses its *représentation*. The judge can accept the sworn statement of X as to the fact in dispute. The reasonableness of such a rule is so obvious as not to require critical comment. There is some interest, however, attaching to the fact that, even before the Ordinance was superseded by the Code, the rule expressed in Article 17 was accepted by legal authorities as well founded. Bornier, commenting on Article X of Title III of the Ordinance, said that if one of whom payment of an

[36] Bédarride, *op. cit.*, p. 490.
[37] *Ibid.*, p. 453.
[38] *Ibid.*, pp. 453–454. See also Goirand, *op. cit.*, pp. 53–54.

alleged debt is demanded should ask the person making the demand to make *représentation* of his books; and if the latter should refuse the *représentation,* then "the judge *should* accept the oath of the defendant."[39] Jousse also used language almost identical with that of Article 17 of the Code: "If the party to whose books it is proposed to give credence refuses to present (*représenter*) them, the judge *should* accept the sworn statement of the other party."[40] The Code said simply: "The judge *can* accept the sworn statement of the other party."

---

[39] Quoted by Bédarride, *op. cit.,* p. 497. Philippe Bornier, jurisconsult, (1634–1711) wrote (*inter alia*) "*Conférence des Nouvelles Ordonnances de Louis XIV avec celles de ses Prédécesseurs.*" Paris. 1678.

[40] *Ibid.*

A. C. Littleton

OLD AND NEW IN MANAGEMENT
AND ACCOUNTING

A. C. Littleton *was born in 1886, and received his bachelor's degree from Illinois (1912), as well as his Ph.D. (1931). He is also a C.P.A. in Illinois. After a stint with Deloitte, Plender & Griffiths (1912–1915), he returned to the University of Illinois to teach and to serve as administrator, where he remained until his retirement. After his retirement at Illinois, he joined the faculty of Arizona State College at Tempe. He was a member of the committee on accounting procedure of the American Institute of C.P.A., and served as editor of* The Accounting Review *from 1943–47.*

Professor Littleton published his Accounting Evolution to 1900 *in 1933. A few years later he collaborated with William A. Paton to produce* Introduction to Corporate Accounting Standards, *which was published in 1940 by the American Accounting Association. In 1953, the Association also published his* Structure of Accounting Theory.

Like Hatfield, Littleton has had a lifelong interest in the history of accounting, especially of the ideas and concepts employed in accounting. The brief essay reprinted here is a mature piece, bridging several centuries of development to give us a renewed sense of the essential unity of accounting and its continual development.

As an approach to comparing the old and the new, we might first take note of some familiar modern ideas about good management and adequate accounting.

In order to operate an enterprise well, management will need to plan future operations and maintain close control over materials and activities. One of the most useful techniques of planning is forward budgeting. Its figures will be based on known intentions decided by high-level authority and on knowledge of the results of prior activities that grew out of prior planning. This necessary knowledge derives from detailed records (i.e. accounting) periodically compacted into summary reports.

Reprinted from *The Accounting Review* (April, 1954), pp. 196–200, by permission.

Of the many techniques of managerial control, several can perhaps be called essential. (1) Set up an operating organization and carefully provide for subdivided duties. It may be helpful if production standards are established as a guide to workers and supervisors. (2) Provide tarined personnel, plus suitable supervision, frequent inspection, etc. (3) Tie record-keeping into the operating activities. This will call for establishing a system of internal check and a systematic testing of the interlocking records. (4) Supplies will need to be kept under lock and key when not under the eye of responsible employees. (5) Separation will be maintained between the activities of recording the collection and disbursement of cash on the one hand and those of reporting on income producing activities and the authorization of payments. (6) Periodical inventories will be taken that can be traced back into cash transactions. (7) Set up internal audit procedures for employees and provide for reaudit of the results by dependable and skilled representatives of management.

This outline obviously is not a complete indication of the relation between modern management and modern accounting. No mention is made above of independent professional accountants. This was premeditated because the period selected to reveal the old ideas is clearly different from the present in this respect. Another notable difference lies in the fact that the factory system and mass production had not yet appeared. Important as the differences are, they nevertheless are overshadowed by many similarities in spite of the intervening four centuries. If the above outline of management planning and control is reasonably indicative of present practice, we are in a position to look for some details about these similarities.

You may be surprised to find the essence of so many modern practices reflected in the activities of so long ago. The elapsed four hundred years would take our thought back to a period centering about 1553. The time would be close to the voyages of Columbus.

The notes which follow about early practices trace back to a bibliography consisting in large part of household account books and estate management instructions preserved from use in sixteenth century England. The records, with some overlapping and empty periods, extend from 1462 to 1640. These old records and much other material were examined more than thirty years ago by Paul V. B. Jones, now professor emeritus of history at the University of Illinois. His analysis was published in 1917 by the University under the title, The Household of a Tudor Nobleman.[1]

I have selected some items from this fascinating account in order to give point to the thought that many of the nobility of that time were good businessmen although they did not operate commercial enterprises. They were forced by circumstances to become good administrators. In maintaining their way of life, they had to make a business out of managing productively

---

[1] Studies in the Social Sciences Vol. VI, No. 4.

their large land holdings and controlling effectively the activities of possibly two hundred employees. Since most nobles of that time had important responsibilities associated with the activities of King and Court, they had to build an organization at home that could operate dependably in their absence. To establish and control an active organization even through trusted officers, calls for an amount of good managerial judgment that is not often revealed to us in our usual sources of knowledge of the people of this era— the books we read, the plays we see.

Note first the chief officers of a typical sixteenth century landed estate. Below the Earl or Duke who owned the estate under the King, were the following. The Receiver-General (a man we probably would call treasurer) collected the land rents, paid cash to other household officers on the Duke's warrant, and kept a record of his receipts and payments. Note that his payments were covered by written authorization and that his collections were made verifiable by the work and records of another officer, the Surveyor. The latter had the duties of judging the character and usefulness of all sections of the nobleman's land, of reporting to the Duke on current and prospective employment of the lands, and of preparing a book of rentals and others incomes.

Just below these officers were Steward, Comptroller, Auditor. The Steward paid the wages and fees as directed, using funds supplied by the Receiver-General. The Comptroller might today be called inspector or perhaps supervisor of internal control. As to the Auditor, he was described in an old record in these words: "He is to bee judge betwixte the lords and his accomptants, and to deale trulie for and between all parties, and upon the determination of his audite, to presente to his lorde by booke or breviate, all his receipts, expenses, imprests, whatsoever, with the remaines of money, if any be. . . ." (from p. 143 regarding accounts audited by Thomas Clay in 1612). More about the auditor later.

These officers were not clerks but executives with clerks to assist them. Frequently they were knights and some were Earls' sons who were in training for managerial responsibilities on their home estate. Many employees with smaller responsibilities, as we shall see, also had clerical assistants. The officers were expected to guard against extravagance and to exercise careful control over supplies. These duties involved a daily tour of inspection into each department—at unannounced hours, let it be noted—and they were to report to the Duke both "misdemeanors" and "zealous painstaking."

Several modern business practices are clearly foreshadowed in this type of organization. There was a carefully selected and experienced group of executives working under a single leader, who was himself active in the affairs at hand. Plainly visible is a logical separation of the duty and the responsibilities of each executive; yet the duties of all dovetail and the responsibilities of all are interrelated. Persons charged with responsibilities kept detailed records of pertinent facts and actions. The records were audited by a third party who, even four hundred years ago, stood without bias between two parties at interest "to deal trulie for and between all parties."

To me the fascinating part of history is found in such spots as these which show us that some of the present is not so new after all; and in those parts which help us to see that the old is not merely reproduced generation after generation. Thus we come to realize that the practices of today are not good or bad because they are old. Then as now, the actions taken in business and accounting were taken because they were judged in their particular setting to be useful and adequate. If judged no longer useful they will be dropped; if no longer adequate, they must be modified. We may well be proud of the present, provided we can know that we are improving when change is made.

We should now look at the lower echelons of the old manor house organization. Most of the names of the work places are self-explanatory and easily converted into the title of the respective workers. Stable, woodyard, granery, butchery, these terms tell of a rural setting, of fields and animals and forest. Here are some others. Armory, wardrobe, larder, bakehouse, brewhouse, kitchen—these are divisions within the manor house itself.

More puzzling terms are those of "buttery," "ewery," "catery." The butler in the buttery was not in charge of butter but beer. The ewerer had the care of towels and basins used at table for washing the hands before and after meals—this being before the day of forks. In addition, the ewerer was responsible for a valuable inventory of pewter and silver plate. The cator (caterer?) was expected to provide and care for the supply of fresh vegetables, dressed poultry, eggs, fish, etc.

These locations were not only work areas (production centers?) but recording centers as well. All provisions brought in, all that were used, and the amounts left at the end of each day, week and year became a matter of record. Would we not call this "perpetual inventory?"

The following is part of an instruction for clerks of the kitchen. "Affore they maik any barganne for provisions (they) shall maik my Loorde privvy thereto...to the entent that they may know whether his Lordship will agre to the said prices or not...." Each day's use of provisions was on specific order, and the instruction book tells us "...none dared under penalty to issue another thing from his stock but by special command." Except during hours of service the supplies were always under lock and key; all "keis" were brought to the counting house after each meal. If any servant's stock issue passed beyond normal he was called to task. Another quotation tells us all supplies "that are boght (must) be entered forthwith in the Journall Booke when their ar boght." Clerks of the kitchen made a constant round of inspection of operations and records. This was to see "that the service that is appointed in the Booke of Direcions...be observed and kept without abridgement."

These old practices clearly have modern equivalents. Our work specialization in production centers has progressed far indeed, but only in extension of a principle. Work in progress is still inspected and checked against production standards, but not always against a "Booke of Direcions" as in the sixteenth century. Control today is execised by a flow of work orders and other directives rather than by a manual of instructions. Perpetual inventories are now commonplace; valuable tools and materials are as carefully safeguarded as ever, although the "keis" will not be delivered into our equivalent of the "counting house."

Perhaps some day historians will bring together in sequence the story of the many stages through which business methodology has passed. It would be fascinating reading, and no doubt would indicate that progress comes less from inspired inventions than bit by bit out of adaptations and improvements.

The remaining topic for these notes touches more closely upon accounting as such. The counting house, as already indicated, was a department in its own right. But lest accountants sigh for the good old days, let me point out that bookkeeping operations began at 7 a.m. and continued to 8:30 p.m.

Today we regard internal check very highly. So did these men of affairs four hundred years ago. It was not unusual for independently kept records to be matched as a test or proof. For example, the gentlemen ushers supervising meal service in the great hall made records of the food used at each meal. These facts could then be compared with issue records kept in the kitchen and other departments. And the issue records could be matched at any time against the same person's record of incoming provisions and unused inventory. Moreover, the records of baker and pantler were expected to agree as to bread delivered and used. Brewer and butler cross-checked as to beer; the slaughterman was checked against the larderer (as to meat), against the glover (as to hides) and the "chaundler" as to tallow for candles. Furthermore, the baker, the larderer, the brewer must produce a predetermined amount of bread, meat and beer out of a stated amount of materials received. Surely this tells of both internal check and production standards.

Faced with managerial craftsmanship such as this, we will not be surprised to see them use budgeting also. We are told it was customary to estimate a year in advance the need for food, cloth, fuel and other commodities. The Duke and his council approximated the price of all supplies and scheduled the times at which stated amounts of money should be transferred to designated household officials. As if this planning (budgeting) was not enough, the Duke and council determined the menus of all meals for the next year, with specified extra dishes for the feast days. These decisions no doubt were the basis for supervisors in the kitchen to calculate daily requirements in provisions issue.

Along with forward budgetting and close control over planned operations, frequent inventories enabled management to observe the extent to which procurement and issue were kept faithful to the budget. Clerks of the kitchen, spicery, granery, etc. made monthly summaries and inventories for their departments under the eyes of the comptroller's clerks. The countinghouse clerks assembled these reports into a total of household expenses and a "Bill of Remainder," the latter being described as "the Remaineth of such Stuf as remains unspent provided and bought in the year aforesaid."

The arrangement of monetary data in statement form prior to audit showed a simple, if detailed, contrasting of receipts and disbursements. First the rents collected from tenants, then receipts from sale of wood, hay, etc. Following these the expenses were reported, the details being grouped in subsections. Under each group of details and for the totals and balance, the auditor indicated his verification by writing "Ex per T.C. auditor" (examined by Thomas Clay, auditor). Part of the year-end procedure was called "declaration of audit" and was carried out in the presence of the Duke, the Receiver, the Surveyor, the Auditor and other members of the domestic council. In attendance were representatives from each department, for example, "the Yoman of the Beddes that staunds charged with my Lord his wardrobe Stuf." Each was presumably present to answer questions and perhaps orally to substantiate the facts of his department from personal knowledge.

It is not unlikely that this assembly was instituted to enable the council to study the cash transactions, serving reports and remaining stock of supplies, in relation to the budget and "Booke of Direcions" provided to guide operations. The scheme of internal check and departmental records led naturally to an inventory report as proof of compliance. And the cash warrants for money transferred to officers, tied the cash reporting to physical facts reflected in the inventory, the latter being that part of authorized disbursements not yet consumed. The whole of the data there assembled not only served for review purposes but also provided the basic information for the Duke and council to use in making estimates for the next year, thus to start the operating cycle once more.

Accountants of today are familiar with the "charge and discharge" form of statement since this is often used now in reporting to the courts on the management of a trusteed estate. It is therefore not difficult mentally to project backward such a scheme of reporting and catch a glimpse of the same kind of reporting four centuries ago.

The kind of recording, of control and audit here described antedated English knowledge of Italian double entry records, although this had been in use in Italy for some time. Even after an English textbook made double entry available (1553) it seems to have been put in use but slowly during the next one hundred years.

Management of the household of the typical Tudor nobleman therefore was skillfully conducted without benefit of the antecedent of modern book-keeping. In some respects, however, the English method was superior to the Italian. In the latter there was at that early day very little of financial statement arrangement, of internal check, or independent audit. After Italian methods were adopted in England came the wedding of English managerial accounting and Italian business accounting. The issue from that union we call "modern accounting" and include in that term not only accounting for mercantile business but for estates, governmental divisions, manufacturing corporations, and other organizations as well.

We may justly take pride in our intricate techniques and the professional status of our independent auditors. Yet we can well afford now and then to acknowledge a large intellectual debt to generation after generation of unknown contributors to our art. Perhaps it is not inappropriate to add that future generations will be able to thank the men of today for striving in their turn to make accounting ever more dependable and increasingly of service to management as well as to investors. Improvements from the past fifty years plainly indicate continuing development. What reason could we find for believing that accounting development is now complete?

Paul Grady

THE INCREASING EMPHASIS
ON ACCOUNTING
AS A SOCIAL FORCE

Paul Franklin Grady *was born in 1900 and educated at the University of Illinois, where he received his B S. in 1923. He has spent his entire career in professional accounting: with Arthur Andersen & Co., 1923–42 (partner, 1932–42), and with Price Waterhouse & Co., from 1943 until his retirement, except for service in the government in World War II. He served as a vice-president of the American Accounting Association in 1954. In 1963 he became director of accounting research, American Institute of C.P.A.*
The article reprinted here sketches the historical relationship between accounting and the society in which it operates, and then dwells on the recent trend in which accounting becomes a positive force in society, with definite responsibilities to discharge over and beyond the immediate task of systematic record-keeping.

In the challenging "Study of History" by Mr. Arnold J. Toynbee the experiences of the human race are analyzed and interpreted in terms of the identifiable species of societies which may be called civilizations. The argument developed is quite convincing that this is the most intelligible unit of historical study as distinguished from the narrower nationalistic approach or the broader approach embracing all mankind. Mr. Toynbee has discovered twenty-one identifiable civilizations which have come into being in the past six or seven thousand years, of which only five remain in existence today. The existing civilizations may be briefly described as follows:

1. Western Christendom, embracing the areas identified with the Catholic and Protestant Churches, principally North and Western Europe, the British Isles, the Americas, Australia and South Africa
2. An Orthodox Christian Society in Southeastern Europe and Russia

---

Reprinted from *The Accounting Review* (July, 1948), pp. 266–75, by permission.

3. An Islamic Society with its focus in the Arid Zone which stretches across North Africa and the Middle East from the Atlantic to the outer face of the Great Wall of China
4. A Hindu Society in the tropical subcontinent of India
5. A Far-Eastern Society in the subtropical and temperate regions between the Arid Zone of Asia and the Pacific

Both Western Christendom and the Orthodox Christian Society, which originated before A.D. 700, were found by Mr. Toynbee to have been affiliated with the Hellenic civilization which developed in the coast and islands of the Aegean before 1100 B.C. and extended to approximately A.D. 400. The oldest identifiable civilization, of course, was the Egyptian which originated in the Nile River Valley before 4000 B.C. and became extinct in the fifth century of the Christian Era, thus existing three times as long as our Western Society has existed to the present date.

Against this extensive background of history it is of great interest to note the comparatively recent origins of two phenomena which we regard as outstanding characteristics of our Western Civilization. I refer to the establishment of responsible parliamentary government since the last quarter of the seventeenth century, less than three hundred years ago, and to the development of the industrial system of economy since the last quarter of the eighteenth century, less than two hundred years ago.

I am certain that accounting, even though elementary in method, served useful purposes in the governmental and economic undertakings through all the millenniums encompassed by the identifiable civilizations. However, an art or science cannot become a social force until the economic and governmental conditions permit an independent professional development which may then use its talents in making a contribution to the public welfare. These favorable conditions for the field of accounting did not arise until after the establishment of responsible representative government and an industrialized economy. Naturally, the conditions favoring independence did not arrive full bloom, and, since the industrial economy itself is less than two hundred years old, it is not surprising that "accounting as a social force" is a relatively new concept even among accountants. Our discussion of the increasing importance of accounting may be limited for all practical purposes to the last hundred years and, as should be expected, the rate of development by which accounting becomes recognizable as a social force is greatly accelerated in the latter portion of the period.

It will be understood, I am sure, that a full coverage of the story of modern industrialism or of accounting, which necessarily travels a parallel orbit, would have to be presented on a world-wide basis. It is necessary to limit this treatise to a narrower scale and, therefore, I shall deal only with a part of the story relating to certain developments of the accounting profession in England, the country which originated the industrial revolution, and in some greater degree with developments in the United States of

America, the country which has carried industrialization to its greatest
effectiveness in production of goods and services.

Growth of Accounting
in an Industrial Economy

In the early period of industrialization business enterprises were modest
in scope and were conducted by individual proprietors. The proprietors
actively supervised and/or performed the functions relating to all phases of
the business—production, sales, finance and accounting. The accounting
problems relating to distinctions betwen capital and expense and income
realization were simple ones and were resolved by the exercise of common
sense and business judgment of the proprietor. Unfortunately, accounting
came to be popularly associated with the scrivener's task of recording the
transactions in books and records rather than with the exercise of judgment
which determined how the items should be dealt with. It is obvious that the
quality of judgment of the proprietor was on no different level for the
accounting decisions than for the other phases of the business, although
admittedly different proprietors would be more proficient in one phase than
another.

As industrialization progressed business enterprises attained much wider
scope and transactions became more and more complex. Under these conditions the proprietors found it necessary to divide duties among personnel in
accord with the logical phases of the activities and to base judgment to a
greater and greater extent upon facts and interpretations furnished by the
accounting process. A well-known contemporary writer has said that when
business becomes too large for one man to see, accounting takes over. As in
most generalities, these words might carry an erroneous connotation and,
therefore, I hasten to add that accounting does not take over in the sense
of running the business or even of creating an end within itself. It is, on the
other hand, an indispensable service function directed toward a dependable
records control over the assets and operations of an enterprise and supplying
essential information required by officers and directors for purposes of
management of the business, which includes the fulfillment of relationships
and responsibilities to governmental bodies and other organizations having
legitimate interests.

The expansion of business enterprises greatly increased the need for capital
which was provided through formation of partnerships and the organization
of limited liability associations or companies, as well as through short- and
long-term borrowings. In this way investor and creditor groups were created
which were not associated in the active management of the enterprises.
Thus management became accountable for its stewardship in utilizing the
capital placed in the enterprise. Furthermore, it soon became apparent that

an independent examination of the financial position and results of operations by persons skilled in accounting and auditing was a practical and essential step in establishing and maintaining confidence in the enterprise and in providing protection to the investing public. This was the basic cause of the development of the independent public accounting profession in countries having private enterprise economic systems and democratic governments.

In Great Britain the public accounting profession had progressed to the point in 1854 of organizing the first Institute of Accountants in Edinburgh. Similar organizations were formed shortly thereafter in England, and the present Institute of Chartered Accountants in England and Wales was incorporated by royal charter in 1880 as an amalgamation of two predecessor groups having approximately five hundred members. The public accounting profession has been fortunate in having as its leaders men of solid character and broad vision. These men through great devotion to their tasks have built the profession on strong foundations of integrity and competence, and by thorough training of an ever-increasing personnel have kept pace with the growing responsibilities imposed by a dynamic private enterprise economy and regulatory legislation enacted by democratic governments in promoting and protecting the public interest. In England some of the Acts were: Regulation of Railroads Act, 1879; District Auditors Act, 1879; Building Societies Act, 1896; Industrial and Provident Societies Act, 1893; Trustee Savings Act, 1893; and various Companies Acts beginning about 1845. All of these Acts contained provisions pertaining to appointment of auditors, and the Companies Act of 1900 required shareholders to elect auditors to report to them on their companies' accounts. The enactment of successive income-tax laws in England beginning in 1799 likewise brought an increase in scope of responsibility to the accounting field.[1]

In the United States industrial development on a large scale came somewhat later than in England due to the conditions inherent in settling a new land and in changing from the status of colonies to an independent republic. A considerable part of the early industrial development was financed by British capital and it was quite natural that the practice of having independent auditors confirm the representations of management regarding their stewardship was adopted in America.

The story of the tremendous growth of industry in America, reflecting qualities of true genius in the organization of human abilities and energies to bring about a maximum use of scientific discoveries and mechanical inventions in the development of our natural resources, is so well known as to require no further comments. It will be sufficient to point out that the industrial development in America has resulted in the highest standard of life for a higher proportion of the population than has ever occurred in the history of the world's civilizations. It is my belief that this result could not

---

[1] See article by Mary E. Murphy in *The Accountant* (August, 1947).

have occurred except under a system of competitive enterprise based upon individual incentives, regulated to the extent necessary to protect the public interest by a responsible democratic government.

The economic development of America has presented broad opportunities for accounting to demonstrate its usefulness. As in Great Britain, successive tax laws beginning in 1913 and various regulatory acts, particularly the Securities Act of 1933 and the Securities Exchange Act of 1934, have had considerable effects. A complete presentation of the manner in which accounting has responded to these opportunities would require volumes. In this restricted treatment it will be necessary to mention only certain highspots of the growth of accounting organizations, and of the services performed. The American Institute of Accountants, through a predecessor organization, was formed in 1887 and the first law authorizing the issuance of Certified Public Accountant degrees was passed in 1896. The American Institute membership has grown to over eleven thousand during the sixty years of its existence and approximately twenty-five thousand persons hold qualifications as Certified Public Accountants.

From the beginning public accountants have stressed the need for placing the accounting function in industry on a higher plane. Managements have increasingly heeded this advice because it has been recognized that a high order of native ability, combined with technical accounting training and experience, are required qualifications for meeting the broad responsibilities of organizing sound systems of internal control in business, and of supplying the information required for intelligent management. It has also become fairly well established that the accounting results must not be dominated by the operating personnel. Accordingly, the controllership position has grown to a coordinate stature with other principal departments of business, and in some instances has been made responsible to the Board of Directors. The need for a national organization of controllers was met in 1932 by the organization of the Controllers Institute of America which has had a phenomenal growth in membership enrollment and in usefulness. The National Association of Cost Accountants had been organized previously in 1919, and embraces both public and corporate accountants who are particularly interested in cost accounting. Further specialization in the accounting field is evidenced by the organization of the Institute of Internal Auditors in 1941 and by the formation of the Tax Executives Institute in 1945. The combined membership of the foregoing organizations at the present time is in excess of twenty-five thousand.

The growth of organizations in public accounting and in corporate accounting has been dealt with at some length because it demonstrates that, from an obscure position at the beginning of the industrial revolution, accounting has progressed to a well-organized body of sufficient strength and independence to discharge fully its responsibilities. The fact that such responsibilities have been appropriately viewed from a broad angle is evidenced by the following quotation from the Committee on Accounting Procedure of the American Institute of Accountants:

> The Committee regards corporation accounting as one phase of the working of the corporate organization of business, which in turn it views as the machinery created by the people in the belief that, broadly speaking, it will serve a useful social purpose. The test of the corporate system and of the special phase of it represented by corporate accounting ultimately lies in the results which are produced. These results must be judged from the standpoint of society as a whole—not from that of any group of interested parties.

Our historical survey will not permit any full development of the functions and usefulness of accounting. However, it is believed that the following brief summary will serve to demonstrate that accounting has fully earned any recognition which may have been accorded it, by arduous tasks faithfully performed in accordance with objective standards:

1. Maintenance of accounting control over asssets, liabilities, revenues and expenses. This includes the broad problem of organizational plan and division of duties among personnel to guard against irregularities and falsification of accounts. It also embraces design and installation of accounting procedures and the provision of effective internal auditing.

2. Supplying information required by officers and directors for the operating and financial management of the business. Effective executive administration requires the establishment of planned yardsticks or standards and the measurement and reporting of performance as a basis for the prompt initiation of any required corrective administrative action. These purposes are accomplished by fixed or variable budgets and operating and financial reports, which are designed to meet all of management's requirements and may involve cost and profit determinations by territories, by plants, by departments, by products and units of products.

3. Accounting and reporting to investors and creditors on stewardship responsibilities, which includes interim and annual reports to stockholders, and interim and annual reports required to be filed with the Securities and Exchange Commission.

4. Supplying information required by management and by governmental bodies for rate-making and other regulatory purposes. This function, of course, has been for many years of primary importance to public utilities. With the extension of government regulation and influence over all business, particularly during the war, this function embraced such matters as costing of production under war contracts, renegotiation, price-fixing, and settlement of terminated contracts.

5. Supplying information required by management and by governmental bodies for all tax purposes, including property, excise, franchise and income taxes. Of these, income taxes have created the greatest demands upon accounting due to the extremely high personal and corporate tax rates in combination with the inexcusably complex determination of taxable income based upon pyramided revenue acts and related regulations and decisions.

6. Supplying the financial and accounting information required for obtaining new or additional capital. In case of public offerings, the registration requirements of the Securities and Exchange Commission under the Securities Act must be met.

7. Supplying information required by management, governmental bodies and labor organizations regarding costs, income or other economic facts or statistics. This is one of the newer fields for accounting service and will be dealt with in further detail at a later point.

The increasing importance of accounting as a social force has been forcefully portrayed by the Hon. James J. Caffrey, Chairman of the Securities and Exchange Commission, as follows:[2]

Perhaps the most striking thing about your profession is the enormous change that has taken place in the position of the accountant. From the simple scrivener tabulating receipts and disbursements, with limited functions and limited responsibilities, he has become the processing plant through which the raw data of finance must pass before it can be compiled in the vast financial encyclopedia of our time. ...

...To these difficulties have been added many others. Not only is the imagination staggered by the growing size and complexity of what the accountant must account for, but it is not always clear even for whom accountants account. The single enterprise is no longer the personal concern of one owner or a small group of owners. Its ownership is likely to be spread among vast numbers of security holders, aggregating into a welter of conflicting legal and economic interests in the single business unit. In any given situation the exercise of an accountant's judgment may vitally affect the ownership interests of one competing group of security holders as against another.

History seems to have an endless storehouse of burdens for the accountant. His presentation must also satisfy the regulatory agencies interested in the operations of the economic enterprises for which he accounts. One group in government is charged with protection of the revenue, another with the protection of rate-payers, another with the protection of employees, and so on. Each of these bodies may approach the balance sheet or the income statement with a different emphasis, and may read it for a different message. Nevertheless, the accountant is expected to produce one single adequate, truthful, and understandable statement.

History has thus thrust the accountant into a crucial role. Management, labor, conflicting groups of investors, potential investors, and governmental interests make vital decisions based on the story told by the accountant. Yet the accountant is no mere reporter who sits by the sidelines giving a play-by-play description of the business. Save in the simplest kinds of business he has been given a task which embraces interpretation as well as mere recording; judgment as well as mere tabulating; art as well as science.

What does this add up to? Perhaps the simplest way of putting it is to say that the accountant's position has become a position of power. In this regard history has an even hand; with power she doles out responsibility.

Growth in Accounting
and Business Education

The development of formal education in accounting and business at the university level has largely taken place in the last fifty years. It is not at all

---

[2] Address, "Plain Talk in Accounting," given at 1947 Annual Meeting of the American Institute of Accountants.

surprising that the majority of classical educators should have resisted the granting of credits in accounting and other business subjects because they have shown the same resistance to practically all new professional fields. The organization of accounting courses was all the more difficult because there were no satisfactory textbooks and on the whole, teachers did not have adequate knowledge of accounting and practical accountants did not know how to teach.

The establishment of the first colleges of commerce which remained in existence was due to the generosity and public spirit of a few businessmen, such as Joseph Wharton and Amos Tuck, and the relatively rapid strides thereafter are a tribute to the broad vision and persistence of a few educational statesmen, one of the outstanding being Dr. Edmund J. James. Dr. James was one of the early professors at the Wharton School; subsequently he was a professor at Chicago University, and later he served a long and distinguished tenure of office as president of the University of Illinois. Throughout his career he was a staunch advocate of a higher level of accounting and business education. The Wharton School of Finance and Economy at the University of Pennsylvania was founded in 1881 and stood alone in the field until 1898. At the close of 1900 there were only seven such institutions in the country. It is of interest to note that one of these, The School of Commerce, Accounts and Finance of New York University, was founded by the trustees principally as a result of efforts of the New York Society of Certified Public Accountants acting through its first president, Mr. Charles Waldo Haskins.[3]

From the one university level College of Commerce which existed in 1897, the passage of fifty years has witnessed the establishment of ninety-five additional institutions which are on the New York accredited list for training prerequisite to qualifying for the CPA examination. The annual enrollment in these Colleges of Commerce aggregates many thousand students of whom a sizable portion look forward to careers in public or corporate accounting. I know there are many other colleges and universities which include comprehensive courses in accounting and business subjects which may not meet the technical requirements of the Department of Education of the State of New York. The American Accounting Association, a national organization of university accounting instructors, was organized in 1916 and has approximately twenty-five hundred members.

In a comparable record of growth, accounting literature has developed from the limited and more or less elementary bookkeeping texts to a well-organized body of knowledge offering a wide variety of volumes in theory or principles of accounting, cost accounting, accounting systems and procedures, auditing standards, auditing procedures, internal auditing, budgetary procedures, etc. In addition the profession can well be proud of its proven periodicals, such as the *Journal of Accountancy, The Accounting Review,* the

---

[3] "Early University Education in Accountancy," by Jeremiah Lockwood, THE ACCOUNTING REVIEW, June, 1938.

N.A.C.A. Bulletins and *The Controller.* By way of indicating a quantitative measure of current accounting literature, the library of the American Institute of Accountants consists of approximately twenty thousand books and pamphlets.

Challenges to Accounting
to Expand Its Usefulness in Society

It is not possible to review the progress and accomplishments in corporate and public accounting and in the closely related educational field without a great deal of justifiable pride. Pride in our profession, if directed into proper channels, must cause us to recognize that the illustrious accomplishments of our predecessors place upon us the full responsibility for meeting the challenges to accounting to expand its usefulness to society in our own generation. The opportunities are great, because no period of history has presented such numerous and complex problems which need independent and objective solutions based upon a careful determination of facts and in the light of the public welfare.

Faithful service to society, of course, embraces the continuous improvements of the various purposes and functions of accounting as previously outlined. I believe that there is little risk that the profession will fail to measure up to high levels of performance of all traditional responsibilities in serving as an intelligence department in an industrial economy. The real risk is whether new challenges will be recognized and successfully met in a timely and adequate manner. Recognition of the challenges to accounting must be based upon an analysis of the major challenges to our country, and on a broader scale to our civilization, to ascertain wherein accounting can make constructive contributions.

Much has been said and written about current moral, political, and economic issues, which are naturally greatly complicated as a result of the destruction, confusion, and stresses and strains engendered by two world wars. It seems to me that the truly major challenges are as follows:

1. Can the people of the world be brought to a recognition of the necessity for, and an active acceptance of, a regeneration of religion? It does not require much imagination to realize how different our world could be if individual, group, national, and international affairs were conducted on the basis of the inspired code of ethics of Christianity.

2. Can the provincialism and prejudices of extreme nationalistic sovereignty be overcome by voluntary means in order to create a world government of sufficient power to prevent war, to abolish mental and physical slavery, and to eliminate artificial barriers to economic welfare? Scientific developments have made close neighbors of all peoples, and effective world government, if it cannot be born of peaceful cooperation, will probably have to be fashioned in the painful forge of military conflict.

3. Can responsible democratic government be organized on a level of efficien-

cy that will reduce the cost of government to a reasonable and bearable overhead charge on our economy?

4. Can the leaders of industrial managements and the leaders of labor be made to see the great mutuality of their interests and the great mutuality of their interests and the extreme need for cooperation in the preservation of private enterprise and in the strengthening of an incentive system of production?

If the third and fourth challenges were successfully met in our own country, its position of leadership would be enhanced to the point where the peoples of other nations would insist on following its political and economic example. The strength and encouragement thus generated might well bridge any remaining difficulties in the accomplishment of world government and religion. In the light of these interesting possibilities, let us explore briefly some of the things that accounting might do to assist in bringing about greater efficiency in government and in promoting a better understanding between labor and management.

A recent newspaper release indicates that tax collections of local, state, and federal governments for the last fiscal year amounted to more than fifty-six billion dollars. While this aggregate may not be comprehensible to the human mind, its significance is quite apparent when we realize that it represents approximately $1,000 per annum for each employed person in the United States. This is a greater burden than can be borne without destroying our way of life. A sizable part of this burden is attributable to the pyramiding of a vast bureaucracy which does not earn its keep. It is difficult to ferret out because, with possible minor exceptions, accounting has not been used in government as a tool for efficient management. Accounting can and should perform all of the valuable functions for government that it now performs for business in establishing standards and in measuring administrative performance. The accomplishment of these purposes would require that the accounting function be placed on a proper organizational level, and that it be administered by competent accounting personnel. Some of the organizational steps which might well be undertaken in the federal government are as follows:

1. Create a position of Controller General, or other appropriate title, as the chief accounting officer in the Executive Department. This position should have Cabinet rank and should be responsible for the establishment of proper accounting systems and reports, and for supervision of the accounting and budgetary activities in all departments.

2. Departmental controllers' offices should be established in each department of the government. The departmental controllers should be responsible to the Controller General for compliance with all required accounting and budgetary policies, but should also be responsible to the respective secretaries for the supplying of all information needed for the administration of the particular departments.

3. The Treasury Department should relinquish its accounting activities for other departments. The Treasury Department would conform to the

general pattern of having a departmental controller to look after the accounting and budgetary problems relating only to Treasury operations.

4. The present General Accounting Office should be reconstituted as the Auditing Office of the Government. It should remain independent of the Executive Departments, should make its examinations on a test basis in the light of existing systems of internal control, and should give particular attention to the efficiency of departmental operations in its reports to Congress. If properly staffed, this office could render invaluable service to the appropriation committees of Congress in consideration of departmental budgets.

While the foregoing is only a thumbnail sketch it will serve to indicate some of many ways in which accounting can serve as useful instrument in helping enlightened management obtain more efficient and, therefore, more economical government. It is the responsibility of accountants to develop fully this theme, and to convince the governmental authorities of its soundness. Our campaign should be directed to high-level executive officers, to the leaders of Congress, and to the Commission headed by Ex-President Hoover which, pursuant to a Congressional Act, is undertaking a comprehensive survey of the Executive Departments of the Government.

During the past year or two there has been a growing realization that facts and an objective viewpoint could serve useful purposes in negotiations between management and labor, and several excellent articles have pointed out the ways in which the accounting profession can help smooth the road to industrial peace. I refer particularly to three articles in the July *Journal of Accountancy*,[4] and to an address delivered by Mr. Donald Richberg at the recent annual meeting of the American Institute of Accountants. No purpose would be served by duplicating the substance of these articles. Therefore, I shall assume that you have studied or will study them, and shall pass on to the development of a few points on a closely related problem.

Much has already been said, and it does not require clairvoyant powers to predict that much more will be said in 1948, about who is to blame for inflation. When we review the splendid control performance of our neighbor to the north, both during and since the war, it is indeed difficult not to indulge in recriminations. However, our efforts may be directed to more constructive channels by a consideration of ways and means of arresting the malady of shrinkage which has attacked our dollar.

Economic statistics indicate that the purchasing power of the dollar is now about one-half of its prewar value. They further show that gross payments to labor have increased more than enough to offset this decrease.

---

[4] *Is There a Field for Accountants in the Future of Labor Negotiations?* by Fred E. King, Executive Vice-President, Munsingwear, Inc.; *Stewardship: Social Contributions of the Accountant to Labor-Management Relations,* by M. H. Hedges, Director of Research, International Brotherhood of Electrical Workers, American Federation of Labor; *An Accountant Shows the Road to Industrial Peace,* by Maurice H. Stans, CPA, Partner, Alexander Grant & Co.

However, a considerable portion, if not all, of this apparent improvement in the position of labor has been offset by the tolls of the tax collector. It should therefore be clear that even labor cannot improve its economic welfare by entering a race in the squirrel cage of inflation. If labor is no better off, think of the dire condition of people who have fulfilled their social contract and who are now dependent on fixed retirement or investment income. The monetary income of this group has been substantially reduced by the decrease in interest rates forced by governmental fiscal policies, and the remainder has then suffered a further 50 per cent reduction in terms of prewar purchasing ability. Surely we have not become so callous as to allow this to happen without trying to find a remedy. Increased production at lower costs is the solution to the problem; and it is the only way labor can raise its own standard of living.

I believe that labor can earn much higher real wages than the present level through the adoption of general incentive plans of production implemented by effective cooperation between labor and management. With this objective in mind, it is suggested that the leaders of labor and industry should reach agreement between themselves—without government help or interference—somewhat along the following lines:

1. Wages should be fixed at present rates for a period of four or five years.
2. There should be no strikes or lockouts during that period; all disputes should be settled by arbitration.
3. In lieu of wage increases employees should receive, quarterly or annually, production dividends representing one-half of the reduction in the current wage component of the cost of products as compared with a similar volume priced at the wage cost per unit of production in the year (or other agreed period) prior to the date of agreement.
4. Selling prices to customers in the succeeding period should be reduced by amounts at least equal to the wage production dividends.
5. Employees should agree to use their best efforts to promote full cooperation in the program of increasing efficiency in production methods. Suggestions for improvements should be rewarded, and loafers should be reported to management and union officers.

No single pattern, of course, would fit all companies and industries. But, if the principle of reducing costs and increasing production with the sharing of the benefits between labor and customers could be generally agreed upon, we would remove most of the conflict from labor-management relations and would reverse the inflationary spiral and the attendant dangers to our economy. Employees would benefit by the production dividends and by lower prices of the goods they buy; customers would benefit by lower prices; and investors would benefit from increased volume of production together with ultimately lowered costs of materials purchased. The accounting profession could readily ascertain the facts and report them objectively and independently in order that there might be a clear understanding of the results obtained under the incentive production plans, both in the aggregate and as to individual employees.

Inflation has brought another important problem to the accountant's door-step by producing a wide disparity between the monetary income reported by traditional accounting methods, and real income as measured by an increment in economic wealth. The disparity arises primarily from stating plant exhaustion provisions in terms of original cost, and from the effect of first-in, first-out inventory methods. The importance of corporate income in our economy is so great that steps must be taken either to bring accounting income into closer agreement with economic income, or to show the latter result in supplementary statements in all published reports. Otherwise appropriate information will not be available to serve in the formulation of many far-reaching governmental and economic policies.

It is hoped that the foregoing will illustrate at least a few ways in which accounting may be of broader usefulness in helping society to cope with current problems. Destiny has fashioned stupendous issues to test the courage and vision of our generation. If we produce the leadership to meet the challenges, we can look forward to the hopeful potentialities of lifting civilization to the dawn of a new millennium morally, politically and economically.

Part Two

Postulates and Principles

Charles Ezra Sprague

THE PHILOSOPHY OF ACCOUNTS

Charles Ezra Sprague *(1842–1912) received a bachelor's degree from Union College in 1860 and a Ph.D. in 1893. He became a C.P.A. in 1896. He was wounded and disabled at the battle of Gettysburg while serving with the Union Army. He spent most of his career with the Union Dime Savings Bank of New York and was its president starting in 1892. He was on the faculty of New York University after 1900, holding the post of professor of the theory of accounts. His writings included* Accountancy of Investment *(1904);* Extended Bond Tables *(1905); and* The Philosophy of Accounts *(1907). He was the first American advocate of Volapük, an international language invented about 1880.*
Four chapters from his Philosophy of Accounts *are reprinted here. The entire book is significant because it is the first successful attempt in the U.S. to present an integrated explanation of accounting. It is couched in terms of "proprietary theory," as the chapters reprinted here demonstrate. Sprague conceived of accounting as "a branch of mathematical and classificatory science...[the principles of which might] be determined by* a priori *reasoning." Many of Sprague's ideas and concepts are still valid, and his influence on subsequent accounting thought continues to the present day.*

Chapter Six

Phases of the Assets.

105. The specific values on the asset side of the balance sheet are of two classes:

    1. Things.
    2. Rights.

Or we may say

    1. Things belonging to us.

        2. Debts owing to us.

Or again,

        1. Possessions.
        2. Expectations.

We shall see upon examination that these classes imperceptibly blend into each other and that every asset may be lookt upon either as a "thing" or as a "right."

    Possession of a thing is merely the *right* to use it and control it.

    Therefore all our "things" may be look upon as merely rights of dominion. We look upon our cash as a thing and as one of our most concrete assets. Yet the greater part of it is usually in bank deposits, which are merely the *right* to receive money on demand or to transfer such right to anyone who will accept it instead of money. But excluding bank deposits as not being money, we may hold bank-notes or greenbacks. These are nothing but printed agreements conferring the *right* to receive money, which is seldom called for. Finally, the coin, even if of the standard metal, is value in possession. Yet, unless we are jewelers, we do not *use* it. We prize it simply because we have the *right* under the law to satisfy contracts by parting with it.

    106. Thus things convert themselves into rights, and the reverse is true: rights are convertible into things. Rights are but the future tense of things. Not only this but they are almost always secured by things. The personal indebtedness which we list in our assets is generally based upon the goods which were ours but which we have sold. We feel that they are still in existence as morally ours until paid for. We have trusted the purchaser for the reason that he owns these and other goods which will more than satisfy our claim. Thus all rights rest ultimately upon things, either present or expected.

    107. But rights are sometimes materialized into a kind of artificial thing, especially when they are evidenced by some material thing, such as a written document. A mere debt is seldom thought of as a thing in possession, while a note, which is a written acknowledgment of the same debt, is lookt upon as something valuable in itself, because it can be toucht and handled. Especially is this true of bonds, mortgages, etc., formal documents, usually transferable, which create the illusion that they are actual property, not merely the symbol of a debt.

    On the other hand, things are sometimes personified into personal debtors, and the whole system of assets and liabilities is converted into a set of debts either receivable or payable. It is feigned that the cash account is the account of the cashier; he is indebted for all the receipts and credited for all the payments. Similarly the warehouseman is regarded as owing for all the merchandise, the land agent for all the real estate; regardless of the fact that there is no actual indebtedness, since these custodians take no title to the things. Neither the shepherd nor his dog is in debt for the sheep.

108. These extremists, who have tried on the one hand to convert all assets into things, and on the other hand to reduce all things to personal debts, have had long discussions, especially in Italy, dividing themselves into the two camps of the *materialists* and the *personalists*. Apparently it has not occurred to these controversialists that in truth some of the assets are of the one and some of the other nature, and that many may be lookt at in either phase; furthermore, that so long as the nature of the asset and its form of account are understood, it is needless to twist it into the shape of some other asset. To seek the truth and follow the facts is safer than to compress everything into the mould of a "theory."

109. Rights always arise from uncompleted contracts. No man owes you unless there has been a contract, tacit or exprest, oral or written, for him to give you something and for you to give him something. If one of you has fulfilled his part of the contract, that one has acquired a right and the other has incurred an obligation. The contract may be a mere understanding without words, or it may be duly signed, sealed and witnest.

110. In another aspect all assets are the embodiment of services previously given; and in still another they are a storage of services to be received. Someone must have given labor in order to produce any wealth; but if it will not in the future command the services of labor, or save the expenditure of labor, or of its embodied results, it is worthless and not wealth at all.

111. Yet the values resulting from these two aspects are only approximately equal. On the one hand, the services which were given may have been sold for more or less than a just price as settled by competition; consequently the assets received for the services may be less or more than the future services receivable. The whole economic struggle (reducing everything to terms of service) is to sell one's own services high and buy the services of others cheap. On the other hand, a disservice (to use Prof. Fisher's word) may have occurred thru various causes, so that the services once anticipated appear impossible of entire realization. It must be observed that the aspect of assets as the present worth of future services is entirely based upon opinion, while the aspect which regards them as the resultant of services given is based upon facts.

112. Capital is defined by economists as that portion of wealth which is set aside for the production of additional wealth. In the balance sheet of a business concern, frequently, all the assets are capital, being employed as tools for its operations. There may be other assets, called investments, where the actual handling of the tools is turned over to someone else and the value receivable for the services is returned in cash or other assets. This is exemplified in the ownership by corporations of the shares or bonds of other corporations. The physical assets underlying these securities are used as tools by the corporation issuing them, rather than by the one owning them.

Yet in a remoter sense such vicarious assets may be considered as capital; for example, their possession may be a safeguard against some contingency or a reserve of strength. Hence it is easy to accept the view of Prof. Irving Fisher, that all assets are capital.[1]

113. To summarize this chapter, the assets comprising the debit side of a balance sheet may be considered in one or more of the following ways:

(1) As things possess, directly or indirectly, or physical assets.
(2) As rights over things and persons, for use, for services, or for exchange.
(3) As incomplete contracts, whereof our part has been performed in whole or in part; or contractual assets;
(4) As the result of services previously given, or *cost;*
(5) As the present worth of expected services to be received;
(6) As capital for the conduct of business operations; or
(7) As investment in the hands of another who uses it as capital.

114. The special case in which certain assets are devoted to the payment of certain liabilities will be treated under liabilities in the next chapter.

Chapter Seven

Phases of Liabilities

115. As we pass from the asset side of the balance sheet we seem to leave the actual and concern ourselves with the ideal, the objectiv gives place to the subjectiv. While the asset side contains concrete actualities, the other side deals with the distribution of these actualities among those who have the title *to* them and those who hold claims *against* them, the liabilities.

116. In algebraic language we may say that liabilities are negativ assets and that proprietorship is measured by the algebraic sum of all the assets positiv and negativ.

Another way of expressing this phase is that the liabilities are postponed decreases of the assets; a future diminution having the same effect on the net proprietorship as a present diminution.

117. The liabilities may to some extent be lookt upon in aspects corresponding to those stated for the assets, altho they never represent concrete property.

As rights, they are the rights of others against us and our property, just as the assets are our right against others.

Considered as uncompleted contracts, they are those in which *our* part of the contract is the part unfulfilled.

---

1 In the "summation of capital," Professor Fisher eliminates, by cancellation, the securities of one concern held by another, as they cannot furnish capital to both; which approximates to the distinction in the text.

As capital, they represent that portion of the total capital which has been furnisht by others, or loan-capital.

118. Ordinarily there is no designation of certain assets as destined to meet certain liabilities, but any or all of the assets may, upon default, be expropriated to a sufficient extent to pay any liability. The word *assets*, meaning enough or sufficient, suggests this view of their nature from the point of view of the creditor. There are cases, however, where definit assets are paired off against definit liabilities, in such a way that these particular assets cannot be parted with unless the liability (which is said to be *secured*) has first been paid. A familiar example is the mortgage on real estate. The title is in the owner; the real estate stands in his balance sheet as an asset; he has full dominion over it; he can collect the rent from it and can even sell the property subject to the paramount rights, or *lien*, of the mortgage. The status of the property would be as follows, for example:

Value of Real Estate $10,000	Mortgage $4,000
	Equity 6,000
$10,000	$10,000

The true proprietorship in the real estate is the "equity" in the above balance sheet, and this is all that the owner can really sell. Hence, instead of calling the entire $10,000 an asset and the $6,000 a liability he sometimes prefers to eliminate the liability and treat the equity as a net asset.

Equity in real Estate.
Value $10,000, Mortgage
$4,000 .... $6,000

The word equity in the balance sheet is taken in the proprietary sense; here, in the sense of an asset.

119. Similarly, other assets are pledged to the satisfaction of liabilities and usually some steps are taken to prevent the owner from alienating the asset to the detriment of the pledgee. The United States Government takes from national banks their bonds as security for the redemption of circulating notes guaranteed by the Government.

Assets.	*Liabilities.*
....	....
....	....
U. S. Bonds to secure Circulation $00,000	Circulation (Notes outstanding) $00,000
....	....

The ordinary loan on collateral is another example of an asset paired against a liability.

120. While there is this correlation between assets and liabilities taken in pairs, there is seldom exact identity of value. The asset is always taken, or

intended to be taken, larger than the liability, for prudential reasons; so that there is a residue above the liability, such as the equity in the mortgaged property or the margin in the loan on collateral.

121. Many seeming liabilities are more properly defined as deductions from certain correlated assets; of this we shall speak more fully under the head of offsets.

122. While assets may shrink in value, that shrinkage affects the proprietorship, never the liabilities, which must be regarded as rigid and inelastic.

Chapter Eight

Proprietorship

123. The proprietorship may, like the liabilities, be viewed in the same phases as the assets, all excepting that of "things." Where there are any liabilities, no list of things can be drawn up which represent the proprietorship because the liabilities may be canceled by disposing of whatever assets are chosen for disposal by the proprietor. But if there are no liabilities whatever, the sum of the assets is the total proprietorship. Let us agree in the balance sheet...that the mortgage shall be stricken out and the value of the equity alone be carried as an asset. There being then no liabilities, the proprietorship is simply the sum of the assets and the balance sheet needs but one side.

Cash	$3,506.74
Merchandise	22,166.73
Personal Debtors	15,972.15
Equity in Real Estate	6,000.00
Capital	$47,645.62

The last line is proprietorship; it is capital in both senses, the bookkeeping sense and the economic sense.

124. As "rights," however, the proprietorship may be viewed. The assets being regarded as composed of rights against others and the liabilities as others' rights against us, the excess of rights in our favor is the proprietorship.

125. Thus the right-hand side of the balance sheet is entirely composed of claims against or rights over the left-hand side. "Is it not then true," it will be askt, "that the right-hand side is entirely composed of liabilities?" The answer to this is that the rights of others, or the liabilities, differ materially from the rights of the proprietor, in the following respects.

(1) The rights of the proprietor involve dominion over the assets and power to use them as he pleases even to alienating them; while the creditor cannot interfere with him or them except in extraordinary circumstances.

(2) The right of the creditor is limited to a definit sum which does not

shrink when the assets shrink, while that of the proprietor is of an elastic value.

(3) Losses, expenses and shrinkage fall upon the proprietor alone, and profits, revenue and increase of value benefit him alone, not his creditors.

For these reasons the proprietary interest cannot be treated like the liabilities and the two branches of the right-hand side of the balance sheet require distinctiv treatment.

126. Considered as the effect of service, the proprietorship is the expression of how much more service has been given than received. Considered as the embodiment of future service it represents the net value of the service which the proprietor has a right to expect without giving any further service of his own.

127. Considering all the assets as capital, the proprietorship is that portion (in value) of the capital, which the proprietor furnishes as distinguisht from the portion which he induces others to place in his hands for utilization, or the liabilities.

128. Before collecting the various phases of the assets, liabilities and proprietorship into a systematic whole, it may be well to mention two somewhat fictitious methods of presentation, each introducing an intermediary element which disappears by cancellation.

129. In the cash theory, every transaction is supposed to pass thru the phase of cash. There is no direct exchange of any asset for another asset, but it is assumed that cash is received for the former and at once paid for the latter. Thus a sale of merchandise on credit is represented as a sale for cash accompanied by a loan of the cash to the purchaser.

Purchaser/Mdse

becomes

Cash/Mdse
Purchaser/Cash.

130. A very large number of the transactions are genuinely cash, and it is evident that the others may be separated into two each, one involving a receipt of cash and the other an expenditure. Without at present dwelling on this, we may conclude that any asset, except cash itself, may be considered to have cost money, and that any liability or proprietorship may be considered as having procured money or as being sources of money. The debit side of the balance sheet is transformed into a statement of cash paid, and the credit side into a statement of cash received—a reversed cash statement.

131. Taking the figures of Figure 23* we thus transform them into the following:

---

* Appears in a previous chapter not reprinted.

Figure 26.

BALANCE SHEET OF JONES & SMITH.

Proceeds of Cash Paid	*Sources of Cash Received*
For Merchandise $39,249.38	From James Jones $47,645.62
// Bills Receivable 7,000.00	// William Smith 23,822.81
// Personal Debtors 24,095.32	// Bills Payable 8,000.00
// Real Estate 10,000.00	// Personal Creditors 5,465.35
// Balance Unpaid 8,589.08	// Mortgage Payable 4,000.00
$88,933.78	$88,933.78

Jones and Smith are supposed to have paid in to the firm's treasury the sums which each was worth, and the firm to have also borrowed the sums of $8,000, $5,465.35 and $4,000, as stated. The firm then bought with the cash thus acquired the assets of each partner, which restored to each enough to replace in his private treasury the cash he had contributed and also to pay the individual debts, which are now replaced by the firm's indebtedness. There also remains unexpended a cash balance of $8,589.08.

132. The application of the cash theory to the corporate balance sheet... may serve to explain several things:

Figure 27.

JONES MERCANTILE COMPANY.

Capital and Liabilities. [Cash received from]	*Assets.* [Cash paid for]
Capital Stock $60,000.00	Merchandise $39,249.38
Surplus 11,468.43	Bills Receivable 7,000.00
Bills Payable 8,000.00	Personal Debtors 24,095.32
Personal Creditors 5,465.35	Real Estate 10,000.00
Mortgage Payable 4,000.00	Cash Balance 8,589.08
$88,933.78	$88,933.78

The facts for which this offers a plausible explanation are the following:

(1) That the English accountants usually place the assets (cash paid) on the right-hand side and *vice versa;* this being the natural form of a cash statement.

(2) That, as remarked in Chapter Four, the proprietary accounts usually come before the liabilities; companies being formed by first paying in cash for shares, in form at least. Often this is effected by the giving of checks which offset each other or are endorsed back, but the form is generally observed.

(3) That the cash stands last in the list of assets, it being regarded as a balance unexpended.

133. The other theory adopts as its intermediary a supposed entity "The Business." All assets are regarded as "owing" to

Assets.	*Liabilities.*	*Proprietorship.*
Property	Deductions from property	Net property
Rights against others	Obligations to others	Surplus of rights
Assets	Negative Assets	Net Assets
Services heretofore given	Services heretofore received	Surplus of services rendered
Services expected to be received	Services which must be given	Surplus of services receivable
Capital	Loan-capital	Own capital

That for which
cash has been given }
Cash
Debtors to the Business

Sources from which cash has been received

Creditors of the Business

The Business and The Business is regarded as owing all the "liabilities" in which are included the proprietary claims. This is a favorit theory in this country, and it has this merit that it recognizes that the proprietor or proprietors may have many other investments and do not in the accounts presented reveal anything more than their worth as to The Business. But I cannot see that it justifies the inclusion of proprietorship among the liabilities. Surely The Business does not stand in the same relation to its proprietors or its capitalists as to its "other" liabilities. It would seem more appropriate to say that it is "owned by" than "owes" the proprietors.

134. The phases, which the three parts of the balance sheet assume from different standpoints, are shown above.

Chapter Nine

Offsets and Adjuncts

135. It is sometimes desirable for some special reason to separate the account of an asset, of a liability or of a proprietor into two accounts, usually in order to present two different valuations. We shall call the supplementary account an *offset* or an *adjunct* to the principal account according as it is intended to be subtracted from or added to the principal account.

136. As an instance of an asset take a set of machinery which cost a year ago $130,000. It is estimated that this machinery will be worthless in a few years, that is, that in those years its value will pass from $130,000 to 0. It is also estimated that the first year of use will depreciate the machinery to the extent of 20 per cent, or $26,000. If it is desired to keep a record of the original cost, $130,000 and at the same time of the present worth, $104,000, it may be done by using two accounts on opposit sides of the ledger.

Machinery at cost, $130,000   Depreciation, $26,000

This depreciation is not a liability, altho it is frequently listed among the liabilities, but an offset to the asset. In a correctly constructed balance sheet it would not appear except indirectly in this form:

Machinery.
Cost $130,000
Depreciation .... 26,000 $104,000 ....

137. In Chapter Six there was a discussion of the relation between a piece of real estate and the mortgage upon it. Two forms of stating the accounts were presented:

(a) Real Estate $10,000	Mortgage $4,000
(b) Equity in Real Estate Value $10,000, Mortgage $4,000 6,000	....

In case (b) the $4,000 is eliminated as being merely an offset; while in (a) it is treated as a liability.

138. It may be noted here that it is not quite a matter of indifference which of these forms is used, but that the facts may be different. If the owner bought this property *subject* to the mortgage, so that he cannot be held for a deficiency-judgment, then it is quite appropriate to treat the mortgage as an offset and the equity only as the true asset. If, however, he gave his note or bond for the $4,000 it would be more correct to keep the mortgage standing by itself as an actual liability.

139. While offset accounts are kept in their current state for convenience, it is proper that at the date of the balance sheet they should be eliminated by subtraction from the opposit side. Adjuncts, being already on their proper side, do not give the same trouble, whether they are left in the main column or added in the margin.

140. As an adjunct to an asset, take the case of a bond purchased at a premium, the par value being $75,000 and the premium paid being $6,131.79. It is desired to exhibit both the par value and the total cost $81,131.79. For this purpose two accounts may be carried and in the balance sheet they may both be exhibited or their sum:

```
(a) Bonds at par ..................................... $75,000.00
    Premium ........................................    6,131.79
(b) Bonds at cost ...................................   81,131.79
```

141. As an offset to a liability we may take the case of a note (Bill Payable) for $6,666.67 which has just been discounted at 3 months at 5 per cent per annum. It is desired to keep an open account of the face of the note (the sum which must be paid three months hence), and also of the actual proceeds. This is done by means of a Discount account, an offset to Bills Payable. The actual proceeds are $5,833.34, and this is all that at the beginning of the three months is owing; as the three months pass, the liability rises till it reaches $6,666.67 at maturity. The accounts at first represent the condition thus:

Discount, $833.33   Bills Payable, $6,666.67

Many bookkeepers consider the discount as lost or "disserved" at once, not gradually. Scientifically, at least in theory, it should be assumed that the liability is at first $5,833.34 and gradually rises, thru the accretion of adverse interest, to $6,666.67, which latter sum is composed of $5,833.34 borrowed + $833.33 interest at 5.0625 per cent.

141. The balance-sheet in Figure 24 gives an example of an adjunct to a proprietary account. The true capital-balance is $71,468.43, but it is divided into the two parts, $60,000 the par value of the shares and $11,468.43 the surplus.

143. On the other hand let us suppose that the nominal capital had been fixt at $75,000 which would really have been nearer the truth than $60,000. The $3,531.57 by which the capitalization exceeds the true value would then be an offset against the $75,000 and two accounts would have to be carried.

Deficiency, $3,531.57   Capital Stock, $75,000.00

144. This is theoretically correct but in practice you will seldom see such a frank confession of impaired capital. Almost universally the assets are hoisted to meet the exigency, or the deficiency is represented as an asset. This receives some euphemistic title such as Good Will, Franchises, Patents. This may not be with any fraudulent intent, but from a feeling that the latent personal assets, spoken of in Article 84 and 101 as "non-ledger" assets, make the concern worth at least par as a revenue producer. There is a natural reluctance to admit the fact of over-capitalization or "watering."

William A. Paton

THE POSTULATES OF ACCOUNTING

William Andrew Paton *was born in Michigan in 1889, and received his bachelor's (1915) and Ph.D. (1917) degrees from the University of Michigan. He has taught at many schools for short periods (e.g., Minnesota, California, Chicago, Florida) but has spent most of his career at Michigan. He was Dickinson Lecturer at Harvard in 1940.*

Paton is a C.P.A. in Michigan, and was a member of the committee on accounting procedure of the American Institute of C.P.A. He has been especially active in the American Accounting Association and its predecessor, the American Association of University Instructors in Accounting, serving as president in 1922, as editor of The Accounting Review *(1926–28), and as director of research (1936–39). He collaborated with A. C. Littleton in writing* Introduction to Corporate Accounting Standards, *published by the Association in 1940. He was editor of* The Accountant's Handbook, *2nd and 3rd editions. Among his other numerous publications are* Accounting Theory *(1922),* Advanced Accounting *(1941), and* Shirtsleeve Economics *(1952).*

The emergence of the "entity theory" of accounting in the U.S. is usually dated from the publication of his Accounting Theory *(1922). The importance he attaches to "entity" is clearly seen in the chapter reprinted here. The assumption of the existence of a distinct business entity is first in the list of postulates he discusses.*

Impressed by the neatly ruled lines and the array of equal footings exhibited by the typical system of accounts and financial statements, the layman is likely to conclude that accounting deals with certainties, with data capable of exact and precise statement; that accounts are either accurate or inaccurate; that the principles and procedures of double entry, if applied without clerical error, will always lead to correct conclusions. Indeed, the accountant at times may be found slipping, somewhat unconsciously, into the same misapprehension. This is evidenced by the attitude of the auditor who spends perhaps several hours of time trying to locate the source of an error of a few cents in the purchases account, and then passes lightly over

Reprinted from Wm. A. Paton, *Accounting Theory* (New York: The Ronald Press Company, 1922), Chap. 20, by permission.

the question of the method of pricing adopted by the management in taking inventory.

Praiseworthy as is an effort to locate and correct clerical mistakes, great emphasis on this side of accounting indicates a lack of an appreciation of its more important purposes and of the inherent weaknesses of the art from the standpoint of literal accuracy. As a matter of fact, the accountant is being constantly faced with the necessity for judgment. Accounting is full of estimate, assumption. At times, unfortunately, the conclusions of the accountant must be well-nigh conjectural. The accountant, it must be remembered, is dealing primarily with economic data, with values, not with physical certainties; and values are highly uncertain and unstable aspects of structures, commodities, rights, services, and situations.

Not only does modern accounting involve estimate and judgment at many points, but the entire structure is based upon a series of general assumptions. In other words, underlying the specific conclusions of the accountant with respect to present values, costs, incomes, etc., are certain fundamental premises and postulates, few if any of which are capable of complete demonstration. It is intended in this final chapter to state and examine briefly the more important of these basic assumptions. In particular, stress will be laid upon their limitations. This does not mean that an attempt will be made to show that some of these postulates should be discarded. Accounting is a highly purposive field and any assumption, principle, or procedure is accordingly justified if it adequately serves the end in view—assuming that end to be reasonable, all things considered. Without certain assumptions, indeed, it would be impossible to proceed very far in accounting practice. On the other hand it is believed that accountants are sometimes in danger of forgetting their own premises and, therefore, the limitations of their work. If the accountant sees clearly the foundation upon which he is standing, with all its implications, he is less likely to fall into the mire of improper applications and erroneous general conclusions.

Several of these underlying propositions upon which accounting is based have been referred to from time to time in the preceding chapters. The present chapter will accordingly involve repetition to some extent. It is believed that it is desirable, however, in concluding this study, to attempt a systematic statement of all the important postulates of accounting. Such a statement will serve in a measure as a recapitulation, and should also aid in indicating the main relationships between the various problems which have been considered.

The Business Entity

To start with, *the existence of a distinct business entity* is something which the accountant almost universally assumes. The unit of organization with which he is chiefly concerned...is the specific business enterprise.

Accordingly, it is convenient for him to assume that this enterprise or business situation has a distinct existence, that it constitutes a real institution through which flows a stream of values and in the operation of which several, perhaps many individuals have a part. It is "the business" whose financial history the bookkeeper and accountant are trying to record and analyze; the books and accounts are the records of "the business"; the periodic statements of operation and financial condition are the reports of "the business"; the assets are the properties of "the business," and the equities are its ownership and obligations.

The assumption of a business entity somewhat apart and distinct from the actual persons conducting its operations, is a conception which has been greatly deplored by some writers and staunchly defended by others. Is it a valid premise for the accountant? Is there any such thing as "the business," a something having an independent and real existence? Or is this postulate unsupported by the facts of the business world?

The business enterprise of course is not a person. Hence to speak of it as a person or to endow it with personal attributes is to make use of a figure of speech. But this does not mean that the particular business enterprise has no real and measurably distinct existence. A particular enterprise is an institution, not a person; but an institution may be a very real thing. We are all living in the midst of a complex system of institutions. The federal government is not a person, but there are few things more real, as most of us have come to appreciate these last few years. A great university is an institution, not a person, but has none the less a distinct existence. Destroy all its current properties, scatter its staff, and the institution would doubtless still persist in some fashion. Similarly the business enterprise may have its reality. It is not always a mere figment of the imagination. It may be a living organism, in some cases huge, powerful, overshadowing, exerting a tremendous influence in the industrial community. The accountant's assumption is based at least in part on fact. There is, in many cases, a genuine business entity.

In the case of the corporation this postulate is validated from the legal standpoint. The corporation is a real entity, endowed by the state with all the privileges of any business person. It may acquire title to property, borrow money, engage in virtually any recognized business operation, hire labor, buy and sell merchandise and other property, etc. In this case the accountant's assumption is given flesh and blood by governmental authority. In general it may be said that the corporation, not its human members, owns the assets, directs the business, borrows funds, establishes dividend policies, and so on. From the legal point of view, evidently, the accounts and statements in this case exhibit nothing more nor less than the affairs of the corporation.

In the case of the sole-proprietorship, so-called, and the partnership, it must be admitted that, in general, the law does not acknowledge the existence of any business entity. The Revenue Act of 1917,[1] it is true, provided for an excess-profits tax upon the income of the unincorporated business, thus recognizing a taxable business entity in this case as well as in that of the corporation; but the view established in this act may be said to be exceptional in American law. For the most part there is no sharp distinction from the legal standpoint between the business affairs of the sole-proprietor or partner and his other interests. . . . There is here no segregation of business assets as in the case of the corporation. The residence of Smith, the grocer, for example, from the standpoint of the satisfaction of creditors in the case of insolvency, is in essentially the same position as is his store building.

But the legal point of view does not furnish the sole criterion. The law may look upon the partnership as merely a contractual relationship between two or more persons, yet there may be a business entity involved from other standpoints. A business need not be incorporated to become a distinct institution. Many an important business has been built upon the sole-proprietorship or partnership plan. Acquiring clientele and business standing, developing characteristic methods, exercising a powerful influence in the business community, swallowing up a succession of owners and managers with scarcely a ripple as affairs changed hands—such a business often has gone on for many decades. The great private banking houses of England and this country are good examples. There is nothing imaginary about the reality and continuity of existence of some of these venerable institutions.

The general proposition requires little argument for its justification. The concept of the business entity is constantly used outside the corporate form of organization by economists and others interested in the business process. The same view is solidly established in the business man's thinking as is evidenced by the fact that the expressions "house," "concern," "company," etc., are applied freely to the unincorporated enterprise.

. . . There are, of course, many situations requiring the use of accounts and other statistical records which are in no strict sense business enterprises. Something in the way of accounts may be needed in connection with the record of an individual's investments and personal property. One meets an occasional enthusiast who is obsessed by the fascinations of household accounting. Clubs, societies, and other organizations outside the business field need a systematic record of their financial transactions. In some of these situations a distinct entity may be involved, but, evidently, they do not constitute business institutions.

Even in the business field, situations so simple and temporary arise that there is little excuse for the conception of a business entity. To conceive of the business of the pop vender at a football game as having any distinct existence, to take an extreme example, would obviously be quite fantastic.

---

[1] That is, the act passed in 1916 as amended in 1917.

The importance of the entity depends upon the circumstances of each case. Enough has been said, however, to justify the statement that the assumption of a business existence is based to an important degree on the actual facts of the business world.

On the other hand, there is a danger that this assumption may be carried too far. The fact of the independent existence of the business entity must not be overstressed. No institution, however real, has any absolute existence. The accountant must remember that human beings are the immediate means by which the affairs of a business institution are conducted and that, in particular cases, it may be necessary to focus attention directly and exclusively upon the individual owners and managers and their acts. . . . The courts have long recognized that the apparent act of the business must sometimes be construed to be the act of an individual owner, and that, in other cases, the apparent act of the individual may be virtually the act of the institution. In order to get at the realities of the situation it is accordingly sometimes necessary to brush aside formal evidences and transactions.

. . . In general it may be said that the relations between the "business" and its individual owners and managers must be considered as being on a different level from those between the business and outside persons or entities. Directors' borrowings, officers' salaries, partners' drawings, purchases by a corporation of its outstanding securities, are cases in point. A blind insistence on the independence of the business entity in such situations is bound to lead to unreasonable conclusions.

Some might contend that the practicing accountant makes no such universal use of this assumption as has been claimed above. The accountant, it might be urged, adopts the viewpoint of the proprietor, the individual or individuals who largely control the business, and constructs his system of accounts and statements on the basis of the relation of the business transactions to this specific person or persons. Now while it is true that many statements of accounting theory have been couched in terms of proprietorship, the writer does not believe that the professional man has ever abandoned the business-entity conception. Consciously or unconsciously he adopts this assumption as a basis for his work. He prepares the balance sheet of the X Co., not of the stockholders of that enterprise. Even the partnership or sole-proprietorship balance sheet is headed with the firm or house name, if there is one, rather than with the names of the individual proprietors. No one would think, for example, of listing at the top of the balance sheet of a certain large publishing concern the names of the more than a score of partners making up its proprietorship. It is the balance sheet of the business, not of its various owners, in which all are interested.

Accounting theory is much less rational than practice at this point, as was pointed out in the preface. In spite of the tremendous development of the corporation in the last few decades, most writers, unfortunately, persist in attempting to state the philosophy of accounts in terms of the conditions of the small sole-proprietorship. The result is a system of concepts and principles highly inapplicable to the facts of modern business organization. This is the day of the *business enterprise* and the accounting theorist must thoroughly realize this fact. It is especially important in view of the emphasis placed nowadays upon the uses to which accounts may be put for managerial purposes. The conception of the manager must be exactly that of the business entity as an economic unit; and if, as is repeatedly said, the most important purpose which modern accounting can serve lies in the rationalizing of business administration, the accountant must of necessity adopt the viewpoint of the manager in large measure.

The " Going Concern "

Not only does the accountant assume the existence of a business entity, but he also, as a corollary, takes for granted *the continuity of this entity*, i.e., he assumes that the business with which he is dealing is a "going concern." This second assumption, it need hardly be said, is largely one of convenience. No one is in a position to predict, with certainty, the future of a specific business. Business in general is reasonably sure to go on in some fashion; but assurance of success in the particular case is not found in this fact. All business involves the speculative element, although in some cases it is much more pronounced than in others.

On the other hand the going-concern assumption is entirely reasonable. In the absence of evidence which gives a definite presumption to the contrary, it is surely fair to assume that the particular business is going to continue, at least for the near future. In the case of large and strongly intrenched enterprises the assumption approaches practical assurance. Further, when the number of business enterprises in the United States is taken into account it is clear that the percentage of failures in a particular year is very small. The accountant accordingly has the right to take it for granted that the specific concern in which he is interested will continue to operate for some time. Conceivably bankruptcy may occur, but it need not be anticipated in the accounts.

The going concern rather than the seriously embarrassed or insolvent business is the normal case. Accordingly, in developing accounting principles and procedures the accountant must keep this in mind. It would certainly be unreasonable to set up the conditions of insolvency as a background in determining present values, effective liabilities, etc. Thus we have the principle that the assets of a business should be revalued for balance-sheet purposes on the basis of their value to the going concern. This rule or standard of measurement is, of course, especially important in the valuation of the fixed properties. The immediate market value of the highly specialized machine bolted to the factory floor is likely to be very much below its cost less conventional depreciation. The liquidation value of a factory building may be even less. A railway roadbed and track furnish a still more extreme case of the discrepancy between use value and immediate selling price. In general, costs less systematic depreciation are considerably higher than immediate selling values in the case of plant and equipment assets.

Similarly the legal liability in the case of insolvency may differ from the effective accounting liability from the standpoint of the going concern. The face or par value, i.e., the amount to be paid at maturity, is usually conceded to be the legal liability and the amount which would become effective—as a base figure at least—in the case of reorganization or complete liquidation. But in the case of a heavily discounted bond issue running for, let us say, twenty years, the true accounting liability at the end of the first period, for example, would be simply the original principal or actual investment plus any accumulated discount (true interest accrued and unpaid). By the date of maturity the accountant would have accumulated out of earnings the difference between original principal and the face or par sum; and the accounting liability and the lump sum payable would then be identical. . . .

The accountant need scarcely be reminded of the profound influence of the conception of the going concern upon accounting principles and practices, especially in connection with valuations. Accounting practice is saturated with evidence of a dependence upon this assumption. It has an especial importance in the two connections already mentioned, but has many other applications as well.

As was implied above, this assumption, although incapable of demonstration in the particular case, is thoroughly reasonable and needs little qualification. The accountant should, of course, keep the possibility of financial embarrassment and insolvency in the background of his consciousness. If the trend of events points toward bankruptcy in a particular case the financial reports should be so constructed that all interested are apprised of the real situation. The chief reason why the accountant and business man should clearly recognize the use of such an assumption is the emphasis thereby given to the provisional character of the balance-sheet statement, even under the most favorable circumstances. A balance sheet is not an absolute statement of fact. The financial history of a business enterprise is a continuous stream, not a succession of mutually independent segments. The accountant, accordingly, in attempting to break up this history into definite periods, setting a balance sheet at either end, must sever many real connections, hazard many judgments. The future is uncertain; and yet the validity of the statement of asset values as of December 31, 1921, for example, depends in a large measure upon the future course of events. In presenting a balance sheet what the accountant says, in effect, is this: "Here, managers, directors, stockholders, creditors, bankers, and others interested, is a balance sheet of the X Co. as of the close of the last fiscal period. Assuming that the company is going to continue operations successfully, I adjudge the statement of the assets and liabilities presented herein to be reasonable."

The Balance-Sheet Equation

We may now turn to certain more specific and technical postulates of the accountant. First among these will be considered the assumption that in every business enterprise an equation exists between the total of the properties and the total of the representations of ownership, proprietary and other elements combined—the assumption, in other words, that the total of the assets of every business is equal to the total of the equities.

This proposition is probably the most nearly capable of a superficial demonstration of any of the accountant's premises. . . . The two classes of the balance sheet, in a sense, are merely different aspects of the same situation. The assets represent a *direct* statement of the value of the properties of the enterprise; the liabilities represent an *indirect* statement of the same values. In one case the accountant is listing the objective properties; in the other he is recording the proper distribution of the asset total among the various individuals and interests having claims therein. In one case attention is being focused upon the objects for which funds have been expended; in the other, upon the sources of these funds. The total of the properties constitutes the total of the wealth or capital of the enterprise; the equities express the dispersion of this capital among the various investors involved. And since the same measuring unit, the dollar, is used in stating both classes of data, the totals are inevitably equal.

Yet this equation is far from being an absolute statement of fact; it is easy to exaggerate its intrinsic validity. It, too, savors of a proposition of convenience. What the accountant is saying in starting with this premise is simply this: "I find the total of the assets of a business situation to be such and such an amount. Next I divide this amount among the various investors in accordance with what seem to be the legal rights and privileges of each. My two lists now constitute a balance sheet."

Evidently the determination of the equities, at least as far as the total is concerned, is a secondary process which is based directly upon the amount ascertained to be the total of the assets. A serious assumption, incapable of any complete validation, is here involved. Why should the legal and economic rights in a particular business situation be considered to equal precisely the sum of a list of asset values arrived at by divers and complex processes of valuation? As a matter of fact they do not, in the absence of immediate and complete liquidation.[2] The equity of the common stockholder, for example,

---

[2] And even in the case of liquidation asset values based upon the going-concern conception would probably not be realized, and hence would not express accurately the various equities in the situation from this standpoint.

is expressed in the corporate balance sheet by what is left over, the residuum of the asset total after all prior equities have been deducted. . . . Does this represent the true equity of the common stockholder in any fundamental sense? Is not this arrangement largely a matter of convenience? To what, precisely, is the common stockholder entitled? Not to what he originally invested nor to this balance-sheet residuum. As far as the assets are concerned, he is entitled in the case of liquidation to any balance available after all other claims are met. In the case of forced insolvency this amount is likely to be nil or negligible and to bear little relation to any previous balance-sheet figures. In addition, he has a right to a share in all the excess future earnings of the company, a right the realization of which, however, is more or less contingent on the specific policy of the board of directors. Is it not evident, under these circumstances, that the usual balance-sheet representation of the residual equity is a very imperfect statement of the situation?

The "book value" of the stockholders' interest in the corporation is a highly conventional thing. It can be explained only as the process of asset valuation is explained, a process which is itself based upon numerous assumptions. No wonder that the market price per share seldom approaches book value and often does not even follow its trends! Because of the control of management vested in the common stockholder and the possibility of future returns, common shares sometimes have a market value when, according to orthodox principles and rules of valuation, there is no book value whatsoever.

In the case of the liabilities the amounts attached by the accountant are likely to be somewhat more reasonable. In general—ignoring unaccumulated discounts, unamortized premiums, etc.—it may be said that the accountant regards the sum due at maturity as the true liability. In the absence of insolvency this is the amount which will finally be realized by the contractual investor; it is likely to approximate the original principal; if the company becomes bankrupt, there is yet some possibility of the creditors receiving the full amount. Consequently, there is a large element of precise fact in the balance-sheet figures which are attached to the contractual equities. Even here, of course, the market value of a particular bond or other similar security may vary noticeably from the amount appearing in the issuing company's financial statement.

It should be emphasized, however, that even if all the liabilities were stated with absolute precision and were shown at figures representing real significance in every case, but the residual equity were shown for convenience as the difference between the asset total and all other equities, the equality of footings of balance-sheet classes would still, to a degree, be a matter of assumption.[3]

In view of the fact that the statement of the stockholder's equity in the balance sheet, as has just been indicated, is likely to be the most questionable

---

[3] The footings as given are, of course, equal. But the question is, are the two classes of data really equal? The accountant assumes an affirmative answer to be correct.

of any balance-sheet item, the stress placed upon the "net worth" figure in current statements of the theory of accounts is perhaps not entirely justified. . . . The implication seems to be that there is something peculiarly valid about this concluding figure. While it is true that this residual figure is of especial consequence to the accountant, its importance, in the case of a corporation at any rate, does not lie in its accuracy or precise validity as an expression of the equity of the buffer interest. . . . It is rather of especial significance to the accountant because it is his doubtful territory. It is the place where all his peculiar estimates, hazards, adjustments, etc., "come home to roost." Its trend is of much more importance than its exact amount on any particular occasion, for, if consistent methods of valuation are followed, its increase is a fairly reliable evidence of operating success and growing financial strength, while its diminution indicates just the reverse situation.

It is not intended to attempt to show by the foregoing that the equation postulate of the accountant is unreasonable or improper. It is instead a thoroughly rational and essential premise, upon which depends, in a sense, the entire technical structure of the accounts. The equation of assets and equities, as has been shown in this study, is the foundation of the double-entry system. And, as was stated at the outset, the equation holds, in the limited sense indicated, for every business enterprise. In the nature of the case the asset total, dispersed among the equities, gives another equal class. The assets are the only objective residence of value. At a certain date they are found to total up to a particular sum. It is then entirely reasonable, indeed unavoidable, to state the evidences of ownership and claims against the business in these terms. There is no alternative. Future earnings are indeterminate; the amounts which will finally be withdrawn are unknown (as far as the residual interest is concerned); a stating of equities in terms of property values is then the only feasible procedure.

It is desired, however, to suggest that the accountant should not take this balancing equity figure too seriously. It behooves him to be fully cognizant of the underlying process by which this figure is ascertained, and thus to realize that it is not an independent and directly determined fact.

Finally, it may be reiterated that there are certain situations outside the business enterprise proper which do not present an equation of assets and equities in the ordinary sense. Perhaps the most important case is the governmental unit, federal, state, or local. A government may owe huge sums far in excess of the value of the assets to which it has specific title. . .and yet ultimately pay 100 cents on the dollar. The state, of course, has the power to tax, and thus ordinarily possesses potential control over sufficient assets to liquidate all its obligations. But since the tax power in itself is not an asset that can be evaluated by ordinary means, it is not ordinarily possible to prepare a conventional balance sheet for the governmental unit.

Similarly, the individual sometimes "mortgages his future" and borrows sums for consumption purposes. A college student, for example, may have liabilities galore but no assets in the usual sense. Yet his creditors may consider him "perfectly good." The liabilities are capable of definite statistical expression in terms of sums due in the future, but there is no way of assaying the future assets. The student has a one-sided balance sheet. No equational statement is possible.

Financial Condition
and the Balance Sheet

This brings us to another, somewhat related, balance-sheet postulate. The accountant commonly assumes that all facts expressing the financial status of an enterprise can be presented in the two classes, assets and liabilities, measured in terms of the dollar. That is, he assumes that *a statement of assets and liabilities in dollars and cents is a complete representation of the financial condition of the enterprise* on the date of the statement.

This proposition not only cannot be demonstrated but it can be pretty thoroughly disproved. . . . The balance sheet, as a true statement of financial condition, should not be taken too seriously; it has very definite limitations under the most favorable circumstances. In the first place, as has just been indicated, the future costs, earnings, and losses of a business enterprise are largely indeterminate; and yet the reality of the present value depends essentially upon the assumption that the business will be at least moderately successful. A balance-sheet statement of asset values is really only provisional; it depends upon the future for its validation.

In the second place, there are many vital considerations and conditions involved in every business enterprise of such a character as completely to escape classification as assets and equities and measurement by the dollar. In the individual's economy, for example, health, energy, resourcefulness, skill, and similar qualifications and endowments, may be of much greater ultimate consequence, even from a strictly economic point of view, than a disposal over a considerable sum of present wealth. These and other "imponderables" are also of the utmost consequence in business. The note of a man of unquestioned integrity, for example, may be better security than a lien upon specific assets. Our college student, as was stated above, may be a "good risk." In the business enterprise a well-organized and loyal personnel may be a much more important "asset" than a stock of merchandise. In other words, the loss by fire, for example, of the goods on hand might not be as serious a matter as the disruption of the staff. Location, trade-name, clientele, and similar considerations are likewise of extreme importance. Such conditions come to definite expression as assets if they are paid for; otherwise they find no place in the ordinary balance sheet.

Until some scheme is found by which these imponderables of the business enterprise may be assayed and given definite statistical expression, the accountant must continue to prepare the balance sheet as he has been doing. At present there seems to be no way of measuring such factors in terms of the dollar; hence, they cannot be recognized as specific economic assets. But let us, accordingly, admit the serious limitations of the conventional balance sheet as a statement of financial condition. How frequently do we note a business which shows a highly favorable "statement of financial condition" and then, within two or three years, because of a change in management, a lapse of demand, the advent of new methods, a decline in labor efficiency, or other reason, we find that the supposed values have evaporated and that the business is insolvent or financially embarrassed! The stockholders and others interested should realize that the balance sheet, even if the underlying accounting is thoroughly sound, is an imperfect representation of the current position of the enterprise and only an indication of its probable position in the near future.[4]

The accountant, of course, commonly recognizes the fact that the balance sheet has serious limitations. In some instances he even tries to allow for the future by appending statements of "contingent" assets and liabilities. That is, if there are potential assets or potential liabilities in the situation, which are sufficiently in sight to be more than bare possibilities, it is considered good practice to indicate these elements, in some supplementary fashion, in connection with the balance sheet.

There is still a further assumption made by the accountant which is of especial importance in this connection. Not only does he commonly take it for granted that the entire financial status of an enterprise can be set up as assets and liabilities measured in terms of the dollar, but in general he assumes that *the value or significance of the measuring unit remains unchanged*. This postulate is, of course, not sound.... The value of the money unit, the accountant's standard of measure, is constantly fluctuating. One of the fundamental limitations of accounting arises here. Since the measuring unit is unstable, comparisons of successive financial statements are likely to lead to erroneous conclusions, unless great care is exercised in making such comparisons. The increase in asset dollars and cents during a particular period, for example, may be unreliable as evidence of increase in the actual stock of structures, commodities, etc.; instead, it may largely reflect simply the application of a less significant measuring unit to an amount of physical goods no greater than the supply at the beginning of the period. Similarly, the net income balance may be a very imperfect indication of genuine improvement in economic well-being; and an enterprise may

---

[4] The balance sheet of the large and complex enterprise is, of course, also likely to be imperfect for various technical reasons. The taking of inventory, for example may consume several weeks, and the final figure placed in the balance sheet will accordingly be no more than an approximation of the value of goods on hand at the precise date of the statement.

build up a huge surplus account in a period of rising prices without increasing its stock of goods or enlarging plant proportionately.

It would not be fair to imply that the accountant does not realize that his measuring unit is unstable. But, nevertheless, he sets up comparative statements of income, surplus, assets, etc.; he values fixed assets on the basis of cost less depreciation; and in many other ways he makes use of the assumption that the dollar has a constant value. Various schemes have been discussed by means of which the accountant might take closer cognizance of the fluctuations in the value of money, but as yet there have been no developments of consequence in this direction.

Cost and Book Value

The accountant makes certain important assumptions in connection with costing and valuation. In the first place, he assumes that *cost gives actual value for purposes of initial statement*. This assumption...is one of the most important premises underlying technical accounting. Its necessity is plain. Cost is the only definite fact available when a property is purchased, constructed, or otherwise acquired. It is accordingly entirely reasonable to charge the appropriate asset account with the amount of this cost in any case. It is a part of the accountant's business to record what has actually happened, to set down a systematic statement of all explicit transactions. It follows as a matter of course that he will assume the original value of an asset in the hands of a particular enterprise to equal its cost.

To put the matter in other words, the accountant, like the economist, postulates a world full of rational businessmen. He assumes that every exchange is fair, that buyer and seller are in every case equally informed and equally gifted in ability to trade. If a manufacturer pays $500 for a unit of equipment, for example, this means that the true value of the unit to him is $500, and that this amount, therefore, should be entered on the books as an asset. Under all circumstances, businessmen are deemed to proceed rationally. Coercion, fraud, bad judgment, carelessness—all these factors are in general assumed to be entirely absent from business transactions.

This is, of course, not literally the case. Business transactions are not actually equal exchanges; for the parties involved are not always equally strong or fortunate. Losses occur in actual purchases as well as in other connections. No one is infallible. How often the individual, in his personal economy, comes to feel that he has dismally failed to get full value for his expenditures! Similarly, the businessman proceeds unwisely in many of his commitments.

But, as was just stated, in the absence of definite evidence to the contrary, the accountant has every right to treat initial value as equivalent to cost. It is difficult to see how he could proceed otherwise. He cannot set himself up as an absolute judge of values. If the transaction is entirely voluntary, and both parties thereto appear satisfied, he is justified in treating the figures that appear in the exchange as bona fide values. Later, if substantial evidence of depreciation or original loss is adduced, it will be time enough to revise the initial figures.

An initial record of total cost would, of course, be necessary even if cost and original value were not identical. However, if it immediately became evident in any case that real value were greater or less than cost, the profit or loss could be recognized at once. But seldom, indeed, does the accountant attempt to pass judgment upon the validity of bona fide purchase price as a determinant of initial asset value.

An asset may occasionally be acquired by gift, accident, "strategy," etc. In such a case the accountant would usually admit that, if the asset were one which had a determinate purchase and sale value, the fair market value of the asset so acquired should be set up in the accounts; for otherwise the existence of a definite property would be concealed so far as the accounts were concerned. On the other hand most accountants would probably agree that cases may arise in practice where cost greatly exceeds initial value. In general, however, the cost-gives-value assumption is rigidly adhered to.

In the second place, the accountant makes the closely related assumption...that the value of any commodity, service, or condition, utilized in production, *passes over into* the object or product for which the original item was expended and *attaches to* the result, giving it its value. This postulate is the essential basis for the work of the cost accountant; without it, there could be no costing.

Just how valid is this assumption? In attempting to answer this question it may be noted first that the physical essence of assets utilized in production does not always literally pass into the product. Even in the case of raw materials there is much waste. The fixed assets, of course, contribute nothing to the product but certain essential conditions. Similarly, supervision and many other services do not attach directly to the physical output. Evidently, then, there is no complete and clear-cut physical connection between cost items and product on which the accountant can base his premise. Further, even if the product were simply an amalgam, physically, of the commodities used in production, this would not mean that the original values had literally passed into the result. A dollar's worth of gold in a watch case may be worth intrinsically somewhere near a dollar. But the value of the recoverable steel from even a new automobile would be much less than the value to the manufacturer of the steel materials used in fabricating the car. In general there is no guarantee that converted materials, in product, will have the same values as when in the raw state.

To the economist this is perhaps the most interesting of all the accountant's assumptions. It constitutes a kind of cost theory of value. The accountant in general assumes that work in process—in all its various stages—and finished stock are worth for balance-sheet purposes the sum of the labor, material, and other costs expended in getting these results. He assumes that in some mysterious manner the values of these original commodities and services, which are worth cost for purposes of initial statement, pass over into and inhere in the object for which they were utilized. This is clearly an application of a cost theory of value to the internal conditions of the specific enterprise. Values are acquired in various original forms; then they are converted into inchoate and, finally, finished goods.

So far as price determination is concerned this is, of course, unsound in most cases. Costs, a partial explanation of supply limitation, undoubtedly influence prices. But in general the influential cost is not the specific cost to the business enterprise in which the accountant is concerned, but rather the cost to the marginal producer (or, in certain cases, the representative producer), whoever and wherever he may be. The specific cost has, in the production of standard goods, little or no influence on selling price.[5] If a particular producer's cost is high, due to labor inefficiency, mismanagement, accident, or other cause, this will not make the product worth any more to the consumer nor enable the producer, who must compete with others in the same field, to advance the price to a point which will cover the unusual expense of production. Further, unless production is directed toward effective demand, output may be of little or no value, regardless of its cost. Or, if demand suddenly lapses, the fact that costs are such and such a figure will not in itself hold up price.

The accountant, however, is not trying to determine selling value but cost value. He is asking the question, what are the costs of this particular enterprise? Evidently this is a matter of fact (although it may be very difficult to get the correct data). It is the accountant's business to report the actual costs, whatever the figure. If he finds at the end of a particular period that a certain fraction of the total costs incurred are still within the business, or at least have had nothing to do with current sales, it is entirely natural, then, for him to conclude that these values attach to work in process and finished stock to the extent that they have entered into production. Since these costs bear no relation to current business, they must be held back; later they will be passed on as expense, conceived to be embodied in finished product sold. To place the deferred amount in the balance sheet as an asset involves, of course, precisely the assumption that we are considering. But since these values are not an expense, or cost of current sales, they must represent either an asset or a loss. If the continued production of the commodity or service in question is in prospect, it is accordingly entirely reasonable to place these values in the balance sheet.

The work in process and finished stock of the manufacturer as well as the

---

5 Many would disagree with this statement, but the writer believes it is essentially sound. On the other hand, in the case of specialized goods and equipment produced to order, specific estimated cost undoubtedly plays an important part in determining selling price.

stock of the trader are sometimes inventoried at "cost or market, whichever is lower." To the extent that this rule is followed by the accountant he is evidently not adhering literally to the assumption we have been discussing. Nevertheless, it constitutes, in general, one of the most important premises of accounting.

Cost Accrual and Income

The accountant assumes, as has just been indicated, that costs *accrue*, that is, that the values of structures and commodities utilized in production gradually expire and attach to work in progress. In general he limits this assumption, however, to costs from the point of view of the particular enterprise, disregarding the margin between this figure and cost to the purchaser, or selling price. In other words, he assumes that expense accrues but that net revenue or profit suddenly appears, full-blown, on some specific occasion, commonly that of the sale. . . . The significance of this postulate may be reiterated here. It means that the accountant's "expense" for the particular business and the economist's "cost of production" are two quite different things. The economist is talking about price-determining cost, the cost to the purchaser. From this standpoint, cost and selling price, at least in the marginal instance, are essentially equal. Cost in this sense includes not only the marginal producer's outlays but his net return as well. Thus, the economist assumes that business net revenue, in part at least, is an essential cost of production, an element which price must cover if production is to continue in satisfactory volume.

On the other hand, the whole scheme of accounting is based upon the plan of showing as costs or expense only the expirations of purchased commodities and services, not the economic value of the services contributed by the business itself in furnishing capital and management. The accounts are organized so as to disclose the difference between expense and revenue as a residuum, a balance. And this margin of value, the net revenue, is assumed to appear with respect to the particular transaction, *in toto,* not to accrue. Purchased commodities and services are assumed to expire steadily and pass into the expense category; services furnished by the business and its owners are assumed to accrue only as sales of finished product are made.

. . . If the value of work in process accrues because of purchased commodities and services utilized, it would seem to be reasonable to assume that the values contributed by the enterprise are likewise accumulating. To admit this, however, would involve the recognition of profit prior to completion and sale; and this the accountant, in general, steadfastly refuses to do.

In the case of rent, insurance, and other costs, where payment is made for the service involved on a time basis, the accountant commonly takes it for granted that the cost accrues with precise uniformity.

That the depreciation of fixed assets is uniformly continuous is an interesting and important subsidiary assumption in this connection. The only method of apportioning depreciation widely used in practice involves the assumption that the values of fixed properties expire continuously and at a uniform rate. In the nature of the case, the accountant must apportion depreciation on the basis of premises of convenience. The whole depreciation analysis must be based upon a series of estimates. In the entire life of a fixed asset but two explicit transactions arise, purchase and abandonment. The situation between is entirely obscure. A machine, for example, is purchased and installed at a cost of $1,000. It is estimated that the service life is ten years. This is the first assumption. Second, it is estimated that the salvage value less demolition expense is $100—another assumption. On the basis of these assumptions, then, the total depreciation during the life of the unit is $900. The accountant is now faced with the problem of apportionment. He has two figures: cost, a known fact; and net salvage, an estimate. It is his problem to bridge the gap in time, estimated at ten years. How shall this total depreciation be spread as a cost of product throughout the period? Evidently his decision will again be based on assumption.

Three or four principal courses at once present themselves. First, shall the depreciation be assumed to be a function of physical product? That is, shall each item, pound, or other unit of product be charged with so much fixed asset cost? Evidently no definite physical connection could be traced on this basis. It might also be pointed out that deterioration is going on steadily in most cases regardless of the number of units of output. In fact, in some instances inactivity accelerates the process of disintegration and decay. Yet this assumption would not be wholly unreasonable. The assets are acquired because their services are deemed to be necessary in turning out product. Why then should not each unit of product bear a proportionate part of this total cost? As a matter of fact the depletion of natural resources is commonly computed and charged in terms of some convenient unit of output.

Or shall depreciation be assumed to accrue in terms of the value of gross revenue rather than its physical volume? This idea again has much to commend it from the standpoint of expediency. And it has been adhered to in business practice to an important degree. Formerly some business managements followed the policy of making heavy depreciation allowances in years of large gross revenues and smaller or even no depreciation charges in lean years. The current practice of incurring heavy maintenance costs in boom years, and of postponing repairs in dull periods, results similarly.

In general, as was stated above, modern practice assumes depreciation of plant and equipment assets to be continuous and uniform. The straight-line method of apportionment is the technical expression for this assumption. Thus, in the above illustration, the depreciation according to this plan would be 10 per cent each year of the total depreciable amount, or $90. This is the scheme now almost universally followed. Yet, obviously, there is no way of demonstrating its validity. True, as already noted, there is evidence that the processes of deterioration are more or less steady and uniform, though not perfectly so. And no doubt these inevitable processes are the important physical expression of value depreciation. But depreciation is lapse in value. It is a value problem and it can never be shown that this value expiration is a direct function of physical processes. If value were a physical essence it would be possible, no doubt, to attach some sort of gauge which would exactly measure its flow. There are still some who believe that valuation will sometime be reduced to an exact physical process. But an appreciation of the true nature of value should make it clear that this is out of the question. Valuation will always involve specific judgments and general assumptions.

Sequences

One further class of assumptions will be discussed. At various points the accountant finds it necessary to adopt certain premises with respect to sequences of data and relationships between series of facts. For example, he commonly takes it for granted that a loss in asset value falls upon or extinguishes the most recently accumulated proprietorship. Thus, expirations are commonly charged first against gross earnings or the otherwise net earnings for the period; in the second place they are deducted from accumulated profits; and they are charged to the accounts showing original investment only as a last resort. In other words, losses are in general assumed not to have any effect upon original investment or capital until the entire amount of accumulated profit is absorbed.

This is evidently purely an assumption. It has been repeatedly pointed out in this study that no particular asset has any direct connection with a particular section of proprietorship. The residual equity simply represents an element in the asset total, it does not represent particular items. Consequently, when an asset disappears it would be just as reasonable, theoretically, to charge the amount against one proprietary account as another. In fact, as it is often the older assets which first expire or are lost, it might be argued that the accounts showing original investments should be used first in the recognition of losses.

This assumption appears entirely proper, however, when attention is focused upon the purposes which the accounts are designed to serve. The investors are interested in seeing the margin by which their original equity is increased. It is accordingly quite rational to retain the original figure unchanged, and show all variations, as far as possible, in supplementary accounts. Even in the case of loss in connection with an original asset—such, for example, as a loss on the sale of the securities of a subsidiary company which were purchased with the stockholders' initial funds—it would be more reasonable, for purposes of financial statement, to charge surplus rather than capital account.

The assumption that all disbursements to shareholders absorb earnings before tapping investment is a closely related postulate. A formal statement of this premise is found in the Revenue Act of 1921. In section 201 (b) it is held that every corporate distribution is made out of earnings and from the most recently accumulated earnings until the entire amount of the undivided profit has been extinguished. Numerous similar assumptions might be cited from this act and its supporting regulations.

Another assumption of this type which is widely adopted by the accountant is that units of raw materials or merchandise consumed or sold are always taken from the oldest in stock, or, to put it differently, that the inventory is always composed of the units most recently acquired. Here we have an assumption which is, quite obviously, not based on literal fact. It is perhaps true to some extent that the trader attempts to dispose of his oldest stock first, especially in the case of perishables; but in other cases quite the opposite holds. The oldest shipment of coal, brass castings, or of other raw materials is quite likely to be at the bottom of the bin.

A justification for this assumption may be found, however, in the fact that the accounts are thereby kept more nearly up to date from the standpoint of sound economics. One of the basic principles of economic reasoning is the law of single price. Another principle is that, in general, cost of replacement is the only cost which has any influence on the determination of price. In view of these laws the most reasonable interpretation of the "cost of goods on hand" is the cost of the most recently acquired lots up to the amount of the physical inventory.

The Bureau of Internal Revenue, it may be noted, has adopted a similar rule of procedure in connection with the determination of taxable income from the sale of securities. The taxpayer who buys and sells securities, unless he can identify specific lots sold, is obliged to treat blocks sold as arising from the earliest purchases.

The accountant makes use of many other assumptions of this type, but the foregoing illustrations will be sufficient to indicate the character of this class of premises.

In conclusion it may be reiterated that many of these fundamental propositions are incapable of any complete proof or demonstration. Indeed, some of them can be disproved from the standpoint of literal accuracy. Yet, in view of the conditions and purposes of accounting practice, they are, for the most part, entirely reasonable. They are largely assumptions of expediency, without which it would be impossible for the accountant to proceed.

The accountant should be thoroughly aware of his assumptions, however, else he is likely to forget the inherent limitations attaching to his exhibits and conclusions. Not only is accounting practice fraught with all kinds of serious technical perils but the entire structure of accounts and the recognized system of procedures is based upon assumptions. In view of this situation, a mild skepticism as to the reliability of accounting data and interpretations, still apparent on the part of some business men, may perhaps be pardoned. Accounting has taken long strides in recent years; the present interest in the subject is unparalleled. It is highly desirable, in the course of this rapid development, that the pillars of theory and practice be occasionally scrutinized and assayed, with a view to discovering precisely how firmly they are grounded.

John B. Canning

SOME DIVERGENCES
OF ACCOUNTING THEORY
FROM ECONOMIC THEORY

John Bennett Canning *(1884–1962) was born in Michigan and educated at the University of Chicago, where he received his bachelor's degree in 1913 and his Ph.D. in 1929. He was on the faculty at Chicago (1915–1917) and at Stanford from 1919 until his retirement in 1946. In World War I, he served as an officer with the U.S. Army in France. While at Stanford he headed the division of accountancy within the department of economics. During the 1920's, he acted as examiner for the California State Board of Accountancy. Among other items, he published* Economics of Accountancy *in 1929, wrote the article on cost accounting in the* Encyclopedia of the Social Sciences, *and wrote "A Certain Erratic Tendency in Accountants' Income Procedure" for the first issue of* Econometrica. *In the 1930's, his interests shifted to fiscal policy, unemployment insurance and social security, health insurance and hospitalization costs, and agricultural policy. He served in various capacities with the U.S. Department of Agriculture during World War II. At the close of the war he went to Berlin as the U.S. representative on the quadripartite council concerning problems of food and agriculture in the occupied zones.*

Canning was primarily a statistician and economist who found accounting of interest because of the wealth of data it provides for analysis and evaluation. He is one of the first to observe that what accountants do is better than what they say about what they do—their actions are better than their explanations. His respect for accounting is evident in the article reprinted here, in which he compares accounting theory and economic theory at various points. His most influential work in the field of accounting is his Economics of Accountancy *in which he brings statistical concepts and methods and the economics of Irving Fisher to bear on the valuation problem in accounting. (For an outline of his general theory, see the reprint of the article by E. G. Nelson, page 158).*

Reprinted from *The Accounting Review* (March, 1929), pp. 1–8, by permission.

Professor David Friday many years ago was, quite unintentionally, the instigator of this paper. In an extemporaneous address to a class in elementary accounting of which I was a member he said in effect that the professional public accountant can lay no more secure foundation for the theory and practice of his profession than by acquiring a thorough familiarity with general economic theory; particularly with the classical theory of value and distribution. For no better reason than that I intended to become a professional economist I believed him; it seems necessary to the beginner in professional study to attach all importance to the subject matter of his profession. No doubt many of you at one time or another have shared Professor Friday's belief. Most economists and some teachers of accounting do.

Even after my chief interest had centered upon instruction for those who meant to become professional public accountants, I continued to preach my belief to all and sundry. And, being in a position not merely to advise and to preach, but also to require conformance, I thrust many excellent students of accounting into courses in economic theory. They were excellent courses in theory. Make no mistake about that. But many of the students came back to me in pained confusion. They would admit that the subject was interesting for itself, but they wanted to know how the theories of production, of exchange, of distribution, of consumption and of public finance and how the history of these theories could throw any light upon the problems of professional public accounting. And, I manufacturing explanations without reflection, told them how. By the look upon their faces I could see that to their confusion I had added disbelief.

I am not wholly insensitive to the opinions of good students. I finally began to consider the matter on its merits and to look for real support to my belief. To my embarrassment I found little. I hardly know now whether to say that my earlier belief was a mere act of faith or that my conception of economic theory is now so different from those brands professed by the classical economists and by Jevons, Marshall, Cannan, Taussig, Seligman, Ely, and a host of others as to constitute an entire shift of ground.

As between the writers in accounting theory and the writers in economic theory of whom I am now speaking it can be maintained: (1) that they adopt wholly different modes of analysis; (2) that they take into account a vastly different scope of subject matter; (3) that their major topical divisions in systematic writings have almost nothing in common; (4) that they concern themselves almost entirely with diverse problems; and (5) that the points of view taken toward method, subject matter, and specific problems have little in common. It is quite possible to discuss the topic to which I have addressed myself under these qualitative divisions. But within the scope of this paper I shall probably convey my ideas more clearly if I consider a series of illustrative cases and hold myself free to point out whatever differences seem most significant.

Both professions, to be sure, deal with the conduct of men in gaining a livelihood—with income getting in that most general sense of the supply of those objective services with which our human, material wants are satisfied—but with a difference. The accountant is concerned with those activities almost exclusively as they manifest themselves in those actual, particular institutions which we call enterprises. His unit group is the business enterprise. With individual human beings he is concerned chiefly to the extent to which they participate in the finances or the operations of the enterprise under review. Even when the accountant prepares an individual's income tax return he is concerned only with those elements of his want satisfying activities that give rise to a tax liability.

Whether the accountant is dealing with an enterprise as an entirety or with the individual as a taxpayer, both the enterprise and the taxpayer are real. The economist, on the contrary, devotes no attention at all to real individuals or to real enterprises. He may appear to be concerned with what laborers do, or what is done by the suppliers of monied funds or by those who exercise managerial powers, or by those who own land, etc. But the appearance is illusory. These are not real laborers, or capitalists, or managers, or landlords. They are functional groupings invested by the economist with standard sets of motives, aims, interests and opportunities. In the over-simplification apparently thought necessary to the analysis and exposition of his subject, the economist passes freely from this large group standardized in his imagination, to the hypothetical individual within the group. He describes the conduct of this imaginary individual in an imaginary market situation. The older economists were content to discuss broad qualitative, type-differences almost exclusively. The acountants have always dealt in classified individual differences of a quantitative character.

Since both professions are interested in income in the most general sense of that term, both are interested in what is called production. But the interests of the two groups are widely divergent. A machine, to the economist, is a specimen capital instrument, an agent possessing certain attributes that confer upon it a capacity to serve society. To the accountant the machine is only a source of immediate technical services and only of technical services the results of which inure to the benefit of, and can be appropriated by, the persons beneficially interested in the enterprise. The economist looks upon *social benefit,* the accountant upon *individual profit,* upon that which can be acquired and appropriated by certain individuals.

Let me present two illustrations. The nurseryman who in his experimental plantings produces a seedling peach of superior flavor, appearance and shipping quality has rendered a service to society. The economist considers this professionally, the accountant, as a consumer of peaches only. For the monetary profit which the nurseryman can appropriate is much less than the benefit conferred. Once grafting stock has passed from his control he quickly loses any advantage that his lucky discovery gave him. His account-ant cannot be professionally impressed by the excellence of the fruit. He can foresee that the profits to the nurseryman are of a different order from the benefits to the consumers of peaches.

My second illustration is the converse of the first. A gold dredge laying waste a valley in the exploitation of a rich deposit can be, and generally is, regarded by the economist as adding nothing to the sum of human utilities.[1] But the mining company's accountants look no further than to the richness and extent of the deposit controlled by the company, to the costs of operating the dredge and to the profits to result from the exploitation. Professionally they are indifferent to the effect of the operations upon the public.

Both professions are concerned with public finance. The economist considers the scope of public control and of public operation of enterprise. He examines the attributes of particular tax measures and of tax systems, he devotes much thought to the incidence and shifting of taxes and to the distribution of the tax burden among elements of the population. He con-siders problems of tax justice, tax convenience, tax economy, etc. The acountant, if his client is a private person, deals specifically only with individual tax incidence, that is, with the tax liability and tax disbursements of his client. If his client is a public person with taxing powers, he considers the client's revenue collections and disbursements in the light of the existing revenue and appropriation acts. The interests of the two professions are almost wholly diverse. Only as private citizens having special knowledge of tax convenience and tax economy do the accountants enter the economist's field at all. Only to the extent that the economist departs from classical theory and becomes a statistical student of public finance does he enter the accountant's field.

But what of the topic, exchange? Surely, one might think, the economist and the accountant meet here on common ground. As the theory of value constitutes the very vitals of economic theory, so also does valuation con-stitute the chief technical pre-occupation of accounting theory. Just so, but note the difference in my terms; for the theory of *value* can be, and is, different from the theory of *valuation* in everything but subject matter under consideration. With ultimate causes of value, with explanations of value, with the primary or ultimate conditions which may, conceptually, determine value in the long run, with normal value or price, the acountant cannot professionally concern himself.

---

[1] In a recent address at Stanford University, Professor Kemmerer expressed a doubt that further present additions to our gold stock would constitute a benefit to the world population. Perhaps a different view might be held if the addition contemplated were great enough to make gold value as low as that of iron, let us say; for then certain of the peculiar properties of gold would allow an enormous expansion of uses in the arts. A gold-plated ship hull would never need painting.

The quantitative effects of the ultimate causes of value cannot be traced with precision or even useful reliability through intermediate causes to the proximate or immediate causes of value in a given specific instance. The accountant does not wish, and has no reason to wish, to explain value. Those primary or ultimate conditions said by the economist to determine value are themselves incapable of being measured statistically; and, on that account, cannot become the foundation for real valuations. The concept of normal value or normal price is almost useless to the accountant. He must, from the nature of his work, set down figures at short run intervals. Before the economists' "long run" has had time to become *long* the thing to be valued will have been consumed or will be in some one else's hands. At any balance sheet date there is always a "long run" still to come. Long runs have a way of continuing to be long. Unless and until the economist finds a *prevalent, reliably measurable chain of related phenomena* running from *ultimate causes* to present *valuation results* his theory of value will be of little use to the accountant. The accountant will have to rely upon proximate, or if you will, superficial, indications of value. If one knows the closing price on a given day of a stock listed upon an exchange he can make a better guess at the next day's opening price than can the most erudite economist who is without knowledge of the stock's quotations and without knowledge of the acountant's reports on the condition of the corporation. As compared with any classical or other purely qualitative theory of value one would nevertheless have to say that the last previous price is but a superficial cause, or explanation, or determinant of the succeeding price.

Taussig, speaking of value in the long run or normal value under conditions of varying cost, says, "Value is then determined in the long run by cost to the marginal producer; but at what point in the varying scale of costs that producer will be, depends on the conditions of demand."[2] If "in the long run a price which will make it worth (a producer's) while to contribute" to supply can barely be expected, he is a marginal producer.[3] This proposition recommends itself strongly to one's common sense. It does more; it recommends itself to the refined and exalted sense of many well informed men. Let us take the proposition into the market place to test its truth—if we can.

Suppose we choose as a specimen commodity for the test a type of cabinetmaker's claw hammer of given design and specification. Some of these hammers are made by concerns that make hammers only, but hammers of many kinds. Others are made by those who manufacture a "full line" of small tools. Still others are made by those who turn out not tools only, but shelf hardware, cutlery, builders' hardware, firearms, ammunition, and so on. Here are conditions of varying cost with a vengeance. Let us ask each of these manufacturers a few questions. What has it cost you per

---

2 Principles of Economics, Vol. I, p. 185.
3 *Ibid.*

hammer in past years to put this tool on the market? What is it costing you this year? What do you expect it to cost you next year, or five years from now? Have you been, are you, or do you expect to be, a marginal producer? Let us ask also upon what evidence the answers are based.

Let us appoint a commission of professional students of cost analysis to weigh the answers made and the evidence produced to substantiate them. Such a jury, of course, will be aware of that intricate and ever changing condition of joint costs that prevails in modern enterprise, and that runs through from expenses of site, of housing, of purchasing materials and supplies, of operating technical equipment, of advertising, of selling, and of collecting the accounts, to expenses of general administration. They will be aware too that this rationally unanalyzable mass of joint costs will be shot through and through with the variables of idle time and inadequate use of men and things and the variable of prices to be paid. They will be aware, too, of the difficulty of writing the schedules of future prices for these hammers and the schedules of future sales volume in them.

This commission can be trusted to view with the utmost scepticism not merely what the manufacturers of these hammers may say about their costs but also the proposition of the economist about normal value or price. They will know that the information and the supporting evidence upon which the economist supposes the manufacturer to act doesn't exist. They will know that the figure representing the economist's cost of production exists only in his imagination. They will know that if a marginal producer exists at all he exists by accident. No one can pick out the marginal producers either by observing their entrance into, or withdrawal from, the market or by any other reliable objective evidence.

When the accountant values the hammers that he finds in a manufacturer's inventory he has before him all the objective phenomena that the economist appears to contemplate, but his contemplations of those phenomena are of a totally different order. His valuation may be superficial, but it works. His valuations, let us hope, may become better, but there is no reason to hope, or to wish, that the accountant will look to this brand of economic theory for light.

The economic theorist not only talks about value, but also appears to talk about valuation as well. He will tell us that a capital instrument, for example, a lathe in a machine shop, derives its value from the value of the lathe's future services and disservices—that the true valuation of the machine is determined by capitalizing its future money-valued service and disservice series. But unless the service of the lathe consists of bringing in a sale price, either for the lathe itself or for a separately sold schedule of its technical services, no series of future services independently valued in money can exist outside the imagination. One may, on the basis of experience, make estimates distributed in time of the disservice series, the outlays for maintenance, upkeep, repairs, power consumed, etc. Like estimates can be made of the cost of obtaining similar services by available alternative means. Such a negative series can be capitalized, but it is only the negative half of the whole series. So also can one make a time schedule of anticipated technical services, that is, of the metal cutting that can reasonably be expected of the lathe. But there is not and cannot be, a coefficient of conversion whereby these metal cutting services can rationally be converted into unit money values. Real capital valuations, i.e., valuations arrived at by discounting cannot exist under the conditions described.

Costs per units of *technical service* can be estimated. On the basis of these, intelligent choice between one mode of obtaining services and another, e.g., through purchase of one machine rather than another, can be made. This rational basis of choice becomes the foundation for a theory and practice of valuation. If a given kind of technical service, for example, metal cutting, is essential to the operations of an enterprise and if this service, together with others, can be had at a price that promises an enterprise profit or the reduction of an enterprise loss, the service is worth what it costs. If a given machine at its purchase price, together with subsequent outlays for maintenance, upkeep, repairs, power consumption, etc., shows promise of rendering adequate service more cheaply per unit than any alternative device, the machine is worth what it costs. No one could sensibly pay more, or value it at more, than he is compelled to pay. Nor can he sensibly value it at less and decline to pay. One might be willing to pay more *if necessary;* one would be glad to pay less if possible, but the fact of *best optional cost of service* is determining. It is the services that are wanted—the buying of a particular machine is but an incident to securing them.

Machine service is bought, and machines purchased are valued by the buyer, with some approximation to this basis of valuation. It is for this reason that the accountant can safely regard actual cost as the best single evidence of going concern value. It is not the fact of cost but the fact of *choice at the cost,* or *despite the cost,* that signifies. The often made charge of the economist that the accountant confuses cost with value cannot be substantiated by the mere fact that accountants so commonly adopt cost as their basis of first valuation and of subsequent revaluations. The backing of a judgment with real money by one skilled in his enterprise is too good an evidence of value to be rejected or departed from lightly.

When the accountant revalues at intervals he finds part of the services gone—either they have been used or the opportunity for using them is lost. The effect of this diminution of residual services is to depress carrying value; it is of the essence of depreciation. But unless there is extraordinarily trustworthy evidence that the best *available* cost per unit of further services is something other than that implied by the purchase price of the machine, the asset will be revalued on the basis of cost.

The accountant's theory of valuation of fixed tangible assets overturns neither the classical theory of value nor the theory of capital valuation, but it does ignore them. It is independent of them. Moreover, it works. It works, yes, but in its workings it does some things that grieve many economists. When this theory of valuation is applied to an enterprise having large holdings of fixed tangible assets, we often see a great discrepancy between the book value of the assets and the investment market value of the stocks, bonds, and floating debt.

Now grant for the sake of the argument, that the investment market price of the securities represents an estimate of the capital value of the securities, i.e., the discounted present worths of the future payments to the holders, and hence represents a capital value of the enterprise. If this security market value differs widely from the sum of the asset valuations found by the accountant, and chronically differs widely, who is wrong? The uninformed person says the accountant is; and says that the accountant's mistaking of cost for value is the cause. I deny this. There is nothing whatsoever in accepted acounting procedure (though there are some mistaken statements in the writings on accounting) to support the notion that accountants are trying to find any figure for the capital value of enterprises. No one knows better than the accountants the difference between cost of the assets and the capital value of the enterprise. Their almost unanimous refusal to recognize goodwill valuations unless these are backed by as good a test as that of having been paid for in a bargain between skilled men who are strangers in interest to one another is, in itself, proof enough of my position. The professional public accountant does not attempt to predict in figures what the present worth of the future earning power of a concern will ultimately prove to be. He does not mentally project the difference between future sales and expenses and capitalize it. Neither will he certify to the soundness of anyone else's mere estimate.

Of those assets that will be directly converted into money he either expresses an opinion of their present worth or gives a figure to serve as an index to their present worth. But of the fixed tangibles which cannot be valued in this way he merely says that their residual services, or services of like kinds, are essential to the conduct of the enterprise. Of each class of these essential services he says in effect that he has no reason to suppose that they could be had for less than their implied cost. He exhibits as a valuation that part of an incurred cost which can be said to apply to unused and available services.

Valuations of this latter kind conform to the valuations upon which skilled men act every day in the conduct of affairs. Good valuations of this kind may be of the utmost importance to all concerned in an enterprise. But there is nothing in the statistical procedure of the accountant that implies either that these valuations are capital valuations or that the sum of them bears any simple relation to the capitalized value of a concern's earning power. These valuations and capital valuations are of such different orders statistically that they cannot be translated by any formula from one form to the other in either direction.

I do not assert that perfection in the accountant's theory of valuation has been achieved. Vastly more remains to be done than has been done. Much less do I assert that practitioners achieve precision in the application of current theory. Some practitioners, perhaps, are not familiar with all theory writings in their subject. Most important of all, the business community is not yet ready always to pay for the best valuation service that accountants know how to render. The improvements in theory and in practice that I confidently expect to occur before the lapse of many years, however, include little or nothing that the classical economic theory of value and of valuation has to suggest.

In my opening remarks I indicated that my change of position on the value of economic theory to the professional accountant might be described as a shift of ground. For I cannot say of all economic theory what I have said of the older, commoner brands under discussion. There is, as you know, a wholly new and wholly different kind of economic theory coming into existence. This new theory is not yet cast into ordered systems. It exists in fragmentary form only. It consists of inquiries into the statistical relations of one real statistical series to another. It is exemplified in the statistical publications of many foundations such as the National Bureau of Economic Research, The Harvard Committee of Economic Research, The Pollak Foundation, The Brookings Institute of Economics, The Food Research Institute, the university bureaus of business and economic research and the publications of many private enterprises of which the American Telephone and Telegraph Company is an example.

This new theory has much in common with accounting theory both in purpose and technique. Its devotees deal quantitatively with the behavior of real people in a real market. Its groups are groups of real units whether of persons or enterprises, or commodities, or services. Its prices are prices actually paid. It is almost purely an objective theory based upon observations of objective phenomena.

It is, perhaps, too soon to decide whether or not this new form of economic theory and its associated techniques should become a part of the professional equipment of the future accountant. It is not too soon for the members of this society to begin considering it. For among the changes in accountancy that suggest themselves as likely to occur few seem more certain than that the academic branch of the profession will play a more important rôle in determining the future accountant's professional equipment.

While we wait for the new economics to prove its worth both in its own field and in ours, shall we abandon all the older theory in our preparatory courses of study? I, for one, hope that we shall not. Professional accountants are to be citizens as well as technicians; and the economists' views upon public problems include much that can ill be spared from the training of the citizen so influentially placed as the professional accountant. The so-called problem courses, such as corporation finance, insurance, money and banking, and so on, despite their being tinged with the old theory, are of undoubted usefulness to the accountant.

Moreover, not all theory writings of the qualitative sort need be cast out of the professional course of study. There is one development of a major part of economic theory in which the accountant ought to feel himself on familiar ground. That development is found best exemplified, perhaps, in Professor Irving Fisher's writings, particularly in his *Nature of Capital and Income,* and in his *Rate of Interest.* Here is a qualitative analysis in a quantitative dress. Fisher, himself, speaks of it as an economic accounting. It is no matter for surprise that his analysis should lend itself so well to quantitative adaptation. His own training as a mathematician, his extremely valuable contributions to the new field of statistical economics and his interest in the theory of accounts show his strong bent for the quantitative method.

From a study of his work much can be learned both by the accountant and by the economist engaged in the newer type of theory formulation. He urges more aptly, perhaps, than anyone else has done the need for keeping fundamental concepts in mind if order is to be brought out of the welter of economic phenomena. In a late paper he says: "I believe that the concept of income is, without exception, the most vital central concept in economic science and that on fully grasping its nature and interrelations with other concepts largely depends the full fruition both of economic theory and of its applications to taxation and statistics."[4]

As a student both of accounting theory and of economic theory I concur fully. Income is not only "the most vital central concept in economic science," it is also the *simplest and most fundamental.* And only by *beginning* with that which is simplest, or most elementary, can we hope ever fully to develop and understand the more complex concepts. Here, if there is one at all, is surely the meeting ground of the accountant and the economist. With what that is more elementary or more vital or more fundamental than income does the accountant concern himself? With what substantive thing, indeed, other than income in its various dresses, does the accountant concern himself at all? For income in essence is services—the desired element in economic events. Change the sign and you have the undesired element in economic events, disservices, or expense. Consider the sources of service and you think of tangible assets. Think of the destination of disservices or expense and you think of liabilities. Value an object and you estimate its residual services, and segregate cost of past services from cost of future services.

---

4 *American Economic Review,* Vol. XIV, p. 64.

If there is to be any work in economic theory required of the university student intending to become a professional public accountant, let it be study in which the sphere of his future professional activity in economic affairs is indicated. Let it be something in which an opportunity of the two professions to join hands in a common endeavor becomes apparent.

Maurice E. Peloubet

IS VALUE AN ACCOUNTING CONCEPT?

Maurice Edouard Peloubet *is a leading accountant who was born in Illinois in 1892 and was on the staff of Price Waterhouse and Co. from 1911– 1919, after which he was associated with the firm of Pogson, Peloubet & Co. Recently he returned to Price Waterhouse. He has lectured at Columbia, Harvard, New York University, Temple, Wheaton, and Rutgers. He has been active in governmental affairs and in the work of the accounting profession, including a term on the committee on accounting procedure of the American Institute of C.P.A. Among other items, he published* Audit Working Papers *(1937);* Costs under Government Contracts *(1942) with Eric Camman; and* Ballads, Songs, and Snatches *(1938). In the late 1930's, he spearheaded the drive to get LIFO accepted for tax purposes. [See his testimony, reprinted later in this book, pp. 450 to 456].*
The article reprinted here sets forth the widely-held view that accounting is not and should not be concerned with changes in values because value itself is not an accounting concept. Whether or not "value" is an accounting concept is an issue that runs through many of the other items reprinted in this book. Peloubet's discussion is significant because it is a clear-cut statement of the views of a respected leader of the profession.

The idea of value is a very old one—probably one of the first ideas, as distinct from sensations or appetites, which entered the human mind. Long before primitive man had conceived the idea of exchange, he had realized that some things were more useful and desirable than others and that he would be wise to store up for future use those which were not perishable. The reason primitive man preserved stores of fuel, flint or bones was because he thought that in the future they would be useful to him. In other words, he decided in his own mind that they had a value to him. Value was thus a subjective idea, and the basic concept of value has never changed from that day to this.

An address delivered at a meeting of the New Jersey State Society of Certified Public Accountants, Newark, New Jersey, February 4, 1935. Reprinted from *The Journal of Accountancy* (March, 1935), pp. 201–209, by permission.

I do not think we are being unduly metaphysical when we say that the only basis of value is what one person or group of persons thinks. There may be compelling reasons for the thoughts of a group, but the reason the value exists is because of the opinion of those who desire the particular material or article.

If the inhabitants of the entire world were Orthodox Jews, pork would have little value. The herring fishery of Holland in the Middle Ages was the result of a religious idea, the obligation imposed on all Catholics to eat no meat on Friday, and dried or salt herring under the conditions of transportation then existing was about the only possible fish for the common people to eat.

The value of real estate is dependent entirely on the consensus of opinion of the inhabitants of a particular city or country. Real estate in the city of New York is immensely valuable because everyone who has thought about the question or has any interest in it has decided, consciously or unconsciously, that New York is the best situation on the Atlantic Coast for a port and the best point for interchange of goods, services and communications in the country. Regardless of the physical facts, if everyone in the United States should suddenly decide that the island of Manhattan was a spot which lay under some sort of curse; if people thought that it was dangerous or unhealthy to visit the island, the value of New York real estate would vanish immediately. We are all well aware—some of us, unfortunately, from personal experience—that security values are largely, if not entirely, subject to the effects of mass emotion and opinion.

There is no value which can exist independently of an opinion or a group of opinions, and these change with circumstances. We think, for instance, that diamonds are valuable and they, for that very reason, are valuable, but if we remember the dramatic scene in *King Solomon's Mines,* where the explorers had finally penetrated into the cave where the diamonds were concealed, we shall recall that just as the men were well inside the cave the old witch who had been their guide slipped outside and the heavy stone slid into place and sealed them in the cave. After that the value of diamonds became non-existent for them. A little water and a few mouthfuls of food and a chance to escape into the open air had more value at that moment than all the diamonds in the cave.

This may sound somewhat remote from the question of accounting and the problems of valuation which are involved in accounts, but a little reflection will show us that it is quite closely related. The very word "account" means, both by present use and derivation, a tale, a story, a record. It must deal with what has happened and, if there is any attempt to estimate or forecast the future, this is a mere projection of present facts and tendencies.

Accounting, I think, must be objective. It is true that this limits its scope, but when we try to enter fields which are entirely subjective in their nature, such as the determination and expression of values, we are trying to use an instrument designed primarily for recording observed, objective facts, to measure the effect and extent of changes in value, which are based primarily on emotions and intellectual reactions. This is the sphere of the politician, political economist, poet, journalist or someone similarly qualified. It is obvious that in the expression of anything dependent on the changing opinions and emotions of men, any order or continuity is almost impossible.

The study of the course of the price of any staple, such as wheat, over the last fifty or one hundred years shows violent fluctuations, some due to physical causes, floods, famine or drought, but more due to the effect of wars, fear of wars, tariffs, quotas, national desire for self-sufficiency and similar forces which are entirely subjective in their nature, that is, those which would not have come into existence at all except for changes in the consensus of emotion and opinion. This would seem to be a most unstable ground on which to build any permanent and enduring records. We see, however, that the record of the changes in price is definite and continuous. The record does not show the causes of the variation and does not attempt to show the effect, either in the past or future, of any change at any particular time. However, anywhere on the scale of change an economist or a statistician could plot a number of curves backward or forward from any point of time to show from that point the effect of the continuance of the values selected or the effect of any assumed change. Such a graphic representation might be of great interest and utility—it might be much more useful than the actual record—but this representation could not be made without the actual record and could not in any way take its place. Here, I think, we have the basis of the general opposition between financial reports and accounts and statistical projections backward or forward from any point of time within the period covered by the accounts.

In the not very distant past, when accounts were first being subjected to really thoughtful analysis, there was a widespread opinion, which is still held in some responsible quarters, that the balance-sheet was "static" and the income account was "dynamic." In other words, the balance-sheet was thought to be an instantaneous photograph of a business at a particular moment of time, and the income account was construed as a sort of symbolic, arithmetical narrative of the happenings in the business between two of the "static" points. This concept, I think, is fundamentally false. It has a certain superficial appearance of truth, because it could have been true in a world where economic changes were so slow as to be almost imperceptible, as, say, in the Middle Ages in Europe. However, we are well aware that we are not living in such a period in the world's history. Economic changes are rapid and devastating. This, I think shows the falsity of the "instantaneous photograph" assumption. What then is the truth? As I see it, the balance-sheet is a continuous narrative, much as the income account is, except that the narrative is told from a different standpoint and covers the entire life of a corporation from its inception to the date of the accounts. The income account is a narrative showing the nature and extent of the transactions involved in the production of income, such as sales, purchases, manufacturing costs and the miscellaneous items of income and expense. The balance-sheet is a narrative of investment. It shows the investment in fixed assets, the estimated wear and tear through depreciation and other deductions, and it shows the amount invested in assets which are to be consumed in the operation of the business. It also indicates how much capital was contributed, who contributed it and the rights to and participation in capital of stockholders, bondholders and various other creditors. From the intending investor's or purchaser's point of view we see, particularly in the fixed assets, a strange jumble of figures, especially when we are working with dollars of different gold content, but from the point of view of a record of investment it is a logical and orderly statement, which, if properly stated, can be used by the economist or statistician for a projection on any assumption he chooses to make. We should not forget that when cost figures, representing investment, are altered to represent some "value" we are not only altering the statement before us, but we are projecting into the future the results of the valuation. When the balance-sheet is prepared on the basis of cost or investment no one who understands accounts will expect a statement which is correct and valid on the basis of economic conditions at any given point of time. The mere statement of the basis precludes any such idea: therefore, a statement which purports to show some "actual" or "real" value assumes a false and impossible validity, both for the present and future.

I have no hesitation in accepting responsibility for the statement that a certain amount of money was invested in fixed assets or that a certain number of shares of stock was issued for them or that they were valued on some other basis by some person or group having the ability or authority so to do, and that a certain amount of money has been provided for their replacement. I am equally willing to accept full responsibilty for the statement that these assets were acquired at certain times and that certain of them have been destroyed or retired. Further than that I hardly wish to go—and I believe the greater part of informed accounting opinion is with me. We are not required by the securities and exchange commission to do more than to disclose the basis on which assets are stated in the accounts. I do not think the accountant has any responsibility under the securities and exchange act for anything further than this, and I do not believe that periodical reappraisal, which is the only logical result of the assumption that accounts should show some sort of value, will be welcomed with much enthusiasm by the commission. When I say that we are absolved from responsibility if we indicate clearly the basis on which assets are valued, I believe we are, nevertheless, responsible for satisfying ourselves that all assets, the cost of which we have stated, are in use or are intended to be used. In other words, the mere statement that so much money was invested in a plant, now abandoned or obsolete, will not absolve us if we have reason to know or could discover the facts by accounting methods. We are, furthermore, not departing from our theory that the balance-sheet is a record of investment if we state that a certain amount of the investment has now passed out of existence so far as profitable production is concerned.

In preparing this paper I made a little search into the meaning of value. This question is one on which three or four ordinary lifetimes could easily be spent before any very definite conclusion could be drawn. I, therefore, decided to drop it after looking into some half-dozen books. The report of the special committee on accounting terminology of the American Institute of Accountants gives definitions of thirty-one different sorts of value which are met in accounting or financial transactions. I do not know how many economic definitions there are of value, but we can all think of a number, such as marginal, scarcity, residual and others. When we go into the domain of the arts we have æsthetic, literary, tonal, both color and sound, and a host of others. It would appear from this mass of definitions that "value" is an opinion and little else. I am quite prepared to admit that this may be more important than facts, but I am not prepared to admit that it is the same thing.

It is a little difficult to find the basis of the contention of those who say that the accountant is or should be responsible for values. No widely used form of certificate with which I am familiar requires the accountant to state that he has satisfied himself as to the value of any of the assets, with the possible exception of those for which there is a ready market, such as securities or basic commodities. Even here "value" is largely conventional, as everyone knows that the quotation on a particular day when, say, five hundred shares of a certain stock were sold and bought, is not a trustworthy index to the value of, say, fifty thousand and a large commodity inventory would generally not have a realizable value equal to the market value as determined by quotations at the end of a period. These are not true valuations, as there is no expression of opinion and there is no evidence that liquidation could be effected at the price indicated. They are useful checks and tend to show, in the case of inventories, whether the company's costs are excessive or otherwise and, in the case of securities, whether the investment policy of the company has or has not been wise and fortunate, but they are not, I think, generally considered as true indications of realizable values.

In the certificates required by the securities and exchange act, which are presumably the most severe and inclusive in their requirements, there is no obligation to go further than to declare that "the statement contained in the attached balance-sheet . . . truly and fairly reflects the application of accepted accounting principles to the facts disclosed."

There is, I think, no accepted practice or principle which requires periodical revaluations; and revaluations made infrequently, either reducing or increasing cost, while permitted in some circumstances, are an exception to the usual rule. The securities and exchange commission apparently does not think it would be of any service to stockholders, investors or the public to attempt periodic revaluation.

A member of the securities and exchange commission, speaking at a recent public meeting in New York, said, in effect, that his concept of accounting was the recording of actual facts, such as the receipt, disbursement or investment of funds, the issuance of stock or some other definite action, and that he did not regard the attempt to evaluate, on any other basis, the assets of the corporation as coming generally within the scope of the accountant's work.

The form of certificate recommended by the American Institute of Accountants, first generally used in 1933, which is now becoming more and more widely accepted, requires only that the accountant shall state that the balance-sheet shows the financial condition of the company. "Financial condition" is a fairly well understood term and covers generally the resultant of rights to receive money, obligations to disburse money and the amount of the investment of money or property to which a money value has been ascribed, less proper reserves at the date of the statement.

The certificate required under the English companies' act states, in effect, that the accounts are drawn up so as to exhibit a correct view of the state of the company's affairs according to the best of the auditor's information and the explanations given him and as shown by the books of the company. Here, again, there is no expression of opinion as to values, nor is there any acceptance of responsibilty for them. All this does not mean that the accountant should be indifferent to the question of value or that he should ignore it when it legitimately affects the position of the company or the books of account.

The accountant, however, is little better qualified than any intelligent layman to pass on these questions. He is concerned with facts which are expressed in terms of money and with the financial inferences which may be properly drawn from them. It might appear from this that while an accountant obviously could not make a valuation of factory buildings and equipment, he would be particularly well qualified to appraise goodwill, as that is generally a question of the present capitalization of expected excess future earnings, and here we have something which seems, at first sight, to be almost entirely a question of figures and records. Past earnings the accountant can ascertain, and from these a reasonable inference as to future earnings would appear to be possible. This sounds quite reasonable, but the statement is untrue, dangerously untrue.

Some years ago an important event in the history of the development of the automobile took place: a practical, cheap and efficient method of lighting and starting cars by electricity was developed. Prior to this the lighting equipment of a car consisted of large lamps which cast a powerful beam from an acetylene flame and smaller lamps in which burned the weaker flame of kerosene oil. Some of the companies manufacturing compressed acetylene for this purpose were highly prosperous. The use of the automobile was expanding rapidly, its mechanical development was making good progress and, so far as the records of such a company would show, there was every reason to believe that a substantial goodwill existed, based on earnings in excess of the usual return on capital in the immediate past. It is obvious that the apparent goodwill of one of the acetylene companies, calculated, say, two years before the introduction of electric lighting and starting, would be substantial in figures, but in fact almost non-existent. A further condition which had much bearing on the state of these companies was the invention and development of methods for cutting and welding heavy metal with an acetylene flame, which, while it did not offset the losses caused by the introduction of electric starting and lighting, did much to mitigate them. It would be most unfair to expect an accountant to be aware of the effects of these inventions, except after they had come into general use. But without making an allowance for their influence, no trustworthy estimate of the goodwill of the acetylene company could be made. It thus appears that even in what seems to be the purely mathematical calculation of goodwill, the accountant should be on his guard against taking responsibility for valuations which may cause him to make statements which later may prove to have been both false and dangerous to those who relied on them. In this case it was clearly the duty of an engineer or a sales executive or both to form an opinion as to the condition of the industry. The accountant fortified with this opinion could then proceed to the valuation of goodwill.

While the accountant cannot make valuations, it is true that his experience, which puts him in the position of a particularly well-informed layman, so far as engineering, economic and legal facts are concerned, makes him a competent critic of such valuations and should enable him to detect anything grossly or substantially inaccurate. When the accountant forms such an opinion of a valuation his recourse is not to attempt to correct it nor to make a valuation of his own, but to bring to the attention of the proper parties his opinion that the valuation submitted is grossly inaccurate, highly improbable or does not take into consideration some important factors.

I agree that it would be pleasanter and would greatly enhance the dignity and increase the profits of the profession if we were able not only to do our own work relative to the accounts, but also to decide the engineering and legal questions as well. So far as my own experience indicates, my entire time and energy are required for the complex and almost impossible, but nevertheless fascinating, task of keeping up with the development of professional accountancy and endeavoring to solve the few problems which clients are kind enough to submit to the firm of which I am a member. There may be supermen who can cover the business field from every angle. If there are such I should be glad to meet them and would follow their careers with great interest—perhaps tinged at first with a little incredulity, as I would naturally hesitate to believe that such creatures could exist. Once, however, they had proved themselves I would follow them with respectful admiration.

Anyone who pretends to such abilities without possessing them is starting on a dangerous course, both for himself and his unfortunate clients. The safe and honest thing for ordinary mortals is to choose one profession, devote the best of their abilities and energies to that and to leave the other professions to their own practitioners. Any accountant who attempts to make valuations other than those indicated by the accounts, or by some definite index, such as a market price, is coming dangerously close to the boundary of his own field and is preparing to step over into that of the economist and engineer. Valuation in any true or important sense is not a matter for the accountant and the more completely this is recognized by accountant and client the better it will be for all concerned.

Gilbert R. Byrne

TO WHAT EXTENT CAN THE PRACTICE
OF ACCOUNTING BE REDUCED
TO RULES AND STANDARDS?

Gilbert Rogers Byrne *was born in Michigan in 1896 and received an A. B. degree, with distinction, from the University of Michigan in 1919. He was with Arthur Andersen & Co., 1922–34, and has been with Lybrand, Ross Bros. & Montgomery since 1934. He edited the 6th, 7th, and 8th editions of Montgomery's* Auditing *(1940, 1948, 1957).*
The article reprinted here was awarded first prize in a contest conducted by the American Institute of C.P.A. in celebration of its 50th anniversary (1937). The contest was for the best answer to the question posed by the title: To what extent can the practice of accounting be reduced to rules and standards? Mr. Byrne stresses the coercive (compelling) nature of "principles," a conception that clearly met with favor in 1937 and that has its adherents today; but it also contrasts with the views of George O. May (among others), who stresses the "conventional" (temporary, expendable) nature of principles.

Modern professional practice of accounting covers a wide range of subjects, and its field, if the experience of the past decade can be taken as a guide, may be expected to widen still further in the future. For example, in 1931 a report of a committee of one of the professional bodies of accountants classified accounting services in six divisions; to this list would now have to be added those services performed by accountants in connection with registrations of securities and other matters for the Securities and Exchange Commission. To discuss the possibility of stating rules and standards relating to all of the matters coming within the practice of the present-day accountant would be quite impossible within the limits prescribed for this article, even if it were agreed that it is practicable to consider the

Reprinted from the *Journal of Accountancy* (November, 1937), pp. 364–79, by permission.

formulation of rules and standards for, say, the installation of a cost system or the prosecution of a tax case.

It probably would be conceded that the major portion of the professional accountant's practice is concerned with the examination of financial statements and the accountant's report thereon; and the discussion which follows will be confined to a consideration of whether and to what extent this phase of the accountant's work can be reduced to rules and standards. As a preliminary to this discussion it will be helpful to recall that, broadly speaking, the accountant's purpose in making his examination is to determine that proper accounting principles have been consistently followed in keeping the accounts, and that clear and truthful financial statements have been prepared therefrom. To assure himself of these facts, he employs a technique of auditing procedures. There are, therefore, really three phases of the accountant's work in connection with the examination of and reporting on financial statements, each of which may be considered potentially subject to reduction to rules and standards:

(a) Accounting principles, and the rules derived from these principles
(b) The practices and conventions relating to the presentation of accounts in financial statements
(c) The technique of auditing

The general question as to formulating and stating the principles, rules, conventions, or standards of the practice of accounting has engaged the attention of a number of writers and speakers on accounting subjects in recent months. There have been developed two quite divergent points of view; on the one hand, those who urge that a statement of accounting principles can and should be formulated, and on the other, those who envisage the impossibility, if not the undesirability, of the task. The following quotations, characteristic of the first school of thought, are interesting:

> After a quarter-century and more of active discussion and experimentation in this country, many of the simplest and most fundamental problems of accounting remain without an accepted solution. There is still no authoritative statement of essential principles available on which accounting records and statements may be based. Public accountants...have been asked to certify to the correctness and adequacy of accounting statements, when no satisfactory criteria of correctness and adequacy have been agreed to.[1]

And another commentator has expressed similar ideas in these words:

> Accountancy has...the tendency to rely on precedent and authority rather than on the scientific method.... It is as if engineers had no agreement on the required strength of foundations, structural steel requirements for skyscrapers, or efficient design for power plants.[2]

---

[1] A Statement of Objectives of the American Accounting Association. *The Accounting Review,* March, 1936.

[2] George C. Mathews—Address before Milwaukee chapter of Wisconsin Society of Certified Public Accountants.

It is perhaps not unnatural that the authors of the above are men of academic or regulatory-body training; expressions of the opposite view given below are those of practicing accountants:

> The field of financial accounting is not one in which guidance is to be found wholly in fixed principles—it is a field of shadowy outlines in which the discovery of a correct course depends upon the possession also of an ability to recognize the essential facts and to appreciate their true significance (distinguishing where necessary between form and substance); upon informed and wise judgment; and upon objectiveness and honesty of purpose. It will be observed that these are not qualities which can be insured by regulation.[3]

Another practitioner comments on the published discussion as follows:

> First, what has frequently been spoken of as accounting principles includes a conglomeration of accounting practices, procedures, policies, methods and conventions relating both to the construction of accounts and their presentation; and second, there seems to be a general agreement among the commentators that the difficulty of any attempt to formulate so-called principles or prescribed rules and regulations on accounting matters is so large and the conditions encountered so diverse that few, if any, sweeping generalizations can safely be adopted.[4]

As indicated previously, there are three phases of the accountant's work in connection with the examinations of financial statements and his report thereon which may be considered potentially subject to reduction to rules and standards. First, the accounting principles which he must assure himself have been properly and consistently applied in preparing the accounts; second, the practices and conventions relating to the presentation of the accounts in financial statements; and third, the technique of auditing employed by the accountant in determining that the accounts and statements have been properly prepared. As indicated by the author of the last quotation above, recent discussions have used the term "accounting principles" to cover a conglomeration of accounting practices, procedures, conventions, etc.; many, if not most, so-called "principles" may merely have to do with methods of presenting items on financial statements or techniques of auditing, rather than matters of fundamental accounting principle. It is not strange, perhaps, that lacking completely satisfactory definition of terms, or clarification of the fields of discussion, there has been little or no agreement among accountants as to what extent, if at all, rules and standards of accountancy practice can be stated.

In fact, the confusion with respect to the matter of differentiating between accounting principles, rules, conventions, practice, etc., is so great that some have despaired of reaching a solution, and have raised the question as to whether, after all, there *are* such things as accounting principles. It is

---

[3] George O. May—Improvement in Financial Accounts. *Journal of Accountancy,* May, 1937.

[4] F. P. Byerly—Formulation of Accounting Principles or Conventions. *Journal of Accountancy,* August, 1937.

proposed, therefore, first to inquire as to the nature of accounting principles, the distinction, if any, between an accounting principle and an accounting rule, and then as to whether accounting principles and accounting rules can satisfactorily be formulated. Some consideration will then be given to the extent to which the accounting practices and conventions relating to the preparation of financial statements and the technique of auditing can be reduced to rules and standards.

The standard form of report used by most accountants in certifying financial statements of corporations whose securities are listed on the New York Stock Exchange is predicated upon the existence of known accounting principles, for it concludes, after an opening paragraph briefly describing the nature and scope of the examination made,

> In our opinion, based upon such examination, the accompanying balance-sheet and related statement of income and surplus fairly present, *in accordance with accepted principles of accounting consistently maintained by the company during the year under review,* its position at December 31, 19—, and the results of its operations for the year.

Such a statement presumably represents the informed and well-considered opinion of an expert in the field of accounting; it presupposes that there are principles of accounting, known to the accountant, which can be applied to business transactions so that the resulting books of account and the financial statements prepared therefrom may fairly reflect the financial position of the enterprise at a given date and the results of its operations for a specified period. There *must* be agreement among accountants that there are recognizable principles of accounting, for if there is not this agreement, accountants have indeed stultified themselves.

It is probably safe to say that all schools of accounting thought would agree that it is desirable to have formulated in an authoritative way the principles of accounting to which reference is made in the form of accountant's report quoted above. While there have been several attempts to enumerate them, to date there has been no statement upon which there has been general agreement. This lack of agreement, it is submitted, results in large part because there is no clear distinction, in the minds of many, between that body of fundamental truths underlying the philosophy of accounts which are properly thought of as *principles,* and the larger body of accounting rules, practices and conventions which derive from principles, but which of themselves are not principles. If accounting, as an organized body of knowledge, has validity, it must rest upon a body of principles, in the sense defined in Webster's New International Dictionary:

> A fundamental truth; a comprehensive law or doctrine, from which others are derived, or on which others are founded; a general truth; an elementary proposition or fundamental assumption; a maxim; an axiom; a postulate.

President Coolidge said, "Laws, whether statutory or natural, are not invented—they are discovered, and discovered only after experience." In the development of any field, principles are discovered which represent the fundamental truths on which the field of knowledge rests. These principles are applied in the working out of problems that arise, and gradually, rules of practice evolve which, over a period of time, become accepted to a greater or less degree as reflecting the effect of the principle in oft-recurring cases. Such rules become the working tools of those engaged in the particular field of knowledge. While the principles upon which the body of knowledge rests cannot, from their nature, be subject to dispute, the rules derived therefrom have validity only to the extent that they properly reflect the principle. Pending complete demonstration of this fact, usually through experiment, there may be considerable disagreement as to whether a particular rule should be followed. Accounting, as well as law, engineering and many other fields, has followed, and is still following this pattern of development. It is probable that there are principles still to be discovered, and certainly accounting rules are still in process of crystallization.

As to the fundamental principles of accounting, there can be no more question of their "general acceptance" than of the moral rightness of the ethical principle that it is wrong to kill. But there are legal rules derived from the moral command, "Thou shalt not kill," which have differed at different times and in different countries. At one time no legal penalties attached to a noble who killed a serf, and even in our own colonial times no jail sentence awaited the Pilgrim Father who shot a stray Indian at sight. At present, legal rules derived from the moral principle are to the effect that an accidental killing is subject to less penalty than killing in the heat of passion without premeditation, and that the latter is considered legally less culpable than wilful, premeditated murder. Legal rules in different states classify differently legal culpability for killing. In short, while there is no difference of opinion as to the moral principle that killing is wrong, there have always been, and still are, differences of opinion as to how the principle shall be reflected in legal rules, and also differences of opinion as to whether the legal rules have been properly applied to the facts in a particular case. The latter is one reason for the popular interest in murder trials.

Another example of the differences between fundamental principles and the effects of their application may be drawn from the engineering profession. There are, of course, principles of engineering governing the size, weight and design of the steel members of a bridge structure. In designing the Manhattan and the Williamsburg bridges, which were built in 1909 and 1903, respectively, and were proposed to span the same stream, presumably sound engineering principles were applied to the problem in each case. In the application of those principles the results, so far as appearance of the two structures are concerned, are quite different, yet no one accuses the engineers of having applied different principles to their respective problems merely because the results of such application have not been identical bridges.

In much the same way, while there may be complete agreement as to the underlying principles of accounting, there may be legitimate and proper—one might say inevitable—differences of opinion as to the effect of the application of a particular principle of accounting to the facts in a particular case, or, in other words, as to the propriety of the accounting rules derived from the principle. Further, while the fundamental principles of accounting remain unchanged, the rules and practices derived therefrom will, and ought to, develop as required by changes in business practice. It should cause no surprise if financial statements a generation hence differ as much from those of the present day as these differ from those of a generation ago. The *principles* of accounting remain the same, and about them there should be no substantial disagreement; as to the body of accounting rules, practices and conventions derived from those principles, there may well be differences of opinion as to their validity in a particular case. As a result of such inevitable differences in opinion, therefore, it is not difficult, in reviewing the work of members of the accounting profession as exemplified by published reports of corporations accompanied by an accountant's certificate, to find instances where apparently similar transactions have been given what appears to be different treatment by different accountants. When analyzed, however, the differences in treatment most frequently reflect, not incorrect nor improper underlying accounting principles, but merely differences of opinion as to the best manner of presenting the accounting effect of the application of such principles.

From the above discussion there begins to emerge, it is hoped, an outline of accounting as an organized body of knowledge resting upon a body of fundamental principles admittedly known to and utilized by accountants in the course of their examinations of financial statements. Certainly, then, these principles can be stated. From these principles, however, have been derived certain accounting rules which have validity only as they correctly reflect the application of the principle on which they depend. Since there may be considerable difference of opinion as to the propriety of accounting rules, the task of stating those rules with respect to which there may be said to be general agreement, is a formidable one. It would seem, therefore, that a long step forward in the solution of the problem which is the subject of this paper would be to establish a basis for distinguishing between an accounting principle and an accounting rule.

Dr. Henry Carter Adams, in discussing the claims of accounting to classification as a science, has said, "The commonly accepted proof that a body of organized knowledge has attained the rank of an established science is the coercive or compelling character of the generalizations to which it gives rise and which come to be known as scientific laws (principles)."[5]

The compelling character of the scientific laws of health is evident, because

---

[5] H. C. Adams—American Railway Accounting.

to disregard them in the long run literally results in death. Engineering principles have a coercive character, because to ignore them in the building of a bridge would probably result in the collapse of the bridge. Such principles are compelling in the sense that they are in effect self-enforcing; they cannot be disregarded with impunity.

The principles of accounting are also characterized by their coercive or compelling quality because inherent in accounting principles are business laws which must be obeyed if in the long run the enterprise is to survive. This does not mean, of course, that adherence to correct accounting principles is, in itself, a guarantee of business success; accounting has to do largely with the financial policies of business, and policies of sales, production, labor, and other management problems are important elements in the success or failure of a business enterprise. It should be apparent, however, that the basing of financial policies upon accounting statements which in turn are not prepared in accordance with fundamentally right accounting *principles,* may lead to courses of action which, if too long pursued, will adversely affect the financial health of the business. It is in this sense that the fundamental principles of accounting may be said to be coercive and self-executory.

Professor Arthur S. Dewing, in describing the financial difficulties of the United States Realty and Construction Company in 1903[6] said as to the causes therefor that "two of these causes were concerned with the methods of accounting tolerated by the company's management...." Both of these methods clearly violated the accounting principle that unrealized and undeterminable profits should not be included in the income account. Professor Dewing[7] gives as one of the causes of the failure of the Consolidated Cotton Duck Company in 1909 the "inadequate allowance for depreciation." Any list of accounting principles would include a statement to the effect that the investment in an industrial plant should be charged to operations over the useful life of the plant. Most experienced accountants will recall other instances where failure to follow correct principles of accounting has led to financial embarrassment.

Accounting principles, then, are the fundamental concepts on which accounting, as an organized body of knowledge, rests. Like the axioms of geometry, they are few in number and general in terms; they possess the distinguishing characteristic of a compelling and coercive nature, and they are the foundation upon which the superstructure of accounting rules, practices and conventions is built. It is not the purpose of this article to attempt a formulation of the principles of accounting, but for illustration, it seems desirable to indicate roughly what, on the basis of the above description, such a statement would include:

---

6 Corporate Promotions and Reorganizations, p. 239.
7 *Ibid.,* p. 374.

(1) Accounting is essentially the allocation of historical costs and revenues to the current and succeeding fiscal periods.

(2) The investment in an industrial plant should be charged against the operations over the useful life of the plant.

(3) In computing the net income (available for dividends) for a period, all forms of expense incurred in the production of such net income must be provided for.

(4) The income shall include only realized profits in the period during which realized; profit is deemed to be realized when a sale in the ordinary course of business is effected, unless the circumstances are such that collection of the sale price is not reasonably assured.

(5) Losses, if probable, even though not actually incurred, should be provided for in arriving at net income.

(6) Capital-stock and capital-surplus accounts, taken together, should represent the net contribution of the proprietors to the business enterprise.

(7) Earned surplus should represent the accumulated earnings of the business from transactions with the public, less distributions of such earnings to the stockholders.

(8) While it is not in many cases of great importance which of several alternative accounting rules is applied in a given situation, it is essential that, once having adopted a certain procedure, it be consistently adhered to in preparing the accounts over a period of time.

It is not suggested that the above list is complete, and certainly not that it is free from all possible criticism. It is urged, however, that it represents, however imperfectly, some of the underlying principles of accounting about which there can be no dispute as to their validity, which possess the characteristic of compulsion in the sense more fully referred to above.

From such principles are derived many of the rules, practices and conventions used in the practice of accounting. Some of these rules are really special cases under, or corollaries of, one of the fundamental principles, and as such have much of the compelling force of the parent principle. Such a rule is the familiar one that inventories should be priced at "cost or market, whichever is lower"; this rule is really an application of principle 5 above. On the other hand, many rules as to the pricing of inventories at "cost" have been developed, such as "first-in, first-out," "last-in, first-out," which cannot be considered as principles, because such rules obviously have no compelling character, of themselves. In the application of the principle that it is necessary to provide for probable losses, the accountant has full liberty to employ any one of these rules as to pricing, according to his judgment as to what is the most appropriate rule in view of all the circumstances, and, whichever one he selects, he should not be charged with violation of any accounting *principle*.

A familiar example is that of the numerous rules which have been proposed for charging to operations the cost of an industrial plant over its useful life. So long as this *principle* is applied, it can make little difference in the long run which of the *rules* for spreading the cost year by year is used. Such rules should not be confused with the principle, for they have not the coercive nature which characterizes a *principle*.

In the application of accounting principles relating to the allocation of revenues and expenses to periods and to the determination of the realization of profits in certain types of contracting business, there have been devloped two accounting rules for use in appropriate cases. Where the contracts comprising the business on hand are few, large in amount, and require long periods for completion or fabrication, an accounting rule is invoked which permits the computation of periodical profits or losses based on the percentage of completion of the contracts in progress. On the other hand, if the contracts involved are numerous, moderate in size and the construction period is less than one year, it is considered that the accounting principles referred to have been correctly applied where profits (and losses) are determined when contracts are completed or deliveries made. It should be apparent that in borderline cases good accounting and business judgment based on long experience are essential for competent decision as to which of the above rules is properly selected. Such rules are not principles, for they are not of themselves compelling, and have validity only as they correctly reflect the principles on which they are based.

A review of the published material relating to the matter of standardization of accounting practices indicates that it is largely the body of accounting rules derived from principles which the academically-minded critics wish to see definitely formulated. They become impatient at the fact that, pending crystallization of accounting practices based on fundamental principles into generally accepted rules, there are differences of opinion among accountants and among business men as to the proper application of a given principle of accounting, or as to which of two or more principles is applicable in a given case, or as to which of several methods of presentation of the effect of the application of a principle is the more logical or informative. They apparently feel that swifter progress would be made if accounting rules were presently established by an accounting authority, or possibly by dicta of government commission. Presumably our democratic political philosophy would then require some judicial body to which appeal could be made for decision between persons of opposite view, so that, following the example of the legal profession, official precedents would be established for future guidance. As to whether such procedure would in fact facilitate the formulation of generally accepted accounting rules, it should be recalled that whereas legal rules have been in process of formulation and definition for many centuries, some of them are still far from final settlement, and differences of opinion are so widespread that they are reflected in five-to-four decisions in our Supreme Court. We may be encouraged, then, in insisting on the present laissez-faire method of development of accounting rules when we consider by comparison the progress made by the accounting profession in its less than one hundred years of experience. As was said by Mr. Justice Holmes:

> ...When men have realized that time has upset many fighting faiths, they may come to believe that the ultimate good desired is better reached by free trade in ideas; that the best test of truth is the power of thought to get itself accepted in the competition of the market; and that truth is the only ground on which their wishes can safely be carried out.[8]

And with specific reference to differences of opinion regarding reporting on accounting matters, Professor T. H. Sanders remarked:

> In the face of these difficulties the main reliance must be on accountants of sufficient experience, disinterestedness, and sound judgment to be able to make that best choices among alternatives. As experience accumulates, however, it becomes possible to embody it in general principles [rules] for the guidance of all concerned. Not that these principles [rules] can ever be a substitute for judgment and experience, but they may serve to supplement these in a helpful way and to reduce the area within which the application of judgment is desirable.[9]

There seems to be no good reason why the experience of the accounting profession to date should not be reflected in a statement of accounting rules, soundly based on fundamental accounting principles, provided it is recognized that such rules have validity in a particular case only if and to the extent that they correctly reflect the underlying principle. The choice between one or more rules, or between methods of applying the rule selected, must always rest upon the skill, experience, and informed judgment of the accountant. It has been well said that these are qualities which are not insured by rules and regulations.

The fundamental principles of accounting followed in keeping the accounts are, of course, reflected in the financial statements periodically prepared therefrom. The manner of preparation of the statements, the classification of the data shown thereon, and the various methods of disclosure of pertinent information have, however, been the subject of many rules, regulations and dicta, which have frequently been dignified improperly with the title of "accounting principles." Such rules are properly designed to produce statements which are convenient and informative, but they are based almost solely on constructive and logical thought as to what presentation will most clearly inform the reader as to the facts desired to be set forth; they have not the quality of compulsion which it is urged is an essential attribute of a fundamental accounting principle.

Many of the rules and conventions relating to presentation of financial

---

[8] *Abrams* v. *United States,* 250 U.S. 616, 630.

[9] T. H. Sanders—Reports to Stockholders. *The Accounting Review,* September, 1934.

statements are so completely logical and have become so imbedded in practice that to disregard them would be to mark the practitioner as inept and unskilled in his art. Compliance with them is assumed by those accustomed to reading financial statements. It is customary, for example, to prepare balance-sheets in statement form, with assets on the left and liabilities and capital on the right; to separate and subtotal current assets and current liabilities, property accounts, long-term debt and the like. But suppose the items, correctly described, were simply listed in alphabetical order on a balance-sheet; the fact that conventional arrangement was not followed might mark an unskilled accountant and might cause annoyance to the reader of the statement, but the violation of the conventions relating to presentation would not cause financial embarrassment; they cannot be said to have compelling or coercive character.

Aside from the conventions as to form, the underlying principle relating to presentation and classification of items and accounts in financial statements is hardly an accounting principle at all but the moral principle that with respect to financial statements the accountant is bound to tell the whole truth. In other words, however an item is listed or classified, it should be correctly described. To include a note due five years from now in the usual balance-sheet under the caption "current notes receivable," to describe an investment "at cost" when it really had been written up 50 per cent, to include extraneous windfall profits in operating earnings, would violate this principle, and this principle is compelling in the sense that those who violate it are subject to moral and even legal penalties.

A number of rules which are really based on this principle are given in the text of section 2 of the bulletin, *Examination of Financial Statements,* issued by the American Institute of Accountants in January, 1936. For example:

> Funds subject to withdrawal restrictions should be so described on the balance-sheet.
> The reserve for bad and doubtful accounts should be shown as a deduction from the corresponding assets.
> The amount of any accounts receivable that have been hypothecated or assigned should be so shown on the balance-sheet.
> Notes payable to affiliated companies and to stockholders, directors, officers and employees should be shown separately on the balance-sheet.
> Any default in the interest or sinking-fund requirements that may exist (as to funded debt) should be mentioned on the balance-sheet.
> Serial bonds, notes and mortgage instalments due within one year should be separately disclosed and, if material, should be included with the current liabilities.

Such rules as the above are essentially suggestions which, if followed, will tend to insure that no material fact is overlooked in the preparation of financial statements. A considerable body of this type of rule has been stated in the bulletin referred to; while others could no doubt be added, it is obviously impossible to foresee and provide rules to cover all possible situations. The busy practitioner knows how very frequently problems of presentation arise which are not covered by any stated rule; his recourse is to apply the moral principle that it is his duty to give the reader all pertinent information in a logical and understandable manner. The result must rest primarily on the integrity and skilled, informed judgment of the accountant. If, in similar situations, equally capable practitioners arrive at different solutions, it may well call for what Dr. Lin Yutang calls a typically Chinese point of view, that "A is right, but B is not wrong either."

There is a large volume of accounting literature dealing with the technique of auditing procedure employed by the accountant to assure himself that correct accounting principles have been employed in arriving at the balances in the accounts, and to afford him the necessary information for judging whether pertinent facts are fully and truthfully displayed in the financial statements prepared from the accounts. Most of this literature represents an attempt to reduce auditing technique to rules and standards. Probably the most successful general statement of the rules of auditing technique is contained in the second section of the bulletin *Examination of Financial Statements* issued by the American Institute of Accountants in January, 1936. The text of the bulletin emphasizes that in determining the nature and extent of the examination, the accountant will necessarily take into consideration, among other things, (a) the purpose of the examination, (b) the amount of detail included in the statements to be covered by his report, (c) the type of business the accounts of which are to be examined, and (d) the system of internal check and control.

It seems apparent that the rules of auditing technique must be limited to rather general statement, such as that contained in the bulletin referred to above, and that the element of personal judgment, competence and integrity of the auditor is far more important than detailed specifications for making audits. With respect to auditing procedures to be undertaken in a specific engagement, however, an audit program written for that particular engagement is a desirable aid to a well-conducted examination, and is a valuable record of just what was done.

To what extent can the practice of accounting, as it relates to the examination of and reporting on financial statements, be reduced to rules and standards? Accountants of the highest abilities and reputation are willing to give their considered opinion, after due examination, that the financial statements under review fairly present the position of a company based upon accounts determined in accordance with accepted principles of accounting. It follows that these fundamental truths upon which such opinion is based, and which may be properly dignified with the term principles, are known to the accountant and are matters with respect to which, by their very nature, there can be no general disagreement. These principles are characterized by their compelling or coercive nature, and this attribute distinguishes them from those rules of accounting which have been derived from principles but, of themselves, have no validity except as they logically depend upon principles. The principles of accounting, as herein defined, are capable of being stated and agreed to; the rules of accounting derived therefrom are subject to gradual crystallization as experience winnows those which are valid from those which are doubtful. The conventions and rules with respect to the presentation of data in financial statements depend on the moral principle that all material facts necessary to the proper and complete understanding of the statements must be given; many of these conventions are so firmly imbedded in practice that there should be no difficulty in enumerating them. As to the rules of auditing procedure, a general course may be charted, as in the American Institute bulletin, and certainly programs of audit for specific engagements are useful tools, but in preparing such a program the first essential is a high type of professional and moral equipment on the part of the practitioner.

A. A. Berle, Jr.

ACCOUNTING AND THE LAW

Adolf Augustus Berle, Jr., *was born in Massachusetts in 1895 and attended Harvard, receiving an A.B. in 1913 and an LL. B. in 1916. He has had a distinguished career as lawyer, government official, and author. He has served as a professor in the Columbia Law School, and is a partner in Berle, Berle & Brunner. He has published extensively, including* Studies in the Law of Corporation Finance *(1928) and* Cases and Materials in the Law of Corporation Finance *(1930), but is probably best known as coauthor, with Gardiner C. Means, of* The Modern Corporation and Private Property *(1932).*

The article reprinted here is significant because it proposes a "Board of Accounting Appeals" as the instrument through which rules of accounting can be established in a systematic but evolutionary manner.

The aim of this paper is to stimulate a more systematic method of evolving standard, but evolutionary, rules of accounting. The conclusion, if sound, follows from two premises. First, rules of accounting have become, in large measure, rules of law. Second, that the present methods by which accounting theory is translated into the accounting rules—or, if you choose, into accounting practices—which thus enter the legal system, are not wholly satisfactory, especially in view of the results which now follow from that translation. By consequence, the task of developing a systematic yet flexible means of arriving at and recording the sound doctrine as it appears in the light of the knowledge of the day, takes the foreground as a major problem in the profession of accounting.

Emergence of Accounting into the Field of Law

John Bauer, writing eight years ago, accurately indicated that accounting development had paralleled, roughly, the enormous growth of business over

Reprinted from *The Accounting Review* (March, 1938), pp. 9–15, by permission.

the past half-century; and he concluded by insisting, also accurately, that the growing control of government over business furnished a powerful spur toward extending the best private practice to all business units in similar fields. He, of course, had in mind the control exercised in the field of rail-roads, utilities, insurance and banking. Two years later, Mr. Frederick Fisher, of the New York bar, with some incidental assistance from the writer, took a somewhat wider base, and attempted to collect the common-law decisions in which guilt or innocence, liability or non-liability, had been predicated upon a pure rule of accounting: the result proving both formidable and a little surprising.† In combination, administrative requirements and court decisions had built a not inconsiderable edifice upon the basis of "rules of sound accounting"; and even had the discussion stopped there, it was plain that this body of doctrine, unsystematized and indefinite, had assumed cardinal importance as—may the phrase be excused?—super-judicial legisla-tion. But the problem became minor by comparison with the results created through the legislation of the next few years. The National Securities Act of 1933, under the guise of the simple phrases requiring disclosure of all material facts and elimination of any facts which might tend to mislead in registration statements and prospectuses, subtended very nearly the whole arc of accounting by the legal rule line. The power given the Commission to indulge its own views as to whether or not a set of accounts met the statutory requirements, very nearly made the newly-formed commission a synthetic czar in the accounting field: access to capital rested on conformity to the rules sanctioned by it; while liabilities, civil and criminal, might follow non-compliance. The Securities Exchange Act of 1934 carried the process still further as did certain strictly judicial determinations—as, for instance, the enlargement by decision of the effect of the Federal statute against use of the mails to defraud.

At all events, the accountant had suddenly come into his own, as a part of the mechanism of government control, though rather by the shot-gun route; and there he is likely to remain for some time to come. As a lawyer, I have to put my accounting books alongside of my Annotated Statutes and my digests of case-law, and so must the judge before whom I argue; at which point the real argument here to be made must begin.

It will not, perhaps, be seriously argued that in 1933—or, for that matter, today—the phrase "sound accounting principles" did not describe a body of accepted doctrine comparable, let us say, to any branch of common law, as, for instance, the law of contracts or corporations. The profession was struggling nobly with the job of bringing the conception into reality. The Federal Reserve system had engaged the interest of A. P. Richardson to edit a report on accounting terminology, and a very capable Special Com-

---

†John Bauer, "Depreciation and Public Utility Valuation" *The Accounting Review* (June, 1930) ; A. A. Berle, Jr., and Frederick Fisher, "Elements of the Law of Business Accounting," 32 *Col. Law Rev.* 573 (1932).

mittee had produced a Preliminary Report, which had been the subject of heavy discussion for some years. The Stock List Committee of the New York Stock Exchange, at which it is fashionable just now to take pot-shots, but without which very little in this field would have been accomplished, had, at the insistence of Mr. Frank Altschul, engaged Mr. George May as accounting consultant, and had begun to render a series of opinions in the field of corporate statements. Progress on many fronts was evident, but objectives were at once undefined and far away. Perhaps the preoccupation of accountants and businessmen with problems of taxation (which are usually too specialized to be of general use in ordinary business accounting) had diverted too much attention to that field to allow of the more general development connoted by the enormous impact of the legal rules which suddenly came into being. In result, the groups of accountants which assisted in drawing the forms and regulations for the Federal Trade Commission as predecessor of the S.E.C. in the Fall of 1933, really found themselves faced with the job of codifying, unofficially, a huge field of accounting in a few weeks—and that in a profession which had only just begun to agree on terminology. It is a tribute, both to the men and to the solid thinking done by writers and students of accountancy, that they were able to handle the assignment. One recalls the plight of a legislative committee in a southern State which was asked to enact a comprehensive statute covering the law of sales. It took the not unintelligent course of adopting as its proposed law, the bulk of Professor Williston's Treatise on Sales, and calling it square. But the law of sales has a history and a body of authority covering several centuries; whereas accounting moved out of the function of a private convenience to businessmen, into the legislative arena within a very few years. Perhaps it is as well that there was this forced evolution from the academic discussion to the legal fact; all discussions do, sometime, have to crystallize. But it leaves for consideration the problem of progress from this point on.

Now we might, to be sure, abandon the collective responsibility for further evolution to the government agencies having power in the field. The banking departments, the insurance commissioners, the F.D.I.C. [Federal Deposit Insurance Corporation], the Comptroller of the Currency, the Federal Reserve Board, the Securities and Exchange Commission, and the Courts, will henceforth be issuing regulations, rulings, informal opinions, formal decisions, and so forth, which, aggregated, will form a growing body of authority; and the accountants' journals can criticize, arrange and group this material. But I venture to question whether this will suffice, and to lay out some of the dangers. Since the S.E.C. is probably the most effective force which today is thrusting accounting rules into the legal structure, let me take that mechanism as illustration.

Every administrative body has a specific job to do, and serves a special interest. That is why it is there. Its views on accounting, accordingly, are conditioned by its desire to reach that result, rather than by any interest in the healthy growth of accounting as a whole. No one who has read Professor Bonbright's classic treatise on judicial valuation can fail to have accepted his major conclusion, namely, that in the realm of valuation, the "sound" accounting rule varied entirely with the purpose for which the valuation was to be used. Consciously or otherwise, the result to be obtained reached backward. For the purpose of a stock issue, the basis of valuation was largely that of historical cost; for rate-making, that of current appraisal, arrived at in any one of several ways; for taxation, still another basis appears; for a reorganization plan, a new set of factors turns up. The illustration is no doubt extreme, because more divergence is possible in dealing with value or worth—largely because it is matter of opinion, and subjective in quality —than in any other; but in greater or less degree, the same situation appears whenever accounting ceases to be a mere record of an historical transaction solely in cash. The theory of disclosure to an investor under the registration provisions of the S.E.C. acts in itself offers a specialized objective. Before the commission can ask what that investor ought to know, it must ask why he ought to know it. Plainly, because he may be asked, or may wish, to buy or to sell a security. At once a theoretical student has to note a reservation.

For instance, it might be entirely in order, as a protection to prospective buyers of utility securities, to insist on a variety of adjustments tending to indicate lower plant values, higher charges to current maintenance, and so forth. This might, at the same time, be the worst disservice possible to existing security holders whose interest in income would lead them to build up the capital account as a basis for obtaining higher rates. It might be of real importance to portray a stock issue as risky to potential buyers at the very moment when another group of public interests was strenuously pressing for equity financing instead of bond—or debt—financing. Even within the investors' field alone there are ineluctable conflicts. Where no-par stock, or nominal-par-value stock is concerned, the existing shareholders who may have paid real value for their holdings, are interested in maintaining their contribution; while incoming shareholders are interested in coming in at the lowest price possible. Instances could be indefinitely multiplied: the point need not be labored. There is always danger, where accounting rules are made by specialized administrative tribunals, that the resulting body of doctrine may be lop-sided, if not positively dangerous, however conscientiously the rulings have been made from the point of view of the administrators making them.

Even more of a problem is the process by which these decisions—now become authoritative—are made.

In practice, accounting points are usually raised by the S.E.C. in the form of a "deficiency letter," which is sent to an applicant who desires to register securities for sale after his registration statement has been filed and gone over by the examining unit. At this point the registrant, or his counsel, decide either that they will comply with the suggestion implied in the deficiency letter, or that someone will go to Washington to argue the matter out with the sub-examiners, carrying the discussion on (if there is failure to agree) with any senior officer of the commission he can get to listen to him. So far, so good; but the next phase is not so simple. If agreement is not had by this informal process, the registrant has only one of three courses open. He may comply, irrespective of what he thinks about it; or he may withdraw his registration and abandon his financing; or he may stand his ground and go to a hearing under Section 8-d of the Act to determine whether a stop-order should issue on the ground that he is trying to sell securities under a fraudulent set of representations.

One need be no fortune-teller to state in advance what the applicant will do. If he can, he will comply. If need be, he will abandon the business. Only if he is a merely irresponsible swindler will he, or can he afford to, try out an issue of accounting in the form of a hearing to determine whether or not he is about to commit a fraud. The result, naturally, is that most questions of accounting are settled by the star-chamber process, and chiefly by sub-examiners. Businessmen who have any reputation do not put themselves in the position of putative swindlers merely to determine matters of accounting. The determinations so taken are non-reviewable. Theoretically, of course, one could fight it out before the Commission, which, in practice, will support its technical staff as a matter of course, and then have the stop-order which has already issued and destroyed the businessman's reputation, as well as the prospect of successful financing, reviewed by the District of Columbia courts. But no sane man would follow that program; for a victory would be as disastrous as a defeat.

Now this, it is submitted, is not a satisfactory state of affairs. Specifically,

(1) Decisions so made are not recorded or available to others as a guide of conduct or a basis of informed criticism and comment;

(2) They are by no means necessarily uniform, reasoned, systematic, or grounded on anything other than the feeling of the examining staff;

(3) They are not reviewed by any competent authority, nor susceptible of being so; and

(4) There is no procedure leading to the conclusion that such decisions are valid precedent rather than purely arbitrary determination, depending on the capability and integrity of the Commission staff at any given moment.

Yet there, at the present writing, is the mechanism by which rules of accounting are determined and, for all practical purposes, written into the living law, by the administrative agency having the greatest degree of control over the accounting profession save in a few specialized fields. Had the common law been developed in any such fashion, its major glory—the constant self-criticism which it engendered, and which has at all times been its safeguard, its forward light and its intellectual fertility—would never have come into existence. The criticism of process is fundamental. It matters not a whit that determinations may have been made (I think they have been made) with a high degree of integrity and competence. It is of little consequence that occasional formal decisions on accounting points have been publicly rendered by the Commission in connection with some fly-by-night who had nothing to lose anyhow and therefore elected the obviously futile course of fighting a stop-order before the full commission, so that we have a few determinations, chiefly by way of *obiter dicta* in fraud cases which should have been stopped in any case. The plain fact remains that effective accounting rules are made *in camera*, without system, without effective submission to criticism, with little guaranty against arbitrary determination, and without the continuous and open self-examination which must go into rulings which attain to the sanction and dignity of law.

Method of Systematic Evolution of Accounting Principles

It is proper, here, to take temporary leave of the S.E.C., which in any case was selected only because it happened to be the broadest mark on an over-full horizon, and to attempt a more constructive attack. Since we are dealing with accounting rules or determinations which serve as a basis for legal action, disability or liability, a lawyer may be pardoned for importing the technique of his own profession, on the chance that it may prove useful to the newer, but sister profession which has thus suddenly converged. Yet a lawyer may as well keep his humility; for we are in an area where the common law itself is making heavy weather. Having come through a crisis of major difficulty in the seventeenth century, the theory of the rule of law (as contrasted with administrative processes, boiling down to government by men) is again under bitter criticism now in the middle of the twentieth century. So it will not do to be dogmatic in the now mixed economico-legal territory which goes by the name of accounting.

Where a government body has power to make an effective rule in any particular case, we have come to expect at least two, and possibly three, safeguards which are also development mechanisms. These are, in order: (1) The opportunity for full argument, afforded both sides; (2) The requirement for a publicly announced, reasoned decision; (3) Review upon appeal to a higher tribunal. It may be granted at once that a conscious attempt has been made, in recent years, by certain influences in the law to eliminate some, if not all, of these safeguards, and to deify the administrative process in and of itself. But this school of thought, is so obviously an extreme as applied to American conditions that it cannot be taken as a permanent guide in building the intellectual framework of the newest branch of law, which accounting really is. In any event, the classic model appears the more useful for our purposes.

There are, taken together, at least several dozen administrative agencies (exclusive of tax or revenue units) which today make law on accounting matters. Beside the S.E.C. in its registration work under the 1933 Act, and under the 1934 Act, there is the New York Stock Exchange, making determinations under its power to list or delist, and more incidental decisions under the little-known but highly useful institution of the Miscellaneous Calendar of the Stock List Committee. There is the Interstate Commerce Commission with jurisdiction over railway accounting; the Federal Communications Commission with less defined but still material power over telephone and telegraph matters; the Federal Power Commission in respect of still other areas. The Federal Reserve Board has considerable latitude in accounting problems of banks and trust companies; and there are endless state commissions in other departments.

It should be within the realm of possibility to create a Board of Accounting Appeals to which accounting questions could be referred, and which, by training, personnel, and equipment was capable of rendering swift decision on such problems. The body might be either formal or informal, provided it were authoritative; for what is needed, here, is not so much a judicial proceeding, as an authoritative statement of the best prevailing thought. It should be so set up that it could decide a specific problem—as, for example, the dispute referred to between an administrative examiner and a registrant who felt he was right but did not care to have the matter tried out by putting his honesty on trial. It should also be so placed that it could render advisory opinions in advance of a controversy; or for general application. It ought not to follow the doctrine of *stare decisis* as do common-law courts; that is, precedent should not be binding. Rather, we ought to borrow from the experience of our European friends who practice the Roman law, and follow the system by which the writers, the scholars, the commentators, are as persuasive authority as are the decisions of the group itself. Just as in older days in England, a jury of merchants was occasionally convened to set out, for the benefit of the law which was then adopting the custom of merchants into its orbit, the actual fact of that custom, so today we could profitably have a continuous mouthpiece for the best applied thought in accounting. To it any body dealing with accounting in the public interest might refer—and, perhaps, should be obliged to refer. We should then get a body of accounting authority which was properly argued, publicly announced, and responsible at the bar of the profession.

If this suggestion seems to take in too much area, we might work out a series of less ambitious, though less satisfactory, experiments. For instance, there is no real need for the S.E.C. to determine accounting questions only as incidents to a stop-order proceeding. In many cases neither the Commission nor any party really believes that there is a question of intent to mislead when in fact the issue is whether this or that item of income was or was not non-recurrent; whether a specific expense cost should be capitalized, or whether a plainly historical entry of cost imparts a present-day appraisal. The dispute in any of these cases may be a difference of opinion. Indeed, in many situations there is a real problem whether the record deals with so-called "facts" at all; for there is no distinct line between fact and estimate or judgment in many of these matters. If, therefore, a central accounting Board seems too visionary, we might make progress, so far as the S.E.C. is concerned by having a special division to rule on problems of accounting and to issue published opinions after hearing argument—thereby at least creating a clear and growing body of available precedent—again, preferably, without the constriction of any rule of *stare decisis* to inhibit further development as new light may appear. To such a division should be assigned the task of ruling on the accounting provisions of new regulations, of new forms, and of changes in old forms. Then, and not until then, will we begin to have something more satisfactory in the way of effective accounting opinion.

Implicit in either the more or the less ambitious plan is the hope that accountants will continue to be fertile in theoretical and professional discussion. Granted open, reasoned decision, and the professional comment, criticism, and review begins to operate. The only places where the United States Supreme Court can be overruled are the Law Schools and the Law Reviews. The only practicable method of checking a foolish or unwise administrative ruling on accounting is in the technical journals and the proceedings of the associations. In the law, we know that the long process of recorded study ultimately serves as a corrective upon the most powerful courts; and the case for that correction is infinitely stronger in a relatively new field like that of accountancy. Wanting that continuous interplay of professional opinion and quasi-legal decision, your profession may well slip into a morass quite as deep as the valley from which it has climbed: having freed itself from the chains of servitude to businessmen, it may, all too easily, find itself merely the ciphering agency for virtually unreviewable bureaucrats. It took time to teach merchants that they could not give orders to accountants as to what their figures should show; and the profession must never drop to the point where its members are in demand primarily because their opinions will change whenever a subexaminer, for reasons not put on the record, wishes a different arrangement of figures.

From the strict legalistic point of view there is real reason for wishing this slow, steady, self-critical erection of accounting theory. For an accountant has both the power and the duty to look behind the strict legal line in drawing his conclusions—a power which lawyers can use only at hazard, and rarely with authority. For instance, a lawyer is taught that corporations are separate entities, irrespective of their stock ownership. If therefore X corporation sells its merchandise to Y corporation, which X happens to control as a subsidiary, the lawyer has to regard the transaction as a sale. From his point of view, title did pass from X to Y, and that settles it. The resulting liability is a debt from Y to X; and that settles that. But the accountant can go behind the returns. He does not, because of that fact, have to assume that the resulting debt is an account receivable; or, for that matter, that the sale is a commercial sale, classifiable with other transactions in ordinary course of business. The lawyer may be right about the technicality of the title-passing and debt-creation; but the legal christening does not make the transaction a true conversion of inventory into collectible liability. Whereupon a good accountant will segregate the item and separately record or explain it. A banker may "pad" his position by accepting a year-end deposit, designed to be kept separate and returned to the depositor after New Year's day. A lawyer may advise that the relation of debtor and creditor —banker and depositor—is thereby created. An accountant, if he knows the facts, knows better, and declines to allow the padding. A lawyer, advising a dividend policy, must rely on the accountant to tell him whether or not there is surplus justifying the dividend. An accountant can and must show him the way, or the limitation. It is not too much to say that in certain directions, the progress of the law is through accounting—just as a century ago, its progress lay through the custom of merchant-bankers, whence comes our entire jurisprudence of banking, negotiable instruments, and what is known as the law-merchant. No, we need the accountant quite as much for our own enlightenment and evolution as for his own peculiar contribution. But we need the cross-fertilization as a schematic, systematic body of doctrine; and that is to be had only by guarding the manner of its growth.

George R. Husband

THE CORPORATE-ENTITY FICTION
AND ACCOUNTING THEORY

George Rosewall Husband *(1896–1958) was born in England but lived most of his life in the United States. He received his A.B. in 1923 from Michigan and his Ph.D. in 1932 from the same school. He taught at Michigan and at Istanbul but is most closely identified with Wayne State University in Detroit, where he taught for many years. He was a vice-president of the American Accounting Association in 1946 and its president in 1952. In addition to numerous journal articles he was coauthor of a series of textbooks.*

The article reprinted here follows through the consequences of applying the concept of entity to the "fiction" of the corporation as a being separate and apart from its owners. Husband uses his analytical powers to show both the uses of such a fiction and the pitfalls in accepting it literally as a description of reality.

The modern business corporation is commonly regarded as a distinct entity,[1] a being separate from the natural persons whose coexistence is essential. It is recognized, of course, that the corporate entity is a fiction, an artificial personality, that it lacks objective reality, and that it possesses no power to act or to direct action. In the final analysis, the corporate entity is a legal concept employed to justify utilitarian conduct. An association of persons, lacking in legal entity, could, and in some cases does, own property in its own name, could sue or be sued, possess a continuity equal at least to that of a large majority of corporations and even be granted the privilege of limited liability without being personified. But it has appeared desirable, in the main, that such privileges be granted to an association only when it takes on the guise of entity, when it comes into being upon the basis of a specific grant by the state, and is to be regulated by special statutory provisions. The corporate fiction was probably first advanced for the benefit of the individual

Reprinted from *The Accounting Review* (September, 1938), pp. 241–53, by permission.
[1] 4 Wheat (U.S.) 518. Kent's *Commentaries*, 267.

participants. That it facilitates the process of regulation and taxation, how-ever, and contributes to the protection of the public appears to be partly responsible for its persistence.

The fiction is most logical when restricted to certain of its legal aspects. While the corporation has contributed much to economic development, it is not fundamentally an economic entity; nor is the legal corporation funda-mentally an accounting entity.[2] For purposes of economics[3] and accounting, the corporation might well be viewed as a group of individuals associated for the purpose of business enterprise, so organized that its affairs are conducted through representatives.[4] Numerous illustrations may be cited of instances in which this latter, or representative, viewpoint has been taken even by the law and the courts, and in its attempt to control the development of trusts, the law has frequently found it necessary to go behind the corporate fiction and prescribe penalities for corporate officers as well as for the corporation.[5] The income-tax law and regulations dispense with the corporate entity in the principle of constructive ownership,[6] in the imposition of a tax upon corpora-tions for improperly accumulating surplus[7] and of a surtax on personal holding companies.[8] And the argument is frequently advanced that the corporate-surplus tax improved the equity of the tax system by reaching wealthy individuals who were incorporating their property as a means of securing lower rates of taxation. The courts, too, have often found it necessary to go behind the theory.[9] The Pennsylvania rule[10] governing the division of a stock dividend between a remainderman and a life tenant pro-vides an excellent illustration. Accounting theory would probably be more

---

[2] From the accounting standpoint, it is the entity of business enterprise which is of importance. In this respect, the accountant's interests are identical in the case of the sole-proprietorship and the partnership. The concept of corporate entity merely lends support to the drawing of a more definite circle than in the case of the sole-proprietorship and the partnership.

[3] The economist's debate as to the identification of the entrepreneur may be referred to in this connection. See Berle and Means, *The Modern Corporation,* Book IV, Chaps. I, II, IV, and Garver and Hansen, *Principles of Economics,* Chap. 4.

[4] Seager and Gulick, *Trust and Corporation Problems,* pp. 28–30.

[5] Among others: The Act to Regulate Commerce (1887) Sections 8, 9, and 10, and its amendment of 1889; The Elkins Act (1903); The Hepburn Act (1906); The Clayton Anti-Trust Act, Section 14.

[6] Section 24, b, 2A (Act of 1937).

[7] Section 102 (Act of 1937).

[8] Sections 351–360 (Act of 1937).

[9] In the Standard Oil Trust case (49 Ohio 137) of 1892, the Ohio Supreme Court declared that "On a question of this kind, the fact must constantly be kept in view that the metaphysical entity has no thought or will of its own; that every act ascribed to it emanates from, and is, the act of the individuals personated by it, and that it can no more do an act or refrain from doing it, contrary to the will of these natural persons than a house could be said to act independently of its owner; and when an act is ascribed to it, it must be understood to be the act of the persons associated as a cor-poration." The courts have discarded the entity mainly when fraud has been involved.

[10] Kerrigan, H. D., "Stock Dividends in Trust Distributions," the *Accounting Review,* June, 1937; Underwood, W., "The Legal Status of the Claim of the Preferred Stock-holder to Dividends," p. 57, Unpublished Master's Thesis, Wayne University.

realistic if it accepted as its basis the fact that the corporation is an association of flesh-and-blood persons who enjoy special privileges because they have complied with certain legal requirements.

Recording the Investment in a Subsidiary

The accountant has eagerly accepted the entity theory, primarily, one suspects, because of its definiteness in circumscribing the business as an enterprise and thus separating business from personal transactions and the transactions of one business from those of another, and because of the situs of legal title. His treatment of various accounting problems has not been entirely consistent with this viewpoint, however. An illustration is found in the accounting procedure sometimes followed in maintaining the record of a holding company's investment in its subsidiaries. It is not exceptional for the accountant to ignore the boundaries of entity and, subscribing to the accrual method,[11] take up a proper proportion of the profits or losses of subsidiaries on the books of a holding company. The accountant denies, however, that the same procedure is justly applied to the records of the small investor. Legal entity is just as real in both cases; in fact the parent company frequently forms subsidiaries to obtain legal benefits attaching to the separate entity. The difference between the two situations is one of practicality. When a holding company owns from 80 per cent to 100 per cent of the stock of a subsidiary, there certainly is a greater degree of justification for treating the two as one accounting identity than for accruing a proportionate share of a corporation's earnings where a stockholder owns only one sixty-fourth of 1 per cent of the total stock outstanding. The accrual method, nevertheless, is consistent with an underlying representative or association viewpoint, while the accounting treatment accorded the investment of the small stockholder is consistent with and justified by the theory of separate entities. The two procedures are therefore theoretically different. This fact in itself is of no significance except for the implications of the two divergent concepts as respects the understanding and treatment of general accounting problems.

Computation of Book Value

The method followed in determining the book value of the stockholders' interests affords a second illustration of a situation in which the accountant

---

11 Finney, H. A., *Principles of Accounting*, Vol. II, Chap. 49; Kester, R. B., *Advanced Accounting*, p. 687; *The Accountants' Handbook*, pp. 1047–48, does not accept the accrual method with enthusiasm; The American Institute of Accountants' "Statement of Accounting Principles" (pp. 69–70) appears to approve the accrual method for losses but not for gains.

violates the logic of the entity theory by an implicit acceptance of the representative or association viewpoint. Consistent with the entity theory, it is usually contended that the income of a corporation does not constitute income to its stockholders; yet, when this same income is credited to surplus, it is added to the stockholders' interest as portrayed by the capital-stock account to secure the stockholders' total equity. But how can that which is not the stockholders' equity as income justly become the stockholders' equity as surplus? Or, to put the question somewhat differently, how can that which is not the stockholders' equity as income become the stockholders' equity as savings or capital? What magic betwixt income and surplus is the cause of such transformation? It would appear that if the income of the corporation is not the income of the stockholder, the resulting surplus is the equity of the corporate entity and not of the stockholders. And consistency with the equity viewpoint would demand that earned surplus be excluded in computing the book value of the stockholders' interest. Obviously, this conclusion is difficult to accept. It is, however, no more fictitious than the corporate entity.

The representative or association viewpoint appears more in keeping with reality. Income of the corporation is income, pro rata, to the respective stockholders,[12] irrespective of the practicality of recording it as such. Surplus is therefore properly considered a portion of the stockholders' equity and is justly included in computing the book value of the stockholders' interests. The situs of legal title to the corporate assets is sometimes offered in opposition to this viewpoint. On the basis of legal title, however, it appears that the stockholders must be regarded as a species of liability, since the legal title to all of the assets is in the corporation. On the other hand, it is also true legally that the stockholders' equity increases as the corporation succeeds. The market recognizes this fact. Further, it is questionable whether the fact that legal title to assets is in the corporation is sufficient to deny the stockholders' claim to income without reifying a legal or metaphysical concept. In the North River Sugar Refining Company case the court stated that the corporation was formed for the benefit of the incorporators as acting and living men and that the benefit of incorporation was theirs.[13] Surely one of these benefits is the receipt of income. A rather satisfactory argument can be set forth to the effect that while the stockholders do not have legal title to corporate assets they do possess a title in equity. In a New York case[14] respecting the fiduciary relationship of directors, the court stated that "The ordinary relation of the directors to the corporation and stockholders is not

---

12 It may be suggested that the representative or association viewpoint is a much more logical and equitable approach to the problem of taxing the corporation where the ability theory of taxation prevails than is the entity viewpoint. The consent-dividend of the 1938 Income-Tax Act is a definite step in the right direction.

13 121 New York 582 (1890).

14 *Kavanaugh* v. *Kavanaugh Knitting Mills,* 226 N.Y. 185, 123 N.E. 148.

a matter of statutory law, or of technical law. It springs from the fact that the directors have the control and guidance of the corporate business, affairs and property, and hence of the property interests of the stockholders. Equity, at least, recognizes the truth that the stockholders are the proprietors of the corporate interests and are ultimately the only beneficiaries thereof."

Conclusions based upon the situs of legal title are logically consistent with the entity theory: the corporation is its own proprietor, assets are the property of the corporation, all income earned is the income of the corporate entity until declared in dividends, surplus is the equity of the corporate entity and ought not be added to the capital stock in computing the book value of the stockholders' equity, the latter should be regarded as a species of liability.[15] Having started with fiction, consistency requires that one continue to deal in fiction. However, such analysis leaves one unsatisfied. It is similar to the philosophical logic by which one disproves one's existence. "The state gave the franchise, the charter, not to the impalpable, and almost nebulous fiction of our thought but to the corporators, the individuals. . . ."[16] Consequently, one feels that the stockholders are proprietors and that the corporation's income[17] is the income of the stockholders, just as one feels himself to be alive after proving philosophically that he is nonexistent. Such also would appear to be the intent of the law in spite of the obstacle for which it is responsible; equity recognizes this fact. The conflict illustrated by the computation of book value is best eliminated by an acceptance of the more realistic representative viewpoint.

Restricted and Unrestricted Capital

Many of the accountant's problems originate in the confused realm existing between the entity and representative or association viewpoints. At the origin of a corporation, the problem arises as to whether par value is capital and a premium, surplus, or whether the total amount received from the investor is capital. This problem is not encountered in the formation of a partnership

---

15 In his *Accounting Theory,* W. A. Paton presents an argument to the effect that the creditors should be considered a part of proprietorship, Chap. III. For a similar conclusion based upon a somewhat different analysis see Berle and Means, *The Modern Corporation,* Book II, Chap. VIII, in which the authors state that "Though the law still maintains the conception of a sharp dividing line recognizing the bondholder as a lender of capital and the stockholder as a *quasi*-partner in the enterprise, economically the positions of the two have drawn together. Consequently, security holders may be regarded as a hierarchy of individuals all of whom have supplied capital to the enterprise, and all of whom expect a return from it," p. 279.

16 North River Sugar Refining Company Case, *op. cit.*

17 The term income is used in the same sense in which the accountant usually accepts it.

or a sole-proprietorship. Obviously, the total amount received, with the exception of forfeitures, etc., is invested capital. The law provides, however, that in return for the privileges which it grants the association, termed corporation, certain safeguards must be provided to meet the requisites, of public welfare, to protect creditors, minorities, etc. It, the law, therefore, stipulates that a certain portion of the total member investment be subjected to restrictions as to withdrawal; any excess investment above the stipulated amount or proportion may be legally construed as unrestricted capital. The restricted portion of the investment is usually termed capital stock or par value; the accountant labels the unrestricted portion capital surplus. It is suggested that the terms restricted and unrestricted invested capital are more in accord with a proper understanding of the legal intent.

Where the law permits the issuance of no-par stock, it frequently applies restrictions to only a small proportion of the amount which the corporation receives.[18] Consistent with what is believed to be self-interest, the corporate directors often credit little more than the minimum amount to the capital stock account; the remainder they credit to capital surplus.[19] Such procedure does not always receive the accountant's approval. But, in the absence of other compelling factors, why should one restrict any greater proportion of his capital than the law requires? At heart, the question hardly appears to involve accounting principles. It is primarily a legal problem with protection of the public's interests the main point at issue. The accountant is merely concerned with recording the facts in such a way as to exhibit their true nature.

It is this latter fact, in all probability, which, from the representative viewpoint, justifies the exhibition of earned surplus as an item separate from capital surplus. Since the income of the corporation is the income of the stockholders, earned surplus constitutes the stockholders' savings, accumulated, admittedly, under compulsion. From the standpoint of succeeding fiscal periods, it is as much capital, economic capital, as is the original investment. As such, it may therefore be combined with capital surplus, the law not declaring otherwise.[20] Consistent with his purpose, however, the accountant properly records earned surplus in a separate account in order to emphasize the respective sources of the two amounts of unrestricted capital. From the entity viewpoint, earned surplus is properly recorded in an account separate from capital surplus since the former, as previously stated, represents the cor-

---

18 Some states are very liberal in this respect. Ohio places the minimum at $500 (Section 8623–37 of the Ohio General Code). Michigan, on the other hand, requires that at least 50 per cent of the amount received shall be credited to restricted capital [P.A. 327, (1931)].

19 Although there can be neither discount nor premium on no-par stock, the amount received can be divided between restricted and unrestricted capital.

20 The corporation codes of some of the states (Illinois, Michigan, Ohio) require that earned surplus and capital surplus be kept separate.

porate entity's equity as distinct from the latter, which is a portion of the stockholder's equity.

Dividends

Charged against capital surplus. The accountant sometimes questions the procedure of charging dividends against capital surplus. He seldom contends, however, that a sole-proprietor should be denied the right to withdraw a portion of his investment from his business when he deems such a step advisable, or that a partner should be denied the privilege of withdrawing a portion of his capital, provided his contract permits. If the law, or the corporate contract, does not, in the interest of public welfare, deny the directors the right to distribute unrestricted capital, why should the accountant complain because of the procedure? Should not the corporation be granted the same freedom to reduce unrestricted capital that a sole-proprietorship or partnership possesses? The decision appears to be a problem for the directors, the stockholders' representatives; the accountant's only concern is to see that the relevant facts are properly exhibited.[21] The accountant's difficulty, however, probably arises from the fact that, in some respects at least, he conceives of the corporation and the stockholder as separate entities. Accordingly, the income earned by the corporation is the income of the corporate entity; it does not become the income of the stock-holding entities until it is declared in dividends. Stockholders have, therefore, come to look to dividends for income and to judge the corporation upon the basis of dividends received. Dividends constituting a return of capital are likely to be interpreted as being paid out of earnings with a resulting misjudgment of the corporate status. Fear of this result has probably influenced the accountant's attitude. The conflict between such reasoning and the logic upon which the computation of book value is based is evident. If the income of the corporation is the income of the stockholders, no dividend can be interpreted as income. Cash dividends are merely a withdrawal of income or capital; stock dividends are indicative of the fact that for one reason or another, unrestricted capital has been transformed into restricted capital.

The stock dividend. The debate as to whether the stock dividend constitutes income is, in part, also the result of confusing the entity and representative or association viewpoints. (In part, it appears to be an expression of conflict between the accountant's cost and the economist's value.) If, from the entity viewpoint, the income of the corporation is not to be inter-

---

21 When dividends are declared out of capital surplus, certain states require that that fact be made known (Illinois, Michigan, Ohio, Pennsylvania). Illinois, Michigan, and Pennsylvania appear to limit the dividends which may be declared out of capital surplus to dividends on preferred stock.

preted as the income of the stockholder, and if the resulting earned surplus is not the equity of the stockholder, the stock dividend would appear to transfer an amount from the corporate entity's equity to the equity of the stockholders and thus to meet the test of income. It should be evident, therefore, that the accountant can not consistently hold the entity viewpoint and deny that the stock dividend constitutes income. From the association viewpoint, however, admitting that the income of the corporation is the income of the stockholder and admitting that earned surplus is a part of the stockholders' equity, the conclusion that stock dividend is not income is logical. The economic status of the stock dividend would seem to coincide more nearly with the decision dictated by the representative viewpoint. The accountant, however, should not be permitted to affirm both the entity and association viewpoints.

In *Eisner* v. *Macomber*[22] the United States Supreme Court held that a stock dividend does not constitute income. This decision is consistent with the association and not with the entity theory. The *Eisner* v. *Macomber* ruling was later modified by the decision rendered in *Koshland* v. *Helvering*[23] in which the Court held a stock dividend to be income if it changed the relationship existing between various classes of stock. This second, or modifying decision appears to be inconsistent with both the entity and representative viewpoints. As previously indicated, from the entity viewpoint all stock dividends appear, logically, to be income. From the association viewpoint, a preferred-stock dividend paid to common stock when nonparticipating preferred stock is outstanding is merely indicative of a transfer of the stockholders' previously unrestricted equity into restricted equity. Thus it does not constitute income. The preferred-stock dividend gives the common stockholders no greater equity than they possessed previously, nor, in general, assuming that the corporation will be sufficiently successful to be able to meet all dividend requirements out of income, need it change future participative relationships. There are three ways, however, in which such a dividend may have economic or income possibilities. First, if future income proves insufficient to meet the full dividend requirements and if the corporation decides to pay only part of the preferred stock's claim, such a preferred-stock dividend will enable the common stock to participate in that payment without having first met the indebtedness to the old preferred stockholders in full. Second, the preferred-stock dividend will enable the common stockholders to participate in dividends without such being specifically declared on common stock. Third, at the time of liquidation, it being assumed that preferred stock enjoys a preference to assets, the common stock may, through the medium of its preferred-stock dividend, participate in asset distributions even though the value of the assets is equivalent only to the stated value of the old preferred stock. From the association viewpoint, however, it is doubtful that these acquired privileges are sufficient to entitle one to conclude

---

[22] 252 U.S. 189.
[23] 289 U.S. 441.

that the preferred-stock dividend constitutes income to the common stock-holders, or to determine the extent to which the dividend constitutes income.

If the previously existing preferred stock and the preferred-stock dividend are participating, a redistribution of the remaining surplus will be effected. The previously existing preferred stock will lose a portion of its equity in earned and capital surplus to the newly issued preferred stock, and thus, actually, to the common stock. Perhaps the Court had this possibility in mind when it announced its decision in the Koshland case. If so, then representatively it is not the stock dividend, or at least not the whole of the dividend, which constitutes income, but rather only that amount which represents the increase in equity gained at the expense of the other class of stock. The gain will be found in part in the dividend itself and in part in the increased equity in the remaining surplus. A stock dividend paid to the common stockholders in common stock constitutes income, also, to the extent, and only to the extent, that it reduces a participating preferred stock's equity in earned surplus.[24]

A stock dividend paid to preferred stock (common stock being assumed to be outstanding) in either common or preferred stock appears to be income from both the entity and association viewpoints if the preferred stock is nonparticipating. If preferred stock is participating, a stock dividend, whether in common or preferred stock, should be construed as income in its entirety if the decision is to be consistent with the entity viewpoint. (From the entity point of view, the term participating would seem to have no reference to the claims of the respective stocks against surplus.) From the representative or association viewpoint, however, if preferred stock is parti-cipating, a stock dividend, whether in common or preferred stock, constitutes income only to the extent that it transfers a portion of the common stock-holders' equity to the equity of the preferred stock. Such transfer need not coincide with the amount of the dividend paid, nor need it be entirely con-tained within the dividend paid. As an illustration of this last point, it may be assumed that the par of the preferred stock outstanding is $1,000,000, that the preferred stock participates equally with the common stock, that the par of the common stock outstanding is $1,000,000, and that earned surplus amounts to $600,000. From the association viewpoint each type of stock possesses a participating equity in surplus to the extent of $300,000. A stock dividend of $100,000 paid to the preferred stock in either common or parti-cipating preferred sock, may be assumed to be charged against the previously existing equity shares to the amount of $50,000 each. Since, therefore, $50,000 of the stock dividend received represents a mere transfer from the preferred stock's unrestricted capital to its restricted capital, it should not be interpreted as income. It is only the remaining $50,000 charged to the common stock's previously participative share in earned surplus which should be construed as income. But this is not the full effect of the payment of such

---

[24] An illustration is presented later in connection with a dividend paid to preferred stock.

a dividend. The preferred stockholders now possess an equity whose par value is $1,100,000; the par value of the common stock outstanding remains the same. The preferred stock's participating equity in earned surplus is, therefore, eleven twenty-firsts of $500,000, or $261,905; the common stock's participating equity is ten twenty-firsts, or $238,095. The declaration of the stock dividend in the form of participating preferred stock or common stock thus transfers an $11,905 greater equity to the preferred stockholders than would be the case if the dividend had been paid in nonparticipating preferred stock. The total income to the preferred stockholders is therefore $61,905 ($50,000 plus $11,905). Had the $100,000 dividend been paid in non-participating preferred stock, the income to the preferred stockholders would have amounted to only $50,000.

Relation of dividends to price paid for stock. The relation between dividends and income is of interest from another angle. If an individual purchases stock just prior to the declaration of a dividend, it is frequently held that the dividend constitutes income, even though charged against surplus in existence at the time the stock was purchased.[25] If the dividend were declared but unpaid at the time of purchase, its receipt may be held to be a return of capital. These conclusions, presumably, are based upon the entity theory. In support of the first conclusion it is held that such a dividend declaration transfers to the stockholders value which previously was a part of the corporate equity; hence, the dividend constitutes income. The fact that the accountant assumes surplus to be a portion of the stockholders' equity, both when computing the book value of stock and in reaching his conclusion respecting the nature of a stock dividend, is ignored. In the second instance, however, the dividend had given the stockholder a creditor's claim, which the new investor acquired with his purchase. Receipt of the dividend is therefore logically a recovery of capital. The more realistic association viewpoint would discard this fiction of fiction and hold the dividend to be a recovery of capital in both cases.

Dividends paid while a deficit exists. Decisions as to the propriety of declaring dividends out of current earnings while a deficit exists have also been influenced by the association-entity analysis. From the representative viewpoint a deficit, assuming no accumulated surplus to exist, depletes capital, unrestricted capital equities first, restricted capital equities subsequently. The operations of succeeding fiscal periods are therefore conducted with a smaller capital. If the earlier losses are not to be capitalized, it would seem that any success attained by the later fiscal periods should be attributed to this smaller capital. This appears to be the logical accounting and, perhaps, the logical economic conclusion. Why, then, should not current earnings be

---

[25] 22 B.T.A. 366. The treatment recommended when a holding company receives such a dividend from a subsidiary is consistent with the association viewpoint, the dividend being credited to the investment account. See also the "Statement of Accounting Principles," by [Sanders, Hatfield and Moore, published by] the American Institute of Accountants, p. 105. Such procedure appears desirable but is inconsistent with the entity theory.

subject to dividend payment? The answer seems to rest with the law[26] (and with management). If in granting the corporation the privilege of entity, the law, in the interest of public welfare, demands that the original restricted capital shall be maintained and that depletion through deficits shall be recouped before dividends may be paid out of current earnings, the accounting procedure is evident. The law establishes the basis for contract and it may justly exact its price. The question is, therefore, not primarily an accounting question but rather a legal one. It is interesting to note that English courts have rendered decisions to the effect that deficits need not be recouped prior to the declaration of dividends.[27] Similar decisions have been made by courts in the United States,[28] although the predominant opinion appears to be on the other side.[29] The argument as to which is the preferable viewpoint lies in the realm of public policy.[30] Accounting theory, however, in the absence of a contrary statement by the law, may logically hold that dividends may be paid from current earnings even though capital has been depleted.

Economic value a limiting factor. The above conclusions respecting the nature of dividends are based upon the hypothesis that accounting costs are acceptable representations of value. But income, in a deeper sense, is economic. Decisions as to the nature of stock dividends, etc., should thus allow for a possible discrepancy between the accountant's cost and the economist's value. In any given case, a considerable gap may exist between accounting procedure and economic reality. The above discussion is intended to refer only to conflicting conclusions made within the accounting framework.[31] If the nature of dividends is to be interpreted in accordance with their economic

---

[26] California, Delaware, Minnesota, at least, appear to permit the payment of dividends while capital is depleted.

[27] *Ammonia Soda Co., Ltd.* v. *Chamberlain*, 1 Ch. 266.

[28] *Borg* v. *International Silver Co.*, 11 Fed. (2nd) 147; *Miller* v. *Bradish*, 69 Iowa 278, 28 N.W. 594.

[29] *Shields* v. *Hobart*, 172 Mo. 491, 517.

[30] From the accounting standpoint, it appears to be a question also of whole-life v. fiscal period viewpoints and of cost v. economic values.

[31] The question of stock rights is subject to an analysis similar to that applied to stock dividends.

The problem of the amount which should be charged against surplus when a stock dividend is declared has also been subject to much controversy. Although the accountant has frequently taken a definite stand in respect thereto (See the *Accountants' Handbook*, pages 941–43, and "Accounting for Stock Dividends Paid," by H. D. Kerrigan in the *Accounting Review*, December, 1937), it is submitted that this is not primarily an accounting problem. The question is one for the law, the courts, management, etc. The accountant's chief concern is to revealingly record and exhibit the transactions taking place. This conclusion appears to accord with the decision of the Executive Committee of the American Accounting Association as set forth in "A Tentative Statement of Accounting Principles," the *Accounting Review*, June, 1936, in which the Committee expresses its approval of the historic purpose of accounting (page 188), but does not agree with the Committee's statement that "It is not necessary to adopt in accounting practice the expedients permitted under any law," (page 191). If the management insists upon capitalizing any amount which it believes to be desirable, it appears that there is little in accounting, *per se*, to the contrary. The corporation is primarily a legal institution. There is nothing in accounting capable of dictating its framework. If reform is desired, it would appear that the accountant should seek it through the proper channels.

status, it would seem that the accountant would have no other recourse than to adopt the procedure of recording values.

Treasury Stock

The treatment to be accorded treasury stock is a third problem affected by the conflict between the association and entity viewpoints. The fundamental issues involved in the debate respecting treasury stock—whether a corporation should be permitted to purchase its own stock, whether purchase should be permitted only when the stock originally issued was fully paid, whether purchase should be permitted freely or only to the extent of an amount equivalent to the accumulated earned, or the earned and capital surplus, etc.—are questions which the law and the courts must decide. The accountant's only concern is to record the purchase of treasury stock and to exhibit it in such a manner as to reveal its true nature. From the representative viewpoint the so-called purchase of treasury stock is in reality a withdrawal of one of the members from the association. The term purchase applies to technique rather than to reality; it has meaning of deeper significance, however, when the corporation is conceived as an entity. The courts have often held that temporary purchases of treasury stock do not reduce the corporate entity;[32] the reduction does not result unless more or less formal action is taken. To subscribe to such a conclusion, however, is to hold that temporarily a corporation may exist as an entity with no other stockholders than itself, that capital which has been withdrawn from a business is still in the business, and that capital which is nonexistent, or nominal only, is as effective in earning profits as that which actually plays a part in the corporation's operations. Obviously, this is adding fiction to fiction. The withdrawal of a stockholder from associate membership reduces the corporate capital and the act should be so recorded as to indicate that fact. In the withdrawal of a member, as in liquidation, the fiction of corporate entity evanesces and reveals the deeper reality of the representative theory. Few accountants would advocate that the withdrawal of a partner from a partnership should be exhibited as an asset no matter how short a period existing between the date of withdrawal and the date of investment by a new partner; yet many accountants contend that treasury stock should be so exhibited.[33]

---

[32] S. A. Woods Machine Co. v. Commissioner 57, Federal Reporter (2nd) 635. See "Treasury Stock and the Courts," by L. L. Briggs, The Journal of Accountancy, Sept., 1933, pp. 185–188.

[33] R. H. Montgomery, while probably recognizing that treasury stock is not an asset, seems to go so far as to advocate that the title of the left-hand side of the balance sheet be changed to "Assets and Other Debit Balances" in order that debit contra balances might justly be exhibited among the assets. See "The Curse of Balancing, or Theory v. Practice," by R. H. Montgomery, The Journal of Accountancy, April, 1937. This appears to be the opposite of accounting progress.

It is possible that the reason for the persistence of this fiction, in addition to the argument that stock outstanding is personal property, is the belief that the corporation ought not to be permitted, by voluntary action, to reduce the stated amount of restricted capital, inasmuch as the latter constitutes the primary buffer behind the creditors' equity. However, if this buffer is to be protected from voluntary reduction, other than that sanctioned by the state, the law should either prohibit the purchase of treasury stock or demand that an equivalent amount of previously unrestricted capital be restricted.[34] The requirement that surplus be earmarked in an amount equivalent to the reduction in restricted capital caused by the purchase of treasury stock is consistent with the state's responsibility to the general public.[35] Where a state has no such provisions it would appear that restricted capital, even though it may not be decreased by the declaration of dividends, may be reduced through the purchase of treasury stock. If such reduction takes place, the accountant ought not to conceal that fact by exhibiting treasury stock as an asset.

From the association viewpoint, the difference between book value and the price paid for each share of treasury stock, assuming the latter to be less, unquestionably constitutes gain to the nonwithdrawing members. Such a differential is not a part of either the remaining members' restricted or unrestricted invested capital. Hence, it appears that it may be credited to earned surplus, although for the sake of information, it may be well to exhibit it separately from surplus earned in the usual business operations. In so far as the remaining stockholders are compelled by law to sacrifice some of their unrestricted equity to a restricted reserve, the crediting of such a gain to earned surplus may be regarded as partaking of the nature of a compensation. It should be noted that the concept gain is based upon the assumption that the book values are representative of a present reality and not of mere historic costs. Economically, it is possible that no true gain is involved, since the purchase price of the stock may represent a fair pro rata proportion of the present value of the business.

From the entity viewpoint the purchase of treasury stock for less than its allocable equity in restricted and unrestricted invested capital represents the retirement of an obligation to an outside entity at an amount smaller than the outside entity's true book claim. Such gain, waiving economic considerations, becomes a part of the corporate entity's equity, as distinguished from the stockholders' equity, just as earned surplus does. It should therefore be credited to earned surplus as a gain to the corporate entity.

The accountant's insistence that the difference between par value and the purchase price of treasury stock, assuming the latter to be less, be credited

---

[34] See the Corporation Codes of the states of California, Michigan, New York, Ohio, etc., Briggs, L. L., "Treasury Stock and the General Corporation Statutes," *The Journal of Accountancy,* May, 1933.

[35] Deinzer, H. T., "This Treasury-Stock Question," the *Accounting Review,* Sept., 1937.

to capital surplus is probably to be explained by his objection to recording any portion of the investment made by a stockholder in the account exhibiting the earnings resulting from operations. This objection is supported by a conception of the business as an enterprise, according to which invested capital and capital derived from business earnings ought not be intermingled, except as a resultant of formal dividend action.[36] It is not consistent, however, with either the association or corporate entity viewpoints. The accountant's attitude receives additional support from the legal prohibition against the payment of dividends out of restricted capital. Crediting such a gain to earned surplus subjects it to possible dividend declarations. This latter is of no consequence, however, where the corporation is required to restrict previously unrestricted surplus upon the purchase of treasury stock.

Consistent with the view that the accounting procedure is based upon an acceptance of the business as an enterprise, the so-called gain from the purchase of treasury stock is in reality a saving. When the accountant speaks of this differential as a gain and at the same time advocates that it be recorded in capital surplus, it appears that he is compromising the association or entity viewpoint and the assumption that his procedure should be based upon an acceptance of the business as an enterprise.[37] To the associate members or the entity, the differential is a gain; to the business, it constitutes capital not contributed by operations.

Charging Stock Discount Against Earned Surplus

A fourth problem which appears to have its roots in the concept of corporate entity is that encountered in charging discount on stock against earned surplus, with or without a motion by the board of directors, thereby capitalizing a part of the latter. It is sometimes held that the stockholding entity must, if called upon, contribute 100 per cent of par value from personal funds held outside of the equity in the corporate entity, prior to being relieved of the assessment liability. This conclusion is in accord with a strict entity viewpoint: the stockholder must fulfill his agreement with the person of the corporate entity through arm's-length transactions. It is questionable, however, whether it is the most practical conclusion and whether it is entirely consistent with the requirements of equity. As previously indicated, par value was probably made a characteristic of stock in

---

[36] The stock dividend merges capital provided by the business and capital provided directly by investors. The accountant could argue with some degree of logic that consistent with his thesis stock issued on the basis of a stock dividend should be exhibited in the balance sheet as "Restricted Capital Provided out of Earnings."

[37] The problems encountered in allocating other items to capital and earned surplus have been subject to a similar shifting of bases and crossing of viewpoints. The treatment of surplus from forfeitures affords another illustration.

order that the creditors might be afforded greater protection and because it was believed to be in line with the requirements of public policy. It is generally conceded that these ends are served by requiring the corporation to restrict a portion of its capital. From the representative viewpoint, however, the creditors are properly protected and public policy is properly served when, by any legitimate means, restricted capital is made equal to the par value of the capital stock outstanding. The trust fund is then complete, the intent of the law appears to be fulfilled, and the constituent owners appear to have made their sacrifice. From the association viewpoint, therefore, charging discount on stock against an honestly accumulated earned surplus would seem to relieve the stockholders of further liability. The requirement that the trust fund, or restricted capital, be maintained complete by earmarking a portion of earned surplus upon the purchase of treasury stock supports this conclusion.

However, the decision as to which of these viewpoints is correct is not within the accounting sphere. The law grants the corporation its privileges for purposes of public welfare. It requires certain corporate procedure, presumably, with the same end in mind. It is therefore the duty of the law to decide whether the welfare of the public is properly protected by permitting the directors to remove the stockholders' discount liability by transferring a portion of earned surplus to the capital account. In the absence of any statement by the law, it appears that the conclusion based upon the association viewpoint meets both the intent of the law and the requirements of justice.

Conclusion

Accounting principles, as frequently presented, are not entirely consistent with either the entity or representative viewpoints. While the accountant subscribes fundamentally to the entity theory, he appears to shift to the representative theory when it suits his convenience. Illustrations of this fact have been noted in connection with various practices, such as the computation of book value, the treatment of a holding company's investment in a subsidiary, and the accounting decision as to the nature of the stock dividend. Both the entity and representative viewpoints are capable of supporting a coherent body of accounting theory. The latter, however, appears to provide a more realistic basis for the development of accounting principles, in spite of the fact that it encounters an obstacle in the situs of legal title. The corporate fiction and the location of legal title should be viewed as being a part of a general arrangement to afford protection both to individuals undertaking business enterprise and to various parties with whom the corporation deals. As such, the situs of legal title does not present an insurmountable obstacle. The theoretical approach to the accounting problems of the corporation should be the same as the theoretical approach to the accounting problems of the sole-proprietorship and the partnership; the entity concept need cause no variation in theory. In practice, however, the procedure followed in accounting for the transactions of the sole-proprietorship and the partnership must be modified to meet the requirements set up by law, the corporate contract with the state, and the various regulatory bodies. Acceptance of such an approach should eliminate much of the debate now found in accounting literature and place it where it belongs—in the fields of law, public policy, and finance. While the statutes of many of our states do not afford satisfactory protection to the public and the investor, reform would seem to depend upon attacking the problem at its source rather than upon the application of so-called good accounting principles.

E. B. Wilcox and R. H. Hassler

A FOUNDATION
FOR ACCOUNTING PRINCIPLES

Edwards Byers Wilcox *was born in Indiana in 1893 and received his B.S. in 1916 from Northwestern University. He was a partner in Edward Gore & Co. (1927–1955), in Wilcox, Harbison & Co. (1955–1959), and in Scovell, Wellington & Co. since 1959. He served as president of the American Institute of C.P.A., 1946–1947, and of the Illinois Society of C.P.A., 1953–1954.* Russell H. Hassler *was born in Indiana in 1906 and received his A.B. from DePauw (1927) and his A.M. from Iowa (1929). He was on the staff of Edward Gore & Co. (1929–1943) and is a C.P.A. in Illinois and Massachusetts. He taught at the Harvard Business School (1946–1962) and is currently financial vice-president of the Hawaiian Electric Company, Ltd. He served as a vice-president of the American Accounting Association in 1951, and as its president in 1953. With Neil Harlan, he published* Cases in Controllership *in 1958. Both he and Wilcox served on the committee on accounting procedure of the American Institute of C.P.A.*
The article reprinted here sets forth "usefulness" as the foundation for accounting principles, a conception which is widely held today. The authors extend their analysis to test four "secondary" principles (truthfulness, conservatism, consistency, and adaptability) by reference to "usefulness."

For years efforts have been made, and are continuing to be made, to state accounting principles, but none of the results of these efforts has been widely accepted. This indicates either that the quest is a hopeless one and should be abandoned, or that the right approach has not yet been found. Assuming that the quest is not hopeless, the task now before us is to find what is lacking in the efforts that have been made and how the problem can be attacked with better chance of success.

Some of these efforts have been directed to specific problems in the apparent hope that sound generalities would emerge. The trouble with such

Reprinted from *The Journal of Accountancy* (October, 1941), pp. 308–14, by permission.

attempts seems to be that they involve tacit assumptions not stated or examined, and therefore not always sound or consistent. Other efforts have been aimed at a coherent structure, although sometimes a limited one. The difficulty here has been that the framework has first been selected, and then the various parts of a living and growing thing have been forced into it as into a strait jacket. Much darkness has pervaded the subject because of such clouds over the issues as the relative merits of the words "standards" and "principles," and the question of whether accounting is an art or a science. All efforts seem to have suffered from too great reliance on either induction or deduction, without a sufficiently happy combination of both, and all have had in common some limitation of scope and an absence of a basis outside of accounting itself.

These object lessons appear to indicate the following criteria for a new approach:

(a) A broad concept of accounting.
(b) A basis for accounting outside itself.
(c) A coherent comprehension of accounting.

What is Accounting?

Accounting, broadly considered, is no simple thing, but it can be generally described under three headings:

(1) A method of recording and an aid in handling current operations of an organization.
(2) A tool of management.
(3) A method of fiscal reporting.

In all these functions accounting adopts, as a common denominator of measurement, the dollar. The first of these is the simplest and the most fundamental. The second provides an extension of the eyes and ears of management. The third includes reports to government for tax and control purposes, reports to creditors and stockholders, the records which underlie these reports, and the machinery for verification of reports and records.

Accounting is thus seen to be a service function in the field of business. By the field of business is meant management, stockholders, and creditors, present and prospective, and government and the public as they are affected by business. In other words, the field is universal as to people, but limited—as distinguished from medicine, for example—by the manner in which it affects people. The sort of service which accounting renders in this field has already been indicated as an adjunct to current operations, a tool of management, and a method of reporting. It will be noted that this first step in reasoning has been an inductive one. Accounting is seen to be a service function in the field of business, after a review of that field and a review of accounting itself. More extensive exploration should be undertaken to afford a clearer, more accurate description of the sort of service function which accounting is and should be.

The First Principle

It follows from the concept of accounting as a service function in the field of business, that the fundamental principle of accounting is usefulness. The only reason for the existence of a service function is that it be useful. The usefulness of accounting must be in that field of business which it serves. The fact that it is useful is the reason why it exists, and the increased need for its services is the reason why it has grown so rapidly in recent years. Everything which follows in any statement of accounting principles must be judged by the standard of usefulness.

The statement of this principle serves to clarify several issues which seem to have been troublesome. It provides a basis for accounting outside itself. We do not have to start with emphasis on the distinction between capital and income, or verifiable objective evidence, or anything else chosen from within accounting itself. The field of business is the objective world in which accounting exists. Accounting may be treated much as a science in this world. Greater discovery of the nature of this world will indicate the direction to be taken in developing the science. But accounting has not only the aspects of a science; its service function, involving, as it does, insight and interpretation, has many of the aspects of art. In approaching this subject, neither scientific nor artistic methods need be avoided as inappropriate.

Recognition that accounting must be useful to business answers those who deplore the influence of business on accounting. Accepting this influence as proper is not equivalent to accepting domination of accountants by businessmen or any admission that such domination exists. It does recognize, however, that accounting must adapt itself to the needs of business. Accounting is like a great tree that has grown in a favorable environment and, by its very growth, has helped to preserve the field that nourished it. It is indigenous in that field, and its roots are deep in that soil. It would be folly to suggest that it be uprooted and replaced by something nurtured in a greenhouse.

The fundamental principle of usefulness goes far to answer the question of whether or not accounting should recognize legal rights and permissions when they sanction treatment not favored by accountants. Law governs by force of police power, not merely because it is useful, and therefore must be recognized as a stubborn fact in the field of business where accounting is to be of service. It is useless to expound, as an accounting principle, that dividends cannot be charged to paid-in or appraisal surplus if the law says they can. If it is legal, and the directors do it, any rule of accounting which denies that it can be done is useless, and therefore to be discarded.

Certain accounting releases by the Securities and Exchange Commission afford an interesting and curious example of what appears sound and unsound in this connection. Releases 15 and 16, issued on March 16, 1940, discuss disclosures in connection with quasi-reorganizations, and No. 16 says, in part:

> I am informed that under the applicable state law it was permissible to effect this restatement without approval of the stockholders...it is my opinion that in such cases sound accounting practice ordinarily requires that a clear report be made to stockholders of the proposed restatement and that their formal consent thereto be obtained. If, however, under the applicable state law it is permissible to eliminate a deficit without obtaining the formal consent of stockholders and if such consent of stockholders is not obtained, it is necessary in my opinion to make a complete disclosure....

Note the statement that sound accounting practice ordinarily requires that stockholders be advised and that they consent in advance. This is not accounting practice at all. It is a requirement which the chief accountant of the Commission thinks desirable, and it probably is, but it isn't an accounting matter. Recognition that it isn't is in the next sentence. If the law permits action without reference to stockholders, all right, but we must disclose the action. That is a proper accounting rule as to what is necessary disclosure in accounts, but it is not proper to say that sound accounting requires advance notice to and consent from stockholders. This distinction is important in recognizing the boundaries of accounting if we are to attempt to describe it.

On May 29, 1941, there was issued release No. 25, which went a step further. This, too, purported to be an accounting release, and it bore the title, "Implications of the Term, 'Quasi-Reorganization.'" It said, in part, "It is...implicit in a procedure of this kind that it is not to be employed recurrently...particularly if the sole or principal purpose of the quasi-reorganization is the elimination of a deficit in earned surplus resulting from operating losses." It is appropriate for an accounting release to define a quasi-reorganization. It is also fairly sound doctrine that recurring losses should not be applied annually to paid-in or other capital-surplus accounts. But the advisability or desirability of recurring application of losses to capital surpluses is not an accounting matter. It is a question of management policy. If it can be done, legally, and the corporation does it, advisedly or inadvisedly, there is nothing left for accounting to do but to record it. It is a transaction just as much as the declaration of a dividend or, for that matter, a cash disbursement. Although the act may be unwise, it is not the function of accounting to refuse to recognize or record foolish acts. In so far as the accounting releases of the Securities and Exchange Commission are contributing to the development of generally accepted accounting procedure, it is unfortunate that they have been extended into the field of management procedure. These fields should be kept separate, and accounting should not set up standards which are at variance with the permissible acts of the entities on whose fiscal affairs it furnishes reports.

This does not mean that accountants must not raise their voices against existing laws or the enactment of new laws when these laws are harmful. It is a natural extension of the service function of accounting that accountants should be of service to their communities in fields where their skill and experience render them most useful. The committee on federal taxation of the American Institute of Accountants has done exactly this for many years, and local bodies of accountants have assisted in framing various corporation and tax laws. A more specific opportunity for similar service was offered a few years ago when the Supreme Court of California held that the administrator of an estate must amortize bond premiums, but could not accumulate bond discount out of income. Accountants know that this is bad practice, and it would be a public service for accountants to be instrumental in introducing sounder accounting into the law. But for as long as that is the law, accounts much be prepared in accordance with it.

Secondary Principles

In the January, 1941, issue of *The Journal of Accountancy* a subcommittee report[1] suggested the following four principles of general application:

> Truthfulness
> Conservatism
> Consistency
> Adaptability

The soundness of these principles will be measured by their usefulness.

It seems clear that no part of the function of accounting can be useful unless it is truthful. Even the apparent usefulness to some interests derived from deceiving others can scarcely be brought in under the governing principle of usefulness, because such advantages are bound to be outweighed by their disadvantages. Fundamentally, the usefulness of accounting depends on the confidence which is placed in it, and this confidence can only be inspired and maintained if it is deserved. Thus the whole subject of ethics in professional accounting fits into the structure based on usefulness, and the soundness of an ethical system can be measured by this principle.

But the principle of usefulness does more than endorse honesty. It also indicates the kind and extent of truthfulness which is appropriate. Literal truthfulness can be quite misleading, and a mass of honest but trivial detail

---

[1] "Reports on 'An Introduction to Corporate Accounting Standards' and 'A Statement of Accounting Principles'": by subcommittees of the committee on accounting procedure of the American Institute of Accountants. *The Journal of Accountancy*, January, 1941, p. 60.

can obscure significant matters. To be useful in accounting, truthfulness must be intelligent and sincere. The much moot question of full disclosure can be answered in any specific case by the criteria of intelligence and sincerity. Full disclosure which really discloses and is intended to do so is quite different from full disclosure which, it is hoped, will not be noticed, and which is primarily intended to enable the accountant to say, "but I told you."

Conservatism means literally preservation in safety, and to the extent that it is employed to this end it is useful. Too often, however, it is confused with understatement. In accounting it must be remembered that conservatism, to the extent of understatement now, generally means overstatement in the future. Thus overzealous attempts at conservatism are not only harmful in their immediate misleading effects, but also involve more deception to follow. The fundamental principle of usefulness, therefore, requires the exercise of skilled judgment in the application of conservatism to accounting.

Consistency finds its chief usefulness in the avoidance of confusion and in increasing the understandability of financial statements, particularly by facilitating comparisons, but it has been aptly described as the hobgoblin of little minds. It has been the downfall of some attempts to set up a coherent structure of accounting standards because the attempt to make all parts of the structure consistent with one another has led to the subordination of usefulness. This generally follows from the arbitrary selection of some aspect of accounting as the immovable foundation on which the rest is to be built, instead of basing the entire structure on something outside itself. Both in such attempts and in the practice of accounting itself, it should be recognized that there is inherently a certain looseness in the joints similar to that which the physicists of today tell us exists in the physical world, and comparable to the inaccuracies in our musical scale. The duty here is to preserve as much harmony as possible by compromising all inconsistencies where they do the least harm, instead of being rigidly consistent in small things, only to be materially inconsistent in others. Primarily, it is important at all times to be consistent with the principle of usefulness.

As to comparison of financial statements, the useful concept of consistency calls for the avoidance of changes based on caprice, but does not preclude departures from established practice which are improvements, or which aid clarity, or which are indicated by changing significance of elements of the statements.

Consistency is sometimes thought to be in conflict with that common application of conservatism which calls for inclusion in a statement of all liabilities but exclusion of doubtful assets. This apparent conflict disappears upon exploration of the field of business, recommended as the basis of a comprehension of accounting. This exploration leads to the discovery that business operates in a field of force wherein assets tend to escape and liabilities tend to adhere. Work must be done against this field of force in order to retain assets and realize profits, and in order to avoid liabilities and losses. Consistent treatment in financial statements would include both assets and liabilities having a comparable degree of probability, and recognition of the field of force shows that inclusion of all known liabilities and exclusion of doubtful assets accomplishes this. Understanding of the fundamental consistency in this application of conservatism will assist judgment in specific cases.

Adaptability is useful to the point of being indispensable in accounting as an adjunct to current operations of a business and as a tool of management. Accounting must be and is adapted to needs of specific businesses. Accounting as a method of reporting should also be adaptable, but not to the extent of serving one set of interests at the expense of another, nor to the extent of being unintelligible to the reader not acquainted with the specific adaptations used. Rules and standards should not be rigid nor be regarded as ends in themselves, but enough stability should be preserved in accounting conventions so that the reasonably informed reader will be able to find his way about and will not feel that he is lost in a strange house.

It will be seen that the four secondary principles of truthfulness, conservatism, consistency, and adaptability all meet the test of usefulness, and are in harmony with one another. But it will also be observed that the principle of usefulness limits and describes the applicability of these secondary principles. They must not be accepted with all the implications and connotations of their dictionary definitions; that is what leads to unsound and impossible conclusions when a word or phrase is chosen and a logical structure is built on it. These secondary principles are incorporated into a statement of accounting principles as aspects of the first principle of usefulness. The preceding paragraphs which have discussed these principles in that light are merely suggestive. The subject, as presented thus far, is good for a volume in itself, and it is not intended that these brief paragraphs deal with it adequately.

The following paragraphs indicate, with similar brevity, the application of the fundamental principle of usefulness to certain problems of current interest.

Periodic Financial Statements

Someone said, a few years ago, that annual financial statements would be utterly indefensible if they were not utterly indispensable. The function of accounting thus seems to include the furnishing of that which cannot be justified, because the world of business requires it. This is an example of that domination of accounting by business which has been previously mentioned. In discharging this function, accounting will attempt to be truthful, conservative, consistent, and adaptable to the extent that these things are useful.

But the goal to be reached is that periodic statements of profit and loss and financial condition be useful enough to justify themselves. In view of the demand for them and the importance attached to them, it must be assumed that, in spite of their faults, they can be justified. Viewed in this light, it is clear why accounting has so often been described as an inexact science. These considerations indicate two basic principles which are particularly useful in statement preparation: compromise and conventions.

In an attempt to serve usefully, by means of so unsound a medium as periodic financial statements, it is necessary to compromise rigid logic and consistency, so that the margin of error in the results will be kept at a minimum of significance, and so that the financial statements will best serve the purposes for which they are intended. At the same time, as much general understanding of statements as is possible by the public should be fostered, and this can best be accomplished by the establishment of widely accepted conventions. Even the most useful conventions will not be in the status of principles, but rather will be like essays on the language of accounting, designed to aid the student of the language in knowing what it means. Writers in this language, however, should be its masters, not its slaves, and should select and modify the conventions so as to convey the most useful information to their readers.

One method of conveying information is by explanatory notes and comments attached to and forming a part of financial statements. It is a generally accepted convention that information be conveyed in this manner. To the extent that it is helpful in making the statements understandable, this method is a useful one. The limit of its usefulness will have been passed, however, when the explanatory words contradict rather than explain the implications of the financial statements themselves.

Another basic set of conventions occurs with regard to the application of the accrual basis of accounting. In general, all costs incurred or likely to be incurred are recorded, and are allocated to periods of time as seems appropriate. Some revenue, such as interest, is recorded as it accrues, but other revenue, such as sales, is recorded when an event occurs and not according to the passage of time. The usefulness of these conventions depends partly on their wisdom, and in general this seems to have withstood the test of time; but the greatest usefulness is in the understandability of financial statements, following the use of generally accepted conventions.

It is frequently stated that cost is the proper basis of accounting, and the advocates of this view regard the balance-sheet more as a list of unclosed items than as a statement of financial condition. The large and important financial interests which attach importance to balance-sheet items and ratios indicate the limitation of the usefulness of this view. Particularly from the standpoint of credit grantors, it seems that current assets and liabilities should be stated on a combination of a current-value and a going-concern basis, whereas fixed assets should be stated on an historical-cost basis. There seems little usefulness in adjusting the recorded cost of plant to a value basis, but there seems to be great usefulness in stating inventories and outstanding accounts on a realization basis, assuming the continuation of the concern in business. There is probably more tacit than overt acceptance of this kind of treatment as conventional accounting, but in the absence of clear pronouncements, the usefulness of established conventions is not being fully realized.

The various methods of stating assets, particularly inventories and fixed assets, in balance-sheets have been the subject of much discussion in recent years.   These methods are conventions which should be selected in the light of judgment as to their usefulness in particular circumstances. Some are definitely of limited usefulness, as, for example, the last-in, first-out inventory method; others may be more generally applicable and therefore offer a wider range of choice. But the important point is that they should all be recognized as possibilities, to be chosen in accordance with their usefulness. Deductive reasoning should not be permitted to elevate one of the possible conventional methods to a place of preference, to the exclusion and discredit of all others. This conclusion is not only in harmony with the basic principle of usefulness, but also illustrates an application of the secondary principle of adaptability.

Summary

Based on a conclusion that accounting is a service function in the field of business, there is deduced the basic principle of usefulness. Four secondary principles are shown to derive their nature and limitations from this first one. Special consideration of financial statements leads to adoption of two principles having special application: compromise and conventions. Some of the more general conventions are mentioned with indications of the necessary compromises.

This discussion purports to do no more than suggest a feasible approach to the subject of accounting principles, and to indicate the place in a statement of principles which some of the more common phases of the subject should occupy. The entire field of accounting in all of its branches and ramifications can be brought within this general structure, and a complete development of it would result in a coordinated library of accountancy. Such a library should be developed, and it will be found that much existing literature will belong in it. Each of various problems such as amortization of bond discount, or depreciation on appreciation, should be approached from the standpoint of usefulness. It may be that answers can be found from this standpoint as to the most desirable treatment of some of these matters. Others will not lend themselves to preferred solutions, but will be seen to be possible of various treatments. If this is so, it should not be regarded as failure, but rather as progress. There is scant usefulness is cherishing a desire for rigidity beyond that of which the subject itself is capable. The task of orienting accounting to usefulness is more difficult than that of forcing it into the strait jacket of a narrower concept, but it is the only task really worthy of achievement.

Roy B. Kester

SOURCES OF ACCOUNTING PRINCIPLES

Roy Bernard Kester *was born in Missouri in 1882, received his A.B. from Missouri Wesleyan in 1902, and his Ph.D. from Columbia in 1919. He taught mathematics at Wesleyan, 1902–1905, and at Denver, 1907–1915. He became a C.P.A. in 1914. In 1915, he joined the faculty at Columbia where he remained until his retirement. He was president of the Colorado State Board of C.P.A. (1915), president of the American Accounting Association (1925), and research director of the National Association of Accountants (then known as the National Association of Cost Accountants) from 1925–1928. He also served on the committee on accounting procedure of the American Institute of C.P.A.'s. He published two widely used and influential texts, which went through several editions—*Principles of Accounting, 1917–1939;* Advanced Accounting, 1918–1947.*

In this article, Kester finds the sources of principles in the bookkeeping system used, in statute law, in accepted trade practices, and in ethical standards of business conduct. He conceives of accounting primarily as a system to furnish information to management, to owners, to creditors, and to the public. "Purpose," "end-product," and "goals" constitute the focus of his discussion.

Introduction

"Accounting principles" is a phrase used to indicate that there are recognized methods, rules, and standards of legal, business, and professional conduct in accordance with which the formal accounting work of a business unit or combination of such units should be carried on. The accounting work of any business unit generally comprises four divisions or kinds:

1. Devising the formal system of records and of supporting documents and papers—often called system work or constructive accounting.

Reprinted from the *Journal of Accountancy* (December, 1942), pp. 531–35, by permission.

2. Making the formal record of business transactions—usually called bookkeeping or, more grandiosely, recordative accounting.
3. Proving the accuracy and propriety of the records—the audit function, both internal and public.
4. Drafting formal reports based on the records—preparation of balance-sheet, profit-and-loss statement, and supporting schedules.

Accounting principles comprise at least all those rules, techniques, basic procedures, or methods, and the broad principles of right and propriety in economic relations, both within the business unit and between the unit and outsiders, in accordance with which the accounting work of the business unit should be carried on.

While accounting work, as classified above, serves many purposes, its goal or end-product is the summarization of the great volume of individual business transactions and the presentation of the summary in such form and with such explanatory notes as will best serve the purpose toward which it is directed. Any approach to the formulation and study of accounting principles may therefore best be made from a consideration of these end-products or goals. These, as just pointed out, take some of their characteristics from the purposes they are to serve. Before consideration of these various purposes, however, the nature and sources of accounting principles may well be treated.

Sources of Accounting Principles

Accounting in a broad sense—classifying, counting, measuring, and recording—has doubtless had an existence coextensive with trade and certainly with organized business life. As business developed and became more involved in character and larger in volume, *systems* of accounting were devised from which came, finally, the system of double entry, now quite generally employed.

Double Entry as a Source

Any system of bookkeeping rests upon a limited number of preconceptions which are analogous to the axioms of mathematics. These preconceptions are in the nature of definitions which the human mind has established in its endeavor to afford the businessman answers to his constant queries as to the status and progress of his undertaking. He is interested in knowing—at least periodically—the amount of his investment and the profit or the loss which has resulted from the employment of his capital in the business unit. For this purpose definitions of the terms assets, liabilities, capital or proprietorship, cost, income, expenses, profit, and loss become necessary to provide the fundamental concepts. Without these concepts no system of bookkeeping is possible of operation, for bookkeeping is concerned primarily with classification, measuring or counting, and summarization. It should be noted that around these definitions has grown up a body of rules to be used in various sets of circumstances for classifying data—e.g., the rules for the differentiation of capital and revenue expenditures.

The chief characteristic of double-entry bookkeeping, as contrasted with other systems, is the use of a class of proprietary accounts—the so-called nominal accounts—attached or adjusted to the two classes of asset and liability accounts—the real accounts—within the mathematical framework of the equation, $Assets - Liabilities = Proprietorship,$ which thus serves as an over-all definition of the term, proprietorship. Use of this equation makes possible a sort of cause-and-effect record of every transaction and so provides to business management a flow of useful information as to both financial and operating status.

Operation of the system of double-entry bookkeeping is an art, and methods of operation are susceptible to statement in the form of rules or principles. Among these may be mentioned the principles of debit and credit; the principles governing the development of labor-saving devices such as special journals, subsidiary ledgers, controlling accounts; rules for periodic tests of the equation of the ledger by means of the trial balance; rules for transfers between accounts, for summarizing or closing the ledger, closing the month's and year's records in journals and ledgers; the techniques or rules for the use of work sheets; etc. All of these are rules and principles based on the mathematics of the double-entry equation and on the experience of careful accountants over the years. These rules, tested and proved by experience, furnish some of the principles or laws of the *science* of accounting as to its mechanical framework, and most of the rules of the *art* of bookkeeping.

The Law as a Source

Inasmuch as business must be carried on within the provision of the law, principles or rules of law have exerted a powerful influence on the principles of accounting; they may well be said to have established some of the principles of accounting. Most of the transactions of business flow from legal contracts, express or implied. It is an important function of accounting to show the legal status of the business unit in relation to its contracts. Traceable to this legal influence are, for example, the method of accounting for contingent liabilities as illustrated by the discounted note receivable; the showing of the debit and credit relationships with customers and creditors, with principals and agents, with owners as partners or stockholders; accounting for the various classes of capital stocks and surplus items; the practice of booking liabilities due at a future time at their settlement or maturity amount instead of the discounted present value of such amount; etc. Specific laws, such as those giving control of public utilities to a governmental agency, may even fix the whole basic scheme of their accounting, the chart of accounts, and their item content, allowable rates of depreciation, form of financial and operating statements, etc. Obviously, accounting principles and rules dare not run counter to established legal principles.

Enlightened Business Management as a Source

From the beginning, accounting has been a service tool of management. Its chief function is to provide a constant flow of information relative to the results of the policies and efforts of management. All events of financial significance must be faithfully recorded so that management may always know what is happening in the business unit and the effects of such happenings. The system of records and, therefore, of reporting, must follow closely the plan of operational organization so that staff responsibilities and results may be appraised. The relations between management and employees, creditors, customers, owners, and the public, as reflected in the interplay of their transactions with each other, are thus recorded in the books of account from which subsequently their propriety may come up for scrutiny and report to all parties at interest. Enlightened management recognizes its obligations to interested parties and will so operate the business unit that the record of its actions will reflect the propriety of all its activities. If, upon periodic review and scrutiny by independent accountants, it should be found that management in performing its accounting work has failed to recognize its obligations or to act in accordance with them, as determined by prevailing standards of conduct, then it is the duty of the reviewing accountant to state that proper principles of accounting have not been adhered to by such management. It is from this conception of the duties of management to each of the parties at interest that such principles of accounting come as, e.g., the following: proper allocations of income and expense between periods, appropriate measurement of income, expense, assets, liabilities, and proprietary equities; the proper item or datum content of the periodic reports to all parties at interest; the proper method of displaying or presenting the significant data in the periodic reports; etc.

Thus, it will be seen that it is an enlightened management which recognizes its obligations and acts accordingly, that fixes or sets accounting principles in this connection. The ethical principles of business and social conduct accepted at a given time, having in view the interests of all concerned—management, creditors, owners, and the public—are the sources from which are formulated the principles of accounting which must be observed in this field.

There are, then, three main sources of accounting principles stemming from the basic concept of private property and its use in satisfying the economic wants of man, this concept giving rise to terms—accounting axioms

—such as assets, liabilities, proprietorship, income, expense, cost, profit, and loss. These three sources are:

1. The adopted system of bookkeeping, usually double entry—the mechanical framework of accounting—from which come all those rules and procedures pertaining to the operation of the system.
2. Statute law and—in its absence—accepted trade practice, from which come all those rules and procedures pertaining to the keeping of the record and the presentation of the summarized results of business operation so as to display properly the status of the business in its legal relationships.
3. Ethical standards of business conduct—currently recognized principles of right and wrong—from which come all those rules and procedures pertaining to the adequacy and propriety of the record, and the reports and statements based thereon, for the purposes to be served by accounting.

Purposes to be Served by Accounting

It is apparent, therefore, that the formulation and statement of accounting principles must never be dissociated from the purposes which accounting is serving at a given time. That accounting is primarily and basically a service tool of management should always be kept in view. Given trained management, success of business operation is largely dependent on the adequacy of the accounting record and of the flow of information from it.

When a management is entrusted with the operation of a business enterprise, its responsibility is twofold, viz.:

1. The maintenance of the integrity of the capital entrusted to it.
2. The earning of a fair average return on that capital for the period of its management.

When management uses only its own capital in the operation of the enterprise—i.e., when the management and ownership groups are identical—its twofold responsibility is self-contained and does not pertain to any other private interests. When management uses other capital than its own, it assumes an additional obligation to report periodically to owners to inform them of the financial and operating status of their business. These reports must give proper recognition to the interests of the owners.

When management borrows funds from outsiders it assumes further obligations to furnish prospective lenders with information to be used as a basis for granting or rejecting the application for credit and such further information during the period of the loan, when granted, as may be necessary to apprise the lender of the condition of his loan as to security of principal, the payment of interest, and any specific legal obligations or conditions made a part of the loan agreement. Human nature being what it is, there may well be conflict of interest here between management and creditor and between owner and creditor. The type of report furnished by management for this purpose gives rise to those principles and methods of accounting deemed appropriate to proper recognition of the special interests of creditors, both short-term and long-term.

Over the years, as many business enterprises have increased in economic power and influence, the public through its various governmental units has found it desirable for its own protection to exercise certain controls over some types of activities. This has been particularly true of business enterprises tinged with a public interest, such as utilities. The use of net earnings as a basis for taxation and the protection of investors through the Securities and Exchange Commission have given the public a peculiar interest in corporate reporting. Reports to serve this purpose must therefore give proper recognition to the special interests of the public.

Accounting is thus called upon to furnish information for reports to at least these four separate groups:

1. Management—a basic group with obligation to report to:
2. Owners who furnish the proprietary capital.
3. Creditors who furnish temporary funds subject to short and long maturities.
4. The public which through suitable governmental agencies has undertaken the exercise of various kinds of control over private enterprise.

It must be apparent, therefore, that the principles, in accordance with which accounting reports must be drafted to serve properly these four parties, must take cognizance of the special interests of these parties. While there are many other miscellaneous purposes which accounting is called upon to serve, these are of relatively infrequent occurrence and will be served by the procedures and principles dictated by the circumstances of each case. For example, for fire-insurance coverage, usually, current market valuations must be taken into account. However, the basic and constantly and regularly recurring purposes to be served by accounting are the four stated above.

General Purpose Reports

While the interests of these four groups are not always identical, and even in some respects may be antagonistic, there is a sufficient core of identity to serve as a basis for the formulation of a body of principles to be observed in keeping the record and drafting reports therefrom. Because of the lack of complete identity of interest, it becomes an important and necessary part of the accountant's work to supplement these reports, termed general-purpose reports, by explanatory notes carrying additional information particularly pertinent to each of the four interests at their points of conflict. Thus, it is not necessary to follow a separate set of principles to serve each of these four interests. However, to serve the miscellaneous interests referred to above, special reports are usually required, because their purposes are too divergent and do not follow with sufficient integrity the core of principles pertinent to the four major interests. In order to be easily identifiable, these special reports must be carefully distinguished from the general-purpose reports formulated to serve the four basic purposes. The general-purpose reports are thus not all-purpose reports; the latter are never possible except within very narrow limits and under conditions seldom existing.

Accounting Principles Not Fixed and Unchangeable

Because of the exactness of accounting processes and thus the *seeming* exactness of the products they give rise to—i.e., accounting reports—the novice, unlearned in the sources of accounting data and their compilation in the reports, all too frequently attributes to the products of accounting an exactness which can never exist and the same unchangeableness of principles as attach to the mathematics of the accounting equation. Reference to the three main sources of accounting principles, as explained above, makes it clear that accounting, except as to the part pertaining to the operation of the double-entry system, is essentially a social science, and in this respect is similar to the law.

As the law, over the period of civilized life, has changed in its concept of equity—right and wrong—in accordance with the needs of the time as reflected largely in the force of public opinion, so has accounting changed in those portions of its principles flowing from the law and from business practice and conduct—the second and third sources treated above. Change—evolution—is the law of life and of all the arts and sciences treating of human conduct.

Accounting principles, therefore, based on economic conduct, are never absolutely fixed, though seemingly so at any given time. While they are subject to change, that change is almost imperceptible until some dramatic happening, such as a nation-wide fraud, focuses public attention and so causes a periodic reëxamination of their foundations. Any statement of principles presented at a given time must be read with this characteristic of change in view and can make no pretense of being more than a fair presentation of best current accounting thought.

Edward G. Nelson

THE RELATION BETWEEN
THE BALANCE SHEET
AND THE PROFIT-AND-LOSS STATEMENT

Edward G. Nelson *was born in the state of Washington in 1904, receiving his B.S. from Southern California in 1926 and his Ph.D. from Stanford in 1931. He taught at Stanford (1931–1941), was with the Office of Price Administration (1941–1944), and, since 1945, has been at Kansas, where he now directs the Center for Research in Business. In 1956, he published* The Company and the Community.

The article reprinted here, based on the work of John B. Canning, is significant because it conceives of accounting as a branch of statistics and, therefore, employs a statistical approach to the problem of the relationship between a statement of financial position and of operating results. This approach "leads" and "lags" cash receipts and cash outlays to determine revenues and expenses. One result is to integrate the balance sheet and the income statement closely togther in a unified accounting project.

Professor Arthur Stone Dewing wrote in the recent edition of his book *The Financial Policy of Corporations*, "...I regard the income statement more fundamental than the balance sheet. This is true for at least two very significant reasons. The business is essentially dynamic in character; its values are forever changing. A statement which depicts the summation of these changes is, therefore, a truer picture of the business than a statement, such as the balance sheet, which seeks to portray only a static condition. The other and perhaps more realistic reason is that the fundamental purpose of the business is to produce an income. The statement of the extent to which it has met this purpose is of distinctly greater importance than a statement representing an arithmetical summation of a series of ledger accounts balanced as of a particular moment of time."[1]

Reprinted from *The Accounting Review* (April, 1942), pp. 132–41, by permission.
[1] Vol. I, pp. 539–50, note n, New York (The Ronald Press), 1941.

Professor Dewing believes that he has found, in contemporary accounting literature, a "steady drift" in support of his position.[2] While this is encouraging, he is greatly disturbed because so many writers still begin their study of accountancy with an analysis of the balance sheet or the so-called fundamental equation of accounts. In view of Professor Dewing's reputation and furthermore, in view of the abundance of material which he believes to lend support to his position, we should examine enterprise accounting with a thought of accepting or rejecting such an attitude.

It is the broad purpose of this study to review the relation between the balance sheet and the profit and loss statement. However, there is a more immediate objective. The present writer believes that we have given far too little attention to particular concepts in our general scheme. An accounting is "correct," as distinguished from "precise," only if it is founded upon realistic, self-consistent concepts. It is therefore proposed that, in addition to a study of the relation between the balance sheet and the profit and loss statement, we will review the general nature of revenue, expense, and asset accounting.[3]

Our analysis properly begins with a list of assumptions about business conditions at the time the statements are prepared and, secondly, with a list of postulates concerning the general nature of enterprise accounting. It is assumed that the business is a "going concern." Generally we mean that the firm will continue to buy and sell goods with a view toward a profit throughout an indefinite future. A more specific statement may be made if it is assumed that the proprietor or proprietors are motivated solely by a desire to maximize their profits, although it is admitted that men have other reasons for continuing their business. A firm is a "going concern" when there is reason to believe that:

1. The present worth of expected receipts exceeds the present worth of expected costs;
2. The amount of the difference is greater for enterprise operations than it is for liquidation; and
3. There is reason to believe that the absolute profit from enterprise operations will be greater than that to be had from alternative employments.

We do not mean that the accountant estimates the amount of these present worths. We do not mean that he should do so. An arithmetical expression of their values is, in most cases, impossible as well as unnecessary. It is sufficient if the proprietors have reason to *believe* that they will continue to buy and sell goods throughout an indefinite future. They should believe that it is distinctly to their disadvantage to cease operations altogether, to liquidate the enterprise, or to employ their resources elsewhere. The above conditions

---

[2] He cites a number of cases from recent periodical literature. His strongest support is found in Stephen Gilman, *Accounting Concepts of Profit* (The Ronald Press), 1939.

[3] This study is founded on Professor John B. Canning's, *The Economic of Accountancy* (The Ronald Press), 1929. It seems practical to give a general acknowledgment rather than the many particular citations.

merely give form to these beliefs when the proprietors are motivated solely by a desire to maximize profits.

A description of a "going concern" tells us nothing about the elements of accounting statements. We must list our postulates—the self-evident truths about profit and loss—before we can describe the methods by which the statements are prepared or the nature of our results. These postulates apply to all transfers of money or money's worth affecting the enterprise except proprietary investments or withdrawals. Accordingly it is asserted that:

1. Over the life of the business, there is a one-to-one correspondence between the amount of revenue and the amount of cash receipts, and between the amount of expense and the amount of cash disbursements;
2. The total profit for that time-interval (positive or negative) is equal to the difference between the total cash receipts and the total cash disbursements;
3. Within any lesser time-interval, the amount of revenue is equal to the amount of cash receipts attributable to bringing enterprise operations to some particular stage during the period; and
4. Within such a fiscal period, the amount of expense is equal to the amount of disbursements necessary to obtain the revenue for the year.

Some of these postulates may be restated as concepts, although they are more important as limits on procedure than as elements of accounting statements. We may speak of *ultimate total revenue* or the revenue for the duration of enterprise existence. The amount is equal to the amount of cash receipts for that time interval. We may also speak of *ultimate total expense* or the expense for the duration of enterprise existence. The amount is equal to the amount of cash disbursements for that time interval. A third concept, *ultimate total profit,* is implied. It is the positive or negative difference between the amount of ultimate total revenue and the amount of ultimate total expense. It is also equal to the algebraic difference between the amount of cash receipts and cash disbursements for the life of the enterprise.

While it is true that there may not be an equality between the amount of revenue and the amount of cash receipts for any period less than the duration of enterprise existence, receipts are the elements with which we construct all measures of revenue. A dollar is received *at some time during the life of the enterprise* for each dollar of revenue exhibited during the fiscal period. The sum of the annual revenues for all fiscal periods is equal to the amount of ultimate total revenue. There may be no equality between the amount of expense and the amount of cash disbursements for the fiscal period and yet the two sums are equal for the life of the enterprise. A dollar is disbursed *at some time during the enterprise existence* for each dollar exhibited as expense of the fiscal period.

The measures of revenue and expense are compiled from receipts and disbursements, although the events—the receipt and the disbursement of money—may occur in some time interval other than that to which they are distributed as an amount of revenue and an amount of expense. The profit and loss statement is designed to express the rate at which money is being received because certain enterprise operations, such as sales, occurred during the year, and to exhibit the rate at which money is being spent in order to effect those operations.

Since money may actually be received during a period prior to or succeeding the one in which the sale occurs, it may be necessary to *lead* or *lag* the receipt through time in order to relate the receiving to a particular year's sales. Similarly it may be necessary to *lead* or *lag* disbursements through time in order to express the rate of spending for the year's sales. Money may actually be spent prior to or succeeding the year in which the purchased instruments contribute to sales. The accountant, in order to obtain his measure of revenue and expense, merely redistributes the events—the receipt and disbursement of money—through time.

Accountants have their own terminology to describe leads and lags and the process of leading and lagging. They *accrue* revenue when a credit sale occurs or, in other words, they *lead* the receipt through time. Wages are *prepaid* when the disbursement occurs before the service is rendered. The expenditure is lagged through time. Receipts may be lagged (prepaid) when the money is received before service is rendered, e.g., when milk and ice tickets are sold before the product is delivered. We may lead (accrue) disbursements when the payment will occur in a period subsequent to the one in which the service is rendered.

The procedure of leading and lagging is warranted because it is assumed that the enterprise is a "going concern." We may lead a receipt of the next year as revenue of this year because we have reason to believe that the enterprise will continue to operate in the future and that it will do so in a manner which indicates that the accounts will be collected. We may lag a disbursement of this year as an expense of the following period because we have reason to believe that the purchased instrument will be used in effecting the next year's sales and, accordingly, its cost or some part thereof is a cost of next year's revenue.

The postulates guide us to "correct" accounting practice. We may use them, for example, as a basis by which we may select the "proper" exhibit of Gross Operating Revenue. Our object is to express the rate at which money is being received from the year's sales. We may use the Gross Sales account, although we know that it may not exhibit the amount of revenue for the period. There may be no one-to-one correspondence between the amount of receipts and the amount of Gross Sales for the duration of the enterprise. Sales returns and allowances are granted and they are seldom reflected in the Gross Sales account. A measured record of these events must be subtracted from Gross Sales if we are to obtain a result that corresponds with our idea of Gross Operating Revenue.

It is not enough merely to subtract Sales Returns and Allowances from Gross Sales. Discounts may have been granted and bad debts incurred. A measured account of these events must also be subtracted from Gross Sales if we wish to determine the amount of Gross Operating Revenue. No money will be received if discounts are granted and if we fail to collect accounts. We must, if we are to express the amount of revenue for the period, adjust the Gross Sales account for such an overstatement. We may do so by subtracting a separate record of Sales Discounts and Bad Debts.

We cannot be content with merely recording the amount of sales returns, allowances, discounts, and bad debts that have been incurred. We must foresee the extent to which *future* events will affect the measure of revenue for a *past* period because that measure contains a lead. The so-called sales valuation accounts—Sales Returns, Allowances, Discounts, and Bad Debts—may be records of past and future events. Their magnitude may be affected by anticipations as well as a knowledge of the past.

The "proper" exhibit of Gross Operating Revenue is as follows:

THE ACME COMPANY

Statement of Gross Operating Revenue
for the Year Ending December 31, 1941

Gross Sales		$100,000
Less: Sales Returns	$1,000	
Sales Allowances	500	
Sales Discounts	2,000	
Bad Debts	500	4,000
Gross Operating Revenue		$ 96,000

Our exhibit is "correct" because it corresponds with our postulates. The amount of gross operating revenue for the period is the accountant's best estimate of the amount of money received or to be received from the year's sales. It is an estimate because, although much of the money has been received, it was necessary to lead some receipts for accounts to be paid during the forthcoming year. We do not know, as a matter of fact, the precise amount of money that will be collected. We can only estimate the amount of returns, allowances, discounts, and bad debts contained in the lead.

Precise accounting is defined as that in which the measurements correspond exactly with the amounts indicated by the postulates. For example, an accounting for gross operating revenue is precise when the amount is exactly equal to the amount of money that will be collected from the year's sales. An accounting for an expense is precise when the amount is exactly equal to the amount of money that has been or will be disbursed in order to effect the year's sales. A procedure, on the other hand, is correct rather than precise. It must be designed to yield the results indicated by the postulates. For example, we chose the method which subtracts Sales Discounts and Bad Debts from Gross Sales as opposed to the method which subtracts Sales Returns and Allowances only because it tends to yield a measure of Gross Operating Revenue. The latter procedure does not. Where two procedures are correct, we chose the one which tends to yield the more precise results. In view of our definitions, we may say that much of orthodox accounting is correct, although very little of it yields precise results.[4]

We have examined the accounting for revenue and we may now turn our attention to the balance sheet. The valuation of Accounts Receivable expresses the extent to which leads appear in the measures of revenue for past periods. Double-entry bookkeeping describes each transaction from two points of view. It is not a description of two separate transactions. The Sales account records the rate of receiving money from the year's sales. The same events—sales—are also described as money received (Cash) or money to be received (Accounts Receivable). Each entry describes only one event, and, consequently, the value of the one term *is* the value of the other. The amount of money received (Cash) or to be received (Accounts Receivable) *is* the amount being received during the year. The value of Cash or Accounts Receivable from the year's sales *is* the value of Sales for the year.

The principles of valuation for Accounts Receivable are, accordingly, similar to the principles of valuation for revenue. The amount of the lead is equal to the amount of future receipts distributed as revenue for the period. The value of Accounts Receivable is equal to the amount of money that may reasonably be expected. The aggregate recorded in the account, like the aggregate recorded in Gross Sales, may overstate the amount of future receipts. The error may be adjusted by subtracting the amount of the over-statement in the several valuation reserves for returns, allowances, discounts, and bad debts.

Any error in the valuation of revenue is an error in the valuation of Accounts Receivable or Cash. Any error in the valuation of Accounts Receivable or Cash is an error in the valuation of the revenue for some period. An error exists in the valuation of Accounts Receivable when the amount exhibited is not equal to the amount of money that may reasonably be expected as of the balance sheet date. An error exists in the valuation of revenue when there is no one-to-one correspondence between the amount exhibited and the amount of money received or to be received from the year's sales. The valuation of revenue is complementary to the valuation of Accounts Receivable and Cash. An error in the one *is* an error in the other.

The complementary relation between the valuation of Accounts Receivable

---

[4] We may say to those who classify Bad Debts and Sales Discounts as expenses that we have not denied the existence of these costs: we merely assert that orthodox records do not exhibit their measure. The cost of Bad Debts, for example, is equal to the amount of money disbursed or to be disbursed for goods sold to customers who will not pay their accounts. The account Bad Debts normally records the sales price. It may over- or understate the amount of Bad Debt expense as the sales price over- or understates the purchase price. It may well be that the difficulty of calculating the expense more than offsets the gain from more accurate records. Under the circumstances sales price may be used as an index of expense. However this use of the account should not be admitted as an excuse for asserting that all debit nominal accounts are expenses. The ruse should be adequately explained.

and revenue is no accident. All elements of profit and loss are similarly related to some balance sheet account. For example, the valuation of so-called "fixed" assets merely completes the record of disbursements which are used to measure depreciation expense. The amount disbursed for an agent of production is lagged and the accountant distributes the lag through time as a rate or rates of spending. The formula for distribution is shaped by our concept of the asset and by the related concept of expense.

The most elaborate definition of the asset is that developed by Professor Canning.[5] The essence of his definition may be restated as follows: Any future service or series of services, in money or convertible into money, that may reasonably be expected by a proprietor is an asset to him. This statement differs slightly from that which appears in Canning's text. The service or services, contrary to the original declaration, need not be legally or equitably secured to the proprietor in order to be an asset to him. The holder of a United States bond may have no legal or equitable security at a given time and yet all accountants would assert that he has an asset. An illegal gambling contract may be an asset to the beneficiary. Legal and equitable security merely add to the reasonableness of the proprietor's expectation, as they provide a means of seeking satisfaction when the service or services are not forthcoming as originally scheduled. They do not assure the flow nor is the flow necessarily dissolved in their absence.

All future services to the proprietor are not his assets, for all are not in money or convertible into money. Policemen, firemen, and some government agencies are useful. It is reasonable to expect much business activity because policemen, firemen, and some government agencies are active. However, their mere existence or the exercise of their powers does not constitute an asset to the beneficiary. The services are not directly in money and the proprietor cannot compound them into a product which will yield him a money return.

The elements of all assets are not listed on all balance sheets. Some are implied. If the enterprise is a "going concern," it may be reasonable to expect future labor services, for example. However, only the relatively minor item, Prepaid Wages, is generally exhibited. The rest is left to the imagination.

Buildings, Machinery, Equipment, and Inventories are commonly listed as assets. These instruments are, in themselves, useless. A building cannot provide shelter for very long without a janitor. Someone must press the button to start and to stop machinery. Salesmen are needed to provide a pleasant atmosphere for customers. When the instruments are listed as assets, the future services associated with their use are implied. Labor, power, heat, light, repairs and maintenance must be had or the instruments are useless and the proprietor has no asset.

We must distinguish between the agent and the asset. The former is

---

5 *Ibid.,* Chapters II and III.

merely an instrument which will render a service. The latter *is* the future service or services. A delivery truck, for example, is an agent. Future transportation is the asset. However, we cannot procure future transportation because we have a delivery truck or the right to use one. We must also have gasoline, oil, tires, repairs, and a driver. Furthermore, we must expect conditions that will favor the *use* of these instruments before we can say that an asset exists. It is possible, for example, that we will discard the delivery truck and the associated instruments in favor of a parcel delivery service. We have, under those circumstances, no asset except salvage.

We cannot distribute the disbursements for agents through time merely because we conclude that an asset exists. We must know the asset's size. Measurement presupposes a unit of measure. For example, we cannot determine the size of a room unless we have available the "foot" or the "yard." Accountants have used a number of different units of measure, e.g., the year-of-use, the unit-of-product, and the machine-hour. The asset Machinery may be 15,000 future machine-hours of use. It is asserted that the proprietor will use his machinery that number of hours and it is accordingly implied that he will acquire the power, labor, and repairs necessary to procure the given quantity of service-units.

When the size of an asset has been determined, we may calculate its total cost.[6] Again, we must distinguish between the agent and the asset, for each has a total cost. The amount, in the former case, is the difference between the amount of the original outlay for the instrument and its salvage value. This sum is the amount actually disbursed. The total cost of an asset on the other hand, is the total amount of money disbursed or to be disbursed for the number of future services indicated by the asset's size. It is the total cost of the agent *plus* the total cost of all services required for the agent's use. We may express the concept algebraically as follows:

$$(1) \qquad\qquad T = V_0 - V_n + \sum_{t=0}^{t=n} 0$$

where T is the total cost of the asset, V_0 the amount of the original outlay for the agent, V_n the amount of the agent's salvage value, and $\sum_{t=0}^{t=n} 0$ the sum of all disbursements for essential related services from the present ($t=0$) until such time as the asset's services have been realized ($t-n$).

The value of T is the amount to be distributed as expense over n years. The amount that may be allocated to any one year depends upon the number of services rendered during the period and the average total cost per unit of service. The latter amount is

---

6 For brevity, we have excluded a study of the methods by which accountants select a particular unit of measure and by which they determine the size of an asset.

(2)
$$U = \frac{T}{\sum\limits_{t=0}^{t=n} S}$$

where U is the average total cost per unit of service and $\sum\limits_{t=0}^{t=n} S$ is the magnitude of the asset. The expense for any period is, accordingly

(3) $E_a = U \times S_a$

where S_a is the number of services rendered during the interval.

The practice of accountancy has produced some unfortunate results. The year-of-use is commonly selected as a unit of measure. The layman is confused. He does not distinguish between the magnitude of the asset and the number of time-intervals over which disbursements are to be distributed as expense. The two quantities are equal and yet they do not express a measure of the same thing.

Unless we refer to the concept of the asset, it is difficult to see why we should distinguish between the year-of-use as a unit of measure and the fiscal period. For example, a machine is said to be three future years-of-use. The total cost of the agent $(V_0 - V_n)$ is $1,000 and the total cost of related services $\left(\sum\limits_{t=0}^{t=n} 0\right)$ is $2,000. The average total cost per unit of service (per year-of-use) is $1,000. No more than one unit of service (year-of-use) will be rendered during any one fiscal period (year) and, accordingly, the amount of the expense per annum is equal to the average total cost per unit of service. A very different result may be obtained if we select some other unit of measure.

It is common practice to select the year-of-use as the unit of measure *for the agent* and to accrue disbursements for related services as if they were separable events. The three future years-of-use are not considered as *stock*. We act as if we needed only to purchase the agent, for we do not say that the total cost of each unit of service is equal to the total cost of every other one. It may be, for example, that the time-schedule for related costs is as follows:

Year	Disbursed
1	$450
2	650
3	900
	$2,000

If the year-of-use is selected only for the agent, we would exhibit the following expenses:

Year	Agent	Related	Annual Expenses
1	$ 333	$ 450	$ 783
2	333	650	983
3	334	900	1,234
	$1,000	$2,000	$3,000

This method yields incorrect results if the year-of-use is the proper unit of measure. The total cost of related services cannot be separated from the total cost of the agent. We imply unrealistic circumstances when we treat the two costs independently. We suggest that the agent may be operated without power, labor, and repairs. As a consequence, we understate the amount of expense for the first two years and we overstate it for the third period.[7]

If the amount of expense is said to be $1,000 for each of the three years, we need not exhibit a single figure. The rate of spending for the machine, power, labor, and repairs may be shown separately in the profit and loss statement. And what is more, the related services may be accrued as they are in common practice. Consistency requires, in the latter event, that the total cost of the agent shall be distributed in a manner that, in view of the accruals, will yield a result for the asset in accord with equation (3). For example, the accrued expenses for the first year may be Labor $200 and Power $250. These accounts may be exhibited in the profit and loss statement. The depreciation expense *for the agent* is $550 or that amount which added to the sum of the accruals will equal the aggregate amount of expense for services from the asset during the period. The concept may be expressed algebraically as

$$(4) \qquad\qquad D_a = E_a - O_a$$

where D_a is the amount of depreciation expense for the agent, E_a is the total amount of expense from the asset during the period, and O_a is the total amount accrued for services associated with the agent during the year.

---

[7] There may be a number of reasons for the difference in the annual costs for related services. It may be that continued use of the machine will require increasing outlays for repairs. We may view an outlay during the third year as a payment for wear and tear of the first and second years. An outlay during the first year will purchase use for the second and third periods.

The annual costs may differ for other reasons. We may pay more in each of the three years for the same amount of service or we may buy more service at the same price. In the former case, we did not pay a different price for each service because we did not buy them separately. When we bought the machine, we were, by implication, committed to purchase all three years-of-use, although we could disburse a different amount in each of the three years. If each instalment on the piano differs from the other, we do not say that we purchased different parts at different prices!

The purchase of an increased amount of power, labor, and repairs may indicate a more intensive or extensive use of the machine during the forthcoming years. It is likely that some other unit of measure should be selected. Each of the three years-of-use must be an equal amount of service.

It may be objected that, to measure E_a, it is necessary to forecast the amount to be disbursed for related services. However, the mere fact that forecasts are made should not be used as an excuse to condemn the procedure. We cannot measure depreciation expense without a forecast.[8] Furthermore, there is no *a priori* reason why errors arising from forecasting the total cost of related services should be larger than that arising from an independent valuation of the asset's component parts.[9]

The valuation of a depreciable agent is another aspect of the measurement of depreciation expense. We describe, by double-entry, the amount of the lag and, secondly, the amount disbursed. There is only one event—the disbursement of money—and it is described in two ways: as a time-lag and as a disbursement. When we "depreciate" Machinery, we are concerned with the distribution of the lag through time. The double-entry describes the disbursement in two ways: as a time-rate of spending (depreciation) and as a deduction from the lag (Reserve), for a part of the lag is no longer to be distributed as expense. Both sets of entries deal with the same event—the disbursement of money. One set indicates the amount of the lag and the other exhibits the amount of the lag distributed as expense of the fiscal period. One set is complementary to the other. If the lag is incorrect, the amount distributed through time is in error. If the wrong amount is distributed through time, the amount to be lagged at the close of the period is incorrect.

For example, the amount of depreciation for the agent may be more or less than $550 during the first year and the value of Machinery at the close of the period is accordingly smaller or larger than $450. When a greater amount is lagged at the end of the year, there is a smaller amount of depreciation expense for past periods. When a smaller amount is distributed as expense, there is a larger amount to be lagged at the end of the year.

While we can say that the value of the agent at any given time is the amount of the lag, we cannot say that asset valuation is an absolute procedure. It is meaningless to say that an asset is 15,000 future machine-hours or three future years-of-use unless we can say that the services are to be had at the lowest available cost per unit.[10] Otherwise the proprietor may abandon

---

[8] We will ignore the fact that salvage value and the size of the asset must be forecast. The amount of salvage is frequently small in proportion to the agent's total cost and the percentage of error arising from mistaken forecasts is negligible. Mistaken estimates of the asset's size are a frequent source of considerable error.

[9] For example, it is admitted that the total cost of related services may be more or less than the estimated $2,000. Depreciation expense for the first year will be more or less than $1,000. However there is no *a priori* reason why the amount of this error should be more or less than error contained in the statement that expense for the period is $783. Certainly there is an advantage in using a method that has defined limits!

[10] The fact that the services are sold at a lower cost per unit is not always evidence that we may obtain them at a favorable price. If it is necessary to close the plant while equipment is replaced, the total cost of a loss in business may more than offset an advantage in purchase price.

his agent and acquire services elsewhere. Our equipment is obsolete. The price to be paid for future services should not exceed the total cost of acquiring the stock in the most economical manner. Algebraically

$$(5) \quad \frac{V_0 - V_n + \sum\limits_{t=0}^{t=n} 0}{\sum\limits_{t=0}^{t=n} S} = U = \frac{V_0 - V_n + \sum\limits_{t=0}^{t=n} 0}{\sum\limits_{t=0}^{t=n} S}$$

where the service-unit formula refers, in the one case, to the asset and, in the other, to the average total cost per unit of service from alternative means. The present valuation of the agent is, accordingly

$$(6) \quad V_0 = U \times \sum\limits_{t=0}^{t=n} S - \sum\limits_{t=0}^{t=n} 0 + V_n$$

where U is the average total cost per unit when the service is provided in the most economical manner available, $\sum\limits_{t=0}^{t=n} S$ the sum of services to be had from the proprietor's agent, and $\sum\limits_{t=0}^{t=n} 0$, the total cost of services related to that agent.

Assume that our proprietor held his agent one year. At the close of the period, the services may be had from an alternative source at an average cost per unit of $900. The value of V_0 is, accordingly, $250. *That amount is the price to be paid for services still to be had from the agent.* At such a price, the asset's total cost will not, in view of the anticipated total cost of related services ($650+$900), exceed the price at which the two future years-of-use may be had in the most economical manner. The amount of the lag at the close of the period should not be greater.

We have indicated that much of the accounting for profit and loss of a *past* period involves forecasting. When we lead receipts, we forecast the amount to be collected. When we lag disbursements, we forecast, among other things, the number of service-units to be had and their total cost. We are not endowed with perfect foresight. Of course we make mistakes. The amount of Bad Debts will frequently be more or less than the amount of the allowance; business men will retire an agent before or after the anticipated time. Each mistake means an error in our estimate of profit and loss for a past period of time. We are in a more difficult position than the proverbial witness: Not only do we have trouble in describing what happened, but we must guess what will happen before we can describe the events of the past!

Mistaken forecasts introduce a new category—capital gains and capital losses. We make the adjustments because we change our anticipations. They are not a part of positive or negative income because they have no time dimension.[11] They are instantaneous. We may make them because we believe that we have incorrectly distributed a given amount of receipts and disbursements through time or that we have mistakenly estimated the amount of receipts and disbursements to be distributed through a given number of fiscal periods.

Accountants are well aware of their existence, for accountants have long been concerned with so-called capital adjustments. A balance sheet valuation is changed and, as a consequence, there is an increase or decrease in the amount of revenue or expense for some period or periods. While accountants do indicate capital adjustments, it is not too much to say that many have concealed them in a maze of bookkeeping. Adjustments to surplus are not always reported in a generally available statement.

Our study suggests that we reject Professor Dewing's conclusion. The income account is not more fundamental than the balance sheet. It cannot be so because balance sheet valuations are generally another aspect of income measurements. When we are concerned with the amount of Accounts Receivable, for example, we are concerned with the amount of revenue for a past period or periods. When we are interested in the valuation of Machinery, we are also interested in the amount of depreciation. It may be that we have more use for the information provided by the profit and loss statement, but we cannot have faith in that information unless we believe in the balance sheet valuations.

All enterprise accounting is, in one sense, profit and loss accounting, for we are always concerned with the distribution of receipts and disbursements through time. All enterprise accounting is therefore dynamic. The fact that we exhibit momentarily the amount of our leads and lags should not distract from the kinetic character of our procedures. We prepare a balance sheet as a check—a revaluation, so to speak—of our distributions between the past and future. The statement contains many elements of profit and loss. It exhibits the amount of future receipts and disbursements which have been represented as revenue and expense of past periods, and it shows past receipts and disbursements which will be distributed as revenue and expense of future years. The balance sheet and the profit and loss statement are complementary: each completes the picture by presenting a different aspect of enterprise receipts and disbursements. Professor Dewing found this to be true when he introduced the subject of obsolescence.[12]

---

11 See Erik Lindahl, "The Concept of Income," *Economic Essays in Honour of Gustav Cassel,* 339.

12 See especially *op. cit.,* 621–623.

George O. May

ACCOUNTING PRINCIPLES AND POSTULATES

George Oliver May (1875–1961) was born in England, where he qualified as a chartered accountant. He transferred from the London office of Price Waterhouse & Co. to New York in 1897, and remained for the rest of his life with the American firm. He became partner in 1902, and served as senior partner, 1911–1936. His book, Twenty-Five Years of Accounting Responsibility, *is his report on the years as senior partner. Mr. May devoted an enormous amount of time and energy to professional affairs. For example, he was active in the conferences between the New York Stock Exchange and the American Institute of C.P.A. (1932–1934), which led to the adoption by the members of the Institute of six principles of accounting. These principles are still in force and were published in* Accounting Research Bulletin No. 1, *and also in Chapter 1 of* ARB No. 43. *He was a leader in the further attempts in the 1930's and 1940's to reduce the principles of accounting to writing, serving as chairman of several short-lived committees of the Institute on accounting principles, and as the guiding spirit of the committee on accounting procedure in its early years. His most ambitious project was the Study Group on Business Income whose report was published in 1952 as* Changing Concepts of Business Income. *Mr. May was the embodiment of the man of affairs, possessed of great intellectual powers and conscious of his role in the midst of rapid and deep-reaching social, political, and economic change.*

The material reprinted here comes from his book, Financial Accounting *(1943). It reflects Mr. May's views that accounting postulates and principles are conventional (tentative) in nature, and that they can only be successfully formulated by getting the cooperation of those who are in a position to enforce them (e.g., the commercial banks, the stock exchanges, the Federal regulatory agencies). In this excerpt he also develops the realization, the monetary, and the permanence "postulates" that underlie so many of the principles and rules of conventional accounting practice.*

The term "accounting principles" has assumed such a wide and varied

Reprinted from Chapter III of *Financial Accounting* by George O. May (New York: The Macmillan Company, 1943), by permission.

importance as almost to demand a chapter for itself. It occurs, for instance, in every auditor's report under the Securities Exchange Act of 1934.

It used to be not uncommon for the accountant who had been unable to persuade his client to adopt the accounting treatment that he favored, to urge as a last resort that it was called for by "accounting principles." Often he would have had difficulty in defining the "principle" and saying how, why, and when it became one. But the method was effective, especially in dealing with those (of whom there were many) who regarded accounting as an esoteric but well-established body of learning and chose to bow to its authority rather than display their ignorance of its rules. Obviously, the word "principle" was an essential part of the technique; "convention" would have been quite ineffective.

Today, we find utility commissions employing much the same device. In their efforts to avert judicial review of their decisions they constantly appeal to "accounting principles," and throw in the adjectival support of the word "fundamental" to enhance the impression of permanence and inevitability of the authority.

The American Institute of Accountants, which is representative mainly of the practicing accountants, has in recent years taken the position that the word "principle," if it is to be used at all, should be used only in the sense of "A general law or rule adopted or professed as a guide to action; a settled ground or basis of conduct or practice" (*The Oxford English Dictionary*).[1] It therefore does not use the word "fundamental," but with more restraint speaks of "generally accepted accounting principles." A committee of the Institute has said that, initially, accounting rules are mere postulates, derived from experience and reason, and that only after they have proved useful and become generally accepted do they become principles of accounting. It has repeatedly recognized that accounting principles are founded on considerations of utility and are subject to modification as criteria of usefulness change.

The American Accounting Association, which is representative rather of the academic accountants, uses the word "principle" without indicating what precise sense it attaches to the word. In a statement, *Accounting Principles Underlying Corporate Financial Statements,* issued in June, 1941, which was a revision of a tentative statement issued in 1936, the Association speaks of "fundamental propositions concerning the functions of accounting in respect to cost, revenue realization, income, and capital." Under the heading of "Cost" it presents eight paragraphs, in commenting on which it speaks of "the cost principle stated above." Perhaps the most crucial of the eight paragraphs is No. 7, which reads as follows:

Values other than costs applicable to future periods should be treated

---

[1] *Accounting Research Bulletin No. 7,* p. 60. [ED. NOTE: This passage now appears in *Accounting Terminology Bulletin No. 1,* "Review and Resumé" (American Institute of C.P.A., 1953), page 11.]

in balance sheets as supplementary data, and then only when supported by substantial evidence. Such data should be adequately described and shown parenthetically, by footnote, or in separate schedules, to avoid obscuring the basic cost figures.

How costs applicable to future periods are to be determined is not made entirely clear, but under such a rule it would certainly not be permissible to carry fixed assets at more than cost or, probably, to carry inventories at market value because less than cost. ... The first part of this rule, although now fairly generally accepted in America, has only recently become established here and is not accepted in England, and the second part is far from being accepted in either country today—indeed, the rule that inventories should be stated at cost or market, whichever is lower, is not only one of the oldest but also one of the best-established rules of accounting.

In a later chapter will be traced the history of the development which has made the precept that fixed assets shall not be carried at more than cost one of the best-established rules of accounting. The fact there disclosed—that the rule of today is the result of a revulsion of feeling, and that it has passed through all the stages from being a postulate to a principle within a decade— illustrates in a most striking manner the nature of accounting principles and the character of accounting. The old rule, which permitted and in some cases encouraged the recording of unrealized appreciation on the books of corporations, fell into disrepute because of the abuses that were committed in its name, and because of a change in the general concept of the major objective of accounting from the determination of net worth to the measurement of income and earning capacity. Newly created regulatory commissions were quick to perceive that a change in the accounting rules might be helpful to them in their efforts to escape from the bondage into which their predecessors had been led by William Jennings Bryan and his associates in the famous case of *Smyth* v. *Ames*,[2] which established the predominance of value over cost in the field of public utility regulation. They have forbidden future, and excoriated past, "write-ups."

It is, perhaps, regrettable that the word "principle" should be used to describe canons or procedures to which it can be applied only in a restricted sense. I must in fairness recognize that the word is used in the standard form of accounting reports, and that its use there grew out of the correspondence between the Institute and the New York Stock Exchange which began with a letter of September 22, 1932*. . . and which was conducted by a committee of which I was chairman. The form of report recommended by that committee was a radical change from the form which had been in use

---

[2] 169 U.S. 466.

* This exchange of correspondence was published in 1934 by the A.I.C.P.A. (reprinted in 1963) in a pamphlet titled "Audits of Corporate Accounts." The rules agreed upon are also found in Ch. 1(A) of A.R.B. 43, "Restatement and Revision of Accounting Research Bulletins," published by A.I.C.P.A. in 1953.

for many years; and since this volume is largely historical in character, it may be appropriate here to discuss its antecedents.

The standard form of audit report or certificate commonly in use prior to 1932 was of English origin. There, the auditor was required to say whether in his opinion the balance sheet to which it related was properly drawn up so as to exhibit a true and correct view of the state of the company's affairs as shown by its books of account. In England, the last seven words had a technical significance and were associated with the general rule that, within wide limits, the methods of accounting employed by a company might be determined by its directors acting within the authority of its memorandum of association. In our country they would have had no such specialized significance, and might have been construed as a reservation which impaired the value of the assurance given; they were therefore almost universally omitted. Moreover, a phrase such as "the financial position of the company" was substituted for "the state of the company's affairs."

When I became senior partner of a large accounting firm in 1911, a conviction that the public generally did not understand the nature of accounts or of audits as usually conducted caused me great concern. I felt that statements on the question by the profession itself would be regarded as self-serving and ineffective, and I was convinced of the desirability of associating responsible authorities with the profession in declarations which would help to define the auditor's responsibilities and enlighten the public.

An opportunity to deal to some extent with the nature of accounting occurred in 1917, when cooperation between the Federal Trade Commission, the Federal Reserve Board, and the American Institute of Accountants led to the publication of the pamphlet *Uniform Accounting,* though that pamphlet dealt mainly with audit procedures. A further opportunity occurred when accountants were called upon to play an important part in drafting the Revenue Act of 1918. They secured the introduction into Section 212 of the provision that returns should be made on the basis on which the taxpayer's books were kept unless that basis did not clearly reflect income, and the inclusion in Regulation 45 of an article (no. 24) which said: "the law contemplates that each taxpayer shall adopt such forms and systems of accounting as are in his judgment best suited to his purpose." While these provisions resulted in a somewhat better understanding, they did not make clear the real and limited significance of any statement that a balance sheet shows the "true position" of a company.

In 1932, the New York Stock Exchange was concerned over the variety in the methods of accounting employed by companies whose securities were listed. A cooperating Institute committee, in its letter of September 22, 1932, sought to do two things: first, to make unequivocally clear the existence of a variety of methods; and, secondly, to suggest a procedure by which the variety could be curtailed and the best methods gradually made practically universal. The latter objective it proposed to achieve by a requirement that listed corporations must explain in adequate detail the basis on which their financial statements were made up, and undertake not to change the basis without due notice to the Exchange and to stockholders. This procedure, it was thought, would insure consistency, or proper disclosure of any inconsistency, and gradually bring about the elimination of the less desirable practices by the pressure of public opinion.

The limitation on the significance of accounts and of auditors' reports thereon was to be emphasized by a change in the form of audit report so that it would become an expression of opinion on the question whether the financial statements were in conformity with the methods professed to be followed, and whether those methods were in harmony with good accounting standards. The question what word should be used to describe those standards was much discussed and finally decided in favor of the expression "accepted principles."

In the correspondence the Committee had used the words "rules," "methods," "conventions," and "principles" interchangeably. The word "methods" was being used in the suggested form of report in another sense; the word "rules" implied the existence of a ruling body which did not exist; the word "convention" was regarded as not appropriate for popular use and in the opinion of some would not convey an adequate impression of the authority of the precepts by which the accounts were judged.

Canons of accounting could not properly be described as "principles" in the more fundamental sense of that word but might be said to be principles in the narrower sense above quoted. It may well be that in agreeing on this word the Committee was resorting to the familiar expedient of securing unanimity by the adoption of a formula which was capable of sufficient variety in interpretation to cover the area of difference of opinion among its individual members. But the object to be sought was of major importance, and unanimity was highly desirable; its achievement was worth a minor ambiguity of this kind.

The response from all quarters to the Committee's proposal was surprisingly favorable and unanimous, and a movement was then initiated which has had lasting effects and might have been of even greater good but for the fact that the powers of the Stock Exchange were shorn by the Securities and Exchange Act of 1934.

Following the publication of the correspondence, the Institute appointed a Committee on Accounting Principles. Immediately the question was raised in what sense the word "principle" was used in the form auditor's report which had been suggested. The new committee recommended adoption by the Institute of certain precepts listed in the appendix to the letter of September 22, 1932. In doing so it spoke of them as "rules or principles." Still later, a Committee on Accounting Procedure superseded the Committee on Accounting Principles and established a research department. In its first bulletin the new committee drew attention to the precepts which had been previously approved by the Institute membership, and in doing so spoke of them only as "rules." Still later, that committee approved a report of the Committee on Terminology in which the opinion mentioned earlier in this chapter was expressed, that the standard dictionary definition that came closest to defining the sense in which the word "principle" was used in accounting was: "A general law or rule adopted or professed as a guide to action; a settled ground or basis of conduct or practice."[3]

The pamphlet of 1917 (which later received the designation *Verification of Financial Statements*) and the correspondence published in 1934 under the title *Audits of Corporate Accounts* are important landmarks in the development of accounting. It is significant of a change in outlook that the earlier pamphlet was the result of cooperation with an institution concerned with the granting of credit, so that questions were viewed primarily from the standpoint of the credit grantor, whereas the latter pamphlet was the outcome of cooperation with a body concerned with the marketability of corporate securities, and problems were considered from the standpoint of those who trade in such markets. It would be difficult to overestimate the importance of the change in emphasis thus illustrated upon the development of accounting.

Returning from this historical digression to a discussion of the question of accounting principles, it may be desirable to deal briefly with the suggestion that the word "principles" has a proper application to accounting as connoting certain fundamental qualities of good accounting, notably conservatism and consistency.

Many years ago, a manufacturer entered my office and said that he wished my firm to displace his former auditors. Upon my asking why, he said feelingly: "I'm through with optimistic accountants." He went on to say that he was himself of a sanguine temperament, and that what he needed in accounting advice was caution. He expressed the opinion that this was generally true of the relation between managements and accountants.

He was, of course, right; the great majority of ventures fail, and the fact that enterprise nevertheless continues is attributable to the incurable optimism (often dissociated from experience) as well as to the courage of mankind. In my experience, also, losses from unsound accounting have most commonly resulted from the hopes rather than the achievements of management being allowed to influence accounting dispositions. To me, conservatism is still the first virtue of accounting, and I am wholly unable to agree with those who would bar it from the books of account and statements prepared therefrom and would relegate it to footnotes.

Consistency is the second great virtue of accounting, and the emphasis

---

[3] Candor requires mention of the fact that the author was chairman of the several committees mentioned; but while this fact may impair the value of the reports as corroborative of the views here expressed, it lends authenticity to the narrative of the course of events.

upon it in the form of auditors' reports that have been in use since 1932 is wholly desirable. However, accounting, like the common law, should have elements of flexibility and adaptability as well as of stability. Therefore, there can be no absolute rule of consistency, but only a general admonition that consistency should normally be maintained, and a rule that any significant departure therefrom and its effects should be adequately disclosed.

Some writers have suggested that the distinction between capital and income is a fundamental principle of accounting. However, the distinction in accounting today between so-called capital expenditures and income expenditures does not rest on any such essential difference in the nature of the property acquired as that between land and other property which is often stressed in the field of economics. The distinction rests rather upon the relation between the length of the useful life of the property acquired and the length of the accounting period for which income is being determined. A capital expenditures is one, the usefulness of which is expected to extend over several accounting periods. If the accounting period were increased from the customary year to a decade, most of what is now treated as capital expenditure would become chargeable to income, while if the period were reduced to a day, much of what is now treated as current maintenance would become capital expenditure.

Indeed, it is a practical test of the utility or significance of an accounting rule to consider the effect of its application if the accounting period were materially shortened or lengthened. For instance, an attempt to allocate the profits of a restaurant for a day to hours, some of which were hours of crowded activity and others hours of idleness, is easily undertaken in retrospect over the entire period and will suggest some of the limitations on the significance of allocations of the costs and profits of a complete business cycle to the individual years falling within that period.

Accounting practices must be considered in relation to the purposes and the principles or conventions which were deemed to be controlling when they were being followed. Moreover, when there is a change in controlling conventions, and some adjustments become necessary, these adjustments should be made upon the basis that a new viewpoint has been adopted—not that errors have been made in the past and are being corrected. Cases will, of course, arise in which revisions of past accounting are needed because methods were employed which were never justified by any accounting theory; but these cases are in a class apart.

The practice of speaking opprobriously of accounting treatments to which no ethical objection can be taken (such as honest revaluation or non-acceptance of straight-line depreciation), and which were in accord with legal and regulatory concepts of the time when they were adopted, is not calculated to inspire confidence in the impartial character of the discharge of quasi-judicial functions by those who indulge in it. Mr. Justice Holmes has pointed out that on occasion it is necessary to revise the judgment of posterity in the light of the judgment of the times. Never is this more necessary than when a change of judgment is the mere accompaniment of a change in interest.

The Postulate of Stability
in the Monetary Unit

In formulating a statement of principles of accounting, as in a general discussion of principles of economics, it is customary to assume that the monetary unit is substantially stable in value; but as Taussig, for instance, points out in accepting this postulate for the purpose of his *Principles of Economics*,[4] it is not universally true, and in dealing with any case it is always necessary to consider to what extent the postulate is valid in the particular set of circumstances, or how its invalidity affects the conclusions to be reached.

Prior to the first world war, the postulate was regarded as accepted in respect of the principal commercial countries of the world. The events of the first world war, and even more, the postwar developments in Germany, France, and other countries, created conditions in which the postulate was clearly inapplicable, and which made the presentation of informative accounts in respect of enterprises in those countries a task of very great difficulty. Subsequent devaluations in Great Britain and in our own country, the concentration of gold in the United States, and the increasing acceptance of the notion of managed currencies have tended further to impair the validity of this postulate; and the prospect that the present war will lead to new developments of the same character makes reconsideration of accounting conventions, in so far as they rest upon it, inevitable.

Now that the main emphasis has shifted from the balance sheet to the income account, the effect of the change in the value of the monetary unit on the balance sheet is not the major question to be considered. The problem is rather to determine the form and content of the income account in such a way as to indicate as fully as possible its real significance. Here again the distinction between long- and short-term transactions is crucial.

...During the decade following the last war there was a considerable movement to reflect the change in the value of the monetary unit in the balance sheet and, indirectly through depreciation charges, in the income account,[5] by restating capital assets on the basis of the then current prices which were, perhaps, roughly 50 per cent higher than immediately before the war and 100 per cent above those at the beginning of the century. In the decade that followed, other forces brought about a situation in which it was apparent that capital assets generally had not appreciated in terms of the

---

[4] *Principles of Economics,* by F. W. Taussig, 4th ed., Vol. I, p. 105.
[5] Cf.*Capital Consumption and Adjustment,* Solomon Fabricant (1938), pp. 213–222.

monetary unit even to the extent of a major fraction of the rise in price indices. . . . The regulatory commissions are making the most strenuous efforts to prevent any reflection of the decline in the purchasing power of the monetary unit in the rate base, by excluding value from consideration and measuring cost in terms of the monetary unit without regard to the fluctuations in its value.

In the light of this history it seems unlikely that there will be any general attempt to reflect a further fall in the purchasing power of the dollar in the capital-asset accounts of corporations generally, unless that fall assumes even larger proportions than it did in the first world war. In the other major phase of the problem—namely, in the valuation of inventories—there is a strong movement, to which the tax law has yielded, to exclude from the income account what may be regarded as nominal profits arising from changes in either the general price level or the price of particular products. It will be recalled that in and immediately after the first world war the index of wholesale prices rose from 100 in 1913 to over 250 in 1921. During this period, many efforts were made to bring about acceptance of the base stock method of inventory accounting, under which normal supplies of raw materials were carried at a fixed price instead of at the latest cost. The result of this method was, of course, broadly to put cost and sales in the measurement of income more nearly upon the basis of current price levels. This movement was successfully resisted by the Treasury, with the result that taxes were collected on large nominal profits due merely to increases in the price level.

In the last decade, a movement to secure the adoption of substantially the same principle was initiated. Its supporters discreetly avoided the terminology of the previous effort, and instead of pleading for the adoption of the base cost principle, asked for recognition of what was described as the last-in, first-out method of allocation in the determination of cost. This movement... requires mention here in connection with the discussion of the historical development affecting the postulate of a uniform monetary standard.

The Postulate of Continuity

It is an almost essential postulate of accounting that it shall be regarded as a continuous process. The emphasis on profits for particular short periods has sometimes led to attempts to isolate an accounting period from its past and future in some important respect. For special purposes, such a procedure may be necessary and practicable.

In the United Railways and Electric Company of Baltimore case,[6] the Supreme Court held that, in fixing service charges, depreciation as well as the rate base should be computed upon present values—not upon costs.

---

6 280 U.S. 234.

Provision for depreciation for a series of years so computed would have no significance as an aggregate, and the method is quite inapplicable to the ordinary accounting processes. For current accounting purposes depreciation must be based on cost. The life of an enterprise, like that of a man, is continuous, and the gains and losses, the successes and failures, of one period are in a large measure the result of acts, omissions, and events of the past, and the results achieved cannot be appraised as successes or failures without regard to the future. The historical character of accounting cannot be too strongly emphasized; and attempts to divorce the present from the past in one respect, even where it may be practicable—as, for instance, by substituting a valuation for cost—are often objectionable because they are at best partial adjustments and because they tend to obscure the true nature of accounting.

The point may be illustrated by assuming a purchase of high-grade securities financed by an issue of secured bonds at a time when interest rates are high. If interest rates fall, the value of the securities will tend to rise, and so will the market value of the bonds issued to finance the purchase. The bonds may then be refunded at a substantial cost in the form of unamortized discount and redemption premium. Current practice would permit the cost to be charged against earned surplus account, and if thereby a deficit were created, that deficit might be absorbed through what is called a quasi-reorganization. Thereafter the income available for the common stock would be determined by deducting from gross income only the reduced interest charge on the refunding bonds, though the gross income itself will be the result of opportunities to invest—which ceased with the advent of the conditions which made refunding of the debt advantageous.

It may be questioned whether this result is altogether sound. No doubt many cases arise where the inheritance from the past is so burdensome that a new start through reorganization or quasi-reorganization is, as a practical matter, desirable. But the concept of continuity should not lightly be discarded, and quasi-reorganizations which relieve a corporation's income account of burdensome inheritances from the past and ignore beneficial inheritances are of doubtful propriety. The whole problem of accounting in relation to reorganizations and quasi-reorganizations is an inviting field for study.[7] There will always remain here, as elsewhere, questions which can be rightly decided only by good judgment and regard for business morality.

---

7 See *Research Bulletin No. 3.* [ED. NOTE: Now appears as Ch. 7(A) of A.R.B. 43]

W. A. Paton

ACCOUNTING PROCEDURES
AND PRIVATE ENTERPRISE

For a biographical sketch of W. A. Paton, *see the headnote to "The Postulates of Accounting," page 64.*

This second item of Professor Paton to be reprinted here was published a quarter-century after the first one on "The Postulates of Accounting." He had witnessed the New Deal in the U.S. in the 1930's and early 1940's and had seen the rise to power of the Labour government in Britain after World War II, with its policy of nationalization of key industries. At the same time, he was aware of the shortcomings of financial reporting, centering on "omission, premature absorption, and understatement in varying degrees" of the assets of private business enterprises. This article pleads for more complete disclosure, based on a recognition that "it is really values that are the basic data of accounting...."

In a preceding paper ["The Accountant and Private Enterprise"], appearing in the January, 1948, issue of *The Journal,* I attempted to indicate the important rôle of the accountant in the system of private enterprise and the need for a more acute realization by the accountant of his obligations to the system. There followed some discussion of the underlying features of the free market economy, with special attention to the relation of costs and prices, and the prevailing misconceptions and fallacies that—coupled with deliberate propaganda—have facilitated the drift toward collectivism. In this continuation of the theme, the technical possibilities available to the accountant of assisting in the effort to maintain private enterprise, in effective operation, are reviewed, with particular notice being taken of the limitations of some of the existing conventions and procedures.

Economic Facts versus Conventions

"The primary function of accounting is to furnish significant, useful information to managers and owners of business enterprises regarding assets,

Reprinted from the *Journal of Accountancy* (April, 1948), pp. 278–91, by permission.

liabilities, revenues, costs of production, income, and so on."[1] Most people are willing to agree to such a generalization, but differences of opinion arise as to what constitutes "significant, useful information." This need not be surprising, in view of the complexity of business activity and the varying characteristics of business enterprises. It is desirable, however, that the bases of particular opinions or procedures not only be understood but be critically examined from time to time. If a procedure has merit, that means that it has something back of it more substantial than the assertion that "we have always done it that way."

It should be possible to secure agreement on two main propositions. First, where the accounting procedures are not providing owners and managers with the economic facts that are admittedly pertinent and significant, accounting is not doing a wholly satisfactory job, and in such circumstances it is up to the accountant to give careful consideration to ways and means of making his activity more useful. Second, if practicable means of supplying the desired facts can be worked out the accountant should not close the door to the possibility of doing a better job simply because some convention or tradition or usage appears to be standing in the way. There is little hope for any contribution to progress from anyone who is unwilling to go that far.

Accounting, like other fields, is plagued with fetishes and sacred cows, and it is high time that homage be shifted from these to the primary objective—furnishing owners and managers with essential economic data. Where recognition of economic realities runs counter to some convention or tradition, perhaps never soundly grounded, tradition should give way. In other words, tradition should not be worshipped for its own sake. On the other hand it should not be assumed that attacking or disregarding established ideas and practices is a virtue in itself. Good reasons may often be found on which to justify a view or a procedure which has become conventional through long adherence or observance. "It must not be assumed," as one teacher of economics put it, "that all our ancestors were damn fools." What is needed, as suggested above, is a clear understanding of function and a critical review of conventions in the light of such function. Such a review is particularly needed at the present juncture.

Conservatism

The most objectionable and obstructive tradition of accounting is conservatism, so-called. Accountants generally, without fully understanding what they are doing, kowtow to this tradition. The textbooks make it a cardinal virtue, and the practicing accountant feels that any proposal seeking to

---

[1] "Restoration of Fixed Asset Values" (second affirmative), *Accounting Review,* April, 1947.

broaden the horizon of accounting is effectively squelched if excuse can be found for referring to it as nonconservative. I recall that some years ago, at one of the meetings of the American Accounting Association, one of the speakers ventured to raise some questions regarding the merits of "cost or market, whichever is the lower" as the last word in inventory valuation. For a few minutes the group seemed to be staggered by the speaker's temerity. Then one of the elder statesmen rose up, solemnly, to rebuke the teacher who had dared question one of the basic articles of faith. He wound up by saying that it was bad enough to have something like this occur at a convention of the Association but he trusted that in no classroom in the country would students be exposed to any such dangerous discussion. No doubt some progress has been made since this episode in the direction of developing widespread and critical consideration of accounting procedures, but there is still too much of a tendency to try to settle controversial issues by reference to "established practice" and "conservatism."

Applying conservatism in accounting apparently means to most accountants on the one hand the understatement of assets by various means and on the other the understatement of net income. As has often been pointed out, these two practices are not always consistent. If, for example, the cost of acquiring a unit of depreciable property is charged to revenues in the year of acquisition, the immediate result is understatement of assets and understatement of earnings, but in succeeding years—during the useful life of the property in question—one effect of the procedure will be to overstate income performance. Aside from the backlash of inconsistency, however, there is no substantive defense—practical or otherwise—for a policy of deliberate understating of any economic measurement in the business enterprise. There is no virtue in either understatement or overstatement. The interested parties want to know the facts of their undertaking as accurately as it is practicable to determine them. They don't want to be confused by an array of data that have been subjected to a process of paring down in varying and often undisclosed amounts.

Far from being something to commend, the habit developed by accountants of leaning in a particular arithmetic direction—the direction of deduction and understatement—is their worst fault. Here is a field in which the end result is a presentation of economic quantities, together with interpretations and evaluations thereof, and yet it is widely considered to be good practice to scale essential figures down by various technical methods. Such an attitude is intellectually crude and professionally stultifying. True, an effort has been made by the profession to limit and control the area of understatement by setting up a structure of recognized devices to be employed, but this sort of thing can never be anything more than a sugar-coating of what is basically the wrong approach.

The stress in accounting should be on careful, competent measurement, not on conservatism in the sense of understatement. An end should be made of the habit of leaning toward subtraction, glorifying the minus sign, condoning and encouraging low figures instead of accurate, reliable, significant data. A basic shift in emphasis is badly needed at this time if accounting is to serve the interests of business enterprise adequately.

In succeeding paragraphs particular attention will be given to the first application of conservatism listed above—the policy of understating business assets.

Suppression of Organization and Financing Costs

Deliberate suppression of certain types of asset costs, in certain circumstances, has long been a feature of business accounting, supported in the name of conservatism. An outstanding example is found in the practice of charging to capital "surplus" the costs of organizing an enterprise and raising the necessary funds. Through this practice a part of the stockholder's investment is immediately suppressed, often with no disclosure whatever. This is misrepresentation, the worst possible kind of accounting. A stockholder, for example, invests $100 and under the authority of a state statute permitting part of this amount to be described as paid-in surplus (incidentally a type of statute for which no reasonable justification exists) half of the investment is designated as stated capital and half as capital surplus. Then the organization and financing costs (legal fees, commissions, printing costs, etc.) amounting, for example, to $5 are deducted from so-called capital surplus and the first balance sheet shows assets and stock equity of only $95. This is the same thing as reporting to the stockholder that five per cent of his investment has been lost in the process of bringing the enterprise into being.[2]

Back of this unwarranted policy is a long-standing misconception regarding the nature of a recognizable asset. There is a persistent tendency in accounting circles to assume that there is something questionable, suspect, about any cost not represented by a specific tangible object, something on which one can stub his toe. Actually all necessary costs incurred are on the same basis; they all have equal validity. Assets for accounting purposes are economic measures, not tangible objects in themselves. The only difference between the cost of organizing and financing and the cost of a factory machine, for example, is that the former is applicable to, associated with, the enterprise as a whole, while the latter is peculiarly applicable to, associated with, a specific material object. It is purely a question of classification, not of validity.

There is widespread popular opinion to the effect that the services of promoters, lawyers, accountants, investment bankers, and various other pro-

---

[2] See *Contemporary Accounting* (Chapter 2, p. 13), American Institute of Accountants. [1945]

fessional groups are less productive than the services of carpenters, electricians, bricklayers, etc., and that the costs of services of the first type are at best a necessary evil and cannot possibly give rise to recognizable property. It is a pity to see the accountant, who should be in the forefront of clear thinking on these matters, employing procedures that put him in the position of chiming in with such mistaken views.

Closely related to the policy of suppressing organizing and financing costs is the absorption of goodwill and other intangibles acquired by reducing the initial equity of the stockholder. Without attempting any discussion of the accounting problems associated with intangibles, it may be pointed out that when intangibles having actual value are contributed by the investor, or when contributed funds are used to purchase intangibles, it is downright misstatement to fail to recognize such property in the accounts. Omission of intangibles is just as improper as failure to disclose the tangible resources, and it is misrepresentation, not conservatism, to do either.

Here is one spot at which the legal tradition tends to be more rational than accounting policy. In the eyes of the law all kinds of intangible assets have just as much standing as the so-called tangibles.

Suppression of Plant and Inventory Costs

But omission of asset costs from the accounts is not confined to intangibles. Suppression of costs of buildings and equipment is common practice, and is generally defended as conservative accounting. We are all familiar with the fact that in many enterprises substantial amounts of true additions are charged directly to revenues as maintenance. This practice arises in part from failure to set up procedures for distinguishing sharply between routine servicing of existing assets and acquisition of new elements, and in part from the notion that the cost of a small item, such as a wastebasket for the office, does not deserve recognition as an asset.[3] Another common practice is to neglect to capitalize part or all of transportation and installation costs involved in acquiring plant assets. In numerous instances a deliberate policy of including the cost of improvements in maintenance is followed. Recently I heard of a case where a company spent $10,000 paving a parking lot and charged the entire cost to repairs. Similar examples are not hard to find.

The result of all such practices is persistent understatement of property to an indeterminate amount. That the amount is often substantial can hardly be doubted. The suppression of the cost of one wastebasket isn't a very serious matter, but it must not be forgotten that a multitude of small items may add up to a total of some consequence.

---

[3] See *Accountants' Handbook* (third edition), pp. 659–661.

Lately we are seeing a recurrence of the practice of suppression of an arbitrary fraction of construction cost. The excuse given is that since present-day construction costs are extraordinarily high it is not desirable to burden future revenues with more than, say, sixty per cent of the total expended for the additional facilities. The balance is charged to surplus or surplus reserves. Such practices, common in earlier periods, have been somewhat discredited, and it is to be hoped that the accounting profession will exert all possible influence to prevent their rehabilitation. That plant costs have increased sharply may be considered unfortunate from some points of view, but the condition is part of the present economic picture, and it is hard to see any justification for an accounting based on an arbitrary scaling down of the actual costs of existing property.

The committee on accounting procedure of the American Institute of Accountants has recently taken the position that, in principle, the recognizable cost of inventory assets is total cost.[4] However, the committee makes it plain that—in common with accountants generally—it does not condemn prevailing practices under which some kinds of overhead costs are excluded from cost of inventories (although the committee states that exclusion of all overheads is not acceptable). In many companies, certainly, the cost of inventories determined for statement purposes is substantially less than the total of the costs of all types incurred in the acquisition or production of goods on hand, and it is safe to assume that seldom is the cost overstated.

It does not follow that the position taken by the committee on this point is objectionable. The determination of total inventory cost in particular circumstances is a difficult matter both in concept and in computation. All that can fairly be urged is that accountants should set up as a goal for inventory measurement the total cost incurred represented by the existing inventory, rather than a varying degree of understatement.

Although all costs are basically on the same footing it is hardly practicable, as a rule, to funnel all kinds of costs through inventory accounts. General administration costs and marketing costs are outstanding examples of types of charges usually regarded as noninventoriable. Accountants might well give further attention to the development of methods of applying noninventoriable costs to periodic revenues, with provision for including in assets—under an appropriate heading—the amount of such costs reasonably applicable to the future.

Some Understatement Unavoidable

Recognition of all costs of existing assets, in the broad sense, is probably impossible or impracticable in many cases. Costs of development, experimentation, and sales promotion, for example, incurred after the period of

---

4 *Accounting Research Bulletin*, No. 29. [Now Chap. 4 of *ARB* No. 43, "Restatement and Revision of Accounting Research Bulletins," American Institute of C.P.A., 1953.]

launching in the strict sense is past, are especially hard to deal with accountingwise because of the difficulty of tracing their relation to revenues. Where any cost is incurred prudently and in good faith for the sake of results expected in later periods, such cost belongs, ideally, in the asset total at the end of the year. However, where such costs are more or less regularly incurred it may be decided, as a practical matter, to treat cost incurred in the current period as the equivalent of cost expired in such period, and omit the asset aspect—the momentum built up for the future—from the accounts and reports. Another example is found in the accounting procedures employed and the accumulated records. Few businesses report an asset of this character, although the developed accounting mechanism is obviously a resource. A perfect treatment of this factor would involve careful sorting out and capitalizing of every item of cost which contributes to the building up of the system and its future use coupled with a scheme of amortization conforming to the "wearing out," expiration, of the component elements of the system. The difficulty of carrying out such a program in a satisfying manner and without undue expense is obvious. A similar situation is found in the training of personnel. Money spent to acquire staff and develop employee skills need not be considered to be wasted, and the effect on production of cost incurred may not all be registered currently. However, few would be willing to urge the desirability of giving definite asset recognition, in all businesses, to the costs of personnel development applicable to the future.

But to acknowledge the complications involved in accounting for all assets is a far cry from a policy of deliberate understatement all along the line. As suggested in the preceding comment relative to inventories, the standard should be full disclosure of all resources, and in general the burden of proof should be on the person suggesting suppression in whole or in part.

Premature Writeoff

Closely allied to practices involving immediate suppression of assets is the policy of initial recognition followed by arbitrary, premature absorption. Before the days of stated value and capital surplus organization, financing, and development costs were commonly set up as deferred charges, and writeoff was undertaken rapidly as soon as revenues appeared in substantial volume. The usual recommendation in the auditing textbooks was absorption in two or three years. In the case of goodwill and allied intangibles, likewise, it has long been common practice to write off the total cost as soon as this could be done without impairing the showing of income too seriously, without regard to the actual status of the assets.[5]

With respect to tangible assets, sentiment in favor of writeoff during a

---

[5] In *Accounting Research Bulletin* No. 24, [now Chap. 5 of *ARB* No. 431], issued by the Institute's committee on accounting procedure, a more sound position is taken.

shorter period than the probable economic life of the property has not been so strong, although numerous cases of overdepreciation are found in practice. There is considerable support for the view that business management should have a wide latitude in the treatment of depreciation for income-tax purposes, and during the recent war years rapid amortization of emergency facilities acquired under certificates of necessity was authorized by Congress.

A distinction should be drawn between (1) deliberate, arbitrary writeoff and (2) a depreciation or amortization procedure, carefully planned, that results in too-rapid extinguishment in view of the actual life of the property. The first is objectionable and should be resisted, not encouraged, by accountants. The second situation is bound to develop from time to time in view of the intrinsic difficulty of predicting useful life in the particular environment with reasonable accuracy.

Restoration of Costs

Where it has become clear that costs have been absorbed prematurely through excessive depreciation or amortization accruals, what, if anything, should be done by way of revising past accounting? A sharp difference of opinion with respect to this question has developed. Some hold that no retroactive adjustment is permissible, under established accounting procedures, but that it is proper to spread the remaining cost, if any, over the remaining life as currently estimated. According to the opposing view, the sound procedure is to reëstimate carefully the over-all service life in the light of the new conditions and adjust the accrued depreciation of amortization appropriately, thus in effect reinstating an amount of cost equal to the past overstatement of depreciation or amortization charges.

To the writer the latter seems to be the only defensible position. It is unfortunate if past accounting has proved to be inaccurate, but it is incompetence if no correcting adjustment is made. The process of determining periodic income is beset with all manner of difficulties and it would seem to be obvious that all available information should be used to the full in carrying out the process. This means that methods and policies employed should be regularly scrutinized in the light of the facts at hand, and that correction and revision are bound to be called for from time to time. The question the accountant should keep in the forefront of his thinking is: how good a job can I do in measuring the performance of the enterprise in the current and future years? If it is definitely known that costs applicable to the current and future have been written off in the past, an adjustment of past reckoning is imperative; otherwise new misstatements, that might be avoided, are added to past mistakes.

In the discussion of this subject at the 1946 annual meeting of the American Accounting Association, H. C. Greer argued that a decision once made as to depreciation or amortization "should be considered irrevocable. . . . The selected assignment may prove to be ill-advised in the light of subsequent events, but the decision, like many others in life, can be made only once."[6] I find it difficult to find any justification for such a position. If the accountant is to furnish owners and managers with the most accurate and dependable measurements possible in view of the available data, he cannot be denied the right to correct errors and revise computations proved to have been "ill-advised." He must not permit the entries of the past to tie his hands; the use of hindsight must not be taboo. No statistician would think for a moment of permitting himself to be strait-jacketed by his past efforts. Why should the acountant? If accounting is to be a professional activity requiring the use of judgment, rather than a rigid formula, the propriety of revising earlier assignments of cost—when changing conditions convincingly demonstrate the invalidity of such assignments—must be recognized.

Everyone admits that when circumstances indicate that costs have not been written off fast enough something must be done about it. In the discussion referred to above, for example, Mr. Greer points out that if the decision as to depreciation or amortization "was not conservative enough the depreciation rate must be accelerated, or a special charge must be made against the current year to increase the accumulated depreciation allowance to the proper figure." If this is sound what is there but sheer prejudice standing in the way of making an adjustment to *decrease* the accumulated depreciation allowance to the proper figure if circumstances develop that demonstrate that costs have been written off too rapidly? If the depreciation allowance can be corrected in one direction, why can't it be corrected in the other?

E. L. Kohler, in opposing restoration, stressed the idea that the results of carefully considered, deliberate accounting judgments "should stand for all time. . . . Decisions arrived at through the exercise of good sense and contemporary good judgment should not be overruled at a later date."[7] Here the implication is present that if a downright error was made at the outset, or if good judgment and good faith were not exercised, correction would be in order. It is hard to find a reasonable basis for distinguishing between blunders or evil deeds on the one hand and good intentions on the other, with respect to adjusting entries, if the effects are the same. Past accounting for costs may be unsatisfactory because of clerical mistakes, arbitrary or questionable policy, or careful procedures that have turned out badly in view of subsequent events, but the problem of revision remains unaffected: shall an adjustment be made that permits presentation of statements of future years uninfluenced by the known defects in such past accounting? Aside from this angle it may be noted again that there is nothing sacred about an accounting judgment

---

6 "Restoration of Fixed Asset Values" (second negative), *Accounting Review,* April, 1947.

7 *Op. cit.* (first negative).

and the resulting measurement, no matter how competent the accountant. Accounting conclusions are reached—or should be—with due regard for the economic environment at the time, and with changed conditions they lose their force and validity. They don't "stand for all time."

Problem of Emergency Facilities

The problem of what to do about amortized "emergency facilities" having substantial peacetime usefulness has been, of course, the principal factor giving rise to the recent discussions of restoration of asset costs prematurely absorbed. At the end of the emergency period in 1945 many companies found themselves with plants the costs of which had been fully amortized from the balance-sheet and had been completely depreciated in the accounts. In some instances these facilities were the major asset of the company. In this situation questions naturally arose regarding the validity of omitting amortized facilities from the balance-sheet and of omitting depreciation thereon from future income statements.

The committee on accounting procedure of the American Institute of Accountants has issued a bulletin[8] dealing with this subject in which the very cautious position is taken that in cases where the facilities have "a substantial usefulness and worth for peacetime production" and as a result of following income-tax amortization in the accounts have been entirely or approximately written off "careful consideration of the conditions may show that an adjustment of the recorded amortization or depreciation of such facilities is appropriate." The committee stresses the point that "useful financial statements are not achieved by an understatement or an overstatement of asset carrying value...accompanied by overstatement or understatement of future income because of materially excessive or deficient prior allocations of costs." The committee also emphasizes the fact that "it does not favor an adjustment of the accumulated amortization or depreciation in cases in which such an adjustment would not have a substantial effect upon the representations that will be made in future financial statements."

In view of the very mild tone of this bulletin it is somewhat surprising that there were six dissents. The general position of those dissenting seems to be that they—like Mr. Greer and Mr. Kohler—are unwilling to recognize a *decrease* in the accrued depreciation total, regardless of the circumstances. They do admit, however, that "a full disclosure of the facts regarding any significant amount of fully amortized emergency facilities or any other fully depreciated fixed assets still in use" is desirable. It is hard to see much difference between the treatment authorized by the majority and "full disclosure."

---

8 *Accounting Research Bulletin* No. 27. [Now Chap. 9(c) of *ARB* No. 43.]

The committee does not specifically suggest how the credit resulting from decreasing the total accrued allowance for depreciation should be handled. Past overstatement of depreciation, of course, means that net income and earnings retained have been correspondingly understated (ignoring the technical possibility that a portion of the depreciation charges may not yet have been charged to revenues). I believe the best treatment is to report the credit arising in the current combined income and surplus statement, specifically labeled as a correction of earnings through the years the excessive charges were recorded.

"Double Recovery"

Aside from prejudice against any adjustment that results in increasing the total of assets recognized, the principal line of objection to restoration to the accounts of any portion of the cost of amortized plant facilities seems to be based on the view that, since the total cost of the facilities was deducted from wartime revenues for tax purposes, and was similarly handled in the accounts (which was usually the case), the total cost has been fully recovered and is not recoverable a second time. The company with a fully amortized plant, so the story goes, should give the interests of the peacetime consumer some thought, and should not expect selling prices to cover asset costs already profitably recovered.

Even in this period of a generally low level of economic thinking this is an amazing position, lacking in justification in terms of either equity or of economic principle, and it is very discouraging to find accountants being taken in by such ideas. If there were only one producer and one consumer, whose activities were controlled by contract or by governmental authority, it might make some sense. This condition could be said to be approached in a state where a single government entity assumed direct control of the production and distribution of all economic goods and set prices in such manner that the total of all prices for all products covered the total of all costs incurred, plus such margin as might be established by government policy. But even in this situation there would remain the practical problems of allocation of resources and efforts between lines of production and preservation of equity between consumers of various products; and I don't think that it is at all obvious that the governmental entity would ignore the existence of valuable resources in its accounting, whatever the previous statistical determinations might have been, or would endeavor to search out the consumers of particular products in the past for the purpose of making rebates to cover errors in the accounting for costs. For example, if in the coal production department of such a state enterprise it was discovered that the cost of a coal deposit and all operating charges had been covered by sales made to customers before the deposit was fully exhausted, I doubt if it would be considered desirable to donate to either past or future buyers of coal the value—in situ—of the remaining coal as it was mined and delivered.

During the recent war many business concerns were producing materials directly or indirectly for government use, and in view of all the circumstances —and notwithstanding the fact that cost-plus contracts as such were not permitted—there is a rough reasonableness in saying that the government consumer undertook to pay prices covering total cost and some "fair" amount of return on investment. This was not the explicit formula but was nevertheless the unexpressed approximate goal of the sum total of relationships and measurements embodied in specific contracts, auditing programs, renegotiation procedure, taxation, and general attitudes and policies. Even so, specific guaranties were lacking, risks were assumed, costs varied, profits were not uniform, there were special concessions and subsidies, and so on. In the case of emergency facilities, constructed under certificates of necessity, it was proposed by some that it would not be inequitable for the government to take title, at the end of the war, to fully amortized facilities, and this idea had merit and was considered by Congress. However, it is important to remember that *this provision was not included;* in other words, the arrangement finally adopted provided for a contingent tax subsidy in the form of any value to the owners the amortized facilities might have in subsequent peacetime operation. Perhaps the wrong decision was made; that's a moot point. At any rate this concession was made; the amortized properties remain the properties of the private owners; there seems to be no likelihood that the government will pass retroactive legislation designed to confiscate such properties. Moreover, if the contingent subsidy that was granted were retroactively canceled, the consumer entitled to the benefit would be the consumer of the wartime products, presumably the government in one form or another. What possible reason is there for the notion that the amount of this subsidy, definitely granted by the government as part of a complex scheme of taxation, should be turned over, gratis, to the consumers of the peacetime products of the converted war plants?

With a return to peacetime operation, and a relaxing of government controls to a considerable degree, the bulk of business activity is being carried on under at least semicompetitive conditions and with a price system which in most cases reflects the attitudes and activities of many producers and consumers. As I pointed out in the preceding paper, in a system of private enterprise, with any substantial degree of competitive operation, prices are not determined by the specific costs of specific producers, either as reflected in their books of account or as otherwise computed. Prices in such a situation are the resultants of many influences operating both from the producing and consuming sides of the market. Producers in the same line have varying costs, varying efficiencies, and varying fortunes, but in general they dispose of their production in the same market at the going market price. It is recognized that some producers may lose money for considerable periods, and may even go to the wall without ever experiencing profitable operation. Risks are assumed; no one is guaranteed either costs or costs plus; particular recorded costs are not the measure of prices to the particular producer. At a particular instant the cost of the particular producer might happen to coincide with the market price of his product, but this condition would only be a coincidence and would presumably not long persist. Cost calculations are useful in many ways, including the general purpose of ascertaining how much the concern is making or losing, but they do not in themselves either control or measure selling prices.

Utilization of Amortized Facilities

War facilities that were fully amortized for tax purposes and in the accounts, but have been found to have substantial usefulness for peacetime production, are valuable private property and should be utilized accordingly. Such assets should not be ignored or neglected, nor put to inferior uses, because of their past tax and accounting history. Surely we can all agree that business management should act prudently and sensibly in the administration of any and all available resources. The origin of particular assets and earlier decisions and interpretations with respect to particular assets should not tie the hands of owners and their representatives when it comes to the very practical question of utilizing such assets to the best advantage in the future. This is just as true of property acquired by gift or subsidy as it is of property that cost something, and it is equally true of property that had a cost but has no present book value because of either outright errors or judgments that have ben proved invalid by subsequent events. The statistical record is only a record; it neither destroys property nor brings it into being. In other words, if for any reason—whether it be a mere fetish or prejudice or something better—continuing omission or statement at less than immediate value is tolerated, certainly we cannot tolerate careless or inefficient use, or decisions of any kind that are based on accounting data alone. If the accounts—in the narrow sense—don't tell the story, the significant data should be available in supplementary statistical form, and should be used wherever needed in internal cost compilations and in all questions involving administration of the available resources. We must not adopt the attitude of the office manager who, when he heard that one of the girls had let a bookkeeping machine roll down a stairway, to its irretrievable ruin, asked frantically if it was one of the fully amortized units or one of those still on the books and, when told it was the former, said, "Thank God for that." Obviously, if the wrecked and previously amortized machine could furnish as much and as good service, for as long a time, as one of the machines which had not been written off, the loss in productive property to the business, and to the investors, is just as great as it would have been if one of the machines which still had a book value had gone down the stairway.

If these observations regarding utilization are sound—and they seem to me to be indisputable—the question may be asked once more: is it reasonable to insist that the vital, essential information regarding property must continue to be omitted from the accounts? Whose function is it to provide the necessary data, if not the accountant's?

Assets Acquired without Cost

Another questionable aspect of accounting practice, often resulting in substantial understatement of property, is the tendency to neglect to recognize assets acquired without cost, or assets having values substantially in excess of related costs. Important resources are sometimes acquired by gift, discovery (e.g., a mineral deposit), invention, and unexpected recovery (e.g., a plant in a foreign country previously treated as lost). It is usually agreed that property received through inheritance or donation should be recorded at fair market value as of date of acquisition, and there is some support for the view that receivables, securities, and other property recovered after having been written off as worthless should be restored to the accounts in terms of recovered values. When it comes to assets acquired through exploration, invention, and development, however, prevailing opinion seems to be that accounting recognition is improper, except to the extent of costs incurred, even where the amount of cost is negligible by comparison with the value of the resulting property. In some cases adherence to this tradition results in omission from the accounts and statements of the major elements of property owned by the enterprise.

Assets originating through physical growth and reproduction—accretion— are likewise generally ignored by the accounting process. As a rule, indeed, not even the applicable costs are capitalized. The result is that the property accounts of nurseries, plantations, lumber companies, and related concerns are often not worth the paper they are written on. Not long ago an important corporation, operating numerous tracts of timber on a continuing production basis, sold a relatively small part of its holdings for more than the remaining book value of all tracts owned. Years of conventional depletion accounting, coupled with a complete lack of recognition of accretion, was of course responsible for this weird condition. It should be fairly obvious that a policy of excluding resources acquired by accretion will in time render the accounts useless in such cases as a basis for managerial conclusions, and that such policy is as inherently unreasonable as it would be for a rancher to refuse to bring the new lambs into the corral because he couldn't find purchase invoices for them.

Limitations of Cost Basis[9]

Where assets are acquired by purchase the cost incurred is the natural starting point for the accounting record; for all such acquisitions cost is generally the best available evidence of the actual market value of the elements acquired. On the other hand, where assets are acquired directly from investors, or in other special ways as outlined above, the proper starting point for accounting is estimated fair market value at date of acquisition (or at the end of the accounting period in which acquired). Thus it is really values that are the basic data of accounting, and costs are important only because they are the most dependable measures of initial values of goods and services flowing into the enterprise through ordinary market transactions.

Subsequent accounting for costs (and values recognized in lieu of costs) depends upon the nature of the resources acquired and other circumstances. In the case of current factors, passing through the business in a relatively short period, cost—initial value—may serve adequately in most cases to represent the economic significance of the factor throughout such period. In the case of long-lived elements, however, passage of time and use in operation may require gradual absorption through depreciation or amortization reckonings, and changes in economic conditions and prices may render the recorded cost data unreliable or even misleading for the purposes accounting is supposed to serve.

The central problem of accounting today is the development of ways and means of making accounting effective to meet the needs of private business enterprise in the face of major movements in the level of prices. And taking the position that the accounting mechanism can deal only with cost data, and that adjustment or revision of recorded figures is improper, is simply evading the issue. In times like these it is more than ever necessary that management and owners be provided with actual, pertinent facts, and that business activity be accurately interpreted to all interested parties. If the accountant is to measure up to the requirements of this situation he must do something more than swear renewed allegiance to prevailing conventions and procedures.

Where recorded cost data are completely out of line with present values it can hardly be denied that such data have largely lost their validity as bases for managerial or ownership decisions. As Professor Dohr points out: "...the *present value* of property is, generally speaking, the measurement of out-

---

9 See "Cost and Value in Accounting," *The Journal of Accountancy*, March, 1946.

standing importance; it indicates...what the owner may expect to realize upon sale; it determines his borrowing capacity...; it fixes his liability for various forms of taxation;...it is the basis upon which the property may be insured."[10]

Current Prices and Depreciation

The particular phase of the problem of cost and value on which attention has been centered in recent months is the question of the basis of the depreciation charge in view of the advance of prices in general and of building and equipment costs in particular. Numerous articles dealing with this subject have appeared in the technical journals and in the newspapers, and statements have been issued by a number of business and professional groups, including the committee on accounting procedure of the American Institute of Accountants.[11] Adjusted depreciation charges have been reported in some corporate statements. There has been considerable discussion of the possibility of a revision of income-tax rules governing depreciation deductions.

Depreciation charges based on recorded dollar costs are undoubtedly subject to serious criticism at the present time, particularly in the case of concerns with important plants acquired at much lower prices than those now prevailing. With labor and materials and most other charges on a current basis, the reporting of depreciation in terms of an earlier price level produces a hodge-podge total of revenue deductions and a questionable if not downright misleading figure of net income. In this situation there is substantial justification for the view that actual cost—in the sense of economic sacrifice—is understated, with consequent overstatement of earnings. If a building, for example, cost $1,000,000 to construct ten years ago, and the same facility would cost $3,000,000 to replace today, it may be urged that depreciation based on $1,000,000 represents only a third of real cost, expressed in the current, cheaper dollar. In other words, there is merit in the proposition that replacement cost measures true cost more reliably than does so-called "actual" cost.

Advocates of adjustment of depreciation under present conditions have made too much of the point that charges based on recorded costs are inadequate to provide for replacement at current prices. Depreciation charges, like other costs, don't "provide" anything. The main objective in setting up any cost is the correct reporting of costs and of net earnings. Funds are provided by the flow of receipts from customers and the amount of that flow—assuming competitive operation—is only indirectly affected, if at all,

---

10 James L. Dohr, "Cost and Value," *The Journal of Accountancy,* March, 1944.

11 *Accounting Research Bulletin* No. 33 [now Chap. 9(a) of *ARB* No. 43]. One of the best discussions available is found in "Depreciation Policy and the Postwar Price Level," issued by Machinery and Allied Products Institute.

by cost reckonings and assignments. Depreciation accounting is required in the case of wasting enterprises, where replacement is not contemplated, as well as in continuing undertakings. Moreover, the ultimate cost of replacement is not known, and is difficult to estimate, particularly where facilities may not be replaced in kind. The matter of real concern, on which attention should be concentrated, is the proper reporting of the cost of using *existing* facilities and of the amount of net earnings. Such reporting furnishes a general guide for those charged with financial administration, but should not be confused with either broad or specific fund programs.

Methods of Handling
Current Depreciation Problem

The accountant should not permit the present anxieties of managers and owners to pressure him into unsound procedures, but he should recognize that there is a serious problem involved and should take steps to deal with it effectively. One possibility is that of reporting supplementary data, with full explanations, designed to bring out sharply the limitations of the conventional, unadjusted figures under existing conditions. By this means the fact that depreciation is understated and net income correspondingly overstated can be pointed out to management, owners, and other interested parties, and a warning sounded with respect to dividend policies and other aspects of financial administration. In fact this is the least that can be done; failure to make such computations and disclosures in current periodic reports is inexcusable. Along with this, in internal departmental accounting, should go the preparation of supplementary cost determinations and analyses designed to provide those responsible with the data required for intelligent decisions as to utilization of facilities and other administrative matters.

Another possibility is the determination of the replacement costs of plant facilities and the introduction of such data into the formal scheme of ledger accounts in such manner as to provide for accruing depreciation in replacement cost and at the same time preserving recorded cost figures. Periodically, under this "compromise" procedure, the amount of "absorbed appreciation" would be charged to the equity adjustment account established when replacement costs were recognized, and credited to net earnings, as a final step in income measurement.[12]

The third available method is essentially that of the thoroughgoing accounting adjustment or "quasi." Under this procedure present values are substituted for recorded costs in the accounts, and the amount of the equity adjustment is either formally or informally capitalized. Thereafter depreciation charges are based on established present values and net earnings are

---

[12] For a complete outline of this procedure see *Accountants' Handbook* (third edition), section 14.

reported on the revised basis without any further adjustment. This treatment, presumably, should be undertaken only where there is a marked disparity between recorded figures and current values and it is clear that the
interests of managers and owners can be best served by making a "fresh
start" as far as plant accounting is concerned.

It should be emphasized that if accounting adjustments are made they
should be handled in an orderly, systematic manner and with complete disclosure. Arbitrary increasing or decreasing of the depreciation charge, with
no concurrent revision of the basic figures on which depreciation is computed, cannot be supported by the accountant.

Misstatement of Assets
and Earning Power

The foregoing discussion boils down to a plea for complete disclosure, at
significant figures, of the total assets of the business enterprise, as opposed
to current policies of omission, premature absorption, and understatement in
varying degrees. A major reason for urging reform in this direction is the
danger at the present time to property rights, and the institution of private
enterprise itself, in persistent misstatement of existing assets. Even in this
country we have gone an amazingly long way down the road of curtailment
of private initiative, impairment of private property, and state control, and
there are many in our midst, including important groups in government, who
are bent on going the whole distance and are quite willing to use any means
at hand—including accounting—to gain their ends. And it has become increasingly evident, during the past ten years, that those who favor complete
governmental control of business, with private ownership hamstrung and
withering away, are stanch supporters—during a period of rising prices—of
rigid adherence to the so-called cost basis of accounting and resist at every
point efforts to make accounts more sensitive to changing economic conditions and hence more useful to managers and owners. These groups, indeed,
are not even willing to permit the gradual adjustment that conventional
accounting provides in its recognition of new costs as a result of transfers
between business entities and continuing substitution of new elements of
property by acquisition on the market. Thus we have seen revision downward of recorded costs—often on very questionable grounds—required of
many utility enterprises, while at the same time restoration of cost factors
prematurely written off was denied simply by attaching the label "reaccount-
ing"; we have seen developed—primarily in the utility field but with some
tendency to spill over into other lines—the idea that a new cost, completely
valid, can't be established by transfer from one owner to another in the
same field of industry; we have seen the fantastic proposition advanced—and
apparently upheld by the "courts"—that if two parties are to any appreciable

degree affiliated, transfers must be accounted for as if made at recorded cost to the vendor without regard to fair market value at date of transfer—although this flies in the face of accounting axiom, sound business administration, and established rules of equity. With these conditions there is some reason for being alarmed by the condition of the property accounts of many business enterprises and the continued use of procedures that result in understatement. There would certainly be a great confiscation of private property if the state were to take over business concerns at present book values.

Assuming for the sake of discussion that there is no immediate danger of wholesale state condemnation of business property, there remains the very obvious fact that regulation of business—outside the utility field—has proceeded apace and that the concepts of "fair price" and "fair return" are becoming more and more potent in business generally, in wage disputes, and in other connections. In other words, the matter of earning *rates,* always intrinsically important to managers and owners, has become one of wide public interest. Now, what does substantial understatement of resources employed do to a computed earning rate? The effect, obviously, is a more or less serious overstatement of earning power. At the present time, it is safe to say, most calculated rates of return based on accounting data are substantially in excess of the returns actually being earned. This is not a good situation, either from the standpoint of the parties immediately interested or from the standpoint of the relation of private enterprise to employees, consumers, government, or the general public.

Interest in earning rates is likely to wax rather than wane, and this is not in itself unreasonable or undesirable. Earning power is perhaps the outstanding fact of any business enterprise. But present accounting data are not satisfactory in this connection, and present accounting methods require improvement if reliable, significant data regarding rates of return for business concerns are to be made available. As has been pointed out many times in recent years, people generally have rather wild ideas about business earnings.[13] It has also often been pointed out that popular sentiment unfavorable to private enterprise is often largely founded on misconceptions and inaccurate data. In the light of these considerations the accountant needs to become more alive to his obligations to business and to the community, and he should undertake to improve his procedures, and abandon unsound conventions, without delay.

It has been popular of late, in accounting circles, to emphasize the importance of the income statement and minimize the financial position statement. This emphasis on income determination is not undesirable, but it must not be forgotten that the income statement alone is useless as a means of computing earning power, rate of return. For this purpose the data of resources employed are just as essential as the income figures.

---

[13] See, for example, Frank M. Surface, "Penalties of Economic Ignorance," an address before 1946 conference of New England Council.

Part Three

Price Level Changes

Max J. Wasserman

ACCOUNTING PRACTICE IN FRANCE DURING THE PERIOD OF MONETARY INFLATION (1919-1927)

Max Judd Wasserman *was born in Missouri in 1895, received his A.B. from Cornell (1918), and a D.Econ. from Lyons, France (1925). He taught at Illinois from 1925–1934 and has been at Kentucky since 1959. In the intervening period he worked with various governmental agencies. He has written extensively in the field of international economics.*

The article reprinted here is an excellent prelude to the next one by H. W. Sweeney. It is valuable mainly for its detailed description of what the French actually did in their accounts and financial statements during the decade following World War I. During the period reviewed by Wasserman, the French price level doubled (approximately), which is about the magnitude of the change in the U.S. price level in the decade following World War II. The French experience is, therefore, closer to our own than the runaway inflations of central Europe and China.

I. Introduction

During and after the World War, France, like many other belligerents, failed to meet her current budgetary expenditures from the revenues arising from taxation. The deficit each year was met by borrowing: the Bank of France made large loans to the government and the state had recourse to borrowing on both the domestic and foreign markets. With each loan which the Bank of France made the government, its bank note circulation was increased. Specie payments were stopped and France was, temporarily at least, on an irredeemable paper money standard. Through this process, as the following table, number 1, will show, the note circulation of the Bank of France increased steadily between 1914 and 1927. This large increase, almost

Reprinted from *The Accounting Review* (March, 1931), pp. 1–29, by permission.

Table I

NOTE CIRCULATION OF THE BANK OF FRANCE IN BILLIONS OF FRANCS[1]

1913	5.7	1921	37.7
1914	7.3	1922	36.4
1915	12.3	1923	37.4
1916	15.6	1924	39.9
1917	19.8	1925	44.1
1918	27.8	1926	53.4
1919	34.7	1927	53.5
1920	38.2		

tenfold, in the emission of irredeemable paper money constituted fiat money inflation of perhaps the simplest and most direct type.

The table, number 2, shows the government borrowing through the emission of bonds and notes. This great increase in the public indebtedness gave rise to indirect inflation, to which some economists have given the name of

Table II

THE FRENCH PUBLIC DEBT IN BILLIONS OF FRANCS[2]

	Consolidated Debt	Floating Debt	Foreign Debt
1913	25.3	1.5	0.0
1918	64.4	33.5	20.4
1919	61.5	56.0	27.3
1920	91.2	79.2	63.4
1921	118.6	86.1	75.2
1922	118.8	87.1	74.9
1923	110.7	89.2	117.0
1924	110.5	87.0	139.0
1925	111.0	86.6	136.0
1926	116.9	93.4	196.0
1927	121.2	93.5	178.0

"credit inflation." Though its action may be indirect, it is none the less real, because, by reason of the loans the purchasing power of the French people was increased. In the case of the domestic debt, both consolidated and floating, we have first a mere transfer of purchasing power from the subscribers to the loan to the government and then from the government to its functionaries and purveyors in the form of salaries and payments for merchandise. But the bonds, once in the hands of the public, were used as collateral to secure loans from the banks, constituting an increase in, or an inflation of credit. Through the operation of the foreign loans, the bonds

---

[1] Source: The *Annuaire Statistique* published by the Statistique Générale de la France, vol. 44, 1928, p. 83 of the section entitled, *Résumé Rétrospectif*. The figures presented show the yearly average circulation.

[2] Source: *ibid*. p. 162. The figures given represent the situation of the public debt on the first of January of each year.

found their way into the hands of foreigners, and the funds received by the French were used largely to pay for goods purchased abroad. But some of the proceeds of these loans were employed in the domestic market thus making for an increase in the French purchasing power and constituting inflation.

The results of this inflation were far-reaching and many new problems were created for the business man. Depending upon the attitude one holds with reference to the quantity theory of money, inflation either created these problems through its effect in bringing about a very rapid increase in prices, or these problems, created by other economic processes than by action on prices, finally resulted in a marked increase in prices. Whatever merits these two opposing views may have, an important problem for the individual business unit was either brought about by this increase in prices, or manifested itself in the form of an increase in prices. Another problem arose from the fact that the franc depreciated on the foreign exchanges, while a third problem was due to the fact that all prices did not respond in the same manner to inflation conditions; that is, some prices rose more rapidly than others. Finally a fourth problem was brought about by the failure of French gold prices to maintain the same level as did prices in countries on a gold standard. Table number 3 shows the movements of various price series during the period 1919–1927. Although, as the preceding tables indicated, inflation existed from 1914 to 1927, the war period, 1914–1918 has been eliminated in this study.[3] Column 1 of the table gives the figures of a general wholesale price index.[4] Column 2 shows an index of Franco-American exchange rates.[5] Column 3 gives the movement of French wholesale prices expressed in terms of dollars[6] for comparison with the wholesale prices in the United States which are given in column 4.[7] Columns 5 to 11 inclusive give the figures for French retail prices,[8] industrial goods,[9] agricultural

---

[3] During the war period French economic life was largely oriented towards the problem of national defense. The effects of inflation on prices were obscured by the heavy demand for the products of the war industries, the light demand for the products of the others, the curtailed supplies of materials and men, the government regulations and price fixing, the heavy imports of goods, and the "pegging" of the exchange rates. It was not until 1919 that the full effects of inflation upon prices could be isolated and studied.

[4] *Annuaire Statistique de la Statistique Générale de la France,* vol. 44, 1928, p. 115 of the section *entitled, Résumé Rétrospectif.* Base: July, 1914.

[5] The index of Franco-American exchange rates is regularly published in the *Bulletin de la Statistique Générale de la France.* This was the source of the index.

[6] Data published in the *Bulletin de la Statistique Générale de la France.* Base is July, 1914.

[7] This is the wholesale price index of the Bureau of Labor changed, for purposes of comparison with the French indices, to a July, 1914 base. In this form, it is regularly published in the *Bulletin de la Statistique Générale de la France.*

[8] Taken from the *Annuaire Statistique de la Statistique Générale de la France,* vol. 44, 1928, p. 116 of the *Résumé Rétrospectif* section. Base: July, 1914.

[9] The figures given were taken from the issues of the *Bulletin de la Statistique Générale de la France* published during the period covered, where they appeared regularly. Base: 1901–1910.

goods,[10] textiles,[11] minerals and metals,[12] domestic goods,[13] and imported goods.[14]

Such inflation is not without its effect upon accounting. Since accounting attempts to interpret the results of business operations in terms of prices, to show, at given periods, the financial situation of a business in terms of prices, and since the only calculus which it employs is cast likewise in prices and the only values with which it deals are price values, the rapid increase in prices rendered the results of ordinary accounting methods unsatisfactory. The usual accounting methods failed to show with any accuracy both the results of business operations and the position of the business unit at given financial dates. Accounting has also the function of furnishing the business enterpriser with precise reports and data for the determination of the policy and the control of his business. The movements of prices at this time rendered the usual accounting data and reports incomplete—often misleading—to such a point that accounting no longer, under its usual methods, constituted a sure guide. The following section will show the nature of these accounting difficulties,[15] while a succeeding section will show the various means devised to meet these new problems, and a final section will indicate the extent to which these various means were used, as well as present briefly the results of their use, and indicate some possible conclusions to be drawn for the general science of accounting as it is at present practiced.

II.   Accounting Problems Presented by Inflation Prices

In general accounting practice it is customary to enter the items in the books at the prices stipulated in the instruments giving rise to the accounting entry or at the current market value for entries which do not result from a transaction. In times of monetary stability this procedure is satisfactory, for the market values expressed in the books of account remain relatively the same over short periods of time, at least. Thus, the financial statements

---

10 The figures were taken from the issues of the *Bulletin de la Statistique Générale de la France* published during the period covered. Base, 1901–1910 = 100.

11 Base: 1901–1910. Source: *Bulletin de la Statistique Générale de la France* issued during the period covered.

12 Base: 1901–1910. Source: *Bulletin de la Statistique Générale de la France.*

13 Base: July, 1914. Source: *Bulletin de la Statistique Générale de la France,* with the exception of the data for 1922, which were incorrectly given in this *Bulletin.* The correct figures for this year were furnished by an employée of the *Statistique Générale.*

14 Base: July, 1914. Source: *Bulletin de la Statistique Générale de la France.*

15 The increase in prices was not the only movement that these indices present. If the monthly data were given, some of them would show a seasonal variation, and all of them would show the cyclical movement of the periods 1919–1922, 1923–1924, and 1925–1927. The upward secular trend of the series was not steady, but tended to move in cycles. It was during the upward swing of these cycles, especially in 1925–1926, that the accounting difficulties were particularly manifest. From a point of view of price theory, however, it is important to notice that the response of prices to inflation did not result in a smooth ascending movement.

Table III

INDICES OF THE MOVEMENTS OF FRENCH PRICES DURING INFLATION, 1919–1927

(Average Monthly Price)

	1	2	3	4	5	6	7	8	9	10	11
Year	General Wholesale Prices	Franco-American Exchange Rate	French Wholesale Prices in Dollars	Wholesale Prices in the United States	General Retail Prices	Prices of Industrial Goods	Prices of Agricultural Goods	Prices of Textile Products	Prices of Minerals and Metals	Prices of Domestic Goods	Prices of Imported Goods
1919	364	141	268	215	260	430	389	520	327	386	323
1920	519	283	187	244	371	635	532	863	538	513	534
1921	352	257	137	155	337	389	410	416	330	389	287
1922	334	238	141	154	301	379	373	457	323	355	295
1923	428	319	134	159	332	506	458	656	470	441	405
1924	499	373	134	155	380	598	523	849	526	489	516
1925	561	410	138	164	425	691	565	951	616	533	612
1926	718	607	119	156	554	876	732	1,095	873	667	810
1927	630	492	129	150	557	732	691	888	687	626	658

at the end of the year ordinarily indicated with reasonable veracity the financial position of the business and the results of the year's operations. In periods of rapidly depreciating paper money accompanied by equally rapidly increasing prices, as was the case in France during the period 1919–1927, this practice ceased to give truthful results. An example will illustrate this fact. A French enterprise founded before the war did business steadily throughout the war and inflation periods. The balance sheet of the firm, as of December 31, 1926, let it be assumed, presented the following figures:

Assets

	francs
Plant	100,000
Equipment	50,000
Inventory	25,000
Accounts Rec.	25,000
Cash	10,000
	210,000

Liabilities

	francs
Capital Stock	75,000
Bonds	50,000
Depreciation	60,000
Reserves	5,000
Accounts Payable	15,000
Surplus	5,000
	210,000

This balance sheet does not give a true picture of the business. In the first place, the plant, acquired before the war, is worth much more in terms of paper francs than 100,000 francs—it would cost six or seven times as much to reproduce. The same remark is also true as regards the equipment. It must be carefully noted, though, that the increase in paper franc value of these two items is not appreciation—it might properly be termed quasi-appreciation—and the readjustment of this account, as will be seen later, should not be handled as real appreciation.

The book value of the inventory, entered at cost, no longer reflects anything approaching the real market value of the stocks, although this account is more accurate than plant and equipment. The degree of exactitude of its book value depends upon the period of turnover of the business in question. The stocks of raw materials, goods in process, and manufactured goods were gradually acquired during the past few months. The book value of those elements recently acquired will be more accurate than that of those acquired at earlier dates. It is evident that a thorough re-evaluation of these accounts is needed.

The book value of accounts receivable is exact. This account is based upon contractual agreements with the customers of the firm who agreed to pay a definite sum in paper francs. No matter how far the franc depreciates, or how high the general level of prices goes, they cannot be obliged to pay more than the stipulated amount.[16] The cash account is also exact. It is evident that the cash on hand does not increase with the general level of prices, and that the bank cannot be forced to pay its depositors any more than they have deposited in terms of paper francs. But the paper franc value of these two accounts tells us very little about their actual purchasing power. The decline in their purchasing power, as will later be seen, constitutes a real loss to the business. The loss on this account should properly be shown in the books. Ordinary accounting methods, as the balance sheet shows, fail to do this.

On the liability side of the balance sheet the capital stock account, expressing a legal relationship, must always remain exact. Further, the nominal value carried on the books is of but little consequence since it corresponds but little to reality. A share of capital stock represents a residual interest in the assets of the business, and in practice the par or book value of a share seldom corresponds to any real value. The movement towards the use of no par value stock in America is an evidence of this fact.

The account for bonds is also always exact since it expresses a legal relation. The corporation can only be obliged to pay back the bonds in terms of nominal francs.[17] However, the depreciation of the purchasing power of the bonds constitutes an element of profit for the business which classical inflation theorists have long stressed. Unfortunately the books do not show this gain and it would be wise to install an accounting method which would bring out this element of profit.

Depreciation presented a different problem which, unfortunately, was not always clearly grasped by business men. If it be assumed that the plant and equipment of this firm were purchased in 1914, and that their life was

---

[16] From a point of view of maintaining the working capital intact this fact was of vital importance to French business enterprises during the inflation period. Whenever credit was extended on open account to the customers during a period of rising prices, the firm was repaid in depreciated francs, that is, in francs having a lower purchasing power. The longer the period of credit, the lower the purchasing power of the francs received finally from the sale of goods. This practice did much to reduce the effective working capital of some firms during inflation. While the nominal value of the working capital was maintained, and in most cases increased, its purchasing power or its gold value declined very steadily. Of course, if the company received equal credit terms from its creditors that it extended its clients, then the working capital showed no depletion, and if shorter terms and amounts were extended than it received, then the working capital increased. It was only those firms who extended larger credit terms and amounts than they received who suffered. It would have been fairer all around to stabilize credit extensions by employing sales contracts drawn in terms of gold francs or other stable monetary units. It is interesting to note that in classical monetary theory, inflation is supposed *always* to benefit enterprisers who are able to repay their debts in depreciated money. This is evidently an incomplete analysis of the real situation.

[17] Almost all the bonds issued by French corporations were drawn up in terms of "francs" which the courts invariably interpreted, as far as domestic corporations were concerned, to mean paper francs. It is also very doubtful if any French court would have sustained a clause providing for the reimbursement of bonds in terms of gold francs, even if this clause had been inserted prior to the war. Naturally, for foreign corporations which had sold bonds on the French market, the courts took a different attitude and generally stipulated for repayment in gold francs, even in the absence of this clause.

estimated at 30 years, then it would obviously be necessary to charge off 5,000 francs a year for depreciation. By December 31, 1926, the date of the balance sheet, there would have been exactly 60,000 francs depreciation reserve (12×5,000 francs) as is shown by the balance sheet. By 1944, the depreciation reserve account would show 150,000 francs, the book value of the plant and equipment. But unless the franc was brought back to its pre-war value (evidently very improbable as the facts since 1926 have shown) the corporation could not replace the plant and equipment with the sum reserved. In all probability, judging by the movement of prices, it would cost close to one million paper francs to reconstitute these items. It is quite evident that depreciation should have been increased. If the plant and equipment were carried on the books at their replacement prices, this discrepancy would stand out at once. Assuming that the replacement or gold value of the plant was six times its cost,[18] the balance sheet should carry it at 900,000 paper francs. In 1926 the plant was 12 years old and therefore should be depreciated 2/5 of its value, or 360,000 paper francs. The depreciation reserve account shows a depreciation amount of but 60,000 francs or but 1/15 of the value. It is quite evident that drastic measures would be needed in order to reserve such a sum as would permit this asset to remain intact as plant. Had such an amount been set aside as soon as prices started to rise, this situation would not have arisen. Accounting, through the use of the usual measures, failed to bring this fact out in the balance sheet.[19] It is

---

[18] This figure was based upon the index number of general wholesale prices which stood at 640 for December, 1926.

[19] It has been assumed throughout this discussion that the purpose of depreciation is to provide the means of replacing exhausted equipment. Space does not permit the discussion of a possible alternative purpose; namely, that depreciation accounting exists only to spread past costs over subsequent periods. A part of the blame for the failure of business men to depreciate the fixed assets sufficiently must be placed at the feet of the fisc. All French business enterprises were subject to the national income tax, levied on the net income of the business. There was naturally much discussion and litigation concerning the deductions to be made from gross profits in order to determine net profits; the business men desiring to make as many deductions as possible, and the officers of the fisc seeking to reduce the permitted deductions to a minimum. Among many other decisions of the fisc which were sustained by the courts the one concerning depreciation was doubtless the most important. The fisc refused to recognize the depreciation of the plant and equipment at its real or replacement value, only allowing the enterpriser to deduct an amount sufficient to amortize the plant at its cost or book value. Of course, enterprisers could deduct any amount of depreciation they desired on their books of account, but the fisc, for purposes of taxation, would add back to get the net taxable income any amount in excess of the book value depreciation. In the case under discussion, the fisc would allow the enterpriser to deduct 5,000 francs depreciation each year, based upon an estimated total life of 30 years and upon the book value or cost of the plant and equipment, 150,000 francs. If the enterpriser desired to depreciate at the rate of 30,000 francs a year, based upon the same life but upon the real or replacement value of the plant, 900,000 francs, it was free to do so, but the fisc then added 25,000 francs to net income in order to determine the tax. It is rather difficult for an economist to follow the legal arguments invoked to sustain this decision. The economic effect, however, was twofold. In the first place business firms were taxed upon income which they had not earned, and in the second place business men were deterred from making proper provisions for the

evident, of course, that these criticisms could not apply to a bond amortization account.

The account, Reserves, expresses a value in terms of depreciated paper francs. If the firm has been setting aside a fixed sum, or a fixed percentage of surplus, each year as a provision for business contingencies it would be necessary, just as was the case with the depreciation, to increase the amount in paper francs at a rate corresponding to the depreciation of this medium of payment. This is especially important in view of the fact that any contingencies which arise are certain to cost more in paper francs than they would have cost in the absence of any inflation. At the date of the balance sheet their cost would have been about six times as great. The need for greater provision is manifest and should be shown by the accounts.

The same remarks which were made with reference to accounts receivable apply with equal force to accounts payable. In this case, however, the rise in prices works to the advantage of the firm, and not to its disadvantage as was the case with accounts receivable.

In view of the readjustments to be made in the balance sheet the surplus can hardly be said to represent with any accuracy the earnings of, or the accretions to, the business. If depreciation was brought up to the amount indicated in a previous paragraph, the surplus account would disappear entirely and a new account, loss, would appear on the assets side. If the plant, equipment, and inventory accounts were brought up to their actual market or replacement value, the surplus account would appear much larger than it actually is, but if surplus be debited for the full amount of the depreciation, its balance would be reduced considerably. It is, however, to be doubted if the increased value of the plant would form a proper credit to the surplus account; it would appear better and clearer practice to create a special account to take care of this increase. Certainly, it would not constitute good or conservative business practice to pay out this quasi-appreciation in the form of dividends—this might result if the quasi-appreciation were credited to surplus.

Some of the French theorists appear to feel that re-evaluation of the plant and equipment might possibly give rise to a credit to the capital stock

---

replacement of their plants. On the subject of depreciation (in French, *amortisation*) during inflation, see the following works among others: Bisson, André, *Le bénéfice réél en periode de dépréciation monétaire,* Paris (Sirey), 1926, pp. 6–9; Ratier, A. E., "L'évolution du point de vue fiscal en matière d'amortissements," *Experta,* no. 33, June 1927, pp. 32–33; Anonymous, "Le calcul des amortissements sur la valeur de remplacement du matériel," *l'Usine,* April 16, 1927, p. 3; Anonymous, "Comment établir un bilan—l'importante question des amortissements," *l'Usine,* March 5, 1927, p. 3; Fain, G., "Amortissements industriels," *La comptabilité et les affaires,* no. 87, March 1927, pp. 74–78; Baudeux, A., *Les charges fiscales des sociétés anonymes commerciales françaises,* Thesis for the doctorate, University of Paris, 1926; Durand, R., "Le fisc dans ses rapports avec les entreprises ayant adopté une comptabilité en francs-or," *Mon Bureau,* no. 150, April 1926, pp. 513–514; Gingembre, L., *De l'imposition des plus-values en droit français,* Paris (Commerce des Idées), 1928; Lefebvre, R., *L'impôt sur les plus-values d'après les récents projets français,* Paris (Rousseau), 1927.

account.[20] It may further be asked if the surplus account as shown on the above balance sheet is a true surplus, or if it has arisen because of the fact that the capital stock and bonds are maintained on the balance sheet at their original or gold value.[21] In the present case this is not true, for the re-evaluated plant and equipment (150,000 francs) would represent a larger sum than the re-evaluated stocks and bonds (125,000 francs), provided, of course, that the same coefficient of re-evaluation is employed throughout. In other cases, however, where the business has a small plant and equipment relative to the capital stock and bonds, a re-evaluation of the balance sheet would give rise to a fictious surplus which is not due to purely business operations. In the present case, the surplus is due in part to a failure to maintain a replacement policy of depreciation.

The surplus is also inexact in that it fails to show the accretions and depletions of the business which are due to the decline in the purchasing power of the nominal amounts inscribed for accounts receivable and payable as well as cash. The variations in the purchasing power of these accounts properly constitute debits and credits to profit and loss or surplus. Ordinary accounting methods make no provisions for this, and therefore the surplus account must remain inexact under these systems.

Due to causes such as this, it is quite conceivable that the balance sheet show a surplus which is a pure fiction, not due even to a failure to maintain the depreciation at its correct amount. This appears clearly when the balance sheet is reduced to its gold value by the method explained in the succeeding section.[22] This can very well the case where the fixed assets are relatively small the liquid assets relatively large, the short term debts small, or the capitalization relatively large.

Another source of deficit comes about through the normal operations of the business by a failure to sell at a remunerative price—which, under inflation, as will be seen in the succeeding paragraphs, consists of selling on a basis of what the French called "replacement prices" (*prix de remplacement*). The accounts, maintained in the usual fashion, and consequently the balance sheet, will show a profit or surplus whenever the goods are sold for more than the total cost. But if this selling price does not permit the business to restock the goods sold, then the profit fails to correspond to any liquid assets, and disappears when the balance sheet is expressed in terms of gold francs.

---

20 Cf., notably, Bayart, Pierre, *Les effets de l'inflation le bilan au point de vue fiscal,* Paris (Sirey), 1926, pp. 166–182. It must be carefully noted that M. Bayart does not recommend this practice; he prefers to reduce the balance sheets to terms of gold francs. The paper franc re-evaluated balance sheets which he gives are merely illustrative examples, or rather proofs, used to substantiate the accounting methods which he advocates.

21 Cf. Bayart, Pierre, *op. cit.*, note 1, p. 173.

22 See the examples given by Bayart, Pierre, *op. cit.*, pp. 166–167, 170–171, and Delavelle, Emile, *La comptabilité en francs-or,* Paris (Nouvelle Librairie Nationale), 1924, pp. 57–63.

The problem of the surplus is, of course, closely allied to the profit and loss accounts and statements as well as to the cost accounts. Under inflation the usual methods of keeping these accounts gave no more satisfactory results than was the case with the balance sheets. A consideration of the following statement may serve to illustrate and explain this point: In this statement it is assumed that all goods produced are sold.

		Paper Francs
Net sales		100,000
Cost of materials	25,000	
Labor cost	25,000	
Prime cost of goods sold	50,000	
Factory overhead	10,000	
Factory cost of goods sold		60,000
Gross profit		40,000
Administrative and selling expense	10,000	
Other expenses and deductions	10,000	
		20,000
Net profit		10,000

This statement, cast in terms of depreciated paper francs, shows a net profit of 10,000 francs. All of the deductions from net sales have been entered at their actual cost at the time that the expenditures were made. As the statement now stands, this net profit of 10,000 may be a pure fiction and not find its counterpart in any of the working capital assets accounts, and it may conceal a real loss.[23] During the manufacturing period (or the turnover period if we are dealing with a trading enterprise) the prices of all the elements which enter the finished product are increasing. The raw materials are increasing in price—as the figures presented in Table 3 would lead one to conclude—especially if they are imported from countries on a gold standard such as the United States or England. Factory labor is fairly well organized and is constantly obtaining wage increases.[24] The elements of factory overhead, light, heat, rent, taxes, power, etc., are being constantly increased as are the other elements of cost. But the profit and loss statement presents these elements at their price at the time that they were incurred. If the statement showed the costs of material, labor, and other expenses, *at the time of the sale of the goods,* the surplus, as shown on the statement, would either be much smaller or would be a negative quantity—a loss. Such a procedure would represent with greater accuracy the net result of the business operations than does the present practice; for the surplus shown does not

[23] See Bisson, André, *Le benefice réél en période de depreciation monetaire,* Paris (Sirey), 1926, pp. 9–11; Faure, Gabriel, *Bilans et comptes en francs-or,* Paris (Nouvelle Librairie Nationale), 1926, pp. 17–22; Raffegeau, P. C., and Lacout, A., *Etablissement des bilans-or,* Paris (Payot), 1926, pp. 40–43; Thomas, Lucien, *La tenue des comptabilités en période d'instabilité monétaire,* Paris (Editions Experta), 1927, pp. 15–19.

[24] For statistics of the increase in wages see, especially, Dubas-Delos, L., *Le prix de revient industriel,* Thesis for the doctorate, University of Lille, 1928, p. 80; *Bulletin de la Statistique Générale de la France,* July, 1926, p. 421, July-Sept., 1927, p. 407.

find its full counterpart in the net working capital assets, since a larger sum of money was needed to replace the goods sold than their total cost as indicated by the cost accounts and, in many practical instances, a larger sum of money was needed to replace the goods sold than was received by their sale. A surplus or profit under these conditions is likely to prove misleading. Profit can only be calculated upon cost of production when the monetary unit is relatively stable—it is only under this condition that the profit will reflect itself fully in working capital. Where money is undergoing a rapid depreciation and where costs are rising with equal or greater rapidity, then profit must be figured on the cost of the reproduction or replacement of the materials and labor sold. This conception may appear false to those accountants to whom gross profits must always equal net sales minus total cost of production, but even the most traditionally minded must admit that profits which have no counterpart in net working capital are purely fictitious. During certain periods profits, in order to possess any reality, must be figured upon cost of reproduction rather than cost of production.[25]

Closely allied to the problem of the correct calculation of profits is the use of accounting statements of cost of production as a guide to managerial price policy. In many lines of business it is customary for the directors or managers of the business to price the product or merchandise on a basis of cost of production. The underlying data for this calculation are furnished by the accounting department in the form of cost statements. During inflation, however, if the working capital of the business is to be maintained intact, prices cannot be based upon cost of production—they must be based on cost of reproduction or replacement (*prix de remplacement*).[26] If prices are based

---

25 From a speculative point of view it would be interesting to note that just the same procedure is needed during periods of price deflation; that is, periods where money is being retired from circulation and credit being restricted. Here we would expect to have a period of falling prices and if profits were determined by deducting costs of production from net sales, the profit account would show smaller accretions than actually would be the case if costs were deducted at replacement prices. Here the net working capital would grow much faster than the profits, indicating a too conservative calculation of profits. If costs were again based upon a reproduction rather than a production basis, since prices are falling, they would appear smaller and the net profits larger. This reproduction costs method is to be recommended since it is in closer conformity to the real results of the business operations than the cost of production methods.

26 This is the famous "replacement price theory" (*théorie du prix de remplacement*) which received so much attention in France during the inflation years. There is reason to believe that this theory was not original with the French; it was probably imported from Germany where German enterprises, working under a much more rapid and severe inflation than the French, were obliged to take vigorous means for the conservation of their affairs. As a matter of fact, many of the French proponents of this theory had studied inflation in Germany prior to their advocacy of the theory in France. Even during stable money times, many enterprises, especially those dealing in imported materials or products for which there was an international market, applied the replacement price theory. See: Fain, Gael, *Comment se défendre contre l'inflation*, printed lecture, Paris (Compagnie des Chefs de Comptabilité de la Région Parisienne, 47 rue Cambon), no date, pp. 4–9; Beaupère, Louis, *Les troubles monétaires et la vie des entreprises,* Paris (Jouve), 1927, pp. 70–80.

upon cost of production or acquisition during a period of rising prices, the monies or credits received from the sale of goods will not permit the business to reproduce or restock the same amount of goods as were sold at these prices. For during the period of manufacturing or stocking the prices of the goods purchased, raw materials, labor, and other costs will have risen. It will evidently take greater funds to restock after this period than it did at the beginning, and if provision has not been made in the selling price for this rise then the working capital will decline.[27] The usual accounting methods cast their cost data in terms of cost of production. This, of course, will permit the business managers to estimate or figure reproduction costs for purposes of pricing, but, in many instances, it would be preferable that the accounting department be able to furnish cost data for any parts of the merchandise based upon the cost of reproduction at a particular moment. The usual cost accounting methods here are incomplete and inadequate for the formulation of a price policy and do not furnish a certain method of control, because they are based upon actual cost outlays.

These are the most important accounting problems which inflation in France conditioned and which usual accounting methods failed to solve. The following section will show the solutions which the leading French theoreticians and practicians proposed for their solution and the modifications which customary accounting underwent under these circumstances.

III. French Accounting Methods
for Inflation

Faced with these accounting problems, the French accounting theoreticians were not long in proposing solutions. In this matter they had the advantage of the earlier German experience, and some of the new accounting methods proposed were but adaptations of German inflation accounting theory and practice while others constituted distinct contributions to the science. M. Lucien Thomas, in his splendid contribution to inflation accounting theory and method, *La tenue des comptabilités en période d'instabilité monétaire*,[28] has classified the French inflation accounting methods in four groups, to which his own must be added, making a total of five groups:

---

[27] The failure to apply the theory of replacement prices cost many French enterprises dearly. In spite of a rapidly increasing market and sales of goods, some enterprisers found themselves with a constantly decreasing working capital. In view of inflation conditions the banks were not inclined to make any large advances to business men for working capital purposes, because the purchasing power of the enterpriser's notes declined as prices rose. Business firms therefore had recourse to the security market. The issues of new securities, especially stocks, were, during inflation, larger than one would expect. These stocks were not issued to augment the fixed plant and equipment; the proceeds were used to replenish the declining working capital.

[28] Published in Paris, 1927, by *Editions Experta,* 71 rue Desnouettes, the publishing branch of the important accounting and business forms company, M. Dequeker et Cie. See pages 31–35 for M. Thomas' classification.

1. Bookkeeping in terms of paper francs with the use of "correcting accounts" (*comptes correctifs*).
2. The use of ordinary bookkeeping methods cast in terms of depreciated paper francs corrected so as to give a balance sheet in terms of gold francs.
3. The use of ordinary bookkeeping methods cast in terms of paper francs supplemented by annual or monthly correcting entries, giving rise to balance sheets in terms of both corrected paper and gold francs at the end of the year.
4. Four column bookkeeping; two columns for paper francs and two for gold francs.
5. Bookkeeping in terms of paper and gold francs with the use of a special "regulating and compensating account" (*compte régulateur et compensateur*).

In the following description the order of presentation indicated by M. Thomas has been changed. The use of ordinary accounting methods in terms of paper francs, supplemented by the creation of gold-franc balance sheets, will be examined first.

1. Paper Franc Accounting
Supplemented by the Establishment of Balance Sheets
in Terms of Gold Francs

This system, widely employed in France during the inflation years, consists of the use of the normal system of accounts in terms of depreciated paper francs with its resulting annual or monthly paper franc balance sheet restated in terms of gold francs. The practice thus required no changes or adjustments in the traditional methods of keeping the accounts. The paper franc balance sheet was simply restated in terms of gold francs. This procedure was followed by many French enterprises which were opposed to the use of any more complete inflation accounting systems.[29] It is a simple matter to translate paper franc balance sheets to gold franc balance sheets: all the accounts on the former, with the exception of the fixed assets and capital, are divided by the coefficient of exchange rates between France and some gold standard country, generally the United States. The coefficient of exchange is obtained by dividing, say, the actual rate of Franco-American

---

[29] This information was obtained by means of interviews with French business men and accountants—public and private—and by the use of questionnaires sent out to the chief accountants of the more important enterprises. In the course of the author's investigation of the effects of inflation in France, more than 500 interviews were held, taken down in shorthand by a secretary, and then transcribed. About 20 chief accountants replied to the questionnaires sent out. The system here outlined was recommended by the Fédération Industrielle et Commerciale de Roubaix-Turcoing, a leading industrial and commercial group representing the woolen goods industry. See Thomas, Lucien, *op. cit.*, p. 32.

exchange by the par of exchange.[30] The fixed assets and capital accounts, unless they were acquired during inflation, are not divided by this coefficient, because they already stand on the books at their gold value. If they were acquired after inflation, they must be adjusted just as the other accounts. The publications which appeared on the subject of inflation accounting methods abound in examples of these restated balance sheets. The following example is taken from Bayart, Pierre, *Les effects de l'inflation sur le bilan au point de vue fiscal,* Paris (Sirey), 1926, pp. 170–176. This is not an imaginary case; the balance sheet was taken from the French financial publication the *Cote Desfossez,* is dated December 31, 1923, and is the actual balance sheet of a French corporation (*Société Anonyme*) which the author does not name. The balance sheet was given in the *Cote Desfossez* in terms of depreciated paper francs. The author, with the collaboration of M. Hilde, professor of accountancy at the Chamber of Commerce School, has reduced this balance sheet to its expression in terms of gold francs using a coefficient of dollar exchange of 4. This coefficient of exchange corresponds to a rate of exchange of 20.7304 francs to the dollar, or 1 franc equals $0.0483— depending upon the manner of quoting the rates. This figure, while not absolutely exact, declares the author, corresponds sufficiently to the actual rate for purposes of illustration.[31]

Assets	Depreciated Paper Francs	Gold Francs	Liabilities	Depreciated Paper Francs	Gold Francs
Plant and Good Will	850,000	850,000	Capital Stock	9,000,000	9,000,000
Lands, material	7,000,000	7,000,000	4% Loan Bonds	7,000,000	1,750,000
Cash and in Bank ..	4,240,000	1,060,000	Legal Reserves	196,000	—
Defense Bonds	760,000	190,000	Litigation Reserve ..	108,000	27,000
5% Rente Bonds ...	972,000	243,000	War Taxes	188,000	47,000
Notes Receivable ...	920,000	230,000	Profit Tax	220,000	55,000
Rent paid in Advance	6,000	1,500	Depreciation	2,800,000	2,800,000
Merchandise	3,600,000	900,000	Accounts Payable ...	3,800,000	950,000
Horses, Wagons, etc..	1,800,000	450,000	Dividends Due	16,000	4,000
Accounts Receivable .	1,800,000	450,000	Interest Coupons		
Due from Share-			Due	168,000	42,000
holders	2,250,000	562,500	Paper Franc Profits	702,000	—
Gold Depreciation ..		2,738,000			
	24,198,000	14,675,000		24,198,000	14,675,000

[30] There was some discussion as to the use of exchange rates or index numbers of prices in this process of reducing balance sheets to their "true value." Most of the French accountants, following in this the ideas of their German colleagues, preferred the use of the coefficient of exchange rates. A few eminent specialists, however, did not share this opinion.

[31] This balance sheet may prove confusing to the American accountant who is not familiar with French accounting practice. In the first place its arrangement does not follow the logical American procedure, based upon liquidity. Then the names of the accounts are unfamiliar. The author has endeavored to translate the French terms by their equivalent American expression wherever this was possible.

In making this conversion the accounts Plant and Good Will, Lands and Material, Capital, and Depreciation show the same amounts in terms of gold francs as they did in paper francs. All the other accounts have been divided by the coefficient 4. The fixed assets, since they were acquired before the war, were entered at their gold value. The capital stock is doubtless regarded in the same way. In view of the fact that the bonded indebtedness of the company is reduced to its gold value, one may well ask why the capital stock was not similarly treated. Had it been reduced to its gold value the new asset account, Gold Depreciation, would have disappeared and a surplus or profits account would be found in the gold franc column. The question does not appear to be a vital one. In the balance sheet of all corporations which have done business for any length of time, the amount set opposite capital stock no longer corresponds to any reality. It is only through liquidation or purchase that the value of this element has any real meaning. In the present case, the book value of the proprietorship would consist of the capital minus the gold depreciation. Had the capital stock been reduced to its gold value, the proprietorship would then be determined by adding the gold value of the capital to that of the new surplus which would appear. The difference in the former case would exactly equal the sum in the latter. We are here faced, however, with a minor problem of principle and procedure, and the author inclines to agree with the solution presented in the balance sheet.[32] This solution has the advantage of presenting the exact result of the business operations which have really resulted in a deficit or loss rather than a surplus. If the capital stock is expressed in terms of gold francs, a surplus will appear on the balance sheet which is the result of mere adjustments. Of course, it can be maintained that the gold depreciation is likewise the result of an adjustment—the translation of the accounts into their gold value. But this adjustment is made with the purpose of determining the true position of the business and results of its operations. An adjustment to the capital account is but a change in the expression of proprietorship, which is unnecessary in order to determine the position or the results of the business.

The depreciation account shows the same amount in terms of gold that it does in terms of paper. This has been done so that the depreciation account will reflect the true depletion of the plant. As was described in the preceding section, the depreciation account should be credited with the equivalent in depreciated paper francs of the gold franc depreciation of the plant. This has not previously been done by this corporation which evidently had been satisfied to credit the same amount in paper francs each year without taking into account the depreciation of the paper money. Assuming that the annual depreciation was correctly determined in the first place, the depreciation account can then be brought to its proper value by placing, in the gold franc column, the same amount as the paper franc column carries.

---

32 Emile Delavelle, in *La comptabilité en francs-or,* Paris (Nouvelle Librairies Nationale), 2d. ed. 1924, pp. 57–63, handles the capital stock account in the same manner.

The asset account, Gold Depreciation, expresses the deficit of the business. It might at first be thought that this deficit arose because depreciation was brought up to the correct amount. A calculation will show that this is not the case. If no change was made in the amount of depreciation charged to profits, the gold franc amount for this account would be 650,000 francs (2,800,000 ÷ 4 = 650,000) instead of 2,800,000 francs. This would reduce the asset account, Gold Depreciation, by 2,150,000 francs (2,800,000 − 650,-000 = 2,150,000) leaving a net gold depreciation of but 588,000 francs. While the larger part of this deficit is due to the adjustment of the depreciation account, 588,000 represents a loss which is independent of any depreciation adjustment.

The account, Legal Reserve, shows in the paper franc column but not in the gold franc column. This is due to the nature of this reserve. French corporations are required to set aside a certain proportion of their net surplus in the form of a reserve to which the name legal reserve (*réserve légale*) is generally given. Since the gold franc balance sheet fails to show any surplus, this account necessarily does not appear in its columns.

While the gold franc balance sheet method recommends itself by reason of the fact that it dispels some of the illusions which ordinary balance sheets are apt to create in times of inflation as well as by the economy of its preparation, it does not furnish business managers with any great fund of information upon which to conduct their affairs during such trying times. The system of balance sheet readjustment does not tell us very much regarding the results of the business as shown by the statement. The manner in which the surplus arose is not indicated. This could doubtless be determined by recasting the profit and loss account in terms of gold francs, debiting it and crediting it, as the case may be, for the difference between the paper and gold balances of each account adjusted on the balance sheet. This procedure groups in one account the results of the operations of the business and the paper money depreciation of the capital and reserves of the period under consideration as well as that of the previous periods.[33] The account, Gold Depreciation, effectively represents this sum and the profit and loss of the period under study does not appear alone on the balance sheet. The net profit and loss of the period can be determined by a comparison of this gold franc balance sheet with the gold franc balance sheet at the end of the last financial period.[34] Unless the balance sheets are thus regularly translated into gold francs, the periodical business profits and loss cannot be determined. This is, of course, a very real disadvantage as such information is indispensable to the business manager.

MM. Raffegeau and Lacout have developed a system of accounting adjustment affording an elegant solution for this problem which they have called

---

[33] See Raffegeau, P. C., and Lacout, A., *Etablissement des bilans en francs-or*, Paris (Payot), 1926, pp. 94–97.

[34] Raffegeau and Lacout, *op. cit.*, pp. 96–97.

"gold money correction by the retrograde method with rectification of the balance sheet for the previous financial period" (*correction en monnaie-or par la méthode rétrograde avec rectification du bilan d'entrée*).[35] In order to grasp this ingenious method it will first be necessary for us to examine briefly what these authors call the "retrograde method" (*méthode rétrograde*).[36] This system includes the correction of the accounts at the close of the financial period through the evaluation of their balances by the use of index numbers or the coefficient of exchange. The accounts are then rebalanced by crediting or debiting, as the case may be, with the difference between the gold value and the paper value of the balances the profit and loss account. The gold evaluation of the accounts' balance is then, *in the French practice,* debited or credited to the new gold franc balance account. Then the profit and loss credit balance—this account will generally show a credit balance during inflation—is debited to a new account called "capital and reserve depletion" (*dépréciation du capital et des réserves*) which in turn is credited with this amount which is carried as a debit to the new gold Balance Sheet account. The authors here have evidently regarded the balance sheet as an account—this is often the case in French accounting practice. According to American practice each account would be evaluated in terms of gold francs and then the difference between the gold and paper value of the account would be carried to the profit and loss account, but the gold value would be simply drawn off as a "balance" after the account was closed, and would not be debited or credited to a Balance Sheet account. The profit and loss account would be closed out, then, to the Depreciation of Capital account which would stand with the assets on the balance sheet. While it would be interesting to trace MM. Raffegeau and Lacout's system through an abbreviated set of accounts as they do in their book,[37] space will not permit this here. The following Raw Materials account will illustrate the principles outlined above.[38] The authors are here dealing with paper and gold marks, since they are here studying a German enterprise during the German inflation, 1919–1923.

---

35 *Op. cit.,* pp. 96–109.

36 *Op. cit.,* pp. 88–96. The authors have also developed, in addition to the "retrograde method," a "progressive method" (*méthode progressive*). See *op. cit.,* pp. 76–88. This method will be described later.

37 *Op. cit.,* pp. 68–76, 88–96.

38 *Op. cit.,* p. 90. In presenting this balance sheet the author has illustrated the working of this account according to both the French and American practices. The translations of the entries have been made as follows: Balance: French, *Bilan d'entree.* Literally this means balance sheet for previous financial period. As explained, the balance sheet has been regarded as an account here by the French authors. Consequently, in order to re-open the books after closing, the balance sheet is debited or credited for the items it shows which are then carried to the respective accounts. Credit Purchases: French, *Achats a terme.* Cash Purchases: French, *Achats au comptant.* Production Account: French, *Livraisons à la fabrication.* Literally, delivered to production. Profit and Loss: French, *Profits et pertes.*

Raw Materials

Debit

	Marks
Balance	900,000
Credit Purchases	4,500,000
Cash Purchases	900,000
	6,300,000
Balance	300,000
(American System)	

Credit

	Marks
Production Account	4,800,000
Profit and Loss	1,200,000
Balance forward	
(American System)	
or to New Gold	
Balance Sheet Account	
(French System)	300,000
	6,300,000

This account shows a total of 6,300,000 mark debits to raw materials and credits, on account of production of 4,800,000, leaving a paper mark balance of 1,500,000. The inventory has been assigned a gold value of 300,000 to this balance using a coefficient of 5. The difference between 1,500,000 and 300,000, 1,200,000, has thus been charged to profit and loss, and the sum 300,000 represents the actual gold value of raw materials on hand. This same procedure is followed with all the accounts which need re-evaluation.

This system, "gold money correction by the retrograde method with rectification of the balance sheet" for the previous period applies the same principles as were illustrated above. A new account, "correction of past (or opening) balance sheet" (*correction du bilan d'entrée*) is introduced, however. Under this system the Raw Materials account, presented above, would take the following aspect:[39]

Raw Materials

Debit

Balance (old)	900,000
Credit Purchases	4,500,000
Cash Purchases	900,000
	6,300,000

Credit

Production Account	4,800,000
Correction of Past Balance Sheet	600,000
Profit and Loss	600,000
Balance (new)	300,000
	6,300,000

---

[39] *Op. cit.*, p. 99.

At the beginning of the period, this account shows a balance of 900,000, the gold value of which is but 300,000—a coefficient of 3 has been used. The difference between the two figures, 600,000, represents the amount which the previous balance sheet must show. This account is therefore debited with this sum which is then carried as an asset, or credit to this previous balance sheet. As in the past case—since we have the same operations—the new balance was evaluated in gold at 300,000, using a coefficient of 5 since the mark showed a smaller depreciation at the beginning of the period than at the end, the account must now be credited with 600,000, which is debited to profit and loss. In the previous example, the profit and loss account was charged with the sum of 1,200,000, whereas in this case it is charged with but 600,000; therefore, there is a difference of 600,000 between the two cases which corresponds exactly to the account, Correction of Past Balance Sheet. This amount represents the decline in the gold value of the opening inventory and should not be charged off to the profit and loss account of the period under study—for it really represents the loss sustained during the previous period. Now under the ordinary system of balance sheet rectification—either by use of the method indicated at the outset of this section or by the retrograde method of MM. Raffegeau and Lacout—the full amount is carried as a loss to the gold depreciation or the capital and reserve depreciation account. Thus the loss due to the period under study cannot be determined. The retrograde method permits this, and therefore constitutes a very real improvement over the simple procedure of balance sheet readjustment outlined at the beginning of the section.

The same procedure that was followed in the raw materials account must also be applied to all the other accounts where a readjustment of paper to gold values is necessary. The amounts shown in the several accounts as debits and credits to the account "Correction of Past Balance Sheet" represent re-evaluations of the old balances and are then carried to an account bearing this name. The debit or credit of each account to profit and loss is determined by the difference between the paper and gold evaluation of the new balance. These amounts are then carried as debits or credits to profit and loss. The account "depreciation of capital and reserves" is then debited or credited with the amounts outstanding in the correction of past balance sheet account. In this way, the balance of the profits and loss account will represent the current results for the period, while the "Depreciation of Capital and Reserve Account" will show the accumulation losses and gains of past periods. The balance sheet will thus normally (under inflation) carry among its assets not only a Depreciation of Capital and Reserves Account, as a sort of past deficit account, but also an account showing the losses of the current period. Of course, this latter account may show a gain, and in this case it would appear with a credit balance on the liability side of the statement.

This method is extremely simple and will not prove very costly to establish. It has the great advantage, over a simple balance sheet restatement, of showing the profit and loss of the period under consideration as well as the depreciation of the capital and reserves. The method outlined by MM. Raffegeau and Lacout implies that entries are made directly to the accounts. In case it is felt to be inadvisable or inexpedient to show these entries on the regular books of account, a special journal and ledger could be drawn up, to which the balances of the paper franc accounts could be transferred, and then all the above outlined adjustments could be made to these accounts, leaving the regular books intact. As will be seen later, this may prove the wiser procedure. However, this does not in any way modify the principles as set forth by these authors.

While this method does show the profit and loss, it gives but little information on the subject of cost of production and would not be particularly recommendable for systems which comprise a set of cost accounts. Although, at the end of the period, the cost accounts would be adjusted so as to show the proper results, it is often desirable to show the cost of a department, of a job, of a unit of production at other than the period when the books are closed. Some costing systems provide for this. Under this system, it would be necessary to make adjustments each time such costing information was desired. Of course, cost accounts would always show the cost of production in terms of paper francs, or in other words, costs based upon the price of acquisition. But during inflation what is really desired is the *cost of replacement*. This is the critical point in the operation of a business—pricing on a basis of cost of reproduction or replacement must form the basis of the price policy if the enterprise is to maintain its working capital intact. Although adjustments could be made at any time to the cost accounts to show this, it might be advisable to construct a set of accounts which would show gold values, or replacement cost values, at all times. The combined method of gold and paper-franc accounting with four columns makes this provision. The method has been styled the continuous method or "continued accounting" (*comptabilité continue*) by some authors[40] in opposition to the periodical accounting adjustments which other methods propose. It is a complete system of accounting procedure rather than a method of adjustment, correction, or restatement.

2. Four Column Accounting: The Simultaneous Use of Two Columns for Gold Francs and Two for Paper Francs

Before examining the system of four column or "gold franc accounting" (*comptabilité en francs-or*) the system of balance sheet adjustment proposed by the well-known French accounting theorist, M. Gabriel Faure, will be described. This system is a hybrid one, possessing some of the characteristics of the balance sheet adjustments outlined above, and some of the features

---

[40] Notably by MM. Raffegeau and Lacout, *op. cit.*, p. 106.

of gold franc accounting of which M. Faure was a fervent proponent. This method provides for the establishment of gold franc balance sheets by the adjustment of accounts expressed in terms of depreciated paper francs.[41] In one of the methods described above the adjustments were made to the balances only of the accounts. Under the proposals of MM. Raffegeau and Lacout, the old and new balances were to be adjusted by the coefficients of exchange for the date at which they were made. According to M. Faure's method the balances of the accounts are not adjusted *en bloc;* the several entries to the account are adjusted separately, using the coefficient of exchange for the date at which the entry was made in each case. The difference between the gold and paper values of the items is then carried as a debit or credit, as the case may be, to either the profit and loss account or to the "loss by inflation" (*perte par dévaluation*) account.

This method presents the same advantages as that proposed by MM. Raffegeau and Lacout; that is, it permits the establishment of profit and loss for each financial period. Further, this method is much more accurate than could be any method of periodical balance adjustment. The exact loss, in reality, is not the difference between totals or round sums but the difference between the paper and gold values on the date of the transaction or entry of each item. The question of accuracy, as it relates to balance sheet adjusting can, however, easily be pushed too far. The present author holds no particular brief as to the absolute accuracy of any method of inflation accounting. The accuracy of any of these methods is purely relative. Their use is favored during inflation because they all give a more accurate picture of the true results of business operations than any system of depreciated paper money accounting alone.

The principal objection to the employment of M. Faure's plan lies in two directions: (1) the possible lack of the business records necessary to the translation of each item in the accounts, and (2) the expense entailed by the required calculations. While a well-managed business may possess all of the necessary records, the enterprisers may well ask if the added accuracy which this system gives will fully compensate the large expenditure which it would entail, and if less accurate methods, much less costly, are not sufficiently accurate for practical purposes. In a large business the amount of detail work, in both time and money, would probably prove prohibitive. For a small enterprise its employment would be more easily envisaged.

Nevertheless, it may be possible to compromise between the periodical adjustment system and the individual entry system, by making periodical adjustments say each month, or each week. This would provide sufficient accuracy for most purposes and would also prove feasible. The author is inclined to take this position in the matter.

The gold franc accounting method applies similar theory. Here the books are kept in both paper and gold francs. Each entry is made in terms of both

---

41 Faure, Gabriel, *Bilans et comptes en francs-or,* Paris (Nouvelle Librarie Nationale), 2d. ed., 1926, pp. 49–66.

gold and paper francs at once. Since all business transactions were carried out in terms of paper francs, it is necessary to carry them to the gold franc columns by using the coefficient of exchange as explained in a previous paragraph. If desired, two separate sets of books could be employed for this method; one set in paper francs and a second set in gold francs. The set in gold francs could eliminate many controlled accounts showing only the controlling accounts and doubtless other simplifications could be introduced without destroying its value or exactitude.

There are three steps involved in gold franc accounting: (1) the evaluation of the past balance sheet in terms of gold francs and the opening of the gold franc books or columns, (2) the technique of bookkeeping under this system, and (3) the closing entries. Each one of the steps will be examined in order.

The evaluation of the balance sheet in terms of gold francs gives rise to no special difficulties but is nevertheless necessary in order to determine the gold value of the amounts outstanding in the accounts before the gold columns or books can be opened.[42] Any one of the methods outlined above can be employed; evidently the method suggested by M. Gabriel Faure is the most accurate, but its cost would perhaps prove prohibitive.[43] Once the gold franc balance sheet is established, it is next necessary to open the gold columns or books by making a set of transfer entries. The balances of the paper franc accounts are naturally left intact. The gold accounts will show one account which is not present in the paper books—"gold depreciation" or "loss by inflation." To this account are carried, as debits or credits, the differences between the paper and gold balances of each account, as was described in the preceding section.[44]

We are now ready to examine the technique of bookkeeping under this system. According to the example of the working of the system which M. Delavelle gives, the entries to the gold accounts are not made to the controlled accounts when there exists a controlling account (*compte collectif*) and apparently the entries are made to the gold accounts but once a month, at the end of the month.[45] The entries were here made by dividing the paper franc values by the coefficient of dollar exchange at the end of the month for which the entries were made. Naturally only the totals of the month for each type of transaction were entered. For instance, each individual deposit

---

[42] Cf. Delavelle, Emile, *La comptabilité en francs-or,* Paris (Nouvelle Librarie Nationale), 2d. ed. 1924, pp. 57–63. Evidently for new enterprises beginning business during inflation the books can be opened at once in terms of both paper and gold francs and the evaluation of the balance sheet, therefore, becomes unnecessary. The illustrative examples given by M. Gabriel Faure are of this nature. See his *Bilans et comptes en francs-or,* pp. 25-36.

[43] M. Delavelle apparently uses the first method outlined. Cf. *op. cit.,* pp. 57–62.

[44] Cf. Delavelle, *op. cit.,* pp. 63–64.

[45] The word "apparently" must be stressed, for M. Delavelle is not very explicit on this point. In the illustrative example that he gives the entries to the gold books are made at the end of the month. It is, however, quite possible that M. Delavelle was employing this method for purposes of illustration only and that he would agree to entries to the gold books at the same time that the entries were made to the paper books.

to the bank was not transformed. Only the total of deposits due to a certain type of receipts was so transformed. Thus the payments made by debtors were transformed *en bloc* and not separately.

Under the system proposed by M. Gabriel Faure the entries are made to the gold accounts simultaneously with those made to the paper accounts. For this purpose the coefficient of dollar exchange is used for the date on which the transaction was made.[46] This system has the advantage of greater accuracy, but the disadvantage of somewhat greater expense. However, it would be easy to greatly simplify the gold accounts. Provided a separate set of gold books were kept, it would be possible greatly to effect combinations of separate accounts which are found in the paper franc books. In other words the gold accounts could represent a condensation of the paper accounts. Then, at the end of each day's entries, the adjustments could be made by daily totals to the gold franc books. Both authors journalize their transactions according to the traditional methods.

The closing entries, in addition to the usual entries made at this time, comprise some special entries due to the nature of this system. In M. Delavelle's method a special account "depreciation of the gold capital" (*dépréciation du capital-or*), which naturally is only to be found in the gold accounts, is created to which are carried as debits and credits the decrease and increase in the real value of the paper franc balances of the accounts. An example may make this point clear. If there were 100 francs in the cash account on June 30th, and the coefficient of exchange stood at 2, while on July 31st it stood at 4, the depreciation of the gold capital account would be debited with 50 francs, the decline in the value of this amount due to the monetary depreciation.[47] In effect, the purchasing power of 100 francs has declined by 50% as shown by the increase of the coefficient of exchange from 2 to 4. This method resembles that proposed by MM. Raffegeau and Lacout as outlined above. In the example which M. Delavelle gives, the paper franc accounts show a net profit. This profit is closed out to reserve, evidently to prevent the books from showing a fictitiously large profit, or to indicate a conservative financial policy. The gold accounts show a profit also, since the decline in the paper balances has already been adjusted, and this amount is closed out by crediting the depreciation of capital account.

In M. Faure's method the principle is similar but the operations, since the gold entries are made simultaneously with the paper entries, vary. An account "loss by inflation" (*perte par dévaluation*), which corresponds to M. Delavelle's "depreciation of gold capital account," is debited or credited for the differences between the balance of the gold value of the paper franc accounts and those of the gold franc accounts. Thus in the example shown by M. Faure,[48] the cash shows a debit balance of 14,310 in the paper francs

---

46 Cf. Faure, *op. cit.*, pp. 25–28, 33–36.

47 Cf. Delavelle, *op. cit.*, pp. 60–64.

48 *Op. cit.*, pp. 33–38.

account, and a debit balance of 30,986 in the gold francs account. The gold value of the actual paper francs on hand, 14,310, is, according to the coefficient of exchange employed, 5,724. Thus the debit to loss by devaluation for this account is found by subtracting 5,724 gold value of the actual paper francs in cash account from the debit balance of 30,986, or net debit 25,262 gold francs. Hence the gold cash account is credited with 25,262 francs which is carried as a debit to "Loss by Inflation." After these entries have been completed, the paper cash account will show a debit balance of 14,310 and the gold cash account a debit balance of 5,724. This latter figure represents exactly the gold value of the actual cash on hand. This same method is applied to all the accounts where any loss or gain by the devaluation of the franc is apparent. The other closing entries employed by M. Faure are in accord with the principles of usual accounting practice.

The results of the operations, as has already been noted, will be more accurately established by M. Faure's method than by those of M. Delavelle, but on the other hand, they will also prove much more expensive to establish. M. Faure's method possesses another advantage of considerable importance— it affords the possibility of maintaining a set of cost accounts, tied up with the regular set of books, in terms of both paper and gold francs, thus enabling the business manager to determine the gold cost of production at any time and without any further calculation.[49] If the gold cost of production is known, the approximate paper cost of replacement or reproduction can be easily determined by multiplying the gold cost by the coefficient of exchange. This would afford a very simple method for the application of the theory of replacement prices, so essential to the life of business enterprises during

---

[49] In the example given by M. Faure the enterprise does not employ a system of cost accounts. In the analysis of cost which M. Faure appends to his discussion of method— *op. cit.*, pp. 40–46—the enterprise has based its prices upon the cost of acquisition and not the cost of replacement. Therefore the suggestions given in the above paragraph must not be attributed to M. Faure, but to the author of this article who must take full responsibility for it. It is a striking fact in the French literature of inflation—which was very large and generally of an excellent character—that the authors so generally insist upon the use of replacement costs, the correct inflation price basis, but that none of the accountants in their various suggestions for inflation accounting methods indicate any inflation cost accounting methods. Their discussions and their examples all deal with the ordinary books of record and never with the cost books. And yet a good system of costing, properly adjusted to inflation conditions, could be of great aid to the business manager in applying the theory of replacement costs. One is tempted to demand the reason for this hiatus; it is probably due to several causes. In the first place the theory and practice of cost accounting is not nearly as well developed in France, as in the United States. This statement is made after a study of French accounting literature and interviews with French chief accountants, public accounts, and business men. Further, such cost systems as one finds in the larger establishments appear to be the results of chief accountants in the regular employ of the company rather than the work of public or consulting accountants. The French public accountant, while perhaps a better theorist than his American colleague, appears to be in general less a practical accountant and to have had a smaller field of experience. The books and articles on inflation accounting were largely prepared by these public accountants. Had they been the work of chief accountants, it is possible that they would have given more information regarding the procedure to be followed in the case of cost accounts.

inflation. While this method does not give the exact cost of replacement, it gives a simple, empirical method of determining it with approximate accuracy—sufficient accuracy, it is believed, for all practical purposes—and will doubtless enable the enterprise to maintain its working capital intact. The exact cost of replacement can only be determined by a knowledge of the real, or market cost of the materials, salaries, and other expenses at the time that the sale was made. These expenses tend to follow very closely the movement of the exchange rates; as a matter of fact they show generally a lag when compared to exchange. If the gold costs, therefore, are multiplied by the coefficient of exchange rates, a sufficient degree of accuracy should be obtained.[50]

The methods of gold franc accounting outlined in this section have been vigorously attacked and defended, and, doubtless, had inflation assumed the proportions that it took in Germany, the question of the advisability of its use would have been threshed out by a study of practical results. We can classify the attacks made upon it into two groups: (1) Attacks by those who favor some kind of special accounting methodology for inflation systems but who prefer the use of another method to that of accounting in gold and paper francs carried out simultaneously, and (2) those who feel that ordinary accounting methods are satisfactory during inflation and that all of the inflation systems give false results. We shall here only examine those objections belonging to the first category.

The objections of MM. Raffegeau and Lacout will first be examined. The difficulties with gold franc accounting, according to these authors, arises from

---

50 The use of the coefficient of exchange rates—preferably Franco-American rates—is here suggested because the paper francs have been reduced to gold values by dividing by the coefficient of exchange. If the paper franc accounts have been reduced by the use of one of the several indices of prices, it will then be necessary to determine replacement prices by multiplying by the same index. One difficulty with the use of indices of prices as means for determining purchasing power lies in the fact that daily "quotations" are not ordinarily available. During inflation the *Statistique Générale de la France* published weekly figures for some of its indices in a supplement to its *Bulletin*. Ordinarily, the indices are established each month. Exchange rates may be had for any day, any hour, or even for a given moment, for they are made on an exchange by buyers and sellers. Thus for purposes of the cost records the use of the coefficient of exchange appears to be the better element. Unfortunately, the question is not as simple as this description might lead one to think. The various levels and movements or rates and the several indices are not the same, and considerable difference will result if one system or another is used. Generally speaking, the level of prices at wholesale was higher than the level of rates of exchange as table 3 shows. The movement of exchange rates, on the other hand, showed a wider scope and prices show, generally, a lag when compare to rates. These considerations must be taken into account when the choice of a coefficient of conversion is made. No definite rule can be laid down here. Each particular enterprise will need to study the movements of its costs and prices and choose a coefficient based upon considerations of this type. It must be noted, as an argument against the use of the coefficient of exchange, that, since the level of this figure is generally below that of wholesale prices, the gold values which result from its use will not bring values down to their pre-war level, but only to their gold level. The other advantages, notably the rapidity of movement of the coefficient as well as the continuous quotations, largely counterbalance this defect.

the incessant variability of the value of the money.[51] The following cash account is used by way of illustration:[52]

Cash Account

Debit

	Coefficient of Conversion	Paper Francs	Gold Francs
Old Balance	4	800	200
Receipts	4	400	100
Receipts	3	300	100
Receipts	6	600	100
		2,100	

Credit

	Coefficient of Conversion	Paper Francs	Gold Francs
Expenditures	5	500	100
Expenditures	8	800	100
New Balance	8	800	
		2,100	

The entries to the above account were made at different dates when the franc was varying in its gold value as is shown by the column of coefficients of conversion. The new paper franc balance is the same as the old, for 1,300 paper francs were received and an equal sum disbursed. Due to the decline of the franc, this balance was worth 200 gold francs at the beginning, while at the end it was worth but 100 francs, for the coefficient has changed from 4 to 8. The balance of the gold accounts, 500 − 200 equals 300 francs. The result of the gold franc columns, showing the balance as worth 300 gold francs, when it in reality is worth but 100 gold francs is, conclude the authors, obviously false.

This criticism is based upon a failure fully to grasp the method criticized. If we close the cash account above, according to M. Faure's method we will debit "Loss by Inflation" with the difference between the gold value of the paper balance, 100, and the gold balance, 300, giving 200. This latter sum represents the loss by devaluation. The difference between this sum and the gold balance, 300, will be 100 francs and represents the new gold balance, an amount which MM. Raffegeau and Lacout recognize as exact. M. Faure, in his reply to these authors, points this out.[53] MM. Raffegeau and Lacout further criticise the method as involving too much work.[54]

A criticism of another order comes from the pen of M. Fernand Leger and,

---

[51] Raffegeau and Lacout, *op. cit.*, p. 106.

[52] *Op. cit.*, pp. 106–107. In reproducing this account the decimal point has been moved three places to the right in order to simplify the figures. Also, the authors use marks instead of francs.

[53] Cf. Faure, *op. cit.*, pp. 78–79.

[54] *Op. cit.*, pp. 108–109.

as he states, it applies principally to the method proposed by M. Delavelle.[55] Effectively, this criticism cannot be applied to the method of M. Faure as a careful study of his method will reveal.[56] M. Leger feels that it is an error to charge the "Gold Capital Depreciation" account with the difference between the gold value of the new and old balances of the merchandise account. If the franc has depreciated in the interval of time between the old and new balances, this practice will show a loss that the business has not really sustained. Let us assume that on December 1, the business has a stock of merchandise worth 100 paper francs and that the coefficient of exchange is 4. The gold value of this stock is thus 25 francs. Let us assume that on December 31 the stock is still intact—its paper value 100—and that the coefficient of exchange is now 5. Its gold value would thus be now 20. It would be an error to debit the gold capital depreciation account with 5 francs, the difference between the two balances, because the stock of merchandise appreciates at approximately the same rate that the franc depreciates. In other words the paper value of the stock on December 31 would be 125 instead of 100 francs. Using the coefficient 5, the gold value of this stock would be 25 francs just as it was on December 1. The account Merchandise must therefore be treated just as the plant and other fixed assets are treated, for the value of the stock appreciates in terms of paper as the franc declines. This holds true, continues M. Leger, of all accounts representing corporal values (*valeurs corporelles*).

The exactitude of M. Leger's criticism is not to be controverted. However, this is less a criticism of the principle of gold franc accounting than it is the technique of handling certain accounts under one of the gold franc methods. It would be a simple matter to change the technique to correctly adjust these accounts and still apply the basic principles. As a matter of fact, M. Leger himself suggests the method to be followed here although he is not a proponent of the method of gold franc accounting.[57] If the enterprise is basing its selling price upon the cost of acquisition, there will be a fluctuation loss upon the merchandise sold. The amount of this loss can be calculated by subtracting from the cost of replacing the merchandise sold, the price with which the merchandise account was credited when the sale was made. This gives the loss which should be carried to profit and loss as a debit. With this correction, the method of M. Delavelle is correct.

M. Leger also criticises the use—by M. Delavelle and the partisans of his system—of the coefficient of exchange at the end of the fiscal period in evaluating the accounts. He believes that it would be more accurate to use a mean between the coefficient at the beginning of the fiscal period and at

---

[55] Leger, Fernand, *Le redressement des bilans en francs-papier,* Paris (Editions Experta), 1926, pp. 29–36.

[56] M. Faure, *op. cit.,* pp. 40–44, in his study of the "result of sales" employs a method similar to that suggested by M. Leger in determining the loss on goods sold, and does not fall into the error committed by M. Delavelle.

[57] *Op. cit.,* pp. 35–36.

the end. This would doubtless be more accurate, but it would not be absolutely so, and would still be less accurate than the method proposed by M. Faure. It must finally be noted that the objections which M. Leger raises against one of the gold accounting methods applies with equal force to the first system of inflation accounting suggested—the preparation of gold-franc balance sheets.[58] This objection is valid, but it does not invalidate the principle of this method any more than it did that of gold franc accounting. It shows a needed change in the technique employed which should not prove, in practice, an insurmountable obstacle.

3. Paper Franc Accounting with Correcting Accounts

M. Leger's criticism of gold franc balance sheets and gold franc accounting methods led him to reject these two systems in favor of one of his own elaboration, at once exceedingly simple and ingenious, and constituting one of the outstanding French contributions to the subject of inflation accounting methods.[59] M. Leger classifies the errors which creep into the accounts during inflation as follows:

1. Insufficient depreciation of the fixed assets.
2. A larger gross profit seems to result than was actually obtained.
3. Loss on the excess of the incorporeal working capital assets over the incorporeal working capital liabilities.

In order to eliminate the errors coming from these three sources, M. Leger proposes three types of accounting adjustments:

A. *Depreciation of Fixed Assets.* The method proposed by M. Leger is essentially the same as that explained in section 2 of this article. The fixed assets must be depreciated upon their gold value so that the enterprise will have placed in the reserve for depreciation account an amount sufficient to replace the physical assets when their theoretical term of life will be at an end. For this purpose the gold value of these assets is multiplied by the coefficient of the exchange rate and the fixed annual percentage of this amount is charged to the Profit and Loss account and credited to the Reserve for Depreciation account.

B. *Re-evaluation of Gross Profits.* Taking the following assumed transaction, M. Leger shows how gross profits, as determined by the accounts, may be inaccurate:

Sales (in paper francs)	1,350,000
Cost of goods sold (in paper francs)	1,000,000
Gross profit (paper francs)	350,000

---

[58] *Op. cit.,* pp. 37–38.
[59] Leger, Fernand, *Le redressement des bilans en francs-papier,* Paris (Editions Experta), 1926, pp. 39–48.

The cost of goods sold represents the actual cost of acquisition. M. Leger then assumes that the franc has depreciated in the interval of time elapsed between the acquisition and the sale of these goods; the coefficient of exchange stood at 4 at the former period and at 5 at the latter. Reduced to gold francs, the statement is as follows:

Sales (gold francs)	270,000
Cost of goods sold (gold francs)	250,000
Gross profit (gold francs)	20,000

The gold franc gross profit of 20,000 francs represents a paper franc profit (with the coefficient at 5) of 100,000 francs instead of 350,000 as shown in the first instance. The paper franc accounting has thus given a misleading result. M. Leger goes on to state that 250,000 francs of the working capital of the enterprise reflect only a paper profit, as the enterpriser will discover when he finds it necessary to renew his stock. If the enterpriser restocks the same quantity of goods sold on the day the sale was made, his new stock will cost 1,250,000 paper francs instead of 1,000,000 paper francs, since the franc has depreciated by 25% since the original purchase.[60]

M. Leger suggests that the situation be handled in this way:[61]

Paper franc price of goods sold		1,350,000
Paper franc purchase price of goods sold	1,000,000	
To reserve account, paper francs	250,000	
Total		1,250,000
Gross paper franc profit		100,000

Thus the difference between the cost of acquisition of the goods sold and their replacement costs is carried as a credit to a reserve account and as a debit to profit and loss. In practice, declares M. Leger, we will not seek out the exact date upon which the goods sold were acquired—this would evidently occasion too much work. The calculations would be made on the ensemble of goods sold during the period, using a mean coefficient for the period under consideration. This mean coefficient would be based upon the period of turnover of the business, and could be calculated in several ways; each enterprise using such a mean as is best adapted to its affairs.

C. *Difference Between Working Capital Assets and Liabilities.* If a French enterpriser purchases a dollar on a given date for 18 paper francs, the rate of exchange on that date, and if the rate of exchange stands at 20 a year later when the dollar is sold, his books will then show a paper franc profit of 2 francs paper. In reality, however, he has made no profit at all. However,

---

[60] $5/4 \times 1,000,000 = 1,250,000$. This will give the approximate cost of replacement, but not the exact. The use of the coefficients of exchange to determine replacement costs assumes that the replacement cost moves in exactly the same way as do rates of exchange. This is obviously inexact for all goods except imports of some goods from gold money countries, but it is nevertheless sufficiently exact for the purpose at hand.

[61] Leger, *op. cit.*, pp. 42–43.

had he set 18 francs aside in his safe deposit box, he would not have been able to purchase the dollar a year later although the books of account would show no loss by reason of this stocking. The purchase of the dollar has simply permitted the business man to avoid a loss. With this remark in mind, M. Leger proceeds with an imaginary example:[62]

Cash and in Banks (paper francs)	300,000
Accounts Receivable (paper francs)	1,000,000
Total Working Capital Assets (paper francs)	1,300,000
Accounts Payable (paper francs)	600,000
Net Working Capital (paper francs)	700,000

If this net working capital is represented by paper money—notes of the Bank of France—it will decline in purchasing power as the franc depreciates. Now if, during a certain period, the rate of exchange passes from 20 francs to the dollar to 25 to the dollar, the gold value or the purchasing power of this working capital will then have passed from 175,000 to 140,000, a loss of 35,000 gold francs or 175,000 paper francs.

Another very important consequence indicated by M. Leger, and one which merits attentive study by enterprisers, is the fact that the several reserve accounts are represented by assets of diverse character, some of them in the working capital assets which are subject to a decline in gold value or purchasing power. If these reserve accounts are maintained at their full value, even taking into account the appreciation in paper franc values, they will be nevertheless represented by working capital assets which are declining in real value. *It is thus insufficient to make proper provision for reserves alone; the asset accounts must also maintain their real value, that is, purchasing power, or gold value.*

M. Leger suggests two remedies for this situation.[63] As far as possible all the assets should be invested in corporeal values which appreciate in value as the franc declines or in the purchase of securities, the price of which rises in the same proportion.[64] For that part of the working capital which cannot be so invested, M. Leger suggests that a reserve be constituted by a debit to profit and loss sufficient to compensate for the decline in the gold value of this element of the working capital. He goes on to state that the various methods used to attain this result might vary. Evidently, each enterprise will need to work out its own formulas and technique.

M. Leger's system is less an accounting procedure than a managerial

---

[62] *Op. cit.,* pp. 43–46.

[63] *Op. cit.,* p. 46 ff.

[64] M. Leger calls attention to the possibilities of the use of several types of security investments for this purpose. He warns his readers that possible future taxation might bring about variations in the utility of certain securities for this purpose, and that foreign securities have already increased so much in value that it is to be feared that they will decline in value in the future. He appears to prefer the use of the new 4 per cent French *Rentes,* the value of which is to be reimbursed in paper francs adjusted so as to maintain their gold value intact.

policy. His proposal makes no fundamental changes in the books of account. These are merely adjusted by the corrections which he has suggested. If these policies were followed by managers—if competition would permit their use—the enterprises would suffer but little from inflation. While the books of account might not present the true situation of the affair as well as M. Faure's gold accounting method, sufficient information would be provided for the management.

M. Leger's proposals do not make any provision for the automatic adjustment of the cost accounts. This will leave the manager the delicate problem of a constant recalculation of replacement cost selling prices. This appears to be the principal objection to the use of this method, which otherwise recommends itself by its economy and simplicity.

4. Paper Franc Bookkeeping with Restated Paper Franc and Gold Franc Balance Sheets

This group of inflation accounting systems includes two methods: The progressive method (*méthode progressive*) proposed by MM. Raffegeau and Lacout, and the "method of heterogeneous accounts" (*méthode des comptes hétérogènes*) or "balance conversion method" (*méthode de conversion des existants*) suggested by M. Gael Fain.

A. The Progressive Method. The principle underlying this method consists in the translation of the old balances of the accounts into their new paper franc values at the end of the financial period.[65] This system does not give a restated balance sheet in terms of gold francs as did the methods previously outlined, but a restated balance sheet in terms of paper francs. The amounts outstanding in the various accounts are brought up to their actual present value, or replacement value. Thus we have a balance sheet in terms of paper francs; the amounts, however, give the approximate present value of the elements represented by the accounts. Two steps are involved in this procedure:

1. The opening balances of the accounts are adjusted on the basis of the value of the monetary unit at the date of these opening entries or, in other words, at the beginning of the financial period. Only those amounts which are undervalued in the accounts are so re-evaluated. The differences in the values which will result from this step are carried as debits and credits to a new account called "Correction of the Opening Balances Evalued in Year X" (*correction du bilan d'entrée valeur annee x*). This account will, in practice, generally receive only credits. The credit balance of this account will then show the paper franc increase in value of the capital and reserves and is closed out to the account "Increment-value of Capital and Reserves"

---

65 Raffegeau and Lacout, *Etablissement des bilans-or,* Paris (Payot), 1926, pp. 76–87.

(*Plus-value du capital et des réserves*). It is clear that accounts such as Cash, Accounts Payable, Accounts Receivable, etc., are not adjusted by entries to the Correction of the Opening Balances evalued in year X. These accounts can show no increase in paper franc value by the decline in the purchasing power of the franc. On the other hand, these adjustments will be made to accounts such as Plant, Equipment, Material, Merchandise, Stocks and Bonds, and the like, for the paper franc value of these accounts will change with the purchasing power of the franc.

2. The second step consists in the reevaluation of the opening balances of the accounts on the basis of their value at the end of the financial period under consideration instead of at the beginning as was the case in step 1. Here the values of the monetary accounts, not so adjusted in step 1 are also adjusted here, because of the fact that, if their face values have not changed or, in other words, if they show no surplus value by reason of the decline in the franc, their purchasing power has declined nevertheless. The differences which will result from this step are carried as debits and credits to an account called "Correction of the Opening Balances, Evalued in Year Y." This account is, in its turn, closed out to the Increment-value of Capital and Reserves account.

The following Raw Materials account shows the application of these principles:[66]

Raw Materials

Debits

	Paper Francs
Opening Balance	900,000
Credit Purchases	4,500,000
Cash Purchases	900,000
Correction of Opening Balance Year X	300,000
Correction of Opening Balance Year Y	1,200,000
	7,800,000

Credits

	Paper Francs
Production Account	4,800,000
Profit and Loss	600,000
New Balance	2,400,000
	7,800,000

The value of the opening balance for the year X, the beginning of the financial year under consideration, was 1,200,000 francs, while the books give the opening balance as 900,000. The difference between the two amounts, 300,000 paper francs, represents the increase in the nominal value of this sum due to the depreciation of the franc. The account is therefore credited with 300,000, which is then carried as a debit to the Correction of

---

[66] *Op. cit.,* pp. 79–80.

Opening Balance, Year X account. In the following year, year Y, the end of the financial period under study, the nominal value of the opening balance, instead of 900,000 or 1,200,000, is now 2,100,000. The increase is here due to the depreciation of the franc during the current year. The sum of 1,200,000 is therefore debited to the Raw Materials account and credited to the account Correction of Opening Balance Year Y.

Profit and Loss has here been debited with 600,000 francs, which represents the difference between the book and replacement value of the new balance. This figure was obtained as follows: The total credits to this account, 7,800,000, less the raw materials charged to Production account, 4,800,000, leaves a nominal balance of 3,000,000 francs. An inventory shows that the material on hand is actually worth but 2,400,000 francs. The difference, then, between the nominal and actual value of the raw material on hand is thus 600,000, which must be charged to the Profit and Loss account, and the Raw Materials account will then show a new balance of 2,400,000 francs. Had the actual value of the raw material on hand been higher than its nominal value, then Profit and Loss would have been credited for the difference between the two values.

The same principles are applied to all the accounts which require these adjustments, and the depreciation and reserves are calculated on the basis of replacement values. No changes are made in the manner of journalizing the entries, nor in the ordinary accounting technique, save those mentioned above. Since both the Corrections of the Opening Balance, year X and year Y, are closed out to the account "Increment-value of Capital and Reserves," the balance sheet will show this account in addition to those found in the usual books. This account will usually, during inflation, show a credit balance, and represents the increase in the nominal value of the Capital Stock and Reserve Accounts. Since this method of accounting adjustment brings the paper franc values shown by the balances of the various accounts up to their present value, or their reproduction value, the credit side of the balance sheet will show a smaller total than the debit side. The difference might be credited to a Surplus account, to a Reserve account, or the values ascribed to capital stock might be increased. Under the method proposed by MM. Raffegeau and Lacout the special account, Increment-value of Capital and Reserves, has been created to receive this credit. This appears to constitute conservative accounting practice, for, in this way, the changes in the values of the accounts will not be ascribed to any of the usual sources as might be the case if they were credited to one of the former accounts. The Profit and Loss account shows not only the results of the business operations for the financial period, but also the gains and losses due to the fluctuation of the franc.

This method is not that which MM. Raffegeau and Lacout prefer and which is the retrograde system with a rectified balance sheet for the previous financial period as outlined in a previous section. The method here presented, however, state the authors, has the advantage of showing the results of the financial period being studied and does not mix these results with those of past periods.[67] They call attention to the fact that this method runs the risk of maintaining the illusion which inflation is apt to create. That is, it shows the net worth of the enterprise in terms of nominal paper francs—it does not deflate values. And since prices are rising, the nominal value of the net worth will appear large to eyes which are not accustomed to the revaluation of paper franc sums in terms of gold francs. The amount of the net worth will *look* larger than it really is because it takes a larger number of depreciated francs to represent it. Translated into terms of gold, the net worth may actually have shrunk.[68]

The method, according to its authors, possesses a second disadvantage. The balance sheets of several financial periods are not directly comparable. Since they are established in paper francs, the value of which was steadily declining, the amounts set opposite the several accounts do not show this depreciation from period to period. Thus the balances for one period may have been established while the coefficient was at 3, the succeeding period may find the franc with a coefficient of 4 or 5.

Some of the objections urged against the methods of balance sheet conversion in the first part of this section also apply to this method. It fails to give much useful data for the costing—the methods of four column gold accounting provide much more usable data. It is also far less accurate than the system proposed by M. Faure. Further, since the adjustments are made to the accounts directly, the books will not show the results of the usual accounting methods; they only show the adjusted results. This, of course, could easily be remedied by drawing up a special set of books to take care of the adjustments. But if this is done it would be almost as easy to establish a simple set of gold accounts. The objections urged by M. Leger concerning the adjustment made to the merchandise account apply to this method since profit and loss is made to support the changes in the value of the merchandise which has not yet been sold. The objection urged by the author of the method, namely, the misleading character of the paper franc statements, constitutes, however, its leading defect.

B. The Method of Heterogeneous Accounts. This method, the proposal of M. Gael Fain, represents a combination of the gold franc balance sheet and the paper franc balance sheet methods and thus avoids one of the difficulties of the method just described—its results are not misleading—and at the same time it gives the business manager more information than either the

---

[67] *Op. cit.,* p. 86.

[68] *Op. cit.,* pp. 86–87. In the example employed by the authors the paper franc value of the net worth stood at 10,580,000 at the end of the period as compared with an original amount of 4,500,000. This might well lead the enterpriser to conclude that his net worth had increased during inflation. Restated in terms of gold, however, there is a shrinkage of 115,000 gold francs in the value of the net worth. It is for this reason that the authors prefer the use of gold franc to paper franc adjustments.

gold or paper franc balance sheet methods used separately.[69] M. Fain does not claim to be the inventor of this method and states clearly that it was developed by the German professors Mahlberg and Schmalenbach.[70]

In M. Fain's demonstration, three forms of each of the accounts are used. The first gives the accounts as they stand on the books; i.e., in terms of depreciated paper francs without any adjustment. The second form shows the account restated (*rédressée*) in terms of paper francs so as to bring the values up to their cost of replacement. The third form restates the accounts in terms of gold francs. The following Merchandise account, taken from M. Fain's example, illustrates the principles which he employs.[71]

Merchandise as Shown by the Books

Debits

Old Balance, 1924	1,200,000
To Accounts Payable	5,000,000
To Cash	350,000
To Accounts Receivable	22,000
To Profit and Loss, 1925	470,000
	7,042,000

Credits

By Accounts Receivable	5,400,000
By Cash	120,000
By Accounts Payable	22,000
New Balance, 1925	1,500,000
	7,042,000

Merchandise Account Restated in Paper Francs

Debits

Old Balance, 1924	1,200,000
To Accounts Payable	5,000,000
To Cash	350,000
To Accounts Receivable	22,000
To Restatement Account, 1925	514,286
	7,086,286

---

[69] Fain, Gael, *Comment se défendre contre l'inflation,* a printed lecture in pamphlet form, Paris (Compagnie des Chefs de Comptabilité de la Région Parisienne, 47 rue Cambon), no date, pp. 22–45.

[70] While M. Fain does not cite the names of the works of Professors Schmalenbach and Mahlberg, he probably has reference to the following contributions: Mahlberg, W., *Bilanztechnik und Bewertung bei schwankender Wahrung,* Leipzig (Glöckner), 3rd ed. 1923; Schmalenbach, *Goldwertausgleich in der bilanzmässigen Erfolgsrechnung,* Leipzig (Glöckner), 1921; Schmalenbach, *Goldmark bilanz,* Berlin (Springer), 1922.

[71] Fain, G., *Op. cit.,* pp. 27, 40–41. M. Fain states that he employs the general merchandise account, criticised by modern accounting technique, only for reasons of simplicity. On the credit side of this account there appears an item "To Accounts Payable, 22,000," while on the debit side there is the item, "By Accounts Receivable, 22,000." These entries refer to merchandise purchased by the customers of the firm and subsequently returned for credit in the first instance, and in the second, to purchases made by the firm and returned to its furnishers for credit.

Credits

By Accounts Receivable 5,400,000
By Cash 120,000
By Accounts Payable 22,000
To Profit and Loss 44,286
New Balance, 1925 1,500,000
                                               7,086,286

Merchandise Account Restated in Gold Francs

Debits

Old Balance, 1924 1,200,000
To Accounts Payable 5,000,000
To Cash 350,000
To Accounts Receivable 22,000
                                               6,572,000

Credits

By Accounts Receivable 5,400,000
By Cash 120,000
By Accounts Payable 22,000
To Profit and Loss 730,000
New Balance, 1925 300,000
                                               6,572,000

The Merchandise Account as shown by the books offers no difficulties. It is merely a reproduction of the account as it stands after the closing entries have been made. The Merchandise Account Restated in Paper Francs has been adjusted to take care of the fluctuations of the franc. The new balance, 1,500,000 francs, shows the same amount as was the case in the former statement of this account. No adjustment need here be made, for this amount is the result of an inventory in which the actual stock on hand was evaluated at its replacement value. The evaluation of the stock on hand at its replacement cost in the first instance, that is, in the account as is shown by the Books, will bring this account to show a larger profit or smaller loss than would have been the case had the account shown the stock at its cost of acquisition. This constitutes doubtful accounting practice, for the Profit and Loss account is credited with an amount which has not yet been fully earned or lost, and will not be earned or lost until the total final stock has been sold, perhaps not even then. It would, therefore, have been better practice to evaluate this stock in the first instance at its cost of acquisition and then make the adjustment to its cost of replacement in the paper franc restatement of the account. This latter method is followed by M. Fain in his arrangement of the other accounts which require a re-evaluation of balances.

In the paper franc restatement of this account the old balance, 1,200,000 francs shows an inflation increase of 514,286 francs. This figure has been obtained by multiplying the original amount 1,200,000 by the coefficient of exchange 5 giving 6,000,000, which amount is in turn divided by the coefficient 3.5 giving 1,714,286 from which the original amount 1,200,000 was then subtracted, leaving the amount 514,286, which is credited to the Restatement Account, 1925. The coefficient 3.5 represented the value of the franc at the beginning of the financial period and the coefficient 5 at the end. Thus M. Fain has multiplied the value of the opening stock of merchandise by the value of the franc at the close of the financial period and has then in turn divided this result by the value of the franc at the beginning of the period. It must be noted that the opening stock of merchandise stood on the books in all probability—although M. Fain is not explicit on this point—at its cost of acquisition. This calculation gives us the figure of 1,714,286 francs for the re-evaluation of the stock of merchandise. This practice would doubtless fall under the criticism made by M. Leger regarding the re-evaluation of the Merchandise Account, and which has already been discussed.[72] The closing balance adjustment to the Merchandise Account has already been made. The method employed by M. Fain, while not absolutely exact in its details, gives a sufficiently accurate global result for practical purposes.

The same principles are applied to all the other accounts which are in need of re-evaluation. The fixed asset accounts have been re-evaluated by using two Restatement Accounts, 1924 and 1925, respectively. To the first is credited the difference between the book and replacement value of the asset on January 1, 1925. The second is credited with the difference between the value of the asset on January 1, 1925 and December 31, 1925. Both of these accounts, probably for the sake of convenience, have been closed out to a general Restatement Account. The closing balances give a figure representing the paper franc replacement cost and are adjusted by entries to profit and loss. The following accounts, and in practice all accounts of a similar character, are adjusted in the same way that the merchandise account was handled: Cash, Accounts Receivable and Payable, and Bank. Since the object of this system is to give a re-evaluated balance sheet in terms of paper francs, it is necessary to "restate" the value of the capital stock and reserves. This is done through the creation of a "Restatement of Capital" Account (*Redressement du capital*). This account is credited with the difference between the book value of the capital stock, which in this case was 2,000,000 francs and the present paper franc value of the capital stock. M. Fain appears to assume that the enterprise was created before the inflation and that therefore this figure, 2,000,000, represents the capital in terms of gold, although this is not explicitly stated. The capital is then brought to its theoretical paper value by multiplying by the coefficient 5 giving a total paper value of 10,000,000. From this amount is subtracted the sum at which the capital stock is carried on the books, 2,000,000, giving a net difference of 8,000,000 paper francs. This amount is carried as a credit to the Restatement of Capital account and as a debit to the general Restatement account.

---

[72] Cf. Leger, F., *Le redressement des bilans en francs-papier*, Paris (Editions Experta), 1926, pp. 30–36.

The final paper franc balance sheet will thus show—generally speaking during inflation—an account, Restatement, with a debit balance, an account, Restatement of Capital, with a credit balance and a Profit and Loss account with a credit balance. This latter account has been debited for the profit and loss entries to the several accounts, in the present example, as follows: Debits: plant, equipment, furnishings, merchandise, accounts receivable, cash, bank, stocks and bonds, general overhead expenses; Credits: mortgage, bonds, accounts payable. The Profit and Loss account thus shows not only the results of the business operations during the period, but also the profits and losses due to the fluctuations of the franc for the period under consideration. The Restatement Account shows the profits and losses accruing to the business on account of monetary fluctuations of the past, with the exception of those changes in the theoretical value of the capital stock.

The restatement of the accounts in terms of gold francs offers little difficulty, for the principles here applied have already been discussed. The Merchandise Account Restated in Gold Francs illustrates these principles. The new balance has been re-evaluated at 300,000 gold francs by taking the paper franc balance of 1,500,000 francs and dividing by the coefficient of exchange at the date of closing the books and which stood at 5. The other amounts in the account were left intact with the exception of profit and loss, which was here debited for the result of the following equation: (the book value of the merchandise on hand at the close of the period in paper francs minus its value in terms of gold) minus the original amount of the unadjusted account debited to profit and loss or, in figures (1,500,000 − 300,000) − 470,000 equals 730,000. This same procedure is followed for all the accounts where an adjustment is found necessary.

Thus the method of gold franc restatement carries no accounts that the books did not originally show. The Profit and Loss Account shows not only the results of the fluctuations of the franc but also those of the normal business operations as well. However, this account groups in one lump sum the results of all the financial periods, whereas with the use of the Restatement Account the results of previous years are separated from that of the one under consideration. M. Fain declares that it would be possible to use a Restatement Account in connection with the gold franc adjustment and thus attain a similar result.[73] The results of both the paper and gold franc adjustments are the same, save that the one is expressed in terms of paper and the other in terms of gold. The objections made by M. Leger concerning the adjustment of the merchandise account evidently apply to the method here described.

M. Fain feels that his results are exact. He declares, however, that the results would have been different had he employed index numbers of wholesale prices instead of coefficients of exchange as the medium of conversion.[74]

---

[73] Fain, G., *op cit.,* p. 43.
[74] *Op. cit.,* p. 45.

M. Fain goes on to suggest that a greater degree of exactitude could be obtained by adjusting the accounts each month instead of each year as was done in the example cited. Further, the Profit and Loss account, he states, does not give us very much information about the detailed results of the operations of the business; that is, the profits and losses upon certain specific transactions or upon a certain type of transaction. Further, if the total result of this account is exact, each of the elements, taken separately, is false, for the operations which tend to compensate themselves have not been separately adjusted. We cannot, therefore, attribute to any one transaction its proper share of profit and loss. It is quite useful to know these detailed results. These can be obtained, according to M. Fain, by a more frequent, say a monthly, adjustment, or by a more frequent adjustment of certain accounts which are of particular importance.[75]

M. Fain's method has the advantage of presenting the results of both the paper and gold franc balance sheet adjustment methods and thus gives the enterpriser more information than will either method taken singly. While his method is more accurate than some which were proposed and which have already been discussed, it is less so than the gold franc accounting system proposed by M. Faure. On the other hand, it is relatively inexpensive and easy to use. It has the disadvantage signalled by M. Leger in the adjustment of the Merchandise Account. The practice of re-evaluating the closing entry in the unadjusted accounts has already been criticised. The defects which are apparent in M. Fain's method can easily be eliminated, and, so corrected, the method should prove useful.

5. Paper and Gold Franc Bookkeeping with a Regulating and Compensating Account

It is impossible, in an article of this length, to give anything approaching a complete description of this method, the proposal of M. Lucien Thomas. This section will, therefore, be limited to a discussion of the principles involved in this method and a brief outline of the procedure followed.[76]

There are two parts or phases to this system: (1) The use of a gold standard money of account (*monnaie de compte a étalon or*), and (2) The use of a regulating and compensating account for the determination of the capital at any time.

---

[75] *Loc. cit.*

[76] Thomas, Lucien, *La tenue des comptabilités en période d'instabilité monétaire*, Paris (Editions Experta, 71 rue Desnouettes), 1927. This work, by reason of the ideas which it embodies as well as the detailed description of the method advocated and the discussions of principle, constitutes one of the outstanding French contributions to the subject of inflation accounting. Its length precludes any attempt here to set forth more than the briefest characterization of the system which it proposes. It consists of 209 quarto format, double column, pages printed in small type. Most of the works already cited give but 20 to 30 pages to the description of the procedure advocated.

The gold standard money which M. Thomas employs—he suggests that any fixed quantity of gold would suit the purpose—is the gold franc as defined by the law passed during the first French Republic, and which, up to the monetary revision of 1929, constituted the French official standard. This is a 20 franc gold piece, 9/10 fine, each piece containing 1/155th of a kilogramme of fine gold. One franc, therefore, will contain 0.290325 grammes of fine gold, and constitutes M. Thomas' standard money of account.

The regulating and compensating account preconized by M. Thomas is destined to correct the accounts for the fluctuations in prices occasioned by the depreciation, *or the appreciation,* of the franc. This account is likened to a clockwork pendulum which is designed to prevent the changes in temperature from effecting variations in the clockwork movement. This account will take, as debits, the amounts set aside to compensate the losses due to the following elements, among others:

1. Losses on account of cash on hand and in banks, accounts receivable, and other sums owed the firm.
2. The insufficiency of the depreciation reserve for the fixed assets.
3. The amounts resulting from an insufficient determination of the cost price of goods sold.
4. Complementary losses, determined at an ulterior date, over the losses ascribed to an anterior period.[77]

This account will take, as credits, amounts set aside to compensate for the following elements, notably:

1. The excessive depreciation reserve for fixed assets.
2. The amounts resulting from an excessive determination of the cost prices of goods sold.
3. Complementary profits, determined an an ulterior date, over the profits ascribed to an anterior period.[78]

The object of this account is to maintain the capital of the business intact, no matter what fluctuations the paper franc may show, nor at what period the business was constituted. The system may be said to be of universal application for periods of monetary variation—all possible fluctuations in prices can be handled by the regular procedure which it institutes. This account is so handled that the detailed loss or gain from all the various sources is kept separate. Thus the loss or gain in accounts receivable, cash, investments, etc., are separated in this account and not grouped together in a total result. This is obtained by maintaining a journal for the regulating and compensating account and appropriate subsidiary regulating and compensating accounts to take care of the detailed adjustments.

This system provides for accounts having separate entries for paper francs

---

[77] *Op. cit.,* p. 37.
[78] *Loc. cit.*

and gold francs, similar to the method of four column gold franc accounting. The regulating and compensating account is also kept in both gold and paper francs. Thus the paper franc records of the business will present the results of the transactions and adjustments in terms of the only legal money (the paper franc), while the gold franc records will reduce these transactions to their gold value and provide for the various adjustments necessitated by the monetary fluctuations. This dual system presents the great advantage of maintaining intact the paper franc records, and at the same time providing for such readjustments as the management of the enterprise may deem necessary.

In order to gain the maximum degree of precision with a minimum of complication in the actual task of bookkeeping, the system provides for the following procedure:

1. The use of only paper francs for subsidiary journals (*journaux division-naires*) and for individual accounts with third parties, as this is the only legal money of contract.
2. If numerous transactions involve the use of foreign monies, separate subsidiary journals will be opened for these transactions, expressed in the money of contract. Separate individual accounts with third parties will also be kept for these transactions in terms of the money of contract.
3. The subsidiary journals will be centralized periodically in the general journal by means of global conversions of total amounts from paper to gold franc expressions and from foreign monies into paper and gold francs.
4. The general and controlling accounts will be kept in both gold and paper francs.
5. In the absence of a perpetual inventory (*inventaire permanent*), the determination at inventory time of the cost price of the merchandise sold.
6. Monthly adjusting entries for the determination and recording of the gains or losses due to monetary variations on cash, accounts payable and receivable.
7. In the presence of a perpetual inventory, the use of gold francs exclusively for the individual accounts of materials and stock.
8. If a cost accounting system is used, the determination of the costs in terms of gold francs.[79]

The length of the adjustment periods referred to above will depend upon the amplitude of the price fluctuations. The gold value of the paper franc is determined by the use of the coefficient of Franco-American exchange rates. The average rate for the period under study is used for this determination. M. Thomas recognizes, however, that the determination of the average rate best adapted for certain types of enterprise is a delicate calculation, and states that no absolute precision in this matter is possible.

The reason may well demand at this point the question: What use is made of the Regulating and Compensating Account in the closing entries? Unfortunately, no single answer can be made to this question. An exact idea of the use

---

[79] *Op. cit.,* pp. 38–39.

of this account can only be obtained by a detailed examination of the examples which M. Thomas gives and which are far too numerous to permit of analysis here.

This account does not appear on either the paper or gold final balance sheets. The paper balance sheet shows an account, "Reserve for Inflation" (*Provision Régulatrice et Compensatrice*), created by a debit to Profit and Loss, and which shows a sum equal to a Regulating and Compensating Account. This entry is made in view of the legal requirements which regard a gold franc as always the equal of a paper franc and which do not recognize profits and losses arising from the fluctuations of the franc. In the gold accounts, this account is closed by entries to the several accounts which show the effects of the fluctuation—each account receiving an adjustment corresponding to its change in value to fluctuation. These changes are brought to the Profit and Loss Account through the employment of a special account "Surplus and Deficits" (*Bonis et Déficits*) for the purpose. The value of M. Thomas' elaboration would have been greatly increased by a more complete statement of the principles governing the use of the Regulating and Compensating Account and of a brief résumé of the procedure to be followed in its employment.

One of the more important advantages of this system lies in the fact that it permits the accounts directly to separate the results of the business operations from the losses and gains due to monetary fluctuations. The books of account here show in detail the results imputable to the various operations of the firm as well as those due to the monetary changes. The system furnishes the enterpriser with a large fund of information for his task of business management and thus constitutes an excellent means of business control.[80] A second advantage, of hardly less importance, is that it permits the accountant, at any time, to furnish the managers with cost data in terms of gold francs, thus enabling the latter to apply the theory of replacement prices wherever competition permits this. A third advantage of this system lies in the method of determination of the results of the business operations. The element, cost of goods sold, is cast both in terms of replacement and acquisition cost. This is, as we have seen, the proper procedure under inflation. Were this element expressed only in terms of cost of acquisition, the profit and loss could not be determined in both bases.

The description provided by M. Thomas takes into consideration many elements which have escaped the attention of the other authors cited, or which these other authors have felt best to leave to the initiative of the accountants who propose to adopt their systems. The one disadvantage of the system lies in the fact that, being so complete, it may prove too expensive to employ, or its use may involve too much added effort on the part of the accounting department. There is always the question of the balance between great precision of results and the cost of exactitude. While M. Thomas' system is well

---

[80] Cf. *op. cit.*, especially pp. 163–173.

adapted to any long and severe period of inflation, other systems might prove satisfactory for shorter and less severe periods.

IV.　Conclusions

Although French inflation was of long duration and fairly severe in its results, the only inflation system used to any extent in France was the establishment of gold franc balance sheets without any changes made either to the entries in, or to the balances of, the ordinary paper franc accounts. The reason why no more complicated plan was followed is to be found in part in the fact that many French business men were not well aware of the nature and effects of monetary inflation. Others failed to understand the principles underlying the more complicated system of accounting and failed to appreciate their utility, or feared that the use of any of these methods would falsify the standard accounting results.

Further, the systems of inflation accounting adjustment, it must be carefully noted, were not universally accepted even by those who understood the nature and effects of inflation.[81] Many thought their results false or at least misleading. Others felt that it was necessary to preserve the accounts intact, free from any inflation adjustments, for they constitute records of far too great importance for any "tampering"; although it must be noted that in the inflation accounting systems, where separate records are kept for adjusted accounts, this objection cannot apply.

One must not expect too much from even the best system of accounts. After all, it is not the task of the accounts to furnish ready-made policy for the conduct of business enterprises. This is, and must remain, the task of the business manager or enterpriser. The accounts furnish some of the fundamental data for the determination of business policy, but they cannot furnish all of the necessary elements; they must be supplemented by much additional data and by the intelligence and business acumen of our industrial, commercial, and financial chiefs. And intelligence is sorely needed by the manager in times of monetary inflation, just as it is—as many American enterprisers are at present learning—in periods of deflation.

But even if inflation accounting methods cannot undertake the whole responsibility for correcting and adjusting the evils of inflation, they can furnish the business man with much useful information and help to dispel some of the financial illusions which may arise in such times. This is the fundamental reason for their use, and it is to be deplored that the French business man did not make a ledger for them in his system of accounts.

The elaboration of these systems by both French and German accounting theorists constitutes a definite contribution to general accounting theory. An understanding of the principles involved may help in settling some of the

---

81 Cf. especially, Sabatier, Charles-Marie, *La Mésure des affaires,* Paris (Sirey), 1927.

controverted questions of principle which attract the attention of accountants to-day. The study of inflation accounting methods further emphasizes the necessity, which thoughtful accountants feel, of some knowledge of economics, especially of economic theory and monetary theory and history. It further shows that the economist has much to learn from the results of accounting. Analyses of accounting results will do much towards lending precision to, to say nothing of correcting the errors of, the classical economist's theory of inflation.

While we are not now in a period of monetary inflation, recurrent periods of that sort are not unknown in our history. It may be possible that at some time in the future we will again pass through such a period. During and after the world war we knew a period of "gold inflation" accompanied by rapidly rising prices. Can we say that our accounts properly interpreted business operations during the period? The archives of American accounting knowledge must be completed by an outline, at least, of inflation practice, so that we will be prepared for any such situation should one arise in the future. And, in closing, it may be well to remember—especially in view of the status of business in America to-day—that the various methods outlined are also adaptable to periods of deflation—periods of severe falling prices. The underlying principles are the same; the methods of application will vary according to the circumstances.

Henry W. Sweeney

MAINTENANCE OF CAPITAL

Henry W. Sweeney *was born in 1898, and received an A.B. in 1919 and a Ph.D. in 1936 from Columbia. He taught at Wisconsin, 1921–1923; he then spent approximately ten years on the staff of Price, Waterhouse & Co. He went to Georgetown to teach in 1936 and stayed until 1958. Since 1958 he has been the head of Henry W. Sweeney & Co., a C.P.A. firm in New York City. He has taught at Columbia as an adjunct professor since 1956.*

His major contribution to accounting is his book, Stabilized Accounting, *published in 1936, and a series of articles preceding the book and dating back into the 1920's, all dealing with the problem of the impact of price-level changes on accounting. The article reprinted here is "the foundation of the book itself," according to Sweeney. It explores the problem of the specific meaning of "maintenance of capital" and does it in a sophisticated fashion.*

Because the fundamental purpose of accounting should consist of an attempt to distinguish clearly between capital and income,[1] the different methods of maintaining capital may well be comprehensively examined and appraised. There are two main views on which maintainance of capital may be based. The first part of this article will briefly judge the more uncommon, less advantageous one. The second part will then evaluate the ramifications of the usual view.

I

According to one viewpoint, the object in maintaining capital should be to preserve the same proportion of the total social capital as was possessed at the time the capital was originally invested.

Reprinted from *The Accounting Review* (December, 1930), pp. 277–87, by permission.

[1] Irving Fisher, "Economics," *Accountants' Handbook* [First Edition], p. 1363; and J. M. Clark, "Valuation for the Balance-Sheet and Profits," *Het International Accountscongres,* Amsterdam, 1926, p. 370.

Accordingly, if capital of $10,000,000 was invested in a concern when the total capital of the community or country was $100,000,000,000, the proportion thereafter to be maintained would be the ratio of the $10,000,000 to the $100,000,000,000—in other words, one one-hundredth of one per cent. If, then, as a result of war or similar disaster, the total social capital shrank to $60,000,000,000, relative capital would be maintained if the particular capital continued to represent one one-hundredth of one per cent of merely $60,000,000,000, i.e., $6,000,000.

Professor F. Schmidt is sponsor of this view. Economic conditions affecting capital and productivity in Germany during the World War and the following years of extreme inflation were so unfavorable, he declared, that to expect absolute maintenance of capital and production on the part of the average business was to expect the impossible. Hence, he advocated maintenance of *relative* capital under such conditions.[2]

What may be said in criticism of this view?

The answer is, first, that such an opinion would seem to be theoretically inaccurate because men usually engage in business to obtain, in the long run, greater command over goods and services than they had when they entered business and not, as a rule to vie with one another for greater relative shares in whatever general economic goods the community may happen later to have. Business is not a race or a game to acquire more goods and services than others have, on the average, acquired. It is an effort to increase power over economic goods and services, regardless of whether others have succeeded proportionately more or less in the same quest.

If, e.g., a man invested capital of $10,000,000 when the total social capital was worth $100,000,000,000, and if the latter declined to $60,000,000,000 while the value of his individual capital was decreasing to $8,000,000, should he feel pleased because he has increased his relative share in the total social capital by one-third, i.e., from .01000% to .01333%? Or should he feel displeased because, other conditions remaining the same, his final capital of $8,000,000 represents only four-fifths as many net assets as his original investments? If, as stated above, the object of engaging in economic activity is to outdo others, he should feel pleased, because he has increased his *relative* economic wealth one-third. But if the object is to acquire increased property and thus, on the assumption, for simplicity, that there has been no change in price levels, greater command over economic goods and services, he should feel dissatisfied, because the changed value of his capital represents, other things being equal, one-fifth less power over property than his original capital.

The second objection to relative maintenance of capital is that it is liable to prove unsafe as a practical basis. Any theory that permits the business man, as this does, to feel satisfied while failing to maintain the original value

---

[2] "Geldentwertung und Bilanz," *Geldentwertung und Unternehmung,* Berlin, 1923, p. 85.

of his invested capital is likely to prove harmful, if not disastrous, to both the individual capitalist and society—much more so than a theory which, like that recommending absolute maintenance, sanctions payments of large dividends from contemporary economic power exceeding that originally invested, even if the general change in the capital of the community has not been *relatively* exceeded or even, perhaps, maintained by the enterprise that pays the dividends.

An ingenious plan that would automatically effect, among other purposes, maintenance of relative capital while utilizing the present system of money is that proposed by one economist.[3] He recommends that the quantity of payment media in a country be made to vary, so far as practicable, directly with the change in population, so that, in the long run, the general price level would, according to his theory, tend to vary inversely with the national productivity and so that fluctuations in prices would then arise from what is known as the "commodity side" of the price equation, instead of from the "money side," which affects prices by variations in the supply and circulative velocity of payment media. With such a scheme in effect, the demands of social justice and business progress would be adequately met, he asserts, by the existing price measuring-unit because changes in the general price level would tend to indicate a productivity change wherein the entire country both should and would share. For, if prices rose, the investor, e.g., a bondholder, would be repaid in money of lower general purchasing power than that which he originally invested, thus partaking *relatively* in the general loss due to lessened productivity; whereas if prices fell, he would receive a larger real equivalent than he initially bargained for —a fair result, however, because he, although bound in this instance to a contractually fixed money amount, should participate in the greater plenty presumably resulting in part from the utilization of the goods and services that he originally contributed, by investment, to the productive process.

Under such a plan, intended to distribute productive shares in the economic process according to a standard of social justice, the individual, at least if acquainted with all the facts, would still, however, probably desire and endeavor to maintain the *absolute* general purchasing power represented by his initial outlay, even if the social point of view would condone distribution, as income, of all his money returned exceeding the amount of his original monetary investment. Hence, stabilized accounting identified with maintenance of real capital, should still be needed. There is, moreover, some doubt as to the social advisability of allowing an economic community to regard its capital as maintained when simply the original money outlay, during the régime of such a plan as that described above, is kept intact; for if, e.g., the price level rose, due presumably to lessened production, the resulting tendency toward non-maintenance of real capital would tend still

---

3 Bradford, F. A., "Some Aspects of the Stable Money Question," *The Quarterly Journal of Economics,* XLIII, 4 (Aug., 1929), 667–696.

more to reduce general productivity and thus further decrease the distributable fruits of industry.

II

The prevalent attitude toward maintenance of capital is that the absolute entirety (but only such) of the original stock or fund of physical objects or value needs to be maintained, regardless of the extent to which economic society in general has meanwhile maintained its capital. There are three major ways in which absolute capital (as well as, incidentally, relative capital) may be maintained. The three following sections will discuss and appraise them.

1. Maintenance of Actual Physical, Material Capital

According to this viewpoint, maintenance of capital means preservation of the same amount of material, physical objects. If, for illustration of this theory, a man has owned a piece of land over a period of years, his capital, in the form of such land, has remained unchanged and thus has been maintained. Or if he has the same quantity and grade of wheat or the same kind of machine in as good condition as he originally invested, his capital has likewise been maintained with reference to such article.

This is the view usually recommended for practical business use when prices are rising rapidly from monetary inflation. In such a time, when money is rapidly decreasing in buying power, maintenance of capital expressed as an amount of money is equivalent to maintenance of a constantly declining stock of the assets used by the business. When the monies of various European nations after the recent war went down rapidly in value, accountants and business men of those countries were not slow in perceiving that the customary accounting method of figuring profit as the difference between sale price and original cost per books led to the preservation of only the money amount of capital.[4] Hence, they recommended basing sales prices, so far as market conditions and governmental restrictions would allow, on the replacement price of each cost element in the good or service sold (depreciation to be based on reproductive cost), plus profit, as of the instant of sale. In this way, they reasoned, the actual physical goods or services entering into the composition of an article sold could be replaced theoretically as of the moment when the sale occurred, and thus the tangible goods and services, i.e., the capital, would be almost exactly maintained and in a very definite, convincing, visible form.

---

[4] Based on the principle that the capital invested in an inventory should be maintained in material quantity and quality, a tabulation of the profit or loss arising under each of the possible interrelationships between original cost, sale price, and replacement price appears in C. Hellriegel's *Der Scheingewinn bei Warenumsaetzen*, Berlin, 1923, pp. 8–18.

There are two objections against maintenance of material capital. The first is theoretical, the second, practical.

The theoretical objection is that maintenance of material capital is not in harmony with the fundamental customary aim of economic endeavor, namely, to maintain original purchasing power over the general field of goods and services while, in the long run, acquiring more. In other words, maintenance of material capital is not necessarily—and usually not actually—maintenance of original general purchasing power because the relative economic desirability or value of an individual item of capital customarily fluctuates.

An example will perhaps clarify this difference and show the importance thereof. Let it be assumed that in the prevalently-horse-drawn-vehicle days of 1900 a man who was engaged in fast (if perhaps unreliable) delivery service owned and operated a one-cylinder motor car. If he may be assumed to have subsequently deducted enough from his gross income to maintain the original car in as good mechanical condition as it was when he bought it (depreciation being ignored for simplicity), he cannot be said, nevertheless, to have maintained his capital on the basis of the usual incentive to business enterprise, up to the present, when the demand for such an object of transportation (aside from possible museum value) is nil. For, although he would have maintained his physical capital, he would be distinctly poorer inasmuch as the car would not possess the same economic command today that it did in 1900, whether such command was based on market value or ability to yield returns for services rendered.

This example likewise illustrates the second, practical objection, which is that maintenance of material, physical capital may lead to maintenance of outward form instead of inner substance and thus to ruin. Clearly, some other view should be adopted.

But does the above argument interpret too narrowly the meaning of maintenance of material capital? Advocates of that maintenance theory may assert that the original motor car should not have been completely maintained while its usefulness was declining, but that instead, provision should constantly have been made for accumulation of sufficient resources to acquire subsequently a more modern car capable of rendering service relatively as good as the first car rendered in 1900. If, however, this amended view is adopted, then *material* capital would not have been preserved; on the contrary, capital would have been maintained according to its general economic serviceability, i.e., its value in producing income.[5] (Incidentally, an inconsistent viewpoint of the reason for the existence of the capital is here exposed. Material capital in the original argument meant a present stock of goods resulting from the past, whereas in the amended argument material capital is transformed into an amount of value determined with reference

---

[5] Or, in the words of Schmidt, as he was reading this manuscript, its "material producing power."

to the future.) If, again, advocates of maintaining material capital declare that the original relationship existing between the cost of the machine and the costs of economic goods in general should be preserved, the material-capital basis is overthrown for maintenance of cost in terms of general purchasing power, i.e., real capital. If, finally, they say that substitution of original material capital is implied, the objection then is that substitution must mean later replacement with physical capital different from the original; that the only way to substitute in accordance with their intent is on the basis of values; and that substitution, i.e., maintenance, based on the value of capital is not maintenance of material capital.

Maintenance of material capital may thus in itself lead to profit or loss. In the example of the motor car it led to loss and so was not conservative enough. In the following case it leads to gain and so is too conservative:

> A plant of 100 machines can have a value of 1,000,000 M in 1910, and in 1920, after its complete replacement in similar technical layout, be worth 1,200,000 M. I cannot comprehend how this difference of 200,000 M, when it has been acquired in these years, is not income. ...[6]

Evidently, therefore, if the economic value, as shown by the price, of an item of capital rises or falls in relation to the average economic value of other goods and services, more or less general purchasing power must be, or remain, invested to maintain the same physical quantity of that capital:

> But...if...the price of the goods and services increases or decreases, it will be necessary, in order to maintain the same volume of production, to invest more and more capital or less and less capital in the successive stages of production.[7]

Relationship Between Maintenance of Material Capital and Depreciation Based on Cost of Reproduction. In a period when prices are rising rapidly and, consequently, maintenance of merely the monetary amount of capital originally invested in a fixed asset is seen to cause eventual decrease in physical productive equipment, computation of depreciation on the basis of reproductive cost is likely to be advocated with increasing frequency. The object is, of course, a preservation of the original, tangible, physical forces of production i.e., material capital, and thus an escape from the rapids of price levels that lead to the whirlpool of ruin when the means of business navigation consists of depreciation based on original cost per books.

But, for reasons previously stated, maintenance of material capital is theoretically and practically objectionable. It, likewise, may lead to ruin. And, therefore, although it may be safer than maintenance of merely nominal capital in times of inflation, some other method should be sought. The foregoing criticism, although perhaps usually overlooked, is fundamentally

---

[6] Schmalenbach, E., *Grundlagen dynamischer Bilanzlehre* (3rd ed. rev., 1925), Leipzig, p. 170.

[7] Dumarchey, J., *Le Bilan Explicite,* Paris, 1927, p. 7.

one of the most severe that can be directed against depreciation on reproductive cost.

But may not depreciation on reproductive cost imply depreciation on *replacement* cost? And may not the inference then be drawn that the depreciation does not, and does not intend to, maintain merely a material capital asset, whose specific value relationship to the field of general values may have been changing very much? For does not depreciation on replacement cost permit depreciation to be based on the contemporary cost of obtaining equipment that, as of the date for which the depreciation is calculated, appears to possess the same productive usefulness to the business as the equipment for which the depreciation is being computed supposedly possessed when originally acquired?

The answer is identical with that previously given to the question of whether the concept of maintenance of material capital can logically permit substitution of original capital to provide a "continuance of the producing and selling processes with the same supply of energy or 'storehouse of strength.'" This answer is negative, at least if "material capital" is synonymous with "identical physical capital," inasmuch as the underlying foundation of the substitution concept is *value to the business*.

2. Maintenance of Nominal Capital

Maintenance of nominal capital—i.e., of a value measured by the worth of the price index of a single good or service, usually money— is subject to the same theoretical and practical objections as maintenance of material capital.

The theoretical objection is that such a way of maintaining capital is unrelated to the usual underlying object of economic effort; the practical objection is that the method is generally either unsafe or needlessly conservative. Because the theoretical objection applies to each form of maintaining nominal capital, attention will be centered upon concrete manifestations of the practical objection.

Maintenance of value that is measured in money ignores the probability of significant fluctuations in the worth of the measuring-unit after the date when the capital was originally invested. If, for example, capital consists of a mortgage during a period when the money in which the mortgage is measured decreases to one-half, the mortgage continues to represent the same amount in money—while the original economic substance is declining one-half. The capital is maintained in nominal amount. But such maintenance may lead either to ruin—much more probably than may maintenance of material capital—if general prices have advanced since the date of original investment or, if general prices have declined, to overmaintenance.

Because paper money is susceptible to much greater and more sudden variations in value than gold money, which is the leading precious-commodity money, maintenance of paper-money capital is exceedingly dangerous. This fact, disastrously experienced by business men in many European nations (especially Germany) after the recent World War, is well illustrated by the following story, which was famous throughout Europe as the "nail anecdote":[8]

During the inflation period a merchant in Germany purchased ten kegs of nails. For them he paid, e.g., 1,000 M. Thinking that he was making a good profit, he sold them for 1,333 M, one-third more than their cost. But when he ordered more nails from his wholesaler, he was startled to learn that the entire proceeds from the sale of the original ten kegs, including the nominal profit of 33 1/3% on cost, would purchase only eight kegs of the same nails. Thinking to prevent a further, similar diminution in his stock of nails, he sold the eight kegs, which cost 1,333 M, at *twice* their cost, namely, at 2,666 M. Upon completion of this second sale he was able to buy, however, only six kegs with the entire proceeds bcause the mark continued its rapid fall in value. In short, after several more similar cycles of buying and selling nails, there remained to him only a single nail. So, in despair, he drove it into the wall and on it hanged himself.

Maintenance of capital expressed in a *gold* monetary unit is, of course, a much safer procedure. Nevertheless, the relatively great fluctuations that have occurred during the last three decades in the worth of even the gold money *par-excellence,* namely, the U.S.A. dollar, demonstrate only too plainly that maintenance of gold capital itself is not a sound way of preserving original capital—unless capital represents merely a specified number of monetary units, regardless of what that sum of money is currently worth. If the general price level remained constant, maintenance of nominal capital would be free from objection. But the general price level has never, so far as economists are able to determine, remained constant very long.

Another measuring unit based on the value of a single commodity or service, and occasionally employed, is a price index representative of the change in such a value as between two given dates or periods. In Germany, for instance, the price index of rye was commonly utilized as previously illustrated to convert the values of one date or period into their equivalents as of another.

At first sight, favor might appear to be well bestowed on measurement of value in terms of the price index of a commodity or service, especially the outstanding one used or produced in a particular business. A concern engaged primarily in steel work, for instance, might measure the values of its assets, liabilities, and net worth by the price index of a ton of steel of specified quality. The changing market value of steel, as reflected in an index number, might seem, indeed, to be a very significant basis for measurement inasmuch as comparative purchasing power over steel is apparently of paramount concern to everybody interested in that enterprise. Why should attention be centered upon the *general* purchasing power of the value of

---

[8] Léger, F., *Le Redressement des Bilans en Francs-Papier,* Paris, 1926, pp. 41–42.

individual capital items if only *particular* kinds of economic goods and services, and primarily steel, are to continue to be the subject matter of transactions?

The answer is, first, that maintenance of capital measured in terms of the price index of a single commodity or service is not maintenance according to the fundamental reason for economic activity; and, second, that it is quite likely to prove either unsafe or too conservative because a single commodity or service, be it money or food or electricity, is much more likely to vary in value than a *combination* of goods and services. When the values of a business are measured, for ascertainment of growth in substance, by the price index of a single commodity or service, one cannot tell "which is hammer and which is anvil," i.e., whether the changed worth of the single commodity currently measures the value changes in the group of business items, or whether the changed values of the items in the group measure the change in the value of the basic good or service.

But if maintenance of relative capital, absolute material capital, and absolute nominal capital, all seem theoretically unsound and practically either unsafe or unnecessarily conservative, how should capital be maintained? The following section will attempt to answer this question.

3. *Maintenance of Real Capital*

Maintenance of individual real capital is effected by preservation of the original absolute command exercised by the capital over the goods and services of most importance to the particular concern. This method necessitates continual current compilation of an individual-concern index, which must then be employed to render properly comparable both the current amount of the capital and the original amount to be maintained.

This basis for maintenance of capital is superior to the material and nominal bases because maintenance becomes judged by preservation of command over the combined values of several goods and srvices, rather than over the quantity or value of only one. Hence, it is more likely to be related to the usual primary object of economic activity,[9] and less likely to be either unsafe or too conservative, as may result if capital is maintaind according to a value that is fluctuating relative to the entire field of values. Maintenance of individual real capital, in consequence of its dependence upon constant construction of a satisfactory individual-concern index, is, however, open to the disadvantages of requiring more work than maintenance of material or nominal capital and of being much more difficult to understand.

---

[9] Voigt recommends multiplying the amount of initial net worth by the subsequent change in the individual-concern index and comparison of the result with the current amount of net worth per balance sheet in order to learn whether the investment has flourished as it could have been expected to. He does not judge maintenance according to preservation of original power over the general field of economic goods and services. *Der Einfluss des veraenderlichen Geldwertes auf die wirtschaftliche Rechnungsfuehrung,* Frankfurt am Main, 1922.

Maintenance of general real capital (or simply "real capital") is effected by preservation of general purchasing power. Inasmuch as the index of general prices is the measure of change in general purchasing power, it may be employed in order quickly and conveniently to convert a current value into its general-purchasing-power equivalent as of the date when the investment was originally made. Comparison of the original amount of capital with the current, subsequent amount then indicates the extent of maintenance of real capital.

If, for example, capital of $100,000 is invested, if the dollar then declines one-half in value, and if the capital at the end of such a period is $190,000, conversion of the $100,000 value, by means of the general index (200), to its equivalent (200,000) in terms of the general price level existing upon termination of this period shows, according to this basis for maintenance of capital, that the value of the original investment has not been maintained— although the nominal basis would recognize an increase of 90%.

Maintenance of real capital, a refinement over the other methods, assures preservation of invested purchasing-power possiblities and means that the capital of the enterprise "can continue to possess its initial, original degree of influence over the whole economic system."[10] Inasmuch as the word "real" means "actual general economic equivalence of," the concept of real capital is deeper than that of nominal capital. It is based on evaluation of the money unit itself, instead of money units, which, because they constantly vary in worth, are themselves of continually changing size.

What judgment may be expresed concerning the merits of maintaining real capital? The answer must rest upon commonly overlooked or misunderstood fundamental principles, which may be summarized thus: Inasmuch as men customarily engage in business with or without capital, to obtain a greater supply of all sorts of scarce economic goods and services,[11] the fundamental purpose of their accounting must ordinarily be to ascertain, as of subsequent specific moments, whether their goal has been attained. If general economic power, i.e., capital, was invested, accounting must be able to determine whether such power has been maintained and, consequently, how much income, if any, has been realized. But to perform these fundamental, related duties, accounting must measure capital in terms of general purchasing power; it must distinguish between capital and income on the basis of *real* capital. Hence, *maintenance of absolute capital measured in terms of general purchasing power* seems most worthwhile and thus is selected as

---

10 Walb, E., *Das Problem der Scheingewinne,* Freiburg im Breisgau, 1921, p. 8.

11 "...the desire to make money does not itself necessarily proceed from motives of a low order...money is general purchasing power, and is sought as a means to all kinds of ends...." Marshall, Alfred, *Principles of Economics* (8th ed., 1920), p. 22.

"...the investment of money is a means to an end; we have no direct use for the dollars received....They must be exchanged for food, clothing, housing and many other things if we are to receive the benefits intended when the original investment was made." Van Strum, K. S., *Investing in Purchasing Power,* p. 4.

the most weighty subject matter available for application of stabilized accounting[12]—although the validity of pure stabilized-accounting theory, which concerns itself only with measurement by units stable in worth,[13] does not depend upon maintenance of real capital.

Probably no one, it is true, anticipates spending all or any of the greater general purchasing power hoped to be obtained from business activity, for acquisition of *every* kind of economic goods and service represented in the general price level. In many cases the purchasing power will be spent, in fact and in expectation, for articles that in the relative proportions of their total costs approximate the weighted prices in an index of the cost of living. In other cases only a minor fraction will be spent on such articles. Part of the purchasing power may be saved. In any event, however, when, as now, many commodities and services bid for the favor of consumers, purchasing power offers to its owner such a constantly widening choice that to predict its eventual use in acquisition of a restricted number of specific articles is likely to be presumptuous. It should, therefore, be regarded as *general* purchasing power.

But may not a man enter into business with the express intention of increasing his economic power over only one kind of good or service, or only several kinds, instead of over the entire general field?[14] May he not, for instance, be so interested in acquiring a home or a motor car that he will risk his capital in the security markets with the intention of using any resulting profit, besides perhaps his original capital, toward acquisition of the one desired commodity? The answer is, or course, affirmative. In such a case, then, should not maintenance of capital be based on the index number of the particular commodity desired, rather than on the general index? The reply is again affirmative. If both the original capital and any gain are intended for

---

[12] As Professor Schmidt points out here, the general index, being dependent upon prices, which, in turn, are determined by productivity, the amount of money in circulation, and so forth, is itself relative. Preservation of capital on the general-purchasing-power basis enables, nevertheless—if, as must, of course, be assumed, the general index is accurate—identical absolute command over economic goods and services to be maintained, as a little experimentation will conclusively demonstrate.

[13] Interesting to observe is the ordinary, orthodox type of current accounting, which uses as the measuring-unit a money stable in purchasing power over the single commodity gold, becomes identical with stabilized accounting if the latter selects as a stabilized unit for homogeneous measurement one that is steadfast in its ability to command the same quantity of gold as the national money. Still, if the value of only one commodity, whether gold or cotton or a particular kind of fixed asset, is to be the basis for the stabilized-accounting unit, gold is preferable to most other goods, although carpets proved, for a time in the United States, more stable in worth than gold. Because, however, the worth of any particular article or service is too liable to become quite divergent from the average value of other commodities and because, more important, men customarily undertake business operations in order to gain enhanced control over the *general* field of economic goods, stabilized accounting chooses to concern itself with measurement by a unit that is of stable value in terms of *all* economic commodities and services in the community.

[14] Regarding the idea that a special index should, ideally, be devised for each individual, cf. Haberler, G., "A New Index and Its Meaning," *Quarterly Journal of Economics,* XLII, 3 (May, 1928); also his *Der Sinn der Indexzahlen,* Tuebingen, 1927.

use in eventual acquisition of a specific commodity, maintenance should be based on the price index number of that commodity. If, however, only the gain is intended for such use, maintenance of the capital should still be based on the *general* index.

Most men who invest capital do not, however, definitely plan to use it or its income, if any, to acquire eventually any particular good or service or any particular combination thereof. And even if they do, they are quite likely to change their minds, under the rapidly moving conditions of modern life, before the eventual date for such use of the purchasing power arrives. Unless, therefore, there is quite definite intention to employ an investment for eventual acquisition of a specific commodity or group of commodities—and not merely the intermediate current acquisition of business goods and services necessary for attainment of the ultimate goal—the most practical assumption in the light of experience is that greater general economic command, which will be available for later expenditure in any direction, is the actual object of business endeavor and that, therefore, maintenance of capital should be based upon the general price index.

If, again, a man invests capital with the intention of *never* withdrawing any of its original amount, should not maintenance be based upon a price index of the commodity or commodities of most importance in the operations of that particular business, rather than upon the general index? A negative answer must be given. The theoretical reason is that if maintenance is not based upon real capital, by means of the general index, there is no precise way of ascertaining as of a subsequent date whether the probable primary object of economic activity has been realized, i.e., whether an apparent subsequent excess over the value originally invested is truly representative of increased command over all goods and services and, as such, consequently withdrawable, in the form of income, without impairment of original capital. The practical reason is that maintenance based upon an index of the commodity or commodities of greatest significance in the particular business operations means maintenance of nominal or individual real capital—and hence either possible disaster or unnecessary overmaintenance.

Real capital should, of course, be ascertained on the basis of the national general index. If, however, the purpose of economic activity in a given case is to obtain greater general *international* purchasing power, strict accuracy in stabilized accounting procedure then requires construction and use of an index representative of the various national general price levels weighted according to expected regions of expenditure. But this is a refinement that may in most instances be disregarded.

Measurement of capital in terms of economic command over goods and services requires, of course, more work and expense than merely nominal measurement of capital. This fact should be considered, however, less an objection to maintenance of real capital, than an additional accusation against a fictitious monetary standard of value and the characteristic concomitant general price fluctuations. If use of a fluctuating dollar for measurement of accounting data makes additional calculation a prerequisite for accuracy in the data so measured, and if such calculation is not performed, the unstabilized figures remain simply incorrect. The extent of such inaccuracy helps determine, of course, the practical need for any remedial procedure.

A concluding objection is that the indispensable instrument for calculation of real capital, namely, the general price index, is itself imperfect. There is truth in this objection, but probably less than there was five years ago, or even one year ago. Price economists and economic statisticians are continuously laboring to perfect the implements that they are using for accurate measurement of the general price level. Presumably these instruments, like most used in science, are becoming more efficacious. In any event, however, if one of them can establish the measurement of economic data on a foundation more stable and more suitable for comparison than the ordinary monetary unit can, then, in spite of remaining imperfection, it should be employed as the best available device for financial measurement.

Important to observe, finally, is that *stabilized accounting is not related to any particular kind of measuring unit.* It attempts simply to measure financial amounts in terms of whatever unit seems most solidly based on the ultimate purpose of the economic activity. If, for example, in a given instance there is satisfactory evidence that such purpose is to acquire greater purchasing power over just one kind of economic commodity or over the kinds commonly supposed to constitute the ordinary cost of living, stabilized accounting priciples require measurement in, respectively, the price index of the one commodity or an index of the cost of living. But because increased purchasing power over the *general* field of goods and services is customarily the primary motive for economic activity, accounting stabilization in the following pages will be based on the general price index.*

III

Maintenance of capital is a subject of great importance because it should be considered a part of the main purpose of accounting.

Capital may be maintained relatively or absolutely.

Relative maintenance is based on a false theoretical concept. Practically, moreover, it is unsafe if the general capital of the nation has diminished during the investment period of the individual capital, and unnecessarily conservative if the social capital has grown.

Maintenance of absolute material capital is based upon an incorrect concept of the purpose of economic activity. Practically, also, it is either unsafe because the individual price level of the capital has decreased in relation to

* "...the following pages..." refers to a manuscript that appeared in book form in 1936 as *Stabilized Accounting.*

the general price level during the period of investment; or too conservative because the specific price level has, on the contrary, relatively increased. To the extent that depreciation on reproductive cost aims to maintain material capital, it is to be condemned.

Maintenance of absolute nominal capital is likewise based upon a false premise regarding the purpose of business activity. It is, moreover, either a very dangerous practical basis—more so than maintenance of material capital —if the general price level has risen since the capital was invested (and prices rise during a greater number of years than they fall); or too conservative a basis if prices as a whole have declined since the date of original investment. Maintenance of capital measured in paper money is an even more unsound and unsafe basis than maintenance of gold-money capital. Maintenance based on the price index of a single good or service, although at first glance a good method, is similar fundamentally to maintenance of monetary capital and consequently both unsound in theory and either unsafe or too conservative in practice.

Maintenance of absolute individual real capital, although superior to maintenance of material or nominal capital, is, nevertheless, theoretically objectionable because based upon a false premise regarding the object of economic endeavor and, practically either unsafe or too conservative. Greater practical objections are, however, the difficulties of understanding and constructing the type of index required for this form of maintenance.

The basis for maintenance probably most often in harmony with the customary fundamental purpose of economic activity is maintenance of absolute *general* purchasing power, i.e., maintenance of general real capital or simply "real capital." It, alone, continually measures capital and income in such a way as to facilitate realization of the usual goal of economic effort, namely, increase of general purchasing power, and thus materially assists accounting to realize its main purpose of accurately distinguishing between capital and income.

Under certain conditions measurement may, with more justification, be based on the price index of a single commodity or service, or a weighted combination thereof, than on an index of the general price level.

Although stabilized accounting customarily employs, with apparent justification, the general price index in maintenance of capital, it is not essentially related to any particular kind of measuring unit.

Ralph Coughenour Jones

FINANCIAL STATEMENTS
AND THE UNCERTAIN DOLLAR

Ralph Coughenour Jones *was born in Illinois in 1897, received a B.S. from the University of Illinois in 1922, and a Ph.D. from Yale in 1929. He is a C.P.A. in Illinois, and has spent his career in teaching, initially at Illinois but mainly at Yale. He served as a vice-president of the American Accounting Association in 1941 and as its director of research, 1950–53. Among his writings are* Price-Level Changes and Financial Statements—Case Studies of Four Companies *(1955) and* Effects of Price-Level Changes on Business Income *(1956).*
The article reprinted here is an early example of the type of analysis of price-level changes that Jones also carried out subsequently. Together with Sweeney's work, it demonstrates that American accountants had solved the price-level problem (at the formal level of analysis) over a generation ago.

The concept of the balance-sheet as a list of assets and liabilities and of the profit-and-loss statement as a summary of income and expense is so simple, and the superficial appearance of mathematical exactness is so reassuring, that many readers, if not the great majority, impute to these statements a degree of accuracy which is seldom attained in practice. Unfortunately for the peace of mind of the accountants who prepare the statements and of the directors, bankers, and investors who must perforce rely upon them, every item in these statements must be expressed in terms of money. The dollar, the pound, the franc or other monetary unit must be used as a common denominator to permit land, buildings, and machinery to be added to inventories, accounts receivable, patents, and goodwill. The process of expressing such diverse items in terms of a common unit is known as valuation, the most important and the most difficult problem of accounting or finance.

The accountant, particularly the public accountant, is inclined to deny that valuation is a function of accounting. The accountant, according to this view,

Reprinted from *The Journal of Accountancy* (September, 1935), pp. 171–97, by permission.

must accept the valuations agreed upon between the parties to bona fide transactions or deals and construct a set of accounts which constitute an accurate historical record. Viewed in this light, a balance-sheet is the cumulative result of all the transactions of a business since its inception and not in any sense a statement of current values. The layman, however, unless he has been initiated into the mysteries of accountancy, undeniably assumes that the balance-sheet is supposed to represent current values, whether it does in fact or not. And many accountants agree with him.

The business man has not been much interested in the theoretical basis of accounts, but under the pressure of financial necessity he has been compelled to recognize important changes in value. Accordingly, appraisals were ordered and plants were written up on an extensive scale after the war period of rising prices. And, during the depression of 1930, plant and property valuations were drastically reduced. As a result, the reports of many companies are a hodgepodge of diverse valuations which indicate neither historical cost nor current values.

Practical men, moreover, have not overlooked the effect of changed valuations on the income account. One motive for the plant write-downs of the 30's was the desire to reduce depreciation charges in keeping with current values. Likewise, various inventory methods, such as the base inventory and last-in-first-out methods, and price equalization reserves, such as that employed by the Procter & Gamble Company, are designed to prevent undue profit distortion as a result of price fluctuations. The theoretical discussions of valuation have dealt largely with balance-sheet aspects, although, as the illustrations to follow will emphasize, the effects, of various methods of valuation on the income account are far more important.

In the past, asset revaluations have as a rule been made and recorded only when the book figures were radically out of line with current values. Write-ups have commonly occurred when the price level was at or near a peak, and write-downs when prices generally were at a minimum. As a result, the changes have been irregular and drastic, and the value of the financial statements for comparative purposes has been seriously impaired. In order to make the accounts reasonably reflect current conditions and to avoid abrupt value changes, numbers of accountants have recommended that fixed-asset accounts be regularly adjusted by means of an index number. Gradual changes thus computed would be better than the irregular revaluations which have occurred in the past, but the recording of index-number adjustments on the books conceals historical costs and at best constitutes only a partial solution to the general problem of valuation. Even though fixed asset values were satisfactorily determined by index numbers, the more important problem of inventory valuation would still remain.

Finding myself substantially in agreement both with the view that accounts should be based on historical cost and with the view that financial statements should reasonably reflect current conditions, I have sought a method of reconciling the two. It is my conclusion that the heart of the difficulty lies neither in the principles of accounting nor in the diverse price movements of different kinds of goods and services, but in the unstable dollar. The dollar serves very well as a medium of exchange but quite inadequately as a measure of value. It is true that the prices of individual commodities or limited groups of commodities may have independent trends, but it is almost inconceivable that the complex properties of a large corporation should deviate far from the general level of prices. If this be true, it will be more fruitful to study the shifting value of the dollar itself rather than the changing prices of various commodities or commodity groups. Accordingly, I shall present three propositions relating to the dollar as a measure of value, then an extended illustration of the effects of a changing dollar on the ordinary financial statements, and, finally, some conclusions to be drawn from the illustration.

I. The Dollar and Other Monetary Units Do Fluctuate in Value

To a generation which has seen the utmost chaos in the foreign exchanges, has seen the German mark vanish into nothing and has seen the gold content of the dollar changed for the first time in a hundred years, the truth of the above proposition should be evident. To some extent the real nature of money is beginning to be understood. In his *Analyzing Financial Statements*, Gilman remarks: "The older concept of the dollar as an unchanging unit has been replaced by an understanding that the dollar itself fluctuates in value." There are many, however, who do lip service to this idea but act at the same time as if the dollar were a fixed unit of value. They say that the dollar changes, and they proceed to compute their profits or losses in the same old way. Even during the period of hyperinflation in Germany, the people within the country thought not of the fall of the mark but of the terrific rise in prices.

This point has been thus belabored because it is fundamental. Everyone is so accustomed to thinking of the monetary unit of his country as a constant that it requires a real mental effort and a marked shift in point of view to accept the idea of a variable unit with all its implications. For anyone who believes, however, that the dollar of 1935 is the dollar of 1932, of 1919 or of 1913, the rest of this article will be meaningless.

II. The Variations in the Value of the Dollar Can Be Measured with Reasonable Accuracy

A dollar is worth what it will buy. This is called its purchasing power. It has no intrinsic value. Formerly, the dollar was worth 25.8 grains of gold; theoretically, it is now worth 15.2 grains. At various times it has been worth one bushel of wheat; at other times, two bushels. If there were dollars and wheat and no other commodities or services in the market, the value of the dollar would be measured in terms of wheat. Since there are in fact many commodities and services, the value of the dollar must be measured by an index number. If all the goods and services, food, clothing, shelter, transportation, entertainment, building materials, hours of labor, stocks and bonds which the American people buy in a year could be listed, and the number of dollars required to buy them in one year could be divided by the number required during the previous year, the reciprocal of the result would indicate the exact purchasing power of the dollars of the second year in terms of the dollars of the first or base year. All the transactions of a year obviously cannot be considered, but an intelligent weighting of the more important elements will provide an index which closely approximates the ideal. Statisticians may argue about the refinements of index-number construction, but even a poor index would provide a better measure of value than the currencies of many, if not all, countries have done during the past twenty years.

Carl Snyder, economist for the Federal Reserve bank of New York, has developed an index of the general level of prices from 1860 to date. The reciprocal of this index indicates the relative purchasing power of the dollar in terms of the dollars of a given year. The index itself is based on the year 1913, but by a simple computation any other year may be treated as the base. This index has twelve components including wages, rents, realty values, security prices, etc., in addition to the usual commodity prices. As a result, it fluctuates less than an index of wholesale prices and gives a more trustworthy measure of general purchasing power.

This index, though less volatile than indexes of basic commodity or wholesale prices, shows important changes in purchasing power. Since 1915 the average purchasing power of the dollar has changed in every year except 1927. In terms of 1926 dollars, the average change has been 8¢, slightly under 8¢ in years of rising prices and almost 10¢ in years of falling prices. In one year the change amounted to 23¢, and in three other years it was from 14¢ to 20¢. These changes, moreover, are as a rule cumulative over a number of years. The purchasing power fell 82¢ (in terms of 1926 dollars) from 1915 through 1920, rose 19¢ in 1921 and 1922, and then fell 13¢ from 1923 through 1929. From 1930 to 1933 inclusive, it rose 38¢ and in 1934 fell 8¢. These changes are too significant to be disregarded in any careful analysis of the financial condition of a business enterprise.

The idea of developing and using a standard and invariable unit of value, distinct from the monetary unit which is primarily a medium of exchange, may at first seem radical. It is, however, very similar to the process by which standards of length and weight were developed. The common unit of measurement in ancient Egypt was the cubit, the length of the forearm from the elbow to the end of the middle finger. The foot originally was the length of a human foot. The yard was the distance from the point of Henry I's nose to the end of his thumb. The inch was the length of three barley corns taken from the middle of the ear. Such rough and ready measurements may have been tolerable in an unscientific age, but today how would interchangeable parts be manufactured or specifications written in terms of such uncertain units? Master gauges now measure to the millionth part of a necessarily invariable inch.

The concept of an abstract unit of length, so familiar and therefore so commonplace to us, was the result of a long process of gradual development. Length at first was measured in relation to such well-known and intimate accessories as hands, feet and arms without the concept of an abstract unit. The dollar is still in this crude stage. Since it must serve as a medium of exchange and be itself affected by the very transactions whose magnitude it measures, an abstract unit for the measurement of value will be necessary, if any but the crudest results are to be obtained. Such a unit we may call a standard dollar, which is merely the dollar of some selected period in terms of which the dollars of other periods may be evaluated. With the experience of the physical sciences before us, we should be able to accept and use this abstract unit of value without a long period of evolutionary development. The inertia of the human mind is such, however, that a catastrophic change in prices must usually occur before the serious errors resulting from the change in the value of the monetary unit are generally recognized. Hastily improvised methods are then introduced after it is too late to deal effectively with the situation. There is evidence that French business men did profit somewhat from the German experience. It would be an unparalleled achievement if American business men, taking their cue from monetary disturbances in other countries, should prepare in advance for important changes in the value of the dollar which may or may not occur as the result of recent monetary and banking legislation in the United States.

III. An Apparent Gain Which Brings No Increase of Purchasing Power and an Apparent Loss Which Results In No Diminution of Purchasing Power Are Both Alike Unreal, Fictitious and Misleading

Regardless of balance-sheet valuations, whether based on historical cost, appraised values, or what not, here lies the key to the correct determination of income. It has long been recognized as desirable to exclude market appreciation and capital gains and losses from the operating income account; but the accomplishment of this result has been rendered difficult by the fact that the dollars in which costs were measured were often larger or smaller than the dollars in which selling prices were expressed. It can hardly be denied that the actual purchasing power involved in a given transaction is more important than the number of monetary units, yet it is the peculiar aptitude of accounting to record only the number of units without regard to their purchasing power. If a man buys a book for ten monetary units called dollars and immediately resells it for one hundred monetary units called dimes, no one would claim that he has made a profit on the transaction. But if he buys the book for $10, holds it for a number of years, and sells it for $100 at a time when the purchasing power of the dollar is only ten cents, he has by all the canons of law and accounting realized a profit of $90. This may be good law, especially if it is income-tax law, but it is absurd economics. The accountant, since he must consider both law and economics, may be compelled to record the transaction in the orthodox way, but he is certainly under no obligation to deceive himself and mislead others in reporting and interpreting the result.

The fact is that income taxes applied to gains of this character are capital levies. Taxpayers who have received no real increment of value are compelled to transfer to the government a part of the purchasing power which they originally held. Since a large proportion of so-called capital gains is of this character, it is no cause for wonder that our income-tax laws hinder and prevent desirable transfers of property. A man might be willing to share his real income but not his capital with the government. There is a possibility, however slight, that the courts may ultimately recognize the fictitious character of such gains. In the gold-clause cases, the Supreme Court denied that the claimants had suffered any damage, on the ground that the purchasing power of the dollar had not fallen. Is it inconceivable that the converse of this idea may at some future time be used for the benefit of the taxpayer? The chances for the adoption of such a rule would be materially improved if it should become the accepted accounting practice rigorously to exclude all such fictitious gains and losses from the income account. The extent to which the effects of these gains and losses permeate the customary financial statements will be brought out in the example which follows.

An Illustration

The fact that financial statements are significantly influenced by the changing value of the dollar is generally admitted, even by those accountants who maintain that nothing can or should be done about it. It is commonly assumed that the expert analyst or business executive who reads balance-sheets and profit-and-loss statements in the light of a broad experience and an intimate knowledge of current conditions can interpret the results with reasonable accuracy. Whether this is true or not will depend in large measure on the degree and kind of variations which the changing dollar introduces into the statements.

The statements of the Hypothetical Manufacturing Company are based on a simple set of assumptions in which the only important variable is the change in the purchasing power of the dollar. During a three-year period it is assumed that the dollar falls in purchasing power at the rate of four cents per quarter or sixteen cents per annum. Stated differently, the price level rises from 100 to 192 in three years—a rapid but not unprecedented change. The average purchasing power of the dollar during each quarter and the purchasing power at the end of each quarter are shown below. The index number of prices is the reciprocal of the purchasing power in each instance.

ASSUMED PURCHASING POWER OF THE DOLLAR BY QUARTERS

Quarters	Average Purchasing Power for Quarter			Purchasing Power at End of Quarter		
	Year 1	Year 2	Year 3	Year 1	Year 2	Year 3
First	.98	.82	.66	.96	.80	.64
Second	.94	.78	.62	.92	.76	.60
Third	.90	.74	.58	.88	.72	.56
Fourth	.86	.70	.54	.84	.68	.52

THE HYPOTHETICAL MANUFACTURING COMPANY

Comparative Profit-and-Loss Statements

	Year 1	Year 2	Year 3
Sales	$871,628	$1,056,296	$1,340,809
Cost of goods sold	584,386	683,424	839,252
Gross profit	$287,242	$ 372,872	$ 501,557
Selling and general expense	196,116	237,668	301,682
Net profit	$ 91,126	$ 135,204	$ 199,875

Surplus Account

	Year 1	Year 2	Year 3
Balance at beginning of year	....	$ 31,162	$ 86,330
Net profit for year	$ 91,126	135,204	199,875
	$ 91,126	$ 166,330	$ 286,205
Dividends paid	60,000	80,000	120,000
Balance at end of year	$ 31,126	$ 86,330	$ 166,205

THE HYPOTHETICAL MANUFACTURING COMPANY

Comparative Balance-Sheets

Assets	Beginning of year 1	End of year 1	End of year 2	End of year 3
Current assets:				
Cash	$ 200,000	$ 239,070	$ 292,210	$ 342,210
Receivables	200,000	232,558	285,714	326,523
Raw materials, at cost ...	40,000	46,512	57,143	74,074
Work in process, at cost ..	22,500	25,320	30,514	38,685
Finished goods, at cost ...	87,500	98,190	117,844	148,792
	$ 550,000	$ 641,650	$ 783,425	$ 930,284
Fixed assets:				
Plant and equipment (including land, $50,000) ..	$ 850,000	$ 850,000	$ 850,000	$ 850,000
Less: reserve for depreciation	250,000	314,000	378,000	442,000
	$ 600,000	$ 536,000	$ 472,000	$ 408,000
	$1,150,000	$1,177,650	$1,255,425	$1,338,284

Liabilities and net worth
Current liabilities:

Accounts payable	$ 50,000	$ 46,524	$ 69,095	$ 72,079
Funded debt—bonds payable	100,000	100,000	100,000	100,000
	$ 150,000	$ 146,524	$ 169,095	$ 172,079
Net worth:				
Capital stock, par $100 ..	$1,000,000	$1,000,000	$1,000,000	$1,000,000
Surplus	....	31,126	86,330	166,205
	$1,000,000	$1,031,126	$1,086,330	$1,166,205
	$1,150,000	$1,177,650	$1,255,425	$1,338,284

Judged by all the usual criteria, this company has made an excellent show-ing. Profits have more than doubled, having risen from 9 per cent of the net worth to over 18 per cent. Sales have increased relative to plant, net worth, inventories and receivables. The percentages of both gross and net profits to sales have increased materially.

PERCENTAGES OF GROSS PROFIT AND NET PROFIT TO SALES

Year	Gross Profit	Net Profit
1	33%	10½%
2	35%	13 %
3	37%	15 %

Liberal dividends have been paid at the rates of 6, 8 and 12 per cent, and yet 39 per cent of the profits have been carried to surplus. The current ratio has risen from 11 to 1 at the beginning to 13 to 1 at the end of the three-year period. The entire indebtedness of the company could be paid off and still leave almost as much cash as was on hand at the beginning.

Those persons who believe that the reader should be left to his own devices in interpreting accounting reports are asked to stop at this time to consider the situation just described in the light of the known facts. The period was one of steadily rising prices in which everyone apparently was making money. No doubt there were complaints about the high cost of living, but business was enjoying a "boom." Let the analyst make such conservative allowances as he deems proper and then compare his results with the analysis which follows.

Before proceeding further, however, it is necessary to state the assumptions on which the figures are based. Hypothetical figures are used throughout for two reasons: first, adequate data for an actual company are not obtainable for a sufficient period of years and, second, such figures if available would contain so many variables as to defeat the underlying purpose, which is to show in bold relief the effect of a changing dollar on the customary accounting reports.

It is assumed, therefore, that the physical volume of purchases, inventories and sales was absolutely constant throughout the entire period. It is assumed further that the costs per unit of product expressed in standard dollars were constant at the following rates:

		Per unit
Material		$ .20
Labor		.20
Burden		
Depreciation	$.08	
Other factory expenses	.22	.30
Factory cost		$ .70
Selling, general and other expenses		.22½
Net profit		.07½
Selling price		$1.00

The further assumption is made that the prices of all goods and services bought and sold by the Hypothetical Manufacturing Company varied directly with the rise in the general level of prices and inversely with the fall in the purchasing power of the dollar. It is recognized that in an actual situation some prices, particularly wage rates, would lag behind others, but such economic phenomena are not pertinent to the present discussion. The lag in wage rates, for example, would throw more profit into the period of rising prices and less into the period of falling prices, but it would in no wise invalidate the inferences to be drawn from the illustration. If wages lag, raw material prices usually precede the rise in the general level of prices and an average of the two may follow the general level rather closely. Inventories throughout are valued at cost on the first-in-first-out basis. Finished goods are priced at the average cost of goods completed during the preceding quarter.

HYPOTHETICAL MANUFACTURING COMPANY

Profit-and-loss statement expressed in standard dollars

	Years 1, 2, and 3
Sales	$800,000
Cost of goods sold	560,000
Gross profit	$240,000
Selling and general expenses	180,000
Net profit	$ 60,000

Surplus account expressed in standard dollars

	Year 1	2	3
Balance at beginning of year	....	$(40,912)	$ (99,996)
Net operating profit	$ 60,000	60,000	60,000
	$ 60,000	$ 19,088	$ (39,996)
Shrinkage in purchasing power of net dollar balances	$ 45,712	$ 58,284	$ 71,744
Dividends paid	55,200	60,800	72,000
	$100,912	$119,084	$ 143,744
Balance at end of year (deficit)	$(40,912)	$(99,996)	$(183,740)

HYPOTHETICAL MANUFACTURING COMPANY

Comparative balance-sheets expressed in standard dollars

Assets	Beginning of year 1	End of year 1	End of year 2	End of year 3
Current assets:				
Cash	$ 200,000	$ 200,819	$ 198,703	$ 177,949
Receivables	200,000	195,349	194,286	169,792
Raw material	40,000	40,000	40,000	40,000
Work in process	22,500	22,500	22,500	22,500
Finished goods	87,500	87,500	87,500	87,500
	$ 550,000	$ 546,168	$ 542,989	$ 497,741
Fixed assets:				
Plant and equipment (including land, $50,000)	$ 850,000	$ 850,000	$ 850,000	$ 850,000
Less: reserve for depreciation	250,000	314,000	378,000	442,000
	$ 600,000	$ 536,000	$ 472,000	$ 408,000
	$1,150,000	$1,082,168	$1,014,989	$ 905,741
Liabilities and net worth				
Current liabilities:				
Accounts payable	$ 50,000	$ 39,080	$ 46,985	$ 37,481
Funded debt:				
Bonds payable	100,000	84,000	68,000	52,000
	$ 150,000	$ 123,080	$ 114,985	$ 89,481
Net worth:				
Capital stock	$1,000,000	$1,000,000	$1,000,000	$1,000,000
Surplus (deficit)	....	(40,912)	(99,996)	(183,740)
	$1,000,000	$ 959,088	$ 900,004	$ 816,260
	$1,150,000	$1,082,168	$1,014,989	$ 905,741

Based on these assumptions, a set of statements expressed in standard dollars, i. e., the dollars in which the original balance-sheet was stated, may be readily prepared. The profit-and-loss statements are, of course, identical for each year.

The surplus accounts are particularly interesting. Instead of the nice surplus of $166,205 shown in the original statements, a deficit of $183,740 standard dollars is shown, a variation of over 33 per cent of the true net worth at the end of the third year. In analyzing this variation it is necessary to explain the concept of net dollar balances. The net dollar balance of an enterprise at a given moment of time is the difference between its money-value assets and its money-value liabilities, or in other words, the difference between the assets representing claims to a fixed number of dollars and the liabilities calling for the payment of a given number of dollars. A net dollar debit balance indicates an excess of dollars receivable over dollars payable and is equivalent to a long position in the dollar. A net dollar credit balance indicates an excess of dollars payable over dollars receivable and is equivalent to a short sale of the dollar. At the beginning of the period, the cash and receivables of the Hypothetical Manufacturing Company amounted to $400,000 and its total liabilities to $150,000. The difference of $250,000 was its net dollar debit balance or its long position in the dollar. At the end of the first year, it was long on dollars to the extent of $325,104, or an average of about $286,000. The shrinkage in the value (purchasing power) of this net dollar balance amounted to $45,712.

It may be argued that this loss is unrealized, which perhaps is true, but it is no more unrealized than that portion of inventory appreciation which corresponds to the change in the general level of prices and, unfortunately, is usually treated as profit. Although the shrinkage of dollar balances has been excluded from the income account, it represents a real decrement in the stockholders' equity. It cannot be denied that dollars carried through a period of declining purchasing power have lost part of their power to command economic goods and services. Money balances carried through the German inflation, for example, were totally lost.

In view of the shrinkage in the value of its dollar balances, the dividend policy of the Hypothetical Manufacturing Company seems fantastic. The facts were:

Standard dollars

Net operating profits		
3 years at $60,000 a year		$180,000
Shrinkage in purchasing power of net dollar balances		
Year 1	$45,712	
" 2	58,284	
" 3	71,744	175,740
Profit available for the payment of dividends without the impairment of real capital		$ 4,260
Dividends paid		
Year 1	$55,200	
" 2	60,800	
" 3	72,000	188,000
Dividends paid out of real capital		$183,740
Per cent of dividends paid out of capital		97 + %

What a contrast to the previous analysis! The one shows that 39 per cent of the profits were carried to surplus, the other that over 97 per cent of the dividends were paid out of capital. Does this variation, perchance, explain the insistence upon conservatism among accountants and financiers? Long experience with the rise and fall of the price level has taught them that, when prices are changing rapidly, accounting reports simply are not to be trusted. It is recognized, of course, that the Hypothetical Manufacturing Company has maintained its nominal or legal capital and that the directors are not liable for the payment of dividends out of capital, but the fact that the real equity of the stockholders has been impaired is beyond dispute. The economic capital of the enterprise is the value of the assets originally contributed by the stockholders. It is this value which must be maintained in terms of real purchasing power if the stockholders are not to suffer a diminution of their equity.

Even more interesting is a comparison and analysis of the net profits of the company. The earnings per share computed without reference to changes in the purchasing power of the dollar were:

	Earnings per share of capital stock
Year 1	$ 9.11
" 2	13.52
" 3	19.99

Adjusted for all changes in the value of the dollar and expressed in standard dollars the earnings were $6 a share in each of the three years. For comparison, however, these earnings must be restated in current dollars. This may be done by dividing $6 by the average purchasing power of the dollar during each year. The results are shown below.

EARNINGS PER SHARE ADJUSTED FOR CHANGES IN PURCHASING POWER OF THE DOLLAR

Year	Average purchasing power of dollar during year	Earnings per share in standard dollars	Earnings per share expressed in current dollars
	(a)	(b)	(b ÷ a)
1	$.9178+	$6.00	$6.54
2	.7573+	6.00	7.92
3	.5966+	6.00	10.06

Compare these results with the unadjusted earnings previously shown. During the third year the earnings per share were $19.99, if computed in the usual way, as compared to a maximum of $10.06 after proper adjustments. If the stock is worth 10 times earnings it would sell on the one basis at $200, on the other, at $100. Of course, an error of a mere 100 per cent in pricing a stock issue is not uncommon, but how can the markets be expected to show any degree of sanity if the reported profits are regularly overstated in periods of optimism and as regularly understated in periods of depression?

A further fact is at once apparent. If the shrinkage in the purchasing power of net dollar balances be deducted from income, the operations of the third year resulted in a loss of $1.97 per share rather than a gain of $19.99.

An analysis of the variations in net profit is enlightening.

ANALYSIS OF VARIATIONS IN NET PROFIT

	Year 1	Year 2	Year 3
Net profit computed without reference to changes in purchasing power	$91,126	$135,204	$199,875
Net profit adjusted for changes in purchasing power ($60,000 ÷ average purchasing power of the dollar)	65,372	79,222	100,560
Total variation in net profit	$25,754	$ 55,982	$ 99,315

Variation due to:

Unrealized or fictitious appreciation of inventories	$20,022	$ 35,479	$ 56,050
Under-depreciation	5,732	20,503	43,265
	$25,754	$ 55,982	$ 99,315

The overstatement of net profit is explained by two factors, of which the more important is inventory appreciation. This is rather surprising in view of the well-established principle of accounting that appreciation must be excluded from income. The insidious way in which it evades the watchful eyes of the accountants and steals into the income account requires careful explanation. At the beginning, two types of so-called appreciation must be distinguished—the one real, the other fictitious. Real appreciation occurs when the value of a given quantity of goods rises more rapidly than the value of the dollar falls. The apparent appreciation which occurs when the value of the given quantity of goods rises exactly in inverse proportion to the fall in the purchasing power of the dollar is, of course, fictitious. There is no true increase in economic value. Only the unit of measurement has shrunk. For example, if the value of an inventory of 1,000 units rises from $1,000 to $2,000 while the dollar falls to 60¢, the apparent appreciation is $1,000, the real appreciation is $1,000 minus $667 or $333, the amount not due to the fall in the value of the dollar.

If the one thousand units in the inventory are simply held throughout the whole period, the entire $1,000 of appreciation is unrealized and will, therefore, not appear in the income account as usually prepared. If, however, the inventory is sold and replaced frequently, both forms of appreciation will by the ordinary methods of accounting be taken up as profit. A strictly accurate statement would be, therefore, that fictitious appreciation rather than unrealized appreciation has been treated as profit. The point as to whether the fictitious appreciation is realized or not hardly merits discussion.

It will be recalled that the inventories of the Hypothetical Manufacturing Company were absolutely constant in physical volume throughout the period, and that the prices of goods bought and sold varied inversely with every change in the value of the dollar. In the circumstances, there could be no true appreciation in terms of purchasing power. The increases in the inventories, therefore, simply measured the fall in the purchasing power of the dollar. These increases were by no stretch of the imagination realized profits.

The point, since it is so necessary to an understanding of possibly the most important cause for fluctuations in industrial profits, can perhaps be clarified by a simple illustration. An enterprise buys 1,000 articles of merchandise for $10,000 when the dollar is worth 100 cents. After the dollar has fallen to 90 cents, 1,000 articles are sold at $15 each and other 1,000 units are bought at $11,111. What was the profit? An ordinary statement would show:

Sales		$15,000
Cost of goods sold		
Opening inventory	$10,000	
Purchases	11,111	
	$21,111	
Less: closing inventory	11,111	10,000
Gross profit		$ 5,000

The correct profit in terms of 90¢ dolars was $5,000–$1,111 or $3,889. The error is not due, however, to the apparent appreciation in the closing inventory, the value of which is both added and subtracted, and therefore cancels out. It was the opening inventory, not the closing inventory, which appreciated in terms of 90¢ dollars, and the failure to recognize this so-called appreciation, which was really dollar depreciation, permitted it to filter unnoticed into the income account. Although the change in value resulting from the 10 per cent shrinkage of the dollar applied in fact to the opening inventory, it was first recognized in the closing inventory. This lag explains the overstatement of profits in periods of rising prices. Likewise it explains the understatement of profits in periods of falling prices.

The second factor which accounts in part for the variation in net profit is inadequate depreciation. Even though the plant in the illustration is large and the rate of depreciation high, this factor is not as large as the inventory factor. In the third year, however, under-depreciation causes an overstatement of $4.33 in the earnings per share, an amount which is far from negligible.

The amount of under-depreciation is computed on the theory that depreciation charges over the life of a fixed asset should provide for the recovery of its original cost in terms of real purchasing power. This is not a replacement theory of depreciation; it is strictly a cost basis with cost defined in terms of purchasing power rather than fluctuating and uncertain dollars. The results in practice might closely approximate those obtained by basing depreciation on replacement costs, but this would not be true in all cases. The correct determination of profit, it is generally held, requires that depreciation be based on cost. If cost is defined in terms of purchasing power, the annual depreciation charges will vary inversely with the rise and fall in the value of the dollar, regardless of the movement of replacement or reproduction costs.

The depreciable property of the Hypothetical Manufacturing Company cost 800,000 standard dollars, i.e., dollars of 100 per cent purchasing power. Depreciation was charged at the rate of 8 per cent or $64,000 a year. The purchasing power of the dollar, however, was only $.9178 during the first year, and as a result less than 8 per cent of the original cost was actually recovered. In order to insure the recovery of the equivalent of 64,000 dollars of the standard or base year, $69,732 (64,000÷.9178) of depreciation should have been charged to cost. Likewise in the other years the formula for computing the amount of under-depreciation is

$$\frac{64,000}{\text{Average purchasing power of dollar}} - 64,000.$$

Although this subject is admittedly a controversial one, the underlying economic facts seem clear. It cannot be denied that an enterprise which recovers less than the purchasing power originally invested in plant currently consumed in service is depleting its real capital. It is true that the full amount may be recovered and kept in the business by building up surplus or reserves for contingencies, but there would seem to be no advantage in the use of erroneous and misleading labels. The simple fact is that either purchasing power equivalent to that consumed in service must be rocovered and kept in the business, or the capital of the enterprise must be depleted.

From this analysis, it is apparent that the net profits of the Hypothetical Manufacturing Company were materially overstated during each year of rising prices as the result of two factors: unrealized or more accurately fictitious appreciation of inventories and under-depreciation. As a result the earnings per share for the three years were overstated by $2.58, $5.60 and $9.93 respectively. The fact that profits are overstated in periods of rising prices is rather generally recognized. It is often assumed, however, that over a period of years the law of averages may be depended upon to produce substantially accurate results and that adjustments for changes in purchasing power may be safely neglected. The fact is, of course, that the law of averages does not apply. It could apply only on the assumption that the values of each monetary unit fluctuate around a fixed base. Recent world conditions have shown that currencies may lose their fixed base entirely or move up or down to a substantially different base. There is no reason to expect the franc or the lira to return to their pre-war values, and such a return of the ruble or the former German mark is manifestly impossible. It should be apparent, however, that even if a currency does fluctuate around a fixed base, the adjustments cannot properly be neglected. Business policies must be formed in the light of current reports and conditions. They cannot await the completion of a cycle. And the losses from unwise policies adopted because of misleading current reports cannot be recouped even if the statements are substantially accurate on the average.

In order to show the effects of falling prices, the statements of the Hypothetical Manufacturing Company have been projected through three additional years during which the purchasing power of the dollar rises from $.52 to $1.00 at the rate of 4¢ per quarter. Conversely, prices fall from 192 at the end of the third year to 100 at the end of the sixth. Physical volume is again assumed to remain constant at the same level as during the first three years. Since no replacements of plant were made during the first three years, these are assumed now to be necessary. Accordingly, one-fourth of the old plant, $200,000, is charged off against the reserve for depreciation, and new equipment of equal capacity is installed at a cost of $384,615. Since this occurs at the beginning of the fourth year when the purchasing power of the dollar is $.52, the cost in standard dollars is $200,000, the same as the original cost of the old equipment.

The statements of the Hypothetical Manufacturing Company prepared without reference to the increasing value of the dollar follow:

HYPOTHETICAL MANUFACTURING COMPANY

Profit-and-loss Statements

	Year 4	Year 5	Year 6
Sales	$1,340,809	$1,056,296	$ 871,628
Cost of good sold	943,128	776,072	647,587
Gross profit	$ 397,681	$ 280,224	$ 224,041
Selling and general expense	301,682	237,667	196,116
Net profit	$ 95,999	$ 42,557	$ 27,925

Surplus Account

	Year 4	Year 5	Year 6
Balance at beginning of year	$ 166,205	$ 202,204	$ 204,761
Net profit for year	95,999	42,557	27,925
	$ 262,204	$ 244,761	$ 232,686
Dividends paid	60,000	40,000	30,000
Balance at end of year	$ 202,204	$ 204,761	$ 202,686

HYPOTHETICAL MANUFACTURING COMPANY

Comparative Balance-sheet

Assets	At end of year 4	At end of year 5	At end of year 6
Current assets:			
Cash	$ 335,385	$ 435,385	$ 438,693
Receivables	267,332	323,628	200,000
Raw materials	60,606	48,780	40,816
Work in process	34,500	28,087	23,814
Finished goods	133,388	109,227	93,055
	$ 831,211	$ 945,107	$ 796,378
Fixed assets:			
Plant and equipment (including land, $50,000)	$1,034,615	$1,034,615	$1,034,615
Less: reserve for dep'n	320,769	399,538	477,308
	$ 713,846	$ 635,077	$ 556,308
	$1,545,057	$1,580,184	$1,352,686

Liabilities and net worth

Current liabilities:			
Accounts payable	$ 42,853	$ 75,423	$ 50,000
Funded debt:			
Bonds payable	300,000	300,000	100,000
	$ 342,853	$ 375,423	$ 150,000
Net worth:			
Capital stock	$1,000,000	$1,000,000	$1,000,000
Surplus	202,204	204,761	202,686
	$1,202,204	$1,204,761	$1,202,686
	$1,545,057	$1,580,184	$1,352,686

Inventories in the above statements have been valued at cost, although cost was higher than market, in order to make them consistent with the statements of the first three years. They may be stated at market by making appropriate adjustments to surplus and establishing a reserve for inventories in the following amounts:

	End of year		
	4	5	6
Reserve for inventories	$ 7,906	$ 7,523	$ 7,685

The net profits adjusted for the declines in inventory would be as follows:

	Year		
	4	5	6
Net profits per statement	$95,999	$42,557	$27,925
Inventory adjustments	7,906	(383)	162
Net profits adjusted for market declines in inventories	$88,093	$42,940	$27,763

The same statements adjusted for the rise in the purchasing power of the dollar and expressed in standard dollars are given below. Since the profit-and-loss statement is identical with that for the first three years, it is omitted.

HYPOTHETICAL MANUFACTURING COMPANY

Comparative Balance-sheets Expressed in Standard Dollars

	At end of year		
Assets	4	5	6
Current assets:			
Cash	$ 228,062	$ 365,723	$ 438,693
Receivables	181,786	271,847	200,000
Raw materials	40,000	40,000	40,000
Work in process	22,500	22,500	22,500
Finished goods	87,500	87,500	87,500
	$ 559,848	$ 787,570	$ 788,693

Fixed assets:
Plant and equipment (including land,
  $50,000) .... $ 850,000 $ 850,000 $ 850,000
    Less: reserve for depreciation   306,000   370,000   434,000
                                          $ 544,000 $ 480,000 $ 416,000
                                          $1,103,848 $1,267,570 $1,204,693

Liabilities and net worth

Current liabilities:
  Accounts payable .... $ 29,140 $ 63,355 $ 50,000
Funded debt:
  Bonds payable   204,000   252,000   100,000
                                       $ 233,140 $ 315,355 $ 150,000
Net worth:
  Capital stock $1,000,000 $1,000,000 $1,000,000
  Surplus (deficit) ....   (129,292)   (47,785)   54,693
                                       $ 870,708 $ 952,215 $1,054,693
                                       $1,103,848 $1,267,570 $1,204,693

Surplus Account Computed and Expressed in Standard Dollars

	Year		
	4	5	6
Surplus (deficit) at beginning of year ...	$(183,740)	$(129,292)	$(47,785)
Add:			
Net profit for year	$ 60,000	$ 60,000	$ 60,000
Gain in purchasing power of net dollar balances	30,448	51,907	70,078
Total gains	$ 90,448	$111,907	$130,078
	$(93,292)	$(17,385)	$ 82,293
Deduct:			
Dividends paid	36,000	30,400	27,600
Surplus (deficit) at end of year	$(129,292)	$(47,785)	$ 54,693

The net profits computed in different ways may now be listed and compared.

Comparison of Net Profits Computed by Different Methods

	Year		
	4	5	6
A. Net profits adjusted for changes in purchasing power annd expressed in:			
1. Standard dollars	$ 60,000	$ 60,000	$ 60,000
2. Current dollars of each year ...	100,560	79,222	65,372
B. Net profits computed without reference to purchasing power			
1. Inventories at cost	$ 95,999	$ 42,557	$ 27,925
2. Inventories at market	88,093	42,940	27,763

Of this variety of methods and results, numbers A2 and B1 may be most readily compared. An analysis of the variations follows:

Analysis of Variations in Net Profit

	Year		
	4	5	6
Net profits (expressed in current dollars):			
Adjusted for rise in purchasing power of dollar	$100,560	$ 79,222	$ 65,372
Computed by customary methods	95,999	42,557	27,925
Understatement	$ 4,561	$ 36,665	$ 37,447
Variation due to:			
Unrealized or fictitious inventory losses ..	$ 33,057	$ 42,400	$ 28,409
Under-depreciation	28,496	5,735	
Over-depreciation			9,038
	$ 4,561	$ 36,665	$ 37,447

Inventory valuations are still the most important cause of variations in net profit. If inventories during the last three years of the hypothetical illustration are valued at cost or market, whichever is lower, the unrealized appreciation of the first three years is exactly offset by the unrealized losses of the last three. But what enormous errors are introduced into the intervening statements! The over-depreciation which appears in the sixth year results from the high money valuation of the plant replacements made at the beginning of the fourth year.

Pity the poor stockholder of the Hypothetical Manufacturing Company! He has seen his profits rise to $20 a share and then fall abruptly to less than one-seventh of this amount. His dividends have been reduced from a maximum of 12 to 3 per cent. The market has fallen and discouragement is in the air. But let us analyze the situation to see how he has fared in terms of purchasing power. During the three years of prosperity the total profits of the enterprise barely exceeded the loss on net dollar balances, leaving, as previously explained, an increment of only $4,260 in favor of the stockholder, less than fifteen one-hundredths of one per cent a year! In the succeeding period of gloom, however, the situation was as follows:

Adjusted net profits		
3 years @ $60,000		$180,000
Gain in purchasing power of net dollar balances		
Year 4	$30,448	
" 5	51,907	
" 6	70,078	152,433
Stockholders' total increment		$332,433

In other words, during the period of depression the stockholders' real economic wealth, measured in the power to command goods and services, increased at an average rate of over 13½ per cent on the net worth of the stock at the beginning of the fourth year. His total gain during those hard years of falling prices was almost eighty times as great as it was during the corresponding period of apparent prosperity!

This seemingly impossible result may, as a matter of fact, be quite simply explained. The capital of the corporation consisted of real wealth, land, plant, raw materials, finished goods, on the one hand, and net dollar balances, the excess of dollars receivable over dollars payable, on the other. Now the inherent usefulness of the real wealth and its relative value in goods and services were not affected by the changes in the value of money. Both the gains and losses on such property were, therefore, apparent only and not real. There was, however, a real shrinkage of the value of net dollar balances as the purchasing power fell and a real gain as it rose. In the financial reports prepared in the usual manner during the first period, fictitious profits were shown and genuine though not necessarily "realized" losses neglected, while in the latter period fictitious losses were reported and real gains omitted. Since the physical volume of business was constant, is it at all strange that the stockholders were really better off in the period of so-called depression than during the boom?

Naturally, this does not imply that corporations as a general rule are more profitable during depressions than at other times. If the debts of the Hypothetical Manufacturing Company had far exceeded its dollar balances of cash and receivables, it might well have been thrown into bankruptcy as a result of the fall in prices. A goodly number of our strongest corporations, however, are affected by price-level changes in much the same way as was the Hypothetical Manufacturing Company. They have large dollar balances and they may have a fairly constant physical volume of business. For such companies particularly the customary methods of computing net profits give misleading results. There can be no doubt that the overstatement of profit when prices are rising and the understatement of profit when prices are falling act as powerful forces tending to increase the severity of booms and depressions.

The influence of changes in purchasing power has many ramifications beyond the computation of earnings per share and the determination of financial policies. It applies with special force to price policies generally. A period of depression is always characterized by price-cutting, which is supposed to be, and may actually become, ruinous. Strenuous efforts, therefore, are made by single enterprises and by whole industries to maintain price scales. It should be apparent, however, that price maintenance in such circumstances produces an actual increase of prices in terms of purchasing power at just the time when economic conditions call for price reductions. By forcing real prices upward, the volume of business is drastically reduced and a basis laid for the ruinous price-cutting which almost inevitably follows. Such problems would be automatically solved in large measure by the permanent stabilization of the purchasing power of the dollar, but until that is accomplished a consciousness of the changes in purchasing power and their effects should enable the managements of business enterprises to avoid most of the disastrous effects.

The shrinkage of net dollar balances, for example, can by careful management be largely avoided. A number of businesses hedge their foreign exchange commitments in order to avoid taking a speculative position. It is likewise possible to hedge their position in the dollar. The company which so arranges its financial plan that its debt is equal to its dollar balances receivable has a perfect hedge on the dollar. Such a hedge may be much more important than a hedge in foreign exchange, since the amounts involved are apt to be larger. The present national administration has pledged itself to raise prices to the 1926 level and laws have been passed which permit, if they do not compel, an increase far above that level. American corporations with large dollar balances are, therefore, particularly vulnerable to a shrinkage of dollar values. They are taking a long position on the dollar, a "commodity" which under existing conditions is peculiarly speculative. Positions in wheat, cotton and silver are regarded as extremely speculative and are avoided by most business concerns. Yet the supply of these commodities is governed by natural laws which definitely limit the quantity which can be made available at a given time. It is hardly conceivable that such commodities should ever become worthless. The dollar, however, can be multiplied, or, more accurately, divided without limit by political action at any time. It could conceivably become as worthless as the German paper mark. Yet many companies do not hesitate to take a long position on the dollar to the extent of many millions.

A continuation of this analysis, however, would take us far beyond the limits of this paper. The implications of a concept of value expressed in units of fixed purchasing power, which we have called standard dolars, are so numerous as to require volumes for adequate treatment. It applies not only to domestic enterprises but to foreign branches and subsidiaries as well. Corporations with extensive operations abroad have in recent years simply been unable to determine their profits or their position. They could have done so with reasonable accuracy if the accounts of both foreign and domestic branches had been converted into fixed value units. The one point, however, which this paper seeks to emphasize is that changes in the purchasing power of monetary units are significant and that such changes must be taken into account if an intelligent understanding of the affairs of a business enterprise, either domestic or foreign, is to be obtained during periods of rapidly changing prices.

It will be urged that the idea of restating financial statements in terms of dollars of uniform purchasing power is highly theoretical, impractical, costly to apply and outside the province of practical men. Such objections can be sustained, however, only by proving one of the following propositions:

1. That the purchasing power of the dollar will not change (though it has changed almost constantly in the past);
2. That the number of monetary units is more significant than their purchasing power; or,
3. That the value of correct information is not equal to the cost of obtaining it.

While it is hoped that the dollar will be stable in the future, the lessons of history are against it. The idea that real purchasing power is less significant than the number of monetary units is so palpably false as to merit no further argument. The additional bookkeeping and clerical costs involved in making adjustments for changes in purchasing power are more indefinite. It cannot be denied that the installation of a system of stabilized accounting, as it has been called by Sweeney, Castenholz and other writers, would be difficult for a corporation with many properties and inadequate plant records. In some cases an appraisal might be necessary. There is reason to believe, however, that once the new system was installed, its operation would be relatively inexpensive. Its cost would certainly be less than that of some elaborate systems of standard costs which attempt to provide more stable criteria by which factory executives may judge their work. Whatever the cost of the new system, however, it could hardly exceed the incalculable costs arising from reliance on biased and inaccurate information at critical periods of economic adjustment.

Part Four

Cost Analysis

A. Hamilton Church

ON THE INCLUSION OF INTEREST
IN MANUFACTURING COSTS

Alexander Hamilton Church *was an English electrical engineer, who worked at one time for the National Telephone Company in Great Britain. He settled in the U.S. about the turn of the century. He was probably the first writer to look at the entire managerial function. He wrote extensively in the technical journals and published several books, among them* Science and Practice of Management *and* Manufacturing Costs and Accounts.

At the time of writing the article reprinted here, Church was a consulting industrial engineer with Patterson, Teele and Dennis. The article is one of a group on the general topic of "interest on investment" that appeared in the Journal of Accountancy *for April, 1913. (Another article from this group, by William Morse Cole, appears later in this volume.)*

The question whether interest should be included in shop costs is frequently obscured by a certain indefiniteness as to what is meant by "interest" in this connection. As a matter of fact, interest as met with in accounting is of two kinds, *viz.*:

(1) Interest paid out by the concern for the use of borrowed capital, as on mortgages, debentures, loans and otherwise. The bearing of this kind of interest on the profits which will ultimately be distributable on the stock of the concern is of course very important. Bad financing may swallow up the profits, but this has nothing to do with the manufacturing efficiency of the shops. Whether or not the proprietors or directors elect to borrow, rather than to invest, capital is entirely a question of how they are willing to distribute profits when earned. In other words, it is a question of finance, pure and simple, and affects revenue account alone.

(2) The second kind of interest is the only one now under discussion, namely, an assessment for the use of capital values in the actual processes

Reprinted from *The Journal of Accountancy* (April, 1913), by permission.

of manufacturing, represented by land, buildings, plant machinery, stores and work in progress, etc. I prefer to call this an "interest charge."

Not only are these entirely separate kinds of interest often confused, but it has happened that concerns have included in their costs percentages designed to distribute the interest incurred for mortages and even for loans, while entirely ignoring any charge for the use of capital in the various forms employed in the shops. Such a practice has neither theoretical authority nor practical advantage.

The general principle that we must apply in discussing this question is that of utility. Older writers on the subject have frequently asserted that one or other of the aspects of the question was more "theoretically accurate," but have generally failed to state the terms of the theory involved. Probably, however, the older practice was on the whole against, rather than in favor of, including any interest charge for the use of capital in costs.

Until recent times, there was a good deal to be said for this attitude, for it must be clearly realized that such an interest charge does not affect the ultimate profits, however handled. If included, it increases costs, but this increase in costs is offset (when the whole course of the transactions is summed up in the profits and loss account) by the accumulation of a balance in the "Interest Earned" account. If not included, costs are lower by just the amount that would have been thus accumulated, and the net trading result is the same in both cases.

In such circumstances it is hardly surprising that many persons, looking at the ultimate result rather than at the intermediate steps, should have preferred the simpler method, and avoided the inclusion of interest in costs. It was of practically no service to the accountant, and from the nature of the methods by which the distribution over costs was made, it was scarcely of more value to the technical man or to the estimating or selling departments.

All indirect expense, including, of course, an interest charge where such was made, was formerly distributed over production in direct proportion to labor involved, or in proportion to time (hourly burden) taken to do the job. The informative value of such methods of distributing burden is very small, and as regards the item of interest-charge included may be said to be nil. The proportion of interest that became affixed to any given job bore no proportion whatever to the call on the use of capital made by that job. A purely hand-skill job might take just as much burden as a job calling for the use of the most powerful machines. All that was really attained was a rough idea of the bearing of indirect expense to direct labor *averaged over all the work*. When this figure was ascertained, the wholly unwarrantable assumption was made that each individual item of work might be safely regarded as taking neither more nor less than such average burden, whereas the truth commonly is that the real absorption of burden by different jobs is very unequal.

Practical intuition discerned this inherent vice of percentage systems long before any remedy was known, and burden figures have as a consequence been under a cloud, and have been treated with perhaps unconscious contempt by the technical men for whom alone they have any significance. If this was the case with all burden, it follows that the inclusion of interest charges in such burden had no practical value whatever.

Some attempts were made at various times, and even very early in the history of manufacturing, to remedy this defect. Machine rates were introduced to give some fairer incidence of the use of capital on individual jobs, but these were crude and arbitrary, and remained unsystematic until the present writer undertook an examination of the whole question of expense burden in 1899–1900. Since the publication of *The Proper Distribution of the Expense Burden*[1] there has been a steady growth of perception among accountants and manufacturers of the desirability of abandoning the practice of aggregating all kinds of indirect expense under the head of burden, in favor of a segregation of such expense into classes or "factors," and observing the relations of such factors to the actual operations of the shop.

Briefly speaking, the method of "production factors" is designed to give, among other things, due expression to the influence on costs of the USE of capital in manufacturing operations. This applies not merely to the capital involved in productive machines and tools, but also to that involved in auxiliary factors of production such as the land-building factor, the power, heating and lighting factors, the stores-transport factor, etc. Each of these factors represents a definite kind of expense, having a particular and definite bearing on the manufacturing processes. The cost of each factor is separately assessed against the productive machines making use of the services involved in, of course, exact proportion to the extent of the service.

Under this arrangement it is evident that each productive machine will be charged with a series of factor rents according to its individual call on the different services (including interest charge on its use of capital) rendered by the factors of production such as the land-building factor, the power factor, the transport factor, and the interest and derpreciation charges on the capital value of the machine itself—the resulting total being expressed as an hourly "machine rent." Large and costly machines, occupying considerable space, using much power, and calling on the transport factor for heavy craneage service, will naturally have a very different machine rent from light, cheap machines, calling in a less degree on any factor. Consequently, also the jobs done on these respective machines will have a very different amount of burden affixed to them.

The method of costing by "production factors" removes what was the main objection to the inclusion of an interest charge in costs under former methods, viz., its inutility. On the contrary, to include it becomes logical and

---

[1] First published in *Engineering Magazine,* 1901. In volume form, 1908. Reprinted, 1912. The subject has been expanded, from a more directly practical viewpoint, in *Production Factors,* published 1910.

even necessary, as soon as we are able to connect its incidence with the variety of processes performed on individual jobs.

While it is obvious that the manner in which capital is *provided* (as by means of stock, mortgages, loans, etc.) cannot affect the cost of shop processes, on the other hand the manner in which capital is *used* must have a strong influence on the efficiency of production from the point of view of cost. Just as soon as two processes are used in the same plant, it becomes necessary to delimit as closely as possible all the elements of cost of such processes. Where more than two are used—and in a modern plant they may be counted by scores and even hundreds—this necessity increases in proportion to the complexity thus introduced. One of the first questions that would naturally arise, if we approached the matter from a logical and natural standpoint, would be to what extent the use of capital is involved in the different processes. This can be shown in the simplest and most convenient way by charging production for the use it makes of capital, in each of the different processes.

It is only by doing so, and consequently by segregating all expense into factors and including a reasonable interest charge for the capital used in the services represented by the factor, that we can obtain the complete story about the cost of any process. Wherever capital is made use of, whether in the power plant, in the erection of buildings, or in the purchase of costly special machinery, the use of such capital has to be paid for, somehow and somewhere. *It is only rational that it should be paid for by just those processes (and therefore those jobs) which involve its use. To exclude interest charge from cost of these jobs is to ignore one of the most important matters that we should know, namely—how far this use of capital is economically justified.*

The matter is rendered more important than formerly owing to the steady increase in the value of plant relatively to the cost of labor. A recent study of manufacturing statistics by Mr. A. C. Popcke (*Engineering Magazine,* September, 1912) shows that the horsepower to drive machines has increased, on the average, 40 per cent per operator in the last ten years. Similarly capital investment in plant has increased 46 per cent per operator in the same period. These changes are significant of the growing size, weight and capacity of modern machinery, and point to the necessity of connecting a charge for the USE of capital with the various factors of production, and so, later, with each individual line or item of product.

In particular, no purchase of new equipment should be made until its call on all production factors has been worked out, and due attention paid to the influence of its use of capital, as represented by a reasonable interest charge.

Ralph C. Jones

SOME ASPECTS OF COST

For a biographical sketch of Ralph C. Jones, see the headnote to "Financial Statements and the Uncertain Dollar," page 262.
The article reprinted here is a plea for more attention by accountants to the complex interrelationships among cost of production (in total and per unit), volume of output, and selling price. It also hints strongly at the direct costing of inventories.

Cost is a protean word. Its habit of shifting its meaning with changes of context makes it a very handy, though rather slippery term. Like "value," to which it is closely related, it is a generic term applicable to a whole family of ideas. A number of definitions[1] could be cited, but they would not be particularly useful. The meaning of the word in the generic sense is well known. Implicit in the cost concept are ideas of sacrifice or sacrificing, of the giving up of something or of something given up, or of time, effort, money, or materials invested in or devoted to the production of goods or services. It would be futile to try to limit this broad concept to a single, precise meaning. Even if it could be done, another term, richer in meaning, would doubtless take the place of cost in common usage.

Reprinted from *Accounting, Auditing, and Taxes—1941* (American Institute of C.P.A.), pp. 102–111, by permission.

[1] Cost: "The amount or equivalent paid, or given, or charged, or engaged to be paid or given for anything bought or taken in barter or service rendered.

"Economics: That which is sacrificed to obtain anything." *Webster's New International Dictionary*.

"Cost, in economics, means the surrender or destruction of value or the performance of some irksome activity as a means to the production of commodities or the acquisition of income. In a voluntaristic capitalist society the cost to an individual who contributes in any way to the processes of production may consist of an expenditure of money, of goods for which money could be obtained, of manual or mental effort irksome at the margin; or it may involve the assumption of a physical or financial risk, the acceptance of a role carrying with it social disesteem, the choice of the less attractive of alternative ways of employing time or resources, although none of the alternatives need be of itself displeasing or irksome." Jacob Viner. *Encyclopedia of The Social Sciences*, Vol. 4, pp. 466–467.

If one were called as an expert witness to define cost in accountancy, the most effective testimony would doubtless be a statement of what accountants do in determining and assigning cost in various factual situations. What accountants typically do, in other words, is more significant than what they say. A study of actual cost decisions made by accountants would reveal certain conflicts and inconsistencies comparable to those found in court decisions, but nevertheless, some well-established and generally accepted practices, standards, or principles would emerge. Since these are at least as well known to you as they are to me, I do not propose to discuss them.

Another approach to the problem before us would be to consider the meaning of cost under various income-tax, fair-trade-practice, and national-defense acts. Urgent questions of cost determination under these laws are doubtless now before you, but the definition of cost for such purposes falls peculiarly within the province of the lawyer and the practicing accountant. In asking an academic accountant to discuss this subject, your purpose, I take it, is quite different. It is your purpose and mine to forget legal and technical details for the moment and to seek some clarification of the general concept of cost as it applies to accounting.

Many people, including perhaps a few accountants, think of cost in the absolute sense and assume that for any article or process there is one correct figure for cost. This, of course, is fallacious. There are different costs for different purposes. The cost, for instance, of driving one more mile in a car already owned, say two cents, is one thing; the average cost per mile of a year's driving, say six cents, is quite another. Both are correct and both are significant. The two-cent rate is pertinent in deciding whether it is more economical to drive or go by train on a given trip. The six-cent rate, however, is pertinent when the question is whether or not to own a car. The use of either rate for all decisions will lead to wrong conclusions.

Few, if any, accountants would admit adherence to the popular view of a single, all-purpose cost. Yet in action they sometimes seem to accept it. A complex cost system, for example, is installed after much argument over methods of allocation. At the time, everyone is acutely aware of the unavoidable compromises and arbitrary decisions made in the interest of feasibility. It is clear, while the system is being planned, that choices made among various plausible alternatives will definitely and perhaps substantially influence the results. The system goes into operation, however, and costs emerge with a superficial appearance of solidity and certainty which they do not in fact possess. To accept those figures as all-purpose costs is the easy way, and the temptation to do so is very great indeed, even among accountants who are aware of the difficulties and uncertainties involved in their preparation. For management, the problem is even more serious, since they must use the reported figures without the accountant's familiarity with the detailed computations.

The accountant on the one hand must recognize the needs of managers, economists, statisticians, and governmental agencies for different sorts of costs for different purposes. On the other hand, these users of accounting data must realize that the accountant cannot reasonably be expected to provide a different set of figures for every conceivable purpose. The accountant, however, since he is strategically situated at the source of the figures by which men act in our industrial society, must accept primary responsibility for the preparation and presentation of data which are really pertinent to the decisions which must be based on them.

While the accountant cannot be responsible for the unintelligent use or intentional abuse of his figures, he can do much to promote a better understanding of them. In more optimistic days, we may have thought that with an increase in the number of college trained men the problem would ultimately be solved if enough accountants had courses in economics, if economists generally had a course or two in accounting, and if business executives had courses in both. It is pretty clear by now that this is not true. A student can, and typically does, take courses in accounting and economics without integrating them in any significant way. What is needed is organized coöperation among mature workers in the various fields. It is just possible that a major function of the universities in the future may be the provision of facilities for such work.

The accountant, since he is interested primarily in the financial events of a particular entity and only secondarily in price determining factors in the economy as a whole, has been able to make little use of the economist's general classification of costs into rent, wages, interest, and profits. In recent years, however, economists have done much of their best work in the economics of the individual firm where the classifications and requirements are much closer to those of accounting. Some of these studies, indeed, are essentially cost accounting with a somewhat more imposing vocabulary. When these newer formulations of economic theory are more generally understood and appreciated by business managements, a demand will undoubtedly arise for accounting data which are more directly pertinent to particular decisions than the figures currently prepared. By anticipating this demand and by helping others to use his data wisely, the accountant now has an excellent opportunitely to increase his prestige and value in the community. If he fails to do so, he may find himself in the company of those generals who still place their chief reliance on the horse. Incidentally, it would help if the economists themselves would gain something more than a superficial knowledge of accounting.

In his book, *Economic Thought and Language*,[2] Professor Fraser of Aberdeen University points out that the word "cost" is commonly used in two senses. He designates one concept as "embodied costs," the other as "displacement costs." Embodied costs are the technical factors of production which

---

[2] Fraser, L. M., *Economic Thought and Language,* London, 1937.

go into the making of an article—the units of material, hours of labor, and units of energy used in producing it and thereby incorporated or embodied in it. These factors may be stated in physical, psychological, or monetary terms. In physical terms they are not commensurable, while in psychological terms they are not even measurable. Psychological or pain costs can be ruled out at once, since they have had limited usefulness in economics and none, of course, in accounting. Standard costs are the best example of embodied costs to be found in accounting. They show the technical factors going into a product and give a sufficient indication of value of make them commensurable. An outstanding characteristic of embodied costs is the extreme difficulty of stating them in monetary terms. They relate fundamentally to technical rather than economic factors.

Displacement costs, in contrast, are what is given up for something, not what goes into it. The displacement cost of having some heavy bags carried by a porter would be the fifty cents paid him. The embodied cost would be the time and energy which the porter devoted to the service. Displacement costs are usually stated in terms of money, since the thing most commonly given up for goods and services is money. They can, however, be stated in "real" terms. In the railroad station perhaps you had to choose between having a cocktail or a porter. If you then decided in favor of hiring a porter, the cocktail in a very real sense was the price of the service received. Neither the cocktail nor the fifty cents, please note, were embodied in the porter or the service. The concept of displacement cost, thus, includes alternative or opportunity costs as well as purchase and exchange costs. Since usually the next best alternative to buying something is keeping the money which it would cost, displacement cost ordinarily is money paid out. Displacement costs, in summary, indicate possible economic consequences or alternatives, while embodied costs furnish information about technique of production. Unsuccessful attempts to fit all ideas about cost into a single concept sometimes produce apparently irreconcilable arguments, both of which are correct: one, in terms of embodied cost; the other, in terms of displacement cost.

The typical accounting cycle consists of three steps: (1) the acquisition of assets, including units of service such as labor, which must initially be regarded as assets no matter how ephemeral; (2) the transfer of these costs within the entity as operations proceed; and (3) the ultimate release of these costs as expenses, the costs of obtaining, or seeking to obtain, revenue.

Acquisition costs, the incurrence of which constitutes the first step in the accounting cycle, are necessarily displacement costs. Each incoming asset "displaces" an equivalent value whether payment is made immediately or later. Since cash or the promise to pay cash in the future is the usual consideration for goods and services acquired, displacement costs for the great majority of business transactions can be determined objectively within fairly narrow limits. This is true even when an assortment of assets is purchased for a lump sum. The cost is what goes out from the entity and that is usually determinable. The allocation of that cost to the individual items acquired, however, is another matter.

In non-cash transactions, difficulties of two types arise. One, of course, is the general difficulty of determining value on any given basis; the other is the problem of selecting an appropriate basis of valuation. The choice of basis in practice is generally between book value and current market value of assets given in exchange. Book value is convenient, and there is a certain plausibility in assuming that the unexpired costs of assets exchanged pass into or are embodied in new assets acquired. The unexpired costs which constitute book values, however, are merely summations of past transactions and may have little relevance to present conditions. The cost of a $25,000 house received in exchange for an oil painting, for example, could not properly be recorded as $10, simply because it was a Rembrandt which you happened to pick up for so little. Reverse the situation and the fountain pen you got for your supposed Rembrandt could not properly be recorded at a cost of $25,000. Even in ordinary situations, involving either depreciable or non-depreciable assets, book values are less reliable than values determined currently and independently, since the information available when an exchange occurs includes both the historical record and current factors as well. On theoretical grounds the book value of old assets exchanged may properly be shown as the cost of new assets acquired only when book value coincides with, or gives the best indication of, probable present value. The generally accepted basis[3] for cost determination, then, is the market value of assets given in exchange.

While the principle that the cost of an article is the market value of the consideration given for it is pretty generally accepted, it is applied with some uncertainty. A large American corporation, for instance, provides a bonus for executives, payable in stock. The total amount of the bonus is determined by formula in relation to the profits of the year. The number of shares to be distributed is then determined by dividing the bonus fund by the daily average market price of the stock during the year. The company pays this bonus by distributing shares of treasury stock acquired some years ago at a relatively low price. Now what is the cost to the company of the bonus? Is it the market price of the stock on the day of allotment, the average market price for the year, or the cost to the company of reacquiring the stock? The company in its reports to stockholders shows the amount of the bonus both on an average-market-price basis and a cost-of-treasury-stock basis, but uses the latter and much lower figure in the determination of net profits. According to the principle just enunciated, the cost of the bonus is the *value* of the stock distributed, not the amount paid out in acquiring it. The excess of the market price of the shares distributed over their cost when

---

[3] "Cost incurred is measured by cash outlay or by the fair market value of considerations other than cash." "Principles Underlying Corporate Financial Statements." *The Accounting Review*, June, 1941. p. 134.

acquired some time ago as treasury stock should, if this analysis is correct, appear as paid-in surplus, not as net profit. In computing taxable net income, the corporation should certainly be allowed to deduct the full amount of the bonus, not merely the cost of the stock distributed.

The second phase of the accounting cycle consists of tracing costs within the entity itself. This involves the original classification of costs and subsequent reclassifications or transfers up to the point of final expiration. From the moment when an asset, whether in the form of goods or services, comes into the entity, the accountant seems to apply a different concept of cost than the one he uses for transactions between the entity and the outside world. A bushel of wheat, for example, is purchased for one dollar. The historical fact, of course, is that at a particular moment in the life of the entity a bushel of wheat displaced a dollar. It would commonly be said that the entity invested a dollar in wheat, or by easy transition, that the entity *has* a dollar invested in wheat. Now the dollar is in the wheat and the entity still has it—an idea rather obviously contrary to fact. Presumably there is nothing in the wheat but wheat, and the entity certainly does not have the dollar. The assumption, however, that the dollar is somehow embodied in the wheat is convenient, useful, and even necessary to the functioning of an accounting system. The real embodied costs of the wheat up to the date of acquisition—the labor of growing, transporting, and marketing it—or their money equivalent cannot be ascertained. The price paid, however, is a fair indication of their probable amount and can, without undue violence to the concept, be used as an embodied money cost. The price paid, a displacement cost, serves in other words merely as a convenient measurement or starting point. The concept after acquisition is that of an embodied cost, and subsequent transfers within the entity regularly follow the pattern of embodied costs.

It is important at this point to distinguish between historical cost and embodied cost. Historical cost is a cost event occurring at a particular moment of time. Embodied cost persists through a period of time. My watch may have cost $50 some years ago. That is a definite historical fact, a closed transaction. But when as an accountant I conceive of fifty dollars as embodied in the watch I endow it with a kind of magic power; namely, the power to transmit that cost to other goods or services. If the watch is used to time a productive process, it is assumed that a portion of the embodied cost is transferred to the new product. Now in the economic sense the only transfer would be the *value* sacrificed in using the watch for the given purpose rather that not using it, an amount not dependent upon original cost. Moreover, when I embody the fifty dollars in the watch, I perform another feat of magic. I apportion this cost to wheels, mainspring, case, crystal, etc. In the economic sense, the only cost of an individual part of the whole watch assembly is the cost which could have been avoided by not buying that particular part, and unfortunately, the sum of such costs would most certainly not be exactly fifty dollars. In the process of applying the fifty dollar cost to the various parts of the watch, I have consciously or unconsciously gone into the technique of watch production. This is generally the case when costs are allocated to an assortment of assets purchased for a lump sum. It is a characteristic of embodied cost as distinguished from historical cost.

In the third and final step of the typical accounting cycle, these embodied costs become expenses, the costs of obtaining current revenues. This step, it should be noted, is exactly the reverse of the first. There goods and services were purchased with dollars; here dollars are purchased with goods and services. It is in this last stage of the accounting process that we find a direct collision between the two concepts of cost and, in consequence, the area of greatest confusion. Here embodied costs so carefully traced through the accounts are measured against revenues stated in displacement terms.

The advocates of the last-in, first-out and base-stock methods of inventory valuation may take comfort from the fact that consistency would require the determination of cost of sales on the basis of present values rather than embodied costs. In deciding whether or not to make a sale at a given price it is the *present value* of the goods or services to be sold, not their original cost, which is significant. This is so obvious in the case of shopworn, damaged, or obsolete goods that it is surprising to find so much doubt about the principle when it is applied to goods which have increased in value. It must be noted, however, that in comparing present costs or values with present sales, attention is focused upon one particular moment of time. The task of accounting is broader than this.

Accounting must report the results for periods of time, not merely successive moments of time. In other words, if cost of sales is to be charged with current or replacement costs, some method is required which will recognize value changes occurring between the moment of purchase and the moment of sale. If a business concern, for instance, sells for $10 an article with an original cost of $6 and a replacement cost of $7, the gain from making the sale rather than not making it may be $3, but that the margin to be accounted for is $4 can hardly be denied. Of this $4 margin it may be useful to call $1 appreciation and exclude it from gross profit on sales, but there is little warrant for neglecting it altogether.

The temptation is very great to make a digression at this point in order to discuss at length the controversial question of inventory valuation. For present purposes, however, it will be sufficient to indicate that base-stock and last-in, first-out methods are rule-of-thumb procedures for adjusting the accounts and statements for price changes of two very different types. Price changes of the first type, probably the more important historically, reflect changes in the general price level. They compensate for inverse changes in the value of the monetary unit and leave unchanged the total purchasing power of a unit of the given commodity. Thus an asset may have been purchased for $1,000 when the dollar contained 100 standard units of purchasing power, however determined. Subsequently it may have been sold for $2,000 when the dollar contained only 50 standard units of purchasing power. It is quite obvious, under the assumed conditions, that no gain in purchasing power occurred and the apparent profit of $1,000 is completely illusory, except for income taxes which unfortunately become capital levies when applied to such gains. It is equally correct to speak of the cost of the asset as $1,000 of the earlier year or $2,000 of the latter year. Both amounts are costs. It is hardly consistent, however, to determine profit by subtracting cost measured in big dollars from selling price measured in smaller dollars. Since it has not been feasible, for legal and other reasons, to recognize such dollar variations in the accounts, the pressure for the adoption of some rule-of-thumb solution has been very great.

Price changes of the second general type represent real changes in commodity purchasing power. In other words, prices of individual commodities vary while the value of the dollar in which they are expressed remains constant. Profits based on costs expressed in stable dollars clearly are real gains in contrast to so-called fools' profits which merely reflect changes in the monetary unit itself. But the base-stock and the last-in, first-out inventory methods treat both kinds of profit exactly alike. They eliminate both from the income statement. Now in all the attempts to rationalize or justify base-stock and related methods, no one has ever shown that price appreciation in stable dollars, realized by subsequent sale, is not profit. It seems reasonable to conclude, therefore, that the exclusion of such gains from the income statement constitutes artificial stabilization of profits which in fact are not stable.

The essence of base-stock and related methods is the substitution of approximate displacement costs for the usual embodied costs in the trading section of the income statement. The effect is substantially to eliminate gains and losses from price changes in inventories whether these are real or illusory. In favor of such methods it can be said that they reduce profit distortion from price level changes without the complexities involved in adjusting embodied costs by means of index numbers, a procedure little understood and strongly opposed. Against them it can be said that they cause some profit distortion by concealing real gains and losses which cannot be ascribed to monetary factors. Since the elimination of one type of appreciation is thoroughly justified, while the elimination of the other is not, and since the separation of the two types is extremely difficult, the argument over methods of inventory valuation may be expected to continue unabated. Base-stock and related methods, it should be noted, apply displacement costs in only one section of the income statement, namely, the merchandise or trading section. It is probably impossible to apply such costs consistently to the whole aggregate of goods and services for which the customer pays in a typical sales transaction.

Which of the two concepts of cost is more appropriate for accounting? The answer is not easy, but it would seem that embodied costs, as defined herein, are the very essence of accounting. By basing his work on the concept of embodied cost, the accountant is able to furnish an account of stewardship, to record all costs incurred, and to trace them to their ultimate disposition. Product costs determined according to this concept are long-run costs representing amounts which must be recovered with some margin for profit if the entity is to remain permanently in business. Such information is of inestimable value. It provides a kind of bench mark for the guidance of management and for the appraisal of their effectiveness.

But even when embodied costs are recognized as essential in maintaining the continuity of the accounting process, it still remains true that such costs are not always appropriate or sufficient for decision making; in other words, for choosing among alternatives. The costs which are effective for a particular decision have been variously called alternative, opportunity, displacement, marginal, differential, or avoidable costs— terms which have some common implications though not identical meanings. In a manufacturing concern, for instance, a question may arise whether to operate a plant or department at reduced capacity or to shut it down completely, or whether to continue to sell a certain product or to withdraw it from the line, or whether or not to continue sales effort in a particular territory. In every case, the pertinent costs are those, and *only* those, which could be avoided by taking one alternative rather than another. Costs which must be incurred regardless of the alternative chosen simply do not exist so far as the particular decision is concerned. They are sunk, lost, or fixed costs—call them what you will— but they simply are not costs at all in relation to the issue at hand.

This principle, simple enough in its general statement, meets much opposition in practice, especially in relation to price cutting. The trouble, however, is not in the principle but in the application of it. A manufacturer estimates, for instance, that by reducing prices 10 per cent he can increase the number of units sold by 20 per cent. If his estimate is based on the assumption that the additional business will be taken away from competitors, it is probably wrong. But if it is based on a study of the elasticity of demand of the commodity, it is probable that the volume of the whole industry would increase 20 per cent at the lower price. If he is now making and selling 100 units at $1, the pertinent costs of the additional business are the additional costs of making and selling 20 extra units. But the revenue with which such costs must be compared is not 20 units at 90¢ or $18; it is $8, the dollar increase in total sales ($120 \times .90$ or $108 minus 100×1 or $100 equals $8). If the additional costs exceed $8, the additional business is not profitable. But this is not all. If the larger volume resulting from the lower price will extend over future years, it may require permanently a larger plant and a larger organization. Under such circumstances certain fixed overhead costs must be considered. The principle of basing decisions on displacement or avoidable costs thus is sound, but the application of it is more complex than is commonly assumed. It is easy to overlook demand factors and certain long-run costs which may be pertinent to what seems on its face to be a short-run decision.

Applications of displacement, alternative, or avoidable costs in relation to any kind of business decision could be recited. A company, for example, is trying in a period of slack business to decide whether to accumulate an inventory or to reduce the rate of operation and lay off a substantial part of the working force. Among other things, the management will want to know how much of the company's funds would be tied up in the enlarged inventory. The plausible assumption that this amount would be the total cost of the inventory, computed in the usual way, would be wrong. The additional investment would include only the avoidable costs of manufacturing the additional inventory; in other words, the total costs, as above, less all apportioned charges which would have to be paid anyway, whether the goods were manufactured or not. As a matter of fact, under such circumstances a pretty strong argument could be advanced for excluding these apportioned charges from inventoriable costs.

A problem involving the same principles arises in the opposite case of a company operating at more than normal capacity and employing labor at high overtime rates. Eighty per cent of the work, let us assume, is done at the regular rate of $1 an hour and 20 per cent at the overtime rate of $2 an hour. Now, if work on a particular order or article is done in overtime, it is apparent that a certain number of hours of work are embodied in the products; it is equally apparent that this work cost $2 an hour. While a strict application of the embodied-cost concept would require the charging of this amount to orders actually worked on in overtime, it hardly seems fair to do so since the selection of such orders is likely to be purely accidental. Many companies, therefore, resort to some sort of averaging by which the extra cost of overtime is spread over all orders. The average cost per hour of labor, assuming 20 per cent overtime at double pay, would be $1.20. The use of this rate as an embodied cost of all goods produced seems reasonable enough, but nevertheless it may be quite misleading. If the sales department uses costs computed at the $1.20 rate in accepting additional business, it may take orders at a loss. The significant cost is $2 an hour for *all* direct labor. If an order for any unit of product requiring one hour's work were canceled or declined, a charge of $2 for labor would be avoided. Any order, therefore, which cannot stand a charge of $2 an hour for labor shows a loss. The $2 rate, thus, properly applies to the total production whether carried out in regular time or overtime. Now, the accountant can hardly use the $2 rate for all goods produced, since to do so would result in the application of labor charges almost double the direct labor payroll. But if his averaging process serves to conceal essential facts from the management, he is rendering no service to them, to himself, or to the accounting profession.

The greater significance of current displacement costs for current decisions has naturally placed accountants under pressure to substitute them for historical costs in the formal accounts. Such substitutions have been made from time to time by revaluations of various kinds. A corporation buys a large tract of land, for example, for lumbering operations and pays $1,000,000 in cash for it. Shortly thereafter a valuable mine is discovered which a mining company tries to buy for $10,000,000, even going so far as to proffer a check for that amount. The lumber company, however, decides to keep the mine, to issue a $6,000,000 mortgage secured by the property, and to use this money to develop and operate the mine. Now, what was the cost of the mine to the lumber company? The orthodox accounting answer would be that some part of the original million dollars paid out is the cost of the mine. In a very real sense, however, the mine cost $10,000,000 cash just as effectively as if this amount of money had been paid out directly. And if the company cannot recover the whole $10,000,000 plus a reasonable profit, the decision to operate rather than to sell must be regarded as a mistake. The management is just as definitely responsible for the $10,000,000 as if this amount had been directly invested by the stockholders. Probably a majority of accountants would recognize this discovery value for balance-sheet purposes, even though under less dramatic circumstances they would insist on original cost. It is probable, however, that they would not think of the higher valuation as a genuine cost, which in fact it is. In this connection it should be noted that appraisals which merely compensate for fluctuations in the value of the monetary unit are also costs, but quite different in character. Properly conceived, they are adjusted historical or embodied costs, not current displacement costs at all. When adjustments of both types are recognized as true costs, many theoretical difficulties disappear, although complete consistency in accounting treatment is not likely to be achieved since the use of index numbers is quite complex and displacement costs are so uncertain and changeable that their general use is not feasible.

In summary, this analysis reveals a need for cost information of two distinct types, embodied costs and displacement costs. Embodied costs make such diverse elements as land, machinery, and labor hours conveniently commensurable. By being attached somewhat permanently to goods and services, they facilitate the process of tracing and matching, which Professors Paton and Littleton have described so well in their *Introduction to Corporate Accounting Standards*. Embodied costs, thus, are part of the continuous, long-run record of the life history of an enterprise.

Displacement costs, however, are needed in choosing among alternatives. They are pertinent and vital until a decision is made; then they become obsolete and die or lose their character by being embodied in particular assets. The decision itself changes the conditions and calls for a recomputation of displacement costs. While accounting can hardly make a formal record of these alternative costs, it can provide the data from which management may compute them.

Standard costs, which are embodied costs in the purest form, can be made especially useful for this purpose. It will be necessary, however, to modify the usual form of presentation in such a way as to separate the variable from the fixed factors. Standard costs typically appear rigid and fixed because they are merely summations of the average or normal costs of the various operations performed in the process of manufacture. As aggregates of averages they are subject to all of the statistical difficulties involved in dealing with averages. They could be used and interpreted with more assurance if they displayed more clearly the technical factors of production, not only the amounts of material and hours of labor, but also kilowatts of electricity and machine hours. By a careful separation of fixed and variable factors, the standards could be made to show costs at various rates of operation and under varying conditions.

Consider power costs, for example. The total requirement in kilowatt hours for all operations in the manufacture of a part could be shown along with the variable and fixed costs of power. Then, if the company buys electric power at usage and capacity rates, the management could ascertain the effect on power costs of manufacturing the part during the peak or off-peak periods. Likewise, if fixed and variable overhead rates were shown, the effect of making a larger or a smaller quantity at various rates of plant operation could be determined. In other words, instead of a fixed and rigid cost applicable only under an assumed normal which is seldom if ever attained, such standards would be a dynamic instrument by which the management could estimate the effect of substituting one material for another, of using higher or lower priced materials, or a change in wage rates, or of a change in the rate of plant operation. Marginal costs, average replacement costs, and other types of cost could be determined within fairly narrow limits, all without complicating the regular accounting process in the slightest. It might be well, as a matter of fact, to furnish the sales department with no other type of cost, since unit costs, when reported in the usual way, have a solid look which tempts the user to forget the unstable averages and doubtful assumptions upon which they rest. Certainly the basic assumption that costs are transferred within the entity according to physical, spatial, and temporal relationships rather than economic consequences or alternatives, although reasonable and necessary for the accounting process, is not valid for all purposes.

Similarly, the behavior of the total costs of enterprise operation in relation to changes in volume deserves more careful study. Analytical reports on such behavior are more vital to management than a mere historical record to be compared with similar records of the past and then filed. Professor R. L. Dixon, Jr., makes the interesting suggestion[4] that the income statement itself be recast to show fixed and variable expenses instead of, or in addition to, the usual classifications. This may not be feasible for published reports unless

---

[4] Dixon, Robert L., Jr., "Fixed and Variable Costs," *The Accounting Review,* June, 1940, pp. 218–222. Also *The Income Statement* (unpublished), Yale University Library, 1941.

some fairly objective method for separating the fixed and variable elements can be developed, but certainly internal reports on cost behavior are desirable. Flexible budgets are used to a certain extent, but the study of cost behavior in general has not been adequate.

Since the word "cost" practically blankets the fields of accounting and economics, it is not surprising that this paper should touch upon widely scattered points. Controversial issues, on which the author reserves the right to change his mind, are strewn along the way. The intention has been to show that the cost concept is broader than is generally recognized and includes much that is commonly spoken of as value. The recognition of certain types of value as true costs should help to clarify their accounting treatment. Further, by recognizing the two broad concepts of cost, the accountant should be able to make them useful servants rather than fertile sources of confusion.

Howard Clark Greer

COST FACTORS IN PRICE-MAKING

Howard Clark Greer *was born in Illinois in 1894 and received his A.B. from Northwestern in 1915. He was on the staff of Arthur Young & Co., 1919–1922. He taught at Ohio State (1922–1927) and at Chicago (1929–1938). He was an executive with the American Meat Institute (1927–1939) and with Kingan & Co. (1939–1949). He was business manager of* The Accounting Review, *1926–1931, and served as president of the American Accounting Association in 1932. He has written extensively, including* Chain Store Accounting *(1924),* Accounting for Retail Furniture Stores *(1926),* How to Understand Accounting *(1928), and, with Dudley Smith,* Accounting for a Meat Packing Business *(1943).*
The article reprinted here is based on the first of Mr. Greer's Dickinson Lectures at Harvard in 1952. This first part deals with the subject in a free economy. The second part, not reprinted here, appeared in the September–October, 1952, issue of The Harvard Business Review, *and extended the discussion to the case of government regulation.*

Price-making is one of management's most important tasks. The success or failure of an enterprise may depend on the ability of its management to select the right prices for its goods.

This is a difficult and delicate operation. The successful price-maker needs a knowledge of economics, an understanding of markets, a familiarity with distribution techniques, and a grasp of the relevant cost facts. This last aspect of the problem is the particular subject of this discussion.

The attempt here is to describe the price-making function as the writer has come to know it, through a quarter-century of close association with such activities, as an accountant, analyst, adviser, executive, and director, serving numerous business enterprises in a variety of industries. The discussion is based on observation and interpretation of what actually takes place in the price-making process. Accordingly the conclusions are derived from practical experience rather than abstract reasoning.

Reprinted from the *Harvard Business Review* (July-August, 1952), by permission.

How does a manager go about the job of establishing a price? What conditions confront him? What considerations influence him? What facts does he require? In particular, what cost information is significant, and what bearing will it have on his decisions?

Part I: In a Free Economy

These questions may be answered first in terms of what happens under a free price system. The problems of establishing prices in a controlled economy require separate consideration and will be treated in Part II of this discussion, in the next issue of the REVIEW.

The Price-Cost-Volume Equation

An understanding of prices requires some understanding of costs. Prices and costs are indissolubly connected. Each affects the other. Both prices and costs, in turn, affect volume. Accordingly, the three factors of price, cost, and volume are fundamental to virtually every business activity, every business decision.

The interrelation of these factors is a subject of great confusion and misunderstanding, in business as well as out of it. Because certain influences are commonly significant, it often is assumed that they are universally controlling. Because simple conclusions are carved, interpretations are oversimplified and become misleading. Thus laymen come to believe that they can comprehend price-cost problems which actually baffle the experts.

For example, it is commonly asserted that costs control prices—that the businessman computes his costs, adds a profit, and establishes a price. Acceptance of this postulate leads to assumptions that prices are controlled by producers, that every cost change will be reflected in a price adjustment, that profit margins are optional with sellers, that inflation stems from cost increases, and so on.

Conversely, it is sometimes contended that costs must be governed by prices—that the producer can pay out for materials, wages, taxes, rents, and other costs only what he can collect from his customers, less a reasonable return on the capital employed. This leads to beliefs that consumers may be exploiting producers, forcing down wages and commodity prices, destroying investments, and so on.

It is not that simple. Costs do influence prices, but seldom control them (in the sense of exercising the final, exclusive dominance over their precise level and variation). Prices do influence costs, but cannot regulate them (in the sense of forcing adjustments of specific amount in any particular component). Both costs and prices influence the volume of goods that will be produced and distributed, and it may be volume that is affected when the cost-price relationship changes.

The fact is that prices and costs are in a continuous process of becoming adjusted to each other, with neither in absolute control. When costs rise, there is a tendency for prices to be raised, provided the conditions which produced the cost increase will also warrant a price increase. In many cases, however, a higher cost (e.g., one due to shrinking volume and higher overhead) cannot be "passed on" to the buyer. Likewise, product price reductions put pressure on cost elements like raw material values, wage rates, and taxes, but some of these are rigid and inflexible charges which yield to pressure very little and very slowly, if at all.

The third factor in the equation, and the one most likely to fluctuate, is the volume of business done. For most products there is no single, uniform, invariable price. Rather there is a range of prices within which some sales can be effected. A limited amount of business can be done at the top of the range, a larger amount at the bottom. The question is how much sales volume can be generated, and how much production stimulated, at any particular price level.

Price-Maker's Choice. What the price-maker must do, when considering the proper adjustment to a change in either the strength of demand or the level of costs, is to decide how much of the gain or loss should be reflected in margins and how much in volume. The combined reaction of all the individual price-makers in an industry determines the change for the industry as a whole.

For example, if demand is strong, sellers may elect to raise prices (widening unit margins) or to seek increased volume (possibly lowering costs and raising total margins). If demand weakens, sellers may choose to cut prices (in an effort to maintain volume, even at lower unit margins) or to "hold the line" and let sales decline (in the hope that maintained unit margins may offset shrinking volume).

Similarly, if costs rise, sellers may attempt to raise prices proportionately (at the risk of curtailing volume if demand is not likewise rising), or may "absorb" the increases (on the theory that lower volume might raise costs even more than higher wage or material costs). If costs decline, sellers may reduce prices to get more business (figuring they can afford it) or may try to reflect the savings in wider margins (accepting current volume as adequate).

Thus the precise effect of a cost change on prices cannot be predicted with assurance. The reaction of sellers will vary with the circumstances. If the cost increase occurs during a generally rising level of wages and consumer incomes, prices are quite likely to be advanced, because a strong level of demand is indicated. If the cost increase occurs in a period of shrinking volume and heavier unit fixed charges, prices are unlikely to be adjusted upward—in fact they are more likely to be reduced.

It is most certainly *not* true, as so often contended, that all cost increases bring about commensurate price increases, or even that costs are the chief element in market-level advances. Growing demand does more to raise prices than do advancing costs. The inflationary effect of wage advances is to give people more money to spend rather than to make products cost more. Prices do not go up and down, and cannot be put up and down, simply because costs have risen or fallen. Many other factors influence the result.

Ceilings and Floors. One reason why prices are not immediately, or necessarily, responsive to cost changes is that for most products there is a fairly wide range within which prices may be established with moderately satisfactory results. There usually is no single, inevitable, "right" price, which cannot be either higher or lower. There is likely to be a top and a bottom for permissible quotations, but often these limits are quite far apart.

This being the case, a cost increase or decrease may not necessitate an immediate price adjustment. An increase can perhaps be absorbed, a decrease retained as profit. Costs change constantly, and prices may have to be quoted for a whole season at a time. When an adjustment is postponed, it may ultimately prove unnecessary.

It is noteworthy that price ceilings are established by consumer demand and the absence of competitive pressure, while only price floors are created by production and distribution costs. If the product is scarce and in strong demand, the price may be pushed up far above the highest conceivable cost. If the product is plentiful and has acceptable substitutes, the price may be driven down close to the out-of-pocket cost of the most efficient producer.

Obviously a cost change is not necessarily a price influence unless prices are already so close to costs that there is no room for absorption. In all other cases the result is speculative, depending on numerous factors, a few of which are mentioned later.

Product-Type Influences

Some of the confusion about price-cost relationships arises from lack of understanding of the price characteristics of products of different types. The controlling factors in the establishment of a price vary according to the nature of the article priced. Attempts at generalization breed confusion, since the principles applicable to one group of products are not necessarily significant in other groups.

A few illustrations may help to clarify this point.

Basic Commodities. This group consists of the primary raw materials obtained from field, forest, mine, and ocean (such as grains, livestock, timber, and petroleum), and the products resulting from their initial processing (like flour, meat, lumber, and oil). While the volume of such products is immense, the number of enterprises in these industries is relatively small, and the nature of their pricing problems is unfamiliar to the average citizen, and even to most businessmen.

For all such products the controlling factor in price determination is the size of the supply and the state of the demand. Except as it influences supply (often remotely and indirectly), cost is not a factor in the short-run price movements affecting such products. They sell for what buyers will pay, irrespective of what they may have cost.

Meat furnishes a good example. The supply is regulated by the amount of livestock produced for market, often determined by producer decisions made a year in advance. The demand is a function of consumer incomes. The product is perishable and therefore must be moved promptly. The composite meat price is the total of the family meat budgets of all households in the country divided by the total quantity of meat available for sale.

The cost to any producer, processor, or dealer has no bearing whatever on the price he will be able to obtain. He is completely at the mercy of his customers. They pay what they wish, and he must accept it. What he offers for his raw materials may be based on what he thinks he can resell them for in processed form; but once he has made his purchase, he is helpless against the decisions of his clientele.

This compulsion of demand-fixed selling prices in controlling costs is more widespread than is generally recognized, though in many lines of activity the effects are obscure, complex, and delayed. With basic commodities the effects are prompt and unmistakable. When flour sales are poor, the price of wheat goes down. When textiles are dull, cotton declines. When gasoline moves slowly, petroleum slumps.

In such industries cost calculations work backward. The seller subtracts his expenses from his obtainable selling prices to determine what he can afford to pay for his raw materials. The collective ability of raw material processors in any such industry to guess right and figure accurately determines the amount of profit they can obtain. The important factor is the margin which the markets afford. All other influences are secondary.

By-Products and Joint Products. Many basic commodities, when processed, yield one major product and several by-products, or a number of joint products. Livestock, for example, produces meat, skins, fibers, greases, and pharmaceuticals. Petroleum is converted into gasoline, fuel oil, and a myriad of basic chemicals. Cotton supplies fiber, oil, meal, and livestock feed.

The ineffectiveness of costs in influencing prices is even more clearly evident where by-products or joint products are concerned. Cattle costs have no bearing on hide prices, and what is paid for cotton has no influence on what can be charged for cottonseed oil. For the individual items in a group of joint products (like ham, bacon, chops, and lard), no true cost can be determined. The price of lard, for example, has varied over the years from double to half the cost of the live hogs from which it was produced.

What *is* true is that the combined price of all the products has a strong and direct effect on the price which will be paid for the raw material. Processors of agricultural commodities make frequent calculations of total prospective realizations, minus probable processing and marketing expenses, to determine what material cost can be incurred with some promise of a profit. The collective result of such calculations is a market influence of no mean proportions. It is not solely controlling, but highly important.

It is noteworthy that in such industries the burden of processing-expense increases tends to fall first on the raw material producer, not on the product purchaser. Higher milling costs are more likely to depress the price of wheat than to raise the price of flour. High transportation costs may hold down raw material values rather than put up product prices. The cost of the box is more important to strawberry growers than to shortcake eaters.

Processed Commodities. When secondary processing occurs, costs (in the form of conversion expenses) begin to be a greater factor in price determination. Here the processor normally has some choice about doing the conversion job. When there is a market for the commodity he owns, he is unlikely to incur the expense of converting it into something different unless the finished product can be sold at a price which will cover the basic commodity value, plus at least the out-of-pocket expenses involved.

Thus, in setting the price on a processed commodity, the manufacturer begins to work forward as well as backward in his cost-price calculations. He reflects the *raw-material market plus processing expense* in his asking price for the finished product, while at the same time he considers the *product price less processing expense* in appraising the raw material market.

When the two markets get out of relationship, as they often do, it suggests that a corrective change may be in prospect, or that an abnormal competitive condition exists, or that the public demand for the article has become exceptionally strong (or weak), or that some other unusual element is present in his situation. Deciding which of these conditions prevails is the essence of successful management in enterprises of this type.

Since most commodity-processing industries are highly competitive, with margins narrow and market fluctuations severe, knowledge of processing-cost data is an indispensable element in the development of sound price-making policies. Often a sequence of processing operations is involved, with the product salable at various stages of completion. Allocation of joint costs among the processes becomes an important factor. The influence of volume is a vital one.

Under normal conditions each stage in the processing will produce an increase in value equal to the conversion cost plus some margin of profit. Manufacturers thus naturally seek to extend their processing as far as possible. Flour millers go into the breakfast-food and bake-mix business; meat packers make sausage and canned meats; cotton oil processors become producers of packaged shortenings; steelmakers turn out rails, pipe, and wire—even fences, bridges, and houses. The price influence of these "integrated operations" is important and particularly difficult for an outsider to comprehend.

Alternative Uses and Sources. Many raw materials have several alternative uses. Animal and vegetable oils, for example, may be processed into edible products (lard, shortening, margarine, salad dressing) or into inedible products (soap, paint, lubricants, cosmetics). Conversely, many needs can be met from alternative sources. Meat, for example, may be replaced on the menu by fish, poultry, eggs, or cheese; for many purposes, metal and wood are interchangeable with glass or plastic.

The availability of substitute outlets and sources is an important influence on prices. Nothing can be purchased for less than it will bring if diverted to its next most valuable use. Nothing can be sold for more than the price of its most acceptable alternate. Gasoline will bring not less than fuel oil, not more than benzene. Rough lumber must command more than firewood, less than finished flooring.

A whole series of prices may be influenced in this way. In the packing business, for example, it is said that the price of grease may affect the price of pork chops, since lard is a substitute for grease, salt pork for lard, bacon for salt pork, ham for bacon, and pork chops for ham. All meats affect each other; cheap beefsteak may mean lower ham prices, high veal chops strengthen lamp chops, and so on.

In transportation the effects of such competition are striking. Barges compete with pipelines, railroads with barges, trucks with railroads, airplanes with trucks. The cost of the service is less significant in its price than the availability of an alternative facility. High cost of an unsatisfactory service will not necessarily raise its price, though it may ultimately eliminate it from competition. The bus and the private automobile put the electric interurban out of business. Labor and materials flow into trucks and planes if freight cars cost too much to be a profitable investment.

For the past generation most agricultural by-products have been under pressure from synthetic substitutes of chemical origin. Petroleum products crowd the inedible oils of animal and vegetable derivation; rubber and plastics push leather aside; man-made fibers elbow cotton and wool in the textile field; oil and gas have ousted coal from its monopoly of the fuel business; and asphalt roofing has made the wood shingle obsolete.

Fabricated Articles. Somewhat different conditions prevail in the broad field of fabricated articles, such as automobiles, appliances, furniture, clothing, personal goods, and industrial equipment. Because of the huge number and wide variety of such items, they tend to be regarded as typifying price formation in all lines of business, which is an unfortunate misapprehension. These products do, however, furnish the most numerous (and therefore the most impressive) examples of price-making activity, and call for extremely careful attention.

With all such products, cost becomes an important factor in price determination. These goods do not exist in nature, merely awaiting cultivation or extraction; they come into being only as created by man to satisfy an apparent need. Since man expects a compensation proportionate to his efforts and risks, he normally will undertake production only if reasonably assured of an adequate return. He must know his costs and their probable relation to his potential selling prices before he devotes his capital and his energies to the undertaking.

This condition exists, however, only at the initiation of the venture. Once facilities are provided, an organization created, and a trade established, the venture becomes subject to all the hazards of competitors' activities, public preference, and cost fluctuations that beset commodity processing or any other form of commercial endeavor. The first price may recover the first cost, but it does not follow that subsequent prices will reflect subsequent costs. Cheaper, more attractive merchandise may appear. Advances in material costs, or wage levels, or tax rates, or promotional services may raise costs faster than values rise. Continuing profit is far from assured.

On the other hand, the value created may be far in excess of the *cost plus normal return on investment*. New discoveries in fields such as chemicals and drugs may provide goods which sell (initially at least) for double or treble their cost. A brand name may create more profit than a brand-new factory. A trade-mark may sell for more than a transit system.

Again it becomes apparent that costs affect prices but seldom control them. For fabricated articles, cost may establish a floor, never a ceiling. Wide profit margins stimulate increased production and attract competitors. More goods and more sellers tend to lower prices until margins shrink to normal or less. Demand, however, is still the most significant factor in determining the price.

Individual Projects. At the far extreme from the basic commodity stands the individual project—the once-and-for-all, not-to-be-repeated job of constructing an object or performing a service on a special contract, unique in its characteristics, beginning and ending with itself.

Here, and here alone, cost normally becomes the solely controlling factor in the establishment of the price. Since no labor, materials, or facilities are committed to the job in advance, it is evident that no one is likely to acquire and supply them unless he feels sure of getting his money back. Since other contractors are normally awaiting the same opportunity, it is unlikely that anyone can include an abnormal profit in his bid without losing the business to some competitor who is willing to work for less.

Unusual conditions (such as labor and material shortages), peculiar circumstances, or extraordinary demand may stretch or shrink the normal margins, and exceptional efficiency or good fortune may lower costs; but on the whole the selling price of construction, investigation, development, and promotion tends to be related very closely to the costs incurred. It is unfortunate that this well-known fact should lead to the conclusion that the same principle applies to the sale of goods and services of other kinds.

Cost Influences

For those industries in which cost calculations form at least the primary basis for determining what prices should be charged (i.e., will be profitable), what cost data are useful and how are they employed?

Here again the answer is far from simple. The "cost" of a product is not some single precisely calculable figure. Cost is a composite of numerous elements—some direct and some imputed, some fixed and some variable, some provable and some theoretical. No two cost-finding procedures are identical, and no one procedure will produce continuously identical results.

Thus cost-finding for pricing purposes is necessarily the assemblage of a variety of cost facts, which can be combined in a variety of ways to produce a variety of answers. The price-maker can use them only as a guide and a point of reference. In constructing his price list, he will apply cost facts more or less conscientiously according to his philosophy and his circumstances.

Every seller would prefer a price list in which the price of each item fully covers the total computed cost of that item. Such a list would consist of "safe" prices, involving no risks of loss if adequate volume is obtained.

In practice, however, it is often found that not all items will carry full overhead. Competition may limit the obtainable price for certain products. Staple items, turning over rapidly, may justify narrow margins. Overhead analysis may indicate that apportionments have been faulty, with some products bearing more than a fair share. It may be even argued that available prices should dictate the overhead distribution. Should by-products carry full costs? The variations are endless.

Price lists ultimately may be forced into patterns established by competition. The question then becomes one of how much cost is recovered by any given price. The slim-margin items are tolerated; the wide-profit numbers are actively pushed. Price-cost relationships must be constantly checked, as a basis of production and sales policy, even when prices themselves seem immune to the influences of cost computations.

Cost Components. Price-making, of course, is not wholly (or even mainly) the job of establishing general price levels or constructing price lists. Almost every seller is constantly confronted with individual selling opportunities requiring him to arrive at a quotation for a particular piece of business involving some one item, or order, or quantity, or customer. Here the knottiest cost-price problems occur.

The normal condition is one in which the seller is anxious to make the sale. In ordinary times, thanks to this country's enormous natural resources and productive capacity, business is conducted in a so-called "buyers' market." The seller must be the aggressor; he must go after the business. To get it he must match, or better, competitors' prices. How low can he afford to go?

This raises the broad and important question of what elements of cost are significant in establishing prices for individual transactions where more volume is needed, competition is severe, and close figuring is essential. The right answer depends on a full knowledge of the components of costs, a shrewd appraisal of the probable effect of the decision, and a generous portion of ordinary good luck.

In the typical enterprise the total of the costs assignable to an individual product or sale comprises cost elements of several types, usually including the following:

1. Costs which are directly connected with that one product or sale and which occur if that product is made or that sale consummated and not otherwise—so called *direct* costs.
2. Costs which are related to the total volume of business done, but not specifically to any individual fraction of that total—sometimes referred to as *variable overhead* costs.
3. Costs which are predetermined and constant, irrespective of individual transactions and even of all transactions combined—commonly known as *fixed overhead* costs.

The first group is made up of such elements at materials and direct labor; the second, of costs of such services as maintenance, power, communications, travel, and operating supplies; the third, of such facility and organization costs as insurance, taxes, depreciation, advertising, and executive salaries. How much of each of these costs must be reflected in an acceptable selling price?

The orthodox answer is that every price should cover the full cost of the article, including not only direct out-of-pocket costs but a full apportionment of fairly allocated variable and fixed overhead. It is argued that unless each sale returns its share of such costs, all sales combined are unlikely to prove profitable. The dangers of below-cost selling are widely advertised.

The trouble with the advocated principle is the impossibility of applying it. Overhead costs relate to individual items only in theory, and the amount properly assignable to some one unit of goods or services is never precisely measurable. Even when the philosophy of cost apportionment can go unchallenged, the size of the overhead burden per unit cannot be determined unless the number of units is known. Getting or losing a particular order may in itself affect the cost of filling it. The manager is almost bound to assume the acceptance of his bid in figuring his overhead, even though his past experience suggests that higher average costs are probable.

Taken by itself any order is desirable if the price will cover its direct costs and contribute something to the overhead. In few cases, however, can an order be taken entirely by itself. A low price on one sale may involve low prices on others. The order which our low price takes away from a competitor may be canceled out by some other order which his low price takes away from us. Too much cheap business may crowd out more profitable orders obtainable elsewhere. The business might ultimately consist of orders which were individually desirable but collectively unremunerative.

In spite of all this, the fact remains that not all business can be obtained at exactly the same price and that some concessions from top prices are commonly necessary to meet many situations. How far such concessions can extend is an ever-present problem of price-making.

Apportionment of Joint Costs. An invaluable aid in the solution of such problems is a clear understanding of the principles underlying the apportionment among products and activities of those costs which apply jointly to many products and transactions. Which will be greater or less if a certain pricing policy is adopted, and by how much? From which classes of business can fixed-overhead costs be recovered, and at what rate?

The first task of the cost accountant confronting a pricing problem is to study all the indirect costs connected with production, distribution, and administration in an effort to determine which ones are positively affected by the amount and kind of business taken. These may then be grouped according to the *factor of variability* influencing each, and a cost *per unit of activity* may be developed.

In a factory, for example, certain costs may vary with the man-hours operated, others with machine-hours operated, others with quantities processed, and others with values invested. In a transportation system, costs may vary with miles of track maintained, with locomotive-hours operated, with car-miles run, with tons hauled, or with passengers carried. In a store or warehouse, costs relate to sales volume, inventory volume, space occupancy, personnel employment, promotion, supervision, and so on.

The cost data so developed are not necessarily those incorporated in product or departmental costs, assembled for bookkeeping purposes. They must consist of basic cost elements—"building blocks" from which any specific cost computation can be made to meet whatever need may arise. Even the contents of a block may have to be varied according to the circumstances. The job must be done over and over, with costs assembled in a variety of combinations, to meet the requirements of each particular situation.

Normally the calculation of total cost is a two-stage operation. The first step is to add to the known direct out-of-pocket costs an appropriate allowance for variable overhead costs of all types—the amounts by which the aggregate expense of conducting the business will be increased if this particular order, or class of orders, is obtained and filled. The second step is to add a reasonable (or perhaps the maximum obtainable) share of fixed overhead costs—those charges which will continue in substantially unchanged amount whether or not this particular business is handled. The resulting figure is the basic "sold" cost which a price must attempt to recover.

Unfortunately the distinction between variable and fixed overhead costs is often difficult to maintain. Few overhead costs are uniformly variable or wholly fixed. The principle is easy to state, often difficult to apply. While the mechanics of applying it cannot be fully described here, at least some further attention to the influence of fixed costs on prices may be in order.

Sunk Costs. Businessmen, apprehensive of price-cutting by competitors, commonly argue that every price quoted should reflect a "fair" share of all costs, including those fixed charges which result from the maintenance of an investment and an organization and which are not directly related to any individual activities in which the business may subsequently engage. Economists, however, recognize that many of these outlays create what are sometimes termed "sunk" costs, irrevocably committed to the enterprise and, therefore, not necessarily an element in the future price decisions of its managers.

While every manager strives mightily to price his goods so that these costs, with all others incurred, will be fully recovered, he usually recognizes that there is no fixed or determinable fraction of the total which is necessarily assignable to, or recoverable from, any individual transaction or group of transactions. While he will use as a guide some possibly arbitrary apportionment of such costs to particular units or classes of products or orders, he must remain conscious that the profitableness of a price, or a price schedule, is not adequately measured by its relationship to costs thus determined.

The reasons are obvious, though they seem often to escape both managers and cost accountants. First, the basis of apportionment is necessarily theoretical and subject to wide variations according to the theory adopted. Secondly, the unit amount of such overhead costs is more closely related to total volume than to the size of the costs themselves. Thus the determination of the fixed-cost component in a total cost involves both a theory as to apportionment and an assumption as to volume. Such a cost factor has no intrinsic veracity, stability, or dependability. It constitutes merely a guide, a measuring stick, or an objective—not a controlling element in price calculations.

The manager's task, broadly considered, is to establish a pricing program which will insure the recovery *in the aggregate* of all costs incurred, plus a maximum of return for the use of the capital employed. Sound pricing usually involves quoting for each item an amount high enough to cover its direct cost, plus its proper share of variable costs, plus its maximum contribution toward fixed overhead and profit. To determine the latter amount it is necessary to estimate the size of the volume obtainable at any level of prices, the probable influence of competition, and many other factors.

Distribution Costs. With attention long concentrated on manufacturing costs, inadequate consideration is frequently given to the expense of marketing the product after its manufacture is completed. Yet distribution accounts for a large percentage of all costs incurred and commonly has more influence on pricing policy than the bare cost of production.

Distribution may include any or all of the following activities: publicity, contact, solicitation, warehousing, display, order filling, delivery, service, credit extension, market research, and the related supervisory and administrative functions. Costs of such activities differ according to products, quantities, channels, locations, customers, and methods of sale. The cost differences vitally affect the price which will be remunerative under varying conditions.

The skillful price-maker must know accurately what cost variations are involved in the offering of goods under the widely differing conditions which may be met in a typical marketing program. One product may differ from another in frequency of sale, rate of turnover, breadth of customer demand, and so on. Unit selling cost for quantity orders is normally far less than for small transactions. Selling to wholesalers is usually much cheaper than direct-to-retailer merchandising. Distance and congestion increase delivery costs. Some customers require more service than others.

Most enterprises develop a pattern of price differentials designed to reflect these cost differences. Quantity discounts are common, and functional (i.e., customer-class) discounts apply in many fields. Delivered prices may include transportation charges. Extra service may rate a special charge.

In no field, however, are there greater temptations toward abuse of the differential cost principle or toward price-cutting of an indiscriminate character. Knowledge of the differences in distribution costs is frequently inadequate; many of the costs are "joint," or seemingly in the category of fixed overhead; the lure of the big order is ever present. The sales temperament plays a part. "If our competitor can do it, so can we" becomes a comfortable excuse for any kind of careless or damaging price-making.

This subject has had intensive study in recent years, but most businesses still have a lot to learn about it. Sound cost calculation is an invaluable aid to sound organization of the selling program. The right selection of customers and channels and the right differentials between classes of service may mean the difference between success and failure for the entire enterprise.

Prior and Current Acquisitions. A particularly perplexing price-cost problem arises from the ownership of materials or facilities acquired at prices substantially above or below those currently prevailing. Should cost calculations (and the related price quotations) be based on actual original costs or on current replacement costs? Should the advantage of the fortunate acquisition be retained by the owner or passed on to the buyer? Should resale prices originally established be maintained even though the goods can now be bought for less?

This is a highly controversial issue, fraught with supposed moral implications as well as real, practical complexities. Is a dealer a "profiteer" if he raises his prices to correspond with changes in replacement costs and sells his low-price inventory for more than he expected to get? Is he a "chiseler" if he marks down his high-cost goods when he learns that lower markets are on the way?

The moralist's response is likely to depend on which theory of price-making appeals to him. If he is a cost-recovery advocate, he may contend that higher replacement costs should not be reflected in higher selling prices till the old low-cost inventory has been sold. This theory comfortably ignores the fact that public demand is expressed in rising prices, and that there is no more justification for denying a seller the advantages of a higher level of purchasing power than there is possibility of protecting him from the penalty of shrinking incomes among his prospective customers. People have to be charged more when they can pay more, and less when they have less to spend.

Oddly enough, sellers often refuse to take advantage of the opportunities for abnormal margins resulting from fortunate acquisitions, using their favorable position instead to "undersell the market" and thus grab some business away from not-so-fortunate competitors. This causes great indignation throughout the trade. The merits and dangers of such a course must be carefully weighed by each seller in the light of his own particular circumstances.

One aspect of this problem is the competitive influence of low-cost and high-cost productive facilities, existing side by side and turning out goods for the same market. Should the owner who acquired his plant at a bargain price—either from a distressed seller or during a period of deflation—use correspondingly reduced depreciation allowances in computing his costs (and setting his prices)? Or should he incorporate in his charges a provision for replacement at current price levels?

The answer again is not properly one of morality or philosophy, but one of judgment, depending on manufacturing conditions, market demand, available trade, volume and profit objectives, and other factors. The utilization of low-cost facilities often involves high operating and maintenance costs, and an inflated depreciation provision may raise the hypothetical product cost to an irrecoverable level. On the other hand, the refusal to recognize a higher level of plant replacement costs may result in "giving away" the economic values inherent in the facilities, when higher prices and wider profit margins are essential to provide the funds needed for replacements.

"Follow the market" is normally the soundest pricing policy. Here again, as in so many other cases, the seller's own actual cost will not constitute the sole (or even an important) determinant of what should be charged. Cost is simply one factor to be considered, receiving greater or lesser weight according to the circumstances.

Incidence of Costs. Despite all the uncertainties as to how much cost can be recovered in any given price, one important fact can never be disregarded, namely, that all costs ultimately burden someone. When the buyer does not pay them, someone else must. Who that someone is depends on circumstances.

It is plainly *not* true that all costs are eventually passed on to the consumers of the products in question. Excessive costs, abnormal losses, and higher income taxes are *not* merely added to selling prices. More than one-fourth of the country's business enterprises normally lose money and thus are obviously not recovering all their costs. Even whole industries may sell their output below the cost of production.

Who takes those losses, carries those burdens?

Most of them, of course, fall on the owners of the enterprises through reduction in, or elimination of, the hoped-for profit—perhaps eventually through dissipation of their capital investment. Others, however, may also be involved.

Unprofitable sales (i.e., those not recovering the costs incurred) in due course put pressure on both volume and costs. The least remunerative business is dropped; special services are discontinued; quality may be lowered. Suppliers are pressed to reduce their quotations for materials and parts. Workers may be forced to accept lower wages, fewer "fringe" benefits. Rents are cut, by using less space or taking cheaper quarters. Tax payments are pushed down, income taxes disappear, and authorities are petitioned for lower property tax assessments.

Thus prices may put pressure on costs as often as costs exert influence on prices. In the long run, for broad segments of the economy, there must be some relationship between the two, but in individual cases it is often difficult to determine which is cause and which effect.

Trade-Position Influences

Costs, then, influence prices, but seldom control them. Costs, moreover, show wide variations according to the basis of computation, which may be altered according to the objectives of the costing process. The conclusion will differ depending on whether the perspective adopted is short-range or long-range, particular or general, aggressive or defensive, complacent or concerned. A price-cost relationship which is acceptable under one set of conditions may be wholly unattractive under another.

It is obvious, moreover, that many considerations other than current and immediate costs have a profound influence on price-making. The trade position of the enterprise is a vital factor. Some of the elements in this position deserve attention.

Competitors' Prices. Run-of-the-mill price-making probably is more strongly influenced by the known (or supposed) prices being quoted by competitors than by any other one factor. Sensitiveness to other people's prices is one of the most marked characteristics of the typical sales representatives. "We can't ask more than they do," the argument runs; "and if they can make money at such prices, so should we."

Persuaded by such flimsy arguments, many enterprises do little more than imitate or adapt their competitors' price lists or individual quotations. Many managers have a blind faith in the soundness and profitableness of a price offered by anyone whom they consider a leader in the field. Others, convinced that competitors are ignorantly or maliciously selling below cost, still feel constrained to meet the price regardless of consequences.

The interpretations of competitors' pricing policies are often unjustified. We cannot assume that any given price is adding to (or subtracting from) a competitor's profits; or that, if adopted, it will add to (or subtract from) our own. There are too many uncertainties, too many differing interpretations, to permit a clear-cut conclusion about the probable effects of a policy on either party concerned.

Competitors' prices may frequently be found unprofitable, in the sense of making less contribution to margins than we consider necessary for the success of our own enterprise. Some concerns consistently underprice their goods, and eventually go broke. On the other hand, the fact that a competitor's price is below *our* cost is far from proving that it is below *his* cost. Some people can and do produce more cheaply than others, and use their cost advantages to establish lower prices, thus either broadening the market or obtaining a larger share of it. Either condition must be presumed possible.

The price-maker's difficulty is in appraising the profitableness of any given quotation he is called on to match. Is it an unwarranted, "flash-in-the pan," loss-leader type of price, which cannot be consistently maintained, or is it symptomatic of someone's ability to make money on a lower price level than our own cost position appears to justify? Should the lead be followed or disregarded?

While few concerns are in a position to know the details of a competitor's costs, it may be possible, from a study of one's own cost experience, to form useful hypotheses as to the facts which may underlie the other fellow's decisions. For example, it is possible to set down all the numerous components of our own calculated cost for the item in question, and then to guess at the probable elements in the competitor's figuring by seeking answers to such questions as the following:

Has he an advantage in raw material cost; and, if so, how much? Are his labor and facilities more efficient; and, if so, what is his maximum saving? What volume may he be enjoying (or seeking), and what fixed-overhead cost per unit would our factory have if operated at the same percentage of capacity? What distribution methods does he employ, and how costly are they? Is this item one of his major products, or a by-product, or a side line? How large a contribution to overhead and profit might he normally be expected to seek from such an item? What is his stock position, and what is that of the trade generally?

The answers may be conjectural, but often even a conjecture is illuminating. Furthermore, our own costs take on additional meaning when viewed in the light of what we believe other people's may be. Much as we may desire to realize a price which will compensate us for all our costs, justified or unjustified, we cannot expect our customers to pay us a premium to cover inefficiency, wastefulness, or disadvantageous position.

If we have bought our materials too high, or employ our labor carelessly, or use obsolete equipment, or fail to attain adequate volume, or spend too much on maintenance or supervision or advertising, we create no values through those expenditures—none, certainly, that a customer will recompense us for if similar goods are being produced for less by aggressive competitors who are willing to work on narrow margins to improve their volume and increase their turnover. Under such conditions an excess cost becomes a loss, not something that can be recovered in a price. When it is one thing and when the other is one of management's perennial $64 questions.

Continuity of Operations. It is significant that just as cost factors influence prices, so also do price decisions influence costs. This is so because the production volume generated by a given price is itself one of the important factors in determining what the product will cost.

This is not merely a matter of the size of the unit-overhead cost, which is strongly influenced by the over-all volume level, but it is also a question of continuity and orderliness in the scheduling of production and distribution. In most lines it is not possible to stay in business by accepting prices (making sales) only when margins look favorable. Continuous, uninterrupted activity is one of the most important elements in effective cost control.

For this reason many concerns plod patiently along through what are sometimes long-extended periods of unremunerative prices, taking business at whatever price level they may obtain, because the penalties of price reductions on business done are less than the penalties of cost increases resulting from business refused. Conversely, the enterprise which tries to protect its margins by refusing orders at substandard prices may find those margins impaired and its maintained prices no longer profitable if its production schedule is too often disturbed by interruptions.

As production has become more highly mechanized, and as labor costs have become more and more inflexible, the effect of this factor has become more pronounced. Set-up and start-up expenses for short runs become prohibitive. Guaranteed minimum weekly pay rates prevent savings from the layoff procedure once widely employed. Labor shortages and high training costs make it essential to preserve a skilled labor force, even when profitable employment for all of it cannot currently be found.

The exact cost significance of these factors can be measured only with great difficulty and considerable uncertainty. Their importance is, however, rather generally recognized, and they become a compelling influence on pricing policy.

Maintenance of Trade Position. Even more important than continuity of operations is maintenance of trade position—that is, holding one's normal share of whatever business is available. For every regular article of commerce there is an established pattern of distribution, and neither sellers nor buyers want it disturbed to their own disadvantage. Normally they will make substantial sacrifices to maintain it.

For a seller, building up trade is a costly and difficult job. He must make his goods known to potential customers through advertising, publicity, promotion, and display. He must form acquaintances, create confidence, solicit orders, and establish a method of transportation and delivery. He must pave the way for repeat orders, provide customer service, and aid in secondary distribution. Eventually he has a heavy investment in his trade position, perhaps comparable in size with his investment in plant facilities.

The position thus established is one not lightly to be abandoned, and an aggressive seller will defend it stubbornly. He is too conscious of the cost of "getting in" to let himself be easily pushed out again. To maintain his position he may have to make price concessions which appear unwarranted from a cost and profit standpoint, but this step may be cheaper in the long run than to let someone else take his place in the market and then try to win .it back at some future date.

The hard choice between selling at a loss and not selling at all may be forced by several different conditions. A competitor's advantage in cost, in location, in service, or in some other factor may make his offerings more attractive and compel us to make a price concession to retain the business. Again, a competitor's willingness to sell at a loss to obtain a "first order" may make our prices look high. The customer may find his own resale margin squeezed by similar competitive factors in his own field, and may demand reductions in the prices he is paying. Substitute goods of a new type may threaten the whole fabric of our trade.

Whatever the cause may be, the effect is often to push prices disturbingly far away from the level which would prevail if current costs and desired profit margins were the only considerations in price-making.

Market-Level Equilibrium. Much of the foregoing has emphasized the pressures toward lower prices which are exerted on the seller by his desire to expand volume, broaden markets, maintain production, and protect trade. These "trade considerations," however, are by no means all on the side of price reductions. Several powerful influences work in the opposite direction.

One of these is the inherent tendency of management to lean to the "high side" in computing costs. Businessmen instinctively fear "close prices." They prefer guides which allow for possible unanticipated cost increases or other contingencies. Accountants are typically conservative. They abhor costs which may turn out to be understated. They like to "forget" possible cost savings in the hope that they will form a welcome, if unexpected, addition to profits.

More important, however, is the disinclination of the average seller to upset an established market equilibrium. Often there is a strong prevailing demand for all the goods currently being produced at prices which are reasonably remunerative to everyone concerned. Why disturb a favorable situation?

True, a lower level of prices might broaden the market, stimulate greater sales, lower costs, and widen the opportunity for profitable employment of capital in expanded plant facilities. When margins are wide and demand apparently insatiable, the pressure for increased competition becomes irresistible. But the typical situation is the one on the border line, where today's prices are barely satisfactory and any reduction seems likely to damage the profit position of the enterprise, perhaps of the entire industry.

Sellers in such cases are characteristically wary. They know that price reductions on their own part may lead to retaliatory price-cutting by others.

Often they see little possibility of substantial expansion in the over-all volume of the industry and fear that lower prices will mean simply lower margins and no improvement in trade position. A sort of trade stigma may attach to a seller who "breaks the line."

The fear of the consequences of price-cutting sometimes has become so great as to encourage collaboration among sellers to maintain existing price levels through formal or informal agreements not to lower them. The foolishness, the ineffectiveness of such joint undertakings has been amply demonstrated, and for half a century they have been legally outlawed, but a wistful desire for "protection" of this sort still lingers in the minds of many businessmen.

Lacking the opportunity for outright price-fixing schemes within the law, apprehensive sellers resort to moral preachments on the evils and dangers of price reductions; and the atmosphere thus created does definitely discourage individual adjustments, thus sometimes offsetting the pressures toward lower prices which come from cost and other considerations previously mentioned.

To cut or not to cut, that is the question. There is no formula which will provide an answer. Each seller must assemble, analyze, and evaluate the available trade information, reaching a solution which seems calculated to give him the best profit possibilities for both the immediate and the long-term future. The decision is likely to be a sound one only if it is based on comprehensive factual data, among which the particulars of costs, both actual and potential, are of prime importance.

Conclusion

Costs influence prices but do not control them, except in a limited and special sense. Goods sell for what buyers think they are worth, whether this price is more or less than cost. Business must recover from its total revenues its total costs, but not every sale will show an adequate individual profit. A contribution to overhead is all that can be expected from some classes of business.

Most enterprises will go to great lengths to maintain volume, continue operations, protect trade position. Sales will be made close to cost (or even below cost) before the operation is abandoned. On the other hand, wide profit margins are eagerly accepted, actively exploited.

In a free economy no seller is "entitled" to a price which will cover his costs. He is entitled only to the price the market affords. He must learn to live on that price, or quit. He cannot burden the buyer with excess costs; he must absorb them himself.

In a free economy the buyer is king. He buys what he wants, pays what he chooses. He must offer enough to bring out the production he desires, but no more. He takes nothing not wanted, and supports no one not needed.

He makes his own price controls, and it is surprising only that he should imagine anyone else could do it better.

This, it should be emphasized, is his experience in a free economy. His experience under the "protection" of government regulations is the subject of Part II of this discussion, to be published in the next issue.

Robert L. Dixon

CREEP

Robert Livingston Dixon, Jr., *was born in Michigan in 1909, received his A.B. from the University of Michigan in 1930, and his Ph.D. from Yale in 1941. He has taught at Yale, Chicago, and Michigan, in that order, and is a C.P.A. in Illinois. He was director of research for the American Accounting Association, 1944–1946, and served as its president in 1949. He edited* The Accounting Review, *1947–1948. He served as a member of the committee on accounting procedure of the American Institute of C.P.A. He is coauthor with W. A. Paton of* Essentials of Accounting *(1958).*

The article reprinted here certainly has one of the most provocative titles in the literature of accounting. It is significant, however, because of its warning against decisions based on an oversimplified analysis of alternative costs. In other words, much of "cost analysis" deals with some of the variables relevant to the problem, but too often omits consideration of other relevant ones.

A business enterprise, typically, is established for a limited purpose, such as the production of a single product or product group, the production of services, or the marketing of certain products. Usually this newly-established enterprise is simple in form, with specialized objectives. The profit motive leads to its creation, and it is expected that profit will be realized through pursuit of this specialized activity.

The case histories of some of the larger corporations, on the other hand, would undoubtedly show that a considerable proliferation of activities accompanies the aging process.

The addition of new activities to the one of initial specialization appears in various ways. Commonly it will appear in the form of integration through taking on the production of component parts formerly delegated to outsiders, or through extending back to the production of raw materials for use in the plant. The sales organization may be expanded to include wholesaling

Reprinted from *The Journal of Accountancy* (July, 1953), pp. 48–55, by permission.

activities and may even be extended forward to include ownership and operation of retail outlets. This process may at the same time be accompanied by a horizontal expansion of activities in which an array of new products is added to the original specialty. In fact, the expansion, diversification, and proliferation may reach the stage where the original objective, through the multiplication of side activities, has become an obscure element in the total activity of the corporation.

Going along with this expansion process one is likely to find another, less spectacular but none the less significant, factor leading to the variegation of enterprise activity. This is the piecemeal attachment of relatively minor activities of service and supply. Examples of this are the establishment of a department for the production of tools; a department for the maintenance of machinery and electrical equipment; a department to service company-owned trucks and automobiles; an engineering department; a legal department; a carpentry and upholstering shop; a printing shop, and so on.

In many instances these accouterments are not added full-grown as the result of a formal analysis and decision, but rather they edge into the picture, starting with the incidental, part-time activity of one or more employees, but ending up later as full-fledged departments of the plant.

In other instances these added activities are undertaken because *they seem to offer cost-saving opportunities*. The reasoning is somewhat as follows: because we have an established plant and organization an important portion of our costs is pretty well fixed; these costs will go on at approximately the same level whether our plant is fully or only partially used; it follows then that we can add odd jobs here and there, call them sideline or self-service activities, *without causing increases in these fixed costs*. In fact, in order to determine whether we should provide our own services and supplies in a particular case, we need consider only the *variable* costs of our existing organization, the variable costs of the added activity and, in cases where new equipment and new permanent personnel are required, certain added fixed costs. But the bulk of the fixed costs can be ignored since they will not be affected by the attachment of the additional operation. In many cases when the addition of a new activity is being considered, the management may go so far as to exclude overhead costs altogether in the computation of the costs to be added. They reason that addition of new activity should not relieve the old activities of any overhead costs.

Under the circumstances of this kind of cost calculation few vendor bids may hope to be successful, since by the self-service activity not only are the middlemen's profits and the distribution costs eliminated, but also the outside producer's profits, and even, in a sense, the producer's fixed costs. In fact, the situation practically offers a bonanza for the manufacturer. The added activities appear to be real bargains.

We are all aware of the advertising slogan, "Direct from the factory to you," but here we are able to go one step farther, in effect bringing the factory right into the home.

In some cases the opportunity for cost saving is so obvious that the self-service activity is allowed to develop, or is taken over in toto, without any preliminary, formal cost studies.

But in other cases the margin of saving may not be so obvious, and the cost accountant may prepare detailed cost studies. In these, if he follows the more orthodox theory, his report will be based on the estimated *incremental* costs, rather than the total costs, of the added activity.

Creep Factors

It was noted above that minor side activities tend in some cases to edge into the operations of a business firm where no special thought has been given to their short-run or long-run effects upon costs and efficiency; it is also true, however, that such activities are frequently added by positive action on the basis of cost studies.

Attention is directed to the proposed exclusion of fixed costs in the decision-making process. Certain observations with respect to this exclusion appear to be in order.

First, if the company is in a position to make permanent additions to its side activities without adding to its fixed costs, something must be out of order. Fixed costs reflect *capacity* to operate, and they appear throughout the entire business organization. Evidently if the fixed costs can be ignored in such a calculation, the company is overequipped and overstaffed for its regular work.

Second, although it is probably impossible to have a condition of absolute balance of staff and equipment throughout the organization, the situation would be rare in which the added activity can be imposed upon the below-capacity segments of the company without in any way impinging on the fully active segments.

Third, equipment to some extent, and human beings to a considerable extent, are capable of being pressed beyond capacity limits for periods of time, but beyond these time limits something must be done to relieve them.

Finally, if idle capacity does temporarily exist throughout the company, the addition of *extracurricular* activities may so pre-empt that available time that it will be difficult to re-establish full-time regular operations when business conditions come back to normal.

All of this means that the fixed costs simply cannot be ignored in making the produce-or-purchase decision, unless one is to be satisfied with a very shortsighted analysis. Fixed costs commensurate with the added activity will inevitably "creep" into the total cost picture, because even though there may be no *immediate* addition to the fixed costs, the added activity will encroach upon the available capacity, and sooner or later this will lead to an actual, though unanticipated and perhaps unrecognized, increase in fixed costs.

The creep effect upon fixed costs can develop in three general ways.

First, if the added activity is allowed to get out of hand in its growth it is obvious that more building space, more equipment, and more salaried personnel must eventually be added. This will be true even though the regular activity of the enterprise is maintained at a fairly fixed level. The question then is, would we have added this activity had we anticipated the fixed cost addition?

Second, even if the added activity is kept at a moderate level, when the main activity is increased fixed-cost increases will again be encountered. Thus, suppose a dozen men and some equipment are added in order that the company can repair its own transportation equipment. This may lead to no immediate addition of employees in the personnel department, the accounting department, or in the other administrative segments of the company; however, the later addition of one person to regular activities can bring into operation a chain of reactions in the form of salaried employee increases, salary increases, and fixed asset additions. The probabilities are that no one will recognize that the factor which really caused the fixed cost increases was the apparently bargain-price addition of the repair operations sometime earlier.

Finally, if the added activity is either kept level, or increased, it will be all the more difficult to cut down on fixed costs should subsequent reductions in the regular operations be necessary.

Side Effects of Creep

The principal aim in the section just concluded was to point out that the exclusion of fixed costs in the contemplation of a produce-versus-purchase decision constitutes a dangerously shortsighted treatment of the problem; that a full quota of fixed costs will almost inevitably creep into the picture, regardless of the subsequent activity trends of the regular and added operations.

What might be called a side effect of creep, although it is actually a direct evidence of creep, is a tendency for the company to compensate unconsciously for overloads resulting from piecemeal additions of "bargain" activities. If, for example, an officer is hired to perform an administrative task under a particular set of conditions, and if then one by one a number of minor, peripheral activities are taken on by the company, the accumulation of these activities may more and more infringe upon the officer's time until through sheer necessity he is forced drastically to neglect his primary responsibilities.

Although no poll of managements has been taken on this point, it is suspected that they are not immune from creep, and one may well wonder if business efficiency and competitive vigor is not often impaired through the accumulation of these barnacles which appear to be bargain activities; in other words, activities which *apparently* do not add to the fixed costs.

Arguments Against Bargain Activities

At this point it may be well, again, to make clear just what sort of activity is being examined. This article does not pretend to weigh the wisdom of a decision to produce rather than purchase where the decision rests primarily (1) upon a question of public relations, or (2) on the basis of guaranteeing adequate supply when needed, or (3) on safeguarding quality, or (4) even decisions to produce rather than purchase during periods of depressed business conditions, where the aim is to keep the working-force intact and to minimize idle capacity losses. Also, it is recognized that new lines of production may properly be undertaken, and old ones dropped, in order to keep pace with changing market conditions. Rather, this is an appraisal of the wisdom of adding an activity, formerly provided by an outsider, on the basis of cost studies which appear to justify the added activity on the ground that fixed costs can be ignored.

The theme of this article is that a major danger in the addition of bargain activities is the creep danger. And this danger is likely to be overlooked in the case of any added activity, whether or not cost saving is the prime motive. In fact it is all the more likely to be overlooked where factors other than cost savings guide the decision.

Another type of danger lies in the fact that the company is not a specialist in the added activity, and that after it has become tied to it, with added personnel and equipment, the discontinued vendor may through research develop cost and sales price reductions which make the decision to produce completely untenable when looked upon with hindsight. Then it may be too late. Reversion to the purchase status is then blocked by prospective sacrifices in the disposal of equipment and the need for discharging personnel.

Public relations may constitute an argument on each side of the question. For instance, an entirely unsupportable contention may be made, particularly in the smaller community, that the local manufacturer should make himself as nearly autonomous as possible, since this means that he will thereby provide more jobs for local labor. Needless to say this is pure bunk. It is a form of disguised charity without the slightest scientific justification.

From the opposite point of view, it is evident that the maintenance of good public relations may actually dictate the avoidance of certain productive activities simply because the good will of the community compels the patronizing of small business firm suppliers.

From the economist's point of view, and unfortunately this argument is not likely to be very compelling with individual businessmen, it may be argued quite conclusively that a decision to produce, when based on a partial cost compilation (that is, with fixed costs excluded), is contrary to the public economic interest. In short, it constitutes mismanagement of economic resources. Just realize that the vendor's price, against which is being matched only a partial summation of costs, is high enough for him to cover not only his variable costs, but also fixed costs, and a profit margin on top of it all. If the vendor's offer, under this assumption, comes within gunshot of meeting the purchaser's variable cost computation, we are doing serious injury to our economic system if we make a decision to produce rather than buy from that vendor.

Another observation is this: activities are usually annexed, with cost saving as the reason, only when they are more or less intimately related to the primary functions of the company. Actually, however, it might be more reasonable, from the standpoint of impact on total profits, to take on completely extraneous operations—again with the assumption that the fixed-cost factor need not be a matter of concern. Thus, the automobile company might just as reasonably open a public restaurant, a dance hall, or a bowling alley, confident that the present executives can soak up such minor administrative burdens as would be involved, and that thereby they have an edge over existing recreational establishments which require a full complement of personnel.

Creep Avoidance

As has been mentioned earlier, some activities are added with clear recognition that no cost saving is attainable, simply because certain non-cost factors are of pressing importance. Others, the ones under consideration here, are annexed because, with fixed costs ignored, bargain rates appear to be achieved. Both kinds cause fixed cost pressures, and lead to unanticipated cost increases—although they may not be recognized in some cases until years later. The important question is then, having brought the nature of creep into the open, what can be done to avoid it?

Among a number of defensive measures undoubtedly existing, four will be suggested here.

First, in the company's organization chart make notations of the number of individuals in each department or other subdivision of the company. From these notations calculate a series of ratios which may be called responsibility indexes. Thus, calculate the ratio of productive and nonproductive employees to foremen in each of the productive and service departments of the plant; then, the ratio of foremen to plant manager or other personnel at the level above foremen. Similarly compute such ratios of responsibility through to top management, in each case using as the numerator of the ratio the number of persons who *report,* or for whom the person reported to is responsible.

Since the number of reporting persons will fluctuate, particularly at the lower levels of the organization, as productive activity fluctuates some judgment must be exercised in establishing certain of the ratios. Whether to use average ratios or ratios to reflect capacity might be debated; however, for present purposes it would seem that the ratios should be computed on a capacity basis. If, for example, the planned description of a given supervisory job is that it shall involve responsibility for receiving and analyzing reports from five persons, or responsibility for supervising the productive activities of twenty-five persons, any contemplation of additional activities should include recognition of probable immediate as well as long-run effects on the responsibility ratios. So far as possible this change should be taken into consideration in arriving at a decision.

A second safeguard in the insurance against creep consists of the exercise of caution that the comparative statement of costs is complete and correct. The costs of purchased supplies, services, etc., are likely to be compiled fairly completely, including an allowance for freight, handling, purchasing, and other incidents of the purchase. Certainly there is no justification for excluding, or overlooking, similar costs which will be incurred if the decision goes in favor of production rather than purchase. Interest on the additional investment should not be overlooked. If the question is one of production of component parts, the acquisition of raw materials is likely to cause a set of costs similar to those incurred in the purchasing of finished parts. A real risk is the likelihood of underestimating even the immediate costs of production.

A third factor to be considered in determining the advisability of adding a new activity is the relative merit of that particular activity as compared with alternatives. It would obviously be illogical to devote available equipment and energies to an operation which would provide a cost saving of a few hundred dollars when the same facilities, otherwise used, could accomplish savings of thousands. Even more foolish would be the addition of an activity of the minor cost-saving variety which might interfere with, or preclude, the later expansion of the company's main operations at a profit in excess of the expected cost-saving. Mistaken decisions of this sort constitute a principal creep danger, leading to a condition of overcrowded facilities and neglected responsibilities.

Creep, as has been emphasized, is not a short-run problem. It consists of the more or less gradual, unrecognized, cluttering up of business activity, accompanied by a parallel deterioration of company efficiency, a building up of fixed costs, and the undermining of profit potential. A fourth factor in the protection against creep is that of flexibility. New activities which are clearly temporary, which can be added and discarded on short notice without significant disruption, are much less likely to cause future trouble than are those which are less flexible. It is pretty well agreed that it is more difficult to dislodge an activity than it is to add one. For the classic object lesson on this point, consider the bureaus of our federal and state governments. But, if an addition is to be made, at least as between two alternative activities which are otherwise equally attractive, the one which can later be abandoned the more easily is certainly the one to be chosen. It is therefore suggested that, among other things, serious consideration be given to the degree of permanence of any new plant, equipment, and especially, personnel, which may be required in undertaking an added activity.

If careful analysis indicates that the proposed activity meets the test of flexibility—that is, if it can be dropped on short notice without serious sacrifice of personnel or of investment in inventories and fixed assets—and if the contemplated addition is purely and unquestionably for a short-run period, then a "partial costs" schedule is appropriate. In other words, under these circumstances it *is proper* to prepare a schedule which is limited to the incremental costs, *the costs which would be added,* and to ignore prorations of existing fixed overhead items. Because of the importance of situations of this class, the point will be considered further under the next section heading.

If, on the other hand, it is contemplated that the new activity may be more or less permanently attached, as where the company will take on its own full-scale printing operations, its own engineering, or toolmaking, or component parts supply, a partial costs schedule is entirely inappropriate. In fact, this point is the crux of the whole situation. For purposes of making the decision to add an activity which may be fairly permanent, the schedule of estimated costs of production should include not only an exhaustive list of the probable added costs, but also a complete assignment of all of the overhead charges, even including administrative overhead, which through regular cost accounting techniques are properly prorated against any regular segment of the enterprise.

Add Allowance for Profit

But this is not all. In addition to the full charge for prorated and added costs, an allowance should be added for profit. That is, in order to justify the addition of a permanent new activity on the grounds of cost savings, the best available supplier's price must be shown not only to exceed the estimated full cost of production, with no apportionable costs omitted, but it should be higher *by an amount at least equal to the rate of profit which the company is able to make through its principal operations.*

The reasons for this fairly extreme view have been expressed earlier in this article, and it should be repeated that the requirement that full costs plus profit be included is, in fact, no more than a minimum protection against creep. Clearly the relationship between today's costs and today's purchase prices may be only a temporary one, and it is altogether too probable that the nonspecialist producer will lag behind the specialist supplier whom he has discarded in the hope of achieving production economies. Thus, the decision can easily turn sour in spite of all of the measures which have been suggested by way of protection.

Justifiable Bargain Activities

It was stated above that where the added activity is clearly intended to be temporary, it is proper to base the decision on a partial list of costs. The point here is that the nonpermanence of the activity tends to insure against the creeping up of fixed costs and managerial overloads. However, resolutions are too often forgotten, and unless positive plans are made in advance for the early abandonment of the activity, it will turn out to be a "sticky," if not permanent, activity, and the fixed costs will flow in to fill up the gaps in the cost analysis.

One form of added activity which, for example, may well be justifiable is that which can be started and stopped repeatedly to serve as fill-in work during periods of temporary lull in the principal activity of the company. Such fill-in work may even extend as long as the depression period of a business cycle, provided it can be stopped conveniently at the time of resumption of normal operations. Under such circumstances the presumption is that the regular working-force should be maintained and, from the cost point of view, the recovery of any portion of costs in excess of variable costs is preferable to their nonrecovery.

One may also justify the addition of activities on a partial cost, or bargain basis, when it is evident that substantial cost reductions will be achieved after a period of experience. In fact, costs during the initial period may be so unrepresentative of the future that they may in effect be disregarded.

Also, where a company is chronically operating below capacity, and has found itself absolutely unable to expand its market, there is justification for taking over certain activities of its suppliers, provided that an already unfavorable position is not further weakened, and provided that existing fixed costs cannot be cut down to a level commensurate with existing activity. Again, however, it should be emphasized that the company should not take over "just any old activity" in which its variable costs will be less than the best outside price. A very careful survey of all opportunities for cost saving should be made before any is chosen.

Elimination of Creep

Assuming that one has already suffered a good case of creep, what steps can be taken to cure the situation? Can we apply the same tests in deciding upon the elimination of activities that we use when consideration is being given to the addition of such activities? Are the same tests applicable in reverse?

Obviously a fringe activity should not be eliminated if the potential cost of acquiring the supplies, services, etc., from outsiders is so far in excess of the costs of self-service that over-all profits would thereby be diminished. But, in exploring this possibility, what costs of production should be included?

It was pointed out above that perhaps the most potent defense against creep is a requirement that outside suppliers be used, in the case of any relatively permanent program, unless it can be proved that their offering prices are higher than the buyer's total costs plus a margin of profit. Does this mean that an existing activity should be dropped in favor of outside supply if it is found that the existing activity when charged with full costs would not show profit if it were given credit for its output at regular market prices?

In general the answer would appear to be *yes,* although subject to one exception. The rule may be expressed somewhat as follows: A company should divest itself of any activity which has been undertaken because of its cost-saving potential if such activity would not be added under the suggested rules for the prevention of creep. The only exception is this: If specialized machinery, equipment, housing, or other specialized fixed assets have been purchased, and are of such nature that they have no alternative full use, the depreciation and other nonseparable costs of such assets can be eliminated from the calculation except to the extent that the assets have a significant present market value. In other words, the cost of such assets is "sunk"; to the extent that such cost cannot be retrieved by sale or through other employment in the business, the cost may be said already to be invested in future production of the related product, and the sacrifice cannot, therefore, be avoided by the discontinuance of the activity. If, with depreciation of specialized assets modified or eliminated, it is found that a given activity, when charged with all costs usually prorated to a routine operation and "loaded" with a profit margin, is not able to compete with the price of comparable service as offered by outside suppliers, the activity should be abandoned.

The term "activity audit" might be adopted to describe a more or less continuous study of the ancillary activities of the business firm for purposes of detecting existing or potential creep.

Summary

A business firm, as it matures, is likely to accumulate an array of productive activities which were never contemplated when the company was founded. Many of these activities are added on a self-service basis as a matter of convenience, or they are added during periods of short supply, or to assure reliable quality, and for other reasons; such activities may well be continued provided that their full costs are adequately recognized and provided that management realizes what cost sacrifices are being made to achieve such convenience, etc. Many other activities, however, may have been taken on solely because of apparent cost savings, and additional activities may from time to time be contemplated. All such activities should be subjected to frequent activity audits to determine whether or not real cost advantages exist. Unless these activities are purely temporary, idle-time fillers, their continuance or addition cannot be justified on the grounds that they need be charged with only a part of the list of costs normally charged to regular, principal operations. This is true because fixed costs commensurate with the activity will inevitably creep in to the operating costs structure.

Equally important, though not examined in detail in this article, are the additions of new lines of products which can be demonstrated to *show a profit* only because they are charged with costs on a partial, or incremental, basis. In course of time they too will cause creep.

Added activities, ranging all the way from minor service items to the production and sale of new product lines, not only create fixed costs but also tend to distract operating management from its principal objectives, and it may be no exaggeration to state that many business firms owe to creep not only the decline in their profit rates but also their ultimate failure.

Part Five

Accounting Under Regulation

Perry Mason

THE SUPREME COURT
ON PUBLIC-UTILITY DEPRECIATION

Perry Mason *(1899–1964) was born in Illinois, and received an A.B. from Michigan (1921) and a Ph.D. from the same school in 1938. In the course of his career he taught at Michigan, Kansas, Antioch, UCLA, and California at Berkeley. He was at Berkeley from 1938–1952. He was a member of the committee on accounting procedure of the American Institute of C.P.A. He left teaching to go to the American Institute of C.P.A. as a member of its research staff, where he remained until his retirement in 1963. He served as a vice-president of the American Accounting Association in 1939 and as its president in 1950. From 1947–1949 he was secretary-treasurer of the Western Economic Association. His major publications include* Fundamentals of Accounting, *an introductory text that went through several editions,* Principles of Public-Utility Depreciation, *which was the first monograph published by the American Accounting Association and* "Cash Flow" Analysis and the Funds Statement, *published by the American Institute of C.P.A. as Accounting Research Study No. 2 in its new research program. The article reprinted here is significant because (a) it provides us with a case study of the interaction between accounting and the law, (b) it serves as background to the rapid developments in regulation in the 1930's and the 1940's, and (c) it contains a discussion of the depreciation problem that has few rivals in the literature. The last point is illustrated in his extended treatment of the decision in the* United Railways *case, starting about a third of the way through this article.*

The opinions expressed by the justices of the Supreme Court of the United States on depreciation necessarily have had a marked influence upon the subsequent decisions of the state and Federal public utility commissions. They constitute an important factor in the formation of regulatory policies for the handling of depreciation problems.

In no case prior to the Knoxville Water Company case in 1909 has there

Reprinted from *The Accounting Review* (September, 1936), pp. 234–70, by permission.

337

been more than an incidental reference to depreciation, or a brief discussion which indicates an entirely inadequate knowledge of its nature and problems. Definite recognition was given of the necessity of a utility keeping its property in good service condition[1] but little or no appreciation was evidenced of the function of depreciation accounting methods.

United States v. Kansas Pacific Railway Co.[2] A statement was made in this case that "Only such expenditures as are actually made can with any propriety be claimed as a deduction from earnings," and the creation of an unspent reserve through periodic charges to operations was prohibited.

Smyth v. Ames.[3] This celebrated leading case on public utility valuation not only presents a curiously confusing, inconsistent, and partly irrelevant set of factors which should be considered in arriving at the "fair value" upon which a "fair return" should be allowed, but it fails to mention the highly important element of depreciation. It is not likely that its use of the term "present value" coincides with the conception of reproduction cost less depreciation. At least subsequent commentators have assumed that its "present value" referred to undepreciated reproduction cost as compared with original cost. The classic formula presented in this case is as follows:

> We hold, however, that the basis of all calculations as to the reasonableness of rates to be charged by a corporation maintaining a public highway under legislative sanction must be the fair value of the property being used by it for the convenience of the public. And in order to ascertain that value, the original cost of construction, the amount expended in permanent improvements, the amount and market value of its bonds and stock, the present as compared with the original cost of construction, the probable earning capacity of the property under particular rates prescribed by statute, and the sum required to meet operating expenses are all matters for consideration and are to be given such weight as may be just and right in each case. We do not say that there may not be other matters to be regarded in estimating the value of the property. What the company is entitled to ask is a fair return upon the value of that which it employs for the public convenience. On the other hand, what the public is entitled to demand is that no more be exacted from it for the use of a public highway than the services rendered by it are reasonably worth.

San Diego Land & Town Co. v. National City.[4] This case is cited most

---

1 See *Union Pacific Railroad Co. v. United States,* 99 U. S. 420 (1878) ; *New York, Lake Erie & Western Railroad v. Nickals,* 119 U. S. 296 (1886) ; *Reagan v. Farmers' Loan & Trust Co.,* 154 U. S. 362 (1894).

2 99 U. S. 455 (1878).

3 169 U. S. 466 (1898). Appeals from a decree of the Circuit Court of the United States for the District of Nebraska, perpetually enjoining the railroad companies from making a rate schedule reducing rates to those prescribed by the state act of Nebraska, approved April 12, 1898, or from conforming to the provisions of said act, and restraining the board of transportation of Nebraska from taking any action to enforce the act or penalize violations.

4 174 U. S. 739 (1899). An appeal from a decree of the Circuit Court of the United States for the Southern District of California dismissing a suit brought by the San Diego Land & Town Co. against the City of National City et al. to obtain a decree that the water rates fixed by the defendant city were void.

frequently in support of the proposition that the proper rate base is the value of the property at the time of the investigation. Depreciation is merely mentioned as one of the factors to be considered in ascertaining fair rates.

> The contention of the appellant in the present case is that in ascertaining what are just rates the court should take into consideration the cost of its plant; the cost per annum of operating the plant... ; annual depreciation of the plant from natural causes resulting from its use; and a fair profit to the company.... Undoubtedly, all of these matters ought to be taken into consideration and such weight be given them, when rates are being fixed, as under all the circumstances will be just to the company and to the public. The basis of calculation suggested by the appellant is, however, defective in not requiring the real value of the property and the fair value in themselves of the services rendered to be taken into consideration. What the company is entitled to demand, in order that it may have just compensation, is a fair return upon the reasonable value of the property at the time it is being used for the public.

San Diego Land & Town Co. v. Jasper.[5] This decision is primarily a restatement of the "fair value" doctrine of *Smyth v. Ames, supra,* as interpreted in *San Diego Land & Town Co. v. National City, supra.* Present value is given priority over original cost and the place of depreciation is left uncertain.

> The main object of attack is the valuation of the plant. It is no longer open to dispute that under the Constitution "what the company is entitled to demand, in order that it may have just compensation, is a fair return upon the reasonable value of the property at the time it is being used for the public." *San Diego Land & Town Co. v. National City,* 174 U.S. 739, 757.... That is decided, and is decided as against the contention that you are to take the actual cost of the plant, annual depreciation, etc., and to allow a fair profit on that footing over and above expenses.... Yet the only evidence in favor of a higher value in the present case is the original cost of the work, seemingly inflated by improper charges to that account and by injudicious expenditures..., coupled with a recurrence to testimony as to the rapid depreciation of the pipes....

An interesting feature of the case, in view of the radically different view which was to be expressed a few years later, is the refusal of the court to insist upon an allowance for periodic depreciation.

> We will say a word about the...contention of the appellant, that there should have been allowance for depreciation over and above the allowance for repairs. From a constitutional point of view we see no sufficient evidence that the allowance for six % on the value set by the supervisors, in addition to what was allowed for repairs was confiscatory. On the other hand, if the claim is made under the statute, although that would be no ground for bringing the case to this court, it has been decided by the Supreme Court of California that the statute warrants no such claim. *Redlands, L. & C. Domestic Water Co. v. Redlands,* 121 Cal. 312, 313, 53 Pac. 791.... We

---

[5] 189 U. S. 439 (1903). An appeal from the Circuit Court of the United States for the Southern District of California to review a decree which dismissed a bill to have an ordinance of a board of supervisors fixing irrigation rates void for unreasonableness.

do not sit as a general appellate board of revision for all rates and taxes in the United States. . . .[6]

Stanislaus County v. San Joaquin & King's River Canal & Irrigation Co.[7] There is no discussion of depreciation in this case other than to mention it as one item to be given consideration in the determination of the reasonable value on which a fair return is to be allowed.

Knoxville v. Knoxville Water Co.[8] This is the first case in which an extended discussion of depreciation appears. The lower court had allowed 2% for depreciation as a part of a total return of 8% on the undepreciated reproduction cost. The comments in the Supreme Court decision in regard to periodic depreciation must be taken as *obiter dicta* although they have been cited frequently in subsequent commission and court cases, but the failure of the lower court to deduct depreciation in the valuation base was one of three errors which led to the reversal of the decision by the higher court.

This case seems to establish the following policies and principles in regard to depreciation:

(a) That when reproduction cost is used as evidence of the proper rate base valuation, a deduction must be made for depreciation in order to arrive at a fair present value.

> The first fact essential to the conclusion of the court below is the valuation of the property devoted to the public uses, upon which the company is entitled to earn a return. . . . . This valuation was determined by the master by ascertaining what it would cost, at the date of the ordinance, to reproduce the existing plant as a new plant. The cost of reproduction is one way of ascertaining the present value of a plant like that of a water company, but that test would lead to obviously incorrect results if the cost of reproduction is not diminished by the depreciation which has come from age and use. . . .

(b) That the depreciation which is to be deducted begins with the use of the property and is the result of age and use.

> The cost of reproduction is not always a fair measure of the present value of a plant which has been in use for many years. The items composing the plant depreciate in value from year to year in a varying degree. Some pieces of property, like real estate for instance, depreciate not at all, and sometimes, on the other hand, appreciate in value. But the reservoirs, the mains, the service pipes, structures upon real estate. . .and appliances of every kind begin to depreciate with more or less rapidity from the moment

---

6 The Redlands case relied upon *San Diego Water Co. v. City of San Diego,* 118 Cal. 556, 50 Pac. 633 (1897) which denied the right of the utility to set up depreciation in addition to charges for repairs.

7 192 U. S. 201 (1904). An appeal from the Circuit Court of the United States for the Northern District of California to review a decree setting aside an ordinance regulating water rates.

8 212 U. S. 1 (1909). An appeal from the Circuit Court of the United States for the Eastern District of Tennessee to review a decree enjoying the enforcement of a municipal ordinance fixing maximum water rates.

of their first use. It is not easy to fix at any given time the amount of depreciation of a plant whose component parts are of different ages, with different expectations of life. But it is clear that some substantial allowance for depreciation ought to have been made in this case.....

A water plant with all of its additions begins to depreciate in value from the moment of its use.....

(c) That depreciation is a determinant rather than an allocation of net income.

Before coming to the question of profit at all the company is entitled to earn a sufficient sum annually to provide not only for current repairs, but for making good the depreciation...

(d) That it is both a right and a duty of the utility to provide for depreciation out of its earnings, and that the utility is not entitled to any special dispensation because it failed to cover depreciation with its charges for service. It is probably fair to assume that the court had in mind cases where the utility had sufficient freedom to permit it to attempt to cover all of its expenses of operation, including depreciation, by its charges for service. Certainly an equitable adjustment of some sort would be in order if the utility had been prohibited from including periodic depreciation as an operating cost by a local commission.

It is not only the right of the company to make such a provision, but it is its duty to its bond and stockholders, and, in the case of a public service corporation, at least, its plain duty to the public. If a different course were pursued the only method of providing for replacement of property which has ceased to be useful would be the investment of new capital and the issue of new bonds or stocks. This course would lead to a constantly increasing variance between present value and bond and stock capitalization —a tendency which would inevitably lead to disaster either to the stockholders or to the public, or both. If, however, a company fails to perform this plain duty and to exact sufficient returns to keep the investment unimpaired, whether this is the result of unwarranted dividends upon over issue of securities, or of omission to exact proper prices for the output, the fault is its own. When, therefore, a public regulation of its prices comes under question, the true value of the property then employed for the purpose of earning a return cannot be enhanced by a consideration of the errors in management which have been committed in the past.

The purpose of making a periodic allowance for depreciation is also described, but the language used leaves one in considerable doubt as to the opinion of the court. It is said in the same breath that depreciation provides for the replacement of worn-out assets and also keeps the original investment intact, two quite different things in periods of changing price levels. At the time this case was under consideration, the great discrepancies between reproduction cost and original investment which characterize later periods were not present and the court probably considered the two values as practically synonymous. The case contributes little, then, to the solution of this problem.

> The company is not bound to see its property gradually waste, without making provision out of earnings for its replacement. It is entitled to see that from earnings the value of the property invested is kept unimpaired, so that, at the end of any given number of years, the original investment remains as it was at the beginning.

The discussion in this case is by no means a complete presentation of the depreciation problems which face regulatory bodies, but it did make an important contribution toward the evolution of commission and court practices and policies. It forced the consideration of depreciation in all subsequent investigations both as a periodic charge to operations and as a deductible item in arriving at the rate base.

Willcox v. Consolidated Gas Co.[9] This decision was handed down by the court on the same day as *Knoxville v. Knoxville Water Company* but it contains little or no direct reference to depreciation. It is frequently cited, however, in support of the depreciated rate base doctrine.

> There must be a fair return upon the reasonable value of the property at the time it is being used for the public. . . .
> In order to determine the rate of return upon the reasonable value of the property at the time it is being used for the public it, of course, becomes necessary to ascertain what that value is. . . .
> The value of real estate and plant is, to a considerable extent, matter of opinion; and the same may be said of personal estate when not based upon the actual cost of material and construction. Deterioration of the value of the plant, mains, and pipes is also, to some extent, based upon opinion. . . .

Railroad Commission v. Cumberland Telephone & Telegraph Co.[10] The discussion of depreciation in this case is difficult to interpret. It centers around the proposition that a utility is not entitled to a return both on its original investment and on funds retained as a result of the depreciation accounting. This could be used to support the policy of segregating funds equal to the depreciation charged off which would not be included in an undepreciated rate base; or it would help to justify the deduction of an accumulated depreciation reserve from the total property values, regardless of the source of the funds used to acquire the property, which would accomplish the same net result. It is not made clear just how depreciation could be charged and set up on the books and result in an increase in the capital investment on which dividends might be paid.

Depreciation is evidently considered as a provision for future replacement costs, and the propriety of a reserve for depreciation, i.e., charging more to operations than is spent during a period for replacements, is recognized.

---

9 212 U.S. 19 (1909). Appeals from the Circuit Court of the United States for the Southern District of New York to review a decree enjoining the enforcement of legislative regulation of gas rates.

10 212 U.S. 414 (1909). Appeal from the Circuit Court of the United States for the Eastern District of Louisiana to review a decree enjoining the enforcement of telephone rates established by the state commission.

It was obligatory upon the complainant to show that no part of the money raised to pay for depreciation was added to capital, upon which a return was to be made to stockholders in the way of dividends for the future. . . . It certainly was not proper for the complainant to take the money, or any portion of it, which it received as a result of the rates under which it was operating, and so to use it, any part of it, as to permit the company to add to its capital account, upon which it was paying dividends to shareholders. If that were allowable, it would be collecting money to pay for depreciation of the property, and, having collected it, to use it in another way, upon which the complainant would obtain a return and distribute it to its stockholders. That it was right to raise more money to pay for depreciation than was actually disbursed for the particular year there can be no doubt, for a reserve is necessary in any business of this kind, and so it might accumulate; but to raise more than money enough for the purpose, and place the balance to the credit of capital upon which to pay dividends, cannot be proper treatment. . . . The evidence is insufficient to show clearly that which complainant is under obligation to show. . . .

The lower court put the burden on the commission of showing how the funds represented by the depreciation reserve were invested. The Supreme Court reversed the decision of the circuit court and remanded the case for a new trial on the ground that the evidence as to the treatment of depreciation funds was insufficient.

Lincoln Gas & Electric Light Co. v. Lincoln.[11] The Supreme Court sent this case back to the lower court for reference to a master, and, in stating its reasons for this treatment, it made a contribution to the interpretation of the nature of depreciation and its calculation. It pointed out that the amount to be allowed for depreciation must be based upon the past experience of the utility and its maintenance and replacement policies, as well as upon the inherent character and probable life of the asset. Depreciation was again considered as a deduction from gross rather than from net income which must be considered before arriving at the "fair return" on the value of the property.

There is some looseness of language which is characteristic of many court decisions when an effort is made to deal with a technical subject. The depreciation reserve is spoken of as a "replacement fund." The depreciation charge is said to "preserve the property from future depreciation."

In this, an in every other legislative rate case, there are presented three questions of prime importance: First, the present reasonable value of the company's plant engaged in the regulated business; what will be the probable effect of the reduced rate upon the future net income from the property engaged in serving the public; and, third, in ascertaining the probable net income under the reduced rates prescribed, what deduction, if any, should be made from the gross receipts as a fund to preserve the property from future depreciation. . . .

---

[11] 223 U.S. 349 (1912). An appeal from the Circuit Court of the United States for the District of Nebraska to review a decree dismissing the bill of a lighting company, which assails as confiscatory the rates for gas fixed by municipal ordinance.

The facts found are not full enough to at all justify this court in dealing with this problem of a replacement fund.

There should be a full report upon past depreciation, past expense for reconstruction or replacement, and past operating expenses, including current repairs. We should be advised as to the gross receipts for recent years, and just how these receipts have been expended. Then the amount to be set aside for future depreciation will depend upon the character and probable life of the property and the method adopted in the past to preserve the property. It can be readily seen that the amount to be annually set aside may be such as to forbid rate reductions because of the requirement of such a fund.

Cedar Rapids Gas Light Co. v. Cedar Rapids.[12] The Iowa Supreme Court allowed five cents per 1000 cubic feet of gas manufactured for depreciation, quoted from *Knoxville v. Knoxville Water Co., supra,* as to the general principles of depreciation allowances, and made the following comments of its own on the subject:[13]

> There can be no doubt as to the justice of some allowance for depreciation. A public service corporation is under no obligation to sacrifice its property for the public good. Nor is it bound to see its property gradually waste by wear and decay without making provision for its replacement. It is entitled to earn enough not only to meet the expenses of current repairs, but also to provide means for replacing the parts of the plant when these can no longer be used. . . .
>
> There is a wide divergence of opinion as to the amount that should be set aside for depreciation. . . .

There is no discussion of depreciation in the opinion rendered by the higher court except the comment: "We perhaps should have adopted a rule as to depreciation somewhat more favorable to the plaintiff. . . ."

It might be said that this case lends some support to the conception of the depreciation allowance as a provision for physical replacement of property when it wears out.

Simpson v. Shepard (The Minnesota Rate Cases).[14] The court quoted with approval a statement of the master which broadened the concept of the causes of depreciation so as to include inadequacy and obsolescence, as well as wear and tear.

> As the master said, "everything on and above the roadbed depreciates from wear and weather stress. The life of a tie is from eight to ten years only. Structures become antiquated, inadequate, and more or less dilapidated. Ballast requires renewal, tools and machines wear out, cars, locomo-

---

12 223 U.S. 655 (1912). In error to the Supreme Court of the State of Iowa to review a decree which, modifying a decree of the District Court of Linn County, in that state, dismissed a bill to restrain the enforcement of an ordinance fixing 90 cents per thousand cubic feet as a maximum charge for gas, without prejudice to a later suit after the ordinance should have been given a fair test.

13 *Cedar Rapids Gas Light Co. v. City of Cedar Rapids,* 144 Iowa 426; 120 N. W. 966.

14 230 U. S. 352 (1913). Appeals from the Circuit Court of the United States for the District of Minnesota to review decrees enjoining the enforcement of intrastate rates of interstate carriers as fixed by the state, and their adoption or maintenance by the carriers.

tives, and equipment, as time goes on, are worn out or discarded for newer types."

The court objected to the cancellation of appreciation against depreciation and insisted that when cost of reproduction new was used as evidence of the rate base, the existing depreciation should be shown and deducted. The term "existing depreciation" was not defined.

But it was found that this depreciation was more than offset by appreciation.... It was said that "a large part of the depreciation is taken care of by constant repairs, renewals, additions, and replacements, a sufficient sum being annually set aside and devoted to this purpose, so that this, with the application of roadbed and adaptation to the needs of the country and of the public served, together with working capital...fully offsets all depreciation and renders the physical properties of the road not less valuable than their cost of reproduction new." And in a further statement upon the point, the "knowledge derived from experience" and "readiness to serve" were mentioned as additional offsets.

We cannot approve this disposition of the matter of depreciation. It appears that the master allowed, in the cost of reproduction, the sum of $1,613,612 for adaptation and solidification of roadbed, this being included in the item of grading, and being the estimate of the engineer of the state commission of the proper amount to be allowed. It is also to be noted that the depreciation in question is not that which has been overcome by repairs and replacements, but is the actual existing depreciation in the plant as compared with the new one. It would seem to be inevitable that in many parts of the plant there should be such depreciation, as, for example, in old structures and equipment remaining on hand. And when an estimate of value is made on the basis of reproduction new, the extent of existing depreciation should be shown and deducted.... If there are items entering into the estimate of cost which should be credited with appreciation, this also should appear, so that instead of a broad comparison there should be specific findings showing the items which enter into the account of physical valuation on both sides.

The court also objected to the recognition of "knowledge derived from experience" as an offset to depreciation.

It must be remembered that we are concerned with a charge of confiscation of property by the denial of a fair return for its use; and to determine the truth of the charge there is sought to be ascertained the present value of the property. The realization of the benefits of property must always depend in a large degree on the ability and sagacity of those who employ it; but the appraisement is of an instrument of public service, as property, not of the skill of the users. And when particular physical items are estimated as worth so much new, if in fact they be depreciated, this amount should be found and allowed for.... If this is not done, the physical valuation is manifestly incomplete. And it must be regarded as incomplete in this case.

Kansas City Southern Railway Co. v. United States.[15] The court again

---

[15] 231 U. S. 423 (1913). Appeal from the United States Commerce Court to review a decree dismissing the petition in an action to enjoin the enforcement of certain regulations of the Interstate Commerce Commission relative to the uniform accounting and bookkeeping system prescribed for interstate railway carriers.

affirms the inevitability of depreciation and the necessity of accounting for it. It approves the regulations of the Interstate Commerce Commission in regard to the treatment of abandoned property—either a profit and loss charge or a deduction from an accumulated reserve for depreciation. Obsolescence is clearly recognized as a cause of depreciation.

> The contention of the appellant that property, originally acquired because necessary in the construction of the railroad, and afterwards abandoned only because rendered unnecessary by the improvement and development of the property, should remain in the property account as a part of the stockholders' investment, will be found, upon analysis, to rest upon the unwarrantable assumption that all capital expenditures result in permanent accretion to the property of the company. This in effect ignores depreciation—an inevitable fact which no system of accounts can properly ignore. A more complete depreciation than that which is represented by a part of the original plant that through destruction or obsolescence has actually perished as useful property, it would be difficult to imagine. . . .

Des Moines Gas Co. v. Des Moines.[16] The master used cost of reproduction less depreciation as the valuation base and the lower court objected to using this basis to the exclusion of other factors. The higher court affirmed the decision of the lower court but made no significant comments on the subject of depreciation.

Van Dyke v. Geary.[17] There is no discussion of depreciation in this case. The court merely refused to interfere with the action of the commission where an annual allowance for depreciation was allowed as a deduction in arriving at the net return.

> The Commission decided that the net return to the owner upon the value of the property employed should be at the rate of at least 10 per cent after allowing an annual depreciation charge of $3\frac{1}{2}$ per cent. Water rates prescribed on this basis obviously cannot be held confiscatory unless either the valuation placed upon the property used was grossly inadequate or the cost of operation greatly underestimated. These elements are largely matters of fact and opinion, as to which both the Commission and the district court, after careful examination, found against the appellants. The case is presented to us on contradictory affidavits dealing with the items of value which go to make up the water system. We cannot say "that it was impossible for a fair-minded board to come to the result which was reached."

Denver v. Denver Union Water Co.[18] Depreciation, as such, was not a

---

16 238 U.S. 153 (1915). P.U.R. 1915D, 577. Appeal from the District Court of the United States for the Southern District of Iowa to review a decree dismissing a bill which seeks to enjoin the enforcement of a municipal ordinance fixing gas rates as confiscatory.

17 244 U. S. 39 (1917); P.U.R. 1917F, 852 (annotation). Appeal from the District Court of the United States for the District of Arizona to review an order which while enjoining the enforcement of the fines and penalties prescribed by a state statute for failure to obey an order of the Corporation Commission regulating water rates, refused to interfere with the enforcement of such order.

18 246 U.S. 178 (1918); P.U.R. 1918C, 640. Cross appeals from the District Court of the United States for the District of Colorado to review a decree made in a suit of equity brought by a water company to restrain enforcement of a rate ordinance.

major point of contention in this case, since the city spent most of its time in an attempt to justify junk value as a rate base on the ground that it could force abandonment of the service at any time. The court, however, made a few observations which conform to previously expressed opinions as to the nature and causes of depreciation as an operating cost, and which lend support to the use of depreciated reproduction cost as a valuation rate base.

> The cost of the service includes the use of the plant, but, ordinarily, not its destruction, except through the slow processes of wear and tear and obsolescence, for which graduated depreciation allowances are made. . . .
>
> What we have said establishes the propriety of estimating complainant's property on the basis of present market values as to land, and reproduction cost, less depreciation, as to structures.

Galveston Electric Co. v. Galveston.[19] The court reaffirmed the doctrine established in *Knoxville v. Knoxville Water Co., supra,* that it is the duty of the utility to provide for depreciation out of its earnings, and that it cannot expect adjustments in future rates to compensate for its failure to make adequate depreciation charges.

> A company which has failed to secure from year to year sufficient earnings to keep the investment unimpaired and to pay a fair return, whether its failure was the result of imprudence in engaging in the enterprise, or of errors in management, or of omission to exact proper prices for its output, cannot erect out of past deficits a legal basis for holding confiscatory for the future rates which would, on the basis of present reproduction value, otherwise be compensatory.

The court approved the allowances made by the lower court for maintenance and depreciation, as well as the deduction of depreciation from cost of reproduction in setting the rate base. An attempt was made to get at a new "plateau" of prices, rather than using "spot" prices in the valuation.

The depreciation reserve was described as "a fund out of which annual replacements and renewals could be made."

Georgia Railway & Power Co. v. Railroad Commission.[20] Depreciation is not an important issue in this case. The use of depreciated reproduction cost in setting the rate base valuation is again approved, but not to the exclusion of other factors.

> The refusal of the commission and of the lower court to hold that, for rate-making purposes, the physical properties of a utility must be valued at the replacement cost, less depreciation, was clearly correct.

The observation is also made that the rate of depreciation is a question of fact and therefore comes under the immediate jurisdiction of the commissions.

---

[19] 258 U. S. 388 (1922) ; P.U.R. 1922D, 159. Appeal from a decree of the District Court for the Southern District of Texas dismissing a bill to enjoin the enforcement of a street railway ordinance alleged to be confiscatory.

[20] 262 U. S. 625 (1923) ; P.U.R. 1923D, 1. Appeal from the District Court for the Northern District of Georgia, denying an injunction to restrain the enforcement of a rate order.

The companies say the rate should be 2½ per cent. The commission and the court allowed only 2 per cent. This question is one of fact, and we are not convinced that it was wrongly decided below.

The case is especially interesting in that the majority opinion is written by Justice Brandeis who had filed a vigorous dissenting opinion in the Southwestern Bell Telephone Company case, 262 U.S. 276, which involved similar issues. In that dissenting opinion he objected to the doctrine that present prices should be given great weight in ascertaining reproduction cost and presented a forceful defense of prudent investment as the most appropriate rate base. Now, in the Georgia Railway case, he is able to agree with the majority opinion since the commission gave consideration to factors other than reproduction cost in arriving at its valuation. Incidentally, Justice McKenna filed a dissenting opinion in this case in which he insisted that the rate base must be the value at the time of the investigation, and that this decision was inconsistent with that of the Southwestern Bell Telephone Company case.

Bluefield Water Works & Improvement Co. v. West Virginia Public Service Commission.[21] This case also approves the use of depreciated reproduction cost at present prices as one of the significant factors in rate base valuation. The court accepted without comment the 2% annual depreciation allowed by the commission.

> The record clearly shows that the commission...did not accord proper, if any, weight to the greatly enhanced costs of construction in 1920 over those prevailing about 1915 and before the war.... This was erroneous.

Pacific Gas & Electric Co. v. San Francisco.[22] This case has frequently been cited in support of the preferential use of appraisal data derived from examination of the physical property in arriving at the accrued deductible depreciation, instead of using an age-life calculation alone. The master in the case had applied a "modified sinking fund method" in order to calculate the accrued depreciation.

> Appellant objects to the application of this method, and insists that depreciation should have been ascertained upon full consideration of the definite testimony given by competent experts who examined the structural units, spoke concerning observed conditions, and made estimates therefrom. As these examinations were made subsequent to the allegd depreciation, for the definite purpose of ascertaining existing facts, we think the criticism is not without merit. Facts shown by reliable evidence were preferable to averages based upon assumed probabilities. When a plant has been conducted with unusual skill the owner may justly claim the consequent benefits. The problem was to ascertain the probable result of the

---

21 262 U.S. 679 (1923); P.U.R. 1923D, 11. Writ of error to review a judgment of the Supreme Court of Appeals of West Virginia sustaining a commission order fixing water rates.

22 265 U. S. 403 (1924); P.U.R. 1924D, 817. Appeal from a decree of the District Court for the Northern District of California dismissing bills filed to enjoin the enforcement of an alleged confiscatory gas rate.

specified rate if applied under well-known past conditions; not to forecast the probable outcome of a proposed rate under unknown future conditions.

There is nothing in the opinion which would seem to preclude the common practices of using inspection to check the assumptions of the age-life methods, and of using "assumed probabilities" when inspection is impossible or impracticable.

The main point at issue in the case was the inclusion of an allowance for obsolescence in the deductible accrued depreciation. The company maintained that the deduction should be limited to depreciation arising from physical causes, and that no deduction should have been made for accrued depreciation which represented a loss of value in property to be abandoned in the near future. The court agreed that more specific information should be available as to the amount and treatment of loss from obsolescence and reversed the lower court, remanding the case to it for further consideration. The majority opinion implies a willingness to consider further whether the obsolescence was sufficiently predictable to have been included legitimately in the estimated accrued depreciation.

> Counsel do not insist that the estimated accrued depreciation is "grossly excessive," if confined to the result of physical causes. But they do maintain that the master should have ascertained and stated what depreciation was due to such causes, and how much followed obsolescence resulting from the introduction of certain patented inventions; and we think such a finding should have been made unless some undisclosed reason prevented. The claim is that, in order to lower cost of production, it became necessary to abandon certain valuable property under conditions not reasonably susceptible of anticipation. The material and relevant facts ought to be disclosed.

There is a reasonable inference in the discussion that if the obsolescence had been predictable it should have been covered in the accounting for depreciation, and a deduction to cover that element in the loss of value would have been appropriate.

A dissenting opinion was filed by Justices Brandeis and Holmes. They felt that the obsolescence was sufficiently predictable to have been included in the accrued depreciation.

> The company's objection is not to the particular method selected, but that, in applying it, the master included as depreciation what is called theoretical inadequacy and obsolescence. Whether he did is a question of fact. The city denies that the reduction in value, made by the master on account of accrued depreciation, includes any sum representing expected loss through future abandonment of the stations. It is clear that, if any deduction was made on account of probable abandonment of the stations, the obsolescence thus provided for was not theoretical. The new process had been introduced two years before the date as of which the valuation was made. On the facts then known, it was expected that the stations would have to be abandoned in the near future. Because it was to be expected (and was not theoretical), the company contended that, to offset it, more of the year's savings should have been charged against the income

of that year. I cannot say that the master and the court erred in their findings of fact as to the amount of accrued depreciation.

The dissenting opinion also reaffirmed the doctrine of *Knoxville v. Knoxville Water Co., supra,* that it is the duty of a utility to provide adequately for depreciation, and presented an interesting philosophy of depreciation accounting as analogous to mutual insurance when associated with the use of prudent investment as the rate base.

> It was settled by *Knoxville v. Knoxville Water Co....*that every public utility must at its peril, provide an adequate amount to cover depreciation. A depreciation charge resembles a life insurance premium. The depreciation reserve, to which it is credited, supplies insurance for the plant against its inevitable decadence, as the life insurance reserve supplies the fund to meet the agreed value of the lost human life. To determine what the amount of the annual life insurance premium should be is a much simpler task than to determine the proper depreciation charge....
>
> Legal science can solve the problem of the just depreciation charge for public utilities in a similar manner [to that of mutual insurance]. Under the rule which fixes the rate base at the amount prudently invested, the inevitable errors incident to fixing the year's depreciation charge do not result in injustice either to the utility or to the community. If, when plant must be replaced, the amount set aside for depreciation proves to have been inadequate, and investment of new capital is required, the utility is permitted to earn the annual cost of the new capital. If, on the other hand, the amount set aside for depreciation proves to have been excessive, the income from the surplus reserve operates as a credit to reduce the current capital charge which the rates must earn. If a new device is adopted which involves additional investment (to buy a new plant or a patent right), the company's investment, on which the return must be paid, is increased by that amount. If the new device does not involve new investment, but the innovation involves increased current payments (like royalties for use of a process), the additional disbursement is borne by the community as an operating expense. The cost of a scrapped plant is carried as part of the investment on which a return must be paid unless and until it has been retired—that is, fully paid for, out of the depreciation reserve. Thus, justice both to the owners of the utility and to the public is assured.

Such a realistic conception of the difficulties of accounting for depreciation, and such a sense of fairness and equity in handling the positions of the utility and the consumer, unfortunately are seldom found in the literature of public utility regulation.

Public Utility Commissioners v. New York Telephone Co.[23] The depreciation accounting methods used by the utility in this case were described with some detail by the court.

> The company's accounts are kept according to the uniform system of accounts for telephone companies prescribed by the Interstate Commerce Commission. Charges are made to cover the depreciation in the elements of the plant which for one cause or another will go out of use. These

---

23 271 U. S. 23 (1926) ; P.U.R. 1926C, 740. Appeal from a decree of the District Court for the District of New Jersey granting a temporary injunction against a Commission from enforcing telephone rates.

charges are made month by month against depreciation in the operating expense accounts, and corresponding credits are entered in the depreciation reserve account. When a unit or element of the property is retired, there is no charge to operating expense, but its original cost less salvage is charged to the reserve account. December 31, 1923, the company's books showed a credit balance in depreciation reserve accounts of $16,902,530. This was not set aside or kept in a separate fund, but was invested in the company's telephone plant. . . .

The point at issue in connection with depreciation was that the Board of Public Utility Commissioners, conceiving the balance in the depreciation reserve as excessive, refused to allow rates which would permit the utility to cover its operating expenses, including an adequate depreciation allowance, and to earn a fair return, and they directed that $4,750,000 of the depreciation reserve should be used to absorb the deficits in any future year when the earnings were less than a reasonable return. The court definitely refused to sustain such an arrangement, although its reasoning is none too lucid. It apparently relied upon the conception of the depreciation reserve as a fund over which the consumer has no control and in which he has no equitable interest. Incidentally, this decision makes ineffective a good many opinions and decisions of state commissions, for the conception of the depreciation reserve as a fund contributed by the consumers in which they have an equitable interest has frequently been used by the commissioners.

It may be assumed, as found by the Board, that in prior years the company charged excessive amounts to depreciation expense and so created in the reserve account balances greater than required adequately to maintain the property. It remains to be considered whether the company may be compelled to apply any part of the property or money represented by such balances to overcome deficits in present or future earnings and to sustain rates which otherwise could not be sustained.

The just compensation safeguarded to the utility by the Fourteenth Amendment is a reasonable return on the value of the property used at the time that it is being used for the public service, and rates not sufficient to yield that return are confiscatory. . . . Constitutional protection against confiscation does not depend on the source of the money used to purchase the property. It is enough that it is used to render the service. . . . The customers are entitled to demand service and the company must comply. The company is entitled to just compensation and, to have the service, the customers must pay for it. The relation between the company and its customers is not that of partners, agent and principal, or trustee and beneficiary. . . . The revenue paid by the customers for service belongs to the company. The amount, if any, remaining after paying taxes and operating expenses including the expense of depreciation is the company's compensation for the use of its property. If there is no return, or if the amount is less than a reasonable return, the company must bear the loss. Past losses cannot be used to enhance the value of the property or to support a claim that rates for the future are confiscatory. . . . And the law does not require the company to give up for the benefit of future subscribers any part of its accumulations from past operations. Profits from the past cannot be used to sustain confiscatory rates for the future. . . .

Customers pay for service, not for the property used to render it. Their payments are not contributions to depreciation or other operating expenses or to capital of the company. By paying bills for service they do not acquire any interest, legal or equitable, in the property used for their convenience or in the funds of the company. Property paid out of moneys received for service belongs to the company just as does that purchased out of proceeds of its bonds and stock. It is conceded that the exchange rates complained of are not sufficient to yield a just return after paying taxes and operating expenses, including a proper allowance for current depreciation. The property or money of the company represented by the credit balance in the reserve for depreciation cannot be used to make up the deficiency.

There can be no quarrel with the court's theory of legal and equitable ownership of the assets of the utility, but this decision does make it difficult to carry out a practically feasible policy of utility rate regulation. While there is nothing in the decision which would prevent the establishment of correct depreciation rates for the future as indicated by the results of past operations, it does make it difficult to work out equitable adjustment of rates of depreciation and rates of return which are admittedly based upon inexact data and estimates. To consider the results of the past as a closed book puts a premium upon the adoption of extreme points of view and unreasonable claims by both the utilities and the commissions, since the opportunity of making adjustments in the future for inevitable errors in estimates is apparently removed. It does not promote that spirit of coöperation between the utilities and the commissions which is essential to successful regulation.

If this utility did charge excessive depreciation in the past, a portion of the depreciation reserve should be transferred to the surplus account where it could well serve to absorb future deficits. The decision of the commission may have been unreasonable, but the principle it appeared to have used was fair and equitable. Justice Brandeis missed an opportunity to add to his list of significant dissenting opinions, for his consideration of depreciation in the dissenting opinion in *Pacific Gas & Electric Co. v. San Francisco, supra,* would have been especially applicable to this case.

It is difficult to reconcile this decision with that of *Railroad Commission v. Cumberland Telephone & Telegraph Co., supra,* where definite objections were made to capitalizing excessive depreciation allowances.

McCardle v. Indianapolis Water Co.[24] This case is best known for its treatment of the more general aspects of utility valuation but there is one significant comment in connection with the calculation of deductible depreciation. The court, following a similar opinion in *Pacific Gas & Electric Co. v. San Francisco, supra,* gives emphatic support to the proposition that the "testimony of competent valuation engineers who examined the property and made estimates in respect of its condition is to be preferred to mere calculations based on averages and assumed probabilities."

---

24 272 U. S. 400 (1927); P.U.R. 1927A, 15. Appeal from a decree of the district court for the District of Indiana enjoying the enforcement of a rate order by the Public Service Commission.

The Commission...deducted approximately 25 per cent of estimated cost new to cover accrued depreciation. The deduction was not based on an inspection of the property. It was the result of a "straight line" calculation based on age and the estimated or assumed useful life of perishable elements. The Commission's report indicates that the property is well-planned, well-maintained, and efficient. Its chief engineer inspected it, and estimated its condition by giving effect to results of the examination and to the age of the property. He deducted about 6 per cent to cover depreciation. Mr. Hagenah made an estimate of existing depreciation based on actual inspection and a consideration of the probable future life as indicated by the conditions found. He deducted less than 6 per cent. Mr. Elmes testified that he made an inspection and estimate of all the actual depreciation. He estimated $443,044 would be required to restore the property as of appraisal date to its condition when first installed and put in practical operation. He deducted that amount. The testimony of competent valuation engineers who examined the property and made estimates in respect of its condition is to be preferred to mere calculations based on averages and assumed probabilities. The deduction made in the city's estimate cannot be approved.

It is not surprising, in view of the evidence presented, that the court followed the opinions of the appraisal engineers, but the decision has several questionable aspects. It would be reasonable to question the desirability of a court entering into the details of a valuation to this extent, for the Commission should be in a better position to work out a consistent and equitable policy for the calculation of deductible depreciation. The typical appraisal report is apt to base its valuations upon the present physical condition and service efficiency of the property, and to give inadequate attention to the length of time during which it can be expected to render the service. Property about ready to be retired is often assigned a value of around 40% of its cost. This policy completely divorces the computation of deductible depreciation from the accumulated reserve for depreciation which, in fairness to both the utility and the consumer, should be taken as the presumptive basis of the deduction. Otherwise the utility may receive a return on property values which do not represent a part of its own investment, or may have values confiscated, the former being more likely since appraisal values are generally considerably in excess of age-life depreciated values.

The result of this decision is to force the commissions to prepare better evidence of inspection of the property which will justify the deductions which they make for accrued depreciation. It becomes difficult to prevent the utility from collecting in its rates an amount to cover expired property values and thereafter earning a return on part of this amounts as well as upon its own investment.

United Railways and Electric Co. v. West.[25] This case is characterized

---

[25] 280 U. S. 234 (1930); P.U.R. 1930A, 225. Appeal by a street railway company from a decree of the Court of Appeals of Maryland sustaining in part a rate order of the Maryland Commission and a cross-appeal by the Maryland Commission from the same decree.

by a short but significant comment on depreciation by the majority of the court and by a set of dissenting opinions which probably constitute the most extensive discussion of depreciation to be found in any court decision. Justice Brandeis contributed the greater portion of the dissenting opinions but he was supported by Justices Holmes and Stone.

The majority opinion supports the proposition that the calculation of the periodic charge for depreciation should be based upon present value or reproduction cost rather than upon original cost. The reason given for this procedure is that it is the duty of the utility to replace property when it is worn out and that unless depreciation is based upon reproduction cost, it will not retain sufficient assets to finance the cost of the replacement.

> The allowance for annual depreciation made by the Commission was based upon cost. The court of appeals held that this was erroneous and that it should have been based upon the present value. The court's view of the matter was plainly right. One of the items of expense to be ascertained and deducted is the amount necessary to restore property worn out or impaired, so as continuously to maintain it as nearly as practicable at the same level of efficiency for the public service. The amount set aside periodically for this purpose is the so-called depreciation allowance. Manifestly, this allowance cannot be limited by the original cost, because, if values have advanced, the allowance is not sufficient to maintain the level of efficiency. The utility "is entitled to see that from earnings the value of the property invested is kept unimpaired, so that at the end of any given term of years the original investment remains as it was at the beginning." *Knoxville v. Knoxville Water Co.*.... This naturally calls for expenditures equal to the cost of the worn out equipment at the time of replacement; and this, for all practical purposes, means present value. It is the settled rule of this court that the rate base is present value, and it would be wholly illogical to adopt a different rule for depreciation.

This method of calculating the depreciation allowance is not only at variance with the methods generally followed in business and accounting practice, and opposed to the opinions and practices of most regulatory commissions, but it cannot, except as the result of a rare coincidence of events, bring about the expected results. Assuming for the moment that it is the purpose of depreciation accounting to finance replacements, and that assets will be retained equal to the depreciation reserve, the mere calculation of depreciation on reproduction costs will not accumulate the right amount of funds in either a period of rising of falling prices. During a period of rising prices, while each successive addition to the reserve will be larger, the total accumulation will necessarily be less than the final cost of replacement unless surplus adjustments are made to build the reserve up to the required amount, or unless charges are made to operations at an accelerating rate. During a period of falling prices more than enough will be accumulated to replace the property in spite of the fact that smaller and smaller amounts are charged to operations unless corresponding surplus adjustments are made or the operation charge reduced below the normal rate.

It may be questioned whether it is reasonable to maintain that the replacement cost of an asset should be covered by charges to operations before or at the time of replacement, when that amount is considerably more or less than the original cost. The conventional business practice is to consider additional costs as an increase in fixed capital requirements which, in the case of a public utility operating under a theory of limited return on the investment, would require an additional investment of capital in the form of capital stock or bonds. If costs have fallen, funds become available for such purposes as additions to the property or a retirement of bonded indebtedness. It would certainly be unreasonable to require consumers to pay rates which would permit the utility to recover more than the depreciation calculated at the normal rate on the then cost of reproduction, but, as was pointed out above, more must be recovered if the full cost of reproduction is to be met in a period of rising prices. The quotation from *Knoxville v. Knoxville Water Company* which speaks of keeping the investment unimpaired rather than keeping the physical property intact is hardly a convincing legal basis for the opinion of the court.

It would be possible to work out a plausible and reasonable argument in favor of basing depreciation on reproduction costs. It could be reasonably maintained, for instance, that present prices for service should be based upon present costs, and that the full benefit of the present value theory of valuation is not received, either by the utility during higher prices or by the consumer during lower prices, unless depreciation is calculated on the same basis. It could be pointed out that when rates have to be set for groups of utilities, the utility with a large investment in new equipment is, in a period of rising prices, at a considerable disadvantage unless its higher costs for depreciation are covered by the rates charged for its services, while in a period of falling prices it would receive an unreasonable advantage if rates were based upon costs which included depreciation on the old basis. The utility with a large investment in old property would receive some contribution toward the excess of replacement over original cost in times of rising prices, and would receive more than enough to replace the physical capital in times of falling prices. These comments do not constitute a complete discussion of the problem but they do indicate some of the factors which should be taken into consideration. The reasons given by the court for its stand are illogical and unreasonable.

From the standpoint of practical accounting the use of present cost as a basis for the periodic depreciation calculation is almost an impossibility, since prices are continually fluctuating. A rough adjustment, such as the use of index numbers of price changes, would not be feasible, for prices of different parts of the physical plant do not change uniformly. Only when depreciation is handled on the crudest of bases, with little or no detailed plant accounting, would such a scheme be practically expedient. There is some evidence that the writer of the decision did not consider depreciation as an operating expense, which may account for the general trend of the comments, for he speaks of "all expenses of operation," and, as a separate item to be covered by the earnings of the utility, "setting aside the necessary sums for depreciation."

One can sympathize, therefore, with the dissenting opinions although they are not wholly free from ambiguities and evidences of an inadequate knowledge of the accounting and financial principles involved in the treatment of depreciation. Justice Brandeis gives an excellent analysis of the nature and purpose of depreciation accounting, emphasizing the point that it is primarily a matter of reasonable and equitable distribution of costs over the operating periods in the life of an asset.

> The annual account of a street railway, or other business, is designed to show the profit or loss, and to acquaint those interested with the condition of the business. To be true, the account must reflect all the operating expenses incurred within the accounting period. One of these is the wearing out of plant. . . . Minor parts, which have short lives and are consumed wholly within the year, are replaced as a part of current repairs. Larger plant units, unlike supplies, do not wear out within a single accounting period. They have varying service lives, some remaining useful for many years. Experience teaches that at the end of some period of time most of these units, too, will wear out physically or cease to be useful in the service. If the initial outlay for such units is entirely disregarded, the annual account will not reflect the true results of operation and the initial investment may be lost. If, on the other hand, this original expense is treated as part of the operating expenses of the year in which the plant unit was purchased, or was retired or replaced, the account again will not reflect the true results of operation. For operations in one year will then be burdened with an expense which is properly chargeable against a much longer period of use. Therefore, in ascertaining the profits of a year, it is generally deemed necessary to apportion to the operations of that year a part of the total expense incident to the wearing out of plant. This apportionment is commonly made by means of a depreciation charge. . . .
>
> The depreciation charge is an allowance made pursuant to a plan of distribution of the total net expense of plant retirement. It is a bookkeeping device introduced in the exercise of practical judgment to serve three purposes. It preserves the integrity of the investment. . . . It serves to distribute equitably throughout the several years of service life the only expense of plant retirement which is capable of reasonable ascertainment—the known cost less the estimated salvage value. And it enables those interested, through applying that plan of distribution, to ascertain, as nearly as is possible, the actual financial results of the year's operation. . . .

The only criticism which could be made of this unusually clear conception of the purpose of depreciation accounting is that it fails to point out that the preservation of the integrity of the investment depends upon the depreciation charge having been "earned," that is, having been covered, together with all the other expenses of operation, by the gross earnings of the utility.

The definition which is given of the depreciation reserve is not adequate for a clear understanding of the significance and use of that account, but at least a careful distinction is made between the reserve and a possible replace-

ment or depreciation fund. Much of the confusion which exists in the literature of depreciation is due to the failure clearly to differentiate between these
two accounts and their functions.

> A depreciation reserve is a bookkeeping classification to which the deprecia-
> tion charges are periodically credited. A depreciation fund is a fund sepa-
> rately maintained in which amounts charged for depreciation are periodically
> deposited. A depreciation reserve does not necessarily connote the existence
> of a separate fund.

It would add to the clarity of this statement if it were pointed out that the
so-called "reserve" for depreciation is merely an offset to the asset account,
or an accumulation of past depreciation less the net cost of retired assets,
and that the general effect of crediting a reserve is the same as crediting the
asset account directly.

Justice Brandeis bases his objections to the majority opinion primarily
upon the contention that the depreciation charge does not and cannot
measure the actual consumption of plant, and that its function must be
expressed in terms of the entire life of the property, each period's charge
merely being an attempt to spread equitably "the only expense of plant
retirement which is capable of reasonable ascertainment—the known cost
less the estimated salvage value."

> It is urged by the Railways that if the base used in determining what is
> a fair return on the use of its property is the present value, then logically
> the base to be used in determining the depreciation charge—a charge for
> the consumption of plant in service—must also be the present value of the
> property consumed. ...But acceptance of the doctrine of *Smyth v. Ames*...
> does not require that the depreciation charge be based on present value of
> plant. For, an annual depreciation is not a measure of the actual consump-
> tion of plant during the year. No such measure has yet been invented.
> There is no regularity in the development of depreciation. It does not
> proceed in accordance with any mathematical law. There is nothing in
> business experience, or in the training of experts, which enables man to
> say to what extent service life will be impaired by the operation of a single
> year, or of a series of years less than the service life. ...
> Where a plant intended, like a street railway, for continuing operation is
> maintained at a constant level of efficiency it is rarely possible to deter-
> mine definitely whether or not its service life has in fact lessened within
> a particular year. The life expectancy of a plant, like that of an individual,
> may be in fact greater, because of unusual repairs or other causes, at the
> end of a particular year than it was at the beginning. And even where it is
> known that there has been some lessening of service life within the year,
> it is never possible to determine with accuracy what percentage of the unit's
> service life has, in fact, been so consumed. Nor is it essential to the aim of
> the charge that this fact should be known. The main purpose of the charge
> is that irrespective of the rate of depreciation there shall be produced,
> through annual contributions, by the end of the service life of the depreciable
> plant, an amount equal to the total net expenses of its retirement. To that
> end it is necessary only that some reasonable plan of distribution be adopted.
> Since it is impossible to ascertain what percentage of the service life is

consumed in any year, it is either assumed that depreciation proceeds at some average rate (thus accepting the approximation to fact customarily obtained through the process of averaging) or the annual charge is fixed without any regard to the rate of depreciation. ...Many methods of calculating the amount of the allowance are used. The charges to operating expenses in the several years and in the aggregate vary according to the method adopted. But under none of these methods of fixing the depreciation charge is an attempt made to determine the percentage of actual consumption of plant falling within a particular year or within any period of years less than the service life.

The point that the depreciation allowance is not and cannot be a measure of plant consumption is somewhat overstated. It is of course true that no precise measurement can be made, but if the results of operations as shown by the accounting records are to be considered as useful approximations of costs and expenses, then the depreciation charge must be considered a reasonable estimate of the operating cost arising from the expired service life of each asset of the utility. The resulting error in connection with any one item of property may be large, but if the available information is carefully accumulated and studied, the average error can be made reasonably small.

The dissenting opinion contains a brief history of business and legal practice in regard to depreciation and presents, with many citations and references, the opinions of business men and accountants, in support of the use of original cost as the basis of the depreciation calculation.

> The business device known as the depreciation charge appears not to have been widely adopted in America until after the beginning of this century.... Its use is still stoutly resisted by many concerns.... Wherever adopted, the depreciation charge is based on the original cost of the plant to the owner. When the great changes in price levels incident to the World War led some to question the wisdom of the practice of basing the charge on original cost, the Chamber of Commerce of the United States warned business men against the fallacy of departing from the accepted basis.... And that warning has been recently repeated. ...
>
> Such is today, and ever has been, the practice of public accountants. ... Their statements are prepared in accordance with principles of accounting which are well established, generally accepted and uniformly applied. By those accustomed to read the language of accounting, a depreciation charge is understood as meaning the appropriate contribution for that year to the amount required to make good the cost of the plant which ultimately must be retired. On that basis, public accountants certify to investors and bankers the results of operation, whether of public utilities, or manufacturing or mercantile concerns. Corporate securities are issued, bought, and sold, and vast loans are made daily, in reliance upon statements so prepared. The compelling logic of facts which led business men to introduce a depreciation charge has led them to continue to base it on the original cost of the plant despite the great changes in the price level incident to the World War. Basing the depreciation charge on cost is a rule prescribed or recommended by those associations of business men who have had occasion since the World War to consider the subject.
>
> Business men naturally took the plant at cost, as that is how they treat

other articles consumed in operation. The plant, undepreciated, is commonly carried on the books at cost; and it is retired at cost. The net profit or loss of a business transaction is commonly ascertained by deducting from the gross receipts the expenditures incurred in producing them. Business men realized fully that the requirements for replacement might be more or less than the original cost. But they realized also that to attempt to make the depreciation account reflect economic conditions and changes would entail entry upon a new field of conjecture and prophecy which would defeat its purposes. For there is no basis in experience which can justify predicting whether a replacement, renewal, or substitution falling in some future year will cost more or less than it would at present, or more or less than the unit cost when it was acquired.

The last paragraph seems to revert to the conception of the depreciation charge as a provision for financing replacements, since it emphasizes the point that because the business man dosen't know what his replacement cost will be, he uses original cost as the only reasonable substitute. This is somewhat inconsistent with the original characterization of depreciation as a matter of equitable expense distribution of the original outlay.

The preceding discussion also overstates the practice of business men. Appraisals frequently are made during periods of rapidly rising prices in order to justify writing up asset values so as to present a better financial picture, and to justify larger mortgage loans; and this inevitably must result in larger depreciation charges in order to amortize the additions to the plant accounts. It is true that a good deal of lip service is given to objections to this procedure, but it is not wholly without authoritative support. The experiences of the last few years, since the writing of this decision, also indicate that the practice is not as uniform as the opinion indicates. Numerous instances can be found in which plant accounts were written down with the direct purpose of reducing depreciation charges and thereby getting costs on a more realistic basis. It is to be noted that in neither case has the business man been concerned about financing his replacements. He is more interested in adjusting his costs of operations and his financial picture to changed conditions.

Evidence is also presented in the dissenting opinion of the practices of the Interstate Commerce Commission, the state public utility commissions, and other governmental agencies which support the use of the original cost basis.

> The business men's practice of using a depreciation charge based on the original cost of the plant in determining the profits or losses of a particular year has abundant official sanction and encouragement. The practice was prescribed by the Interstate Commerce Commission in 1907, when, in coöperation with the Association of American Railway Accounting Officers, it drafted the rule, which is still in force, requiring steam railroads to make an annual depreciation charge on equipment. It has been consistently applied by the Federal Government in assessing taxes on net income and corporate profits; and by the tax officials of the several states for determining the net profits or income of individuals and corporations. ...In 1923, it was adopted by the depreciation section of the Interstate Commerce Commission in the report of tentative conclusions concerning depreciation

charges submitted to the term railroads, telephone companies, and carriers by water. . . . A depreciation charge based on original cost has been uniformly applied by the Public Utility Commissions of the several states when determining net income, past or expected, for rate-making purposes. . . .

There is no doubt that the original cost basis greatly simplifies the problems of the regulatory commissions and that this is a highly significant argument in its favor, especially if care is taken to use it consistently so that equitable results will be obtained over periods of both falling and rising prices.

Justice Brandeis also felt that the majority opinion is in conflict with the decisions of the court in income tax cases and with the general trend of legal opinion.

In 1927 the business men's practice of basing the depreciation charge on cost was applied by this court in *United States v. Ludey* (1927) 274 U. S. 295, 300–301. . . . , a Federal income tax case, saying: "The amount of the allowance for depreciation is the sum which should be set aside for the taxable year, in order that, at the end of the useful life of the plant in the business, the aggregate of the sums set aside will (with the salvage value) suffice to provide an amount equal to the original cost." I know of nothing in the Federal Constitution, or in the decisions of this Court, which should lead us to reject, in determining net profits, the rule sanctioned by the universal practice of business men and governmental departments. For, whether the expense in plant consumption can be more nearly approximated by using a depreciation charge based on original cost or by one based upon fluctuating present values is a problem to be solved, not by legal reasoning, but by the exercise of practical judgment based on facts and business experience. The practice of using an annual depreciation charge based on original cost when determining for purposes of investment, taxation, or regulation, the net profits of a business, or the return upon property, was not adopted in ignorance of the rule of *Smyth v. Ames*. . . . That decision, rendered in 1898, antedates the general employment of public accountants; and also antedates the general introduction here of the practice of making a depreciation charge. The decision of the court of appeals of Maryland here under review, as well as State ex rel. *Hopkins v. Southwestern Bell Teleph. Co.*, 115 Kan. 236, P.U.R. 1924D, 388 . . . and *Michigan Pub. Utilities Commission v. Michigan State Telephone Co.* (1924) 228 Mich. 658, P.U.R. 1925C, 158 . . . were all decided after this court reaffirmed the rule of *Smyth v. Ames*. . . in Missouri ex rel. *Southwestern Bell Teleph. Co. v. Public Service Commission* (1923) 262 U. S. 276 . . . P.U.R. 1923C, 193 . . . But since this decision, as before, the Bell Telephone Companies have persisted in basing their depreciation charges upon the original cost of the depreciable property. . . . And they have insisted that the order of the Interstate Commerce Commission requiring a depreciation charge . . . should be so framed as to permit the continuance of that accounting practice. The protest of the railroads . . . against basing the charge on cost was made for the first time in 1927. . . . And this protest came only from those who insist that no depreciation charge whatsoever shall be made.

In a footnote he points out that the company involved in this case will have to use one figure of depreciation for its report to the public utility commission and another for its income tax report. This point of inconsistency is well taken, but to the layman, at least, it is not especially convincing, since the income tax law and regulations often seem to have evolved away from the accounting conceptions of income and expense and are using the amount of taxes which a given procedure will yield as the principal criterion of correct principle.

The practical difficulties of using present cost as the basis for the depreciation calculations are given a brief but pointed discussion.

> To use a depreciation charge as the measure of the year's consumption of plant, and at the same time reject original cost as the basis of the charge, is inadmissible. It is a perversion of this business device. No method for the ascertainment of the amount of the charge yet invented is workable if fluctuating present values be taken as the basis. Every known method contemplates, and is dependent upon, the accumulation or credit of a fixed amount in a given number of years. The distribution of plant expense expressed in the depreciation charge is justified by the approximation to the fact as to the year's plant consumption which is obtained by applying the doctrine of averages. But if fluctuating present values are substituted for original cost there is no stable base to which the process of averaging can be applied. For thereby the only stable factor involved in fixing a depreciation charge would be eliminated. Each year the present value may be different. The cost of replacement at the termination of the service life of the several units or of the composite life cannot be foretold. To use as a measure of the year's consumption of plant a depreciation charge based on fluctuating present values substitutes conjecture for experience. Such a system would require the consumer of today to pay for an assumed operating expense which has never been incurred and which may never arise.

The practical difficulties of using a fluctuating depreciation base are admittedly great, and, again, this is of especial significance in the matter of effective public utility regulation. The point, however, that the consumer may be asked to pay for an expense which may never occur because prices may change in the opposite direction by the time replacement becomes necessary, is not significant. There is no good theoretical reason why public utility rates should not be based upon present costs, or why a plant using old equipment should have to charge higher or lower rates than one using new equipment. But the practical difficulties are extremely great, and if the same base is used consistently there is no long-run inequity.

Justice Brandeis took the opportunity of restating his conception of an analogy between depreciation and mutual life insurance, and again defended his favorite rate-base—prudent investment. (See *Pacific Gas & Electric Co. v. San Francisco supra,* for a similar discussion.)

> The depreciation charge is frequently likened to the annual premium in legal reserve life insurance. The life insurance premium is calculated on an agreed value of the human life—comparable to the known cost of plant— not on a fluctuating value, unknown and unknowable. The field of life insurance presented a problem comparable to that here involved. Despite the large experience embodied in the standard mortality tables and the relative simplicity of the problem there presented, the actual mortality was found

to vary so widely from that their rate was found to work serious injustice either to the insurer or to the insured. The transaction resulted sometimes in his securing profits which were extortionate; and, rarely, in his receiving only the intended fair compensation for the service rendered. Because every attempt to approximate more nearly the amount of premium required proved futile, justice was sought and found in the system of strictly mutual insurance. Under that system the premium charged is made clearly ample; and the part which proves not to have been needed enures in some form of benefit to him who paid it.

Similarly, if, instead of applying the rule of *Smyth v. Ames...*, the rate base of a utility were fixed at the amount prudently invested, the inevitable errors incident to estimating service life and net expense in plant consumption could never result in injustice either to the utility or to the community. For, if the amount set aside for depreciation proved inadequate and investment of new capital became necessary, the utility would be permitted to earn a return on the new capital. And if the amount set aside for depreciation proved to be excessive, the income from the surplus reserve would operate as a credit to reduce the capital charge which the rates must earn. If the Railways should ever suffer injustice from adopting cost of plant as the basis for calculating the depreciation charge, it will be an unavoidable incident of applying in valuation the rule of *Smyth v. Ames*. This risk, if it exists, cannot be escaped by basing the charge on present value. For this suggested escape, besides being entirely conjectural, is instinct with certainty of injustice either to the community or the Railways. The possibility of such injustice admonishes us, as it did in deciding the constitutional questions concerning interstate commerce...that rate regulation is an intensely practical matter.

The adoption of Justice Brandeis' prudent investment and mutual insurance principles would do a great deal to make public utility regulation more effective. Unfortunately, the trend of court opinion seems to be precisely in the opposite direction—toward present costs and values, and the treatment of depreciation in valuation as a problem independent of the accounting for original costs.

The dissenting opinion also contains a summarization of the arguments frequently presented by the utilities in opposition to the depreciation charge and presents a footnote statement concerning the "Retirement Reserve" method advocated by the National Association of Railroad and Utilities Commissioners. Although Justice Brandeis makes plain his disapproval of these proposals, he points out that they are not at issue in this case.

> Public officials, investors and most large businesses are convinced of the practical value of the depreciation charge as a guide to knowledge of the results of operation. Many states require public utilities to make such a charge. But most railroads, some gas and electric companies, and some other concerns deny the propriety of making any annual depreciation charge. They insist that the making of such a charge will serve rather to mislead than to aid in determining the financial result of the year's operations. They urge that the current cost of maintaining the plant, whether by repair, renewals, or replacements, should be treated as a part of the maintenance account, at least in systems consisting of large and diversified properties intended for continuous operation and requiring a constant level of efficien-

cy. They insist that, in such systems, retirements, replacements, and renewals attain a uniform rate and tend to be equal each year; that, therefore, no great disproportion in revenues and operating expenses in the various years results if the whole expenditure made for renewals or replacements in any year is treated as an expense of operation of that year and the retirements of property are not otherwise reflected in any specific charge. They admit that it may be desirable to create a special reserve, to enable the company to spread the cost of retiring certain large units of property over a series of years, thus preventing a disproportionate burden upon the operations of a single year. But they say that such a reserve is not properly called a depreciation reserve. Moreover they contend that when a large unit is retired, not because it has been worn out but because some more efficient substitute has been found, the cost of retirement should be spread over the future, so that it may fall upon those who will gain the benefit of the enhanced efficiency. . . . Under the replacement method of accounting advocated by the railroads and others there is no depreciation charge and no depreciation reserve. Operating expenses are charged directly with replacements at their cost. This method does not concern itself with all retirements, but only with retirements which are replaced.

Despite the seemingly unanswerable logic of a depreciation charge, they oppose its adoption, urging the uncertainties inherent in the predetermination of service life and of salvage value, and the disagreement among experts as to the most equitable plan of distributing the total net plant expense among the several years of service. They point out that each step in the process of fixing a depreciation charge is beset with difficulties, because of the variables which attend every determination involved. The first step is to estimate how long the depreciable plant will remain in service. Engineers calculate with certitude its composite service life by applying weighted averages to the data concerning the several property units. But their exactitude is delusive. Each unit has its individual life dependent upon the effect of physical exhaustion, obsolescence, inadequacy, and public requirement. The physical duration of the life depends largely upon the conditions of the use; and these cannot be foretold. The process of obsolescence is even less predictable. Advances in the arts are constantly being made which would require retirement at some time, even if the unit were endowed with perpetual physical life. But these advances do not proceed at a uniform pace. The normal progress of invention is stimulated or retarded by the ever changing conditions of business. Moreover, it is the practical embodiment of inventions which produces obsolescence; and business conditions determine even more largely the time and the extent to which new inventions are embodied in improved machines. The march toward inadequacy, as distinguished from obsolescence, is likewise erratic.

The protestants point out that uncertainty is incident also to the second step in the process of fixing the appropriate depreciation charge. A plant unit rarely remains in service until consumed physically. Scrap remains; and this must be accounted for, since it is the net expense of the exhaustion of plant which the depreciation charge is to cover. Such scrap value is often a very large factor in the calculation of plant expense. The probable salvage on the unit when retired at the end of its service life must, therefore, be estimated. But its future value is never knowable.

And, finally, the protestants show that after the net expense in plant consumption is thus estimated, there remains the task of distributing it equitably over the assumed service life—the allocation of the amount as charges of the several years. There are many recognized methods for calculating these amounts, each method having strenuous advocates; and the amounts thus to be charged, in the aggregate as well as in the successive years, differ widely according to the method adopted. Under the straight line method, the aggregate of the charges of the several years equals the net plant expense for the whole period of service life; and the charge is the same for all the years. Under the sinking fund method, the aggregate of the charges of the several years is less than the net plant expense for the whole period; because the proceeds of each year's charge are deemed to have been continuously invested at compound interest and the balance is assumed to be obtained from interest accumulations. Other methods of distributing the total charge produce still other results in the amount of the charges laid upon the operating expenses of the several years of service.

The dissenting justices expressed the opinion that the above arguments need not be considered in this case, since, in their opinion, the allowance already provided by the company was adequate under any interpretation of the proper theory of the depreciation charge. The company had charged 5% of gross revenue for depreciation, and in nearly every year the allowance had exceeded the charges for retirements.

We have no occasion to decide now whether the view taken by the Interstate Commerce Commission...or the protest of the railroads, gas and electric companies should prevail, for in neither event was the court of appeals justified in directing an increase in the allowance. The adequacy of a depreciation charge is dependent in large measure upon the practice of the individual concern with respect to its maintenance account. The Commission found that the Railways' property was well maintained and that the allowance of $883,544, together with the usual maintenance charges, would be adequate to keep the property at a constant level of efficiency. It found further, on the basis of the company's experience, that the charges previously allowed had served "fairly well" to take care of current depreciation and retirements. ...

The estimated charge of $883,544 was thus clearly ample as the year's share of the expense of plant retirement based on cost. But even if the annual depreciation allowance could be made to correspond with the actual consumption of plant, there was nothing in the record to show that the value of the part of plant to be consumed in 1928 would exceed that amount. Nor is there anything in the record or in the findings to show that $883,544, together with the usual maintenance charges and under the improved methods of construction, would be inadequate to provide, at the prices then prevailing, for the replacements required in that year, and also for the year's contribution to a special reserve under the plan advocated by the railroads before the Interstate Commerce Commission. On the contrary, the company's history and the present advances in the street railway industry strongly indicate that, by employing new equipment of lesser value, the Railways could render more efficient service at smaller operating costs. Neither the trial court nor the court of appeals made any finding on these matters. The Commission's finding that $883,544 was an adequate depreciation charge should, therefore, have been accepted by the court of appeals, whether the sum allowed be deemed a depreciation charge properly so called, or be treated as the year's contribution to a special reserve to supplement the usual maintenance charges.

It is clear that the management of the Railways deemed the charge of 5% of gross revenues adequate. On that assumption it paid dividends on the common stock in each year from 1923 through 1927. If the addition to the depreciation charge ordered by the court of appeals was proper for the year 1928, it should have also been made in the preceding five years. Upon such a recasting of the accounts, no profits were earned after 1924; and there was no surplus fund from which dividends could have been paid legally. If the contention now urged by the Railways is sound, the management misrepresented by its published accounts its financial condition and the results of operation of the several years; and it paid dividends in violation of law.

There is also a significant comment in a footnote of the dissenting opinion in regard to the deduction of the amount of depreciation accumulated in the reserve in arriving at the rate base. While no opinion is expressed, it at least indicates that such a proposition would meet serious consideration by these members of the court.

Nor need we express an opinion on the relation between a utility's depreciation reserve and the valuation of the accrued depreciation of its property. . . . While it is true that the annual depreciation charge does not purport to measure the current actual consumption of plant, it may be that the credit balance in the depreciation reserve is good evidence of the amount of accrued depreciation. . . . It may also be that so much of the depreciation reserve as has not been used for retirements or replacements should be subtracted from the present value of the utility's property in determining the rate base, on the theory that the amounts thus contributed by the public represent a part payment for the property consumed or to be consumed in service. . . .

Justice Stone agreed with the opinion prepared by Justice Brandeis, but also presented a brief statement of his own views. He elaborated the point that it was the function of the depreciation accounts to accumulate a fund for financing the replacement of property, but that the probable cost of replacement was too uncertain to justify the adoption of present prices as the basis of the calculation.

I will assume, for present purposes, that as a result of *Smyth v. Ames . . .*, the function of a depreciation account for rate-making purposes must be taken to be the establishment of a fund for the replacement of plant rather than the restoration of cost or value of the original plant investment. But what amount annually carried to reserve will be sufficient to replace all the elements of a composite property purchased at various times, at varying price levels, as they wear out or become obsolete, is a question, not of law but of fact. It is a question which must be answered on the basis of a prediction of the salvage value of the obsolete elements, the character of the articles which will be selected to replace them when replacement is necessary, and their cost at the time of replacement.

Obviously, that question cannot be answered by *a priori* reasoning. Experience is our only guide, tempered by the consideration of such special or unusual facts and circumstances as would tend to modify the results of experience. Experience, which embraces the past fifteen years of high price levels, and the studies of experts, resulting in the universally accepted practice of accountants and business economists...have demonstrated that depreciation reserve, calculated on the basis of cost, has proven to be the most trustworthy guide in determining the amount required to replace, at the end of their useful life, the constantly shifting elements of a property such as the present. Costs of renewals made during the present prolonged period of high prices and diminishing replacement costs tend to offset the higher cost of replacing articles purchased in periods of lower prices. I think that we should be guided by the experience and practice in the absence of proof of any special circumstances showing that they are inapplicable to the particular situation with which we are now concerned.

Such proof, in the present case, is wanting. The only circumstance relied on for a different basis of depreciation, and one which is embraced in that experience, is the current high price level, which has raised the present reproduction value of the carrier's property, as a whole, above its cost. That, of course, might be a controlling consideration if we were dealing with present replacements at their present cost, instead of replacements to be made at various uncertain dates in the future, of articles purchased at different times in the past, at varying price levels. But I cannot say that since prices at the present moment are high, as a result of postwar inflation, a rate of return which is sufficient to yield 7.78% on present reproduction value, after adequate depreciation based on cost of the carrier's property, is confiscatory because logic requires the prediction that the elements of petitioner's property cannot, in years to come, be renewed or replaced with adequate substitutes, at less than the present average reproduction cost of the entire property—and this in the face of the facts that the cost of replacements in the past fifteen years has been for the most part at higher price levels than at present, that the amount allowed by the Commission for depreciation has been in practice more than sufficient for all replacement requirements throughout the period of higher price levels, and that the company has declared and paid dividends which were earned only if this depreciation reserve was adequate.

To say that the present price level is necessarily the true measure of future replacement cost is to substitute for a relevant fact which I should have thought ought to be established as are other facts, a rule of law which seems not to follow from *Smyth v. Ames*... and to be founded neither upon experience nor expert opinion and to be unworkable in practice. In the present case it can be applied only by disregarding evidence which would seem persuasively to establish the very fact to be ascertained.

These dissenting opinions are interesting, not only as a significant addition to the literature on the subject of depreciation, but as an indication of a substantial difference of opinion among the members of the court. It seems highly probable that a well prepared brief which was presented effectively would stand a good chance of establishing many of the practices and principles followed by accountants, business men, and many public utility commissions.

Smith v. Illinois Bell Telephone Co.[26] The lower court, in its consideration of this case, objected to the inconsistency in the contention of the Illinois Commerce Commission that a deduction should be made for the full amount

---

[26] 282 U. S. 133 (1930); P.U.R. 1931A, 1. Appeal by the members of the Illinois Commerce Commission from a decree of a Federal district court setting aside an order fixing telephone rates in the city of Chicago.

of the depreciation reserve in arriving at the rate base even though the depreciation rate on which this accumulation was based was reduced for the determination of the future periodic allowance. (The following quotation is from the decision of the lower court.)[27]

> The Commission in defense of its order now asserts that the deduction of $26,000,000 was proper as representing the deduction to be made on account of depreciation in valuing the property, despite the fact that the order specifically finds that the property was in 90% condition. But if the basis on which the $26,000,000 was accumulated is the correct basis for measuring depreciation, then the order is clearly erroneous in reducing by $1,800,000 the allowance for expense of depreciation. It is inconceivable on any theory consistent with equity and fair dealing that both acts of the Commission can be right. If, indeed, the unreasonable and arbitrary method of the Commission in handling depreciation and property paid for out of the reserve does not make its order void,...it certainly operates to destroy any presumption which may have existed in its favor.

The district court seemed to rely to a considerable extent upon the principles expressed in *Public Utility Commissioners v. New York Telephone Co., supra*, as to the absence of any legal or equitable interest of the customers in the assets of the utility, whether contributed by them to cover depreciation or not, and as to the error in using past profits to justify confiscatory future rates.

The higher court did not approve the action of the district court and the case was remanded for further consideration; it attempted to clarify its previous statements by pointing out that there was no intention to prevent the determination of a correct allowance for the future, based upon past experience, and the lower court was asked to make a more definite determination of an appropriate depreciation allowance. No comment was made upon the inconsistency stressed by the lower court.

> There is also the question of the annual allowance for depreciation. The Illinois Commission concluded that the accumulation of a large reserve (26,000,000) despite the fact that the property had been maintained "in at least 90% condition," showed that the reserve had been built up by annual additions that were in excess of the amounts required. The Commission by its order provided for a "combined maintenance and replacement allowance" which it deemed to be adequate "to fully protect the investment in this property and permit the company to accrue a reserve in the anticipation of property retirements." The court found that by this method the amount as charged by the company to operating expenses in 1923 with respect to depreciation had been reduced by the Commission to the extent of about $1,800,000. It was on the assumption of this reduction, that the court, without finding as to the proper annual allowance for depreciation, reached its conclusion as to the inadequacy of the rates.
>
> While it has been held by this court that property paid for out of moneys received for past services belongs to the company, and that the property represented by the credit balance in the reserve for depreciation cannot be used to support the imposition of a confiscatory rate..., it is evident that

---

[27] *Illinois Bell Telephone Co. v. Moynihan.* 38 F. (2d) 77, (1930); P.U.R. 1930B, 148.

past experience is an indication of the company's requirements for the future. The recognition of the ownership of the property represented by the reserve does not make it necessary to allow similar accumulations to go on if experience shows that these are excessive. The experience of the Illinois Company, together with a careful analysis of th results shown, under comparable conditions, by other companies which are part of the Bell system, and thus enjoy the advantage of the continuous and expert supervision of a central technical organization, should afford a sound basis for judgment as to the amount which, in fairness both to public and private interest, should be allowed as an annual charge for depreciation.

It is unfortunate that the court did not comment upon the "90% condition" of the property. There is a definite conflict between the engineering concept of condition per cent and the economic concept of value. The "condition per cent" usually refers to the physical condition of the property, its ability to render efficient and satisfactory service. Forty or fifty per cent condition is the absolute lower limit for the use of the crudest of tools, and delicate electrical equipment such as that used by telephone companies can hardly be used at all unless its physical condition approaches one hundred per cent. A unit about to be retired from service might still be in "90% condition." The value of an asset is a function of both its physical condition and its remaining service life. There is nothing necessarily inconsistent between property in 90% condition and an existing reserve for depreciation of 90% of the cost of the property. The implication in the case is that the reserve was suspiciously large because of the high degree of physical condition. A definite interpretation and decision on this point would greatly facilitate the work of the regulatory commissions.

Los Angeles Gas & Electric Corporation v. Railroad Commission.[28] This case is particularly interesting because it approves the unusual methods followed by the California commission in its treatment of depreciation. This commission has consistently used the sinking fund method of calculating both the perodic allowance and the accrued depreciation, and has used an undepreciated rate base. The court recognized a distinction between the 'fair value," to obtain which there must be a deduction for depreciation, and the "rate base" which is used to test the reasonableness of the rate of return and which may be undepreciated. The calculations of annual and accrued depreciation were undisturbed.

> Although the accrued depreciation was...treated by the Commission as deductible, in order to arrive at fair value, the Commission thought that operating results under the fair value theory could best be shown by using an undepreciated rate base. . . .
>
> No ground appears for challenging the findings of the Commission, made upon inspection and appraisal, that the accrued depreciation of the property amounted to $7,650,000. While not admitting the accuracy of the finding, the Company does not undertake to contest it here, but takes the amount

---

[28] 289 U.S. 287 (1933) ; P.U.R. 1933C, 229. Appeal from a district court decree refusing to restrain enforcement of an order of the California Railroad Commission reducing rates.

as the maximum which can be allowed upon the evidence. In determining present value, deduction must be made for accrued depreciation. . . . But the Commission made its calculation of the company's return. . . upon the rate base it fixed, undepreciated.

This decision appears to involve a contradiction of terms and concepts, for "a fair return on a fair value," or the identity of the rate base and the fair value, has been a canon of public utility regulation ever since *Smyth v. Ames*. The explanation is arithmetical rather than philosophical. When the sinking fund method is used, the periodic depreciation on an asset is a constant figure, equivalent to the deposit which would be required at a given rate of interest to accumulate to the cost of the asset at the end of a given period of time. The income from the fund plus the constant assessment against operations builds up the reserve and the fund to the required amount. Under the plan used by the California commission, if there is an actual fund, it is not included in the inventory of property on which a rate of return is expected, and the earnings of the fund are credited to the reserve; if there is no fund, but the assets representing the reserve for depreciation are invested generally in the operating property of the utility, a deduction is made from the net income equal to the amount which would be earned on a special fund and this amount is credited to the reserve. The net income is compared with an undepreciated rate base, but the net effect of this policy is the same as though the fund had been included in the rate base and a corresponding deduction made for accrued depreciation, with the entire earnings being taken into account and the total additions to the reserve being treated as an operating expense. In other words, the California undepreciated rate base method gives the same net results as the depreciated rate base method, if the same data are used for comparison.

"Inspection and appraisal" was again mentioned as the appropriate method for arriving at accrued depreciation.

Clark's Ferry Bridge Co. v. Public Service Commission.[29] The principal evidence used to establish the rate base was cost of reproduction less depreciation. The lower court did not make a specific deduction for depreciation accrued since a prior appraisal, but it used this omission to offset items which were not included in the original cost figures, so the effect is the same as though a specific deduction had been made.

> It does not appear that the court made any deduction from the amount of the fair value as determined in 1926 by reason of the depreciation accrued during the succeeding years. There was controversy as to the extent of that depreciation. Appellant's engineers allowed for the four and one-half years which had elapsed to the time of their survey the sum of $16,282. The commission's engineer estimated the accrued depreciation for six years at $41,403. The court thought that the latter figure was "nearer the actual

---

[29] 291 U.S. 227 (1934). Appeal from a judgment of the Superior Court of Pennsylvania affirming an order of the Pennsylvania Public Service Commission prescribing a tariff of tolls to be charged on a certain toll bridge.

accrued depreciation than the estimate of the company," but the court apparently treated such accrued depreciation as largely offset by the "extra allowance, over the contractor's bid, for concrete and cofferdams." The court decided that no harm was done the appellant by leaving the fair value at $767,800.

Much of the discussion centered around the annual allowance for depreciation, the company having claimed an allowance considerably in excess of that allowed by the commission and approved by the lower court. Depreciation was conceived as a protection against impairment of investment resulting from age and use.

> There is no question as to the fact of depreciation. It was established, as respondent admits, that concrete bridges deteriorate from the moment of their completion; that there are chemical changes in their structure... which cannot be stopped in their process or their effects removed. With this understanding, the question is as to the amount which should annually be allowed which will serve adequately to protect the investment from impairment due to age and use. ...

Except for the fact that the commission used one of the smaller estimates of the life of the bridge, there was no recognition, implicit or explicit, of the factors of obsolescence or inadequacy which are frequently the primary causes of bridge replacements.

One of the most interesting points in the case is the opinion of the court that the accrued deductible depreciation and the annual allowance for depreciation need not be mathematically consistent. The doctrine stated in *Smith v. Illinois Bell Telephone Co., supra,* to the effect that future depreciation allowances should be based upon past experience is reaffirmed.

> Respondent urges that the annual allowance asked by appellant was plainly too large and contrasts it with appellant's claim for accrued depreciation; that is, as the court stated, appellant's engineers "allow an accrued depreciation for the four and a half years elapsing to the time of their survey of $16,282, but claim a yearly depreciation allowance thereafter of $21,210." While it is recognized that accrued depreciation, as it may be observed and estimated at a given time, and an appropriate allowance of depreciation according to good accounting practice, need not be the same, there is no rule which requires an allowance to be made or continued which in the light of experience is shown to be extravagant. ...

These comments of the court on the inconsistency between the calculation of depreciation for the rate base and for the periodic allowance are not very satisfying, and the same criticism can be made of the discussion in *Smith v. Illinois Bell Telephone Co.* where the point made by the lower court as to the inconsistency was ignored. It is difficult to see how equitable results will be obtained if a utility is allowed to charge periodic depreciation on one basis and have the deductible depreciation for rate base purposes computed on another basis. It will either receive a return on capital contributed by the consumers to cover depreciation or it will be deprived of a return on its own capital investment, depending upon whether the annual depreciation rate is larger or smaller than the rate used to calculate the accumulated depreciation. It may not be possible to correct past errors by manipulation of future rates, but policies for the future can be made consistent.

The decision comments at some length upon the point that the Supreme Court is concerned only with the constitutionality of the depreciation provisions made by the commissions and not with the particular method of calculation. We cannot expect, for instance, that a decision will ever be rendered in favor of the straight line method over the sinking fund method of calculating the periodic charge. The commission allowed depreciation on a basis which involved the calculation of interest on a fund and this was approved by both lower and higher courts.

> After reviewing the testimony, and the methods of calculation which the parties advocated, the court thus stated its conclusion: "The commission allowed $7,678 annually. This sum set aside each year, with 4 per cent simple interest will in fifty years produce approximately $767,800 sufficient to rebuild the bridge as now valued. The straight line method advocated by the company will in fifty years with 4 per cent simple interest produce a fund twice as great as that necessary to replace the bridge. The straight line method is often used for short-lived structures, or plants of a character that they can be restored from time to time to the original condition of efficiency. . . . It is not so fair or equitable when applied to a long-lived structure or one that is disintegrating gradually and continuously and not capable of being restored to its original condition. The company may not be required to apply the income received from the depreciation fund to make up any deficit of operation (*Board of Public Utility Commissioners v. New York Telephone Co.,* 271 U. S. 23 . . .), but it is not entitled to an allowance which, exclusive of interest earned on the fund, will be sufficient to rebuild the bridge, when its life is done, but only to such an allowance as will with reasonable interest added make a fund sufficient to replace the bridge, when it requires replacement." In this view, the court thought the amount allowed by the commission to be "fair and reasonable in the circumstances.". . .
>
> The question of the amount which should be allowed annually for depreciation is a question of fact. . . . In reviewing the findings of the state court we are not required to enter a debatable field of fact and to choose and prescribe an invariable method of computation. To justify the overruling of the determination of the state court we must be able to see that what has been done will produce the result which the Constitution forbids. Considering the nature of the property, and upon facts shown by the evidence, the state court has allowed appellant to reserve annually, and use for its own purposes, an amount which according to common experience may be expected to produce a sum adequate to replace the property on the expiration of its life. We find it impossible to say, from a constitutional standpoint, that another method should have been employed or a greater amount allowed.

It is noteworthy that the court again thinks of the depreciation reserve as a financial provision for replacing the property, even though replacement is by no means essential and the probability of a fund being created equal to the amount required by replacement is far from certain; and it ignores the possibility that depreciation would continue and have to be accounted for, even though earnings were not large enough to cover depreciation.

Lindheimer v. Illinois Bell Telephone Co.[30] This case is supplementary to *Smith v. Illinois Bell Telephone Co., supra.* The former decision remanded the case to the district court for further proceedings and the present case is an appeal from the final decree of the lower court.[31] The district court, following its instructions from the Supreme Court, revised its previous estimates of depreciation "to place them on the basis of the present value of the property."

> The court found that the fair rate of depreciation to be applied to reproduction cost new was 16 per cent for the years 1923 to 1928, inclusive, and 15 per cent for the succeeding years. . . .

The amounts allowed by the district court were about 95% of the charges made by the company on its books, which were based upon original cost, and the company claimed that still larger allowances should be permitted on the reproduction cost basis.

Depreciation is an important issue in this case and it is discussed at some length by the higher court. There is a concise statement of the nature and causes of depreciation, and of the purpose of including a periodic charge in the operating expenses. Obsolescence and inadequacy are definitely included as factors to be taken into account and the maintenance of the integrity of the investment is again emphasized as the major purpose of the regular allowance.

> Broadly speaking, depreciation is the loss, not restored by current maintenance, which is due to all the factors causing the ultimate retirement of the property. These factors embrace wear and tear, decay, inadequacy, and obsolescence. Annual depreciation is the loss which takes place in a year. In determining reasonable rates for supplying public service, it is proper to include in the operating expenses, that is, in the cost of producing the service, an allowance for consumption of capital in order to maintain the integrity of the investment in the service rendered. . . .

The court describes with considerable detail the straight line method, using original cost as the basis of the calculations, which has been followed by the company in the past.

> The amount necessary to be provided annually for this purpose is the subject of estimate and computation. In this instance, the company has used the "straight line" method of computation, a method approved by the Interstate Commerce Commission. 177 I.C.C. pp. 408, 413. By this method the annual depreciation charge is obtained by dividing the estimated service value by the number of years of estimated service life. The method is designed to spread evenly over the service life of the property the loss which is realized when the property is ultimately retired from service. According to the principle of this accounting practice, the loss is computed upon the

---

[30] 292 U. S. 151 (1934). Appeal from a decree of a district court in favor of the plaintiff in a suit to restrain enforcement of telephone rates prescribed by the Illinois Commerce Commission.

[31] *Illinois Bell Telephone Co. v. Gilbert,* 3 F. Supp. 595; P.U.R. 1933E, 301.

actual cost of the property as entered upon the books, less the expected salvage, and the amount charged each year is one year's pro rata share of the total amount. Because of the many different classes of plant, some with long and some with short lives, some having large salvage and others little salvage or no salvage, and because of the large number of units of a class, the company employs averages, that is, average service life, average salvage of poles, of telephones, etc.

While property remains in the plant, the estimated depreciation rate is applied to the book cost and the resulting amounts are charged currently as expenses of operation. The same amounts are credited to the account for depreciation reserve, the "Reserve for Accrued Depreciation." When property is retired, its cost is taken out of the capital accounts, and its cost, less salvage, is taken out of the depreciation reserve account. According to the practice of the company, the depreciation reserve is not held as a separate fund, but is invested in plant and equipment. As the allowances for depreciation, credited to the depreciation reserve account, are charged to operating expenses, the depreciation reserve invested in the property thus represents, at a given time, the amount of the investment which has been made out of the proceeds of telephone rates for the ostensible purpose of replacing capital consumed. . . .

It is then pointed out that the test of the acceptability of any particular method of calculating depreciation is experience, that is, whether the resulting accumulations are too small or too large to accomplish their purpose. The burden of proof is placed upon the company to show that its charges have not been excessive.

If the predictions of service life were entirely accurate and retirements were made when and as these predictions were precisely fulfilled, the depreciation reserve would represent the consumption of capital, on a cost basis, according to the method which spreads that loss over the respective service periods. But if the amounts charged to operating expenses and credited to the account for depreciation reserve are excessive, to that extent subscribers for the telephone service are required to provide, in effect, capital contributions, not to make good losses incurred by the utility in the service rendered and thus to keep its investment unimpaired, but to secure additional plant and equipment upon which the utility expects a return.

Confiscation being the issue, the company has the burden of making a convincing showing that the amounts it has charged to operating expenses for depreciation have not been excessive. That burden is not sustained by proof that its general accounting system has been correct. The calculations are mathematical, but the predictions underlying them are essentially matters of opinion. They proceed from studies of the "behavior of large groups" of items. These studies are beset with a host of perplexing problems. Their determination involves the examination of many variable elements and opportunities for excessive allowances, even under a correct system of accounting, are always present. The necessity of checking the results is not questioned. The predictions must meet the controlling test of experience.

The company weakened its case for its usual annual allowance by claiming much smaller deductible depreciation than the annual provisions accumulated in its reserve for depreciation. It denied any necessary relationship between the balance in the reserve and the "actual" depreciation.

In explanation of this large difference, the company urges that the depreciation reserve in a given year does not purport to measure the actual depreciation at that time; that there is no regularity in the development of depreciation; that it does not proceed in accordance with any fixed rule; that as to a very large part of the property there is no way of predicting the extent to which there will be impairment in a particular year. Many different causes operating differently at different times with respect to different sorts of property produce the ultimate loss against which protection is sought. As the accruals to the depreciation reserve are the result of calculations which are designed evenly to distribute the loss over estimated service life, the accounting reserve will ordinarily be in excess of the actual depreciation. Further, there are the special conditions of a growing plant; "there are new plant groups in operation on which depreciation is accruing but which are not yet represented, or are but slightly represented, in the retirement losses." Where, as in this instance, there has been a rapid growth, retirements at one point of time will relate for the most part to the smaller preceding plant, while the depreciation reserve account is currently building up to meet the "increased eventual retirement liability" of the enlarged plant.

The court did not deny the validity of the proposition that there need not be complete correspondence between the actual or deductible depreciation and the amount in the reserve, but did feel that in view of the high degree of maintenance in which the property continuously was kept and the high percentage of physical condition found by the appraisers, the discrepancy was too large in this case and that the depreciation allowances had been excessive.

Giving full weight to these considerations, we are not persuaded that they are adequate to explain the great disparity which the evidence reveals. As the company's counsel say: "The reserve balance and the actual depreciation at any time can be compared only after examining the property to ascertain its condition; the depreciation, physical and functional, thus found can be measured in dollars and the amount compared with the reserve." Here we are dealing not simply with a particular year, but with a period of many years—a fairly long range of experience—and with careful and detailed examinations made both at the beginning and near the end of that period. The showing of the condition of the property, and of the way in which it has been maintained, puts the matter in a strong light. In substance, the company tells us: The property in Chicago is a modern Bell system plant. Through the process of current maintenance, worn, damaged, or otherwise defective parts were being constantly removed before their impairment affected the telephone service. The factors of "inadequacy" and "obsolescence" were continuously anticipated by the company, so that the telephone service might not be impaired, "and no depreciation of that character was ever present in the plant, except to the slight extent that obsolete items of plant were found," as stated by the company's witnesses. One of these witnesses testified that, in his examination of the plant to determine existing depreciation, he understood "that anything that was obsolete or inadequate was to be depreciated accordingly." We are told by the company that in that investigation "Condition new was assumed to be free from defects or impairment of any kind, that is, perfect or 100% condition, and the thing as it stood in actual use in the plant was compared with the same thing new." "All existing depreciation, both physical and functional, was reduced to a percentage, and subtracted from 100 per cent." The service measured up to the standards of the telephone art at all times. The plant cpable of giving such service "was not functionally deficient; in any practical sense. This is not to say that parts of the plant did not from time to time become inadequate or obsolete, but that the Company continuously anticipates and forestalls inadequacy and obsolescence. Before a thing becomes inadequate or obsolete it is removed from the plant." But little variation was found in the percentage of existing depreciation during the years 1923 to 1931. The company points out that the commission found, in its order of 1923, that the property was then "in at least 90 per cent condition." "The weighted total or over-all condition," the company shows, "is 90 per cent for the years 1923–1928 and 92 per cent for subsequent years.". . .

In the light of the evidence as to the expenditures for current maintenance and the proved condition of the property—in the face of the disparity between the actual extent of depreciation, as ascertained according to the comprehensive standards used by the company's witnesses, and the amount of the depreciation reserve—it cannot be said that the company has established that the reserve merely represents the consumption of capital in the service rendered. Rather it appears that the depreciation reserve to a large extent represents provision for capital additions, over and above the amount required to cover capital consumption. This excess in the balance of the reserve account has been built up by excessive annual allowances for depreciation charged to operating expenses.

The discussion of the maintenance charges of the company contains a good presentation of the theoretical difference between maintenance and depreciation as expense charges, and some indication of the practical difficulties involved in making such a distinction.

In the process of current maintenance, "new parts" are "installed to replace old parts" in units of property not retired. Such "substitutions or 'repairs' " are separate from the amounts which figure in the depreciation reserve. The distinction between expenses for current maintenance and depreciation is theoretically clear. Depreciation is defined as the expense occasioned by the using up of physical property employed as fixed capital; current maintenance, as the expense occasioned in keeping the physical property in the condition required for continued use during its service life. But it is evident that the distinction is a difficult one to observe in practice with scientific precision, and that outlays for maintenance charged to current expenses may involve many substitutions of new for old parts which tend to keep down the accrued depreciation. . . .

The court felt that the excessive amount of depreciation accumulating in the reserve destroyed the validity of any claim of confiscatory rates.

In answer to appellants' criticism, the company suggests that an adjustment might be made by giving credit in favor of the telephone users "in an amount equal to $3\frac{1}{2}$ per cent upon the difference between the depreciation reserve and the amount deducted from the valuation for existing depreciation." The suggestion is beside the point. The point is as to the necessity for the annual charges for depreciation, as made or claimed by the company, in order to avoid confiscation through the rates in suit. On that point the company has the burden of proof. We find that this burden has not been sustained. Nor is the result changed by figuring the allowances at the somewhat reduced amounts fixed by the court below.

We find this point to be a critical one. The questionable amounts annually charged to operating expenses for depreciation are large enough to destroy any basis for holding that it has been convincingly shown that the reduction in income through the rates in suit would produce confiscation.

Justice Butler, in a special concurring opinion, pointed out that the straight line method of calculating depreciation used by the company was not "in harmony with the principle of our decision in *United Railways & Electric Co. v. West...supra* which requires replacement cost to be taken as the basis of calculation." He presented a table which showed that the balance in the reserve for depreciation remained around 26 or 27% of the cost of the property, including land, throughout the years 1923 to 1931, even though the cost of the property increased rapidly during that period. He also presented several tables of statistics to show the relation between maintenance and depreciation charges. He drew the conclusion that depreciation charges were not necessary to equalize maintenance charges in proportion to income. He definitely refused to approve a method of depreciation calculation based on expired service life, and accepted the proposition that the plant as a whole rather than the individual parts must be taken into account. In general, he supported the "retirement reserve" philosophy of depreciation accounting.

This comparison serves to test the claim that the depreciation reserve is needed in order to equalize annual cost of upkeep in relation to revenue. If the period covered is typical, the last statement strongly suggests that no reserve account is necessary for that purpose. . . .

From the foregoing it justly may be inferred that charges made according to the principle followed by the company create reserves much in excess of what is needed for maintenance. The balances carried by the company include large amounts that never can be used for the purposes for which the reserve was created. In the long run the amounts thus unnecessarily taken from revenue will reach about one-half the total cost of all depreciable parts of the plant. The only legitimate purpose of the reserve is to equalize expenditures for maintenance so as to take from the revenue earned in each year its fair share of the burden. To the extent that the annual charges include amounts that will not be required for that purpose, the account misrepresents the cost of the service.

The company's properties constitute a complex and highly developed instrumentality containing many classes of items that require renewal from time to time. But, taken as a whole, the plant must be deemed to be permanent. It never was intended to be new in all its parts. It would be impossible to make it so. Expenditures in an attempt to accomplish that would be wasteful. Amounts sufficient to create a reserve balance that is the same percentage of total cost of depreciable items as their age is of their total service life cannot be accepted as legitimate additions to operating expenses. In the absence of proof definitely establishing what annual deductions from revenues were necessary for adequate maintenance of the property, the company is not entitled to have the rate order set aside as confiscatory.

There seems to be plenty of evidence that the reserve for depreciation kept on the books of the company had been accumulating too rapidly, but the general tone of the decision goes to the other extreme of accepting physical condition as a measure of value. Under the interpretation of accrued depreciation as a measure of expired service life, a reserve equal to 20 or 30 or even 50% of the cost property would not necessarily be excessive, although it is of course true that in a period of expansion the reserve should not remain at such a high percentage. An inconsistency between the reserve and the deductible depreciation is accepted uncritically by the court, but it does not appear that a good brief on this point has ever been presented to the court. In this case the utility adopted the usual tactics of claiming a high annual allowance and a low deduction for accrued depreciation and the court was forced to render its decision without the assistance of a well-organized presentation of the depreciation policies involved in the situation.

Dayton Power & Light Co. v. Public Utilities Commission.[32] There is little discussion of depreciation in this case. There is, however, evidence that the court treats the rates and methods adopted by the commissions as presumptively correct.

One unusual procedure, which is approved by the court, is the establishment of a reserve for maintenance, with a corresponding fund of assets.

> The commission allowed as a charge against the operating expenses of the affiliated seller an annual reserve of $667,612 to be placed in a sinking fund and devoted to the maintenance of the plant, with the exception of the wells and their equipment which had been separately cared for in the allowance for depletion.
>
> The appellant has failed to show in any conclusive or convincing way that this reserve will be inadequate.

The provision for a periodic depreciation allowance discloses little as to the basis of the calculation other than its consistency with the past practice of the company as shown on its annual reports to the commission.

> The commission also allowed as a charge against the appellant's operating expenses an annual reserve in the amount of 2 per cent of the "depreciable property" employed by the appellant in the business of distribution.
>
> The percentage so fixed is stated to be in accord with the practice of the appellant as disclosed in its annual reports on file with the commission.
>
> The contention that the percentage of allowance should have been 4 per cent instead of 2 has no basis in the evidence.

The deduction for depreciation in the rate base was a considerably higher percentage than is usually approved for other types of utilities. (In general more liberal allowances and larger deductions are made for the gas utilities, since the end of the life of the principal assets—gas wells and their equipment—is more apparent than in the case of other types of utilities where the assets can be replaced and the enterprise apparently go on indefinitely

---

[32] 292 U. S. 290 (1934). Appeal from a decree of the Supreme Court of Ohio affirming a rate order of the Ohio Public Utilities Commission.

in the same location.) The court did not meet directly the objection made by the utility of excessive deductions but merely said that the expense allowances for depletion and amortization of leases were sufficiently excessive to make up for any possible extravagance in depreciation deductions.

> In determining the price to be paid for gas delivered at the gateways, the commission appraised the wells and equipment of the affiliated seller as having suffered a depreciation of 58.1126 per cent. The appellant insists that the depreciation is excessive.
>
> There is evidence that the method of computation adopted by the commission is in accordance with the accepted practice of mining engineers. The practice is to ascertain the rock pressure at the initial flow of the gas and again at the time of the appraisal, and to measure the depreciation by the reduction thus disclosed. The wells and their equipment have only a scrap value after the exhaustion of the gas, and contents and containers thus depreciate together.
>
> The appellant, though complaining that the percentage of depreciation is excessive, has had a benefit, more than equivalent to any injury, in the enhancement of the allowance for amortization and depletion.

The court approved the principle of an allowance of an operating charge for amortization and depletion, although it thought the particular amount allowed might be excessive. Its defense of the necessity for such a charge is found in *Columbus Gas & Fuel Co. v. Public Utilities Commission, infra,* where the lower court had definitely prohibited such an allowance in testing the fairness of the rates.

Columbus Gas & Fuel Co. v. Public Utilities Commission.[33] This case is noteworthy in that it clears up a confusion which has long existed between the treatment of depletion and depreciation. The court points out that a state may prohibit an allowance for depletion in arriving at a taxable income, but that it cannot prohibit the deduction of an allowance for depletion in arriving at a constitutionally valid return on the value of the utility's property. The depreciation doctrines developed in *Knoxville v. Knoxville Water Co., supra,* are cited in support of this opinion, so the conclusion may be drawn that depreciation and depletion are to be treated alike in rate regulation.

> We have seen in the Dayton Case that, in determining the price to be paid for gas delivered at the gateway, the commission included among the operating expenses of the affiliated seller an annual allowance...to amortize the value of leaseholds...and of the well-structures and equipment used in connection therewith, and thus provide a fund that would restore the depleted capital when the gas had been exhausted. The same allowance was made here.
>
> Upon the appeal by the city of Columbus to the Supreme Court of Ohio, the item thus allowed was excluded altogether. The court did not deny that without the creation of a fund to replenish wasting assets the affiliated seller would be left with only a salvage value for leases, wells, and fittings after

---

33 292 U.S. 398 (1934). Appeal from a decree of the Supreme Court of Ohio setting aside a rate order of the Ohio Public Utilities Commission.

the exhaustion of the gas. It puts its judgment upon the ground that the statute of Ohio defining the powers of the commission and the method of appraisal makes no provision for depletion...and that the statute, and nothing else, gives the applicable rule. We may assume in submission to the holding of that court that the amortization allowance must be rejected if the rate-making process is to conform to the rule prescribed by statute, irrespective of any other. That assumption being made, the conclusion does not follow that the statutory procedure may set at naught restrictions imposed upon the states and upon all their governmental organs by the Constitution of the nation.

To withhold from a public utility the privilege of including a depletion allowance among its operating expenses, while confining it to a return of 6½ per cent upon the value of its wasting assets, is to take its property away from it without due process of law, at least where the waste is inevitable and rapid. The commission has found that the life expectancy of the operated gas fields is only three years and two months. If that holding is correct, the owner of the exhausted fields will find itself in a brief time with wells and leases that are worthless and with no opportunity in the interval to protect itself against the impending danger of exhaustion. Plainly the state must either surrender the power to limit the return or else concede to the business a compensating privilege to preserve its capital intact. *Knoxville v. Knoxville Water Co.* ....There is nothing to the contrary of this in cases such as *Burnet v. Harmel,* 287 U. S. 103...; *Stratton's Independence, Ltd. v. Howbert,* 231 U. S. 399...; and *Goldfield Consolidated Mines Co. v. Scott,* 247 U. S. 126. ....The profits of a mine may be treated as income rather than as capital if the state chooses so to classify them and to tax them on that basis. This is far from saying that in the process of rate making depletion of the capital may be disregarded by the agencies of government in figuring the interest returned on the investment. "Before coming to the question of profit at all the company is entitled to earn a sufficient sum annually to provide not only for current repairs, but for making good the depreciation and replacing the parts of the property when they come to the end of their life." *Knoxville v. Knoxville Water Co.* ...It is idle to argue that a company using up its capital in the operations of the year will have received the same return as one that at the end of the year has its capital intact and interest besides.

We hold that a fair price for gas delivered at the gateway includes a reasonable allowance for the depletion of the operated gas fields and the concomitant depreciation of the wells and their equipment. ...

There being error in the deduction of the appellant's operating expenses by the refusal to make provision for replenishing the wasting assets of its affiliated companies, the decree is reversed and the cause remanded to the Supreme Court of Ohio for further proceedings not inconsistent with this opinion.

This treatment of depletion and depreciation in the same way is logically and practically sound. One could wish, however, that the court had not been so positive in its assertion that a charge to operations for depletion will "provide a fund that would restore the depleted capital" when such a result could occur only under the assumption that the depletion charges, together with other operating costs, were covered by the earnings.

The court considers an objection to the allowance for depreciation on property other than well structures and equipment, and it points out that the depreciation allowance assumes a going concern, that it is not a problem of providing for abandoned property.

> Objection is made that the annual depreciation allowance...for depreciable property other than well structures and equipment is less than is necessary to maintain the property intact.
>
> We considered this objection in the Dayton Case and overruled it. In this case, however, the appellant submits a computation which is intended to prove that in measuring depreciation certain items of property, such as land and rights of way, have been omitted altogether. The record tells us nothing as to the location of this property or its present or prospective uses. Whether it has relation to the operated fields or the fields to be opened in the future there is nothing to inform us. Certainly land and rights of way may not be characterized as wasting assets in the absence of explanation that would stamp that quality upon them. In saying this we do not forget that an abandonment of the business might bring about a sharp reduction in the value of the plant, aside from well structures and equipment. There is nothing to show, however, that any such abandonment is planned or even reasonably probable. On the contrary, the course of business makes it clear that, when the fields in use shall be exhausted, the business will extend to others, and this for an indefinite future, or certainly a future not susceptible of accurate estimation. We find no reason for a revision of our conclusion that the depreciation reserve has not been proved to be inadequate.

At another point, when considering a further objection to the depreciation allowed by the commission, the court again indicates its unwillingness to interfere with the work of the commission in its arrangement of the details of the periodic depreciation calculation.

> Objection is made that there was an inadequate allowance...for the annual depreciation of the physical assets in Columbus.
>
> The value of those assets, together with general overheads, as fixed by the commission, was $3,927,647. The depreciation reserve at the end of 1929 was $1,166,762.30, and at the end of 1930 $1,251,886.77. On the other hand, the accrued depreciation (which was taken at the company's own figures) was only $710,659 as compared with a reproduction cost new of $4,633,326.
>
> The commission determined that, in view of the large reserve and the good condition of the plant, the allowance asked for by the company ($174,880.24) was too high, and that $68,196 was adequate.
>
> This is slightly less, it is true, than the amount ($88,695.03) suggested by a witness for the city, but the commission was at liberty to form its own judgment. In any event, the rule of de minimis is applicable where the difference is so trivial in its effect upon the rate. . . .

It may be noted that, as in other cases, the court does not assume any necessary equality between the reserve for depreciation and the accrued depreciation on the property.

Summary and Conclusions

The United States Supreme Court has not had occasion to pass upon all of the theories and practices which have developed in connection with depreciation of public utility property, but it has given consideration to a good many of them. The following propositions indicate the position of the court on several important issues.

Accounting for Depreciation

Depreciation is an operating cost, a determinant rather than a distribution of net income. Knoxville v. Knoxville Water Co., 212 U.S. 1 (1909); Lincoln Gas & Electric Light Co. v. Lincoln, 223 U.S. 349 (1912); Denver v. Denver Union Water Co., 246 U.S. 178 (1918); Lindheimer v. Illinois Bell Telephone Co., 292 U.S. 151 (1934). This interpretation of depreciation is especially significant in view of the common practice of the utilities to treat depreciation as a deduction from net income.

The principal purpose of depreciation accounting is to provide for the financing of replacements of property. Knoxville v. Knoxville Water Co., 212 U.S. 1 (1909); Railroad Commission v. Cumberland Telephone & Telegraph Co., 212 U.S. 414 (1909); Lincoln Gas & Electric Light Co. v. Lincoln, 223 U.S. 349 (1912); Cedar Rapids Gas Light Co. v. Cedar Rapids, 223 U.S. 655 (1912); Galveston Electric Co. v. Galveston, 258 U.S. 388 (1922); United Railways & Electric Co. v. West, 280 U.S. 234 (1930); Clark's Ferry Bridge Co. v. Public Service Commission, 291 U.S. 227 (1934). Until 1930 the provision for replacements could have been interpreted as merely providing for the original cost of retired assets, but in *United Railways & Electric Co. v. West* there was a definite recognition of the price fluctuation factor and the recording of depreciation was expected to finance replacements at the increased price level. There is some suspicion of the validity of sizeable depreciation reserves as being unnecessary for replacement requirements.

It is unfortunate that the court has adopted this conception of the function of depreciation accounting. [The financing of replacements is an important problem in financial management toward which the recording of depreciation can often make an important contribution, but depreciation must be accounted for. Whether specific items of property are to be replaced or not, assets are retained in the business as a result of the depreciation entry only when there is no net loss, and the depreciation entries alone cannot provide adequately for the replacement cost in a period of rising prices.] It is difficult to conceive the court's taking a consistent position during a period of falling prices, that is, that less than the original cost of property can be recovered in the earnings, that depreciation charges must be reduced if the cost of reproduction of the property falls.

Another purpose of depreciation accounting is to prevent the impairment of capital investment. Knoxville v. Knoxville Water Co., 212 U.S. 1 (1909); Galveston Electric Co. v. Galveston, 258 U.S. 388 (1922); Clark's Ferry Bridge Co. v. Public Service Commission, 291 U.S. 227 (1934); Lindheimer v. Illinois Bell Telephone Co., 292 U.S. 151 (1934). This point is emphasized with sufficient frequency to give it some significance, but just what constitutes the capital investment which is to be protected is none too clear. In *Knoxville v. Knoxville Water Company* the expression "original investment" was used, but, if this means the original cost of the property of the utility, it is incompatible with *United Railways & Electric Co. v. West* in which the proper basis for the depreciation calculation was said to be present or reproduction cost, so that provision would be made for the replacement cost. In *Lindheimer v. Illinois Bell Telephone Company,* however, as Justice Butler pointed out in a special concurring opinion, the court did not insist upon the use of reproduction cost and approved the calculation made on the original cost basis. It seems quite likely, therefore, that the conception of depreciation accounting as a provision for replacements has often been considered as the equivalent of the maintenance of original investment, which would be true only under the assumptions of static prices and of literal and inevitable replacement.

The prevention of impairment of original capital investment is a much more feasible proposition than the provision for replacements. It still depends for its fulfillment upon sufficient earnings to cover all of the expenses including depreciation, but otherwise it is a workable concept which avoids the impracticable features of the replacement doctrine.

The provision for depreciation should cover losses caused by obsolescence and inadequacy as well as wear and tear from age and use. Simpson v. Shepard (The Minnesota Rate Cases), 230 U.S. 352 (1913); *Kansas City Southern Railway Co. v. United States,* 231 U.S. 423 (1913); *Denver v. Denver Union Water Co.,* 246 U.S. 178 (1918); *Lindheimer v. Illinois Bell Telephone Co.,* 292 U.S. 151 (1934). In general, the attitude of the court seems to be that the depreciation charge should cover any reasonably predictable factor which will bring about the retirement of an asset from use.

It is both a right and a duty of the utility to provide adequately for depreciation. Knoxville v. Knoxville Water Co., 212 U.S. 1 (1909); *Galveston Electric Co. v. Galveston,* 258 U.S. 388 (1922). Unearned depreciation in the past cannot be recovered by charging higher rates in the future.

The maintenance policy and the accounting methods followed by the utility in handling repairs and replacements help to determine the appropriate depreciation allowance. Lincoln Gas & Electric Light Co. v. Lincoln, 223 U.S. 349 (1912); *Lindheimer v. Illinois Bell Telephone Co.,* 292 U.S. 151 (1934). A policy of keeping the property in a state of good repair will tend to extend the physical life of property and lower the periodic charge for depreciation. The practice of charging the cost of many replacements directly to operating expenses will reduce the amount which has to be covered by the depreciation allowance. In *Dayton Power & Light Co. v. Public Utilities Commission,* 292 U.S. 290 (1934), the use of a reserve for maintenance and a special maintenance fund was approved.

The allowance made for depreciation assumes that the property is being used by a going concern. Columbus Gas & Fuel Co. v. Public Utilities

Commission, 292 U.S. 398 (1934). This eliminates the confusion of second-hand or liquidation values, and permits rates for depreciation to be set which take into account the particular circumstances of the property and of the utility under consideration.

The Supreme Court is interested only in the constitutionality of depreciation provisions and not in the details of methods, rates, etc. Van Dyke v. Geary, 244 U.S. 39 (1917); *Georgia Railway & Power Co. v. Railroad Commission,* 262 U.S. 625 (1923); *Clark's Ferry Bridge Co. v. Public Service Commission,* 291 U.S. 227 (1934); *Dayton Power & Light Co. v. Public Utilities Commission,* 202 U.S. 290 (1934); *Columbus Gas & Fuel Co. v. Public Utilities Commission,* 292 U.S. 398 (1934). The court has said several times that the depreciation rate and the method of calculation are questions of fact with which it is not directly concerned; it treats the rates and methods prescribed by the commissions as presumptively correct. No preference is shown for the straight line, sinking fund, or annuity methods of calculation.

Experience is the best test of the acceptability of depreciation methods. Lincoln Gas & Electric Co. v. Lincoln, 223 U.S. 349 (1912); *Smith v. Illinois Bell Telephone Co.,* 282 U.S. 133 (1930); *Clark's Ferry Bridge Co. v. Public Service Commission,* 291 U.S. 227 (1934); *Lindheimer v. Illinois Bell Telephone Co.,* 292 U.S. 151 (1934). It is said that depreciation allowances should be based upon a study of past requirements. Depreciation reserves are considered excessive if they accumulate so rapidly that they obviously have more than provided for property replacements. Even the definite statement in *United Railways & Electric Co. v. West,* that depreciation should be calculated on the basis of cost of reproduction, was ignored and the original cost basis approved in *Lindheimer v. Illinois Bell Telephone Company* on the ground that the reserve was more than adequate.

Errors in past depreciation rates cannot affect rates for the future. Galveston Electric Co. v. Galveston, 258 U.S. 388 (1922); *Public Utility Commissioners v. New York Telephone Co.,* 271 U.S. 23 (1926); *Smith v. Illinois Bell Telephone Co.,* 282 U.S. 133 (1930). A utility cannot be forced to omit or reduce its depreciation allowance and charge rates for its services which would otherwise be confiscatory in order to offset an excessive past accumulation of depreciation; and it cannot ask for rates which are high enough to make up past deficiencies in depreciation. It is usually maintained that the consumer has no equitable interest in the depreciation reserve.

This doctrine seems highly legalistic and unless interpreted liberally will place a considerable handicap upon effective regulation by the commissions. It forces the utilities to try to charge excessive depreciation, while the commissions, in order to protect the consumer's interests, are forced to be niggardly in their depreciation allowances, since neither side can expect to have an equitable adjustment made for past errors.

Depletion and depreciation are to be treated alike in judging the adequacy of public utility rates. Dayton Power & Light Co. v. Public Utilities Commission, 292 U.S. 290 (1934); Columbus Gas & Fuel Co. v. Public Utilities Commission, 292 U.S. 398 (1934).

The dissenting opinions contain a number of ideas concerning the depreciation allowance which either do not appear in the majority opinions or are in conflict with them. Justice Butler definitely approves the "retirement reserve" method of accounting for depreciation whereby the reserve is kept at a minimum estimated to meet the requirements of the retirements in any one period, and the additions to the reserve are made irregularly either by appropriations of surplus or charges to operating expenses. *Lindheimer v. Illinois Bell Telephone Co., 292 U.S. 151 (1934).* Justice Brandeis thinks of the depreciation provision primarily as an equitable distribution of costs, analogous in principle to mutual insurance. He presents a strong and lengthy support for the use of original cost as the proper basis for the depreciation calculation, emphasizing the practical difficulties of using the present value basis. He makes a clear distinction between the depreciation reserve and depreciation fund, and believes that the depreciation claimed by the utilities should be consistent with that shown in their published statements. *United Railways & Electric Co. v. West, 280 U.S. 234 (1930).* Justice Stone, in the same case, supports the use of original cost as the basis for the periodic calculation.

In conclusion, it may be said that the Supreme Court recognizes the necessity of some systematic recognition of depreciation as a cost of operations of public utilities. It does not sponsor any particular technique, but merely insists that a method and rates be prescribed which will adequately maintain the capital investment, or provide for replacements, and which will permit the charging of rates for the services rendered by the utility which are neither so low as to be confiscatory or so high as to permit the earning of an unreasonable rate of return. The present attitude of the court may be criticized as giving undue emphasis to the provision for financing replacements, as failing to recognize the necessity of having earned the depreciation in order to bring about the expected financial results, and for its unnecessary rigidity in connection with the adjustment of past errors in depreciation estimates.

Depreciation in Rate Base Valuation

Some deduction for depreciation is generally required in rate base valuations. "Fair present value" is usually interpreted so as to require a deduction for "accrued" depreciation. The only exception is found in *Los Angeles Gas & Electric Corporation v. Railroad Commission, 289 U.S. 287 (1933),* where the court approved an undepreciated rate base in connection with the use of the sinking fund method, and drew a curious distinction between "fair value" and the rate base instead of justifying its decision on more obvious and reasonable technical grounds.

Reproduction cost less depreciation is used most frequently as the rate base. Denver v. Denver Union Water Co., 246 U.S. 178 (1918); Galveston Electric Co. v. Galveston, 258 U.S. 388 (1922); Clark's Ferry Bridge Co. v. Public Service Commission, 291 U.S. 227 (1934). In some cases this basis is mentioned as only one factor to be taken into account, but it generally appears to be the most significant figure in the final valuation. *Des Moines Gas Co. v. Des Moines, 238 U.S. 153 (1915); Georgia Railway & Power Co. v. Railroad Commission, 262 U.S. 625 (1923); Bluefield Water Works & Improvement Co. v. West Virginia Public Service Commission, 262 U.S. 679 (1923).*

The calculation of periodic depreciation need not be consistent with the calculation of deductible depreciation. Clark's Ferry Bridge Co. v. Public Service Commission, 291 U.S. 227 (1934); Lindheimer v. Illinois Bell Telephone Co., 292 U.S. 151 (1934). This doctrine is also implied by the discussion and methods followed in other cases. *McCardle v. Indianapolis Water Co., 280 U.S. 234 (1930); Columbus Gas & Fuel Co. v. Public Utilities Commission, 292 U.S. 398 (1934).* There are a few indications of the desirability of consistency. *Railroad Commission v. Cumberland Telephone & Telegraph Co., 212 U.S. 414 (1909); United Railways & Electric Co. v. West, 280 U.S. 234 (1930),* in both the majority opinion in support of basing depreciation on reproduction cost, and Justice Brandeis' description of the prudent investment base in his dissenting opinion.

A distinction is usually drawn between the reserve for depreciation and the "accrued" or deductible depreciation. The former is treated as merely a matter of technical bookkeeping procedure, of making periodic charges to operations so as to take care of replacement requirements; while the latter may be determined independently of the reserve whenever an appraisal of the property is made, and it should take into account the condition of the property at the time and any other relevant factors. This "accrued" depreciation would be deducted even though no depreciation reserve had been set up on the books of the utility, or regardless of the size of the reserve.

Accrued depreciation determined by inspection is to be given preference over age-life calculations. Pacific Gas & Electric Co. v. San Francisco, 265 U.S. 403 (1924); McCardle v. Indianapolis Water Co., 272 U.S. 400 (1927); Smith v. Illinois Bell Telephone Co., 282 U.S. 133 (1930); Los Angeles Gas & Electric Corporation v. Railroad Commission, 289: U.S. 287 (1933); Lindheimer v. Illinois Bell Telephone Co., 292 U.S. 151 (1934). This proposition is closely associated with and is perhaps one reason for the approval of the inconsistency between the bookkeeping and appraisal calculations of accrued depreciation. The members of the court have been impressed with the testimony of engineers as to the physical condition of the property and yet have felt that the accounting procedures were also in conformity with good business practice, so the conclusion was reached that they were dealing with two procedures which were not necessarily intimately related. At any rate, a calculation of accrued depreciation has to be supported by good evidence of having been checked by a careful inspection of the property before it becomes acceptable.

The principal objection to this emphasis upon the importance of inspection is that the typical engineering calculation of "condition per cent" ignores the fact that the value of property to its owner depends not only upon its physical condition and the efficiency of the service it is rendering, but also upon the length of time in the future during which the service will be forthcoming. The physical inspection is valuable in ascertaining what will be the probable remaining life of an asset, but an asset in 90% service condition with ten years of remaining life is certainly worth more than an asset in the same condition with only five years of service left in it. These appraisals tend, therefore, to overvalue the property and to give results which cannot be incorporated into any systematic scheme for accounting for depreciation.

A blind acceptance of an age-life calculation, however, is equally objectionable. The conditions surrounding the use of the particular asset should be given adequate consideration, and the depreciation rates should be changed whenever a careful inspection reveals that the original estimates of service life were inaccurate. Each method should give the same results if all the relevant factors are taken into account and if the same basis, such as original cost or reproduction cost, is used in the calculation.

Appreciation and going value must be treated separately and not be allowed to offset accrued depreciation. Simpson v. Shepard (The Minnesota Rate Cases), 230 U.S. 352 (1913).

Obsolescence should be taken into account in the deductible depreciation. Pacific Gas & Electric Co. v. San Francisco, 256 U.S. 403 (1924). The appraisals made solely on the basis of inspection of the property and the calculation of the condition per cent tend to minimize the effect of probable obsolescence.

The attitude of the court on the deduction of depreciation in arriving at rate base valuations can be criticized for its undue rigidity and for the failure of most of the members of the court to appreciate the financial and accounting implications of the various methods and proposals.

The policy of computing the deductible depreciation without regard to the accounting practices and records of the utility tends to create an inequitable situation. Almost inevitably, either a deduction is made for depreciation which the utility has not been able to charge and earn under the rules of the commission, or, what is more frequently the case, a deduction is made for considerably less than the amount accumulated in the reserve, thereby giving the utility the right to ask for earnings on a greater amount of property than that represented by the invested capital. From the legal point of view it may be valid to maintain that the consumer has no interest, equitable or otherwise, in that portion of the assets represented by the depreciation reserve, as the court does in *Public Utility Commissioners v. New York Telephone Co.*, 271 U.S. 23 (1926), but the court would do well to give more weight to Justice Brandeis' observation that "rate regulation is an intensely practical matter," give some recognition to the fact that depreciation is at best a crude estimate, and allow for equitable adjustments of past errors and of discrepancies between recorded and observed accrued depreciation. Certainly some such approach to the problem is highly desirable in order to prevent the problem of rate regulation from developing into a feud between the commissions and the utilities with each side spending more time and energy in maneuvering toward strategically advantageous positions than in working out practical schemes for handling the many complex problems of valuation and accounting.

The adoption of reproduction cost as the most significant factor in valuation complicates the treatment of deductible depreciation and probably accounts to a considerable extent for the development of the independence of the treatment of depreciation in valuation cases from its treatment as a periodic operating charge. If prices have risen, the deductible depreciation should be proportionately increased in order to arrive at a figure which can legitimately be called "present" value. If the operating charge for depreciation is not raised to the same basis, the utility does not receive the full benefit of the new price level in its operating costs and receives no assistance in financing the higher replacement cost. (It previously has been shown that raising the depreciation charge to the new basis cannot provide completely for the higher replacement cost.) But the utility, since much if not most of its capital is obtained with the use of fixed obligations which do not vary with changing price levels, will receive a disproportionate increase in its corporate surplus from the use of the increased values. The appreciation of the old assets will provide the increase in the stockholders' equity and the depreciation of these higher values, if earned, will enable the utility to finance an investment in total property in the future which is greater in dollars and cents than the original capital investment. There will have to be some additional investment from some source, however, to make up the difference betwen the replacement cost and the amount recovered by depreciation charges. If, on the other hand, prices have fallen, the deductible depreciation should be proportionately decreased. The total recovered depreciation, if reduced to the new basis, will be greater than the cost of replacement but not as great as the original cost. But the fixed indebtedness was used to purchase assets at their original cost and all of the loss will fall on the stockholders' share.

If the rate of return is based upon present or reproduction cost but the regular depreciation charge is left on the original cost basis, the reserve for depreciation and the amount of deductible depreciation would necessarily be different in amount, but they could be kept consistent on a proportionate basis, that is, each one using the same estimates of life, scrap value, etc. But, in a time of rising prices, new capital would have to be found for all of the excess of the replacement cost over the original cost and the operating charges would be understated in the sense that they would not reflect current conditions. In a time of falling prices, the entire excess of original cost over replacement cost would be recovered, if earned, by means of the depreciation charges and this would be available to the utility as additional working capital. The operating charges would in the sense mentioned above be overstated. In either case, however, the original capital investment in dollars and cents would presumably be recovered and be available to meet the fixed obligations of the company.

Few, if any, of these considerations have been given the attention of the court, probably because they have never been presented adequately by the attorneys of either side. Justice Brandeis is apparently the only member of the court who has worked out anything like a consistent and complete philosophy of the situation, but his prudent investment theory seems to stand little chance of acceptance by the majority of the court. In view of the numerous complex and conflicting problems and interests involved in the entire situation, the writer is inclined to favor the use of original cost as the basis of the periodic depreciation calculation regardless of whatever basic principle may be used for the rate base valuation. It would seem highly desirable, however, to introduce enough consistency, so that the reserve for depreciation and the deductible depreciation would otherwise be comparable.

LIST OF UNITED STATES SUPREME COURT CASES REPORTED

U. S. Reports Vol. Page Year	*Title*
99 455 1878	United States v. Kansas Pacific Railway Co.
169 466 1898	Smyth v. Ames.
174 739 1899	San Diego Land & Town Co. v. National City.
189 439 1903	San Diego Land & Town Co. v. Jasper.
192 201 1904	Stanislaus County v. San Joaquin & King's River Canal & Irrigation Co.
212 1 1909	Knoxville v. Knoxville Water Co.
212 19 1909	Willcox v. Consolidated Gas Co.
212 414 1909	Railroad Commission v. Cumberland Telephone & Telegraph Co.
223 349 1912	Lincoln Gas & Electric Light Co. v. Lincoln.
223 655 1912	Cedar Rapids Gas Light Co. v. Cedar Rapids.
230 352 1913	Simpson v. Shepard (The Minnesota Rate Cases).
231 423 1913	Kansas City Southern Railway Co. v. United States.
238 153 1915	Des Moines Gas Co. v. Des Moines.
244 39 1917	Van Dyke v. Geary.
246 178 1918	Denver v. Denver Union Water Co.
258 388 1922	Galveston Electric Co. v. Galveston.
262 625 1923	Georgia Railway & Power Co. v. Railroad Commission.

E. L. Kohler

THE DEVELOPMENT OF ACCOUNTING
FOR REGULATORY PURPOSES
BY THE FEDERAL POWER COMMISSION

Eric Louis Kohler *was born in Michigan in 1892, and received his A.B. from the University of Michigan in 1914, and his M.A. from Northwestern in 1915. He is a C.P.A. in Illinois, and has been a partner in Arthur Andersen & Co. and in E. L. Kohler & Co. He has taught at Northwestern, and was comptroller of the Tennessee Valley Authority, 1938–1941. He edited* The Accounting Review *from 1928–1944, and served as president of the American Accounting Association in 1936 and again in 1946. He is the author of books on income taxes (1924), accounting principles (1927), advanced problems (1939, 1947, 1959), auditing (1947, 1954), and accounting in the Federal government (1956). He is also the compiler of* A Dictionary for Accountants *(1952, 1956, 1963).*
The title of the article reprinted here summarizes its significance—it is a study of the use of accounting as a tool or implement of public policy rather than as a tool or implement of private enterprise. In such a setting, the consumer becomes the focus of attention rather than the investors in the enterprise or its management.

A few months ago a series of three articles entitled "Power Price Fixing,"[1] by James L. Dohr, appeared in the *Journal of Accountancy*. Purporting to be "a dispassionate review of the questions involved," these articles are prefaced with the following statement:

> The proceedings in the *Montana Power Company* case before the Federal Power Commission involve an accounting reclassification under section 301 (a) of the Federal Power Act. In its decision (February, 1945) the Commission reiterates its oft-made statement that its classification of accounts for public utilities is based on a "cost" as distinguished from a "value" basis.

Reprinted from The George Washington Law Review (December, 1945), pp. 19–31, by permission.
[1] Vol. 79, pp. 432–439; Vol. 80, pp. 15–22, pp. 111–117 (June-August, 1945).

What it seeks to convey by this statement is indicated more clearly by other statements in its opinion. On page 16 it says "Our system of accounts is firmly rooted in the cost concept, which has been generally recognized as the proper basis for regulatory purposes"; on page 17 it suggests that the position taken by the company would "enable regulated utilities to utilize accounting as an instrument for imposing an effective check on regulations"; on page 8 of the concurring opinion the testimony of the company's accounting witnesses is rejected as being an attempt to support the claims of their clients "rather than an expression of sound accounting principles consistent with the purposes of the Federal Power Act." It is to be observed that in the foregoing statements there is a hopeless confusion between accounting principles and regulatory mandates and objectives.[2]

The articles then discuss at some length the Commission's decisions and those of the Montana and Arkansas utility commissions on the accounting practices of the Montana Power Company and the Arkansas Power & Light Company. At the end of his last article Mr. Dohr concludes:

> The Commission's treatment of the company's accounting witnesses in the Montana Power Company case is a bungling attempt at besmirchment. It is inaccurate; it is lacking in an understanding of accounting; it is at variance with the obvious facts; it is wholly unwarranted...the Commissioners' lack of understanding of accounting principles is a severe handicap....[3]

Mr. Dohr's indignation is shared, possibly for other reasons, by Joe Bond, a certified public accountant formerly associated with the Arkansas Public Utility Commission. Mr. Bond states:

> The present program of the Federal Power Commission, as revealed in "original cost" proceedings which followed the initiation of this system of accounts, shows conclusively that this system of accounts, together with the arguments advanced for its adoption, were, to this authority, a well-planned Trojan horse, within the shell of which was concealed an economic philosophy utterly foreign to the American system of private enterprise.[4, 5]

Following the Hope decision,[6] it has been generally agreed that the Federal Power Commission, acting under a blanket authority from the Congress, has an exceedingly free hand in establishing a rate basis. But Justice Jackson, in a dissenting opinion, commented thus on the propriety of leaning too heavily on costs and the accounting records which are built up from costs:

> To make a fetish of mere accounting is to shield from examination the

---

[2] *Ibid.*, p. 432.

[3] *Ibid.*, p. 117.

[4] "Accounting Policy or Economic Philosophy?" Accounting Review, January, 1945, pp. 24–30. Mr. Bond quotes Karl Marx' *Values, Prices and Profits,* in an attempt to demonstrate that the Federal Power Commission, by denying a return on "intangibles," has adopted Marx' labor-value theory.

[5] The same quotation, cited by Henry A. Horne in "Utility Regulation," Chapter 20, p. 1, of *Contemporary Accounting* (New York: American Institute of Accountants, 1945), is referred to by Mr. Horne as "an interesting answer to...some surprising assertions about accounting [which] have come from the regulatory authorities."

[6] *Federal Power Commission* v. *Hope Natural Gas Co.* 320 U. S. 591 (1945).

deeper causes, forces, movements, and conditions which should govern rates. Even as a recording of current transactions, bookkeeping is hardly an exact science...it uses symbols of certainty to express values that actually are in constant flux...our quest for certitude is so ardent that we pay an irrational reverence to a technique which uses symbols of certainty, even though experience again and again warns us that they are delusive.[7]

From these quotations—and there are many more like them—it appears that accounting as it has been practiced by the Federal Power Commission in recent years has inspired a good deal of angry rhetoric. The vocal chorus emanates not only from those who imagine that their interests have been adversely affected, but from accountants themselves, the validity of whose traditional practices has been put to the test. It is the purpose of this paper, within the limitations of brevity, to examine the basic questions of accounting which the Commission has raised, and to appraise very generally some of the Commission's accounting practices.

What the Commission has Required

Sec. 301 (a) of the Federal Power Act[8] obliges every utility to keep accounts in accordance with whatever system therefor is prescribed by the Federal Power Commission. A similar provision appears in the Natural Gas Act of 1938. By virtue of the earlier authority, the Commission devised a uniform system of accounts for electric utilities which was made effective January 1, 1937, and a comprehensive annual report based on the uniform accounts. The average utility has had little trouble in conforming its records to the Commission's requirements, except for the analyses and reclassifications made necessary in the "property" accounts (i.e., land, buildings, equipment, intangibles). Most utilities had maintained property accounts without supporting detail, and it was not unusual to find a variety of tangibles and intangibles therein with credits for retirements on varying valuation bases or with no credits at all, and widely differing methods for capitalizing new construction and equipment. Among the Commission's accounting requirements, as outlined in the uniform system, were the following.

1. A grouping of properties was required through the use of subaccounts whereby items of the same type would appear under a common head, the purpose being to facilitate comparisons of property investments with those of other utilities, make possible better retirement entries, and establish a more intelligible rate base.

2. Cost to be recorded for each grouping and subgrouping was the total of the "original" costs of the property items on hand, original cost meaning that "incurred by the person (including any preceding owner) who first devoted the property to utility service." This led in many instances to an

---

[7] *Ibid.,* p. 643.
[8] 49 Stat. 838 (1935).

investigation of the books of predecessor organizations, and sometimes resulted in estimates if old records were unavailable.

3. The excess of purchase cost over the original cost of an asset already in use was to be segregated in account 100.5, pending a disposal order from the Commission. In most instances the Commission has recommended an amortization period of 15 years or less.

4. "Write-ups" in original cost resulting from "book entries" and not bona fide investment in physical equipment were to be segregated in account 107. One would expect to find under this head "appreciation" entries, profits paid to promoters in cash or capital stock and charged to plant, intercompany transfers and profits on construction, and other "paper" transactions—arbitrary increases having no justification under conservative financing and accounting procedures. This class of items the Commission has directed to be removed immediately from the accounts.

5. Property having a limited life (which means all fixed property except land and a few minor intangibles) was to be depreciated in such a manner as to spread cost over useful life. The Commission has tended to favor straight-line-depreciation methods, in accordance with prevailing practice in competitive enterprise.[9]

What has Happened in
the Industry

Each year the Commission has published in a single volume the financial statements of the principal privately owned electric utilities of the country.[10] An epitome of these statements was published for the year 1943[11] which brought out the striking changes that had taken place in the industry since January 1, 1937, the date when the Uniform System of Accounts became effective—changes for which the uniform system and the controls established thereby had been at least in some measure responsible. Several of these changes are worth noting:

1. The segregation in accounts 100.5 and 107 of the excess of book values of property over original cost has up to a recent date (August, 1945), amounted to $870 millions, and the full amount eventually to be segregated is estimated by the Commission at $1,500 millions. Since on January 1, 1937, the total book value of fixed properties over which the Commission has jurisdiction was approximately $6,500 millions, an ultimate adjustment of at least 20 per cent is indicated.

2. Depreciation reserves between 1937 and 1943 increased from $1,500 millions, to $2,500 millions, or 70 per cent. By the end of 1945, at the present rate of accumulation, the reserves will have increased 100 per cent over their old level and their ratio to fixed properties should exceed 20 per cent.

---

9 *Uniform System of Accounts*, pp. 33, 37–83.

10 *Statistics of Electric Utilities in the United States*. The last volume to be published at this writing covered the calendar year 1943. On the basis of gross reserves, the combined figures of these companies represent 98 per cent of the country's privately owned electric utilities.

11 *The Financial Record of the Electric Utility Industry 1937–43* (1944).

3. Reported annual net income, ranging from $487 to $548 millions (or from $392 to $497 millions if reduced by net surplus charges of all kinds), and showing no observable trend in either direction, was sufficient to yield annual dividend payments on preferred stock averaging 6 per cent and on common stock averaging 7 per cent, and to absorb more than $1,100 millions in surplus charges, an undisclosed portion of which consisted of write-up eliminations and amortization provisions against excess purchase costs.

4. Structural and other property additions of approximately $1,300 millions, reductions of long-term debt and paid-in capital of $260 millions and $60 millions, respectively, and increases in working capital of $330 millions were made possible by the reinvestment of depreciation reserves and of earnings in excess of dividends.

During the seven-year period, the number of domestic customers (excluding rural) rose from 18,900,000 to 22,100,000, annual consumption increased from 783 to 1,052 kwh, the rate declined from 4.3¢ to 3.6¢ per kwh, and the annual domestic bill increased from $34 to $38. The number of commercial and industrial users declined slightly because of the war (1 percent from 3,630,000), but average annual consumption increased from 17,900 to 32,400 kwh, the average rate decreased from 1.7¢ to 1.3¢ per kwh, and the annual bill increased from $304 to $427. A part of the decrease in average rates may of course be attributed to the lower brackets into which higher consumption falls. Again, much of the increased consumption was caused by the war. Nevertheless, the fact remains that the rate of output increased 65 per cent, the number of customers 15 per cent, and gross revenue 38 per cent, while net income displayed but little average variation. In future years further trends in the same direction may be expected.

It would be rash to impute to the Commission, to management, or to circumstances beyond the control of either, such as the war, any specific portion of the credit for this favorable showing. The results have been produced by a combination of forces which has included numerous elements. But one can agree with the *Wall Street Journal* in saying that "the fundamental position of the electric-utility industry has been strengthened by the Federal Power Commission's program of eliminating intangible items and write-ups from the property accounts of many companies."[12] One result has been a lowered rate for both interest and dividends in the case of utilities which have complied with the Commission's rules on the valuation of their properties, thus bringing about ultimately a saving to ratepayers.

Trends in Accounting

In the broad areas embraced by financial and business controls, accounting principles and policies have played a role that has increased greatly in

---

[12] Issue of March 14, 1945, quoted in a letter dated August 3, 1945, from Basil Manly, chairman of the Commission, to Edwin L. Davis, chairman of the Federal Trade Commission.

importance during the past ten years. Accounting has become firmly entrenched as the language of business and of businessmen. Total assets, gross volume, net income—these are among the many terms that accountants have been able to keep within the confines of their art. Accounting terms and the practices they reflect have universal implications and applications, notwithstanding the technical variations among situations in which they are employed.[13] The result has been a series of strong moves both within and without the profession: first, to define and improve accounting terms and standards; and, second, to use accounting as the basis not merely for interpretation but for action as well.[14] The rapid growth in the use of accounting as a basis for action has often dismayed and confused accountants themselves, particularly public accountants, who have been all too conscious of the shortcomings of their art: the discrepancies between principles and practice; and the not infrequent absence of principles altogether, accompanied by the cheerful if not always consistent and qualified certification by themselves and their fellows of widely opposing practices. What is more, formal statements of principles often lag far behind practice.

Cost has commanded the attention of accountants for many years.[15] The recent pronouncements by the Federal Power Commission and the Supreme Court appear to the writer and to many of his fellow practitioners as a natural outgrowth of this extended consideration. In the 20's much reliance was attached by business enterprise to appraisals of properties and their expression on the books of account and in financial statements. There was a good deal of magic in appraisals, for they were often the basis for new loans, and, in the case of utilities, higher rates. Economists there were who justified appraisals as lessening the distinction between "mere accounting"[16] and cherished notions of "value," but these same economists have been wholly uncritical of the method of obtaining the result in individual cases; their continued presence in regulatory bodies has been a factor in protracting the use of present-value concepts to this day. In June, 1938, the executive committee of the American Accounting Association, in a

---

[13] "We cannot refuse to use the only available tools because they are imperfect; we must recognize their value and their limitations and seek to improve them...the era of accounting has arrived." George O. May, "Accounting in the Light of Recent Supreme Court Decisions," *Journal of Accountancy*, Vol. 77 p. 375 (1944).

[14] During the war accounting was the basis for decisions, controls, and actions of an amazingly wide variety. Cf. E. L. Kohler and W. W. Cooper, "Costs, Prices and Profits: Accounting in the War Program," ACCOUNTING REVIEW, July, 1945, pp. 267–308.

[15] The writer, for example, in 1931 participated in an informal panel discussion of "original cost" as a possible basis of valuation for any type of business enterprise. The occasion was an annual meeting of the American Society of Certified Public Accountants. Interest in the subject at that time was prompted by the collapse of the Insull empire and its overstuffed balance sheets. One of the conclusions drawn at the end of the panel discussion was that adherence to depreciated original cost or less on books of account and in reorganizations would have an important influence in discouraging inflation.

[16] A phrase which seems to be persistently employed by those who fear the consequences that will follow the "oversimplification" of economic concepts.

"Statement of Accounting Principles" strongly advocated the adoption of a basic cost principle for all accounting;[17] this was followed in 1940 by a statement of the Committee on Accounting Procedure of the American Institute of Accountants that "any attempt to make property accounts in general reflect current values is both impracticable and inexpedient."[18]

The reasons for this trend are not difficult to find. Assumptions made by appraisers who compute costs of reproduction are always so unreal that the assumptions, if revealed to the reader of financial statements, would largely if not wholly offset the impression of value increment which it is the purpose of enhanced figures to convey. Another reason is that costs are the only "value" that can be understood with any certainty by stockholders, and it is primarily from the stockholders' point of view that financial statements are prepared. Finally, there is a growing feeling that costs must be kept as low as possible in order to keep the business on the favorable side of the competitive picture. The lower the asset valuations, the lower the price to consumers; and the lower the price to consumers, the larger the sales volume and the more stable the net profit for stockholders—objectives now recognized as necessary to the successful operation of any business enterprise. These objectives have in some measure been reflected in the operations of the power industry, as already pointed out.

Another trend has been in the direction of eliminating intangibles, which has taken two forms: the amortization of existing intangibles and the avoidance, whenever possible, of new intangibles. It was once the custom, when a business enterprise changed hands or was reorganized, to issue capital stock having a par or stated value in excess of the book value of net assets, to call the difference "goodwill," and to regard the intangible as a permanent fixture on the balance sheet. With the recognition that goodwill in its usual form is represented to be the discounted value of future excess earnings, has come the conviction that it should be charged off over the periods to which such earnings are ascribed, that after a few years following the purchase of goodwill, the goodwill then existing is dependent on factors of comparatively recent origin, and that the goodwill factors originally present have largely disappeared.[19] Further, in the purchase of a business enterprise as a whole, there has been a declining emphasis on the worth and transferability of any excess earning power. The hazards inherent in estimating future prices, and the urge from various quarters to lower prices in order to add solidity to the operational foundation have had the effect of minimizing goodwill transactions.

More attention has recently been given to depreciation rates and depreciation reserves. At one time the feeling persisted that any measure of depreciation was at best a rough guess—a bookkeeping device which

---

17 ACCOUNTING REVIEW, Vol. 11, p. 103. The principle was reiterated in the Association's reissued "Statement of Principles" in 1941; see ACCOUNTING REVIEW, Vol. 16, p. 134.

18 *Accounting Research Bulletin No. 5,* p. 37.

19 Paton, *Advanced Accounting* (New York: The Macmillan Co., 1941), p. 409.

warranted the time of management only when not agreed to by the Bureau of Internal Revenue. This has been followed more recently by the development of methods by which the adequacy of depreciation rates and reserves may be tested. Group or composite straight-line-depreciation methods have become almost universal. The standard of depreciation procedure in commercial enterprises has required the application of composite straight-line rates which may be compared with those developed elsewhere in industry and changed when experience indicates the accumulation of a reserve that is too large or too small. The adjustment has been usually limited, however, to the alteration of the future rate, leaving the over- or under-provided-for reserve for the moment undisturbed. Under the newer procedure, retirements, less salvage, are charged in full against the reserve. Reserve balances now tend to reach their theoretical 50 per cent level in relation to the assets against which they apply, although remaining at 35–40 per cent in expanding enterprises. The war has increased many reserves to as much as 80 per cent of asset cost; many plants having doubtful utility in peacetime have been depreciated 100 per cent. It may be that reserves will be found to be excessive in war plants which continue to be useful. Consumers in some instances are certain to benefit from lower prices.

These trends in commercial accounting have doubtless had the effect of stimulating better standards of performance in the electric-utility industry, and they both explain and fortify the efforts of the Federal Power Commission in seeking more intelligible property accounts.

The Commission's Accounting Policies

For its extension of the cost principle, now so well established in accounting practice, to transactions of predecessor or affiliated companies, the Federal Power Commission has been compelled to face such attacks as those appearing at the beginning of this paper. The specific charges have been that the Commission has violated "generally accepted accounting principles" and has set up in their place an arbitrary "formula." "Management," says Mr. Dohr, "cannot exercise sound judgement in the operation of a public utility if the accounting rules are laid down by an outside agency for some special purpose.... [Management] must determine what is desirable for purposes of finance, taxation, replacement of obsolete equipment, etc. The accounts must be kept accordingly."[20] Why these purposes would not be served as well or even better by the "rules" of the Commission, Mr. Dohr does not state. Like critics of the Commission, Mr. Dohr entertains dire forebodings when he contemplates the upsetting effect of the Commission's controls over accounts.

If it were not for accounts 100.5 and 107 and their disposition, the accounting profession would probably have remained silent and wholly

---

[20] Dohr, *loc. cit.,* p. 22.

complaisant, since recent decisions and regulations have so greatly extended the importance of accounting and accountants. The violence of the reactions of a number of prominent accountants has, however, raised questions as to the nature of the motives that lie behind the Commissions' actions. To the writer these motives seem to have been derived from some such approach as the following.[21]

(1) During the 20's the financial practices of public utility holding companies were completely out of hand; accounting followed fantastic standards—standards that would be damned today by numerous groups, including the holding companies themselves. Fixed-asset values in dozens of cases investigated at the end of the decade by the Federal Trade Commission were found to be based on the par or stated amount of capital stock, which was always greatly in excess of their cost; or values had been increased almost at will by management, with resultant surpluses absorbed by stock dividends; and there had been wild scrambles on the part of the holding companies to buy up independents, often ending with cash purchases of fixed assets at prices amounting to several times their cost.[22] Only one or two of the holding companies and their subsidiaries escaped the mad rush in the direction of fixed-asset inflation. In its report to the Congress, after a five-year investigation, the Federal Trade Commission recommended drastic remedies and the establishment of a Federal agency to cope with the problem, with broad powers to fix a basis of accounting for that portion of the industry engaged in interstate business. The Congress followed the recommendation, and the Federal Power Act of 1935[23] and the Public Utility Holding Company Act of 1935[24] were the consequences. From the beginning, therefore, the Federal Power Commission has been charged with the responsibility of untangling and recasting the industry's grotesque valuations and valuation methods, and of establishing a simpler basis for accounting, reporting, and rate making.

(2) Investors, as well as the utility companies themselves, have been on notice since the commencement of the Trade Commission's investigation that a day of reckoning was approaching. Many companies quickly complied with the Commission's rules and regulations as they were issued, recognizing that their goodwill in the community was dependent on the elimination from their financial set-ups of speculative values and swollen equities of stockholders. The gradual, often voluntary, reduction in electric rates throughout the country during the last fifteen years, and the steady improvement by the industry of its financial practices and position, as noted above, testify

---

21 It should be emphasized that these are the writer's surmises, not necessarily the views of the Commission.

22 Further examples appear in the series of reports issued from 1928 to 1935 by the Federal Trade Commission; a brief analysis and comment from the point of view of the accountant was made by the writer in an editorial in the ACCOUNTING REVIEW, Vol. 7, p. 301 (1932).

23 49 Stat. 838.

24 Administered by the Securities and Exchange Commission.

to its awareness of the public demand for reform. The many recapitalizations downward, made necessary by the elimination of imaginary values and the insufficiency of capital surplus and earned surplus, have thus been necessary, long-postponed, deflationary acts.

(3) Value appreciation, even though reflected in arm's-length transfers of utility properties for cash, or for capital stock having or not having a market value, is always difficult and in most cases impossible to prove on an objective basis. The writer has had occasion to examine a large number of appraisal and engineering reports on utility valuations, and to discuss with appraisers, and engineers the methods they have followed in obtaining reproduction costs and present values. Many of their assumptions involve what are commonly referred to by accountants as intangibles: the greater worth of an asset as a part of a coordinated and functioning plant; the price of materials and the cost of labor at rates or in amounts which no prudent operator would consider paying; the use of general price indices having no application to the community in which the property is located; contractor's profit on construction undertaken by the utility itself; overhead containing many elements and allowances approved at different times and under different conditions by various state regulatory commissions; capitalized excess earnings of an "efficient" plant, combination, or use of an asset or group of assets; in short, value increments that would never be incurred in practice by a management which had regard for the interests of investors and consumers. When such increments are stripped from the valuation report, cost of reproduction is not infrequently found to be no more than original cost—sometimes even less, since the deterrents which hindsight suggests cannot be applied to current transactions. In time, the Commission may develop standards for prudent construction costs which, if applied to past extravagant outlays or projects undertaken and completed without adequate supervision, might well raise serious questions as to the validity of a significant portion of original costs. Accountants who have criticized the Commission have apparently been unaware of the nature of such costs and of appraisals whose purpose so often is to justify profits to promoters as a part of the rate base. Even the Supreme Court, relying in past years on many an appraisal report to sustain a high rate base, seldom stopped seriously to question the assumptions of the value-makers.

(4) Although particular items of equipment may cost more today than when originally purchased, there seems to be no reason why such an increase in price should be assumed to have any relation to the present costs of the individual enterprise which has paid a lower price. To the asset's owner the price increase has significance only in pointing out the possibility that more money may have to be retained in the business for replacement. Every manager knows that when the time for replacement comes, a cheaper or more efficient substitute may be available, or perhaps the replacement may be avoided altogether. Replacement of exactly the same type of asset is a rarity, particularly if price changes may have the effect of bringing

about a different return on the investment. The revaluation of an asset or of a plant attempts to give reality to events that never occurred and to events that never could occur simultaneously except in the mind of an appraiser. In actual business life, assets are acquired at different times and under different conditions; and management, investors, and consumers alike know the meaning of varying costs, and the effects costs are prone to have on rates when they tend to move in the same direction for any protracted length of time. Fortunate indeed for all three interests is the utility that can ride through a period of high prices without purchasing major items of new equipment. No basic economic reason seems to warrant contributions by the ratepayer to the investor during such a period, however.

(5) Without the leavening effect of competition, a business enterprise such as a public utility tends to neglect its customers. Regulatory bodies fill the gap. They superimpose accounting and other policies on management, just as corporation laws sometimes do. Their purpose is to see that the best possible deal is given ratepayers. This necessitates a fair deal also to investors, else an adequate supply of capital will not be available and the capital now invested in the industry will be withdrawn. But the fairest deal for both interests is to cut out inflation and return to the simple basis of costs. No harm has been done to investors, since they have been expecting capital reductions and have even looked forward to the day when a fully stabilized valuation policy of cost will lend a larger degree of certainty and security to their holdings. Public-utility securities should then have the lowest yields in their history; the investment risk will have been minimized; there will be no lack of capital available for refunding and new financing; and the market price of a utility security will tend to remain at its original selling price. Investors have more confidence in utilities under strict regulations than in those subject to the hazards of speculation and promoters' profits.[25]

(6) One of the chief virtues of the prudent-investment theory long advocated by Justice Brandeis is the unity it gives to valuation for capitalization, accounting, reporting, taxation, and rate making. If the public interest is to be regarded as paramount, the theory cannot be

---

[25] A good example may be found in the interest rates which are now being paid by the more than 80 municipal power departments in the TVA area. Although these obligations are income bonds and are not secured either by a mortgage or by the municipalities' taxing power, 20 public refinancings during the fiscal year ended June 30, 1944 (the latest year for which statistics are available) reduced interest rates from an average of 2.67 to 1.69 per cent, or more than one-third, and most of these issues are currently selling at a premium. Municipal-bond dealers in Chicago who have participated as underwriters in these refinancings have frequently stated to the writer that a plentiful supply of capital will always be available for publicly or privately owned projects under rigid government regulation, particularly when the borrower is pledged to follow the conservative financial policy involved in an original-cost-less-straight-line-depreciation basis for accounting, reporting, and rate-making.

adopted in part. Freezing valuations[26] before a certain date is a poor remedy, for in fairness to more conservative organizations each member of the industry should be permitted a revaluation as at that date; for if that were done, all the questions of padded, nonobjective valuations would again be raised. Less risk to investors would be incurred by excluding from the common base every element of increment above original cost. Whatever portion of the current market price of a security may be imputed to the hope for a return on something exceeding original cost will be more than compensated for by a secure, nonspeculative rate base. The investor, of course, takes the risk that the venture will fail in whole or in part; but, under the present and any conceivable future policies of the Commission, that risk will recede to the vanishing point, with rates attuned to straight-line depreciation and the recovery of unforeseen losses.

(7) No violation of accounting principles occurs when the Commission's rule of "original cost" is applied. The Commission is still adhering to cost, notwithstanding its denial of the validity of a portion of a subsequent sales, or other write-up, figure, once the asset has been put to public use. In many cases accrued depreciation, properly computed, would reduce the acquisition cost to original cost or lower, and the net figure is still commonly referred to by accountants as cost. In other instances, extraordinary obsolescence may justify the write-down of an original cost figure, the reduced amount also being commonly referred to by accountants as cost. The Commission, imposing a policy on the management, may very properly require that a write-up be eliminated, as in the *Northwestern* case[27], in which a utility was compelled to amortize gradually an intangible created by the issue of common capital stock. Each year, until the intangible had been completely eliminated, the company was required to apply against the intangible the annual net income remaining after preferred-stock dividends. The Court lightly brushed aside the objection raised in a brief filed by the American Institute of Accountants that the Court's approval of this method of disposal "would have a detrimental effect on all accounting." The only detrimental effect implied by the brief was that an accounting principle would be violated. Yet the principle itself—that a write-up[28]

---

[26] Freezing old original costs, as the Commission has done, appears to be a reasonable modification of the basic principles laid down by Justice Brandeis, who would have excluded cost elements that would not have been incurred by a prudent management. Lack of records has made it necessary, however, to start with the cost to the first person employing an asset in the public service, notwithstanding the possible inclusion in such costs of intangibles and other items of doubtful propriety.

[27] *Northwestern Electric Company and American Power & Light Company vs. Federal Power Commission,* 321 U. S. 119 (1935).

[28] Henry A. Horne, chairman of the Institute's Committee on Public-Utility Accounting, in a communication relating to the same case and addressed to the chairman of the Federal Commission in January, 1943, sought to limit the term "write-up" to valuation changes accompanied by credits to surplus. In conventional usage, however, "write-up" means any amount added to the cost of an asset which does not involve a physical change in the asset.

ought to be eliminated from the books—was only half-heartedly accepted by the Institute's counsel. In fact, he quoted an authority as opposing it, but a careful reading of the authority indicates that he was dealing with stock discount, not an intangible created by a stock write-up, and his recommendation was that the discount be retained on the books for record purposes and that it be subtracted on a published balance sheet from the related stock issued.[29] The brief then attacked the opinion of the Commission's chief accountant "that the Commission would be fully justified from the standpoint of accounting principles in ordering the amount written off or disposed of at once," but that "policy" might "call for spreading the amount over a reasonable period of years in the future," the attack presumably resting on the assumption that the two statements quoted are in conflict with each other. Actually, there is no conflict. The principle, at least as the chief accountant stated it, asserts the need for the elimination of the write-up, not the method of elimination: a statement with which most accountants should readily agree, since all fixed assets except land are subject to depreciation. An immediate write-off or a write-off over a series of years becomes a matter of policy, within the framework of the principle. Many accounting principles have been thus variously applied.[30]

(8) Accountants make frequent use of the expression "generally accepted accounting principle" in objecting to the Commission's write-off of what it regards as inflation. The generally accepted accounting principle referred to is that cost, or fair value at the time assets are acquired in an exchange, should govern accounting entries and thereafter accounting reports. The rule was intended, however, for commercial enterprises, in which management restraint, induced by the compulsion of remaining in a competitive market, establishes a natural deterrent to excessive valuations. No such deterrent exists in public utilities, and it thus appears that a modified principle is essential for such organizations. The Commission's definition of original cost has already had the effect of establishing a new principle, and the new principle has for many years been recognized by professional accountants who, in reporting on the financial statements of public utilities, have always disclosed any failure to comply with the Commission's requirements as to fixed-asset analysis, valuation, and depreciation. Compliance, on the other hand, has invariably been followed by the omission of such

[29] Paton, *op. cit.*, p. 506–9. The reason that the discount should be retained in the records, according to Professor Paton, is to indicate the obligation of the stockholder to the corporation for the full amount of his subscription. In the *Northwestern* case, however, the common stock was presumably "fully paid" despite the conditions of its issue; at least there was no suggestion that an alternative would have been the creation of an unpaid-subscriptions account. Further, the Company's contention was that it should be permitted to continue to show the write-up as "actual asset value."

[30] See "Accounting Principles Underlying Corporate Financial Statements," prepared by the executive committee of the American Accounting Association, in the ACCOUNTING REVIEW, Vol. XVI, p. 133 (1941), wherein each *principle* is followed by a series of applications.

comments. Whether or not the disclosure or its omission conforms with pronouncements the American Institute of Accountants has made on the subject of "principles," what accountants have actually done, and done deliberately over a period of time, appears to offer more realistic evidence of the principles they are observing. What is more, private opinion among public accountants closely associated with the annual audits of utility enterprises should leave no doubt as to the "generally accepted accounting principle" involved. Their beliefs, as expressed to the writer, are reflected in their reports.

(9) The Congress did not impose on the Commission a formula requiring the use in rate cases of values other than cost or depreciated cost; it imposed only the duty of determining "just and reasonable rates." In the Natural Gas Act, for example, it permits but does not require the Commission to "investigate and ascertain...when found necessary for rate-making purposes...the fair value" of property, thus seemingly leaving to the Commission's discretion the admission or exclusion of evidence relating to reproduction cost or present value. On the other hand, the refusal of the Congress to commit itself to the prudent-investment theory during its consideration of the Natural Gas Act of 1938 does not mean that it rejected the exclusive application of that theory should the Commission so elect. It simply referred the whole task of valuation to the Commission without any restriction.

(10) In the Montana case,[31] a number of professional accountants, in testifying for the company, brought out clearly the lack of principles and standards among accountants in interpreting the meaning of "value" at the time of an exchange of assets for stock. The witnesses indicated their approval of recorded amounts at the time of the transfer, with but superficial evidence in support of figures in excess of original cost. They indicated no distinctions between the judgments that should be applied to the paid-in values of utilities, particularly in transactions between affiliates,[32] and those of competitive commercial enterprises. To one familiar with the subject matter developed during the investigation of the Federal Trade Commission, it seems all too obvious that, prior to the enactment of the 1935 legislation, the appearance of arm's-length transactions between either affiliates or unrelated companies more often than not gave no clue to their real meaning, and that to accept them unquestioningly at their face value would surely defeat the purposes for which the Federal Power Commission was established—that purpose being to rid the industry of its existing write-ups and to see to it that no more of them occurred. If at times the remedy

---

[31] In the matter of Montana Power Company, Docket No. IT-5825, Opinion No. 120 (February, 1945).

[32] Paton would put the transactions of affiliates on the same basis as those of independent parties. "Transactions between Affiliates," ACCOUNTING REVIEW, Vol. XX, p. 256. He gives no weight to consumer interest in such transactions.

adopted has seemed a bit too drastic, especially when the significance of transactions has been dimmed by age, it should be recalled that the evils which the 1935 legislation sought to correct were so widespread as to be almost universal, and that, at the same time, the practical effects of applying the remedy will not be found to be so severe as at first supposed.

The practical judgment that may follow a review of the Commission's actions, if, indeed, the writer's surmises reflect with any accuracy the approach of the Commission to the accounting problem with which it has had to deal during the first ten years of its existence, can be expressed thus: The Commission has given ample evidence that it understands accounting, even though it does not exhibit reverence for the pronouncements on accounting principles which have been issued from time to time by the American Institute of Accountants and certain of its members. It has demonstrated its courage and persistence in the efforts it has made to purge write-ups from utility accounts. It has succeeded in inaugurating an "era of accounting" by removing ratemaking from the obscurities and myths[33] of an esoteric "valuation" process and placing it in the clear light of original cost less depreciation.[34] By that act it has imposed on accounting and accountants a much larger responsibility than they have faced before. It has understood well its social objectives—and management, investor, and consumer have each profited from its activities thus far. The objectors to and the harsh critics of the Commission have had their say, but the Commission has been firm in its convictions and has successfully resisted their attacks. Our economic system has not crumbled in the process, and the Commission has given no evidence that it means to do other than its utmost to preserve that system.

Some Defects
in the Uniform System

In must not be inferred from this seeming extollation that the Commission has been without fault. Now, after nine years' experience with the uniform system of accounts and the annual reports based on the system, the Commission should make some needed changes. One should be to omit the allowance of interest on construction which, over the seven-year period

---

33 Such as those voiced by Justice Jackson in his dissenting opinion in the *Hope* case, footnote 7. It has always appeared to the writer that those jurists, economists, and accountants who defend cost of reproduction or other forms of present value as an accounting or rate base have never made even superficial inquiries into the valuation methods of appraisers. Not a few public accountants have found, however, that a trustful acceptance of an engineer's valuation report does not discharge their responsibility in arriving at an opinion of financial position.

34 Plus, possibly in some instances, unamortized balances of a portion or all of the intangibles remaining in account 100.5. The Commission's policy in this respect has not yet been determined.

previously referred to, has averaged about 2 per cent of interest expense and 1 per cent of net income. In justification it is sometimes said that during a period of construction a portion of the utility's borrowed money is tied up unproductively. But more funds on the average are also tied up in current assets, not temporarily, but permanently; and no one suggests an allowance in the accounts for interest thereon. Again, there is no necessary connection between borrowed funds which have been outstanding for some time and the funds that are used for current construction; the assets of a typical utility, whether liquid or fixed, originate in about equal proportions from long-term obligations, contributions of stockholders, and reinvested earnings and reserves. There may be some justification, in a utility just starting out, for charging interest to construction accounts, but not after the proceeds have been invested. It is a fiction of the first water.

Other unfortunate accounting procedures which the Commission has tolerated are carrying forward as quasi assets: (a) losses from the disposal or destruction of property on which insufficient depreciation has been accumulated; (b) stock discount and expense; (c) discount and expense on refunded issues of stocks and bonds; and (d) securities reacquired. The losses and the discount and expense may eventually be absorbed through high enough rates, and in the end the repurchased securities will be deducted from the liability for issued securities: yet none of these items are assets by any stretch of the imagination, and their presence in the balance sheet distorts whatever meaning may be assigned, for statistical purposes, to balance-sheet totals. Again, three sorts of charges against earned surplus have been permitted: miscellaneous reservations of net income (e.g., provision for sinking-fund reserve), direct debits to earned surplus during the year, and debits direct to the previous year's earned-surplus balance which are not reflected in the current year's surplus analysis. Thus, in the Commission's epitome, "The Financial Record of the Electric Utility Industry, 1937–1943," these amounts for the seven-year period average $3, $92, and $6 millions, respectively, per annum, the total of $101 millions representing what may be a serious overstatement of net income of as much as 20 per cent a year.[35] The details of these surplus charges, many of them undoubtedly write-offs of the sort previously noted, are, however, important enough to be revealed even on a summary statement. Finally, the form of balance sheet needs to be modernized so that it may be more easily understood by the average investor: assets and liabilities arranged in the order of their liquidity, valuation reserves subtracted from the assets to which they relate, capital stock and surplus accounts brought together, standards established for surplus charges and credits, if, indeed, any are to be allowed at all, and so on.

---

[35] P. 8.

DR Scott

ROLE OF ACCOUNTING
IN PUBLIC UTILITY REGULATION

DR Scott *(1887–1954) was born in Missouri, and, except for a brief tour of duty with the* Detroit Times *(1912–14), spent most of his life there. He received an A.B. from the University of Missouri in 1910, and a Ph.D. from Harvard in 1930. He taught at Missouri from 1914 on. He published his* Theory of Accounts *in 1925 and his* Cultural Significance of Accounts *in 1931.*

Scott was especially interested in accounting as a social or cultural force. One aspect of this interest is seen in the attention he pays to ethical norms in his theoretical discussions. Concepts such as truth, justice, and fairness hold the center of the stage. Another aspect is his view of accounting as a control device in economic life. This latter aspect is illustrated by the article reprinted here. Essentially, Scott maintains that the use of accounting in regulation is normal and natural, fitting in perfectly with the role accounting has played over the centuries.

The role of accounting in public utility regulation is merely one aspect of the role of accounting in the broader field of economic control.

Of course, the general development of accounting is a process of evolution which has gone on for many centuries, whereas the use of accounts in public utility regulation is a matter of recent origin. It is, in fact, considerably less than 100 years old. Nevertheless, the use of accounts as a tool of regulation is, in a sense, a forerunner of the current dominant trend in general accounting.

Our procedure in the present discussion will be to consider first, public utility regulation and some of the accounting problems associated with it. On the basis of that discussion we shall turn to the broader problem of

Reprinted from *The Accounting Review* (July, 1947), pp. 227–40, by permission.

general economic control in the expectation that the broader view will help us to appraise better the place of accounts in public utility regulation.

Early Regulation

The regulation of public utilities developed as a practical expedient designed to correct certain injustices and abuses which had arisen in the prevailing economic system of competitive control. Economists, students of government, and accountants alike recognized no need for any theoretical adjustments to accompany this practical buttressing of the existing social structure. The responsibility of regulating agencies was essentially negative in character. They were expected to prevent the abuses which had called them into being.

Positively stated, this responsibility of the regulating commission was to enforce competition or, at the very least, achieve by direct regulation the results which would be afforded by effective competition. Economists long had recognized that the market was surrounded and supported by a complex system of laws and conventions. Regulation was intended to be an extension of this underlying support. The regulating commission was to be a kind of dyke on the economic system, guiding and directing the currents of competition. The yardstick to be applied by it clearly was the competitive market and the principles summarizing the market's operations.

Regulation in fact has been quite another matter. It has not followed either the spirit or the theoretical outlook which accompanied its inception. That spirit and that outlook came from the abstract analysis of an idealized individualistic society, whereas regulation has been a practical adjustment worked out in the sphere of concrete, everyday affairs.

As agencies for the realization of justice between the owners and patrons of public utilities, and to prevent discriminations between different patrons, regulating commissions faced immediate and practical situations. The utilities were going concerns with investments already made in operating assets. The primary initial problem was one of setting and enforcing reasonable rates. As a basis for the solution of this problem, commissions turned their attention to the valuation of properties used by the public utilities.

Two theories of valuation promptly developed. These were cost of reproduction, and original cost. The latter, in the course of time, was superseded by the prudent-investment theory which took its name from the fact that it excluded from the rate base costs which could have been avoided by the exercise of reasonable judgment.

The clash of opinions of the supporters of these two schools of thought occupied a prominent place in the early discussions of regulation. The issue, however, has become somewhat less acute as regulation has become more mature.

The essential difference between the two theories is in their treatment of changes in the values of assets in use arising from causes outside the operations of the utilities, such as those from changes in the general price level or from growth of the urban community served by a utility. Under the application of the cost-of-reproduction theory such increases would be included in the rate base. Thereby a higher income would go to the investors or owners. Conversely, a decrease in values would lower the rate base and give owners lower incomes. If the original-cost or prudent-investment theory were used the consumers or users of service would benefit when prices went up by continuing to receive service at rates determined when competitive values were lower. They would pay for this gain, however, by continuing to pay rates based on the cost of assets even when competitive values for such assets had declined.

Under the cost-of-reproduction theory, therefore, the owners stand to gain from increases in the values of assets used and at the same time they bear the risk of losses in such values. For the consumers, this would mean that in each situation they would be paying for the service received a price approximately what they would pay in that situation if the service were being rendered under competitive conditions. Hence, the cost-of-reproduction theory represented an application of the competitive market yardstick which was implicit in the spirit in which regulation was adopted. This fact meant that in the early period of regulation the cost-of-reproduction theory enjoyed a strong initial bias in its favor. The reasons it has not been able to retain this initial advantage will appear in the following discussion.

The Accounting Yardstick

From the start regulating commissions have been heavily dependent upon accounts. Uniform accounting systems for the different classes of utilities have been a basic standard requirement as a minimum starting point in regulation. In their day-to-day decisions, commissions have been concerned with asset values, the determination of what expenditures may properly be capitalized, the disallowance of good will, the approval of certain other intangible assets, the rate of return to be earned, and a host of other problems all running in accounting terms.

To understand why regulating commissions were so dependent upon accounts from the start of their activities we need to go back still further in the evolution of our economic system.

In a thorough-going individualistic society in which economic activities were carried on exclusively by individuals, the market would be the means of adjustment of economic interests as between all of those who resorted to it as buyers and sellers. Such was, in fact, the essential nature of the early market economy. Adam Smith predicted that the corporation would never be an important factor in economic affairs because of the lack of a personal interest in its management. How much mistaken he was needs no demonstration.

When the corporation, operating in the market as a legal person, became large and relatively complex, various groups of interests developed within it. In the very nature of the situation the market could make no distinction between those interests which were internal to the business unit. The variety of such internal interests has become still greater with the appearance of supercorporate units in the form of holding-company organizations.

Inability of the market to adjust conflicts of economic interests internal to the business unit has necessitated a resort to other agencies of adjustment and control. In general, the task of supplying this necessary supplement to the market method of adjusting economic interests has been assigned to accounting. Beginning with the problems of partnership accounting, even before the advent of the modern corporation, it has been an ever-growing responsibility.

As the corporation has become larger and much more complex in its organization and activities, the stockholders have been excluded from any effective participation in its control. In the first place, they have become too numerous and too widely distributed geographically for any considerable portion of them to assemble for even an annual meeting. But more important still, is the fact that the problems of management of such an enterprise have become so technical and complex that the stockholders would be quite helpless even if they could be assembled in an annual meeting.

The failure of stockholders' control has brought with it a corresponding breakdown of control by directors. Control of the so-called annual meeting of stockholders by the officers of the company has meant in fact that the directors have come to be selected by the officers. At the same time, even general policies of such enterprises have become so much a matter of technical administration that the outside directors frequently have found themselves as completely dependent upon the judgment of the officers as stockholders would be. The resulting tendency has been for the board of directors to become a rubber stamp in the hands of the officers of the company. The fact that some large companies have been compelled to reduce the legal quorum for directors' meetings to a minor fraction of the board's membership is an index of this trend.

This concentration of power in the hands of the management of large business enterprise has highlighted the growing responsibility of accounting and the accounting profession. The way in which the accounts of a large corporation are kept has long since become a matter of vital interest to stockholders. And since this includes potential as well as actual present stockholders, it means that the question is one of vital public concern. In consequence, practicing accountants are called upon to certify that the published statements of corporations have been arrived at by keeping records in accordance with the accepted principles and practices of accounting.

The purpose of this somewhat commonplace analysis has been to show how accounting has become a yardstick by which the conduct of business enterprise is measured and controlled. Accounting has become as much a part of the social and legal machinery of economic control as is the market itself. And, while the *de jure* status of the regulation of public utilities was in its initial stages tied up with the competitive market yardstick, the *de facto* practices of regulating authorities have always been more closely tied up with the increasingly important accounting yardstick. It should be pointed out also that while the cost-of-reproduction theory of valuation of assets has represented an application of the competitive market principle, the original-cost or prudent-investment theory has, with equal aptness, fitted in with the accounting basis of control.

Some Accounting Problems

When regulating commissions turned to accounting for help, they often added to their difficulties even while arriving at workable decisions on the particular cases in hand. Because accounting had developed as a tool of private business enterprise, its outlook and its rules did not always meet the needs of a regulation commission.

One of the immediate problems confronting regulating authorities was the problem of depreciation. How ready accountants were to help with the problem is indicated by the fact that after nearly three-quarters of a century of regulation, accountants are not yet agreed upon a definition of depreciation. In fact, the action of regulating commissions was one of the factors which helped to standardize the accounting practice of allowing for depreciation before arriving at a statement of profits available for dividends.

Early in regulation there developed the concept of a value level of depreciable assets in use at a point halfway between the cost new and composite scrap value. This is the point around which the depreciated value of the group of assets would fluctuate after the plant passed the initial period of declination from cost new, assuming the use of the straight-line method. This concept has exercised an influence in the field of regulation which is out of proportion to its real merit. It has been a significant factor in the thinking of those who have been charged with regulating authority but its more important contribution has been in the promotion of controversy. One of the controversies which it has promoted has been over the question whether or not straight-line depreciation is excessive.

The period of public utility regulation has been one in which accounting has made rapid progress in the direction of more accurate methods of accounting for costs. It would be illogical to expect precision in accounting for a newly recognized cost like depreciation before we had achieved a high level of accuracy in cost determination generally. Undoubtedly in the vast majority of cases in which the straight-line method has been used by accountants, its use has been justified by the fact that the different inaccuracies involved in it have come within the general margin of error of cost determination. It would be a waste of effort to attempt meticulous accuracy in figuring depreciation cost when other costs are not determined with a comparable degree of precision. But as cost methods generally improve we can expect a corresponding attention to increasing the accuracy of depreciation cost. That we have not yet achieved even a reasonable degree of precision in depreciation accounting is indicated by the report on depreciation of the American Institute Committee on Terminology.

The question whether straight-line depreciation is excessive is meaningless when stated as an abstract proposition. Applied to groups of some kinds of assets the straight-line method would give too little depreciation rather than too much. The turbines in a hydroelectric plant, a machine used exclusively to produce a style good, a dairy cow, and an airplane engine depreciate in strikingly different ways. To apply a single method of calculating depreciation to all of them would be very crude accounting.

If a given enterprise makes use of a large volume of assets which require large investments of capital, have relatively long useful lives, and require relatively small expenditures for repairs, it should select a method of calculating depreciation which will take these basic conditions into account. If at the same time such an enterprise uses relatively small amounts of labor and raw materials, its capital costs, including depreciation expenses, will make up a correspondingly large proportion of its total operating costs, and a premium is thereby placed upon the accurate determination of operating costs which are associated with the capital used. Such an enterprise should use a method of calculating depreciation which takes into account the effect of interest upon depreciation.

Whether or not the straight-line method will result in excessive depreciation in public utility accounting depends upon the kind of assets used by the public utility. A public utility enterprise should not be limited to the use of any one method. Business enterprises, both inside and outside of the public utility field, should adapt their methods of calculating depreciation to the types of assets to which the methods are to be applied. They will do so increasingly as the standards of accuracy achieved in accounting practice are raised.

Likewise, regulating authorities, in their valuations for rate-making purposes, should assume the use of methods appropriate to the assets of regulated companies.

Should Reserves be Deducted in Arriving at a Rate Base?

In the valuation of assets, as a basis for rate making, should reserves for depreciation be deducted or should the assets used be included at an undepreciated valuation? The controversy over this question has been due largely to the uncertainty of accounting authority on the problem of depreciation.

It has been argued that a public utility property does not depreciate so long as it is kept in condition to render a constant volume of service. The argument is invalid. A new plant is worth more than an old plant because the new plant enjoys a period in which replacements are fewer than they will ever be again on account of the fact that it starts out with all assets new. If $500,000 is spent in replacing an asset in a public utility property, it would be foolish to say that the operating assets are worth no more after the expenditure than they were before. One might just as well say that a new asset is worth no more than one which is at the point of being scrapped.

Our discussion of this topic will be clarified if we make the artificial assumption of a public utility enterprise which is called upon to render a constant volume of services without either growth or loss of patronage. Let us assume that its necessary plant cost $10,000,000. At no time after the original construction of the plant will all of the assets be new at the same time. And the depreciated value of the assets in use will not be a constant figure. When replacements are relatively few, they will not offset accruing depreciation, and the trend of the total depreciated value of the plant will be downward. When replacements are more than enough to offset accruing depreciation, the trend of the depreciated value will be upward. The point around which these changes in value will fluctuate will be determined by the composite scrap value for the plant, the amount of nondepreciable assets, and the rate of interest used in methods which call for a rate of interest.

Let us suppose that in the above case, after the passing of the initial period, fluctuations are around a mean point of $7,000,000, reaching at the maximum $8,000,000 and at the minimum $6,000,000. Under these circumstances, what should be the rate base upon which the owners should be allowed to earn a reasonable rate of return? The answer to this question is $8,000,000.

Still holding to our assumptions of an original investment of $10,000,000 and a constant volume of operations, let us assume that at a given time the utility shows a depreciated value of properties in use of $7,000,000 and $3,000,000 of invested reserve funds which are earning on the average 3%. Of the reserve funds, $1,000,000 may properly be considered as part of the investment in the enterprise, since they will be needed to help finance replacements when they again run ahead of accruing depreciation. However, the other $2,000,000 of reserve funds are not needed in the business and could be returned to the owners. If the reasonable rate of return were 7%, consumers could, with propriety, be charged rates which would afford 7% upon the depreciated value of assets used, plus enough to bring the 3% upon $1,000,000 of necessary reserve funds up to 7%. However, it would not be equitable to ask consumers to subsidize the investment return upon the $2,000,000 of reserve funds not needed in the enterprise.

In actual practice, the problem of returning capital to the owners does not arise because depreciation funds are used to finance the growth of the business. The usual practice of competitive business may be followed. It is to keep no invested depreciation funds but to follow the more profitable course of investing the funds in the business itself. If this course is followed, the proper rate base is still the maximum depreciated value of assets in use. Our conclusion, therefore is that reserves are deductible only down to the point of the maximum depreciated value of assets in use.

Interest Foregone During Construction

One of the problems of regulation in which accounting has not been very helpful is the treatment of intangible assets. This was inevitable in view of the traditional accounting treatment of intangibles.

By ruling out monopoly profits, regulating commissions have disposed of the problem of good will in the ordinary sense. However, they have been compelled to recognize the propriety of including in the rate base various costs which do not result in the acquisition of tangible assets. For example, during the initial period necessary to build up the business to a profitable basis, they have allowed the capitalization of costs which in later periods of operation must be charged to expense. Among the costs capitalized under regulation but not under general accounting practice is one which constitutes what might be called an intangible element in the value of a tangible asset. This is interest foregone on owner's capital during a period of construction.

Suppose, for example, that a utility constructed a building at an out-of-pocket cost of $300,000, and that a reasonable allowance for interest foregone while the capital was tied up in the building during construction, was $15,000.

How should this item of $15,000 be entered in the accounting record? Under the influence of conventional accounting, the Interstate Commerce Commission sets up a special account for such charges. If the charge were included in the cost of the building, it would be spread over the life of the building as part of the depreciation charge. In the case of initial construction, a rational analysis of the situation and conservatism would both suggest closing the credit item to capital surplus as part of the investment put into the enterprise.

Let us suppose further with regard to the above case that the $15,000 was charged to the building; that at the end of its life the building was depreciated to zero; that a wrecking company removed it for the salvage; and that a new building was constructed under the same conditions as the first one. On these terms, depreciation during the life of the old building will have made available $315,000, and the new building will be placed on the books at $315,000. The credit item, "Interest Foregone During Reconstruction," may properly be closed to income rather than to capital surplus since funds to match it have been made available by the depreciation charges on the old building.

If the interest-foregone cost were charged to a special account and not amortized over the life of the asset, we would find ourselves accumulating additions to the special account and to capital surplus each time the asset was reconstructed. This would make it appear necessary to sink an additional investment of interest foregone in the enterprise each time such an asset was rebuilt.

Charging interest foregone to the depreciable asset, therefore, would accomplish three different things, as follows;

1. It would afford a more accurate costing of operations in which the asset was used.
2. It would permit the treatment of "Interest Foregone During Reconstruction" as an income and thereby would help to relieve the financial stress of reconstruction periods.
3. It would avoid a spurious capitalization of interest foregone costs.

If an asset were replaced at a higher cost with a consequent larger cost of interest foregone, the excess interest-foregone cost should be added to capital surplus.

The Experimental Character of Regulation

It is not the purpose of this discussion to present an account of the positive and indispensable contributions of accounting to the process of regulation. The foregoing problems have been presented, not as typical of the role played by accounts but as illustrative of ways in which halting and uncertain accounting practice and theory have helped to keep regulation equally uncertain and tentative.

Another factor in the situation which has helped to keep regulation tentative and experimental is the wise refusal of the Supreme Court to give exclusive approval of any one theory of valuation. A different course by the Court might well have led to a doctrinaire regulation running in much less flexible terms.

Still another factor which has made for uncertainty has been the wholly opportunistic policies of the utilities and the representatives of consumers. They have not hesitated to espouse one theory of valuation when prices were rising and an opposing theory when prices were falling.

Regulation has been highly experimental in fact, even if it has not been so in the conscious actions of those who have administered it. The greatest factor in the preservation of its experimental character has been the fact that regulation has proved to be in practice something different from what it was thought to be by those who introduced it and from what was implicit in the public opinion which sanctioned it.

In the beginning it was generally assumed that the regulation of public utilities applied to a very small segment of our economy, called the natural monopolies. Because of special conditions under which they operated, competition could not be depended upon to control those natural monopolies. Hence, regulating commissions were set up to fix rates and protect consumers from exploitation, while allowing the investors or owners a reasonable rate of return on their capital. The standard for the reasonable rate of return to be allowed, quite naturally, was drawn from the larger economic area in which profits were still regulated by competition.

This conception of regulation was due to the fact that regulation was set up to apply to going enterprises with investments already made in operating assets. Practical experience, however, soon disclosed that the regulation of free enterprise capital in public utilities did not focus on the rate of return on investment. If regulation were liberal, that is, favorable to investors, capital tended to flow into the regulated enterprise until returns on it were comparable to those in competitive enterprise. If regulation were strict, and rates were set too low, the regulated industry was starved and stunted because capital went elsewhere. Consequently, the focal point of regulation became the problem of determining the proper development of the regulated industry. This is a much more positive and constructive responsibility than is contained in the initial conception of regulation. It also is a problem which cannot be answered by an appeal to the competitive market.

Not only has public utility regulation changed from a negative and restrictive outlook to one which is positive and constructive; at the same time it has been extended over more lines of activity. The early natural monopolies have given way to a broader conception of "business affected with a public interest." And more recently the question has been raised as to whether all big business is not affected with a public interest.

Government Regulation in General

The regulation of public utilities has been followed by many other forms of government regulation. All of these forms of regulation, in one respect at least, have followed the pattern set in the public utility field. The logic of circumstances, implicit in the problems confronting them, has compelled those in charge of the regulation to move in the direction of more positive responsibilities and a more positive control. An examination of the discussions leading to the adoption of the Federal Reserve System in the first Wilson administration discloses that many of those who were supporting the change believed they were merely improving the machinery of a system of competitive control in the field of banking. Those in charge of the system have been slow to recognize or admit the positive character of their responsibility. Nevertheless, the administrative policies of a central bank do not subordinate themselves to the competitive market. The central bank is not primarily a money-making institution.

Government regulation of our economic system is not confined to the work of administrative boards and commissions. Antitrust legislation adopted by Congress and enforced by the courts exhibits a change of policy which is not unlike the trend in regulation by commissions. When the Supreme Court adopted the rule of reason by which it allowed good trusts to continue because they had not indulged in bad practices, its action was a concession to the trend towards large-scale business enterprise. It held that mere bigness was not a violation of the law, even though the big enterprise had come to dominate the market which it served. This concession to current economic facts was made at the expense of the principle of market control. It received the sanction of popular opinion.

As a people, we are proud of the bigness of our economy which performs miracles of production every year. We are proud and jealous of the high standard of living which we enjoy. We associate the bigness of our economy and the abundance which it affords with the bigness of individual business organizations. And rightly so. Our present-day economy could not have been achieved by the mere multiplication of little businesses.

If our robust economy bursts out of its harness (consisting of the rules of the game developed back in the horse-and-buggy period) we undertake to mend the break by putting in a stronger part—a stay chain for a broken leather tug. We prefer results to the preservation of a nice set of harness. We believe in progress anyway. Such is the spirit which lies back of our frequent resort to regulation.

The Depression and the War

In the depression crisis of the last decade, the Federal government used its power and its credit to furnish relief on a large scale in order to prevent widespread suffering. This action had the support of a large majority of the people in spite of the fact that it reversed a long standing principle of basic law which forbade the use of public funds for the benefit of private individuals.

With a recurrence of such an emergency, the government will take similar action again. In adopting a program of social-security legislation the government has acknowledged its responsibility and has undertaken to forestall the necessity of again resorting to an outright dole. The general principle at stake is that if our economic system breaks down, the government is responsible to take whatever emergency measures are necessary to protect the welfare of the people. This principle has been approved by the will of the people and is as much a part of our constitution as if it had been incorporated in the written document.

Social-security legislation is, therefore, another example of government interference in or regulation of economic affairs. It is understandable only in the light of a long period of development of numerous other forms of regulation.

When war broke out in Europe at the close of the 'thirties, it was a relatively simple adjustment for our government to shift its relief and "pump priming" expenditures into the channels of a preparedness program.

When we were catapulted into the war by the Japanese attack at Pearl Harbor, the people of the country were just about as nearly one hundred per cent behind the war effort as could ever be possible. With a popular president in office; with a background of depression experience in which people generally turned to the Federal government for leadership as well as economic assistance, and with an unprecedented unanimity of patriotic support to back it up, the government was able to organize and carry out a mobilization of manpower, materials, and productive resources never before equalled in any country. Taking advantage of its strategic position, the government did not compete with private interests in the traditional competitive market. It set up controls over the use of basic materials and thereby diverted the productive facilities of whole industries to war work. This virtual taking over of the nation's industrial plants was supplemented effectively by a system of rationing which limited still more rigidly private consumption.

The size and effectiveness of the armies we put in the field, the navy we put on the ocean, and the wealth of material with which they were supplied were not due solely to the courage and ingenuity of the fighting men, the know-how and energy of business men, and the skill and industry of industrial workers. The miracles of production, which so impressed other peoples of the world with the power of the United States, would not have been possible without a highly effective psychological mobilization.

This psychological mobilization was crystallized and solidified overnight by the sneak attack on Pearl Harbor. However, its foundations go back to three-quarters of a century of government regulation. They go back particularly to the dramatic early days of Franklin D. Roosevelt's first administration. The Federal government's role in the depression of the 'thirties, its shifts of expenditures from relief to a preparedness program, and its later conduct of the war were all involved in a single build up of psychological mobilization. Of course, no one planned this sequence of major events. It was a fortunate but fortuitous combination of circumstances. In a very real sense the psychological mobilization was the foundation upon which the mobilizations of manpower and productive resources were built.

The cessation of hostilities brought immediate psychological demobilization with military and economic demobilization following closely in its wake. The immediate problem which faces us now is to take stock and find out just where the demobilization of our wartime economy leaves us. One would need to be very naive indeed to believe that removal of wartime controls automatically places us back in the simple, self-regulating, individualistic economic system from which we had been drifting away for several generations before the war came on.

Inventory of Economic Control

Our current economy shows not one but many forms of control over economic activities. In spite of its many failures, competition is still the largest single factor in the control of our economic affairs. However, the other agencies of control have developed at the expense of the competitive market and it continues to lose ground to them.

As was indicated earlier in this discussion, the principles of accounting and the practice of professional accountants have come to play a significant part in the guidance and control of business activities.

Government regulation is a factor in economic control which has grown rapidly. Its typical form is administrative control through state and federal boards and commissions. It includes also, however, regulatory legislation such as antitrust laws and social-security legislation. It has shown a general trend from less to more positive control. It has two distinct aspects. One is concerned with the regulation of particular activities or particular areas of our economy. The other is concerned with responsibility for, or regulation of, the operation of our economy as a whole.

Another significant form of control in our present-day economy is the voluntary control by business exercised through trade associations. This form of control was temporarily elevated to a high place in the system by the N.I.R.A. [National Industrial Recovery Administration]

A form of control which is hard to appraise accurately is that exercised by the managements of business enterprises which have become so large and powerful that their operations are affected with a public interest. The way in which such managements exercise the economic power vested in them is a matter of vital public concern.

This inventory would be incomplete if it did not include also the power exercised by labor leaders through the collective action of organized labor. This power has been fostered by the Federal government as a parallel to the power of big business management. It has grown to the point of challenging the Federal government itself.

Finally, the management of large business enterprise is carried on under conditions which can be expected to shape the development of a professional attitude on the part of those who are responsible for it. Already we have moved a considerable distance in that direction since the time when the lack of any sense of social responsibility on the part of business management was characterized by that famous dictum "the public be damned." The professional business school has become a regular feature of institutions of higher education. Such schools of business, however, can be counted upon to follow and to standardize the movement rather than to shape its development.

An unbiased appraisal of our present situation shows us an economy which is capable of a tremendous volume of production. Under modern conditions of production and exchange it tends to operate as a closely articulated organization as if it were a single vast machine. When it operates smoothly the output is large, but when it breaks down or is stopped the losses are equally large and soon bring hardship to large numbers of people.

What we need is an integrated system of dependable control which will keep our economic machine running smoothly, and that is what we do not have. Instead, we have a system of multiple agencies of control which often work at cross purposes and sometimes stop the machinery rather than help to keep it working. We cannot look to the competitive market for an integrated system of control. It was not devised to control the kind of economic machine we now have. Among all the agencies of control enumerated above it is the one which steadily is losing ground.

Higgling of the Market

In the free market economy, the higgling of the market, the bargaining between buyers and sellers, was what determined prices and kept the market functioning. The modern counterpart of higgling in the labor market is the negotiation of a new labor contract. When there is serious difficulty in reaching an agreement, this involves a strike which is a part of the higgling process duly recognized by law. It is the seller's freedom of choice to sell or not to sell. But whereas in the original market higgling kept the economic system going, in the modern version it leads to a stoppage of economic processes. And when the stoppage involves coal or steel or railroad transportation the effects of the stoppage are tragic. Under these circumstances, the need for some kind of machinery which will make possible the negotiation of a new contract while work goes on is becoming more and more imperative. If the government, acting in the interests of the general public, proposes compulsory arbitration, management protests against such an interference with the free enterprise system and labor raises the cry of involuntary servitude. The situation calls for intelligent cooperation on everybody's part in working out a constructive solution of the problem. Yet neither management nor labor has any suggestions to offer. Indeed, for the most part they do not recognize any responsibility. If they continue in this attitude and the problem continues to grow more critical, the government will in time impose an arbitrary, unilateral solution in the name of its responsibility for the economic welfare of the people.

The above described problem is typical of our current economy. A host of problems of the same general character head up in the problem of evolving an integrated system of over-all control. We are learing much about the economic society in which we live, about the technique of managing big business, about accounting and statistical methods of control, about the operations of a credit system, and about many other things. The most effective method of solving both our particular problems and the problem of general control is to work them out together. What we need above everything else is to keep the problem of over-all economic control upon a tentative and experimental basis as the problem of regulating public utilities has been kept. Our greatest danger lies in the possibility that unwise leadership or untoward circumstances may throw us into a doctrinaire and half-baked solution of the problem. When John L. Lewis seized upon a mine disaster as an excuse to throw his weight around in defiance of the Federal government, he was engaging in a dangerous practice. If the Federal government should throw its weight around and destroy the power of organized labor, it would impose a role of martyrdom on the labor group. Such action might well set the stage for the people to throw their weight around and that would be a real social catastrophe.

Western civilization is in the midst of a transition which is changing even the philosophical foundations of the law itself. We have fought through two world wars which are incidental features of the transition period. It is to the everlasting credit of the English-speaking democracies that, in the midst of so much stress and world confusion, they are still working along under governments of law.

Unfortunately we are involved in processes of change which run in terms broader than those in which we habitually think. Changes affect different peoples differently. Since those peoples do not think in terms broad enough to find a common ground, irreconcilable conflicts develop. Such is the character of the present conflict between the United States and Russia.

The Russians are engaged in trying to build the kind of society which they think is best suited to the utilization of a modern industrial system such as we have, and they are developing as rapidly as they can. Because of historical and social influences which do not affect us, they have elected to proceed by way of a dictatorial form of personal government and the application of a radical, doctrinaire method of social reform. But, granting the success of their experiment, they still have before them the whole task of building up the social machinery necessary to administer modern large scale processes of production and distribution. They have yet to build a regime of law along with the simpler task of developing an industrial plant.

We, in contrast to the Russians, have elected to proceed under a regime of law and to content ourselves with a slow, tentative, experimental process of evolution. If we can maintain continuously our government of law, and we have every prospect of doing so barring untoward accidents, then in another hundred years the Russians will be borrowing from us our machinery of social control just as assiduously as they now are borrowing the technology of industrial development.

If the English-speaking democracies can succeed in preserving their respective governments of law throughout the current period of cultural transition, they will have demonstrated a degree of cultural maturity not heretofore achieved. The advantages of such a process of orderly change under the constant rule of law are obvious. It saves those who must live through the process a great deal of hardship and also avoids much of the loss in social organization which is inherent in more violent forms of change. For example, a price system and a credit system are extremely valuable tools of social organization. They represent a peculiar and distinct combination of control and freedom which the human race could ill afford to lose. However, our price system developed in a situation which called for flexibility and adaptability in the social control of economic processes. Since that time we have developed a productive system which calls for steadiness and regularity of control rather than flexibility and adaptability. This inconsistency has given rise to numerous frictions. We already have made much progress in adapting our price system to the needs of the current situation, but it is a slow and complicated process. It is a problem which cannot be solved by a blind faith in traditions or by an equally blind faith in a process of radical reform. It will be solved automatically, however, if we have the patience and the insight to work out gradually an integrated system of control adapted to the conditions under which we live and the ways in which we now think.

Students of the process of social change through which we are passing have been too prone to suggest solutions of our economic problems running in terms of some kind of personal control. If we work out the change under a continuing regime of law there will be no problem of translating our results from the terms of personal government into the terms of a government of law.

We have not yet learned enough about our current social problems to proceed with a constructive integration of control. However, we are justified in pointing out the fact that accounting is a connecting bond running through the different agencies of control enumerated at an earlier point in this discussion. It is the only one of those agencies, except the market, which brings to the problem a comprehensive body of relevant theory. Also it may be pointed out that through the decisions of regulating agencies, through the decisions of courts of law, and through the position of trusteeship which the law vests in the accounting profession, the principles of accounting are being absorbed into the law of the land. This process constitutes a suggestive parallel to the absorption of the law merchant into the common law of England in the

Elizabethan period. Through that absorption of the law merchant into the common law the free market acquired its position as the focal center of economic organization among English-speaking peoples.

Federal Power Commission Accounting

Among the many regulating bodies, the Federal Power Commission has made the most positive application of the accounting yardstick to public utility regulation. In consequence it has been praised as having placed regulation upon a sound basis for the first time by its adoption of an accounting approach to the problem. By other critics it has been condemned for undermining free enterprise; for carrying on a program of "wiping out a substantial portion of the investment in public utility property as it now stands on the books"; and, for elevating accounting to the role of a new kind of economic system.

The distinctive policies which have called forth such emphatic views of approval and condemnation have been the commission's adherence to the original-cost or prudent-investment theory and its specific interpretations of the theory in setting up and administering the uniform set of accounts prescribed for power companies. It has set up as a basic concept the cost of an asset to the first owner who devoted it to public utility service. It has required utilities to charge costs of assets in excess of the cost to the first user to an adjustment account and has reserved to itself control of the treatment of the adjustment account. Since the commission has the power to say when and to what degree the adjustment account shall be amortized, and whether the amortization shall be charged to expense or against profits, it retains a continuing accounting control over management of the utility.

One of the difficulties of regulation has been the crudeness of rate-making control. In setting rates for specific utilities, commissions have faced the necessity of forecasting the probable volume of business of the regulated company. If the actual volume of service rendered runs much above expectation profits are greatly increased. The technique of readjusting rates has been a somewhat unwieldy method of control.

The subterfuge involved in the Federal Power Commission's application of the already overworked cost principle is quite naturally irritating to accountants. It is reminiscent of the many fictions by which the law has permitted evolution of the established machinery of social control. It does no more violence to the realities of the situation than, for example, the legal conception that a corporation is an individual person. However, the essential issue involved in the situation is the commission's continuing accounting control. It can allow profits with its right hand by the regulation of rates and can take them away with its left hand by its control over the treatment of account 100.5. Whether this twofold power will receive the final verdict of public approval will depend upon the standard of equity with which it is applied. It is a matter of public policy which must be judged on its merits. It does not violate any sacred principle, accounting or otherwise. If regulation were so severe as to discourage private capital from entering the power industry, it might be bad policy but it would not be a violation of principle. However, there is no evidence as yet of the flight of private capital from the field.

General Conclusions

The conclusions to be drawn from the foregoing discussion are relatively clear.

There is no separate solution of the problem of public utility regulation. When we have worked out a generally integrated scheme of control over our economic affairs, it will cover public utilities along with other forms of business enterprise.

However, the public utility field has been and still is an area of experimentation in which we are trying out techniques of social control.

Whatever the precise form of the system of integrated control which we shall evolve it is clear that accounting will play a vital part in it. Both the scheme of control and the role of accounts in it will be shaped in part by the intelligence and insight with which accountants and others approach the problems of cultural readjustment. As the problem of necessary integration takes form out of the conflict, complexity, and confusion which typify present day society, accounting will move toward a definitely more social point of view. It will be less dependent upon tradition and convention and will be a more logical and constructive organization of theory and techniques built around the functions served by accounts.

Herbert F. Taggart

TROUBLES THAT ARISE
WHEN GOVERNMENT CONTROL AGENCIES
TRY TO PRESCRIBE ACCOUNTING PROCEDURES

Herbert Francis Taggart *was born in South Dakota in 1898, and received an A.B. (1920) and a Ph.D. (1928) from the University of Michigan. He has taught at Kansas and at Michigan, and has had extensive governmental experience, serving with the National Recovery Administration, the Department of Commerce, the Office of Price Administration, and the Federal Trade Commission. He is a C.P.A. in Michigan. He served as director of research for the American Accounting Association, 1939–1941, and as its president in 1942. Among his published works is* Cost Justification *(1958), which deals mainly with accounting issues raised by the Robinson-Patman Act.*
In the article reprinted here, Taggart points out the pitfalls in having laymen (e.g., judges, members of regulatory commissions) make decisions on accounting matters and attempting to use accounting to implement their missions.

Almost always, when the relationship of government to accountants is mentioned, the brighter aspects are stressed—the fact that thousands of accountants obtain their livelihood from tax practice, that the sixteenth amendment and the acts regulating securities and exchanges have stimulated the adoption of adequate financial recording and reporting procedures, and that many other governmental activities in the areas of trade regulation, procurement, and social legislation have greatly increased the reliance of business upon accountants and their records. The purpose of this article is to point out that not all of the contacts between government and accountants have led to wholly desirable results, either for accountants or for the standards by which their functions are guided. It should not be accepted as a truism that public

Reprinted from *The Journal of Accountancy* (March, 1953), pp. 296–304, by permission. [*This article was inspired by, and much of the material in it was taken from an address by the author before the Federal Government Accountants Association, Washington; the address was published in the journal of that association. Editor.*]

accountants should be indiscriminatingly greatful to a benign government for adopting the Federal income tax, thus assuring the profession of an ever-expanding livelihood, or that private and industrial accountants should take unalloyed pleasure in the job-insurance guaranteed by such governmental activities as renegotiation, price-control, and the Robinson-Patman Act. It cannot be denied that all of these enactments have made work for account-ants, but they have not necessarily been good for accounting as an art or a science, nor for the esteem in which accountants ought to be held by the community at large.

In citing a few ways in which accounting and accountants are misused for governmental purposes we find that legislatures, courts, and administrative bodies are all guilty. In many cases their actions do make work for account-ants, but too often it is work in which the accountant can take little satisfac-tion, and which does not further the best interests of the profession.

The general area of government regulation of business is that in which legislators are most likely to set impossible tasks for accountants. Pending before a recent session of Congress were several bills, the primary and laudable purpose of which was to separate the pay for carrying air mail from the subsidy for the support of that portion of the airline industry which is not able to make its own way. In the past, these payments were so inter-mingled that no one could be sure what part of the payments was for services rendered and what part was intended to benefit national defense. It is only good business and sensible budgetary procedure to make this separation. The larger airlines no longer need a subsidy, but they must, of course, be paid for the services they render to the Post Office Department. Subsidy payments to the smaller airlines should be designated for what they really are, so that the taxpayer may be in a position to decide whether he is getting his money's worth.

What was required in the circumstances was a simple Congressional direc-tive to the Civil Aeronautics Board to negotiate a price for air mail carriage with the air lines, so that the separation could be made. There seems to be little doubt that such a directive could be carried out. Certain members of Congress, however, apparently felt that the CAB could not be trusted to do a good job of rate-making, and there were introduced several bills which would base the rate on the cost of the service. One bill, for example, provided that air mail rates "shall in no event exceed reasonable and necessary cost to the air carrier...of the mail-transportation service rendered...including a fair return." To the uninitiated this provision sounds innocuous enough, but it was not well received by the airlines. One of them even went to the trouble of asking a couple of witnesses to testify against it before the Senate Committee on Interstate and Foreign Commerce. The chief trouble with this provision, according to one of the witnesses, is that "no...determination" of the cost of transporting air mail "is possible, and any figures purporting to represent such cost which might be prepared as a result of such legislation would be misleading and fallacious."

The reason for this conclusion is that the air transportation industry, like meat packing and oil refining, is a joint-product industry. It is universally recognized by accountants and economists that actual individual product costs in such industries can never be objectively determined. In several hundred well-chosen words the accounting witness explained this elementary truth to the committee, pointing out at length and in detail that the only cost which could be ascertained would be an average cost, which would not and in the nature of things could not take into account the many imponderable differences between the transportation of air mail and the transportation of freight, express, and passengers.

Witnesses then pointed out that this would be the first time Congress had ever directed an administrative agency to set a price for a public utility service on a cost basis. Individual railroad rates are not so set. Even the rate for rail transportation of mail is not set on the basis of cost to the carrier. Thus the Congress would be venturing into new and untried territory.

Some of the bills also contained language which would apparently force the airlines to establish elaborate and complicated bookkeeping procedures to determine costs. One bill, for example, required the CAB to "prescribe standards by which air carriers, in keeping their accounts, records, and memoranda, shall allocate receipts from, and expenditures for, the air transportation services rendered by them." Just what this might involve in the way of detailed cost bookkeeping is hard to say, but the airlines envisioned tons of additional paperwork, brigades of additional clerks, and acres of additional floor space devoted to this unproductive task. None of them had ever tried to allocate costs among services rendered, since such allocation would obviously serve no useful commercial purpose.

The truly sad part of this whole affair is that if such a bill should pass, the staffs of the CAB and the airlines would be duly increased, the paper work would be carried through, cost figures of a sort would be prepared, and rates would be set which would conform to the letter of the law. Any privately employed accountant knows that if the boss insists on having certain figures he will get them, whether they make sense or lead to proper decisions or not. This fact does not make it any more pleasant to see the taxpayers' and stockholders' money wasted by such ill-conceived legislation. Nor, though jobs for accountants are provided, can the profession take much comfort in such prostitution of the art of accounting.

Not everything that happens to accounting and accountants in their relationship to government can be laid at the doorstep of the legislature. After laws are passed, they must be administered and adjudicated. Judges are ordinarily lawyers, and not expert in accounting or business procedures, and, although it must be granted that they often exhibit great acuity in passing on accounting matters, they have been known to render decisions which leave much to be desired.

The Robinson-Patman Act is a good example of a law which involves accounting determinations of a peculiarly difficult type. This law forbids sellers "to discriminate in price between different purchasers of commodities of like grade and quality...where the effect of such discrimination may be substantially to lessen competition. ...." It provided, however, that "nothing herein contained shall prevent differentials which make only due allowance for differences in the cost of manufacture, sale, or delivery resulting from the differing methods or quantities in which such commodities are...sold or delivered." The result of this law is what has been called "ordeal by cost accounting."

Ordinarily, the Federal Trade Commission is the authority which passes on the complex cost analysis problems which arise under this legislation. The commission has a staff of accountants who are in a position to evaluate the procedures used and to cast an expert eye at the intricate calculations which are necessary. The commission has shown an extraordinary ability to penetrate to the heart of the most complex situations and to come up with well-reasoned conclusions. Courts of appeal seem inclined to accept the commission's findings with respect to these matters, as well they might. Where such problems are placed before a court *de novo*, however, a different situation arises.

In two recent cases, Federal district judges have been confronted with the problem of determining the adequacy of an accounting defense against charges of violating the price-discrimination provisions of the Robinson-Patman Act. These cases both involved the same defendant and very similar sets of facts. For the purpose of granting discounts, the defendant classified its customers. In compiling cost data, the same classification was used. In view of the fact that there were between 2,200 and 3,000 customers during the period involved, some classification for both purposes seems inevitable. In both cases, however, the district judges were of the opinion that only a cost analysis in terms of individual customers and even of individual delivery points, where customers received goods at more than one point, would suffice. As one judge put it, "A literal interpretation of Section 2(a) would appear to call for a consideration of the sales costs to individual customers and to individual plants of customers who operate more than one. It is difficult to see in what other manner price differentials can be limited to the sphere of actual costs." This judge modestly admitted that he did not pretend to "function as an expert in the field, as does the Federal Trade Commission," which has accepted cost analyses derived for classes of customers. It seems obvious that, if this opinion should prevail, no defendant in such a case could ever avail himself of the cost-justification provision. Complex and unsatisfying as cost analysis results often are when dealing with customers in groups, they would be infinitely more complicated, as well as impossibly expensive, when applied to individual customers. If Congress meant to give sellers a practicable method of justifying price differentials by cost analysis, such intention would be effectively nullified if the requirement for analysis in terms of individual customers were to become the rule.

How Cost Procedures Can Confuse Laymen

One of these cases furnished an excellent illustration of how the layman can be confused by even the most elementary cost accounting procedure. The defendant kept track of the "contact" time of its salesmen and sales supervisors and charged the cost of such time directly to the customer classes contacted in accordance with daily time reports made by the employees in question. Noncontact time, such as travel time, vacations, etc., of salesmen was allocated to customer classes in proportion to contact time. The company employs salesmen to contact customers. Quite obviously all of the salesman's pay and expenses are chargeable on some basis to the customer classes with whom the salesman deals. Yet the judge's comment on this accounting procedure was as follows: "This resulted in the allocation of numerous hours of working time that was never actually consumed in work and further resulted in an arbitrary allocation to the various [customer] classes of costs that were not expended." The final remark was wholly gratuitous, since no evidence was presented which would tend to show that imaginary costs were included in the analysis. The judge made particular note, however, of the fact that one employee had actually been paid by the company for time spent at a golf tournament!

Another aspect of this incident is particularly disturbing from the standpoint of accountants. The complainant introduced no testimony to the effect that the method of accounting for salesmen's time was invalid. Counsel for the plaintiff had dug through voluminous records and had unearthed several time reports which showed little contact time and much noncontact time during the particular periods covered. These reports were shown to two of the company's accounting witnesses on cross-examination, and each was asked if the cost analysis method used in these cases was good accounting. The answer was in the affirmative. The plaintiff's one accounting witness was not questioned on this point. Having thus only favorable testimony before him, from persons who had qualified as expert accounting witnesses, the judge nevertheless chose to substitute his own unsupported opinion and to condemn the method as bad accounting, even while admitting that he was not "an expert in the field."

Government Can Refuse to Face Facts

The executive branch of government is no more guiltless of sins against accounting and accountants than the legislative and judicial. Many examples could be cited. Instances of distortion and perversion of accounting data by governmental boards, bureaus, and commissions are so numerous as almost to give the impression that this is standard operating procedure.

An example in the area of accounting semantics, which in itself is of no great importance, nevertheless shows with what utter unconcern for established accounting concepts rulings may be made by governmental authority. By order dated March 12, 1942, effective January 1, 1943, the term "unearned surplus" became a part of the accounting classification for steam railroads, prescribed by the Interstate Commerce Commission. This term had apparently originated in utility regulation in New York, and had caught the eye of one of the commissioners, who had taken an understandable dislike to the older and not wholly satisfactory term, "capital surplus." Adoption of the new term was protested by the Association of American Railroads, but the protest was ignored and the change went into effect and was incorporated in the revised Uniform System of Accounts for Steam Railroads published in May, 1943.

This matter was brought to the attention of the committee on terminology of the American Institute of Accountants, in the hope that that organization might wish to lodge a protest with the commission. The committee was interested, and properly shocked by the term. A good bit of correspondence was exchanged, but we were at war and everybody had more weighty problems. Nothing ever came of it.

Some of the comments with respect to this term indicate what competent and experienced accountants thought of it. One letter characterized the term as "not only stupid and meaningless but positively dangerous." It was held to be "improper and undesirable for use in any financial statements of any kind." Another prominent accountant pointed out that, "apart from its general undesirability...the use of the term 'unearned surplus' might give the impression that the surplus could at some future time...become 'earned.' In other words, confusion between 'unearned surplus' and 'deferred income' might arise." A more important basic difficulty with the term is that it implies that the surplus in question is somehow undeserved, or improperly acquired. The term "surplus" itself is bad enough in this respect without adding to the confusion by tacking on an ambiguous and invidious adjective.

Needless to say, no accountant or accounting organization was consulted with respect to this change—not even the accountants on the commission's own staff. Fortunately, the use of the term does not seem to have spread, even in regulatory circles, and the harm, if any, has been confined to industries regulated by the ICC.

An example which is of much more vital concern to the industries affected is the so-called "aboriginal cost" rule of the Federal Power Commission and a number of other utility regulatory bodies. This is the rule which requires that utility assets acquired by one operating company from another must be recorded at the cost which they bore at the time they were first dedicated to public utility use, and that any difference in the purchase price must be recorded in a separate account. A thorough discussion of this matter is not possible here. It should be pointed out, however, that whatever merit this rule may have as a regulatory device, it should under no circumstances be defended as good accounting. The adoption of any such procedure in commercial accounting is unthinkable, and in a free economy what is good accounting is determined in business enterprise and not by governmental authority.

A Misuse of Standard Costs

Incidentally both the ICC and other utility classifications contain numerous examples of accounting procedures, terminology, and concepts which are archaic and outmoded in comparison to the best in commercial accounting. Many of these matters are relatively harmless, and perhaps one should not complain. The Securities and Exchange Commission, in contrast, has been criticized for a tendency to lead the way in accounting innovations. Apparently it is difficult for governmental bodies to find the golden mean.

Even when government departments are doing their best to adapt the principles and procedures of modern industrial accounting to their own operations, they are not wholly to be trusted. Spurred on by the Hoover Commission report, one segment of the executive branch decided to adopt standard cost procedures in order to encourage efficiency in its operations. For this purpose activities at each location were subdivided into functions. Costs of each function were obtained at each installation and unit costs were computed, the activity of each function being measured in terms of appropriate units, such as the man-day for subsistence. Then the unit costs by functions of all installations were arrayed, from the lowest to the highest, and weighted average unit functional costs were calculated. These averages were adopted as the tentative standards in the early stages of this control procedure.

Each installation was provided with a complete set of reports showing its own unit costs for each function, the unit costs of other installations, and the weighted average unit costs which were designated as tentative standards. These reports conveyed the implication that all installations whose unit costs were higher than the weighted average were doing badly and should set about putting themselves in order. Those installations whose unit costs were less than the weighted average were, on the other hand, inferentially commended.

The most elementary precept of standard cost procedure is that an average is not a standard. This is particularly obvious when the average is that derived from a number of establishments of differing sizes and operating under different conditions. Installations included in this compilation ranged from small ones with a few hundred employees to large ones with several thousands. In general, the unit costs varied inversely with size, as might have been expected. As a matter of fact, the person responsible for a particular function at a small establishment might be doing an outstanding job of good management, even though his unit costs were far above the weighted average. On the other hand, the supervisor of a similar function at a large unit might be conducting a shamefully wasteful operation, and yet show a unit cost substantially below the weighted average.

Even though these weighted average standards were presented as tentative, irreparable damage to the cause of cost control through the use of standard costs had been done. Sooner or later, standards for each establishment would have to be determined in terms of its own conditions and its own capabilities. By that time, however, the operating personnel would be convinced that standard cost procedures were just another foul-up on the part of the top brass, and the usefulness of the whole program would be questionable. It is difficult enough to enlist the support of employees and supervisors in the most logical and admirable system of cost control, to say nothing of one which on its face is unreasonable and impractical.

Income Tax's Contribution to Accounting

There can be no doubt that the Federal income tax has made a very great contribution to the development of accounting in this country. It has required the sharpening of concepts of income and the distinction between income and capital charges and credits. It has put the force of necessity behind the development of adequate business accounting, both as to principles and as to the maintenance of adequate records. Together with the laws which regulate the issuance of securities and their trading on the exchanges it has been of far more basic importance to accounting and accountants than is reflected merely in employment statistics.

Nevertheless, the income tax is responsible for some bad accounting, and might easily become the cause of more, if care is not taken. Everyone is familiar with many of the points at which the income-tax computation of income differs from the definition of income in terms of accounting concepts alone. Such things as the rule that there can be no gain or loss in the exchange of one piece of equipment for another and the failure to recognize unaccrued but definitely foreseeable liabilities, such as those for guarantee of product, are among the familiar examples. The Federal income tax is, more than any other factor, responsible for the wide adoption of LIFO, with its attendant calamitous effect on the balance-sheet.

The case of the Montreal Mining Company suggests how still other departures from accepted accounting practices by the Bureau of Internal Revenue might easily have an upsetting effect on commonly employed and entirely satisfactory accounting techniques and procedures. This company mines iron ore and for many years had treated certain taxes as cost of its product and included them in inventory valuations thereof. Among these taxes were Wisconsin real estate, personal property, and income taxes, Federal and state social security taxes on mine employees, and Federal capital-stock tax. A similar accounting practice was followed by the bulk of the iron-mining industry and, indeed, is followed by a very high proportion of all industry, at least as to some of the taxes involved.

For some reason not disclosed by published reports of the case, the Commissioner of Internal Revenue decided that this particular taxpayer should not be permitted to follow his accustomed practice, but should instead be required to deduct all such taxes in the year paid or accrued. This ruling was appealed, and the Tax Court upheld the Commissioner. The reasons for concurrence were both because the Tax Court agreed with the accounting doctrine thus applied and also because the Internal Revenue Code gives the Commissioner the right to determine the basis of valuation of inventories, and the court is unwilling to interfere as long as he does not act in a capricious and arbitrary manner.

Many questions about this case remain unanswered to the casual observer. Among them is why the ruling was ever made in the first place. Also, why was the Commissioner's apparent conviction that no taxes should be included in production costs placed in effect only in this case, and not applied generally? The effect of such an application is easily predictable. As a practical matter, taxes would be universally excluded from inventory valuations, regardless of their nature and the obvious accounting justification for their inclusion. Although there are some cases in which taxpayers report income to the government on one basis and to their stockholders on another, this would not be one of them. Taxpayers would simply take the easy way and treat all taxes as a direct charge against revenues, no matter whether logic might demand their treatment in another fashion. Just as the income-tax law has in general been a compelling force in the direction of adequate income accounting, so in matters of detail it can be an overwhelming argument against a thoroughly sound accounting practice.

Many of the deviations from accepted accounting procedures which have been adopted by the Bureau of Internal Revenue may be traced to the exigencies of practical administrative necessity. The "bird-in-hand" principle accounts for some departures from the accepted accounting definitions of income. The Montreal Mining Company ruling cannot be ascribed to administrative necessity. It appears to be a purely gratuitous attack on established accounting procedures, and it is to be hoped that its like will not often be encountered.

The instances cited are but a few of the many examples which could be given of the less happy aspects of the relationship between government in its several capacities, and accountants and the art of accounting. From these examples a few generalizations may be drawn.

The Examples Point to Generalizations

The first, and rather obvious generalization, is that accounting concepts and standards which are reasonably well recognized by accountants and the business community in general are all too frequently given little consideration by lawmakers, jurists, and administrators. Doubtless this is in part the fault of the accountants themselves. They have not attained stature as a professional group to the extent that they should. For many years accountants did little or nothing in the way of formulating standards or principles which could be presented to society as the rules by which the profession guided itself. Accountants operated as individualists and as opportunists. Many of them still do. Fairly recently an article by a lawyer appeared in a law journal claiming that, since accounting rules were of the utmost importance in our economy, and since accountants had shirked the job of formulating them, the legal profession should take over and prepare a set of principles and standards which would meet the important social needs which depend on accounting statements and financial statistics.*

Still more recently a financial writer in a New York newspaper, commenting on the fact that financial statements presented by public accountants are not always accepted by all parties at face value (*Journal of Accountancy*, September 1952, p. 295), says that the accounting profession has "a long way to go" in lifting its ethical standards if "their figures cannot be accepted by management, labor, and the investing public." This writer continues:

"One of the primary difficulties encountered is that corporate management is unwilling to have labor accountants or government accountants go over their books. This attitude is not unreasonable. But the standard of ethics in the accountancy profession should be so high that labor or government accountants should be able to accept the word of the independent accountancy firm after it has made an inspection of a corporation's books.

"It should be possible for the accountancy profession to put its own house in order. That, in fact, would be the ideal way. But the public is not without recourse if it fails to do so. So-called independent firms could be placed under government license and such a license could be revoked if any firm failed to abide by accepted standards."

These are strong indictments of the accounting profession. In earlier years they would have been deserved. As of today, however, the activities of the committees on accounting procedure and on auditing procedure of the

---

* The reference is to Ralph Wienshienk," Accountants and the Law," *Univ. of Penna. Law Rev.* (Nov., 1947), pp. 48–65.

American Institute of Accountants and the formulations of accounting standards by the American Accounting Association have made long strides in the direction of establishing standards and concepts which deserve recognition as the authoritative voice of the profession. The fact that articles of the sort quoted above can yet be written is an indication that the profession cannot regard the progress thus far made with complacency. The standards thus far adopted do not yet have the full support from the profession which they must have if they are to be recognized by the public as constituting complete assurance of the objectivity and reliability of accounting statements.

A related general observation is concerned with the compulsion exerted by government rules and regulations with respect to how books are to be kept and statements prepared. This is obvious in the case of such agencies as ICC and FPC, which actually prescribe account classifications and reporting forms. It is, however, almost as apparent in connection with such authorities as the Bureau of Internal Revenue and the SEC. As a practical matter, it is impossible to any material extent to keep two sets of books, one for the government and one for the stockholders. Except in the most extraordinary circumstances, one set of records must suffice. If the accounting procedures required or permitted by governmental bodies are in accordance with sound accounting doctrine and do permit recording and presenting accounting facts in an adequate way, no fault can be found. If the government, however, by a law, a court decision, or an administrative ruling, requires a method of accounting which does not reflect the best procedure, the undesirable method will nevertheless prevail, simply because the taxpayer or the security issuer, or whoever the victim may be, will not go to the trouble and expense of maintaining two sets of records. Where good accounting becomes a luxury, it will be sacrificed on the altar of necessity. This fact should make government officials think twice before they adopt arbitrary methods and procedures merely for their own convenience or out of their own prejudices.

Will Government Dictate Accounting Rules?

A corollary of the preceding is the observation that there exists a very real danger that the governmental accounting prescriptions will become the accepted rules of the game. Whenever anyone points out that a different principle or another procedure has more logic or produces more reliable data, the suggestion is likely to be shrugged off by the remark, "What's the use? The government requires us to do it this way, so this is the way we do it." Constant repetition of this theme will cause the government rule to become the accounting principle, and not only government accountants but other accountants will accept it for what it is not.

More basic and more serious, in some ways, is the final observation. It goes to the heart of why accountants exist—what their function is in society—and the basis for the esteem, if any, in which they are held. As taxes become more complex and take an ever greater share of the income dollar, as government control over business activity increases in the fields of competition, pricing, labor relations, and issuance of securities, a greater and greater proportion of the accountant's time is taken up by these matters. He must do his bit in minimizing taxes, in interpreting price regulations, in preparing materials for hearings before this governmental body and that, in trying to keep his employer in business and out of trouble. In its every essence this is negative activity—it is preventive; it is defensive. It makes no positive contribution to business success or human welfare.

Accountants have always been considered overhead. They have been thought of as a necessary evil. Perhaps there is no escape from this condition, but in recent years accountants have at least seen the desirability of making positive contributions rather than negative ones. They have been trying to point the way, instead of merely taking notes on history. They have begun to participate positively in the functions of the managers of sales and production, instead of being a wet blanket on the making of decisions and risk taking.

Standard Costs a Positive Contribution

The development of standard cost procedures is an outstanding example of this new place in the sun for accountants. Recently the following appeared in THE JOURNAL OF ACCOUNTANCY: "Standard costs, say some knowledgeable accountants working with procurement, are being killed by unwillingness of procurement authorities to accept figures produced by the standard cost system...they insist on auditing themselves, seeking actual, not standard, costs. Result: many companies are abandoning standard costs. It's too tough to keep two sets of cost records. These accountants fear that standard costs —so useful to management—will suffer a nearly fatal blow as a result of being driven out by government auditors."

That there is much truth in this statement is attested to by a speaker at the 1952 conference of the National Association of Cost Accountants. Though this speaker laid part of the blame at the feet of accountants who were satisfied with inadequate and unreliable systems of standard costs, his observations, nevertheless, bring the point into sharp focus. Just when the accountant is succeeding in his effort to become a positive business force— to make real contribution to human welfare by promoting business efficiency and economy—he is relegated to the status of bookkeeper by the necessities of the relationship of business to government.

A somewhat different facet of the accountant's place in the business world, and the esteem in which he is held by his employers and clients, relates to his function in connection with government regulations. All too often he is placed in the unenviable role of policeman, or that despised policeman's helper, the stool-pigeon. He is a policeman if he works for the government, checking up on tax liabilities, infractions of laws and rules. He is a stool-pigeon if he keeps his employer's records honestly and the employer is thereby convicted of cheating. Some of this is inevitable, of course, but it is one of the less pleasant aspects of the accountant's existence. And the bigger the bite of taxation, and the more points at which government regulation touches business, the more accountants could be looked upon as enemies rather than friends of the businessman. In spite of this possibility, however, most good accountants manage to earn the gratitude of their clients for assisting them to manage their affairs so as to mitigate the harmful effects of some regulations.

This article does not advocate repeal of the Federal income tax nor abandonment of all efforts to regulate economic conduct. What is needed is more understanding of and regard for sound accounting doctrine on the part of legislators, jurists, and governmental functionaries, and no bland assumption that accounting and accountants can be made to serve any desired ends, no matter what distortions of accounting principles and procedures may be involved.

Part Six

Specialized Topics

Stephen Gilman

ACCOUNTING PRINCIPLES
AND THE CURRENT CLASSIFICATION

Stephen Gilman *(1887–1959) was born in Illinois and attended the University of Wisconsin, where he took an engineering degree. His interest in accounting began when he used his engineering background to help his father prepare a book on cost accounting. From 1913 to 1916 he worked for the Tennessee Coal and Iron Company. He then moved to Chicago to prepare accounting courses for the LaSalle Extension Institute. He became a C.P.A. in 1917. Shortly after the end of World War I, he and John Tanner acquired the International Accountants Society (Chicago) and converted it into one of the leading correspondence schools in the field of accounting. He edited* The Accounting Review *from 1944–1946, and also served a term on the committee on accounting procedure of the American Institute of C.P.A.*

He published Analyzing Financial Statements *in 1925, and is best known for his* Accounting Concepts of Profit, *published in 1939. This long book reviewed critically and in detail all the significant work in accounting of the preceding decade. It emphasized the increased importance of the income statement and the related increase in importance of accounting practices designed to determine periodic profit. Gilman paid a great deal of attention to terminology, attempting to distinguish among terms like principles, conventions, rules, doctrines, precepts, procedures, practices, and methods.*

The article reprinted here is a sketch of the leading ideas in Accounting Concepts of Profit. *In addition to serving as an introduction to the book, the article illustrates the way in which form (specifically, the classification of certain assets as current) may influence the more substantive problem of the appropriate valuation rules to apply in a particular case.*

One minor bright spot in the whole tragedy of global war is to be found in the temporary silencing of arguments about accounting principles. Some of these arguments with which we busied ourselves before Pearl Harbor seem now to be comparatively trivial. Obviously, it would require high moral

Reprinted from *The Accounting Review* (April, 1944), pp. 109–16, by permission.

courage to promote a theoretical accounting argument in these days when clients are trigger-tempered and engrossed with grave issues. In time of war we concern ourselves but little with the comparability of profit and loss statements, with technicalities relating to distortion of figures, and similar trivia. The industrialist who faces the certainty of a swollen inventory at the end of the war is in no mood to ponder finespun theories of inventory valuation. Nor does he see any advantage in arguing pro and con as to the theoretical legitimacy of offsetting, when the relationship between his current assets and his current liabilities has become entirely askew from the impact of terrific taxation.

Fortunately for the writer, however, there is one justification for a discussion of accounting principles at this time. That justification is to be found in postwar planning—a most useful phrase which invites us to philosophize in the midst of stark realities.

One of the early postwar tasks to be faced by the accounting profession is that of resuming the search for accounting principles. That this is a "must" item seems apparent upon consideration of the alternative, namely, elimination of the phrase "accepted principles" from the standard form of audit certificate or, even worse, the adoption of some definition of the word "principle" which does not conform to common usage.

Debatable Accounting Principles

Assuming that the search for accounting principles must be continued, it seems worth while to consider briefly a few remaining areas of disagreement which still require exploration and discussion.

Several of these are secondary in importance. For example, some of us do not believe that there are any principles of accounting according to our own understanding of the word "principles," and yet we might be willing to cease arguing on that point if agreement could be reached on more important issues.

One stumbling block in the prewar search for principles was related to coercive legal influence and the extent to which laws or the rulings of regulatory bodies could be said to control accounting principles. In spite of some evidence to the contrary, I gravely doubt whether any of us has ever really admitted that so-called accounting principles depend on the pronouncements of technically uninformed legislatures or courts. Under forecasted conditions of postwar controls and taxes this particular problem may settle itself by *reductio ad absurdum*. The difficulties of reconciling accounting principles with tax laws and rulings, for example, have already become insurmountable.

The long-continued argument as to whether certain losses and gains should be reported in the profit and loss statement or carried to surplus still remains open for discussion. The current trend seems to favor their inclusion in the profit and loss statement. The combined statement of profit and loss and surplus, which diminishes the importance of the issue, is also becoming more popular; hence we need expect no insuperable difficulty in obtaining a reasonable final settlement of this particular controversy.

Principles Affected
by Current Classification

More serious, in my opinion, than any of the matters just referred to is the unfortunate influence of the current asset and current liability classification upon accounting theory and practice. In this area we find a problem which, if not solved, will effectively prevent any satisfactory codification of principles of accounting.

The fundamental difficulty here seems to be one of viewpoint. It relates directly to one controversy which many of us thought had been settled, namely, the relative importance of the balance sheet and the profit and loss statement. Certainly most of us have given lip service at least to the dominance of the profit and loss statement. Official publications of accounting bodies and considered opinions of leading accountants have supported the conclusion that the profit and loss statement is the primary report and that the balance sheet, to use another's phrase, is but a link between two successive profit and loss statements.

Actions, however, often speak louder than words, and we now find ourselves in the uncomfortable position of having been detected in the simultaneous worship of both God and Mammon. It is suggested that no final agreement as to accounting principles can be obtained until we as accountants decide which is the true god. More specifically, it is suggested that the traditional balance-sheet classification of current assets and current liabilities conflicts with two of our most fundamental profit and loss concepts, namely, the concept of matching costs with revenues and the concept of realization of revenues.

Origin of Current Classification

In approaching the problem it seems necessary first of all to decide whether the current classification is an accounting classification. It seems to require little more than a superficial study to reach an adverse decision on this point. The current classification is primarily a classification for credit granting, which was popularized to meet the needs of credit men many years ago, at a time when single-entry bookkeeping was probably more prevalent than double-entry, when there was no well-organized internal accounting worth mentioning, and when the statement of assets and liabilities furnished to creditors consisted substantially of estimates unsupported by anything approaching modern accounting records.

For brevity of discussion we must be content with only a passing reference to the small utility of the current classification to such groups as investors, vendors, and managers in comparison with a large usefulness for the more influential bloc of credit analysts, namely, bank credit men.

In the early days referred to, the granting of credit on the basis of the representations of an applicant involved first of all the identification and measurement of all the applicant's assets which were capable of speedy realization, and the comparison of such values with debts of early maturity, the result being expressed in terms of net working capital or, percentagewise, as a current ratio. Current assets usually, but not necessarily, consisted of (1) cash, (2) receivables, and finally (3) merchandise and other salable inventories.

To the credit grantor, the inventory classification has been particularly troublesome. The value of an inventory, using the word "value" from the peculiar viewpoint of the creditor, was definitely influenced by style factors and by varying degrees of marketability. Credit grantors looked to the accountant for informative help in these two respects but looked in vain, the accountant being neither an appraiser nor an expert in merchandising.

We have almost forgotten how savagely the credit man of the preceding generation scaled down the inventory values reported by a credit applicant. That same credit grantor was a great believer in audits; but he was never able to persuade accountants to report the same kind of realizable or liquidating values that the credit grantor wanted to know about for his ultimate protection in the contingency of customer insolvency.

The cost-or-market rule of inventory valuation, which already had some dubious accounting significance, seemed to offer the best compromise between the viewpoint of the credit grantor and that of the accountant. Possibly from the credit viewpoint the accountant's idea of market values as going values was none too realistic and yet it has usually been satisfactory enough, since credit granting was, and to some extent still is, upon a rule-of-thumb basis. Thus, the arbitrary one-year requirement is a headache-causing hangover from the older days. The two-for-one current ratio was then, and still is, little more than a factor of safety to protect against overvalued inventories.

Credit men, it should be noted, were excellent friends of the accounting profession in its early days. The insistence of credit men upon audited statements contributed mightily to the growth of our profession. It is far from strange, therefore, that the concept of current assets and current liabilities fastened itself upon accounting practice so early and so firmly. And yet, if we take a detached viewpoint toward the current classification we find it faulty in several respects.

Faults of Current Classification

The classification of current assets is bad classification from almost any viewpoint. The total of current assets is not homogeneous, for it is built up of unlike elements and unlike values.

While it has been generally accepted that figures for net working capital or percentages representing current ratios possess significance, such significance has never been satisfactorily proven. In fact, the few studies ever made of this subject seem to indicate that such ratios possess little significance except from the peculiar short-term-liquidation viewpoint of the credit grantor. An important survey made some years ago by the University of Illinois should be disillusioning to those who worship such credit indexes.*

Their value has become even less during these recent years of high taxes. Some of our leading corporations are now showing current ratios of less than two-to-one, a phenomenon which results from the inclusion among current liabilities of swollen tax accruals with offsetting cash funds or tax anticipation notes among the current assets—a development of importance in relation to the occasional current-ratio requirements of some bond indentures.

The most serious accusation, however, which can be leveled at the current classification is that the concept of value rather than that of cost is still inherent therein, a concept which disregards distortion of periodic profit and loss statements.

Time permitting, numerous other accounting complaints against the current classification could be made, particularly with respect to the illogic of including certain kinds of items and excluding certain others.

Accounting Influence
on Current Classification

Accountants have not been unaware of complaints against the current classification nor have they been unaware of the need for reconciling this specialized credit concept with general accounting theory. Remedial measures which have been or are being proposed, however, do little to improve the situation from the accounting viewpoint, while at the same time they do much to diminish the credit utility of the current classification. For example, the word "market," as used today in the phrase "cost or market," often has

---

* Several studies of this type were made and published in the 1930's by the Bureau of Business Research of the University of Illinois.

little reference to the market value of interest to the credit man who is
wondering what he could realize by dumping a customer's inventory if that
necessity should arise. What credit man can truly express a passionate
interest in any so-called market value which merely represents replacement
cost?

To the accountant it seems logical under certain conditions to exclude an
early maturity of a long-term debt from the total of current liabilities.
Similarly, it seems logical to eliminate from current assets any cash held
in anticipation of purchasing a fixed asset, even though that cash may be
free cash and dedicated to its ultimate purpose only by intent. It seems
equally logical to exclude receivables arising from the sale of fixed assets.
Finally, there is logic underlying the proposition that inventories in excess
of one year's normal requirements should be excluded. These, however, are
accounting viewpoints and are influenced by the concept of the going
business. They disregard the fact that a good banker is a pessimist who
dislikes to admit, even to himself, that a customer's debts will be paid as the
normal result of operations and who expects to impound cash from any
source or liquidate inventories of any size if the occasion demands.

This seems to be a point worthy of some amplification.

When we listen to credit men talk in public or when we read their technical
publications we are apt to get a false impression of credit granting. Such
verbal or written evidence tends to mislead us into thinking of the typical
credit man as being a kindly soul who is interested primarily in performing
a public service and in assisting his customer to grow and prosper. Thus, bank
publicity presents a picture of banking in terms of a service to business.
While it would be both untrue and unkind to suggest that the banker is not
a benevolent man or to imply that he does not hope that the borrower's
obligations may be paid as the result of successful operation, nevertheless
there is one fundamental concept which absolutely controls every banker
who is worth his salt.

That concept refers to the banker's responsibility for his depositors'
funds.

He regards himself, quite properly, as occupying a singular position of
trust, and when he is in the process of negotiating a loan his sincere desire
to render a service to business and to his community is somewhat dwarfed by
an even greater desire to insure recovery of the funds he passes out. This is
reflected in his eager interest in cash and near-cash assets, and in overhanging
liabilities. It is reflected in his coolness toward plant, machinery, and fixtures
which cannot be quickly converted into money, and his tepid disinterest in
the profitability of a customer's operations in which his depositors cannot
share.

Long experience with over-optimistic borrowers has caused him to look
with some suspicion upon their figures and rosy predictions. It would not be

too unjust to say that in the process of negotiating a loan the banker often exhibits a faint trace of skepticism which finds expression in vigorous demands for collateral, including everything from the borrower's life insurance down to his wife's gold teeth.

No real banker is going to surrender good dollars in anticipation of a meager 3 per cent or 4 per cent return until he has satisfied himself that recovery of the funds depends upon something more tangible and more certain than figures, projected operating results, or promises. It is impossible to conceive of any lending transaction in which prayerful consideration is not given to the possible necessity for liquidation of the borrower's affairs through conversion of collateral or forced sale of inventories.

Accordingly, the banker wants to know about the cash value of insurance, about money dedicated to plant expansion, and about all marketable inventories regardless of whether they represent more than a year's normal supply. Quite logically he considers such items as current assets without regard for the borrower's intent or the accountant's rules.

Commendably, the accountant attempts to reconcile the irreconcilable, to justify the current classification as an accounting classification; but, less commendably, he ignores the fundamental fact that his actual or proposed modifications of the current concept rob it of some of its remaining credit value.

And what, in a large way, has been the result?

Credit Utility
of Accountants' Figures

Almost any credit man will admit that he uses the accountant's classification of current assets and current liabilities merely as the beginning of his own personal computation, which may involve bringing into the figures certain items such as the cash value of life insurance, which the accountant has omitted, or excluding from the figures certain items, such as inventories of work in process in highly specialized enterprises in which salesmanship is the dominating factor. The credit man's computations may, and often do, involve a substantial scaling down of values, particularly of inventory values in the case of style goods or other items for which there is no broad market capable of absorbing large quantities of goods on forced sale.

Thus, plain white paper in a publisher's inventory may have a credit value far in excess of that same paper after printing. Because of the conventions of cost accounting, we as accountants impute an added value to a publisher's printed inventory. But unless the final product should turn out to be a best seller, like Carnegie's *How to Win Friends and Influence People,* or Willkie's *One World,* the credit man will suspect a lowering in the credit value of that same inventory. White paper, untouched by printer's ink, can be sold and sold quickly under distress conditions. Printed books are notoriously difficult to dispose of at forced sale.

A Substitute Classification

It has been suggested that the current classification is not good classification, considered either on its own merits or from the special viewpoint of accounting. A better classification, one which is mutually exclusive and which has accounting authority, is a classification which divides assets into three and only three major divisions: cash, deferred charges to cash, and deferred charges to revenue.

I hasten to deny any thought that such a classification should be employed in the actual preparation and presentation of balance sheets. If the classification possesses merit it is only the merit of aiding clearer thinking.

It appears that such a classification harmonizes with the modern emphasis upon the profit and loss statement rather than contradicting it as does the current classification. The classification helps to simplify certain problems of matching, both theoretically and practically. It is of special value in relation to the two important categories of receivables and inventories since it is in tune with generally accepted concepts of realization of revenue, emphasizing rather than ignoring the important elements of (1) transfer of title, and (2) the creation of a legal claim to cash. It distinguishes sharply between those assets which are directly or indirectly intended for sale and those assets which result from a sale.

A common example of a deferred charge to cash is the ordinary trade receivable. Characteristic of this particular asset is an assertion which might be questioned by a collection agency but which, for purposes of accounting reasoning, may be considered true, namely, that the transition from a legal claim in the form of a receivable to actual cash itself is, generally speaking, an automatic transition.

While trade receivables represent the most important example of deferred charges to cash, others, such as notes receivable and bonds, deserve mention.

Similarity of Inventories
and Fixed Assets

The proposed asset classification groups inventories with fixed assets as being deferred charges to revenue. Fundamentally, both have the same relationship to revenue and income. Both represent costs "held over" to be applied against future revenue. Both have the same ultimate effect upon income, hence are logically of the same family; they should be valued consistently on a cost basis and should be matched against revenue according to the same general theory, even if not by the same procedure.

Disregarding sudden obsolescence, spoilage, theft, and similar types of loss, it seems clear that inventories and fixed assets make the same kind of negative contribution to income, a contribution which should be reasoned about on a harmonious and consistent basis.

Following from this assumption that the resemblances between inventories and fixed assets are more important accountingwise than the differences, it seems that (1) the cost of a necktie which is sold is not too different from the depreciation of the dealer's showcase, and (2) the allocation of such costs to fiscal periods should be made not only on a strict cost basis but also without being influenced by the probability or improbability that such treatment may result in a net loss in any one accounting period.

This assertion is almost certain to arouse indignant protest. In fact, I am quite sure that I would have little stomach for arguing the point with a war contractor with swollen inventories, who wishes to establish an inventory reserve from his war profits. I am wondering, however, whether such reluctance might not be due to lack of the courage to press such an issue with a man whose emotions are strongly excited, rather than to any lack of conviction. Years ago depreciation was booked on the basis of expediency and the amounts thereof were controlled by the size of profits. In many cases, if there was no profit there would be little or no charge for depreciation. Had it not been for the helpful assistance of the income tax laws we might still be arguing with clients regarding the propriety of charging off depreciation according to a predetermined plan. But this bridge, fortunately, has been crossed.

We do not, or should not, over-depreciate fixed assets in one year merely because we think that the succeeding year may show a loss. By the same token it is difficult to understand why we should justify, as an accounting principle, the absorption of part of the cost of an inventory prior to its sale because of a similar anticipation of future loss.

It is submitted that we do so in the case of inventories not entirely because we do not recognize the essential similarity between inventories and fixed assets, but because of an overemphasis upon conservatism in relation to inventories that arises merely from the fact that inventories are in the current classification. Such overemphasis leads to the absurd result that a dollar of cost representing a fixed asset and a dollar of cost representing merchandise are applied against revenue according to radically different theories.

Matching Costs With Revenue

Thoughtful accountants have long been disturbed over the contradiction between (1) balance-sheet conservatism, and (2) the fundamental doctrine of matching costs and expenses with revenues.

These men have seen how the balance-sheet conservatism of one period is offset by a lack of profit-and-loss conservatism in a succeeding period. It is suggested that this serious problem is, at least, half solved if balance-sheet conservatism is properly recognized in many cases as being the conservatism of a credit grantor rather than the conservatism of an accountant.

It is further suggested that we can never complete a structure of accepted principles of accounting without basing such principles upon a logical, consistent convention of matching costs with revenues, and furthermore that the matching problem cannot be satisfactorily solved so long as accounting is under the domination of the current classification.

Realization of Revenue

Of less practical value perhaps, but still important because any sound body of theory must give effect to extreme cases, is the problem of realization.

Deliberately simplified, the problem may be stated thus: Is revenue realized by the passing of title and the corresponding creation of *any* legal claim to cash, or must such a claim to cash conform to the credit man's idea of a current asset? Eminent authorities have intimated that *liquidity* of a resulting receivable is a necessary prerequisite to the reporting of revenue. Eliminating from present consideration the special treatments permitted in installment sales, long-term contracts, and the like, it seems safe to say that most accountants would regard liquidity of the receivable resulting from a sale as an essential factor in the recognition of realized revenue. And yet it is difficult to see why it would be proper to recognize revenue when the sale resulted, let us say, in a note receivable for 11 months and refrain from doing so if the life of the note was 13 months. The distinction between the two notes is purely a credit distinction based upon the familiar one-year rule of thumb.

In fact, liquidity has been held so important in relation to revenue realization that some authorities have gone so far as to recognize revenue and income as being created by certain transactions which are no more than barter.

Barter

As an extreme case, consider the merchant who sells a suit of clothes to a customer and for some obscure reason of his own accepts in exchange a share of General Motors stock. Because General Motors stock is listed and has an active market, it can definitely be characterized as a liquid asset. However, no revenue results from such a transaction, income tax authorities notwithstanding. It is barter pure and simple, hence it is utterly impossible to determine which of the parties thereto is the seller and which the purchaser. Since it has been long recognized that income never can be realized by the act of purchasing, it should be clear that any transaction of the type referred to cannot result in income. And yet we may infer from some of our technical reading that because the General Motors stock is so highly liquid it would be proper to recognize the realization of income in connection with such a transaction, but improper to do so if the suit of clothes had been exchanged for a long-term promissory note.

As justification for spending even a few minutes upon a point which appears to have so little practical value, it may be repeated that at times theory can be tested only by an extreme example. If theory does not stand up under such a test, suspicion is aroused that the theory does not furnish a sound foundation for any superstructure of accounting principles.

Conclusion

While we may conclude that the current classification is poor classification, and furthermore that it is not inherently an accounting classification; while we may agree that it has exercised a disturbing influence upon two of the most important accounting fundamentals, namely, the concept of matching and the concept of realization; nevertheless, we are not left with the undesirable alternative of abandoning it entirely. Such an alternative invites rejection, the current classification having so long been featured in corporate balance sheets. It has been suggested, however, that the current classification may be retained at the same time that its disturing effect upon profit and loss statements is eliminated.

The use of parenthetical disclosure has previously been mentioned as one method of accomplishing this end. A survey among bank credit men, reported by me in the *Journal of Accountancy* a year or so ago, indicated little opposition to parenthetical disclosure of values other than cost.*

It is believed that equally satisfactory results might be obtained by reporting current assets and current liabilities in the form of a schedule accompanying, and reconciled with, the balance sheet. It is likely that such an exhibit might be welcomed by credit grantors and investment analysts, since the items and the values shown in such a schedule could be so presented as to provide the greatest credit utility.

The adoption of such a plan would justify elimination of the current classification on the balance sheet itself, would permit the exercise of sane conservatism consistently applied to all asset items, particularly fixed assets and inventories, and would thereby remove one important cause of distortion in periodic profit and loss statements.

---

* See "Bankers Look at the Cost or Market Rule," *The Journal of Accountancy* (May, 1941), pp. 418–21.

Maurice E. Peloubet

STATEMENT OF MAURICE E. PELOUBET,
NEW YORK CITY,
THE COPPER & BRASS MILL
PRODUCTS ASSOCIATION

For a brief biographical sketch of Mr. Peloubet, see the headnote to his article, "Is Value an Accounting Concept?" page 95.

The testimony reprinted here is significant because it is probably the first extended public explanation of the need for the last-in, first-out method of pricing inventories and of determining cost of goods sold. It also represents one of the few cases where a group of prominent accountants in practice lobbied openly, persistently, and successfully for a change in the income tax law. (The next article reprinted [page 457] is an extended critique of LIFO.)

Mr. Peloubet. I am Maurice E. Peloubet, a member of the firm of Pogson, Peloubet & Co., certified public accountants, of New York City. I am speaking for the Copper and Brass Mill Products Association, a group of manufacturers who produce copper and brass sheets, tubes, rods, and other shapes, principally for further fabrication by other manufacturers but to some extent for use as finished products. The members of this Association wish to have that section of the proposed Revenue Act which corresponds to section 22 (c) of the Revenue Act of 1936 so worded as to permit members of the association to use, for purposes of computing income subject to Federal income and excess profit taxes, the same accounting methods which are generally accepted as correct for reporting to the Securities and Exchange Commission, reporting to their stockholders and for other corporate purposes. This method is the last-in, first-out method of applying current costs to current sales and is not now permitted by the United States Treasury Department to be used as a basis for determining taxable income.

I appeared before this committee at the hearings on the Revenue Act of

Reprinted from U.S. Senate, *Hearings Before the Committee on Finance,* 75th Congress, 3rd Session, on H.R. 9682 (Revenue Act of 1938), March 17, 18, 19, 21, and 22, 1938.

1936 to request legislation in that act to permit the use of this method and was told that it was within the power of the Commissioner of Internal Revenue to permit the use of the last-in, first-out method and that legislation was not, therefore, required. Those whom I represented were advised that appropriate action could be obtained from the Treasury Department, but while they have been in almost continuous touch with the Department since the passage of the Revenue Act of 1936, the Treasury has continued to require the use of methods of determining income which are not generally considered to be correct for the copper and brass mill products industry.

The copper and brass mill products industry conducts its business so as to avoid loss and thereby preclude gain from market fluctuations, which is accomplished by matching purchases and sales in the following manner:

Orders are customarily taken for delivery some time in the future—generally 90 days, sometimes more. The price at which the orders are taken is a combination of the fabricating charge, generally known as the fabricating differential, and the price of the metals used in the product on the day that the order is taken. Promptly thereafter a purchase commitment is made for copper, zinc, or other metals required to fill the orders taken.

The products may not be delivered and the metal may not be received for several weeks or months, but the manufacturer knows that he can obtain metal to cover the sale he has made and that he will neither gain nor lose on the metal but will make his profit on the difference between his fabricating cost and the differential charged the customer, which is the basis on which his business is done.

The prices of copper and brass mill products are increased or lowered as the prices of copper and zinc change. Price changes on products are made within a few hours after a change in metal prices, and it is of the utmost importance to each fabricator to have a system and organization by which these prices can be changed and made effective promptly. If this were not done, heavy losses could result.

Thus, on the metal itself, which is bought for and included in the products sold to customers, the brass manufacturer neither gains nor loses. It is not possible, however, to run a mill solely on the metal which the manufacturer has contracted to deliver to his customer in the form of finished products. He must, in addition, maintain a substantial inventory of metal. This inventory is in many different forms. Beginning at the casting operation, an excess of metal must be provided to allow discarding of unsound metal and dross. Similarly, in the rolling, drawing, and extrusion operations, unsound surfaces, edges, and ends must be removed. In finishing operations the product is reduced to proper dimensions by cutting off surplus material.

In other words, to produce a given quantity of a product a substantially larger quantity must be processed, the difference being mill scrap which is reclaimed and constitutes a constantly revolving inventory within the mill. Besides this, quantities of partially processed material must be kept at various points in the mill to permit economic production of the stream of orders which vary widely as to their individual quantity requirements. Altogether, therefore, the manufacturer must keep on hand an inventory which in metal content may equal several months' production. The inventory must always be kept on hand; a mill could no more operate without this inventory or so-called metals in process than it could operate without its plant or any of its equipment. And its practice, as I have explained to you, recognizes this fact. Sales are not made against this inventory; they are made against purchases of metal which occurred at approximately the same time as the sale.

In spite of this, the regulations of the Commissioner under section 22 (c) compel the fabricator to apply his current sales against an inventory deemed to be the earliest purchases when this, in fact, is exactly contrary to the fabricator's business practice. This results in inclusion in the computation of income, for income-tax purposes, profits or losses which are not the result of actual transactions.

The resulting distortion becomes particularly important in the copper and brass mill products industry because of the nature of their manufacturing operations, the relatively high cost of the metals they use, and the fluctuations in price to which those materials, particularly copper, are subject and over which the mills have no control. Their manufacturing operation is a complicated process bristling with physical and technical difficulties, and such a long period is involved that changes in price of inventory have a maximum effect. The cost of the metal is the principal single cost of their product—often representing 60 percent or even more of the price which they receive for the product. Furthermore, copper is subject to wide fluctuations in price. During 1937, for example, copper rose from 12 cents at the beginning of the year to 17 cents, then declined again to $10\frac{1}{8}$ cents at the end of the year. The reflection of this market fluctuation in the manufacturer's taxable income for that year might either double his actual profits for tax purposes, or result in a loss for the year, depending solely upon when his fiscal year ended. Certainly uniform and equitable taxation cannot be predicated on such an unreal base.

The taxation of fictitious incomes cannot be justified by the allowance of fictitious losses. The taxation of profits based on assumed transactions which do not occur in periods of rising prices and expanding business forces a taxpayer, at the time when his working capital is most fully employed and most urgently required, to provide money for tax payments at effective rates double, triple, or quadruple those nominally in force. No matter how much benefit he may receive later in periods of declining prices and declining business, when through contraction of operations his needs for working capital are less and his position more liquid, he will still have no relief from his present compulsion to obtain by any means and under any terms money to pay the taxes then assessed on income assumed to have been realized. Over a period of years total income will be the same under any method of accounting consistently applied, and if taxed at a flat rate the aggregate tax will be the same.

What the members of the Copper and Brass Mill Products Association want is an amendment in section 22 (c) which will permit them to determine the cost of current sales by using the cost of the metal which they buy currently to cover such sales. This is the system which I have described as "last-in, first-out"—that is, metal which is sold is deemed to be the last acquired instead of the first acquired, as the Treasury Regulations now provide. This method corresponds with the mills' actual practice in conducting their business and is the method which many of them now use for their corporate accounts, although they are not allowed to use it for tax purposes. It determines all of the profit which they have actually realized, but it does not tax them upon profits or allow them losses which have not occurred as the present method does.

There can be no doubt that the last-in, first-out method is an approved accounting practice. Statements filed on this basis have been accepted by the Securities and Exchange Commission and the special committee on inventories of the American Institute of Accountants approved this method in a report dated May 7, 1936. In A Statement of Accounting Principles prepared by Professor Sanders, of the Harvard School of Business; Professor Hatfield, of the University of California; and Professor Moore, of the Yale University School of Law, the authors expressed their approval of last-in, first-out or similar methods. This study was prepared under the auspices of the Haskins & Sells Foundation, an organization formed for research into accounting matters, and was published by the American Institute of Accountants.

I have here letters from members of nine of the most prominent accounting firms in the United States approving the use of this method.*

---

* The letters were received from the following: Paul K. Knight, Arthur Andersen and Co.; Deloitte, Plender, Griffiths & Co.; Edward A. Kracke, Haskins & Sells; Joseph J. Klein, Klein, Hinds & Fink; Walter A. Staub, Lybrand, Ross Bros. & Montgomery; Samuel J. Broad, Peat, Marwick, Mitchell & Co.; Rodney F. Starkey, Price, Waterhouse & Co.; C. Oliver Wellington, Scovell, Wellington & Co.; Victor H. Stempf.

Mr. Peloubet also submitted the following list of corporations using last-in, first-out, or similar methods (probably base-stock) in their financial statements:

	Auditors	Date of first use of method
American Smelting & Refining Co.	Scovell, Wellington & Co.	1906.
National Lead Co.	Bieth & MacNaughton	1913
Chicago Frog & Switch Co.		Previous to 1916.
Continental Can Co., Inc.	Deloitte, Plender, Griffiths & Co.	Do.
American Can Co.	Lybrand, Ross Bros. & Montgomery	1917.
International Harvester Co.	Haskins & Sells	1917.
U. S. Smelting, Refining & Mining Co.	Lybrand, Ross Bros. & Montgomery	1924.
Graton & Knight Co.	Arthur Andersen & Co.	1925.
Anaconda Copper Mining Co.	Pogson, Peloubet & Co.	1927.
Anaconda Wire & Cable Co.	do.	1929.
Cerro de Pasco Copper Corporation	Lybrand, Ross Bros. & Montgomery	1929.
The American Oak Leather Co.	Ernst & Ernst	1932.
American Metal Co., Ltd.	Lybrand, Ross Bros. & Montgomery	1933.
Bridgeport Brass Co.	R. G. Rankin & Co.	1933.
Consolidated Oil Co.	Arthur Young & Co.	Previous to 1934.
Vulcan Detinning Co.	Loomis, Suffern & Fernald	1934.
Standard Oil Co. of California	Price, Waterhouse & Co.	Previous to 1935.
Phelps Dodge Corporation	Pogson, Peloubet & Co.	1935.
Revere Copper & Brass, Inc.	Scovell, Wellington & Co.	1935.
Gulf Oil Corporation of Pennsylvania	Price, Waterhouse & Co.	1935.
Swift & Co.	Arthur Young & Co.	Previous to 1936.
Endicott Johnson Corporation	Touche, Niven & Co.	1936.
Surpass Leather Co.	Price, Waterhouse & Co.	1936.
Socony Vacuum Oil Co., Inc.	Arthur Young & Co.	1936.
St. Joseph Lead Co.	Haskins & Sells	1936.
International Paper & Power Co.	Arthur Andersen & Co.	1937.

The members of the association which I represent do not ask for any special consideration; they do not wish any preferential treatment; they merely ask to be placed on a par with other industries which are permitted to determine taxable income on the basis of accounting methods recognized as correctly determining income in the industries in which they operate. No one inventory method is suitable for all industries, and the members of the Copper and Brass Mill Products Association merely ask that they be permitted to pay income and profits taxes on income actually realized rather than on the basis of a method which is not applicable to their particular industry, which shows profits in periods of rising prices which are not and can never be realized and which show losses in periods of falling prices which are equally fictitious.

The copper and brass mill products industry is being subjected to discriminatory treatment by the United States Treasury Department because other manufacturing industries are permitted to use their recognized accounting methods to determine taxable income and are taxed on income which is admittedly realized or realizable, while the copper and brass mill products industry is taxed on unrealized and unrealizable income determined by methods not recognized by the industry.

Other industries are permitted to determine income and inventories by methods substantially similar in purpose and effect to the method the use of which is denied to the copper and brass mill products industry.

Industries dealing in a product such as cotton textiles or flour, where the conditions are similar to those in the industries described above, apply "hedging" transactions to their inventories and are thus able to get for themselves the same sort of results as the industries under discussion obtain by the use of the "last-in, first-out" method. The cotton and flour milling industries are permitted to use their "hedging" methods for tax purposes. The leather, nonferrous metal and other industries are not permitted to use an accounting method producing the same results. The entirely fortuitous circumstances of the existence or absence of an effective futures market is thus made the basis of discrimination between various taxpayers similarly situated. (See general counsel's memorandum 17,322.)

The high rates of tax which are generally considered to be inevitable for many years in the future magnify the importance of using accounting methods which reflect only such income as can actually be disbursed in taxes. A nominal tax rate of 5 percent, which by the inclusion of fictitious income becomes an actual rate of 10 percent, is unfair but will not ruin an industry. A nominal rate, however, of 20 to 30 percent levied on the fictitious income may easily become an actual rate of 40, 60, 80, or 100 per cent on realized income. The members of this association do not wish to pay an effective rate of 3 or 4 times that of most industries and I cannot believe that it is the intention of Congress that they should do so.

I ask, therefore, that the section of the proposed act which deals with inventories should be so worded as to make it possible for the members of this industry to determine their taxable income on a basis which is generally accepted as that which shows as nearly as possible the actual results of operations and the actual realized income. They ask relief from the arbitrary imposition on their industry of a method which is clearly unsuited to it and which shows results which are demonstrably at variance with the facts.

To accomplish this I suggest the addition of the following language to section 22 (c) of the revenue act now under consideration:

> Goods remaining in inventory which have been so intermingled that they cannot be identified with specific invoices may be deemed to be the goods first purchased or produced during the period in which the quantity of goods in the inventory has been acquired and the cost of goods most recently sold may be deemed to be the cost of those most recently purchased or produced, if in conformity with the taxpayer's method of keeping his books or records and with the best accounting practice in the trade or business.

The CHAIRMAN. You say it is a question then of regulation by the Department?

Mr. PELOUBET. I think not, because the Department has refused to recognize an accepted method.

The CHAIRMAN. I understood that the Treasury Department, in 1936, had stated that they had the power to effect it by rules and regulations.

Mr. PELOUBET. They now say no.

The CHAIRMAN. Is that the only question you discussed in your brief?

Mr. PELOUBET. That is the only question.

The CHAIRMAN. When was the last time you had a conference with the Treasury officials?

Mr. PELOUBET. A few days ago, with no results whatever.

The CHAIRMAN. With whom did you talk?

Mr. PELOUBET. That was not a conference at which I attended personally, but I understand they spoke with Mr. Kent and with some of the other officials working under him.

The CHAIRMAN. You did not get very far?

Mr. PELOUBET. We got nowhere, I think there is no question about that.

The CHAIRMAN. I might say to you that this is not a new question. I remember it was presented in 1936.

Mr. PELOUBET. Yes.

The CHAIRMAN. The committee will inquire into it very definitely and will take your brief in connection with it. I was going to suggest, if you had not talked to these experts it might be well to bring it up to date, because we have some experts at one time and at another time we have different experts. They change them at times.

Mr. PELOUBET. We haven't gotten very far with them.

There is one thing that I might bring out. Of course we are not asking for privileges, we are not asking for anything exceptional, and there is nothing in this method which will reduce revenue over a period. As a matter of fact, in the year 1937 the revenue would have been increased if we had been permitted to use this method, for the year 1937 there would have been more taxable income in a number of industries than there are. Of course that will always happen in a period of declining prices. It works both ways. Our people are perfectly willing to take the consequences either way. The only thing is we do not want to pay taxes 2 or 3 years before we make any profits just because we must write up inventories which we cannot sell.

The CHAIRMAN. I will ask the representative of the Treasury to bring those matters to their attention.

Maurice Moonitz

· THE CASE AGAINST LIFO
AS AN INVENTORY-PRICING FORMULA

Maurice Moonitz *was born in Ohio in 1910. He received a B.S. from
California in 1933 and a Ph.D. from the same school in 1941. He has taught
at Santa Clara (1937–1942), Stanford (1942–1944), and at California since
1947. He is a C.P.A. in California, having been on the staff of Arthur
Andersen & Co. from 1944 to 1947, and again in 1955–1956. He served as
a vice-president of the American Accounting Association in 1958 and as
chairman of its committee on accounting theory in 1958 and 1959. He was
the first director of accounting research for the American Institute of
C.P.A.'s new research program, serving from 1960–1963. He is currently
a member of the Accounting Principles Board of the A.I.C.P.A. His publications include* Entity Theory of Consolidated Statements, *published as Monograph No. 4 by the American Accounting Association 1944;* Accounting:
An Analysis of Its Problems *(first edition, 1951, with C. C. Staehling; revised
edition, 1963, with Louis H. Jordan);* The Basic Postulates of Accounting,
published by A.I.C.P.A. as Accounting Research Study No. 1 (1961); and
A Tentative Set of Broad Accounting Principles for Business Enterprises
*(with Robert T. Sprouse), published by A.I.C.P.A. as Accounting Research
Study No. 3 (1962).*
*The article reprinted here reviews the first fifteen years of experience with
LIFO, and should be read in conjunction with the preceding testimony of
Peloubet (page 450).*

In recent years, the LIFO method of inventory pricing has increased in
popularity as a result of the tax advantages it confers; at the same time, its
inadequacies as a measure of assets and of net income have become more
prominent. This article seeks to review the history and rationale of LIFO in
this country in order to lay bare the reasons for the rising tide of opposition

Reprinted from *The Journal of Accountancy* (June, 1953), pp. 682–90, by permission.

457

to its continued presence in the goodly company of generally accepted accounting principles.[1]

In order to narrow the area of discussion and to minimize misunderstandings as to what is being attempted, it should be emphasized that this article does not attempt to encompass the whole area of the accounting treatment of price level changes. For example, a method of reflecting "replacement cost of goods sold" has long been described in the literature.[2] More recently, the use of index numbers to convert accounting data to a common-dollar basis has been urged.[3] These and other similar devices are not the central preoccupation of this article; it is immediately concerned with LIFO, as that method is described in the Internal Revenue Code and the Income Tax Regulations.[4]

Developments prior to 1938. Until the middle and late 1930's, LIFO was not an important method of pricing inventories and cost of goods sold. According to testimony submitted to a Congressional committee, six companies had used "LIFO of similar methods" in their corporate accounts prior to 1920; five additional companies appear in the 1920's; fifteen more are included in the list during the early 1930's.[5] That more than these 26 companies used or had used LIFO prior to 1938 is probable, since the list referred to was compiled from readily available data, and was restricted to the larger companies. But the evidence is unmistakable that LIFO was of no consequence until the Great Depression had run its course. As careful and painstaking an author as Hatfield, for example, does not even mention

---

[1] The types of objections raised to LIFO can be traced in one or more of the following items: W. A. Paton, *Advanced Accounting* (New York, 1941), pp. 145–147; G. R. Husband, "The First-In, Last-Out Method of Inventory Valuation," *Acctg. Rev.,* Vol. 15, No. 2 (June, 1940), pp. 190–196; E. B. Wilcox, "The Rise and Fall of LIFO," JofA, Feb48,pp.98–103; J. E. Walter, "Last-In, First-Out," *Acctg. Rev.,* Vol. 25, No. 1 (January, 1950), pp. 63–75; J. Pagani and W. O. Jones, "Price and Mortality Expectations and Valuation of Inventories," *Acctg. Rev.,* Vol. 25, No. 3 (July, 1950), pp. 315–319: Study Group on Business Income, *Changing Concepts of Business Income* (New York, 1952). LIFO is discussed throughout this report, and, on balance, is mildly censured. A careful reading of pages 39 to 44 should be required of anyone seeking a license to discuss LIFO.

[2] C. F. Schlatter, "Market Profits on the Operating Statement," *Acctg. Rev.,* Vol. 17, No. 2 (April, 1942), pp. 171–178. A similar discussion is also contained in Dean Schlatter's books on cost accounting.

[3] Committee on Concepts and Standards Underlying Corporate Financial Statements of the American Accounting Association. Supplementary Statement No. 2, "Price Level Changes and Financial Statements," JofA,Oct51,pp.461–465; also *Acctg. Rev.,* Vol. 26, No. 4 (October, 1951); Study Group on Business Income, *op. cit.*

[4] Regulations 111, Sec. 29.22(d), "Gross Income—Inventories under Elective Method." The "elective" method now includes the "dollar-value" method of adjustment by the use of price indexes as well as "LIFO" in the older sense. See Sec. 29.22(d)-1. In Section 29.22(d) of the regulations is found the requirement that a taxpayer must employ the "elective" method in his records, accounts, and financial statements if he wishes to employ the same method in his tax return.

[5] Senate Finance Committee, Hearings on the Revenue Act of 1938, 75th Congress, 3d Session, on H. R. 9682 (Govt. Printing Office, 1938). Pages 143 to 167 of these hearings contain the statements of M. E. Peloubet and others on behalf of LIFO. The statistics cited appear on page 164.

the method in his *Accounting,* published in 1927.[6] The 1934 edition of Finney's *Principles* is likewise silent on this topic.[7]

The clearly discernible features which distinguish the 1930s from earlier decades all center around the federal income tax. Although income taxation has been an integral part of the American scene since 1913, the rates of tax applicable to business corporations were not of sizable proportions until the 1930's. An excess-profits tax had been in effect during World War I, but it was short-lived, and the 1920s were years of relatively mild taxation. The rise in rates after the Great Depression was great enough to constitute a qualitative as well as a quantitative change in terms of the impact of the tax on business.

Against a backdrop of fluctuating prices, the problem assumed sizable proportions. Prices had risen sharply during World War I, had dropped abruptly a few years thereafter, had held reasonably stable during the twenties, had broken catastrophically in the Great Depression, were on the rise in uneven fashion after the spring of 1933, and were expected to drop again in the near future, as they did in fact in 1937 and 1938. It is significant that there was no averaging provision in the tax law in the early and middle thirties, such as the carry-back or carry-forward of operating losses. As a consequence, a company which paid taxes on large profits during a price rise could look forward to no "relief" or offset if a subsequent price decline should result in net losses.

In 1936, permission to use LIFO had been requested of the House Ways and Means Committee and of the Senate Finance Committee, but the petitioners had been referred to the Commissioner of Internal Revenue who, they were told, had authority to legalize the use of LIFO for tax purposes. But the Treasury refused to budge in its traditional opposition to the "normal stock" methods of inventory pricing in general, and to LIFO in particular.[8]

The problem of an inequitable tax burden could have been solved by a change in the tax rules (i.e., averaging of gains and losses over a period of years, for tax purposes, according to some workable formula) or by a change in the accounting rules (i.e., a new theory or formula for determination of profit). Taxpayers got both. The Revenue Act of 1938 permitted the use of LIFO by a few types of businesses; the scope of LIFO was liberalized somewhat in the Revenue Act of 1939. The latter act also restored the "net operating loss deduction." Both features have been in the federal tax structure ever since. The root of the difficulty created for accounting is the unique provision of the income-tax law which requires that LIFO must be used for reporting purposes if it is to be accepted for tax purposes. In other words, a generally applicable accounting rule was formulated by act of Congress.

In order to obtain some perspective on later developments, the conditions

6 H. R. Hatfield, *Accounting: Its Principles and Problems* (New York, 1927).

7 H. A. Finney, *Principles of Accounting: Intermediate* (New York, 1934).

8 Hearings, *op. cit.,* p. 143.

under which LIFO was originally thought to be appropriate, according to its proponents, are summarized at this point.[9]

1. The investment in inventories must be large, relative to other assets.
2. The inventory must consist of a few basic materials which form a substantial part of the cost of the product sold.
3. The spread between raw material cost and selling price must be relatively constant.

(The discussion of Statement 4 in *Accounting Research Bulletin 29,* as originally issued in July, 1947, contained the following sentences: "These methods recognize the variations which exist in the relationships of costs to sales prices under different economic conditions. Thus, where sales prices are promptly influenced by changes in reproductive costs, an assumption of the 'last-in first-out' flow of cost factors may be the more appropriate. Where no such cost-price relationship exists, the 'first-in first-out' or an 'average' method may be more properly utilized." The committee on accounting procedure, in the process of codifying the *Accounting Research Bulletins,* voted some time ago to eliminate these sentences from Bulletin 29.)

4. Inventory turnover must be slow because of the length of the period of process.
5. The company involved must customarily make purchases of raw materials to fill specific orders.

Furthermore, it is abundantly clear that LIFO was viewed, in 1938, primarily as an adaptation to cyclical price movements. Witness the following statement by Peloubet:

"Over a period of years total income will be the same under any method of accounting consistently applied, and if taxed at a flat rate the aggregate tax will be the same.... There is one thing that I might bring out. Of course we are not asking for privileges, we are not asking for anything exceptional, and there is nothing in this method which will reduce revenue over a period.... Our people are perfectly willing to take the consequences either way (i.e., rising prices or falling prices). The only thing is we do not want to pay taxes 2 or 3 years before we make any profits just because we must write up inventories which we cannot sell."[10]

Inflationary Trend Since 1938

Developments since 1938

Instead of a series of cyclical price movements about some reasonably stable norm, the last decade or so has witnessed a marked inflationary trend.

---

9 Hearings, *op. cit.,* pp. 154–55.
10 Hearings, *op. cit.,* pp. 145, 147.

Prices have moved unevenly upward, with only minor and sporadic interruptions. During the same period, income-tax rates moved to levels formerly unknown, the peak being reached during the war period under the excess-profits tax. Especially during the war years, liquidation of a part of the basic or normal LIFO inventory became extensive enough to constitute a new problem. This liquidation occurred because of the disruption of usual sources of supply and the consequent difficulty of replacing inventories as fast as they were consumed. It is significant that liquidation occurred even among companies which had asserted that their basic or normal inventory was essential to operations, that it was "fixed" by technical considerations and could not be liquidated without suspension of activity. Still they continued to operate, and on a high level. It is also significant that these companies were *not* willing to take the consequences, taxwise, of their use of low-valued inventories in a period of high prices. The result was an extension of LIFO to include "next-in first-out," to permit the deduction of the cost of units *subsequently* acquired from revenues *previously* realized and wholly unrelated to the replacement of the "involuntarily-liquidated" basic stock.

In 1947, the Tax Court handed down a decision, later accepted by the Commissioner of Internal Revenue and incorporated in his regulations, which removed the last legal barrier to the use of LIFO by any taxpayer in any line of activity in which inventories were used for tax purposes.[11]

The combined effect of these developments has been to stimulate the adoption of LIFO—adoptions which have been dominated by tax considerations. This point is made crystal-clear by an analyst of the LIFO method:[12]

"Since 1939 few management decisions on LIFO have been made without reference to their tax effects. Decisions as to whether to use LIFO, how to apply it, and even as to the industries in which the method constitutes acceptable accounting practice, have been dominated by tax considerations. It would be difficult to cite other instances in which management considerations on matters of broad policy and general economic significance have been more strongly influenced by tax requirements.

"Undoubtedly the opportunity to reduce tax liabilities has been by far the most powerful motivation leading to the widespread adoption of LIFO during the past decade. The combination of sharply rising prices and high excess-profits taxes gave managements in many industries a strong tax incentive to shift to LIFO during the early war years. The large postwar price increases caused some companies to make the shift as late as 1946 and 1947, though the risk of ultimate tax penalties was then greater because of the height to which price levels had already risen."

---

[11] *Hutzler Bros.*, 8 T.C. 14 (1947).

[12] J. Keith Butters, *Effects of Taxation: Inventory Accounting and Policies* (Boston, 1949), pp. 6, 8. See also R. W. Button, "The LIFO Bonanza?" *The Balance Sheet*, February, 1948, and subsequent articles on LIFO in the March, 1948, and April, 1948, issues of the same journal, published by the Controllers' Congress of the National Retail Dry Goods Association.

As to non-tax reasons for electing LIFO, Butters states (p. 9), that "many executives who recalled the severe inventory losses of 1920 and 1921 were also anxious to provide a 'cushion' to protect themselves from the necessity of reporting similar losses in the event of a price collapse at the end of World War II. They saw in the availability of LIFO an opportunity to accomplish this objective and at the same time to make substantial tax savings."

Why More Companies Don't Adopt LIFO

Why haven't more companies adopted LIFO for the tax advantages involved? Apparently there are two main reasons (other than inertia). The first reason is based on the fact that in a period of rising prices, and all other things being equal, reported profit under LIFO will be less than reported profit under FIFO or average cost. As a consequence, a shift to LIFO may involve less income, less dividends, less management compensation where that compensation varies with reported profit, and may result in a default under a bond contract. The second reason stems from expectations as to price movements in the near future. If prices are expected to decline sharply, any advantages under present rules and regulations obtained by a shift to LIFO will be minor, or nonexistent.

But this is not the end of the story. Under existing tax regulations, LIFO is a "cost" method; a taxpayer who elects LIFO must stay on LIFO. He cannot employ "cost or market, whichever is lower," as can a taxpayer on FIFO or average cost. In other words, as long as prices are stable or are rising, real or potential tax advantages exist; but if prices should fall substantially, the LIFO taxpayer will at that time report higher profits and pay higher taxes than a taxpayer not on LIFO, but otherwise in identically the same situation. For the time being, then, those who expect price declines will stay away from LIFO. Meanwhile, representations are being made to the appropriate Congressional committees to amend the Internal Revenue Code to permit LIFO cost or market, whichever is lower.

The recommendations for amendment of federal tax laws, submitted to Congress by the committee on federal taxation of the American Institute of Accountants, contained the following statement, as summarized in *The Journal* of *Accountancy* (December, 1952) p. 720:

"Section 22(d). The Code should be amended to permit taxpayers using the LIFO inventory method for income-tax purposes to value their inventories at the lower of cost or market while the Excess Profits Tax Act of 1950 is in force, and for five years thereafter."

If Congress obliges, first-in first-out can then be added to the list of "generally accepted accounting principles."

Analysis of LIFO

Later the arguments for and against LIFO are to be considered. The discussion in this section remains on the descriptive and historical level in order to round out the picture of LIFO in actual operation.

The salient effect of LIFO is the smoothing of reported profits in the face of continued changes in prices. Technically, the relative stabilization of profit is obtained by an increase or decrease in recorded cost of goods sold as prices rise and fall. Two effects of the relative stabilization of reported profit are immediately apparent. One is the failure to report all gains (and losses) from changes in prices; the result of buying cheap and selling dear, or of buying high and selling low is not recorded. Good merchandising is obscured. It is not a question of isolating or earmarking these gains or losses for special treatment or disclosure; the LIFO method simply ignores them, and leaves no trace of them in the financial statements. The other effect, in terms of actual experience since 1938, is the gross understatement of inventory values among the assets in the balance-sheet. This attribute of LIFO has long been recognized by its advocates. Indeed, as long ago as 1934, W. A. Staub commented that "if such a cost formula or method (i.e., LIFO cost or market) were generally adopted in an industry, it would be desirable to show as a memorandum on the balance-sheet the current replacement market-value for the inventory."[13] But to date, the instances in which companies reporting inventories on LIFO also disclose current replacement costs are all too few.

A further result of LIFO, then, is to weaken, if not to destroy, comparability among the published financial statements of different companies, or indeed, the comparability of financial statements of one company over a period of years. For example, the calculation of inventory turnover involves a comparison of cost of goods sold or of sales, on the one hand, with inventory, on the other. But the inventory figure, under LIFO, bears no relationship to current conditions; consequently, the calculation of inventory turnover in such cases is a useless exercise in arithmetic. A similar effect is observable with respect to the current ratio, and other analytical devices involving inventory data. In this respect, then, the usefulness of published financial statements has diminished in recent years.

Despite the high hopes of its proponents that LIFO would reduce the inequities in the federal tax structure, the method has actually increased them. In the face of rising prices and rising tax-rates, the LIFO companies have been a favored group; a substantial burden has been shifted from them to

---

13 Quoted in *Hearings, op. cit.,* pp. 157–58. Staub pointed out that replacement value would be needed to assist credit-granters, and to facilitate comparison among industries. He also urged the disclosure of replacement value under other methods of inventory pricing.

taxpayers not on LIFO. This is no reflection on the taxpayer who elected LIFO and was permitted to use it for tax purposes; under the prevailing rules of the game, anyone may use every available legal means to see that someone else foots the bill. But the experience with LIFO and the federal tax bill should serve as an object-lesson to the accounting profession. No one will seriously maintain that the size of the federal tax load on the whole community has been reduced by LIFO, or by any other scheme of tax "minimization." The profession should be wary, now and in the future, of new "principles" of accounting whose major objective is to shift the burden of the income tax from one group of clients to another group.

Rationale of LIFO—Pro and Con

Over the years, the arguments advanced in support of LIFO as a superior method of inventory pricing have changed. As the current euphemism has it, there has been "evolution" in the concept of LIFO, and the process of evolution is not yet complete.

Originally, much was made of the point that LIFO reflected results of operations as though "hedging" had been practiced successfully. For example, assume that, at the time a contract for future delivery of metal products is made, a quantity of metal is purchased to replace the amount which will be consumed in filling the order. The assertion is made that, under this set of circumstances, fluctuations in the price of metal as raw material are irrelevant to the calculation of gain or loss on the contract.[14] In a perfect hedge, the facts bear out the assertion; gains and losses on the simultaneous sale and purchase of commodities cancel each other. But a perfect hedge requires, by definition, no speculation in commodities. In the cases, however, in which LIFO was urged as a more appropriate method of pricing, substantial quantities of basic commodities were carried, against which there was no offsetting "hedge." As a consequence, to the extent of these basic stocks, the business was exposed to the effects of price fluctuations. In order to bolster the "hedging" argument, the further point was made that the fabricator, in effect, acts as a buying agent for his customer, and not as a dealer in metal; as a consequence, it is alleged, no gain or loss on the metal accrues to the fabricator.[15] To accept this argument, however, is to ignore the actual relationship between the dealer and customer and to substitute a fictional relationship. If the agency relationship is in actuality more realistic, it would appear to be a relatively simple matter to change the formal contracts and other arrangements to bring it into being; if this were done, there would be no need to invoke LIFO, since the fabricator would have no materials' inventory to price.

---

[14] *Hearings, op. cit.,* p. 143.
[15] *Hearings, op. cit.,* p. 152.

In these days of "dollar-value LIFO" for department stores, the points just discussed appear archaic, and are no longer relied on as major elements in the theory behind LIFO. Instead, three other points appear more frequently as buttresses of the structure:

1. To an extent varying with technical conditions in each industry, inventories represent an involuntary, fixed commitment, analogous to a fixed asset.
2. LIFO is a method of adjustment to price level changes.
3. Increases in the unit prices of inventory items represent unrealized and unrealizable inventory profits, and therefore should be excluded from the accounts, by means of LIFO.

The first point, the one with respect to an "involuntary commitment" of inventory, need not detain anyone long. Even if the point is accepted as valid, its impact is with respect to the classification of the inventory item, not its pricing. If it were decided to show some basic quantity of materials, for example, among the fixed assets, the problem would still remain as to the appropriate pricing formula. No one has ever, in a published statement, so treated inventories; consequently, there is no evidence as to the concrete, operational meaning of the assertion that some portion of inventories are "fixed."

LIFO Does Not Adjust Price Level Changes

For obvious reasons, the second point asserting that LIFO is a method of adjustment of price level changes, is in vogue these days. But the point is invalid, for two related reasons.

First, LIFO fails miserably and completely in making adjustments of inventory values for *any* type of price change. Arthur Dean has this to say on the point under discussion:

"There are, however, obvious shortcomings to LIFO as a solution of the problems presented by the decline in the value of the dollar. While it does in certain circumstances. . .have the effect of revaluing goods *sold* in terms of depreciated dollars, it does so by ascribing to *unsold* goods the old monetary costs, resulting in a corresponding undervaluation in terms of current dollars of inventories on hand."[16]

Witness also the following comment of Gilman:

"While both LIFO and accelerated depreciation may accomplish a desired effect on the income statement, they influence the balance-sheet oppositely, and conceivably, below the limits of reasonable conservatism.

---

[16] Arthur H. Dean, *An Inquiry into the Nature of Business Income Under Present Price Levels* (New York, 1949), p. 24 (Emphasis supplied).

"This effect contradicts our general thesis relating to decreased purchasing power of the dollar. It is inconsistent in that it provides 'inflated' costs in the income statement and correspondingly 'deflated' asset values in the balance-sheet—a paradox which should cause concern to the certified public accountant who is requested to give as his opinion that his client's balance-sheet presents fairly the client's financial position."[17]

In the second place, LIFO does not even adjust for price level changes in the income statement. What LIFO does do under the procedures usually prescribed by its advocates is to reflect in cost of goods sold the latest costs paid for the *specific* commodity dealt in.

These latest costs may or may not be close to the current replacement costs of the commodity involved; in the case of seasonal buying the last cost paid may be quite different from current replacement cost. As a consequence, LIFO eliminates only an undetermined part of the effects of specific price fluctuations.

But even if it is conceded that LIFO, on the average, does eliminate the effects of fluctuations in the prices of specific commodities, the problem of the effect of price level changes is still left unsolved. The price movements of any given commodity bear no necessary relationship to the movements of the general price level or of its reciprocal, the purchasing power of the dollar.[18]

As to the "unrealized profit" argument, an early proponent of LIFO has made the following statement:

"These inventory profits may be called unrealized inventory profits—that is, profits represented by unsold inventories rather than cash. In fact, to a going concern, most of the inventory profits are not only unrealized but they are also unrealizable if the concern is to continue in business. Even though inventories are constantly being turned over, a certain quantity of inventories is a part of the capital equipment of the business. Increases or decreases in inventory values are analogous in every essential to unrealized capital gains or losses. Inventory profits, as here defined, cannot be converted into cash profits without a net liquidation of inventories."[19]

This quotations makes abundantly clear the extent to which LIFO depends upon a crude "cash balance" concept of profit, without reference to changes in other assets or debts. The quotation also makes clear that the primary

---

17 Study Group on Business Income, *Changing Concepts of Business Income,* (New York, 1952), p. 120.

18 For more detailed discussion of the problems involved in adjusting for price level changes, see Supplementary Statement No. 2 of the American Accounting Association's Committee on Concepts and Standards, "Price Level Changes and Financial Statements," *Accounting Review,* Vol. 26, No. 4, (October, 1951), and the report of the Study Group on Business Income, *Changing Concepts of Business Income* (New York, 1952).

19 H. B. Arthur, "Inventory Profits in the Business Cycle," *American Economic Review,* Vol. 28, No. 1, (March, 1938), p. 28.

technical objective of LIFO is to avoid the credit to balance-sheet net worth which would result if inventories were to be carried at a figure close to their current value, as measured by prices actually prevailing in the market in the current period.

What About " Unrealized Profit " ?

But what is to be made of the point as to "unrealized profit"? Observe that the unrealized profit is "represented" by unsold inventories. Accordingly, in a period of rising prices, inventories must, under LIFO, be progressively understated as compared with the same inventories stated at current prices actually prevailing in the market; total reported assets and reported proprietary investment are also correspondingly and progressively understated. The defense of LIFO must then take the uncomfortable form of a defense of a statement of financial position which is known to be inaccurate, and, what is worse, wherein the approximate magnitude of the inaccuracy is known but usually undisclosed. This type of defense is put forward in many forms and under numerous guises; probably the most common form is the oft-repeated assertion that the income statement is more important than the balance-sheet, and therefore it doesn't make too much difference what appears in the latter statement. But this leaves unanswered the important query as to how it is possible to have reasonably accurate statements of income accompanied by a series of admittedly inaccurate balance-sheets. Where is the difference buried, and of what significance is it? In other words, the advocates of LIFO have formulated no theory of income or of financial position which will meet the practical test of making understandable that which is going on in the real world.

One type of argument frequently advanced in defense of LIFO states essentially that a ton of steel, for example, has the same economic and business significance today as a ton of steel did last year, and in 1940, and in 1890. If, then, a concern has need for at least 1,000 tons of steel at all times in order to operate, the corresponding inventory valuation should not be affected, so it is asserted, because of increases or decreases in the price of steel. This type of primitive economic argument is advanced despite the clearcut recognition of changed buying prices for steel, of changed selling prices for steel products, of changed market conditions confronting the industry of which the concern is a part, of changed technology, wage rates, labor relations, and so on. The plain fact of the matter is that the economic or business significance of any given quantity of any specified commodity changes from day to day, in response to a whole constellation of forces; any accounting procedure which fails to reflect in some degree the effect of these forces cannot claim to be realistic and practical. The manner in which accounting can, and usually does, reflect the effect of these forces can be sketched in broad outline, somewhat as follows.

How Accounting Reflects Economic Forces

By definition, units of inventory are acquired, processed, and held for sale to customers; each repurchase is an independent decision, as to time, type, and quantity, or whether to repurchase at all; at each turnover of the inventory, the resultant receipts from customers restore the liquidity of the investment in inventories, thereby making possible a new set of decisions as to the amount and direction of investment. If the proceeds of sale are used to acquire, process, or hold additional units of inventory, it is because management expects future sales to be at a price equal to or (usually) greater than current cost; to assume otherwise is to postulate deliberate dissipation of resources by management. Any inventory is worth what the quantity of goods actually on hand will bring on the market at orderly sale; under the cost rule, then, and in the absence of physical deterioration or obsolescence, an inventory is realistically priced when it is carried at some cost prevailing in the last turnover period (e.g., FIFO and possibly some forms of average costing) or at some net selling price expected to prevail in the next turnover period (e.g., cost, not in excess of net realizable value). In brief, profit emerges not later than the time of sale or collection from customer; reinvestment in similar items has no bearing on whether a profit was or was not realized on the investment and liquidation of items previously held.

The validity of the preceding observations is independent of the movements of the price level. That is to say, inventories should always be reflected in terms of prices currently prevailing; if the price level has changed appreciably then *all* relevant statement data should be adjusted in some systematic manner. The assault on common sense offered by LIFO, which requires the assertion on a balance-sheet that an inventory is "fairly presented" at three cents a pound when the level of prices actually prevailing in the current period is around fifteen cents, is thereby avoided.

Summary and Conclusion

The case against LIFO as an inventory-pricing formula can be readily summarized:

1. On historical grounds, the original reasons for its adoption are no longer present; a reading of the early testimony before the pertinent Congressional committees amply demonstrates this point.
2. As it has worked out, LIFO is primarily a device for reducing or

deferring the amount of income tax payable by a given concern, not a device for measuring its business income.

3. LIFO does not even have the virtue of adjusting for price level changes; in fact, it has a perverse effect on the inventory figure appearing in the balance-sheet.

4. LIFO suppresses realized market gains and losses; it assigns a non-existent stability to earnings and to inventories.

In fact, LIFO presumes a type of business and economic system which does not exist. In the world in which we live, prices do go up and down, profits do change from year to year, dividends vary; as a result, stockholders, trade union leaders, and tax collectors may misunderstand what is going on. Therefore, says LIFO, let us write down the story as it does *not* happen; if we shut our eyes to reality, maybe it will go away.[20]

But despite all the marshalling of facts, arguments, logic, and analysis, the popularity of LIFO increases. Given permission, as seems more than possible at the moment, to use "LIFO cost or market," many more taxpayers will adopt LIFO. This "popularity" rests solely on the unique provision of the Internal Revenue Code requiring the use of LIFO in all published statements and reports if a taxpayer wishes to use LIFO for tax purposes.

What is sorely needed is a declaration of independence by the profession from the exigencies of income taxation as the arbiter of business income. Specifically, two recommendations are submitted:

1. For the immediate future, the current cost of inventories on LIFO should be revealed in financial statements.

2. For the longer term, LIFO should be abandoned for reporting purposes, provided the mandatory provision of the Internal Revenue Code is modified, as it should be in order to restore to accounting its function of defining and measuring business income.

These steps seem to be the least that can be taken in order to preserve the rational basis of modern accounting.

---

[20] "To summarize, if one grants that the traditional accounting statement of profits is subject to dangerous misinterpretation, the alternatives are to change present accounting practices or to change the public. The former would seem to be infinitely more feasible than the latter." Butters, *op. cit.*, p. 136.

Seymour Walton

SINKING FUNDS AND RESERVE ACCOUNTS

Seymour Walton *(1846–1920) was educated at Williams College. He was an organizer of the Fort Dearborn National Bank (Chicago), and taught at Marquette and Northwestern. He left Northwestern in 1912 to become head of the Walton School of Commerce, a leading correspondence school with headquarters in Chicago. He was the author of materials used in the correspondence courses of the Alexander Hamilton Institute and the Walton School of Commerce. He served as president of the Illinois Society of C.P.A. He edited the Student's Department of the Journal of Accountancy until his death in 1920; he was succeeded in this influential post by his associate, Harry A. Finney.*
The article reprinted here is a straightforward, incisive analysis of the meaning of a sinking fund "out of profits." It is typical of most of his writing and helps explain the influence he had on thousands of men and women preparing for the C.P.A. examination in the first quarter of the twentieth century.

There is no subject on which there seems greater need of clear thinking than that of sinking funds and their relation to reserve accounts. While most of the authorities have given a clear and absolutely correct definition of the sinking fund as a fund set aside of assets and accumulated at interest for the purpose of meeting a debt, as Lisle says, followed exactly by Tipson, or, according to another writer, a species of financial arrangement by means of which a fund is created to reduce or extinguish a debt either already incurred or about to be incurred, they have unfortunately not been content to stop there, but have gone on to say that this fund must be charged against revenue. There seems to be a complete failure to discriminate between a fund and a reserve account. This is shown by the fact that some of the state boards of examiners have asked for definitions of various funds and

Reprinted from *The Journal of Accountancy* (October, 1908), pp. 394–99, by permission.

for their classification as assets or liabilities. Dicksee as usual is so uncertain in his utterances that it is difficult to know exactly how he intends the matters to be handled, but he seems to make a distinction between the sinking fund and the sinking fund account, making the latter a credit, but not explaining why the debit item is not just as much an account as the credit one is.

A. Lowes Dickinson expresses the general view when he says, "sinking funds or debt extinguishment funds are not in theory a charge against profit and loss, for the reason that they do not represent a loss or expense, but the extinction of an existing liability. Inasmuch, however, as in most cases the only source out of which such redemption fund can be provided is the surplus earnings, it is usual to insert a provision in trust deeds that the sinking fund is to be provided out of the profits of the year." From this he goes on to reason that the sinking fund installments should be charged to profit and loss.

The expression "out of profits" seems to have been the cause of the confusion in the minds of all the accountants who have placed themselves on record on this subject. It has been taken for granted that because accumulated profits must usually be the source from which is obtained the money necessary for the purchase of the sinking fund securities, therefore profits must be charged with it. Since the charge to profits necessitates a corresponding credit and since the credit to sinking fund would extinguish that account and leave nothing on the books to represent the securities actually on hand, various devices have been resorted to, to represent this fictitious credit, such as sinking fund account, sinking fund reserve, or the recommendation that the amount be charged off of fixed assets, ignoring the patent fact that there is no necessary connection between the sinking fund requirements and the amount of depreciation that should be charged off from any of the assets. Dicksee in one place seems to realize the difference between a charge against profits and a sum set aside out of profits, but he apparently quickly forgets it.

The truth seems to be that there is no relation whatever between a reserve account and a sinking fund. A reserve account is a device to put on the books the judgment of the accountant as to the probable or certain loss to be expected, or at least guarded against it, in respect to certain assets. As it represents a diminished value it is of necessity chargeable to profits. In the case of a wasting asset, such as a coal mine or a building on leased ground with reversion to the owner of the fee, it may be advisable to establish a sinking fund with which to reimburse the stockholders when the company is eventually liquidated, but the advisability of doing this is entirely a question of financiering. If any other disposition is made of the money accumulated, it will make no difference in the amount or the character of the reserve set up to provide for the loss in value of the mine or the building. In other words, in such a case, the reserve is the essential thing, the disposition of the money is a secondary and immaterial element from the accounting standpoint.

In the case of a sinking fund to provide for the redemption of bonds, there is absolutely no reason for any reserve account as a credit against it. The provision of the trust deed that the sinking fund shall be provided out of the profits means no more than that a sufficient portion of the money which results from the profits must be dedicated to the eventual redemption of the bonds. It is a measure intended to protect the bondholders from directors who might be willing to squander all the money obtainable by declaring excessive dividends, but it is purely a financial measure and consists entirely in a change in the form of assets from cash to securities. That it has not changed the actual amount of the surplus profits is evidenced by the usual requirements that the securities must be placed in the hands of a trustee where they will be out of the reach of the directors. If it were correct to charge the amount of the sinking fund against surplus, there would be no danger of the directors using the securities as a basis of dividends since they can declare dividends only out of surplus earnings.

An analysis of the real nature of a sinking fund to provide for bonds not yet due will strengthen the reasoning. If the money thus accumulated is used to buy up some of the bonds for whose payment it is eventually intended and those bonds are charged directly to the bond account, it hardly seems possible that any one should advise that a reserve account should also be set up. The establishment of the sinking fund is in reality only a division of the bond account into two parts, bonds representing the gross credit, and sinking fund the debit side of the account. If in the case of the direct charge to bond account of the bonds bought, there is no occasion for a charge to revenue, it is difficult to understand why the charge to revenue should be necessary when the charge to bond account is temporarily suspended, for it must not be forgotten that the eventual charge is against the bond account, and that the device of the sinking fund is a temporary one only, resorted to so that the interest on the fund may be properly cared for, and also because the securities in the fund are not always nor necessarily the identical bonds that are to be redeemed.

Taking up the question practically, it will be found that the theoretical reasoning is entirely justified. If the reserve account has been set up, we would have at the maturity of the bonds, say for $100,000, the following accounts upon the books:

Bonds, Cr.		$100,000
Reserve for Bonds, Cr.		100,000
Sinking Fund, Dr.	$100,000	

Realizing on the sinking fund and with it paying off the bonds, we would have still remaining a credit of $100,000 to reserve for bonds, with no bonds outstanding and therefore no necessity for the reserve. The only way it can be disposed of is by a credit to profit and loss but no explanation has ever been vouchsafed as to why it was ever charged to profit and loss at all. Tipson says that when bonds are paid "the sinking fund account then becomes a surplus," but he neglects to say what magic is responsible for "the sea change into something rich and strange." If our $100,000 reserve for bonds is a liability on June 30, what weird transformation has taken place during the silent watches of the night to make it appear as a surplus on July 1? The conclusion is irresistible that it has always been a surplus and that it was an error of accounting principle to call it anything else. The contention is put forward that if it is left in the surplus account, there will be a temptation to declare dividends against it. The answer to this is, that since so much money has been tied up in the sinking fund there is none left with which to pay a dividend based on this portion of the surplus, a financial and not an accounting reason as we have already seen. This is also shown by the fact that if, in any way, perhaps by the sale of some of the assets, the company should be put in funds sufficient to pay a dividend that would reduce the total accumulated surplus below the amount dedicated to the purchase of sinking fund bonds, it would be perfectly competent for the board of directors to declare and pay such a dividend.

The surplus account should show the total undivided net earnings of the company to date, regardless of the manner in which the funds realized from this total surplus are represented in the assets, whether in cash, in new plant or in sinking fund bonds.

If any further argument were needed to show that no reserve account should be set up against a sinking fund for the redemption of bonds, it may be found in the consideration of the real nature of the bonds. There is no essential accounting difference between bonds and ordinary bills payable secured by the deposit of collateral. The bonds run for a longer time and are more formal in character so that they may be easily transferred, but they are both promises to pay at a future time and nothing else. No one would think of charging the partial payments on a six month's note to revenue, and there seems no adequate reason why such charge should be made when the note is divided into bonds and runs for perhaps forty times six months.

It might seem as if this were only a question of names with no practical bearing whatever, but it is really of vital interest to the stockholder in estimating the book value of his stock. For instance, in the balance sheet for December 31, 1907, published by the United States Steel Corporation, there appears among the liabilities an item of bond sinking fund with accretions $31,503,976.45, while the undivided surplus appears as $122,645,243.62. A note states that this sinking fund is represented by bonds held by the trustees and not treated as assets, and yet the bonds outstanding are shown reduced from the original amounts by the deduction of the exact amount of the bonds so held. It has usually been considered that the reduction of a liability was the equivalent of an asset, but this corporation does not seem to take this view.

If a stockholder inquires as to the profits accumulated by this corporation up to the date of this balance sheet, it seems manifestly unfair to say that they are only $122,000,000 and to ignore the $31,000,000 which differ from the rest of the surplus only in being empirically offset by specific assets instead of being represented by the general excess of all the assets above the capital and active liabilities. If the capital of the subsidiary companies is included in the capital of the corporation, the book value as shown by the balance sheet in its present form would be a little over 114, whereas the actual value should be nearly 117¾. If the corporation could be liquidated without expense and the full book value of the assets realized, it cannot be denied that each stockholder would receive the larger value per share, therefore the larger value must be the true book value of the stock.

In order to meet the views of those who claim that a portion of the surplus corresponding to the sinking fund has been rendered unavailable for dividends owing to the financial exigencies of the situation, and yet preserve the true nature of the surplus, it would be entirely proper to divide the surplus account into two parts, fixed surplus, representing the portion whose proceeds had been locked up in the sinking fund, and free surplus which is available for dividends, both from a financial and an accounting standpoint. The balance sheet which has been quoted would then stand as follows:

SURPLUS:
    Fixed, by dedication of proceeds to
        sinking fund .... $ 31,503,976.45
    Free, available for dividends 122,645,243.62
        TOTAL SURPLUS $154,149,220.07

a statement which would give the true condition of affairs from any standpoint.

The advisability of calling a credit account a fund instead of a reserve is merely a question of the correct use of English words and has no real bearing on any accounting principle.

William Morse Cole

INTEREST ON INVESTMENT IN EQUIPMENT

William Morse Cole *was born in Massachusetts in 1866, the same year as* Henry Rand Hatfield. *He was educated at Harvard, receiving his Bachelor's degree in 1890 and his Master's in 1895. He taught at Harvard until his retirement in 1933.*
Among his published works are Accounts: Their Construction and Interpretation *(1915), and* The Fundamentals of Accounting *(1921).*
The short article reprinted here was written while Cole was an assistant professor. It appeared in the issue of The Journal of Accountancy *(April 1913), devoted mainly to the problem of interest as a cost. Cole's article followed the one by A. Hamilton Church, also reprinted in this book (see page 287).*

Though it is common to speak of cost accounting as if it were different in nature from other kinds of accounting, virtually all accounting worthy of the name has for a prime purpose the determination of cost. Accounting should serve as a guide in three ways: in fixing prices so that they shall be adjusted properly to costs; in eliminating waste of material, of labor, and of burden charges; and in determining what had best be undertaken in the establishment itself and what had best be purchased or ordered outside. Since these three purposes are the recognized fundamental purposes of cost accounting, it is necessarily true that whether an enterprise is concerned with manufacturing, distribution, or service, its accounting should be, in a sense, cost accounting.

Let us examine these three aims in turn.

Prices must be fixed at such a point that they shall at least cover (1) materials, or goods; (2) labor, or service; and (3) expense burden, or what are commonly called "overhead charges." Obviously, if the last of these is not quite fully covered, the continuance of production or service is not economically advisable (unless, of course, the work serves other purposes

Reprinted from *The Journal of Accountancy* (April, 1913), pp. 232–36, by permission.

than those which are immediately connected with the initial enterprise). If, again, the income provided by the price gives less than a proper amount as interest on the investment—investment in the form of capital locked up in machinery, facilities, material, or waiting product—the return is not economically sufficient to make the enterprise self-supporting. If this interest is not included in the expense burden, therefore, it must be added later, somewhere, before one can know whether the return is adequate to make the enterprise self-supporting. Since one of the purposes of accounting is to show whether the return is adequate, the interest would seem necessarily to be involved somewhere in the accounting.

Efficient management always attempts to eliminate as much as possible of excess consumption of material, excess expenditure of labor—both mental and muscular—and excess investment in machinery, in other facilities, and in supplies. The best guide for such elimination is an analysis of these various elements, so that comparison may be made between different methods and between different managements. To use a simple illustration, there may be a choice between two methods as follows: machinery at a cost of $35,000, materials at a cost of $5, and labor at a cost of $20; or machinery at a cost of $5,000, material at $5, and labor at $30. We may know, perhaps, that the maintenance, insurance, and taxes on the machinery, while the article is in machine process (that is, the share of maintenance, insurance, and taxes chargeable on this particular production), will be $10 in the first case, and $1.50 in the second case. These figures give us with the expensive machinery a production-cost of $35.00 (that is, $5 for material, $20 for labor, and $10 for maintenance, etc.), and of $36.50 ($5 for material, $30 for labor, and $1.50 for maintenance, etc.), with the less expensive machinery. Taking no account of the interest, therefore, the investment in the expensive machinery appears worth while—if, at least, our production is so large that a margin of $1.50 reduction in cost on each article of product is worth while when set against the possibly greater error in our estimate of depreciation, etc. Yet we have clearly left out of account one element of the problem, for, until we know the length of time for which the different equipments are involved in production we do not know whether interest on the greater capital in the first case will more than eat up the margin of saving over the second. If, for example, the machinery is employed a day in producing this article, even though we use as low a rate of interest as 3 per cent, there is in the expensive machinery an additional element of $3.50 in interest for the one day involved (on a 300-day basis), but there is an additional charge of only 50 cents in interest, on the same ground, for the inexpensive machinery. This difference in favor of the less expensive machinery turns the scale of advantage; for the costs are now $38.50 compared with $37. If, on the other hand, the machines were employed in this production only one hour, on the basis of a 9-hour day, the more expensive machinery with the lower labor cost would be a more economical means of production; for, since the interest element is now only

39 cents, its total is $35.39, but the total for the other machine, with interest of 6 cents, is $36.56. It is absolutely essential, therefore, that interest be taken into consideration in determining which of two methods of production is more economical.

The same sort of consideration of interest is essential in attempting to determine what we shall make in our own establishment and what we shall order outside; for if work at home involves investment in machinery, or other facilities, so that we must get a return of $38.50 from our ultimate product or service, but we can purchase the same product or service outside for $37, it is obviously foolish to do the work at home—unless, indeed, our freedom from outside dependence is worth to us more than the difference in cost, or unless we can find no employment for our capital elsewhere at a rate as high as that which we have used in our calculation.

No comparison is possible between different establishments, between different periods in the same establishment, or between different methods in the same establishment, if capital investment in labor-saving or material-saving machinery is neglected; for the very purpose of such investment is to save cost in other directions, and to neglect the capital sacrifice, made in saving other costs, is to neglect in part the very aim of cost accounting.

Opponents of treating interest as a cost may admit the need of knowing the figure of interest but may deny the desirability of showing it on the books. The function of an accountant is to analyze a situation and learn the facts; and the function of a bookkeeper is to record the facts which, if not recorded, will be forgotten. It seems, therefore, as if it is the function of a cost accountant to learn regarding interest the facts which will serve as a guide in determining prices, in eliminating wastes, and in determining what may best be undertaken; for one cannot otherwise easily get a safe guidance in these particulars. It seems, too, as if it is the function of the bookkeeper to record the results of such study, for surely they will be forgotten if they are not recorded.

Possibly some persons admit that, for such purposes as those just discussed, interest must be considered, but deny that it is a cost. Discussions of terminology are quite as likely to be fruitless as fruitful. Any practical value that they may have must lie in a possible better common understanding of one another's meaning when men use the terms in question. Today the word "profit," which is the complement of "cost," is used in many senses. Under many partnership agreements, salaries and interest on investment are charged as expenses, and net profit is the gain arising from proprietorship pure and simple—from the *circumstance of responsible ownership,* aside from the salary of the manager as manager (not financially responsible) and from the income of the capitalist as capitalist (not personally responsible). The happy conjunction of ownership and personal responsibility often results in a gain not otherwise realizable, and that gain is profit. When there is no provision for interest and salaries, on the other hand, the term "profit" is commonly applied to the difference between the gross income and the charges incurred for purchases and outsiders' (non-partners') services; so that the profit shown is a compound of return for proprietors' services, for interest on partners' investments, and for the circumstance of responsible ownership. In corporation accounting, again, salaries are always included in expenses, and net income is the return to the stockholders as owners of capital. In common parlance, therefore, the word "profits" means much or little.. Knowing this, men always interpret it with a mental footnote.

On the announcement of the figure of profits under an agreement which makes no provision for interest, the first mental act of anyone interested in the business is to see what relation those profits bear to the capital—so as to see what are the excess profits over a reasonable return on the investment. Instinctively interest is a first deduction—partly because it has a definite basis that can be figured, and partly because it is the one thing that everyone counts on. One does not think of terminology: one thinks only of the fact. Virtually everyone admits that in partnership or other settlements the most satisfactory agreement is one that provides for a definite interest charge. This is mere practical convenience. Though the accountant is not much concerned with theoretical economic distinctions, he is at least interested when he sees that economists use a term in a sense that happens to be, for his own practical purposes, most convenient for him. Professor F. W. Taussig, in his *Principles of Economics,* a recently published and standard authority used in many universities, says, "So much only of a business man's income is to be regarded as profits as is in excess of interest on the capital which he manages."[1]

We have seen that for analytical purposes, in studying operations, practical necessity requires us at least to consider interest in virtually all calculations when investment is involved; and we have seen that in financial statements practical convenience is served by the treatment of interest as a charge, or cost, rather than as a residue, or profit. It seems reasonable, therefore, for accountants to adopt a terminology that will serve their own ends, will agree with the terminology of economists, and will mislead no one. Business men are likely to be misled in the future, as they have been in the past, by statements of profit which assume that no cost is involved in the use of capital.

---

[1] Vol. II, p. 179.

Paul-Joseph Esquerré

GOODWILL, PATENTS, TRADE-MARKS, COPYRIGHTS AND FRANCHISES

Paul-Joseph Esquerré *(1872–1934) was a practitioner of accounting who was also a prolific writer and a leading force in the field in his day. Among his published works is* Applied Theory of Accounts *(1917), widely used in advanced courses in the 1920s and 1930s.*
The article reprinted here raises the relevant issues concerning "intangibles" in a clear and forthright manner.

Goodwill

One of the most commonly quoted definitions of goodwill, so far at least as accounts are concerned, is the one given by Lisle in his book on *Accountancy in Theory and Practice*: "Goodwill is the monetary value placed upon the connection and reputation of a mercantile or manufacturing concern, and discounts the value of the turnover of the business in consequence of the probabilities of the customers continuing."

Another definition, is the one appearing in the opinion of Lord Elton in the English case of *Crutwell* v. *Lye,* which is about one hundred years old: "The goodwill which has been the subject of a sale is nothing more than the probability that the customers will resort to the old place."

Lord Elton's definition gives the impression that goodwill is a purely local matter, and that if a concern having acquired the business of another, subsequently transfers it to a different locality, it loses the right to expect that the old customers will continue. This is indeed the stand taken by a Pennsylvania court in the case of Elliott's appeal,[1] in which it was held that the goodwill of an inn or tavern did not exist outside of the premises where the business was conducted at the time of the sale.

Reprinted from *The Journal of Accountancy* (January, 1913), pp. 21–34, by permission.
[1] 60 Pa. St., 161.

479

Still, Lord Elton's definition has been the subject of much criticism in and out of American courts, owing to its narrow conception of the valuable asset goodwill. Nor does it seem that English courts have shared his views. Vice Chancellor Sir W. Page Wood, says: "Goodwill, I apprehend, must mean every advantage . . . that has been acquired by the old firm in carrying on its business, whether connected with the premises in which the business was previously carried on, or with the name of the late firm, or with any other matter carrying with it the benefit of the business."

Purely local as the character of goodwill is under certain conditions, as for instance in the case of a hotel whose attractive and convenient location is primarily responsible for the vogue which it enjoys, it may be said to be more commonly personal. If Steinway and Sons were to sell their business and their name to a firm who found it advisable to transfer the plant and the selling agency from New York to Boston, it is certain that the goodwill of the musical world would not be affected by the change.

It is precisely that element of personality, possessed by goodwill, which links it so naturally to types of organization in which the names of the supposed proprietors are known, that is to say, sole proprietorships and copartnerships. It is also on that account that the courts have ruled that the goodwill of a partnership does not inure to the benefit of the surviving partners, but belongs to the purchasers of the firm name,[2] and that the goodwill of a market stand or stall, the lessee of which has died, is independent of the stand itself, and belongs to the estate of the decreased.[3]

Goodwill is very frequently referred to as an "intangible asset," that is to say something the existence of which is spoken of, but is not palpable. Intangible as it may be by itself, it must nevertheless rest upon something tangible; it is not conceivable, for instance, that a skilled surgeon, whose fame is far-reaching, could sell the goodwill of his practice to an unknown confrere whose skill has yet to be demonstrated. There is nothing tangible in the assurance of the vendor surgeon that his patients will be willing to entrust their lives to his successors. Goodwill, in this case is nonexistent as a marketable value, since it depends upon personal skill, which is not to be acquired through purchase. On the other hand, a physician practising without competition in a rural district could in all propriety place a value on the goodwill of his practice, provided he were to agree to recommend the purchaser to his patients as fully capable of giving them equally skilled service, the vendor at the same time agreeing to retire, or to move to another state or to another part of the same state. Goodwill, in this case would rest upon the monopolistic prerogative of the vendee. This is so true that if the vendor subsequently performed an act which would tend to defeat the certainty of monopoly—such for instance as announcing the resumption of his practice in the field of his former activities—the courts would invalidate

---

[2] *Slater v. Slater*, 175 N.Y., 143, 1903.
[3] *Journe's Succession*, 21 La. Ann., 391.

the contract, and relieve the aggrieved vendee of his pecuniary obligations under the contract of sale.[4]

The nature of the goodwill of corporations appears to be quite different from that of the goodwill of sole proprietorships and of copartnerships. When corporations sell their assets, it often happens that the identity of the vendor is lost in that of the vendee. In this case the purchaser does not expect that the customers of the vendor will resort to the old place. He acquires the earning power of an established business whose products will sell, no matter who offers them for sale. He may also, perhaps, figure that with more up-to-date methods of conducting the business, through the application of scientific economy and the union of forces which, up to now, have been antagonistic, larger profits will be obtained than could be had before the consolidation of interests took place. For this he is willing to pay a sum of money which may be far in excess of the value of the tangible properties acquired.

In the absence of a better term accountants as well as laymen are generally satisfied to call their excess price goodwill; but the frequency with which the excess of cost over the intrinsic value of the properties acquired is distributed by boards of directors over the value of the individual property units included in the purchase, no mention whatever being made of goodwill, indicates that there is some deep-rooted objection to the term, at least from the point of view of corporations.

There are, in fact, many instances of consolidations of corporations, where the application of the word goodwill to the excess price paid by the consolidating interests over the intrinsic value of the properties acquired would be equivalent to an attempt to mislead, or to an admission of ignorance of the conditions which brought about the combination. The earning power of, say, three corporations to be consolidated, may have been reduced to a negligible quantity by the keenness of the competition in which they have engaged. If that earning power were to be used as the basis for the computation of the value of goodwill in accordance with the rules which are said to prevail in such cases, there would remain a minus quantity to express it; and yet the stockholders of the three competing companies may not feel disposed to combine, unless they receive a considerable amount over the intrinsic value of the properties which they control. Thus, so far as earning power is concerned, the bonus paid does not apply to past performances, but to confidence in the future. If the word goodwill applies to anything, under these conditions, it must be to that harmony which the consolidation has brought about among forces which up to now were only desirous of destroying one another.

It should be said, however, that while any reference to goodwill may properly be eliminated from the books of a corporation which absorbs other

---

[4] *Townsend* v. *Hurst,* 37 Missouri, 679.

interests in such a manner as to cause the identity of the vendor to be entirely lost, it should be retained as an asset of a corporation which takes over a copartnership or a sole proprietorship, principally when the vendee concern retains enough of the name of the vendor to preserve the personal character of the goodwill purchased.

The importance of the asset goodwill, when it has been acquired by purchase, cannot be overestimated. There is no other asset of a concern, the sale of which would be so effective in bringing operations to an end. In some instances it has been held by courts of law that under the terms of a contract for the sale of goodwill, the vendor has no subsequent right to solicit trade in the section of the country in which he previously operated, even among people who were not his customers at the time of the sale.[5] The sale of goodwill may even prevent an individual from using his own name in connection with the line of business in which he was engaged prior to the sale. Judge Bates (*Law of Partnerships*) quotes a case in which Beatty and Gage formed a partnership whose most valuable asset was a series of copy books, known as *Beatty's Head Line Copy Books*. They dissolved, Gage buying out Beatty's interest for $20,000.00. It was shown that a large part of the price was for the right to the copy books. A publishing company, with Beatty's assistance, got out a new series called *Beatty's New and Improved Head Line Copy Books*. This was held to be an infringement of Gage's rights, the word Beatty, as applied to the books, being a valuable asset which passed to Gage.[6]

Why goodwill, having been acquired at a cost which is somewhat considerable, and constituting in some instances the only truly valuable asset of a concern, should be outlawed, and sentenced to gradual expulsion from respectable books of account, is one of the perplexing puzzles which accounting offers to its students. Accountants who would never permit the reduction of a physical asset by the estimated amount of depreciation which it may or may not have suffered during a given period have no scruples at all when it comes to goodwill. Still, it seems that if a concern has paid a large sum to acquire the goodwill of another, and has not only retained it, but even increased it, there is no apparent reason why so-called conservation should demand the writing off of the asset, to the detriment of the very profits which its purchase gave the right to expect.

One of the reasons frequently advanced in favor of this writing off policy is that the valuation of goodwill, being based on a given number of years' average net profits of the vendor concern, less a fair return on capitalization, its cost is consumed concurrently with the effluxion of the period for which it has been purchased. This is, indeed, an extreme view. It is unequivocally expressed in Day's *Accounting Practice*: "Goodwill is a legitimate asset in

---

[5] *Munsey* v. *Butterfield,* 133 Mass., 492.

[6] *Gage* v. *Canada Pub. Co.,* 11 Ont. App., 402; aff'g, 6 Ont. Rep., 68.

an industrial enterprise and the most accepted method of computing the amount of goodwill is to take the total profits for the last five years and deduct from them five years' interest on the capitalization at seven per centum per annum; the balance is goodwill. The rate of interest is based on the assumption that no capitalist would invest in an enterprise unless he were assured at least seven per cent annual return. Goodwill should be written off the books during five subsequent years, by charging off one-fifth against each succeeding year."

As opposed to this view, which we have characterized as extreme, the following quotation from Dicksee's *Auditing,* American edition, may be of interest: "Goodwill does not depreciate. On the other hand, it will generally be conceded that it is liable to fluctuations both continual and extreme; . . . as a matter of fact goodwill is not written down because its value is supposed to have become reduced—such a course is all but unknown. The amount at which goodwill is stated in a balance sheet is never supposed to represent either its maximum or its minimum value; no one who thought of purchasing a business would be in the least influenced by the amount at which goodwill was stated in the accounts; in short, the amount is absolutely meaningless, except as an indication of what the goodwill may have cost in the first instance. Inasmuch, therefore, as nobody can be deceived by its retention, there is no necessity for the goodwill account to be written down. On the other hand, the practice is not unusual, where sufficient profits are being made. The question is not, however, one upon which the auditor is required to express an opinion."

It is generally recognized that the question of the value of goodwill does not arise until a sale is contemplated. Thus, it does not seem possible for a concern, which has organized otherwise than by purchase of an already established business, to create the asset goodwill during the course of its operations as a going concern. Still, if it is considered proper to set aside the expenses of organization in an account which will be reduced periodically during the years to which the benefit derived therefrom applies; if, further, it is agreed that corporations have the right to spread the loss incurred through discounts on bonds over the life of the bonds, there does not seem to be a valid objection to the operating shortcomings of what might be called the "probation period" of a newly established business to an account which would record the cost of obtaining the goodwill of the community.

We often hear of concerns which expect to lose money during the first five years of operation, owing to the heavy advertising which they will have to do in order to call the public's attention to the value of their goods. If the cost of such advertising is charged to expense, together with other lavish expenditures which a newly-established business is bound to make at the start, to win the favor of those whom curiosity alone attracts to the establishment, a considerable deficit may be shown. Would it not be better to raise an account with goodwill, which would be made to reflect the extraordinary cost of establishing the business, and to distribute that cost over the future periods which are to be benefited thereby?

Patents

Black's *Law Dictionary* defines a patent: "A grant made by the government to an inventor, conveying and securing to him the exclusive right to make and sell his invention for a term of years."

Thus a patent is nothing short of a monopoly granted by the state, presumably as an inducement to the inventor to disclose the secret of his invention for the benefit of the public at large. The territory over which the monopoly extends is mentioned in both the letters patent issued to the inventor and in the statute authorizing the issue of patents. United States patents apply to all the states and organized territories, as well as to American vessels on the high seas. They do not, however, apply to foreign vessels in American ports. In certain foreign countries—England for instance—a patent which has not been operated for four years may be revoked, but in the United States the right of the patentee is not thus affected. In England, the crown reserves the right to use the patented invention in return for fair compensation. While the United States government does not reserve that right to itself, it is within its power to use the invention by paying therefor reasonable fees to the inventor. No injunction can be obtained against the government.

In the United States the term of a mechanical patent is seventeen years from the date of grant; the term of a design patent is three years and one-half, or seven years, or fourteen years, according to the application. In England, the patent expires with any foreign patent granted before the English patent; in Canada, it expires with any foreign patent granted during its life. In the United States a patent can be extended by special act of Congress.

The value at which the asset "patents" is carried on the books depends upon whether the concern which owns it is at the same time the inventor, or has acquired it from the inventor. In the former case its value is the cost of conducting the experiments which have led to the invention, as well as the cost of the fees paid in connection with the search as to the validity of the claim for the patent, and with the filing of the said claim. In the latter case its value will of necessity be what the concern which acquired it paid for it.

Since patents grant what may be termed a legal monopoly, it is clear that they convey a sort of a title to the goodwill of the community in which the right to exclude everybody except the government from the use of the invention is exercised. This is why so many corporations which acquire the business of other concerns where a patent is included among the assets, carry the excess price paid over the intrinsic value of the property acquired under the term "patents and goodwill," or merely spread it over the value of the patents.

If the monopoly granted by the patents lasts only for a term of years, it would seem that the asset should be written off during the life of the grant. This can be done in two ways:

(a) Credit patents and debit profit and loss with equal installments corresponding in number to the number of years during which the patent is to be operative.

(b) Credit patents, or reserve amortization of patents, and debit one of the components of the cost of goods sold with periodical amounts representing the probable royalty which would have to be paid on the sales if the patents were leased instead of owned.

If the reserve account has been created, debit it and credit patents as soon as the two accounts are equal in amount.

It will be noticed that method (b) makes the cost of manufacture bear the loss sustained through the natural extinction of the very asset which made operations possible, and created a legal monopoly; and, further, that it leads to the peculiar conclusion that the income from sales becomes larger as soon as the asset patents have been eliminated.

It should be stated that, instead of being written off, patents have frequently been appraised on the basis of the saving in royalties which their possession affords, precisely as waterpower rights have been appraised on the basis of the saving in fuel and power producing machinery which the privilege to use natural forces guarantees.

There exists another theory, to the effect that while it is true that patents expire within a certain number of years, the benefit derived from them by the business does not expire concurrently. It is pointed out that the species of monopoly granted by patents is bound to create a considerable amount of goodwill, the existence of which is appreciated by would-be competitors, and deters them from engaging in a line of business which has been for so many years the exclusive domain of an established concern. Under this theory it would be possible to retain the asset patents long after its legal termination by transferring its value to the account goodwill.

Trade-marks

A trade-mark is nothing more than a conventional sign which, for commercial purposes, has the same effect as the signature has upon a written document—both certify to the genuineness of the thing to which they are appended.

Trade-marks make it possible for their owners so to earmark their goods as to make them easily recognizable by buyers. In other words they guarantee that whatever goodwill attaches to the product will be certain to revert to the proper party. In the case of *Liedersdorf v. Flint,* 15 Fed. Cases No. 8,219, it was said: "The court proceeds upon the ground that the complainant has a valuable interest in the goodwill of his trade or business, and that having appropriated to himself a particular label or sign or trade-mark, indicating that the article is manufactured or sold by him or by his authority, or that he carries on his business at a particular place, he is entitled to protection against any other person who pirates upon the goodwill of his customers or of the patrons of his trade or business, by sailing under his flag without his authority or consent."

Since an unauthorized use of trade-marks constitutes an infringement of the owner's right to exclusiveness, it may be said of them that they confer a monopoly different from the one obtained under patents only in that its duration is not limited by statute, and can be exercised as long as one desires to use the marks for trade purposes. Thus, the main distinction between patents and trade-marks is that the former need not be used to remain in force, whereas the latter must be.

While the cost of trade-marks may be insignificant when acquired otherwise than by purchase from former owners their value may be considerable, because the very success of the goods which they protect means the acquisition of the goodwill of the trade, to which these goods are offered for sale. If trade-marks have been acquired from another concern, their cost may be high, owing to the goodwill which they convey. No matter what their cost may be, their influence upon the prosperity of the business is so well defined that they are entitled to a place among the invested values of the enterprise. If kept in force their value should not be written off. If abandoned they may be closed by debit to profit and loss, precisely like all other assets which have outlived their usefulness; or they may be written off gradually during a period of years, upon the theory that, although given up, they have brought goodwill to the business of future years; or again their original cost may be transferred to goodwill, to be written down with that asset if such is the policy of the concern.

Copyrights

BOUVIER's *Law Dictionary* defines copyrights as follows: "The exclusive privilege, secured according to certain legal forms, of printing, or otherwise multiplying, publishing, and vending, copies of certain literary or artistic productions."

Like trade-marks and patents, copyrights give a monopoly; but in this country the privilege is limited to a term of twenty-eight years from the time of recording. The term can be extended for a further term of twenty-eight years, upon request by the author, his widow, or his children, within six months of the termination of the original grant of twenty-eight years. This privilege of extension is not conveyed to the assignee, unless so provided in the contract of assignment.

Copyrights are personal property and as such, they may be willed. In the absence of a will they descend to the natural heirs.

The nature of the species of monopoly granted by copyrights consists in the privilege enjoyed by the owner or his assignees or full licensees to prevent any unauthorized sale of the copyrighted works, and the publication of mutilated parts thereof.

The question of the value of the asset copyrights is a complicated one. The original cost of obtaining the grant is insignificant, unless the value of the time consumed in the preparation of the work be capitalized, together with the expenses incident thereto and the cost of such preliminary advertising as may have been deemed necessary.

In the case of copyrights which are valuable only to the original grantee— such, for instance, as catalogues, price lists and advertisements—the cost of plates, etchings, half-tones, etc., may be added to the value of the asset as stated above. But in the case of assignable copyrights, the plates, etchings and half-tones are so independent of the right itself that they can be sold without giving the purchaser the slightest claim upon the copyright, unless the contract provides to the contrary.

The probable value of assignable or salable copyrights depends to a great extent upon an estimate of the vogue which they will enjoy; their real value depends upon past performances so far as public favor is concerned, as well as upon an estimate of the continuation of their vogue.

Copyrights, being a monopolistic grant, raise naturally the question of goodwill. A copyrighted work may have proven a financial failure, and yet have obtained an artistic success such as to lift its author and its publishers to a very high plane in the favor of a certain class of readers. If the defects which made it commercially unprofitable can be remedied in future works of the same author, the goodwill which the first production has acquired may enhance greatly the commercial success of subsequent copyrights. Hence, the losses sustained by the poor seller might be capitalized under the name of goodwill, or added to the value of the copyright, at least until such time as the retroactive effect of subsequent successful works upon the unsuccessful one has been ascertained.

Franchises

Franchises have been defined thus: "A branch of the sovereign power of the state, subsisting in a person or in a corporation, by grant from the state." This definition has been assailed, upon the ground that it fails to establish a proper distinction between "primary franchises," and "secondary franchises,"

Primary franchises are special privileges, not generally possessed by individuals, which are granted to them by the state in pursuance with a well-defined policy of government or of business control. They include the right of perpetuity of purpose and of life, which corporations obtain by virtue of their charter; the privilege of limited liability which certain forms of organization receive from the state, as well as all the other special privileges which their legal status conveys and the rights and privileges which all citizens enjoy under existing statutes, or in accordance with the spirit of the common law.

Secondary franchises, at least under the American system of government, originate through a contract made, upon valuable consideration, between the sovereign power and individuals or corporations. The consideration for the contract may be monetary, or it may be only the public value of the services to be rendered by the party seeking the grant. They include in the language of the Supreme Court, "rights and privileges which are essential to the operations of the corporation, and without which its road and works should be of little value such as the franchise to run cars, to take tolls, to appropriate earth and gravel for the bed of its road, or water for its engines, and the like."[7]

The main distinction between the two classes of franchises, so far as organized business codes are concerned, is that the former (primary) cannot be alienated, assigned, mortgaged, or otherwise disposed of, while the latter (secondary) may be, if proper authorization is given by the sovereign power which made the grant.

Generally speaking, secondary franchises are monopolistic and permanent rights "to do an act, or a series of acts of public concern."[8] They constitute a contract between the grantor and the grantee, which cannot be revoked unless the grantor specifically reserves to himself the right of revocation.

The characteristic feature of franchises is that they must be granted by a sovereign power. Under this interpretation of the nature of the grant, it has been claimed that the privileges conferred by the municipalities are not franchises but merely licenses.[9] On the other hand, it has been held if the grantee of the municipal licenses has given adequate consideration, (such as a promise to pay to the municipality a certain proportion of its earnings or of its net profits), the grant ceases to be a license and becomes a franchise which is in the nature of a binding contract, and cannot be revoked at the will of the grantor.[10]

The legal doctrine which attempts to establish a difference between franchises granted by the state and those granted by municipalities is generally thought to be unsound, upon the ground that municipalities, being state corporations and part of the body politic, are mere subdivisions of the sovereign power. The question as to whether or not the grant of a franchise

---

[7] *Morgan* v. *Louisiana*, 93 U. S., 217, 23 L. Ed., 860.
[8] *Southampton* v. *Jessup*, 162 N. Y., 122, 126, 56 N. E., 538.
[9] *Chicago City R. R.* v. *People*, 73 Ill., 541.
[10] *Chicago Municipal Gas Light, etc., Co.* v. *Lake*, 130 Ill., 42, 22 N. E., 616.

by a city is an infringement of the right of the state appears to be one of legal proceedings, and not a question of facts.[11]

In connection with the components of the book value of the asset franchises, when possessed by public service corporations, the public service commission of the first district of the state of New York has ruled:

> To this account shall be charged the amount (exclusive of any tax or annual charge) actually paid to the state or to a political subdivision thereof, as the consideration for the grant of such franchise or right which is necessary to the conduct of the corporations. If any such franchise is acquired by mesne assignment, the charge to this account in respect thereof must not exceed the amount actually paid therefor by the corporation to its assignor, nor shall it exceed the amount specified in the statute above quoted. Any excess of the amount actually paid by the corporation over the amount specified in the statute shall be charged to the account "other intangible street railway capital." If any such franchise has a life of not more than one year after the date when it is placed in service, it shall not be charged to this account but to the appropriate accounts in "operating expenses," and in "prepayments" if extending beyond the fiscal year.
>
> Payments made to the state or to some political subdivision thereof as a consideration for granting an extension for more than one year of the life period of a franchise shall be classed as renewals. Those made as a consideration for franchises or extensions thereof covering additional territory to be operated as a part of an existing system shall be classified as betterments. If the franchises cover separate and distinct new enterprises, the payments therefor shall be classed as original. *Note*: Annual or more frequent payments in respect of franchise, must not be charged to this account, but to the appropriate tax or operating expense account.[12]

This debars a public service corporation, which falls under the commission's supervision, from charging to the account "franchises" the cost of obtaining the consent of the property owners, and the cost of the legal expenses incurred in connection with obtaining the grant. Generally speaking, however, such expenses are thought to be properly capitalized under the heading "franchises" by companies not controlled by the commission, together with the consideration for the contract between the grantor and the grantee, i.e., the amount paid to the state or political subdivision thereof. As to the propriety of capitalizing legal expenses, the question remains an open one; some accountants claim that such capitalization is faulty whenever the company which is the beneficiary of a franchise has a permanent legal department as part of its administrative organization.

Any other cost incident to or necessary for the enjoyment of the franchise, such for instance as the cost of paving between tracks, may be capitalized in some other property account, such as paving, track and roadway, etc.

The payment to a municipality of a portion of the earnings from operations, in accordance with the terms of a franchise grant, is considered as a burden of the asset, and cannot enter into its valuation.

---

[11] *East Cleveland R. Co.,* 6 Ohio Cir. Ct., 318.
[12] §55 of the Public Service Commission Law.

Charles E. Sprague

PREMIUMS AND DISCOUNTS

For a brief biographical sketch of Colonel Sprague, see the headnote to the excerpts from his Philosophy of Accounts, *reprinted in this book (page 53). The short piece reprinted here (actually it appeared as a letter to the editor of* The Journal of Accountancy*) is included for two reasons. First, it is part of an exchange between two of the great figures in the field, the elder Sprague (then 66 years old) and the younger May (then 33 years old). Second, it is timely. Accountants and their clients still have difficulty comprehending the nature of premium and discount on bonds, despite the lucid analysis and explanation available in the standard literature of accounting, at least since 1906.*

I desire to express my high appreciation, which will be shared by all readers of THE JOURNAL, of Mr. George O. May's most able and lucid article in the July number on the treatment of premiums and discounts on bonds. Not only are his principles sound, but their clear and logical presentation is a model for those discussing accounting problems.

He exposes the unsoundness of many judicial opinions on the subject, wherein the judges have tried to take the ground that premium is something different from what Mr. May so appositely states it to be: "the capitalization of an increase of the rate of interest."

Judge (now Chief Judge) Edgar M. Cullen of this State is one of those whom Mr. May has not cited because he is one of the few lawyers and judges who apprehend the actuarial law governing prices of securities. It is a great pity that Judge Cullen has not adjudicated a case involving discount as well as the one respecting premiums. I believe his logical mind would have forced him to the conclusion that discounts as well as premiums were subject to the law of amortization, and that a discount was *always* "the capitalization of a reduction of the rate of interest."

Reprinted from the correspondence section of *The Journal of Accountancy* (August, 1906), pp. 294–96, by permission.

Mr. May seems to me a little faint-hearted on the side of discounts, if I may be allowed to find a single fault in so admirable a whole. He concedes too much to the lax, unscientific point of view of the populace, and finds excuses, rather than reasons, for that position. Having laid down the perfectly sound view of both phases, above par and below par, he immediately recedes from this high ground, and makes a distinction in practice between discount and premium, which I think is unfounded and unsupported by facts.

By the very mail which brought me the July JOURNAL, there came an offering of bonds, literally as follows:

> $100,000 Chicago, Burlington and Quincy, Illinois Division, 4% Bonds, due January 1, 1949; interest payable January and July, at 101½ and interest, to net about 3.95%.
> $50,000 Chicago, Burlington and Quincy, Illinois Division, 3½% Bonds, due January 1, 1949; interest payable January and July, at 91⅝ and interest, to net about 3.91%.

Here are two lots of bonds identical except as to rate of interest; issued on the same security under the same mortgage, which, if foreclosed, would satisfy each in equal amount; one is absolutely as certain of payment as the other. Yet Mr. May considers that a different rule of income may apply to each because there is greater certainty of the vanishing of the premium than of the accretion of the discount. In his own words: "The case of bonds bought at discount differs from that of bonds bought at a premium in that there is not the same certainty of the discount being eventually earned as of the premium being lost."

"Earned" and "lost" are not happy expressions here. The premium is not lost at maturity, but has gradually (on Mr. May's own authority) been refunded to us; and the discount is not lost but gradually withheld from us.

If there should be a loss on either lot by default at maturity it would be loss of capital, not of income, and the distribution between capital and income is precisely what we are considering.

If we discount one note for $100 and take another note of the same amount "with interest," are we not rather more, than less, secure from loss in the former case? The case of the bond at a discount is similar to that of a bill discounted with the exception of the (partial) collections of interest.

Mr. May remarks that, probably, "Comparatively few bonds sell below par because the interest is lower than the normal rate for well-secured investments." This is a very ill-chosen moment to assert this. Take the published quotations of railroad bonds (which is the largest class), and you will find that all the 3½% bonds, even the best, are at a discount, while three years ago the same bonds were almost all at a premium. "The market value of bonds selling at a discount is seldom affected by the fact that they are nominally redeemable at par." For "seldom" read "always." Does Mr. May believe that Steel 5's, when they sold at 83, would have sold at the same price had they been irredeemable? Is it not absolutely certain that the value must in every case be affected by the nominal rate, and by the time of redemption, no matter how great the effect of other causes?

There is no line to be drawn between bonds above par and those below par which will enable us to judge them by different criteria. It is purely a question of how much each dollar actually invested will earn. Eighty may be a high price for one bond because it is a 2% and long to run; another bond may be very cheap at 120 because it bears 7% for the same time. The former may be even more certain of redemption than the latter, and we cannot say arbitrarily that in the former case only 2% income is gained, while in the latter it is 7% less amortization.

The time, the nominal rate and the price must all be combined whether above par or below; we cannot ignore any one of these. These taken together produce as a resultant the effective rate; and the effective rate is affected by belief in security or insecurity of capital.

"Usually the annual interest actually received constitutes a fair return to the life tenant and no real injustice is done him in not crediting any portion of the discount to him." This might do for a lawyer, but is no argument for an accountant. Then if a client of Mr. May's, as trustee of two funds, should invest equal sums in C. B. & Q. bonds, that in trust for A in 4's of 1949 and that in trust for B in $3\frac{1}{2}$'s of 1949, would he advise paying to the latter only $3\frac{1}{2}$% and not even crediting him with the 4 1–100? Would there be "no real injustice" in withholding over a tenth of B's income, while A would get his full 3.95?

The qualifications "usually" and "seldom" will not do in mathematics and accounts. Principles are principles, and deviations can only be excused by the minuteness of the deviation in a particular case.

What is said about discounts being offered to attract purchasers is true, but it is only another version of higher interest. Psychologically, some purchasers are more attracted by the presentation of a low price and others by a high nominal rate of interest; but the reasoning in both cases is the same: "In proportion to the amount put in, I get big returns; I can afford to risk loss." It is true that all interest is partly insurance of risk; but insurance premiums are always payable out of income, never out of capital.

Let us stand for correct accounting principles in legal matters and resist as far as possible the crude tendencies of the unmathematical lawyer, or even judge. He will listen to us after a while. Perhaps he may in time grasp the idea of compound interest, and admit that interest for four consecutive years ought to be more than four times the interest for one year; or he may even reach that further height which not even all accountants have attained, to admit that the interest for three months ought to be less than one-fourth of the interest for a year.

James L. Dohr

CAPITAL AND SURPLUS
IN THE CORPORATE BALANCE SHEET

James Lewis Dohr *(1892–1961) taught for many years at Columbia University, both in its business school and its law school. He was a vice-president of the American Accounting Association, 1932–1933, and served as its president in 1934. He was also Director of Research for the American Institute of C.P.A. for a short while in the early 1940s, served on the Institute's Committee on Accounting Procedure, and was one of the original members of the Accounting Principles Board when it was established in 1959. Among other works, he was author or coauthor of a textbook in cost accounting, and a case book on accounting and the law. In the article reprinted here, Dohr draws upon his accounting and legal background to free the owner's equity section of the balance sheet from narrow, specialized influences.*

The past decade has witnessed much writing and discussion as to the nature of the corporate balance sheet. As a result, I think I may say, substantial progress has been made in balance sheet practice. There is still a good deal of confusion, however, due largely to the lack of uniformity and definition in balance sheet terminology, and to the use of narrow or "specialized" methods of approach in our efforts to solve the problem. This is particularly true of the third, or what I shall for the moment designate as the "net asset" section of the corporate balance sheet. Here the reader encounters a wide variety of inadequately defined and misdescriptive terms such as net worth, capital, surplus, undivided profits, undistributed earnings, proprietorship, equities, investment, reserves, invested capital, liabilities, appropriations, paid-in or donated surplus, revaluation surplus, etc., to say nothing of those time-honored atrocities, "debits and credits to surplus." In addition, the thoughtful reader is frequently confused by an apparent conflict of economic, legal, and accounting considerations. Further progress is, therefore, dependent upon a

Reprinted from *The Accounting Review* (March, 1939), pp. 38–42, by permission.

greater accuracy in the use of terms and the adoption of a broad or general point of view.

If our ideas in this connection are to be clarified and our practice made more effective, we must agree as to the starting point. While it may seem to be almost fantastic, it appears that we can get different results depending upon whether we start with a balance sheet in the "account" as compared with the "statement" form.[1] The point is well illustrated in a very able article by Professor Littleton in the ACCOUNTING REVIEW of December, 1932. While Professor Littleton reaches his conclusions as to the presentation and description of corporate "capital and surplus" on the basis of the "two-sided" character of the balance sheet, he recognizes that the so-called right-hand side is merely a regrouping of the *economic capital* which is itemized on the left-hand side.

I have long been suspicious as to the influence of the double entry method on the reasoning of accountants. I am afraid that the quality of their logic has on occasion been impaired by their passion for balance. In no other way, for instance, can I explain the showing of a loss as an asset. I prefer, therefore, to start with the corporate balance sheet in statement form, i.e., a showing based on the formula of assets minus liabilities as representing net assets. To me the balance sheet is not (to use a phrase of Professor Littleton) "two-sided" like a coin; it is "three-layered" like a cake. The first "layer" shows the gross economic capital, i.e., itemized *individual* assets and their total; the second shows itemized and *individual* liabilities and their total; the third must of necessity represent net assets, i.e., the *net economic capital* of the enterprise. The net assets are, of course, not itemized as such but are shown as a "collective," i.e., it is not possible to identify any portion of the aggregate as representing a particular asset such as cash, accounts receivable, plant, etc.

Starting then with the proposition that the third subdivision of the balance sheet reflects the net assets collectively, the question is how that aggregate of economic capital may or should be divided. That, I take it, is the problem involved in the topic "Capital and Surplus in the Corporate Balance Sheet." In considering the possibilities along this line, I think it advisable in the first instance to refrain entirely from the use of the customary accounting terms. If we can agree as to the classifications of the indicated net economic capital, the terminology question may then be dealt with.

I submit that the subdivision of net economic capital is to be made on the basis of origins, restrictions on withdrawal, and administrative control.

As To Origins

The fact of outstanding importance in connection with the net economic capital is that of its origins, i.e., whether contributed by way of an investment

---

[1] Witness the struggle of an economist with the "accounting equation." John B. Canning, *The Economics of Accountancy,* pp. 50–56.

of capital in the enterprise or whether "earned" or "accumulated" or resulting from the profitable conduct of business. This conclusion is inescapable whether the matter be approached by an economist, a lawyer or an accountant. From the standpoint of economics, the distinction as to origins is the distinction between "capital" and "income" and is obviously of major significance. From the legal point of view, the statement of capital resulting from earnings is a representation as to the profitability of the business enterprise, and the financial statement must show correctly the extent to which the present economic capital of the enterprise has been built up through the profitable conduct of business.[2] From the accounting standpoint, the distinction is of overwhelming importance as a matter of business administration and of information to stockholders and others interested.

Starting with this basic proposition, two important points may be made. The account or accounts showing the net economic capital resulting from earnings during the life of the enterprise must be accurately maintained, and no "juggling" or distortion may be permitted. Mr. Howard C. Greer has shown vividly the possibilities of variation in the income statement under current accounting practice and the manner in which some of these practices fail to preserve the integrity of the undistributed profits account.[3] Secondly, as a matter of law, a corporate distribution made without characterization as to its source is a representation that the payment is a distribution of profits.[4] Every distribution, other than of profits, should therefore be accompanied by a statement as to origins, and it is possible that we should require some sort of governmental consent before such a distribution be made.

In the matter of origins there is possibly a third category in the form of "revaluation surplus." Here again I find myself in a suspicious mood. I question whether the device of revaluation is worth, in a few cases, what it costs in the way of misleading statements in a majority of cases. Certainly no economic capital is created by the mere changing of the price tag. In any event, this item should be shown by itself and as a separate category.

As To Restrictions on Withdrawal

The next point in order of importance is that of withdrawability. In return for the privilege of doing business with limited liability we require a permanent dedication of a portion of the corporation's net economic capital. While this may be, and generally is, viewed as a "legalistic" consideration, I submit that it is equally a matter of sound economics and sound business

---

[2] See *In the Matter of General Income Shares, Inc.,* 1 S. E. C. 110, for an early indication, by the Securities and Exchange Commission, of the importance of showing correctly the "earned surplus" of the enterprise.

[3] See *Proceedings of the First Institute of Accounting,* Ohio State University Publications No. 3, pp. 133–154.

[4] See *Ottinger v. Bennett,* 144 A. D. 525; 203 N. Y. 554; *Lockhart* v. *Van Alstyne,* 31 Mich. 76; *Hill* v. *International Products Co.,* 129 Misc. 25.

administration. If the corporate form of business enterprise is to function satisfactorily, some such restriction there must be. As a matter of fact, my criticism of the present situation is that the restriction is not as effective as it should be, and the only criticism I have of the New York statute making it a misdemeanor to violate the restriction is that the statute is not enforced. Whatever the restrictions are, they should be adequately portrayed; in this connection I disagree with the implications of the "Tentative Statement of Accounting Principles."[5]

The foregoing classifications based on origin and restriction may, at first glance, seem to be in conflict because of the fact that capital resulting from earnings may, under some laws, become restricted as to withdrawal. They can, however, be combined as is suggested by Professor William A. Paton in the *Journal of Accountancy* for April, 1938.[6] The result would be a basic classification as follows:

1. Contributed Capital
   A. Restricted as to withdrawal
   B. Not so restricted
2. Accumulated Capital
   A. Restricted as to withdrawal
   B. Not so restricted

This classification might be simplified by either one of two changes in the law of corporations. We could provide that all *contributed* capital be *restricted,* in which case item 1B would not appear. As an alternative, we might provide that increases in restricted capital be made *first* from item 1B so that item 2A would not appear until item 1B had been completely transferred to item 1A.

As To Administrative Control

The control of the corporation is vested generally in its directors. The investment and employment of corporate capital is, subject to the charter and by-laws, within their discretion, and if the conduct of business results in an increase in economic capital, theirs is the decision, subject to the rule of restriction as to withdrawal, as to whether such capital shall be distributed or whether it shall be appropriated to the furtherance of the enterprise. To what extent can the portrayal of net economic capital reflect the exercise, in times past, of their discretion?

This is obviously more difficult, and since there is no identity between the

---

[5] See Reprint, page 16 "It is not necessary, however, to adopt in accounting practice the expedients permitted under any given law." [See *The Accounting Review* (June, 1941), pp. 133–39 for the complete "statement."]

[6] See pp. 285–289.

collective net economic capital and specific assets, some assumption must be made. Logically, it would seem to me, we should associate with contributed and restricted capital the more permanent type of investment, i.e., land, building, machinery and equipment, etc.[7] Let us assume, then, that the first three of the above categories (1A, 1B and 2A) are so invested, and from that point classify the unrestricted accumulated capital in accordance with the facts. In a majority of cases the results would be somewhat as shown in the "Third Stage" on the accompanying illustration.

Analysis of the Net Economic Capital of a Corporation

First Stage

The net economic capital of this corporation was derived from the following sources:

1—*Contributed* by way of investment (for shares or otherwise)

2—*Accumulated* during the lifetime of the corporation (less any distribution thereof)

Second Stage

1—Contributed Capital as above:
  A. Restricted by law as to withdrawal or return to the stockholders
  B. Not so restricted

2—Accumulated Capital as above:
  A. Restricted by law as to withdrawal or return to the stockholders
  B. Not so restricted

Third Stage

1—Contributed Capital as above:
  A. Restricted by law as to withdrawal or return to the stockholders
  B. Not so restricted

2—Accumulated Capital as above:
  A. Restricted by law as to withdrawal or return to the stockholders
  (All of the foregoing three items are invested in fixed assets.)
  B. Not so restricted
  (a) *Appropriated* by the directors for the following purposes (itemized) fixed assets, working capital, debt retirement, contingencies, etc.
  (b) *Unappropriated* and available for expansion, dividends, etc.

If the net fixed assets are less than the total of items 1A, 1B and 2A, the difference may, for instance, be working capital and may be so indicated; if

---

[7] The assumption would vary, of course, if the history of the enterprise indicated that the suggested assumption was not in accord with that history.

the net fixed assets are more than the total of these three items, the excess is an appropriation of item 2B.

Conclusion

Having established a classification of the net economic capital in the third section of the balance sheet, two important questions remain. How shall the various sections be designated? As to this question I suggest a complete reexamination of the situation as to terminology; the possible abandonment of such terms as capital, capital stock and surplus; and the adoption of terminology which will better describe the facts of the situation. Secondly, having established a classification along the lines indicated, the question arises as to the extent to which the directors should be permitted to indicate, in the case of dividends, purchases of the company's own stock, write-downs, write-ups, items relating to prior years, etc., which classification is to bear the charge or receive the credit.[8] In this connection it is obvious that the utmost caution should be exercised. One rule must be adopted. Whatever the charge or credit be, it must be so handled as to preserve the integrity of the account reflecting accumulated as distinguished from contributed capital. Perhaps we should also adopt the tax rule on dividends to the effect that all such distributions be regarded as having been made from the most recently acquired accumulated capital. Beyond this there are numerous problems, a discussion of which would unduly prolong this paper.

---

[8] See W. A. Hosmer, "The Effect of Direct Charges to Surplus on the Measurement of Income," THE ACCOUNTING REVIEW, March, 1938.

Arthur Lowes Dickinson

SPECIAL POINTS IN CORPORATION
ACCOUNTING AND FINANCE

Sir Arthur Lowes Dickinson *(1859–1935) was born in England and educated*
at King's College, Cambridge. He practiced as a chartered accountant in
London from 1888 to 1901. He then came to the U.S. to become senior
partner of Price Waterhouse and Co. in this country, a post he held until
1913. He returned to London in 1913 as a partner in the English firm of
Price Waterhouse and remained active there until his retirement in 1924.
Dickinson wrote extensively, mainly on the technical and professional prob-
lems of the new profession of public accountant. The Dickinson Lectures
at Harvard were established in his honor.
The material reprinted here is a chapter from his Accounting Practice and
Procedure, *published originally in 1913. The bulk of the chapter is devoted*
to the problem of consolidated financial statements, that peculiarly American
invention in whose creation the Englishman Dickinson played such a major
role from his vantage point as senior partner of Price Waterhouse.

(1) Accounting for Holding Companies

The now common practice of forming large aggregations of capital on the
basis of a control by one corporation of the whole or the majority of the
stocks of a number of others, raises important accounting questions.

It has generally been considered that the balance sheet of any corporation,
prepared from its books and records properly kept, would disclose its true
financial position; but the development of this system of control has shown
that such a balance sheet will no longer suffice for this purpose.

It is important in this connection to realize the difference between an
investment in a company when this investment represents only a small proportion of its capital stock, and an investment representing the whole or
practically the whole, and carrying with it the absolute control of the opera-

Reprinted from *Accounting Practice and Procedure,* Second Edition, 1918, by Arthur
Lowes Dickinson, Chapter VIII (New York: The Ronald Press Company), by permission.

tions. Thus, corporation "A" may own the whole stock of corporation "B," both carrying on a similar business. Stockholders in "A" may know this fact, but have no means of ascertaining the real position of corporation "B." "A," having the control of "B," may turn over to "B" all its unremunerative work, with the result of showing large profits on its own accounts, while the accounts of "B" show correspondingly large losses. Corporation "A" in its balance sheet may carry its investments at cost, probably merged under the general head of "Cost of Properties," with all its other capital assets. Corporation "B" may obtain loans from corporation "A" which largely exceed its current assets, and may be expended in construction work, or even lost in operations, while corporation "A" may carry in its balance sheet these same loans as current assets recoverable on demand.

The Consolidated Balance Sheet and Income Account

By reason of the misleading character of the ordinary balance sheet in such cases, there has been evolved the consolidated balance sheet; the basis of which is the recognition of the common-sense fact that a network of companies connected with each other by control of stockholdings is still in effect one undertaking, and that if the stockholders in the holding company are to have before them a clear statement of its position, legal technicalities must be brushed to one side, and the position of the holding company shown in its relation, not to these subcompanies, but to the general public. The position of the holding company can only be changed by outside influences affecting itself or its constituent companies, and not by any change in the relation between itself and these companies, or in the relations among the latter. The consolidated balance sheet represents the true position of the whole group of the constituent companies to the outside world, and is thus not the balance sheet of a corporation, but of a condition after eliminating all the relations of the constituent companies one to another. Debts due by one company of the group to another; stocks of one company owned by another; earnings of one company at the expense of another—are all eliminated. The amount by which the value of the stocks of any company on the books of another exceeds or falls short of the par value thereof, represents an addition to or diminution of the asset of goodwill in the final balance sheet; and as a result the capital assets in the consolidated balance sheet consist of the total physical assets of all the companies (that is, land, buildings, plant, machinery, etc.), and in addition an item of goodwill represented by—

(a) The goodwill asset in the balance sheets of the separate companies, and

(b) The amount by which the aggregate book value to the holding company of the stocks of subsidiary companies exceeds the par value of that stock and the surplus at the date of acquisition.

Similarly, the capital liabilities represent the stocks and bonds of all the companies in the hands of the public, those owned between companies being eliminated.

The consolidated earnings account is made up on the same principles. Profits resulting to one company out of sales to another are eliminated. Only sales and purchases to and from the outside public are included, so that no profits are considered such except those made on deliveries outside the organization.

In other words, the whole organization is considered as merely a series of separate works under the same ownership; and the same accounting principles which would apply to a corporation owning several factories, are applied to the one owning the whole stocks of a number of subsidiary companies, which in turn own the stocks of other subsidiary companies, all the companies in the group themselves owning and operating their own factories. It will readily be understood that in practice the preparation of a statement of earnings exactly on the basis here laid down is a difficult matter; but inasmuch as a neglect of these principles, so far as the Income account is concerned, only means the swelling of the totals both of gross earnings and cost of operation, it is not of so much importance; provided that the valuation of the stocks of goods on hand is made on the basis of actual labor, material, and expense involved therein, without including any proportion of the profit of the different companies in the organization through which these products may have come, and provided also that capital expenditures do not contain any intercompany profit.

A balance sheet of a corporation, whose only or principal assets are stated to be investments in other companies, should be looked upon with suspicion, unless the names of the other companies are given, and clear statements are also given of their financial position; and even then a collection of balance sheets cannot show the true financial position of the whole group until they are all combined into one and the intercompany interests eliminated.

In respect of the earnings of such a consolidation similar considerations prevail. Legally, the earnings consist of the results of the operations of the holding company, together with any dividends which may be declared on the stocks which it owns in the subsidiary companies; and so long as those stocks represent only minority interests in companies which are not in any way controlled or operated by the directors of the holding company, an Income account prepared in such a way would be a correct and proper statement from an accounting as well as from a legal point of view.

Under the conditions, however, of majority or complete ownership, as they so commonly exist, no statement of earnings can be considered correct which does not show in one account the profits or losses of the whole group of companies, irrespective of whether dividends have or have not been declared thereby. If this principle be not insisted upon, it is within the power of the directors of the holding company to regulate its profits according not to facts, but to their own wishes, by distributing or withholding dividends of the subsidiary companies; or even to largely overstate the profits of the whole group by declaring dividends in those subcompanies which have made profits, while entirely omitting to make provision for losses which have been made by other companies in the group.

Legal Status of Consolidated Balance Sheet

It is doubtful whether there is any existing law which could legally require a corporation to make up its statement of profits on the basis here suggested; but possibly it may eventually be found that the ordinary rule, of a reasonable valuation of assets, may be made to cover this point, for the following reasons. It is clear that whatever the value of an investment in a corporation may be at a particular date, its value at any subsequent date (other things being equal) must be greater or less by the amount of the profits or losses made and not distributed during the intervening period. Even if other conditions at the two dates are not the same, and—quite apart from any consideration of the earnings or losses during the intervening period—there is a considerable appreciation or depreciation in the investment, that appreciation or depreciation must undoubtedly be more or less, respectively, by reason of profits earned or losses incurred. The change in value of the asset is at any rate partly due to the result of the operations for the purpose of which the investment is held. On the general principle, therefore, that an Income account should take into account all profits or losses resulting from the trading operations, but should not take into account the profits or losses arising from a revaluation of capital assets, it may eventually be held, on legal as well as on accounting principles, that the statement of earnings presented by a holding company is not correct unless it takes into account, by way of either a reserve or a direct addition to or deduction from the capital value of the investment, the profits or losses made in operating the subsidiary companies.

Intercompany Profits and Accounting

In a large consolidation, when the subsidiaries are carrying on business as separate entities, and contracting and dealing with each other as independent concerns, the elimination of profits on sales or transfers between companies is a somewhat difficult and complicated matter, particularly having regard to the fact that each subsidiary company is legally entitled to take up the profits on such sales, and, if there are substantial minority interests outstanding, has no right to exclude them. This difficulty has been overcome by means of an elaborate system of accounting which provides for carrying the intercompany profit through the operations as a separate item from the original cost, until such time as the finished product is sold to parties outside the consolidation. The method by which this result is accomplished may be shortly outlined as follows:

Company A produces a raw material and sells it to company B at a profit of, say, 10 per cent; company B converts this raw material into a partly finished product and ships it over a railroad C, owned by the consolidation, to company D, by whom it is further manufactured and finally sold to outside parties. Company A produces material to the cost value of $100,000, and sells $20,000 of this to outside parties, $60,000 to company B, and has the remaining $20,000 in stock. Company B buys material from company A, costing $60,000, for $66,000; spends $34,000 in further manufacture; ships $70,000 of the manufactured product over railroad C to company D; sells $20,000 to outsiders, and has $10,000 in stock. Company D purchases products from company B, costing, $70,000, for $77,000; pays $5,000 freight to railroad C—which costs the latter $3,500; expends $18,000 in completing its manufacture; sells $80,000 of the finished product to outsiders, and has the remaining $20,000 in stock.

The books of company A require no special entries.

In company B's books its Manufacturing account will stand as follows:

	I. C. Profit	1st Cost	Total
Cost of material	$6,000	$60,000	$ 66,000
Manufacturing cost	.....	34,000	34,000
	$6,000	$94,000	$100,000
Cost of Sales:			
To outside parties	1,200	18,800	20,000
To Company D	4,200	65,800	70,000
Balance in stock	$ 600	$ 9,400	$ 10,000

In company D's books the Manufacturing account will be dealt with similarly, as follows:

	I. C. Profit	1st Cost	Total
Cost of material per Company B	$11,200	$65,800	$ 77,000
Freight	1,500	3,500	5,000
Manufacturing cost	.....	18,000	18,000
	$12,700	$87,300	$100,000
Cost of Sales:			
To outside parties	10,160	69,840	80,000
Balance in stock	$2,540	$17,460	$ 20,000

The subsidiary companies will take up in their Income accounts the whole of their profits on their sales, and will declare dividends in the usual way. Out of the dividends it receives, the holding company will set up $600 in respect of B's profits, and $2,540 in respect of D's profits, or a total of $3,140, which will be credited to an inventory reserve. In this way, all stocks on hand of all companies are, on the consolidated balance sheet, carried at net cost within the consolidation, and the consolidated income takes up no profit except on sales made to outside parties. If any of the product is used for construction work within the organization, the net cost only is used, so that no profit of subsidiary companies enters into capital expenditures.

The actual process, by reason of the magnitude of the business and number of transactions, is necessarily more complicated than the simple example given, which, however, is sufficient to show the principles involved.

What is a Constituent Company?

One other difficult point is the determination of what is or is not a constituent company whose Profits and Losses or Assets and Liabilities should be brought into account in this manner. It is suggested that this depends partly on the proportion of stock owned, and partly upon the degree of control exercised by the holding company. When the latter owns at least a majority of the stock, operates the company, dictates its policy, and practically treats its property as its own, subject only to the right of the minority stockholders to receive a share of the profits, the conditions would appear to be such as to require the proportion of profits and losses corresponding to the stock owned to be taken up. In order to justify a consolidated balance sheet, in addition to the other conditions just mentioned, the ownership of at least the common stock should be substantially complete; or the balance not owned should consist either of shares left in the hands of managers or others for business purposes, or of shares the ownership of which cannot be traced. On the other hand, a mere majority ownership of stock, without any effective control of the management and operation, should properly be treated as a permanent investment, subject to the same rules as other investments of a similar character.

The conditions under which any stock of a subsidiary company remains outstanding are of some importance, not only in determining whether the ownership of the holding company is sufficient to justify or require consolidated accounts, but also in determining what proportion, if any, of the surplus should appear on such a balance sheet as appertaining to the minority stockholders. The proper practice is to take up as a liability the par value of the outstanding stock, together with its relative share of surplus; but when the amount involved is small, the proportion of surplus is not always set aside.

If minority stock is left outstanding by deliberate intent, as, for instance, to give managers of the company a substantial interest in its results, then a share of any undistributed surplus clearly appertains to this outstanding stock, and the liability to be taken up, therefore, is the par value of the stock, together with the proper proportion of the accumulated surplus.

Other Forms of Consolidated Statements

While the consolidated balance sheet already discussed is on the whole the best method of stating the accounts of a holding company with a group of controlled subsidiaries, it is not necessarily the only one. It must be remembered always that the object of accounts is to show facts, and that any form of statement which discloses all material facts is equally permissible and proper; whether one or other of these forms should be adopted, is largely, but within limits, a matter of individual preference.

Such statements are frequently prepared in a form in which there is shown, as one item in the balance sheet of the holding company under the heading of "Investments in Subsidiary Companies Controlled," the total cost to the holding company of the stocks of its subsidiary companies. This is supported by a columnar statement, each separate column of which contains the assets and liabilities of one subsidiary company under the usual and proper headings; while the total column contains a summary of all the detail columns, eliminating intercompany items, and adding or deducting the amounts by which the prices paid by the holding company for the stocks of the subsidiaries exceed or fall short of the par value of their stocks and surplus.

The consolidated balance sheet shows to shareholders of the holding company the position of the interests they own or control through these shares, but it does not perhaps answer this purpose so well for either creditors of, or minority stockholders in, subsidiary companies. The consolidated balance sheet, being a grouped balance sheet, does not distinguish between the liabilities of different companies in the group, and does not show separately the assets to which the creditors must look for the discharge of these liabilities. Similarly, the stocks outstanding in the hands of the public are shown as representing all the assets in the consolidation, and no separation is made of those appertaining to the stocks of any particular subsidiary company outstanding in the hands of the public.

Such objections apply in a lesser degree to the balance sheet of any single company which has different classes of bonded debt, each secured on separate assets. The objections in the case of the consolidated balance sheet, as in the case of any ordinary balance sheet, can be met by subsidiary schedules giving the information required, or by publishing the balance sheet of each separate company as well as the consolidated one.

(2) Profits Earned Before
Date of Consolidation

A question of considerable importance in its bearing upon the determination of profits in a holding company, or in any corporation which has acquired a going business, is that of the proper disposition of the profits of the consolidating companies, or of the purchased business, earned prior to the date of consolidation. There is a clear rule of common sense, and probably also of law, that a corporation cannot earn profits before it exists; when, therefore, a corporation at its organization purchases an undertaking, together with the profits accrued from a certain prior date, the whole of such profits earned prior to the date of purchase must be treated as a deduction from the purchase price, and not as a credit to Income account available for dividends.

This proposition is the more evident if it be remembered that these profits exist in the form of assets included among those purchased, and that any realization thereof is merely a return to the purchasing company of a portion of the purchase money, i. e., of the capital of the corporation. Similar reasoning will show that where a holding corporation purchases the stocks of several others, all profits of the purchased corporations accruing up to the date of the purchase must be treated by the holding corporation as a deduction from the price paid. The subsidiary corporations can legally declare dividends therefrom; but these dividends, when received by the holding corporation, are merely a transfer to it of some of the assets included in the value of the stock it purchased, and are therefore a return of capital; and dividends declared and paid by the holding corporation to its stockholders out of such profits would clearly be paid out of capital. It is important to note that the date of purchase should be taken as the date of the contract for purchase, and not the date of completion. If the purchasing corporation was in existence at the date of entering into the contract, it is to be presumed that the price fixed had relation to the conditions existing at that date, and that the corporation is entitled to treat as profits all earnings of the subsidiary corporations subsequent to that date, less any consideration, such as interest, given for those profits. But if the holding corporation had no legal existence until a later date, it is submitted that, as it cannot earn profits when it is not in existence, it is only entitled to distribute as dividends profits of the subsidiary corporations earned subsequent to its own incorporation, or to the purchase of the property, whichever is the later date.

(3) Questions Arising on the Organization of a Corporation

Initial Surplus

It frequently happens that a corporation contracts to purchase property at an agreed price, which on the face of the contract is declared to be its value, and that by another clause in the contract, or by another contract, the vendors agree to provide, in addition to the property, a certain sum in cash for working capital or even for free surplus. It is sometimes maintained that this free sum so provided is a profit or surplus of the new corporation available for payment of dividends if the directors so determine. It is submitted that this contention is entirely unsound. Vendors are men of business, and it is not their practice to give something for nothing. A contract must be assumed to be the result of a bargain between purchaser and seller, and whatever the purchaser is to receive under the contract must be set off exactly against what the vendor is to receive; and although, in the formation of a large number of modern corporations, the vendors and purchasers, through the intervention of syndicates, are one and the same, the only safe and sound method of accounting is to assume that the same principles apply as in the case of an ordinary sale. It is difficult to believe that, if such a contract formed the subject of legal proceedings, any other view could be taken than that the so-called gift for working capital was merely a return to the purchaser of a portion of his purchase money, and should be so treated in the accounts. If the reverse principle were upheld, and this gift were treated as a clear profit to the corporation and distributed in dividends, it would seem that a portion of the subscribed capital would in effect be returned to the stockholders.

In a few exceptional cases properties are transferred to corporations at appraised values, and for some reason the stock and other securities issued for the properties have an aggregate par value less than the appraised value of the properties and all other net assets. Assuming that the appraisals are genuine, it would seem that in such a case the corporation commences business with a real surplus, which, however, is clearly a capital and not an income one. Such a condition can only exist when the appraisals cover substantially all the assets.

Losses on Current Assets Acquired

Other accounting questions relating to the formation of consolidating corporations have relation to losses that may occur on current assets taken over from the vendors. The valuation of inventories for purposes of transfer from a vendor to a purchaser is frequently made on a higher basis than would be usual for a going concern, the vendor in effect stipulating for some profit on his unsold product. The excess over the fair, going value of the inventory must in such cases be considered as an addition to the fixed capital investment in the shape of goodwill.

Similarly, if debts and liabilities, as is sometimes the case, are taken over without any guarantee from the vendor, and a loss occurs on final realization and payment, this loss may also be treated as an addition to the amount paid for goodwill. These principles are in accord with those heretofore laid down, that profits and losses of a corporation are such as arise out of its operation subsequent to the date of its formation or of the purchase of its properties, and that profits and losses appertaining to a period prior to these dates are capital items.

Adjustment of Inventories on Purchase and Sale of a Business

It frequently happens that the vendors have many contracts in force for the purchase of materials or supplies or manufactured articles, at prices differing widely from the market price at the date of sale. It is, therefore, fair both to the vendor and the purchaser in such cases that some regard should be paid to such contracts. If the vendor has made advantageous contracts a long way ahead at a time of low prices, the puchaser is certainly getting something more than the mere business contracted for; on the other hand, if such contracts for purchase are above current market prices, then the purchasing company is in a worse position than it otherwise would be. It is, however, doubtful whether it is a fair proposition as between the vendor and the purchaser that the market price on the date of the transfer should necessarily form the basis of a settlement between them. Some allowance must be made for the good judgment of the purchasers, and they should not be required to take over large quantities of materials on the fixed date of acquiring the property, at prices which in the ordinary course of business they might not have considered, when the transfer of such an inventory at the top market price may have a considerable effect on the future prosperity of the business. It is certainly, therefore, a material fact to the intending investor that he should be clearly informed on what basis of price the inventories will be acquired, and what contracts for purchase of materials or manufactured articles have been entered into at prices differing from those current. Another material factor is the amount of orders on hand for future delivery, and the prices therefor, and the proportion such orders might bear to the possible capacity of the works. As a rule a large number of orders on hand may be regarded as a source of strength, if they have been obtained in the ordinary course of business and at reasonably remunerative prices. It is, on the other hand, an easy matter to obtain orders if no regard be paid to the prices, and it might happen that an unscrupulous promoter had built up a large prospective business, at totally unremunerative prices, for the sole purpose of transfer to the purchasing company. Even without any fraudulent intent it may be that, owing to a considerable rise in costs, either of raw materials or labor, or both, the vendor concern may have on hand contracts taken when the range of prices was much lower, which can be filled only at considerable loss to the purchasing company. Similarly, orders on hand—to be completed by a fixed time—to an amount largely in excess of the actual or contemplated factory capacity, might easily be a source of loss rather than of profit to the purchaser.

These are some and perhaps the more important of the questions that may arise in practice when a new corporation is formed to take over one or more businesses as going concerns.

Walter A. Staub

MODE OF CONDUCTING AN AUDIT

Walter Adolph Staub *(1881–1945) was born in Pennsylvania and attended Girard College. He spent his entire professional career with Lybrand, Ross Bros. and Montgomery, joining their staff in 1901 and becoming a partner in 1911. He served as president of the New York State Society of C.P.A., and was chairman of the American Institute of C.P.A.'s committee on accounting procedure for several years just before his death. He gave the Dickinson Lectures at Harvard in 1941. He was the author of technical books on auditing and taxes.*

The article reprinted here won a prize as the best paper at the first International Congress of Accountants held in St. Louis in 1904 in conjunction with the St. Louis Exposition. It appeared in the October 22, 1904, issue of the Accountant (London) and also in the New York Accountants' and Bookkeepers' Journal for November, 1904. It was reprinted in The Accounting Review in April, 1943. This essay is the earliest authoritative description of the typical American audit program, with its mixture of the technical process of verification with the problem of compliance with "principles." By contrast with a contemporary audit program, Staub's paper emphasizes the detection of fraud as a primary objective of an audit.

Before proceeding to the consideration of the mode of conducting an audit, it may be well to inquire as to the purpose and object of making an audit. The reasons clients may have for wishing audits made are many and diverse.

Periodical examinations of the accounts of commercial and financial institutions, special examinations for prospective investors, investigations on behalf of creditors and trustees in bankruptcy, examinations to ascertain the cause of decreasing profits, exhaustive audits preparatory to installing improved systems of financial and cost accounts, and investigations of the accounts of public officials at the behest of dissatified citizens are but a few of the many purposes which clients have in mind when desiring to have the accounts of an undertaking audited.

Reprinted from *The Accounting Review* (April, 1943), pp. 91–98, by permission.

509

The object of the auditor should be, in the main, threefold: (1) detection of fraud, (2) discovery of errors of principle, (3) verification of the mechanical accuracy of accounts. As has been pointed out by other writers, the attempted concealment of fraud must be accomplished by commission of either an error of principle or one in the mechanical work of the accounts; owing, however, to its importance, and often its predominating importance, the detection of fraud is conceded a separate place among the objects of an audit. From first to last it is the auditor's duty to be on the lookout for fraud. Nine times out of ten the client who determines upon an audit suspects no one in his employ in the slightest of dishonesty, and yet experience teaches that in nine cases out of ten it is where they are least expected that fraud and dishonesty are discovered. This should not be taken to mean that all the employees in a client's office are to be suspected of being rogues masquerading as honest men—on the contrary every man is held to be innocent until proven to be otherwise—but it does mean that the auditor must be vigilant and not forget that occasionally, or we may even say frequently, "appearances are deceitful." Errors of principle are as often found to be errors of omission as of commission, and it is here that an initial audit most often bears its fruit. As regards verifying the mechanical accuracy of accounts, it would be preposterous of course to suppose that an auditor in the limited time at his disposal could be expected to verify every footing, every posting, and all the other routine details of a set of accounts. The verification incident to and necessitated by the attainment of the first two objects is usually sufficient reasonably to satisfy him of the correctness of the accounts from this standpoint.

Having very briefly considered the purpose and object of making an audit, we may now profitably proceed to the question of the mode of conducting it. In the treatment of such a general subject as this, it is necessary to deal largely in generalities, leaving the particulars and their application to be determined by individual practice and experience. It is not the intention of the writer to pronounce any dictums or to lay down any hard and fast rules, but rather to touch upon the general lines of procedure which suggest themselves as being essential to a satisfactory investigation of a set of accounts.

When an audit is being made for the first time it will be of great advantage to the auditor to go thoroughly over the system in force, the methods employed to gather the information necessary to the proper administration of the accounting department, the manner in which it is treated after obtained, whether intelligently or otherwise; he should observe the safeguards, if any, against error, intentional or unintentional; and further note whether in the case of manufacturing and mercantile enterprises any system of stock accounts is kept (in the case of the former whether there is a cost system) and whether they fit into the scheme of the general accounts or are in any way of assistance. It is also desirable that he familiarize himself, at least in a general way, with the business of his client, ascertaining in the case of a commercial undertaking, for instance, the article manufactured or handled, the average rate of profit which is expected to be earned, and the numerous other matters that will suggest themselves.

Succeeding this preliminary survey, the mode of procedure should be mapped out in considerable detail. It will, of course, not be possible to determine in advance all the work that should be done, as the results and observations made during the progress of the audit will call attention to much of the detail which it may be desirable to go into, but there is no question that a well laid out plan will greatly facilitate and simplify the the work in hand.

Ordinarily, the work of the audit will naturally run in two channels, viz., the verification of a balance sheet on a date specified and the examination of the profit and loss or equivalent account for a period or a number of periods ending with the date of the balance sheet.

A balance sheet is a statement of assets and liabilities as of a given date, hence an audit of it will embrace, (a) the verification of the existence of the assets, ascertaining whether any have been omitted, and, as far as it lies within the province of the auditor, judging their values, or at least determining the bona fides and the methods of derivation of those items whose statements of value are open to question; (b) the verification of the existence and amounts of the liabilities and ascertaining most particularly that there have been no omissions, either of contingent, accrued, or direct liabilities.

Of the assets the cash naturally suggests itself as the item which should be verified at the earliest possible moment. Bank balances should be proved by reconciliation of the balance per check book with the bank pass book which should be settled at the time of the audit, or, if there is any doubt as to the authenticity of the pass book, by procuring a certificate from the bank. Cash and checks on hand should be counted, the latter being carefully scrutinized as to date and also as to entry in cash book; if this precaution be omitted it is possible that a shortage may be concealed by submitting as part of the cash balance certain checks which have not yet been entered. Memoranda, I.O.U.'s, etc., should be noted, attention being given to the question of the authority of the cashier to make advances or other payments on memoranda. Where cash is on hand in several different departments, as for instance in a bank, it is important that, as far as practicable, the counting of the cash proceed simultaneously in all the departments; otherwise cash already counted in one department might be very easily transferred to another department, and, unknown to the auditor, be included as part of the balance in the latter, and thus be used to conceal a shortage.

Accounts receivable are, in many instances, very trying to the auditor and call for special attention as to both their genuineness and value. Where it is practicable for the auditor to send out to the debtors, or examine before they are sent out, statements of their accounts, this is the most satisfactory way of verifying them, and especially so if provision is made for acknowledgment (addressed to or marked for the auditor) of their correctness, although there is almost a certainty of some recipients not making any acknowledgment. In some cases, such as that of stockbrokers, this method is absolutely essential, as in no other way can the auditor satisfy himself that the accounts are correct as stated on the books, particularly in the item of collaterals which are carried on the accounts.

In a mercantile business the balances should be earmarked as consisting of certain specific unpaid bills of recent due date. "Slow pay" and overdue accounts and those on which payments are made in round sums with very infrequent settlements should be closely scrutinized, as it is possible that the operation of "washing" is being carried on. That is to say, payments are being received when due, but the earlier collections having been misappropriated, such cash credits as appear on the books are made from subsequent collections, or in rare instances, where the use of misappropriated funds is successfully followed up, from restitution. Bad or doubtful accounts should be investigated before being charged off to make sure that they have not been collected and the moneys misapplied. The old practice of charging off bad accounts to profit and loss without keeping any further record of them is a poor one and is being gradually abandoned. Where bad accounts are charged direct to profit and loss instead of to a suspense account, they should be entered in a memorandum book, together with all particulars relating to them, so that they can readily be followed up and any possible future value be realized.

As has already been noted, accounts receivable should be examined for their value as well as genuineness and a suitable reserve provided for such as are bad or doubtful. It is best to err on the safe side and make the reserve too large rather than the reverse. In "lean" years clients are very apt to omit making any reserve for doubtful debts, contending that they will be collected "some time," and the auditor cannot urge too strongly the necessity of making proper provision for them.

Where accounts consist mainly of instalments payable on sales made on the lease agreement plan—the article sold to become the property of the lessee upon payment of the final instalment—a tabulated record of these sales showing total amount of each sale, terms of payment, etc., is much more convenient and lends itself more easily to an intelligent examination than the ordinary form of ledger. To confirm the existence and amount of the accounts the agreements themselves, which are signed by the customer, may be examined and compared with the record. The question of doubtful debts is especially important here, as, with few exceptions, there is sure to be loss on some of the accounts.

Bills discounted and time and call loans, which form the largest item of a bank's assets, should be scheduled together with the collateral pledged with them, both the notes and collateral themselves being examined or verified by letter as to such items which may be in the hands of correspondents for collection or other cause. The bills discounted should be separated into one-name and two-name paper, and indication made of the customer for whom discounted. The value of collateral on loans should be shown as far as practicable; where it consists of securities listed on a stock exchange this is comparatively simple, but in the case of securities which are not listed, such as those of closed corporations, or warehoused goods other than those dealt in on an exchange, it is not so simple a matter and in some instances not practicable for the auditor to attach any value.

The subject of inventories of materials and manufactured products is one of great importance in those businesses of which they form a part. Their verification seems to be somewhat akin to that of payrolls in so far as the most efficient check is to have a number of different people concerned in and held responsible for their make-up. Generally speaking, it is not possible for the auditor to verify the quantities of materials on hand, and he is, to this extent at least, at the mercy of those preparing the inventory. In some very unusual instances the auditor is requested to have one of his assistants present to verify the counting and weighing of the stock on hand, but even in such a case he cannot vouch for the quality of the materials or products. Where the force of clerks is large enough to permit it, the work of taking count of the quantities, pricing, and making the extensions and footings should be assigned to separate employees who should be required to certify separately in writing to the work performed by each of them. The footings should be checked by the auditor's staff and the extensions as well, at least roughly.

The inventories should be analyzed and compared with those of previous periods, as to both prices and total values, and any marked changes inquired into. Prices of raw materials can be verified by comparison with purchase invoices; where cost accounts are kept the prices of finished goods can be readily verified; if no cost accounts are kept it may be somewhat more difficult, but at all events it should be seen to that there is a margin between the inventory and selling prices of finished goods. The items forming the basis of valuing manufactured products should be scrutinized to see that no expenses which have not been actually incurred are included. For instance, in the case of a publishing house it is usually the rule to pay royalties to authors only on the books actually sold; to include the royalty as part of the cost of unsold books would not be correct unless the royalty had been credited on book account.

Under the heading of "Plant," which may be expanded to include rights of way and tracks of railway companies, together with locomotives, cars, and other equipment, we have a subject which from its very size attracts much attention. It is the consensus among accountants that an auditor can-not be expected to act in the capacity of an appraiser and determine the actual value of the plant of the concern he is auditing. He should, however, examine very carefully all entries in the books relating to this account; the minutes should be consulted regarding all issues of capital stock which may be charged to it for purchase of plant or equipment; charges for extensions and additional machinery, etc., during the period under review should be looked into to make sure that no replacements are being charged to this account because they may happen to run into large amounts; sales of worn-out plant items, such as old boilers, must be verified as having gone to credit of plant account and not to some operating account, unless the original cost or depreciated cost (if depreciation has been provided for) be charged off at the same time. Extensions are, at times, very difficult of verification when the concern does its own construction work, as is largely the case with railway companies, and the materials and labor charges are of exactly the same nature as those for repairs and renewals. In such cases, the character of the extension and the value should be certified to by the engineer or other competent authority.

Depreciation must be considered in relation to any statement of property values. The number of instances in which depreciation is properly provided for forms an exceedingly small percentage of the grand total of business enterprises. The auditor cannot, of course, compel his client to provide for depreciation, but he should certainly call attention to its great importance for both a properly stated balance sheet and a correct report of earnings; and if no provision is made, attention should specifically be called to the fact in the report submitted. The amount or rate of depreciation to be allowed in various undertakings cannot, of course, be gone into in the limited space available nor under such a general heading as that of the subject under discussion. That must be left to the writer who has more space and time at his disposal.

Investments in mortgages, stocks, bonds, etc., should be verified by examination of the securities or by correspondence if pledged as collateral on loans. Their cost can be verified by the vouchers for the expenditures made for their purchase. It is well to note the numbers of registered securities, so that at the time of the succeeding audit, if no change appears in the book accounts of the same, the auditor may satisfy himself that there has been no unauthorized use of them in the interval. It would be found convenient, when the investments are not likely to be disposed of for some time, to place them in envelopes sealed with the auditor's private seal and their contents marked on the envelopes by him. The unbroken packages do not then have to be examined during every audit.

Prepaid and accrued expenses, such as insurance, taxes, wages, etc., which may rank as either assets or liabilities, are usually not very difficult of verification. The unexpired insurance may be readily proven by scheduling the policies in force with the total premium paid on same and calculating the value that the unexpired portion of the term bears to the whole. When the fiscal year of a business subject to taxation is not coincident with the calendar year, or the period under review is not an even year, prepaid or accrued taxes form an item in the balance sheet; if prepaid, their verification is a matter of simple arithmetic; if accrued and the amount of the assessment and the tax levy be known, it is likewise quite simple; if the current year's taxes are not yet known, the preceding year's will have to be taken as a basis of calculation, due allowance being made for any expected increase in assessment or levy. Accrued wages may be roughly checked by comparing them with the proportion which the accrued period bears to the whole payroll period, and so on ad libitum.

The audit of the liabilities is not of less importance than the audit of the assets. This aspect of the examination demands that great care be taken, as liabilities are more often omitted from the balance sheet than assets. The usual items of liabilities are accounts and bills payable, bonds, mortgages, revenue collected in advance of being earned, such as discount on unmatured notes held by banks, subscriptions paid in advance, etc., and accrued expenses. The proving of accrued expenses has already been spoken of in the preceding paragraph and need not be dealt with again, except to say that the auditor should be certain that all accrued accounts of whatsoever nature have been included; the verification of revenues collected, but as yet unearned, is in general not very complicated and is generally more a matter of arithmetic than anything else.

As regards accounts payable, the most frequent error in practice is one of omission, and consists of bills for goods actually received and included in the inventory of stock on hand that are not entered in the books during the same fiscal period. Where a good system of stock accounts is in use or a method exists of checking back a record of goods received with the purchase book or the invoices themselves, this is not so liable to occur; but in a concern where neither of these systems obtains, especial vigilance is needed on the part of the auditor to satisfy himself that no bills have been omitted. A good way of verifying the accounts payable is to check back the vendors' statements with the ledger, any bills appearing on the statements but not entered on the books being carefully scrutinized as to their dates and the dates of the receipt of the goods, which latter should be subsequent to the date of the taking of the inventory; otherwise the bills should have been entered.

Unpaid notes per the bills payable book should be totaled and the aggregate compared with the ledger account. In the case of collaterals being pledged on the loans, the holders should be communicated with for confirmation of the loans and the collateral. This is especially important in the case of stockbrokers and similar houses where the balancing of the stocks is an important feature of the audit.

In the matter of bonds or mortgages the minutes of the concern, if it be a corporation, should be consulted for authority bearing upon their issue, rate of interest, etc. The bond and mortgage should be read through to see what provisions regarding sinking funds, redemption, etc., may be contained therein, and, further, the auditor should see whether the provisions are carried out. It might also be well to examine the county records for any other encumbrances on real estate appearing among the assets, although it is still an open question how far an auditor's duty extends in this direction.

Contingent liabilities, such as endorsements on bills receivable discounted, should not be overlooked. They sometimes become direct and very live liabilities in short order.

Examination of the books and records pertaining to the issuance of capital stock should, at least, extend to the checking of the stock ledger trial balance and inspection of the stock certificate stubs and preferably also the transfer records. This latter is, however, sometimes of such volume that it is necessary to have it made the subject of a special examination. As with the issuance of bonds, the minutes should be examined for any action relating to issuance, retirement, or exchange of capital stock.

The articles of co-partnership in private firms should be examined for the provisions relating to the investments to be made by the several partners, interest on capital and on withdrawals, division of profits, etc.

The audit of the accounts constituting the profit and loss account is partially covered by the work incident to auditing the items of the balance sheet. It is in this part of an audit that the greatest amount of detail is usually encountered. While this cannot always be said of financial institutions, the verification of those accounts constituting the balance sheet often requiring a more extended examination of detail than the profit and loss section, yet of manufacturing, mercantile, and enterprises of like character this is undoubtedly true.

Limited space permits of only some very general remarks in this connection. The entries in the cash book should be vouched; when the payments are all charged to personal accounts or for such of them as are charged when this is only partially the case, paid checks may be accepted as sufficient vouchers. Invoices for purchases should be examined and used to vouch the credits to the personal accounts. These latter usually come through a purchase book or voucher register, or where the system is antiquated are found in the journal. Checks which are drawn to "Bearer," "Cash," or to order of a bank in such form that the funds could be obtained by the bearer either in cash or due bill, should, of course, not be accepted as final vouchers. A check to the order of payroll is of no value as a voucher for wage payments, except in so far as it might imply that the drawer held himself responsible for the correctness of it; such a conclusion would, however, be rather farfetched, as the person signing a check is not unusually one upon whom the examination of the payroll would devolve.

In the case of very large concerns it is not practicable for the auditor to examine all the vouchers. Even in such cases, however, it is well to vouch all payments which are charged direct to operation accounts. The best plan is to have all payments charged to personal accounts or a controlling account such as "Vouchers Payable," to have all vouchers entered in a voucher register to the credit of personal accounts or the controlling account, and to have the cash book and the voucher register kept by separate persons. By this method the voucher for each payment, except such few as it may be desired to charge direct in the cash book, and which can be readily examined by the auditor, is submitted to the scrutiny of a second person, who has no connection with the cash or bank account and who, except in the event of collusion with the cashier, would have no interest in putting through any fictitious vouchers.

In connection with the subject of vouching payments, that of payrolls may be spoken of. It is generally conceded that, as regards payrolls, the only safety is in numbers, that is, in a good system designed to use a number of different people in preparing the figures. An auditor may verify the footings and in some cases be able to check back the payroll to the original time reports from which it is made up, but to accept any responsibility further than this is foolish in the extreme. Even in the instances where it might be possible to verify the payroll by other documents, the time required to do it would usually entail much greater expense than clients would care to pay.

The person making up the payroll time reports should not be the same one who affixes the rate and makes the extensions, nor should either of these, where it is possible to avoid it, be concerned in the filling of the envelopes or the actual paying off. In some parts of the country, such as in the South...the question of unclaimed wages becomes quite important. A good plan to take care of these items is for them to be turned over to the treasurer, or some other authorized person, immediately upon completion of the paying off, to be entered by him in a book ruled to permit of the workman signing for his envelope when he calls for it subsequently. After a sufficient lapse of time those still uncalled for should be returned to the general cash, being credited to an "Unclaimed Wages" account. From the book before mentioned, the auditor can easily see that no unclaimed wages are lost to the company or proprietor.

In practice the satisfactory auditing of the income will be found more difficult than that of the expenses. Here, too, a good system is the best assurance of the integrity of the accounts. The recording of the sales should not be committed to the charge of the same person who handles the cash collected. This will go far to insure the correctness of the sales record and obviate any intentional omissions. Where possible the auditor should verify the sales independently for at least a portion of the period under review. The circumstances of each particular situation must, of course, govern. In some cases the shipping book, which is kept in the factory or store, can be compared with the sales book. If a stock account of the production is kept or can be constructed, as for instance at coal or ore mines, the sales can usually be verified, as to quantities at least, quite satisfactorily.

In this connection the matter of "internal check," which is dwelt upon at length in most works on auditing, may be mentioned. Briefly stated, it consists largely in so disposing the office staff that there will in reality be an internal audit continually going on. In some cases this is arranged by changing the duties of the various clerks from time to time; e.g., in a bank where there is more than one individual bookkeeper, it is well to change the bookkeepers from one ledger to another; where there is only one, it is not always practicable to vary his duties, but the trial balances can occasionally be taken off by some one other than the bookkeeper.

In other instances this is accomplished by having the work so divided that the work of one person is incomplete by itself and must dovetail into that of another before being complete, the theory being that only by collusion between two or more persons would it be possible to conceal dishonesty. In still other instances the duties of one of the office force may be those of an auditor, that is, he would verify much of the detail which would not be practicable for the professional auditor to go into. A case in point is the auditing of the income of railway companies. Here there is need to have auditors constantly checking the income from freight and passenger traffic. The safeguards to be placed about payrolls and sales, which come under this head, have already been touched upon.

Income from securities presents no especial difficulty, as that collectible on bonds and mortgages can be determined from the securities themselves, while the dividends declared on stocks can usually be quite easily ascertained.

Miscellaneous income must be dealt with as the occasion demands; there are hardly any two businesses in which it can be verified in exactly the same way.

Regarding the footings and postings to be verified, this will, of course, vary with circumstances. As a general rule, the footings of all the books of original entry and of the nominal ledger accounts should be verified. All postings to the impersonal accounts and, at least, the credit postings (particularly the cash) to all other accounts should be checked. It goes without saying that the trial balance and its footings, as well of subsidiary ledgers as of the general ledger, should be verified.

A few words concerning the report upon the audit may not be out of place. The report should be clear and concise. Qualifications pertaining to the work or to any financial statements which may form a part of the report should be definitely expressed without any ambiguity. It may be noted that qualifications are not very desirable from a client's point of view and should only be made where there is good ground for so doing.

In conclusion, there will in the course of many audits be assets or liabilities, or classes of income and expenses, to be verified which have not even been mentioned in this dissertation. The aim of the writer has been to illustrate the mode of conducting an audit by touching upon the methods of auditing the items which commonly appear in the balance sheets and profit and loss accounts submitted to the auditor for examination.

Robert H. Montgomery

PROFESSIONAL STANDARDS:
A PLEA FOR CO-OPERATION
AMONG ACCOUNTANTS

Robert Hiester Montgomery (1872–1953), lawyer and accountant, was born in Pennsylvania. He was a partner in Heims, Whelen, Lybrand and Co. in 1896–1897, and in Lybrand, Ross Bros., and Montgomery from 1898. He was admitted to the bar in 1900. From 1912 to 1931 he was on the faculty at Columbia. He was president of the American Association of Public Accountants, 1912–1914, of the New York State Society of C.P.A., 1922–1924, and of the American Institute of C.P.A., 1935–1937. He fought in the Spanish-American War, and in World War I, emerging as a lieutenant colonel. He saw active service on several boards and commissions during both World Wars. He was the author of books and articles on taxes and on auditing. "Montgomery's Auditing" was for years the most authoritative source on auditing standards.
The article reprinted here is a clarion call for the members of a young profession to band together to weed out the incompetent and the unfit and to upgrade the remainder. Some of the specific issues of 1905 are no longer with us, but the underlying problems are as fresh and challenging now as they were then.

Until quite recently an article on professional standards would have seemed out of place, unless found in a journal read largely if not exclusively, by clergymen, doctors or lawyers. The recognition of accountancy as a profession, while gained in a marvelously short time when we consider its history, is yet so new a matter that it is difficult to define accurately the conditions which exist, and a far more onerous task to outline ideal standards. At first thought we might take it for granted that a code of ethics generally followed or at least particularly fitted to the legal or medical profession might with

Reprinted from *The Journal of Accountancy* (November, 1905), pp. 28–39, by permission.

519

propriety be recommended to the accountant, but there are so many inherent peculiarities which differentiate the professions named that accountants find themselves forced to compile a new code.

It is not too much to say that more is expected of a professional accountant in these youthful years of the profession than was exacted from the lawyer or doctor when their professions were centuries old. The law, perhaps, made the most rapid strides, although the standards have been raised considerably in comparatively recent years. We frequently hear of attorneys who are not faithful to their trusts, but the total number of recreants is very small, and the ever vigilant bar associations honestly strive to rid the ranks of those who have violated their rules. The medical profession has been rather slow in its advance to universal public respect. Not so many years ago the barber applied the leech without thought of punishment for practicing without a license. We cannot take the time to examine the progressive steps made by these two great professions, nor follow in detail the gradual growth of their codes of ethics, but a cursory look is sufficient to convince the observant student that legislation has not been responsible for their present high standards. The moving cause has been the careful education and training of the juniors and constant supervision over their early practice; not supervision by state boards, but through school societies, and state and national organizations.

Co-operation among the practitioners is responsible more than any other thing for the high standing of these two professions to-day, and while we ask for the same measure of legislative protection, we must not lose sight of their history and the keynote of their success, which, after all, is largely explained when we consider the definition of the word "profession," viz., "An employment requiring a learned education." Let education, then—in its broadest sense—be our watchword.

Before we attempt to lay down rules of conduct for the professional accountant, we should review briefly his qualifications, for it would be a waste of time to make suggestions as to what the accountant should *do* unless we agree as to what he should *be*.

Assuming that he is skilled in accounts, there are other desirable and, in fact, necessary qualities. Mr. Dicksee, in his "Auditing," mentions the following: tact, caution, firmness, fairness, good temper, courage, integrity, discretion, industry, judgment, patience, clear-headedness, and reliability; "in short, all those qualities that go to make a good business man contribute to the making of a good accountant; while that judicious and liberal education which is involved in the single word, 'culture,' is most essential for all who would excel. Accountancy is a profession calling for a width and variety of knowledge to which no man has yet set the limit." If this a fair portrait of an ideal accountant, it is obvious that he will be expected to conduct himself on a much higher plane than if he were subject to less onerous rules of conduct. But as he is measured by the community at large, so must he regulate his own relations (1) to the public, (2) to professional brethren, and (3) to himself.

Relations to the Public

Unquestionably the public demands a high standard in accountants, *but only in particular cases and at particular times*. That is, the average financier, lawyer, or business man cares little and thinks less about a *general* standard of efficiency, and is unwilling, as a rule, to accord proper support to the accountancy profession *as a profession;* but if a specific instance arises involving error or misconduct on the part of anyone purporting to practice as a public accountant, he awakens to the importance of requiring the maintenance of a high standard, and the good name of the whole profession is thereby involved without any means whatever being provided for punishing or disciplining the guilty party. No one can hold himself out as a lawyer and practice law unless he is admitted to the bar. No one can hold himself out as a doctor nor practice medicine unless he has been licensed by a state board. And either the lawyer or the doctor may be disqualified if he fails to maintain the proper standard.

But anyone can call himself a public accountant or an "expert" accountant without having a single qualification for the profession, and such a man frequently receives generous support from the public. His severest punishment for malpractice is usually merely the loss of the one particular client who has suffered through him.

The remedy for this condition is clear. What the public demand in specific cases should apply in all, and a system of registration or certification similar to that required in law and medicine should be compulsory. The certified public accountant legislation so far effected has not accomplished the best results. We are in exactly the same position as the legal profession would be if certain lawyers were admitted to the bar and called themselves "admitted" lawyers, while a great many other persons, although not admitted, enjoyed the same priviledges, practiced in the same courts, and were permitted to sit on the bench.

We are advised that the state of Ohio is about to enact accountancy legislation which embodies not only the usual clauses governing the certification of public accountants, but in addition prohibits anyone practicing in any form as a public accountant unless certified according to the requirements of the proposed bill, which, incidentally, has been approved by prominent lawyers and business men in that state.

In this connection we have been advised by our brethren from over the sea that a plan of registration which would restrict the practice of public accounting to qualified accountants has been presented to Parliament several times and has been defeated, not because the public object, but because of disputes between rival societies. Happily the latter condition no longer exists with us, and the experience of the members of the profession in Ohio would seem to justify the assertion that the business public welcome rather than oppose legislation which promises to limit the practice of accounting to responsible persons. It is to be hoped that the ability to arouse public sentiment along these lines is not confined to one state.

It would seem, therefore, that those states which have certified public accountant laws that do not protect the public from unqualified practitioners should amend them as suggested above. It is quite true that in several states it would have been impossible a few years ago to pass any such restrictive law, and it may even now be urged by some, who have learned by bitter experience the difficulty of securing regulative legislation, that in view of the objections which might be raised, any agitation along this line would be a mistake. Such a position, however, entirely ignores the great advance made in recent years, especially in the last year. Indeed, within the last month, some of the foremost men in the United States—including President [Theodore] Roosevelt—have paid a tribute to public accountants, which is direct proof of the change in sentiment over several years ago. If, then, public accountants are needed, who is to pass upon their qualifications? Surely not the man himself, as is now the case.

We need, however, to do far more than attach the letters C.P.A. to our names. The certificate must be made to *mean* something, and to accomplish this, constant vigilance will be necessary.

Let us take advantage of the public recognition so far accorded to accountancy as a profession, and use it as a basis to secure proper legal safeguards, and the benefit which accrues will not only inure to those properly qualified, but the largest benefit will flow to the public.

The Relations of One Accountant to Another

Reference to the qualifications of a professional accountant easily convince us that the possession of a part only would suffice to make him not only an ideal accountant from the standpoint of his clients—the public—but he would also possess those qualities which would endear him to his competitors. The latter term is used in its broadest sense, of course, and is used advisedly, for it has been found by experience that, as a rule, the professional accountant who has finally lodged in a place where he no longer competes for general business from the public has also lost all interest in the advance of professional standards, and cares but little for friendly contact with fellow practitioners. He has lost the professional spirit and with it fraternal feeling.

Fifty years ago several Scottish accountants, imbued with both professional and fraternal feelings, organized the first society of public accountants.

Thirty-two years elapsed before a society was formed in the United States —the year 1887 witnessing the formation of the American Association of Public Accountants. Let us put the accountancy profession to a test and, by examining the history of the last eighteen years, form an opinion as to whether representative accountants in the United States have acquitted themselves well, and whether those qualities which we mentioned as essential have, as a matter of fact, been manifest.

I unhesitatingly answer that accountants *have* borne themselves well, they *can* stand a hard test, and I believe I can prove it. In the first place, the most severe test of a man's technical ability, fairness, good temper and courage are found in his intercourse with his competitors. An unskillful, mean, ill-tempered, weak man does not want to rub up against his fellow practitioner. It follows, therefore, that the formation of a society in which are found practically all of the leading professional accountants in a given community is proof that those in question measure up, approximately at least, to the ideal standard. Furthermore, while there are several medical societies, and many societies of engineers in the same neighborhood, there is but one society of professional accountants in any one state in the Union, and no state in which there are a dozen reputable practicing accountants is without a society.

But it may be said that the formation and success of a society, while it may be ample proof of a high standard in several particulars, is not evidence of other necessary qualities. For instance, what does one accountant have to say about his fellow society member when the latter is not around? I answer that, as a general rule, the most kindly feelings prevail. The heartiest praise I have heard of some accountants has come from the lips of competitors. Of course, we occasionally hear criticism, and we shall doubtless always hear it, for it is a debatable question whether or not the accountancy code of ethics should prohibit any criticism of a competitor whatever, whether merited or unmerited. Physicians are notoriously careful about this and the result has been at times that incompetent doctors have killed off their patients by reason of the fact that the incompetency of their doctors has been carefully concealed by their fellows, the patient having mighty little opportunity to discover it for himself. Still another test which, it might fairly be supposed, could not be passed by the majority of public accountants is the practice of soliciting or undertaking work which has been done in the past by a competitor. To my positive knowledge accountants have declined to undertake work which they have had offered them after ascertaining that it had been formerly intrusted to fellow accountants whose services had been satisfactory. The latter, of course, is a necessary element, because under any code of ethics it would be the clear duty of an accountant to undertake work which had not been satisfactorily performed by another. It is not claimed, of course, that the above conditions are without exceptions, but the claim is made in all sincerity that with respect to the attitude of one member to another no other profession in the history of the world has made such rapid strides in a few years toward attaining a high standard, and, if there are those who fail to measure up to their opportunities, it is believed that lack of knowledge rather than indifference is responsible for such failures. This lack of knowledge is easily explained, for it must be remembered that in some communities the accountancy profession has but one representative, who can hardly be expected to originate or uphold a high standard of professional ethics "all by himself." With all his difficulties, nevertheless, we will usually find that in theory, at least, an accountant who strives to be independent has set up for himself most commendable ideals. Undoubtedly this accounts for the comparative ease with which practically all the accountants in every large city "get together." Were it not for the true professional spirit that has grown up unawares in the heart of each one, the present satisfactory condition of the profession would have required a half-century of cultivation.

Advantage should be taken of the present era of good feeling to bring the profession still closer together, and correct any defects that may still be apparent. One of the most important points is the desirability of enlisting the support of all reputable accountants to their local society. A strong society not only carries great weight with the public, but is of incalculable benefit to a man individually. It broadens his vision generally, and, if accountancy questions are discussed by his society, it gives him an opportunity to get out of a beaten path.

It must be remembered that no one of us is free from error. The best lawyers make mistakes and lose cases which they should win; the best doctors, through errors of judgment, kill patients whom they should save, and so even an accountant will sometimes make a mistake and the last, the very last, one who should criticise him or attempt to profit thereby is his fellow practitioner.

Incidentally, it is worthy of note that incompetent assistants are responsible for the majority of mistakes which have been attributed to professional accountants. Serious consideration should be given to this question, because it is not only highly desirable that our assistants should be above reproach, it is more than desirable, it is vital. The hope of the future lies in the proper education of a sufficient number of young men to fill the ranks. Schools are accomplishing much in this direction and can confidently be counted upon for more. The English custom of article clerks might well be established here, and it is hoped that before long young men from the colleges and universities will be found eager for an opportunity to enter the office of public accountants, and instead of expecting compensation out of all proportion to their usefulness, will consider the experience they are getting ample pay and will depend for their advance upon the intelligence they display. Apprenticeship is practically in effect in the legal and medical professions and corresponds very closely with English methods. Time will no doubt solve this problem, but some definite step should be taken immediately to improve present conditions.

The Accountant's Personal Standard

The personal element in a professional accountant is necessarily a prominent one. In fact, a man who embodies one-half the qualifications named as desirable must possess the strongest kind of personality. Fortunately this portion of my subject needs little discussion. While we may occasionally find an accountant who criticises too freely or unfairly, we rarely find one who has not set for himself a high personal standard of professional conduct. How many instances have come to us where a confidential communication has been divulged? Who has heard of one? And is it not a fact that of the hundreds of practicing accountants in this country almost each one is in constant receipt of information, the disclosure of which would frequently be of great pecuniary advantage? Have we ever heard of a case of a professional accountant who has failed to account for funds intrusted to him? And is it not a fact that tens of millions of dollars are turned over to them monthly for inspection?

Of course, there are exceptions, but I claim that the proportion of those who fail to measure up to their responsibility is smaller than with any other like number of men occupying positions of responsibility. The moral responsibility of the accountant is largely personal, and the insistence on a high professional standard implies a full measure of moral accountability. It is hardly necessary to dwell at length on this phase of the question. Several of the speakers at the recent banquet of the American Association referred to the necessity for a high personal standard, and while too much can hardly be said on so important a topic, yet it may safely be said that the present state of affairs is highly encouraging.

It has been urged that two necessary steps in the progress of the accountancy profession toward complete recognition and establishing high standards are (1) exemption from jury duty and (2) the right to regard confidential communications from clients as privileged, thereby furnishing the means to prevent undesired disclosures.

As to the first point there seems to be little real merit in the claim. The Anglo-Saxon regards the jury system as one of the bulwarks of his liberty and he will continue to think so until something better is devised. Jury service is a clear civic duty which should never be avoided unless some reason better than the usual selfish one is present. It is conceivable that occasionally, in the course of years, an accountant might be engaged on some particular work the cessation of which would be injurious to the general community, but such occasions are so rare that it certainly would be unwise to attempt to secure universal exemption to fit an unusual and individual case. The classes now exempt are few and the reasons therefor are so good that their cause needs no support. With respect to accountants, however, it is my opinion that there are dozens of other classes of men as to whom personally equally important reasons could be urged for exemption in particular cases, and if we consider family and business hardships reasons for exemption, the list of those available would be narrowed down to the most worthless classes of the community.

It must not be forgotten, moreover, that where service on a jury will work real hardship it is comparatively easy to be excused, and unless an accountant is able to show good cause for his unwillingness to serve the state, he certainly does not deserve special privileges. I am of the opinion that any agitation along this line will be harmful to the profession at large and result in a diminished respect for individual accountants who would thus seek to avoid a public duty.

The second point mentioned above is far more difficult of solution, for there are many arguments in favor of the extension of legal "privilege" to public accountants with respect to such matters as are laid before them in a confidential capacity by clients. It cannot be disputed, however, that the necessity for such procedure seldom arises and the cases of accountants being called as witnesses and forced to disclose confidential communications are few, if, in fact, there have been any.

As a matter of fact, it is hardly conceivable that such a case will ever occur, unless it is discovered by a prosecuting attorney, that a guilty defendant has destroyed incriminating books and papers, or, having confessed his crime to an accountant, refuses to incriminate himself on the stand. In such cases it is submitted that the welfare of the public would be better served if the accountant witness is compelled to testify than if he is permitted to screen himself behind a technical privilege. He is not at all in the position of a doctor or a lawyer. He is supposed to be an independent public accountant, and if he has had submitted to him books and papers which contain information to which others than his client are legally entitled, why should the law interpose to prevent justice being done and the truth known? The books and papers, if they can be found, are the best evidence, of course, but if they have been secreted or destroyed, why should the guilty parties be protected?

It will, of course, be urged that the information which an accountant might be forced to disclose might not be of such a character, and that no public service would be accomplished by compelling its publication. The answer to this is that under our laws refusal to testify is not in itself a crime, and if an accountant were called upon to divulge matters which he deemed to be confidential and refused to answer, it would be the duty of the court to pass upon the effect of such disclosure; and I venture to express the opinion that accountants need never fear, even under present conditions, that any judge will require them to disclose confidential matters unless the case is a grave one and public interest demands it. In all cases the testimony sought would have to be pertinent to the issue.

If this is a fair presentation of the case it would hardly seem wise, for the present at least, to make any serious effort to secure a privilege so rarely granted that the legislatures in the majority of our states have not been willing to extend its protection to the secrets of the confessional.

Legal Responsibility

In my opinion the quickest way to weed out the incompetent men who now hold themselves out as public accountants would be to make them understand the civil responsibility of a professional accountant. Naturally, an unreliable, incompetent man cares nothing about his moral responsibility, and so long as he knows that American courts have never laid down specific rules regulating the duties or obligations of public accountants, he probably feels safe from any legal responsibility. One sure and very desirable result of the weeding out process would be the raising of the professional standard, for a few irresponsible men can offset the good work of ten times their number.

As is well known, there are numerous English decisions dealing with the rights and liabilities of professional auditors. In view, however, of the total number of accountants in practice and the number of years the decisions cover, the number does not seem at all appalling. While the fact that we have no reported decisions speaks well for the integrity and good judgment of our accountants, yet it is felt that occasions have arisen where a test case would have been made had it not been known that any judgment involving money damages which might have been rendered would have been worthless so far as the possibility of collection were concerned. It is unfortunate that anyone should be permitted to practice as a public accountant, who, in case of gross negligence or malpractice, has so little financial responsibility that a judgment against him would be worthless, and who, moreover, is beyond the legal reach of his fellow practitioners, who at present have no opportunity to prefer charges against one who is neither a member of a state society nor certified by a state board.

The absence of decided cases, however, does not alter the principle of law that anyone who holds himself out to be skillful in any trade or profession and who is negligent in the performance of what he undertakes, becomes responsible in damages for such failure. This civil responsibility is settled and cannot be debated, but it should not be passed over lightly and should be emphasized on all occasions. The measure of legal responsibility, however, is much too low for a conscientious accountant. The law only requires of him the skill of an ordinary skillful accountant; the law gives him the privilege of assuming the accuracy of many things unless he has definite suspicions to the contrary, and, as already stated, the law never requires one to measure up to the standard of the most skillful in the same profession or trade. In this respect accountants are to be congratulated, for it is common knowledge that the majority of professional accountants in the United States seek to do more for their clients than the law requires, and every year witnesses a more general desire to advance the quality of services rendered.

It is earnestly hoped that further progress will be made in this direction. Since the wish for high standards is general, let each individual accountant do his part toward maintaining them. Public opinion should be aroused so that unqualified practitioners will gradually cease to practice and in their place a united certified body will control all accountancy matters—not because the law grants them exclusive privileges, but by reason of the fact that they can be depended upon at all times and under all circumstances, while the others cannot.

The Future

This is a critical time in accountancy. Much has been accomplished recently, and we may be pardoned for feeling gratified at results little short of wonderful, but for the very reason that public sentiment is now strongly in our favor; for the very reason that many individual differences of opinion have been harmonized; for the very reason that many accountants, stimulated by encouraging words from men high in authority, have, with the highest purposes, resolved to meet the exacting obligations imposed upon them; for all of these reasons I say that a solemn obligation lies upon each one of us not only to maintain past traditions as to what an ideal accountant should be, but also to raise the standard up to the highest ideals.

To accomplish this, some self-sacrifice will be required. It will be necessary for some who do not belong to their state or district society to join forthwith, and by so doing indicate their interest in and jealousy for the good name of the profession. It will be necessary for some who belong to societies, but who have taken no active part in their work, to sacrifice a part of their time to the meetings, lectures, addresses and discussions. Such work will have its reward, for while it will be of great service to the younger members of the profession who need advice and encouragement, the reflex benefit is considerably greater than is generally supposed.

It will also be necessary to eliminate, almost, if not entirely, adverse criticism of a competitor's work or professional standing, unless the facts at issue are known and perfectly clear. Good fellowship is not only desirable as a manly virtue, but it pays from a selfish standpoint in that it results in greater respect and confidence on the part of the public.

Another consideration of recent growth is the practice of competitive bidding. It cannot be defended, and unless direct action is taken to put an absolute stop to it, great harm will result both to client and practitioner. Not only is the whole idea wholly unprofessional, but, strange as it may seem, there is absolutely no compensation to offset the harm done. For example: Client A requests B, C and D to bid for stated work. Assuming that an effort is made by each to secure the work (and otherwise they should not bid), it is only natural that steps will be taken to do the least work actually called for, and that as low a fee as the contract will stand will be made. The successful bidder surely does not render any service to his chosen profession when he accepts the contract, for Client A is now furnished a basis for future work and he can be depended upon to advise all of his associates to adopt his method of securing low prices.

The inevitable result of a few such instances would be the general lowering of professional standards. This is highly undesirable if we expect to work together, not only for our present good, but for posterity, to which we wish to transfer an honorable and respected profession.

Let us then thoroughly appreciate the importance of compiling a code of ethics for the accountancy profession that will embody the essential elements of the highest skill and include the broadest principles of fraternal co-operation.